PATERNOSTER THEOLOGICAL MONOGRAPHS

The Possibility of Salvation Among the Unevangelised

An Analysis of Inclusivism in Recent Evangelical Theology

PATERNOSTER THEOLOGICAL MONOGRAPHS

A complete listing of all titles in this series and Paternoster Biblical Monographs will be found at the close of this book.

PATERNOSTER THEOLOGICAL MONOGRAPHS

The Possibility of Salvation Among the Unevangelised

An Analysis of Inclusivism in Recent Evangelical Theology

Daniel Strange

Foreword by Gavin D'Costa

Wipf & Stock
PUBLISHERS
Eugene, Oregon

Wipf and Stock Publishers
199 W 8th Ave, Suite 3
Eugene, OR 97401

The Possibility of Salvation Among the Unevangelised
An Analysis of Inclusivism in Recent Evangelical Theology
By Strange, Daniel
Copyright©2002 Paternoster
ISBN: 1-59752-776-9
Publication date 6/10/2006
Previously published by Paternoster, 2002

This Edition Published by Wipf and Stock Publishers
by arrangement with Paternoster

Paternoster
9 Holdom Avenue
Bletchley
Milton Keyes, MK1 1QR
Great Britain

Unless otherwise stated, Scripture quotations are taken from the
HOLY BIBLE, NEW INTERNATIONAL VERSION
Copyright © 1973, 1978, 1984 by the International Bible Society.
Used by permission of Hodder and Stoughton Limited. All rights reserved.
'NIV' is a registered trademark of the International Bible Society
UK trademark number 1448790

PATERNOSTER THEOLOGICAL MONOGRAPHS

Series Preface

In the West the churches may be declining, but theology—serious, academic (mostly doctoral level) and mainstream orthodox in evaluative commitment—shows no sign of withering on the vine. This series of *Paternoster Theological Monographs* extends the expertise of the Press especially to first-time authors whose work stands broadly within the parameters created by fidelity to Scripture and has satisfied the critical scrutiny of respected assessors in the academy. Such theology may come in several distinct intellectual disciplines—historical, dogmatic, pastoral, apologetic, missional, aesthetic and no doubt others also. The series will be particularly hospitable to promising constructive theology within an evangelical frame, for it is of this that the church's need seems to be greatest. Quality writing will be published across the confessions—Anabaptist, Episcopalian, Reformed, Arminian and Orthodox—across the ages—patristic, medieval, reformation, modern and counter-modern—and across the continents. The aim of the series is theology written in the twofold conviction that the church needs theology and theology needs the church—which in reality means theology done for the glory of God.

Series Editors

David F. Wright, Emeritus Professor of Patristic and Reformed Christianity, University of Edinburgh, Scotland, UK

Trevor A. Hart, Head of School and Principal of St Mary's College School of Divinity, University of St Andrews, Scotland, UK

Anthony N.S. Lane, Professor of Historical Theology and Director of Research, London School of Theology, UK

Anthony C. Thiselton, Emeritus Professor of Christian Theology, University of Nottingham, Research Professor in Christian Theology, University College Chester, and Canon Theologian of Leicester Cathedral and Southwell Minster, UK

Kevin J. Vanhoozer, Research Professor of Systematic Theology, Trinity Evangelical Divinity School, Deerfield, Illinois, USA

To Elly, Noah and Isaac

Contents

Foreword   xv
Acknowledgments   xvii
Preface   xix

Part 1 – The Question of the Unevangelised in Recent Evangelical Theology 1

Chapter 1 - Evangelicals and the Question of the Unevangelised: Establishing Working Definitions and Parameters of Study 3
Evangelicalism and Three Strands of Evangelicalism 3
    Towards a Working Definition
    Three Strands of Evangelical Theology
       THE REFORMED/CALVINIST TRADITION
       THE ARMINIAN TRADITION
       POSTCONSERVATIVE EVANGELICAL THEOLOGY
Defining 'Pluralism' and the 'Theology of Religions' 14
The Question of the Unevangelised in Recent Evangelical Theology 16
    Introduction: The Impact of Religious Pluralism on Evangelical Theology
    The Question of the Unevangelised: the Current State of the Issue
       A THEOLOGICAL TENSION
       AN ORTHODOX EVANGELICAL 'POSITION'?
    The Organic Nature of Doctrine
    Evangelical Parameters of Study on the Question of the Unevangelised
Towards a Working Definition of the Unevangelised and Inclusivism 32
    Delineating 'the Unevangelised'
    Defining Inclusivism

Part 2 – The 'Pneumatological Inclusivism' of Clark H. Pinnock 41

Chapter 2 - An Introduction to the Thought of Clark H. Pinnock 42
Introduction 42
Reasons for Study
Methodology
A Synopsis of Part 2
Theological Presuppositions: Pinnock on the Nature of Freedom and Trinitarian Openness 47
Pinnock's Pilgrimage Concerning the Nature of Freedom
Pinnock's Espousal of 'Trinitarian Openness' and his New Understanding of Divine Sovereignty

Chapter 3 - Two Foundational Axioms: Universality and Particularity 56
The Scope of God's Salvific Will and an Optimism in Salvation 57
Universality and Biblical Revelation
Universality and Western Theology
Universality and the Doctrine of the Trinity
The Finality of Jesus Christ: Universality through a Particular Act of Representation 67
The Person of Christ
   MODELS OF INCARNATION AND *KENOSIS*
   A 'SPIRIT ENRICHED' CHRISTOLOGY
The Work of Christ
   THE REJECTION OF PENAL SUBSTITUTION AND THE SEARCH FOR A NEW MODEL OF ATONEMENT
   RECAPITULATION AND THE ROLE OF THE SPIRIT IN ATONEMENT
Summary 83

Chapter 4 - The 'Cosmic Covenant': God's Universal Saving Presence 85
From Universality to the Principle of Universal Accessibility 86
The Spirit and Creation

The Spirit and Prevenient Grace
   A WESLEYAN UNDERSTANDING OF PREVENIENT
   GRACE
   PINNOCK'S UNDERSTANDING OF PREVENIENT GRACE
   PREVENIENT GRACE AND THE 'SUPERNATURAL
   EXISTENTIAL'
The Spirit and Christ
   CHRISTOLOGY FROM THE PERSPECTIVE OF
   PNEUMATOLOGY
   THE REJECTION OF THE *FILIOQUE*

Chapter 5 - 'The Cosmic Covenant': Humanity's Free Response to God through the 'Faith Principle' **108**
Introduction 108
The Cognitive 'Faith Principle' 110
   The Analogy with Premessianic Believers
   The Nature and Efficacy of General Revelation
   The Nature of Faith in the 'Faith Principle'
The Ethical 'Faith Principle' 116
   Excursus: An Outline of Pinnock's 'Theology of Religions'
   Pinnock's 'Theology of Religions' and the Ethical 'Faith Principle'
   Discerning the Spirit
Motivation for Missions, the Post-Mortem Encounter with Christ and Related Issues 127
   Motivation for Missions
   The Rejection of the Gospel by 'Not-Yet Christians'
   The Post-Mortem Encounter with Christ
   The Analogy of Children who Die in Infancy and the Mentally Incompetent

Part 3 – An Analysis and Critique of Clark H. Pinnock's 'Pneumatological Inclusivism' **137**

Chapter 6 - The Covenant, Christ, and Confession of Christ: A Redemptive-Historical Critique of Pinnock's Inclusivism **139**
Introduction: Aims and Objectives 139
Setting Out an Evangelical Theological Framework 140

    Sola Scriptura
    Towards an Evangelical Framework
    A Redemptive-Historical Approach
    An Outline for Chapters 6-9
Introduction: Approaching the Biblical Texts on these Issues 142
Dispensationalism 153
Covenant Theology 155
    Outlining Covenant Theology
    Defining Covenant
    Unity and Diversity within the Covenantal Structure
        CONTINUITY
        DISCONTINUITY
Pre-Messianic Believers and the Nature of Saving Faith: Issues of
Unity/Continuity 163
    The Israelite Confession of Christ
    The Analogy with 'Holy Pagans'
        THE SALVATION OF ANTE-DILUVIAN SAINTS
        THE USE OF YAHWEH ('LORD') IN THE PATRIARCHAL
        NARRATIVES
        THE NOAHIC COVENANT
        GENEALOGICAL SUCCESSION AND THE CONCEPTS OF
        'PRUNING' AND 'INGRAFTING'
        THE CASE OF MELCHIZEDEK IN GEN. 14:18-24
Post-Messianic Believers and the Nature of Saving Faith: Issues of
Discontinuity/Diversity 189
    The Preparatory Nature of the Old Testament
    No Other Name?
    The Case of Cornelius in Acts 10
Conclusion 197

Chapter 7 - Universality, Particularity and Incarnation: A Christological Critique of Pinnock's Inclusivism 199
Universality, Particularity and the Person of Christ 199
    Problems Concerning Christ's 'Derivative Uniqueness'
    Problems Concerning 'Spirit-enriched' Christology and Kenosis
Universality, Particularity and the Work of Christ 206
    Understanding Pinnock's Model of Atonement

Contents   xiii

    Understanding the 'Penal Substitution' Model of Atonement
    The Spirit's Role in Atonement as Regards the Unevangelised
Summary 224

Chapter 8 - The Spirit and Son in the Accomplishment and Application of Redemption: A (Binitarian) Trinitarian Critique of Clark Pinnock's Inclusivism 226
Spirit and Son in the *Historia Salutis* and the Accomplishment of Redemption 226
    Three Fundamental Trinitarian Truths: Homoousios, Autotheos, and Perichoresis
    The Filioque
    A Functional Economy: The Glorification of the Son by the Spirit
        WORD AND SPIRIT IN CREATION
        WORD AND SPIRIT IN RE-CREATION
    The Spirit and Word Agraphon and Engraphon: Pinnock's Inclusivism and Sola Scriptura
Spirit and Word in the *Ordo Salutis* and the Application of Redemption 256
    Salvation as Union with Christ
    The Centrality of Justification by Faith
Summary 263

Chapter 9 - The Universality Axiom and the 'Problem' of the Unevangelised 265
The Universality of Sin 266
    Two Different Harmatologies
    Defining 'good'
    An Optimism in Salvation?
Understanding the Wider Context 274
    Relating Universal Accessibility to a Universal Salvific Will and a Universal Atonement
    The Case for an Effective and Particular Atonement
    The 'Problem' of the Unevangelised?
Concluding Remarks 286
    Assessing Pinnock's Inclusivism

Towards an Evangelical 'Theology of Religions: Tasks and Topics Ahead
The Universality of Mission

Appendix 1 - Evangelical Responses to the Fate of the Unevangelised 294
Introduction 294
John Sanders' Typology of Evangelical Responses on the Fate of the Unevangelised 297
A Typology and Description of Evangelical Responses on the Fate of the Unevangelised 304

Positions of Particular Accessibility
THEME: REFORMED 'HARD' RESTRICTIVISM
VARIATION I: REFORMED 'AGNOSTIC' RESTRICTIVISM
VARIATION II: REFORMED 'SOFT' RESTRICTIVISM
VARIATION III: JOHN PIPER'S REFORMED *PREPARATIO EVANGELICA*
THE IMPLICIT-FAITH VIEW: 'SOFT' INCLUSIVISM/ 'OPAQUE' EXCLUSIVISM
EXCURSUS: PARTICULARITY AND PARSIMONY IN SALVATION
NON-REFORMED RESTRICTIVISM

Positions of Universal Accessibility
POST-MORTEM EVANGELISM / DIVINE PERSEVERANCE
MIDDLE KNOWLEDGE
MIDDLE KNOWLEDGE AND UNIVERSALLY ACCESSIBLE SALVATION
MIDDLE KNOWLEDGE AND THE FAIRNESS OF GOD
POSITIVE AGNOSTICISM

Bibliography 332

Index 351

FOREWORD

In the twenty first century, the question of whether there is salvation outside Christianity and Christianity's relation to other religions is a major issue pressing all Christian communities, both in traditionally 'Christian countries' and in what used to be traditionally the 'mission fields'. The debate in mainstream Roman Catholic and Protestant circles has been rapidly developing since the Second World War and it is precisely in this vigorous current of discussion that Strange's work is to be located. What is quite is remarkable about Strange's book is the careful argument that undermines some of the major assumptions that have fuelled the debate such as (using Karl Rahner and John Hick's conundrum): how could a loving and good God in effect consign the majority of humankind to perdition in so much as most people in history have not been Christians? While both Roman Catholic and some Protestant theologians have tended to give degrees of qualified affirmation to the possibility of salvation outside Christianity, Strange cuts across the growing consensus, asking very difficult and pertinent questions that will unsettle the entire field as it has so often been cast. Strange turns the table, and asks, how is it that anyone is saved given the depths of human sin? – and rather than questioning the ways of God in their particularity, he calls for Christian celebration for the particularity of the gift of unmerited salvation.

Strange enters the fray via his own evangelical Calvinist tradition. In this book, readers will find one of the best comprehensive surveys of the debate within Protestant evangelical circles. Strange is a reliable and fair narrator and will help entry-level students engage with the complexities and varieties of question. Besides locating the many contours on this map, Strange focuses on a major volcanic eruption within evangelical circles: the work of Clark Pinnock. Those who are familiar with Pinnock's wide range writings will gain greatly from Strange's careful outlining of Pinnock, and his equally careful and in depth critique of Pinnock. In his critique, Strange helpfully throws light on many questions and assumptions within the wider debate, so that even those not interested in Pinnock as such, will learn from following Strange's devastating critique.

This critique allows Strange to eventually move into his own original creative contribution to the debate – and readers will, I am sure, eagerly anticipate further work from the pen of such a fine young theological mind. As a Roman Catholic theologian, I found myself in serious disagreement with much of Strange's final position. But I must also gratefully acknowledge that Strange's work has caused me more self-questioning and challenge on these questions than many a well established writer. The reader will be privileged to engage with a fresh young theologian who is one of the sharpest and most able of his generation writing in England. The fields of theology of religions and the exploration of salvation within dogmatic theology will be greatly enhanced by this book, and all those who continue to work in these fields, those in or out of sympathy with Strange, will have to respond to his argument before they continue in their own reflections on this vexing and monumentally important question.

Dr Gavin D'Costa
University of Bristol
Department of Theology and Religious Studies

ACKNOWLEDGMENTS

The Whitefield Institute for enabling me to get the whole thing started by financially supporting me in the first year of my study, but more importantly their constant prayer support and fellowship throughout my research. The British Acadamy for their financial support. Dr. Gavin D'Costa for being a wonderful supervisor and for his sympathetic fairness to my study and my confessional community. Professor Clark H. Pinnock for his willingness to talk to me and read portions of the study despite my severe criticisms of his theology. Dr. Chris Sinkinson for looking after me at the beginning. Ms Evelyn Cornell for all the books from King's College and especially for all the proof-reading. My Mum and Dad for their constant love, support and faith in me. The late Jean Bateson who first asked me about the fate of the unevangelised. Noah and Isaac, my two boys. My wife Elly who has supported me unswervingly over the last few years and who has put up with me and the rollercoasters that are research and life in general.

Finally, and in the words of King David:

> Give thanks to the Lord, call on his name;
> make known among the nations what he has done.
> Sing to him, sing praise to him;
> tell of all his wonderful acts.
> Glory in his holy name;
> let the hearts of those who seek the Lord rejoice.
> Look to the Lord and His Strength;
> seek his face always.
>
> (1 Chronicles 15:17-11)

Soli Deo gloria

PREFACE

Steering a safe course between the Scylla of particularity and the Charybidis of universality has long posed a Herculean challenge for the Christian theologian.[1] While there is evidence that this challenge is not recent in origin,[2] the phenomenon of 'empirical pluralism,' that is the seemingly incontrovertible 'fact' that in the post-Christian West we live in an age of ethnic and religious diversity, has brought an intense urgency, theological, philosophical, and emotional, to the challenge of mediating particularity and universality. The question of the 'unevangelised,' that is those people who have never heard of Christ through no apparent fault of their own, possibly highlights the challenge in its most acute form.

The focus of this study can be delineated as follows: through a detailed description, analysis and critique of a specific representative (Clark H. Pinnock) of a specific theological position (inclusivism), my primary aim, using Pinnock as a facilitative vehicle, is to examine a cluster of issues surrounding the question of the 'fate of the unevangelised,' of which 'inclusivism,' or more accurately Clark Pinnock's 'version' of inclusivism, is but one possible answer. This question itself must be contextualised as being subsumed under, and generated by, a more generalized area of systematics; the so-called 'theology of religions.' However, as I will demonstrate, the

---

[1] In Greek mythology, an infamous stretch of the Sicilian Sea contained two dangers that terrified sailors: the Scylla was a sea-monster, and Charybidis a whirlpool. Hercules had to steer a course through these straits when he brought back Geryon's herd.

[2] For example St. Augustine in a letter to Deogratias, quotes from the third century philosopher and critic Porphryry, "If Christ declares Himself to be the Way of salvation, the Grace and the Truth, and affirms that in Him alone, and only to souls believing in Him, is the way to return to God, what has become of men who lived in the many centuries before Christ came? ...What, then, has become of such an innumerable multitude of souls, who were in no wise blameworthy, seeing that He in whom alone saving faith can be exercised had not yet favoured men with His advent?" in *Nicene and Post-Nicene Fathers* Series 1, vol.1, ed. Philip Schaff (1866; reprint, Grand Rapids, 1974), p. 416. Quoted from John Sanders, *No Other Name: Can Only Christians be Saved?* (London, 1994), p. 11.

seemingly abstruse nature of this question does not imply a theological insignificance, for this question has necessary implications for many fundamental areas of systematics, most noticeably the doctrine of revelation, Christology and soteriology. With this in mind a second aim of this study is to highlight the organic nature of systematic theology and to analyse the question of the fate of the unevangelised not as an end in itself, but as a gateway to explore these other areas, for this question appears to be a nub where many lines of theology converge. All of this analysis will be focused within the boundaries of a particular theological community (evangelicalism) where the significance of the destiny of the unevangelised is particularly acute and where discussion of it generates some interesting tangential questions concerning the definition and nature of this community, questions which receive added potency and tension by the 'reputation' of certain evangelical theologians (e.g. Pinnock) who are at the forefront of the debate and who propose new ways of answering the question. I hope to bring out all these differing dynamics throughout the study.

PART 1
The Question of the Unevangelised in Recent Evangelical Theology

CHAPTER 1

Evangelicals and the Question of the Unevangelised: Establishing Working Definitions and Parameters of Study

In this opening chapter, I wish firstly to establish some parameters of study by proposing working definitions of several terms that I shall be using throughout the study, and secondly, outline the background of the question of the unevangelised in recent evangelical theology. This will provide the context for looking in detail at the inclusivist position of Clark H. Pinnock.

Evangelicalism and Three Strands of Evangelicalism

Towards a Working Definition

The theological community within which this study will be focused is the evangelical community, and so defining the parameters of this community would appear to be a necessary task. The problem of defining evangelicalism is a constant preoccupation of so-called 'evangelical' theologians. Carson notes: "Giving definition to evangelicalism is not only difficult, but is growing even more difficult as a wider and wider group of people apply the label to themselves... The term is exceedingly plastic and runs into many moulds shaped by local history."[1] Noll, Plantinga and Wells also comment somewhat polemically on the problem of definition: "...it is usual nowadays to find 'evangelical' used as a mute substantive that gains its voice only when coupled to another, and more clarifying, adjective... The concept *evangelical* has become so promiscuous, has enjoyed so many bedpersons, has been equally and unequally yoked so often, that its self-concept has broadened into that of a commune."[2]

---

[1] Donald A. Carson, *The Gagging of God. Christianity Confronts Pluralism* (Leicester, 1996), p. 444.
[2] Mark Noll, Cornelius Plantinga, Jr., David Wells, 'Evangelical Theology Today' in *Evangelical Review of Theology* 21/2 (Oct. 1997), p. 176.

The debate over defining evangelicalism is complex and cannot be entered into in detail here.³ Suffice it to say, different scholars employ various fields of study to make a definition: the doctrinal, historical, sociological, denominational, and others. Naturally the danger of reductionism is always inherent in defining a community in only one way. One of the more useful analyses is that of George Marsden who identifies three different but overlapping axes to define the phenomenon known as evangelicalism. The first axis is that of a conceptual unity which fits a certain definition. The second designates evangelicalism as a more 'organic movement' with common traditions and experiences. Thirdly, "within evangelicalism in these broader senses is a more narrow, consciously "evangelical" transdenominational community with complicated infrastructures of institutions and persons who identify with "evangelicalism."⁴ As this study is primarily interested in evangelical theology, the working definition of evangelicalism I propose to use is Marsden's first type which is that of a conceptual unity. As Anderson comments: "Only when one looks at evangelicalism from the perspective of conceptual unity (Marsden's first sphere), does a coherent basis for a theological structure to evangelicalism emerge. While the relation between evangelical theology and evangelicalism as a movement is an uneasy alliance, both need each other."⁵

---

³ For a more detailed look at the debate on definition see Carson, op. cit., pp. 444-461; Noll, Plantinga and Wells, op. cit., pp. 176-188; Mark A. Noll and David F. Wells, 'Introduction: Modern Evangelicalism' in ed. Mark A. Noll and David F. Wells, *Christian Faith and Practice in the Modern World: Theology from an Evangelical Point of View* (Grand Rapids, 1988), pp. 1-23; Klaas Runia, 'What is Evangelical Theology?' in *Evangelical Review of Theology* 21/4, April 1997, pp. 292-304; R. Albert Mohler, Jr. '"Evangelical": What's in a Name?' in ed. John H. Armstrong, *The Coming Evangelical Crisis* (Chicago, 1996), pp. 29-45; Alister E. McGrath, *Evangelicalism and the Future of Christianity* (London, 1994), pp. 9-80; idem *A Passion for Truth. The Intellectual Coherence of Evangelicalism* (Leicester, 1996), pp. 9-50; David Bebbington, *Evangelicalism in Modern Britain* (Grand Rapids, 1989), pp. 1-17; Millard J. Erickson, *The Evangelical Left. Encountering Postconservative Evangelical Theology* (Grand Rapids, 1997), pp. 11-33; George M. Marsden, *Evangelicalism and Modern America* (Grand Rapids, 1984); Derek J. Tidball, *Who are the Evangelicals? Tracing the Roots of Today's Movements* (London, 1994), pp. 11-14,19-24; Richard Turnbull, 'Evangelicalism: the State of the Scholarship and the Question of Identity' in *Anvil* 16/2 (1999), pp. 95-112.
⁴ Marsden, op. cit., p. ix.
⁵ Ray S. Anderson, 'Evangelical Theology' in ed. David F. Ford, *The Modern Theologians* Vol. 2 (Oxford, 1993), p. 133. I should note here the attempt of Tidball, op. cit., who illustrates the variety within evangelicalism by using the picture of a "Rubik's cube" which "allows us to make distinctions on a number of different dimensions and to create a variety of identikit pictures of evangelicals" (p. 20). His three dimensions are the Church (established, denominational, Pentecostal, new church, ethnic, separatist),

Although it is perhaps ultimately unsatisfactory, I wish to propose a working definition of evangelicalism and evangelical theology which if anything errs on the inclusive side.[6] Fundamentally I will define evangelicalism as a transdenominational community that is brought together by a number of family resemblances, both historical and theological. Adapting and developing the outline of Klaas Runia, I wish to note four layers of tradition whereby one can trace the main contours of evangelical theology.[7] Firstly, and a layer not mentioned by Runia, is that evangelical Christianity is historic orthodox Christianity. This may seem obvious, but it is worth noting that all evangelical theology adheres to the Ecumenical Creeds: The Apostles' Creed, the Nicene Creed, the Athanasian Creed and the Creed of Chalcedon.[8] Secondly, evangelical roots can be traced to the Reformation and the theology of the Reformers: "evangelicals like to speak of the *solas* of the Reformation: *sola fide, sola gratia, solus Christus* and *sola Scriptura*."[9] The third layer of tradition is the movement known variously as Pu-

---

Spirituality (Reformed, Holiness, Pentecostal, Renewal, Radical), and the World (introversionist, conversionist, thaumaturgical, reformist, transformationalist, adventist).

[6] Ideally I think I agree with Carson that: "'evangelical' and 'evangelicalism' are most useful when they are held to their etymology in the evangel, "the gospel [God] promised beforehand through his prophets in the Holy Scriptures regarding his Son" (Rom. 1:2-3), on the assumption that an 'evangel' is held with sincerity and firmness of heart. In this light, evangelicalism as a movement must be seen to be determined by its center, not by its outermost boundary-and even that center must, in the light of its own confession, constantly be held up to the examination of Scripture." Carson, op. cit., p. 448. A recent attempt to define the evangel has been attempted by a group of prominent evangelical scholars including D. A. Carson, David Neff, J. I. Packer and R. C. Sproul and entitled 'The Gospel of Jesus Christ: An Evangelical Celebration'. For a copy of this statement and the evangelicals who have endorsed it, see 'A Call to Evangelical Unity' in *Christianity Today* (June 14th, 1999), pp. 49-56.

[7] Klaas Runia, op. cit. Runia notes three layers of tradition whereas I feel it is necessary in this context to add a more primary layer. It should also be noted that as well as his three layers, Runia also mentions two twentieth century movements which he believes have deeply influenced certain areas of the evangelical community. The first is the reaction against liberal theology between 1910-1930 known as 'Fundamentalism,' and the second is the Pentecostal/Charismatic movement. See Runia, op. cit., p. 295. Noll and Wells, op. cit. pp. 2-4, outline a similar typology connecting *evangelical* to: 1) the Protestant Reformation; 2) Revivalism of the 18th century; 3) theological conservatism of whatever heritage; 4) a 'denomination' joined together through a network of evangelical theological seminaries in North America (e.g. Trinity Evangelical School, Gordon-Conwell, Regent College and Fuller), publications (e.g. *Christianity Today*), and evangelistic and social agencies (e.g., World Vision).

[8] These creeds can be found in Wayne Grudem, *Systematic Theology* (Grand Rapids, 1994), pp. 1168-1171; and Gerald Bray, *Creeds, Councils and Christ* (Fearn, 1997), pp. 212-216.

[9] Runia, op. cit., p. 294.

ritanism in the English speaking world, Pietism in the German speaking context, and *'Nadere Reformatie'* for the Dutch speaking. Finally, and most recently, contemporary evangelicalism can trace its roots back to the various revival movements of the 18th and 19th centuries, for example, the ministries of John Wesley, George Whitefield, and Jonathan Edwards to name but three.

Commenting on these layers of tradition, McGrath notes that it is important to appreciate that:

> while these...streams merge, as contributries, to form a single flux in modern evangelicalism, their mingling produces eddies and vortices. Like great rivers cascading at their point of juncture, their merger causes tension and disruption. The resulting flux is greater; yet it is also more disturbed, with a number of disagreements and debates featuring prominently within the evangelical heritage. This inherent theological and spiritual tension is supplemented by additional factors, including the cultural contexts in which evangelicalism finds itself.[10]

This last sentence of McGrath's is important in understanding the geographical and cultural parameters of the use of 'evangelical' in this study. McGrath notes that while evangelicalism's origins can be traced to "the later European Renaissance in France, Germany and Italy, it appears to have consolidated itself in England and North America."[11] McGrath puts this down to the rise of Puritanism which gained influence in England and North America in the seventeenth century and which merged the intellectual rigour of the Reformers with the experiential aspects of Pietism. He notes that as a result of this "evangelicalism emerged and developed primarily within an English-language context."[12] While realising that the evangelical movement is present all over the world, the focus of this study is primarily on the North American and British evangelical theological scene.[13]

---

[10] McGrath, *Evangelicalism and the Future of Christianity*, p. 17.
[11] Ibid.
[12] Ibid., p. 18.
[13] Noll and Wells, op. cit. speak of "an American-British-Confessional Coalition" (p. 7), which emerged from four parallel developments in the 1930's and 1940's: 1. The emergence from within American Fundamentalism of a group of thinkers like Harold John Ockenga, Edward John Carnell and Carl F. H. Henry, who "valued responsible education and an intellectually responsible expression of the faith"(p. 8); 2. Theological conservatives who never became fundamentalists; 3. The conversation and assimilation between American evangelicals and the Dutch Reformed Church who added "a heritage of serious academic work and experienced philosophical reasoning"(p. 9); 4. The emergence of British evangelicalism around the Inter-Varsity Fellowship and led by figures

Evangelicals and the Question of the Unevangelised 7

Within this historical context, and noting McGrath's comments concerning theological tensions within the movement, I would like to state six doctrinal convictions which make up the evangelical identity and which are referred to in some way in many of the doctrinal definitions of evangelicalism. Here I will quote McGrath's own formulation:

1. The supreme authority of Scripture as a source of knowledge of God, and a guide to Christian living.[14]
2. The majesty of Jesus Christ, both as incarnate God and Lord, and as the saviour of a sinful humanity.
3. The lordship of the Holy Spirit.
4. The need for personal conversion.
5. The priority of evangelism for both individual Christians and the church as a whole.
6. The importance of the Christian community for spiritual nourishment, fellowship and growth.[15]

I will be referring to the details of all of these convictions throughout the study.

---

such as Martyn Lloyd-Jones, F. F. Bruce, David Wenham and John Stott: "The British connection served also as a conduit for establishing relations between Americans and evangelicals further afield. British evangelicals reached out to confessional Protestants on the continent, to the Commonwealth, and to mission efforts in Africa and Asia. Through these connections American evangelicals were drawn into even wider orbits" (p. 10).

[14] I will be commenting on the place of Scripture in evangelical theology at the beginning of Part 3. It can be argued that evangelicalism can be solely defined regarding its position on the Bible. One example of this is brought out in the effort to establish a core definition of evangelicalism attempted by Carl Henry and Kenneth Kantzer at the 1989 conference on Evangelical Affirmations (the proceedings of which are published in eds. Carl F. H. Henry and Kenneth Kantzer, *Evangelical Affirmations* (Grand Rapids, 1990)). Mohler, op. cit., notes that Henry and Kantzer "produced three 'marks' of evangelical authenticity: 1. belief in the gospel as set forth in Scripture, 2. commitment to the basic doctrines of the Bible set forth in the Apostle's Creed and other historic confession, and 3. an acknowledgment of the Bible as the authoritative and final source of all doctrines" (p. 32f).

[15] McGrath, *Evangelicalism and the Future of Christianity*, p. 51. I do note with Turnball, op. cit., p. 101, that this set of tenets is theologically quite broad, and says nothing of the centrality of the cross nor emphases concepts such as justification and faith, traditionally seen to be evangelical shibboleths. However, and again noted by Turnball, these terms are used by McGrath when he gives a more detailed exposition of the tenets in pp. 54-80.

Three Strands of Evangelical Theology

Having broadly defined evangelicalism, I wish to specify three traditions within evangelicalism to which I will be frequently referring throughout the study. Again the debates over defining these strands are detailed and complex, and I am only dealing here with quite simple working definitions that will help to understand certain theological issues contained in this study. With this in mind, I believe it will be helpful if I define these traditions by highlighting two of the relevant areas over which these three positions disagree, namely issues of soteriology and providence.

THE REFORMED/CALVINIST TRADITION

By the Reformed/Calvinist[16] tradition, I am referring to those theologians who place themselves within the tradition represented by the Magisterial Reformers especially John Calvin and his followers.[17] Defining this strand is made somewhat easier by certain creedal affirmations that the majority of Reformed/Calvinist theologians adhere to depending on their denominational preference. The most important of these confessions are: the Thirty-Nine Articles (1571, Anglican); the Westminster Confession of Faith (1643-1646, Presbyterian); the so-called 'Three Forms of Unity' which

---

[16] It should be noted that for my basic definition, I am using Reformed and Calvinist as synonymous terms because I wish to include some traditions which, while not agreeing with the ecclesiology of the Reformers and Calvin (e.g. Baptists) still hold to the teaching of them in terms of the sovereignty of God and the so-called 'Five Points' (see below). I realise that there is a case to be made for distinguishing Reformed (which is linked strongly to a presbyterian form of government) from Calvinist (which is generally associated with those who believe in the 'five points').

[17] I should distinguish between what could be called 'classical' or 'paleo' Reformed theology and 'reformed' Reformed theology. Clark H. Pinnock brings out this distinction well in his response to Alister McGrath's particularism in eds. Dennis L. Okholm and Timothy R. Phillips, *More Than One Way? Four Views on Salvation in a Pluralistic World* (Grand Rapids, 1995). Commenting on McGrath's claim that his theology lies within the Reformed tradition, Pinnock questions whether McGrath is Reformed in a classical sense of the term: "Most Reformed believers in Europe, including McGrath, have accepted what was enshrined in the *Agreement of Leuenburg* (1973), which involved a drastic revision of Calvin's thought. It tossed out double predestination and spoke of God's election of humankind in Jesus Christ, as Barth does. In a nutshell, McGrath is Reformed like Hendrikus Berkhof or Vincent Brummer but not paleo-Reformed likes James I. Packer or R.C Sproul"(p. 191). In this study I will be using 'Reformed' in the 'palaeo' sense of the term although I am well aware that the term is used more broadly to refer to those theologians who interpret the Reformers through a 'Barthian' prism such as T. F. Torrance, Eberhard Jüngel, Wolfhart Pannenberg and Jürgen Moltmann. A good example of this type of Reformed theology can be found in a recent collection of essays eds. David Willis and Michael Welker and entitled, *Toward the Future of Reformed Theology* (Cambridge, 1999). On Karl Barth's relationship to evangelicalism in general see below p. 31f.

consist of the continental creeds (The Heidelberg Catechism (1563), The Belgic Confession (1561), and The Canons of Dordrecht (1618-1619)); the Augsburg Confession (1530, Lutheran); the New Hampshire Baptist Confession (1833, Baptist); and the Baptist Faith and Message (1925/1963).[18]

In terms of soteriology, the Reformed/Calvinist position is often summarised by the so-called 'five points of Calvinism' that are a summary of the Synod of Dort (1618). Packer summarises them as follows:

> (1) Fallen man in his natural state lacks all power to believe the gospel, just as he lacks all power to believe the law, despite all external inducements that may be extended to him. (2) God's election is a free, sovereign, unconditional choice of sinners, as sinners, to be redeemed by Christ, given faith and brought to glory. (3) The redeeming work of Christ had as its end and goal the salvation of the elect. (4) The Work of the Holy Spirit in bringing men to faith never fails to achieve its object. (5) Believers are kept in faith and grace by the unconquerable power of God till they come to glory. These five points are conveniently denoted by the mnemonic TULIP: Total Depravity, Unconditional Election, Limited Atonement, Irresistible grace, Preservation of the saints.[19]

What should be noted though, is that the Reformed/Calvinist tradition cannot be defined solely on these points of soteriology. The 'five points' must be seen as being a microcosm of a broader paradigm. As Packer notes:

> Calvinism is a whole world-view, stemming from a clear vision of God as the world's Maker and King. Calvinism is the consistent endeavour to acknowledge the Creator as the Lord, working all things after the counsel of his will... Calvinism is a unified philosophy of history which sees the whole diversity of processes and events that take place in God's world as no more, and no less, than the outworking of His great preordained plan for His creatures and His church. The five points assert no more than that God is sovereign in saving the individual, but Calvinism, as such, is concerned with the much broader assertion that He is sovereign everywhere.[20]

A development of the main tenets of the Reformed tradition will be brought

---

[18] The Thirty-Nine Articles, Westminster Confession, New Hampshire Baptist Confession, and Baptist Faith and Message, can be found in Grudem, op. cit., pp. 1171-1207. The Three Forms of Unity can be found in *The Three Forms of Unity* printed by the Mission Committee of the Protestant Reformed Churches in America, 1996.
[19] J.I. Packer, 'Introductory Essay' to John Owen's *The Death of Death in the Death of Christ* (Edinburgh, 1959), p. 4.
[20] Ibid., p. 5.

out as the study progresses.[21]

THE ARMINIAN TRADITION

Whereas Calvinism often refers to the theology of John Calvin, the same cannot be said of Arminianism that takes its name from James Arminius (1560-1609), an Amsterdam clergyman and pupil of Theodore Beza, Calvin's successor in Geneva, whose studies led him

> first from supralapsarianism to infralapsarianism and then to settle for a position like that of Melanchthon and Nicholas Hem(m)ingius, Lutheran professor of theology at Copenhagen and once Melanchthon's student - namely, conditional predestination of individuals based on a synergistic view of how, through grace, men have faith.[22]

'Arminianism' today tends to refer to a spectrum of positions that differ from Calvinism on issues of freedom, predestination and election. However it is worth briefly noting the historical roots of Arminianism. Packer writes:

> Historically, Arminianism has appeared as a reaction against the Calvinism of Beza and the Synod of Dort, affirming in the words of W.R. Bagnell, "conditional in opposition to absolute predestination, and general in opposition to particular redemption"... Arminianism was born in Holland

---

[21] For a recent collection of essays on Calvinism in general see eds. Thomas R. Schreiner and Bruce A. Ware, *The Grace of God, the Bondage of the Will. Biblical, Practical, Historical and Theological Perspectives on Calvinism* 2 Vols. (Grand Rapids, 1995); ed. John H. Armstrong, *The Coming Evangelical Crisis* (Chicago, 1996). For a basic exposition of Calvinism against other views see R. K. McGregor Wright, *No Place for Sovereignty. What's Wrong with Freewill Theism* (Downers Grove, 1996). Wayne Grudem's *Systematic Theology* (Grand Rapids, 1994) is written from a Calvinist perspective and is helpful for his bibliographies at the end of each chapter, which outline how major evangelical systematic theologies have dealt with each issue of doctrine. Those who would come under this Reformed/Calvinist category include, from a Baptist perspective: John Gill, *Complete Body of Practical Divinity* 2 Vols. (first published 1767-1770) (Grand Rapids, 1978); Carl F. Henry, *God, Revelation and Authority* 6 Vols. (Waco, 1976-1983); Millard Erickson, *Christian Theology* (Grand Rapids, 1985); Gordon Lewis/Bruce Demarest, *Integrative Theology* 3 Vols. (Grand Rapids, 1987-1994); from a Presbyterian perspective: John Calvin, *Institutes of the Christian Religion* 2 Vols. (Ed. McNeill. trans. Ford Lewis Battles. Philadelphia, 1960. Trans. from 1559 text); Jonathan Edwards, *The Works of Jonathan Edwards* 2 Vols. (Edinburgh, 1974. Reprint of 1834 edition); Charles Hodge, *Systematic Theology* 3 Vols. (Grand Rapids, 1970. First pub. 1871-1873); B.B. Warfield, *Biblical and Theological Studies* (Philadelphia, 1976); John Murray, *Collected Writings of John Murray* 4 Vols. (Carlisle, 1976-1982); Louis Berkhof, *Systematic Theology* (Grand Rapids, 1958).

[22] J.I. Packer, 'Arminianisms' in eds. Godfrey and Boyd, *Through Christ's Word: A Festschrift for P.E. Hughes* (New York, 1985), p. 128 n.10.

at the turn of the seventeenth century, and synodically condemned by the whole Reformed world at Dort in 1619. In England, an Arminian tradition of teaching lasted into, and right through, the eighteenth century. Arminianism was part of the Wesley family heritage, and John and Charles fought the Calvinists by prose and poetry throughout their evangelical ministry. The Arminian evangelical tradition has been maintained by Methodists and others up to the present day.[23]

In 1610 a group of Arminius' followers published a *Remonstrance* which has become known as the 'five points' of Arminianism and to which the Synod of Dort responded shortly afterwards in 1618. So for Arminians:

(1) Man is never so completely corrupted by sin that he cannot savingly believe the gospel when it is put before him, nor (2) is ever so completely controlled by God that he cannot reject it. (3) God's election of those who shall be saved is prompted by His foreseeing that they will of their own accord believe. (4) Christ's death did not ensure the salvation of anyone, for it did not secure the gift of faith to anyone (there is no such gift): what it did was rather create a possibility for everyone if they believe. (5) It rests with believers to keep themselves in a state of grace by keeping up their faith; those who fail here fall away and are lost.[24]

Again such views are but one small part of a wider theological perspective. In very broad terms, Arminians believe that human responsibility and accountability entail a 'libertarian' view of human freedom and that God cannot cause human decisions: "Therefore they conclude that God's providential involvement in or control of history must *not* include *every specific detail* of every event that happens, but that God instead simply *responds* to human choices and actions as they come about and does so in such a way that his purposes are ultimately accomplished in the world."[25] Again I will refer in more detail to Arminianism throughout the study especially in reference to Clark Pinnock.[26]

---

[23] J.I. Packer, 'Arminianisms,' p. 122,124. The quotation by W.R. Bagnell comes from *The Writings of Arminius* tr. James Nichols and W. R. Bagnell (Grand Rapids, 1956), I:iii.
[24] Packer, 'Introductory Essay,' p. 4.
[25] Grudem, op. cit., p. 338.
[26] Two recent collections of essays by evangelical 'Arminian' writers which promote Arminian theology over and against Calvinism are ed. Clark H. Pinnock, *Grace Unlimited* (Minneapolis, 1975); and ed. Clark H. Pinnock, *The Grace of God and the Will of Man. A Case for Arminianism* (Minneapolis, 1995). For an historical account of Arminianism (although from a critical perspective) see Packer, 'Introductory Essay,' pp. 1-25; 'Arminianisms,' pp. 121-148; Richard A. Muller, 'Grace, Election, and Contingent Choice: Arminius' Gambit and the Reformed Response' in eds. Schreiner and

POSTCONSERVATIVE EVANGELICAL THEOLOGY

This is a strand of evangelicalism that has received much attention in the last ten years. Postconservative evangelical theology is mentioned here because Clark Pinnock, whose position on the unevangelised will be focused on in this study, is arguably the most prominent advocate of this theology. We will be dealing with Pinnock's views in detail in subsequent chapters. However it may be helpful to briefly outline the genesis of this movement and list some characteristics of this position. To do this I refer to Millard Erickson in his recent book, *The Evangelical Left: Encountering Postconservative Evangelical Theology* (1997).[27]

Erickson traces the roots of postconservative evangelical theology back to the 1960's and the move to the theological left by evangelicals including Daniel P. Fuller, George Ladd and David Hubbard who started to question and redefine the notion of biblical inerrancy. This trend was confirmed by Richard Quebedeaux[28] and given more empirical evidence by James Davidson Hunter.[29] Erickson notes that it is only recently that the movement has become more defined and developed, the most prominent institution of the movement being Fuller Theological Seminary and the central figures being, Clark Pinnock, Bernard Ramm,[30] and Stanley Grenz.[31]

Ware, pp. 251-279. Again Grudem is helpful in his bibliographical lists. Those evangelicals who fall under the 'Arminian' category include: James Arminius, *The Writings of James Arminius* 3 Vols. (Grand Rapids, 1956); Jack Cottrell, *What the Bible says about God the Creator*, (Joplin, 1983); John Miley, *Systematic Theology* 2. Vols. (New York, 1892-94); Wiley H. Orton, *Christian Theology* 3 Vols. (Kansas City, 1940-43).

[27] (Grand Rapids, 1997).

[28] See Richard Quebedeaux, *The Young Evangelicals* (San Francisco, 1974); idem *The Worldly Evangelicals* (San Francisco, 1978).

[29] See James Davidson Hunter, *Evangelicalism: The Coming Generation* (Chicago, 1987). Hunter surveyed teachers and students at nine evangelical liberal arts colleges and seven evangelical seminaries.

[30] See Bernard Ramm, *After Fundamentalism: The Future of Evangelical Theology* (San Francisco, 1983). The inclusion of Ramm in this group of evangelicals opens up the debate over the relationship between Karl Barth and evangelicalism as Ramm's theology is strongly influenced by the theology of Barth. Erickson, op. cit., pp. 33-38 outlines the contours of Ramm's theological methodology and writes that Ramm noted three elements in Barth's theological programme: "1. He rejected the Neologians' criticism of historic Christian orthodoxy 2. He accepted the positive accomplishments of the Enlightenment. 3. He rewrote his Reformed theology in the light of the Enlightenment. Ramm says that...for those who believe that the Enlightenment has precipitated a crisis for evangelical theology, the best option available" (p. 37)." There has always been interest in Barth's theology from within evangelicalism although it is a matter of definition and debate as to whether Barth can be included in the evangelical camp. I have already stated that my own use of 'Reformed theology' would not include Barth in its definition. However from within postconservative evangelical theology there is definitely more of an openness to Barth's theology and neoorthodoxy in general especially concerning

Erickson notes the following characteristics of this theology:

1. Eagerness to engage in dialogue with nonevangelical theologians. Indeed, "they seek opportunities to converse with those whom conservative evangelicals would probably consider enemies."... 3. Broadening of the sources used in theology. This frequently includes an emphasis on "narrative shaped experience" rather than "propositional truths enshrined in doctrines." The sources may include, in addition to the Bible, Christian tradition, culture, and contemporary Christian experience... 6. An open view of God, in which God limits himself and enters into relationships of genuine response to humans, taking their pain and suffering into himself. God is a risk-taker, not one who controls everything so that nothing contrary to his desires can occur. 7. An acceptance, rather than a rejection, of the realm of nature. Nature, although fallen, is never abandoned by grace, which then pervades it. 8. A hope for a near universal salvation. 9. An emphasis in Christology on the humanity of Jesus. While retaining belief in the divinity of Christ, this is thought of in more relational than in substance and person categories. 10. A more synergistic understanding of salvation. These theologians are, overall, more Arminian than Calvinistic.[32]

---

matters of revelation. In *No Other Name? A Critical Survey of Christian Attitudes Toward the World Religions* (Maryknoll, 1985), the Roman Catholic theologian Paul Knitter, shows something of this ambiguous relationship between Barth and the evangelicals. Although he notes that Barth is not a classical evangelical and notes the opposition to his theology by evangelicals such as Carl Henry, Francis Schaeffer and Cornelius Van Til because of his use of biblical critical methods and his views on revelation, Knitter ends up using Barth as an "eloquent and sophisticated"(p. 80) advocate of his 'conservative evangelicals model' of the relationship between Christianity and other religions, and appears to legitimize this on the basis that there is a trend within evangelicalism towards a more sympathetic reading of Barth: "Today, ..Barth is being 'reinstated' among Evangelicals, 'Evangelicals now find their theological insights in those neoorthodox theologians...condemned so vehemently by their predecessors in the 1950's and 1960's' [Quebedeaux, *The Worldly Evangelicals*, p. 100]. Evangelicals, both conservative and ecumenical, are, "finding real potency and balance in the neoorthodox approach to critical issues" [Richard J. Coleman, *Issues of Theological Warfare: Evangelicals and Liberals* (Grand Rapids, 1980), pp. 4-5].
[31] See Stanley J. Grenz, *Revisioning Evangelical Theology: A Fresh Agenda for the 21st Century* (Downers Grove, 1993).
[32] Erickson, op. cit., p. 29f. Erickson adapts this list from Roger Olsen's paper, 'Postconservative Evangelicals Greet the Postmodern Age' in *Christian Century* 112.15 (May 3, 1995), p. 480. Erickson's book appears to be the only detailed analysis of postconservative evangelical theology. For an analysis of this movement from within its boundaries see Clark H. Pinnock, 'Evangelical Theologians Facing the Future: An Ancient and a Future Paradigm' in *Wesleyan Theological Journal* 33 (Fall, 1998), pp. 7-28; Robert Brow, 'Evangelical Megashift' in *Christianity Today* Feb. 19th, 1990, pp. 12-17. Inter-

As I will demonstrate, some of the above characteristics are very relevant in my discussion of the unevangelised.

Defining 'Pluralism' and the 'Theology of Religions'

The focus of this study is a specific doctrinal area concerning the 'fate of the unevangelised.' I believe this question to be a subset of a wider area of systematics known as the 'theology of religions,' for while this study does not directly deal with evangelical responses to other religions, the fate of the unevangelised is a question generated by and inextricably linked to religious pluralism and questions such pluralism raise for Christian theologians. When I refer to the term 'religious pluralism,' I do not only mean 'empirical pluralism,' the seemingly incontrovertible 'fact' that in the West we live in an age of ethnic and religious diversity, but more controversially, the notion of 'cherished' pluralism: "It has become commonplace to say that we live in a pluralist society - not merely a society which is in fact plural in a variety of cultures, religions and lifestyles which it embraces, but pluralism in the sense that this plurality is celebrated as things to be approved and cherished."[33] To this I could also add the idea of 'philosophical pluralism.' For a basic definition of this term I refer to a remark made by Harold Netland to Don Carson in Carson's book, *The Gagging of God. Christianity Confronts Pluralism* (1996):

> Netland...says that 'philosophical pluralism' is, an umbrella term that embraces a variety of contemporary positions that are united in their opposition to the idea that we can know objective truth: e.g., ontological non-realism (there is no objective reality 'out there' to be experienced and known); constructivism ('reality' is merely a construct of social experiences); perspectivism (we can never know reality as it is; the most we can know is reality from our perspective); various forms of relativism (truth, rationality norms, and the like are all relative to, or internal to, particular contexts.)[34]

---

estingly in his brief outline of evangelical theology, Paul Knitter in *No Other Name*, op. cit. subdivides evangelicalism into three groups: fundamentalists; conservative evangelicals; and ecumenical or new evangelicals. This third group corresponds to what I have called postconservative evangelical theology. Knitter notes that new evangelical concerns revolve around three areas: 1. ecumenical co-operation; 2. a move away from the insistence on the absolute inerrency of the Bible; 3. that "political involvement and efforts of all the oppressed is part of living the gospel" (p. 75).

[33] Lesslie Newbigin, *The Gospel in a Pluralist Society* (Grand Rapids, 1989), p. 1.

[34] Don Carson, *The Gagging of God: Christianity Confronts Pluralism* (Leicester, 1996) p. 19 n.19.

The pressure of pluralism has generated a number of questions for the Christian theologians pertaining to the relationship between Christianity and other religions: "Why are there so many diverse religions? If Christianity is the true religion, why is it that so much of the world rejects it in favour of diametrically opposing religious traditions? Is it theologically and morally acceptable to maintain that one religion is uniquely true and that the others are at best incomplete or even false?"[35]

It has become standard to note three main approaches by which theologians have responded to religious pluralism: exclusivism, inclusivism and pluralism.[36] For the moment and in order to contextualise the focus of this study, I wish to persist with these three paradigms while noting that there appears to be a degree of fluidity between these three 'types' of response.[37] Rather than seeing these three positions as being tightly defined, it is perhaps more helpful to see them as three points of reference on a wide spectrum. Such an approach takes into account many positions that appear to fall in between the three defined points. Netland provides a concise summary of these reference points:

> *Exclusivism* maintains that the central claims of Christianity are true, and that where the claims of Christianity conflict with those of other religions the latter are to be rejected as false. Christian exclusivists also characteristically hold that Jesus Christ is the unique incarnation of God, the only Lord and Saviour. Salvation is not to be found in the structures of other religious traditions. *Inclusivism*...holds that [although] God has revealed himself definitively in Jesus Christ and that Jesus is somehow central to God's provision of salvation for humankind, they are willing to allow that God's salvation is available through non-Christian religions... *Pluralism* parts company with both exclusivism and inclusivism by rejecting the

---

[35] Harold A. Netland, *Dissonant Voices. Religious Pluralism and the Question of Truth* (Leicester, 1991), p. 8.

[36] See for example Gavin D'Costa, *Theology and Religious Pluralism* (Oxford, 1986); Gavin D'Costa, Theology of Religions' in ed. David F. Ford, *The Modern Theologians* Vol. 2. (Oxford, 1989), pp. 274-290; Netland, op. cit., pp. 8-35; Alister McGrath, *Christian Theology. An Introduction* (Oxford, 1994), pp. 458-464; eds. D. Okholm and T. Phillips *More Than One Way? Four Views on Salvation in a Pluralistic World* (Grand Rapids, 1995); Ronald H. Nash, *Is Jesus the Only Savior?* (Grand Rapids, 1994).

[37] I should note that this threefold typology has recently been challenged by Gavin D'Costa, one of the theologians who championed the typology in the first place. In his book *The Meeting of Religions and the Trinity* (New York, 2000), D'Costa argues, I think persuasively, that rather than representing separate paradigms, both pluralism and inclusivism are actually just different forms of exclusivism. For example, commenting on several manifestations of pluralism D'Costa wants "to suggest that 'pluralism' represents a tradition-specific approach that bears all the same features as exclusivism-except that it is western liberal modernity's exclusivism" (p. 22).

premise that God has revealed himself in any unique or definitive sense in Jesus Christ. To the contrary, God is said to be actively revealing himself in all religious traditions... Christian faith is merely one of many equally legitimate human responses to the same divine reality.[38]

Having defined some key themes to which I will be referring throughout the study, we are now in a position to look at the area of the 'theology of religions' within evangelicalism and more specifically to introduce the central focus of our attention: the question of the unevangelised.

The Question of the Unevangelised in Recent Evangelical Theology

Introduction: The Impact of Religious Pluralism on Evangelical Theology

Over nineteen centuries of Christian Missionary activity hinged on this belief alone: that those who did not believe in the salvific capabilities of Jesus Christ had no hope of receiving eternal life. It followed that the unevangelised...would also be damned to an eternity in hell.[39]

The rise of religious pluralism as an empirical fact, and as a philosophical and hermeneutical ideology to be encouraged in twentieth century Western culture, has challenged evangelical theology in two distinct yet related ways. Firstly, from the outside and in the context of the discipline called 'theology of religions,' evangelical theologians have had to re-assert their own statement of the exclusivist paradigm that affirms the *solus Christus* in terms of truth, revelation and salvation. This has uniformly entailed a repudiation of pluralism and more specifically the work of its most prominent proponent, John Hick.[40] However in this re-assertion of exclusivism, evan-

---

[38] Netland, op. cit., p. 9f.
[39] James Hunter, *Evangelicalism. The Coming Generation.* (Chicago, 1987), p. 34.
[40] See for example, Netland, op. cit., pp. 157-162,198-233; Ronald H. Nash, *Is Jesus the Only Savior?* (Grand Rapids, 1994), pp. 29-92; R. Douglas Geivett, 'John Hick's Approach to Religious Pluralism' in *Proceedings of the Wheaton Theology Conference. The Challenge of Religious Pluralism: An Evangelical Analysis and Response* (Wheaton, 1992), pp. 39-55; Carson, op. cit., pp. 319-325; Norman Anderson, *Christianity and the World Religions.* (Leicester, 1984); Alister McGrath, *A Passion for Truth. The Intellectual Coherence of Evangelicalism,* pp. 220-240; E. David Cook, 'Truth, Mystery and Justice. Hick and Christianity's Uniqueness' in eds. Andrew D. Clarke and Bruce W. Winter, *One God, One Lord. Christianity in a World of Religious Pluralism.* (Grand Rapids, 1992), pp. 237-246; eds. Dennis L. Okholm and Timothy R. Phillips, *More Than One Way? Four Views on Salvation in a Pluralistic World.* (Grand Rapids, 1995), pp. 60-81; Chris Sinkinson, *John Hick: An Introduction to his Theology* (Leicester, 1995).

gelicals have had to face squarely certain perennial questions asked and criticisms made by both inclusivists and pluralists, questions which earlier had formed the grounds for their own paradigmatic shifts out of exclusivism. Unable to satisfactorily deal with these problems and the tensions they created, the only answer for the inclusivist and pluralist had been to question the very foundations on which these problems arose: the *solus Christus*.

It appears though, that almost independently, evangelicals have come across these same problems without them being raised from outside the community. Evangelicals have seen themselves that the implications of such questions threaten the whole meaning and interpretation of the *solus Christus*. Ironically, therefore, in light of these new nuanced exclusivist responses to pluralism,[41] the very argument evangelicals have put forward, have generated some difficult questions and tensions for themselves that are only now being tackled.

It is not only the academic evangelical community that is struggling with these questions, for within the broader evangelical community, these same questions have been constantly asked. Although they have always been implicitly present, it is only now in the context of the pluralistic society in which evangelicals live that they have become explicit questions and a major stumbling block. The phenomenon known as 'globalisation' that recognises and acknowledges other cultures outside our own, can bring us instantly into contact with adherents from other religions who appear to be holy and devout people. This means that instead of abstract theorising, an emotional element has been added which influences theologians' doctrinal formulations no matter how much they say it has not.

Analysing the results of the evangelical Academy Project that interviewed evangelical students from sixteen institutions of higher learning from 1982-1985, James Hunter found that many evangelicals were giving certain qualifications to questions of soteriology that had not previously existed. He notes that "the introductions of these qualifications tempers the purity of the theological exclusivism traditionally held."[42]

Secondly, and as alluded to in the Introduction, evangelicalism as a movement appears to be displaying elements of pluralism in its identity and definition. Carson tellingly calls his chapter which deals with a definition of evangelicalism: 'Fraying, Fragmented, Frustrated: The Changing Face of Western Evangelicalism.'[43] Hunter comments that in moving out of the sociocultural ghetto which evangelicals had fashioned for themselves in order to maintain an orthodoxy, now it is the whole concept of orthodoxy which is threatened: "Certainly, in its move out of the ghetto, it has risked the un-

---

[41] See for example Netland, op. cit. and Carson, op. cit.
[42] Hunter, op. cit., p. 38.
[43] See Carson, op. cit., p. 443.

intentional contamination by the very reality it has tried to keep out. That this process has begun, there is little doubt."[44] For some, this fragmentation is appearing in the formulation of the *solus Christus*.

What then are these questions which have been asked from the *outside of* evangelicals and which have been generated from *within by* evangelicals? I would say that in the context of exclusivism, three questions are constantly generated. The first concerns the 'fate of the lost,' and is mainly concerned with the nature and duration of hell.[45] The second concerns an evangelical 'theology of religions': how should evangelicals assess and judge other religions in light of the *solus Christus*?[46] The third concerns the fate of those who have never heard the gospel through no fault of their own: the 'unevangelised.'

Some points need to be borne in mind when looking at these questions. Firstly, and as already stated, at both an academic and popular level these are not new questions nor are they wholly new responses. Rather they have always been seen as 'difficult' questions that were hard to ask, calling for answers that were hard to accept. However they were not seen to threaten the very nature of Christian exclusivity because what was meant by the *solus Christus* was clearly understood. It could be said that these questions remained on the periphery of theological thinking. It is only recently that these questions have been moved to the forefront of debate. Their importance has been increased as they are all inextricably linked to any evangelical formulation of exclusivism. Indeed the way one answers these questions has become a mark of orthodoxy. For example, it is significant that Carson in *The Gagging of God*[47] devotes a whole chapter to the question of the nature and duration of hell. While the question is important in itself, Carson uses this chapter to say something about the nature of contemporary evangelicalism. He writes that this particular chapter "picks up one particular doctrinal area, final punishment - an area in which current developments within evangelicalism doubtless reflect greater diversity, greater pluralism if you will, than anything the movement experienced half a century ago."[48] In Carson's treatment of the debate surrounding the nature of hell, he remarks on those who have moved from the traditional position of hell being

---

[44] Ibid., p. 48.

[45] For a good survey of the issues involved see Carson, op. cit., Ch. 13; ed. Nigel M. de S. Cameron, *Universalism and the Doctrine of Hell. Papers Presented at the Fourth Edinburgh Conference on Christian Dogmatics, 1991* (Carlisle, 1992); ed. William Crockett, *Four Views on Hell* (Grand Rapids, 1992).

[46] For a good representative survey of positions see Netland, op. cit.; eds. William Crockett and James Sigountos *Through No Fault Of Their Own* (Grand Rapids, 1992); and eds. Andrew Clarke and Bruce Winter *One God, One Lord. Christianity in a World of Religious Pluralism* (Grand Rapids, 1992).

[47] op. cit.

[48] Carson, op. cit., p. 443.

a conscious and everlasting punishment: "Despite the sincerity of their motives, one wonders more than a little to what extent the growing popularity of various forms of annihilationism and conditional immortality are a reflection of this age of pluralism."[49] Such discussions have highlighted the widening of the evangelical theological spectrum from so-called 'liberal,' 'progressive,' or 'neo-' evangelicalism right through to 'conservative' and even 'fundamentalist' positions.[50]

Secondly, all three questions mentioned impinge on each other and stating a position on one necessarily points the way forward to answering the others. For example, in discussing the unevangelised, it is impossible not to comment on other religions, as this is usually the cultural and religious context in which the unevangelised person lives. Similarly, when discussing the justice of God in view of the unevangelised, one must reflect on the nature of judgement and hell. Despite this inter-linking, all three questions can be dealt with separately and all have their distinct features. Most commonly the question of other religions has served as a gateway to discuss the unevangelised that has been dealt with as a secondary issue.[51] However more recently the question of the unevangelised is being treated in its own right (see below). This study will concentrate specifically on the question of the unevangelised and will analyse all other questions (e.g. the 'theology of religions') through this particular one. What will quickly become apparent is that any position one takes on the unevangelised will colour the response one gives to the other questions. So 'inclusivism' (an important position concerning the unevangelised), does not remain a narrow position on the unevangelised but becomes a position on other religions in general. Bearing in mind all this preliminary discussion, it is to the question of the unevangelised that I now turn.

The Question of the Unevangelised: the Current State of the Issue

A THEOLOGICAL TENSION

The question that will be the focus of this study can be expressed as follows:
If one believes that: 1) God has revealed Himself uniquely and definitively in the incarnation; 2) that Jesus Christ is Lord and Saviour and that there is no other name by which one can be saved, Jesus Christ being the only

---

[49] Carson, op.cit., p. 536. 'Annihilationism' and 'conditional immortality' are two different arguments concerning the nature and duration of hell.
[50] I briefly mentioned the plethora of 'evangelicalisms' in my introduction to Part 1, pp. 3-7. The paper which shows the great diversity of evangelicalism is Noll, Plantinga, Jr. and Wells, 'Evangelical Theology Today' in *Evangelical Review of Theology* 21.2 April, 1997, pp. 176-188.
[51] See e.g. Netland, op. cit., pp. 262-277; Anderson, op. cit., pp. 145-155.

way of salvation, and; 3) that explicit faith in Jesus Christ is necessary for this salvation, then what is the eschatological destiny of those who live and die having had no opportunity to hear about the life and work of Jesus? Are they by definition 'without hope of salvation'?

The acute nature of this question threatens Christian exclusivity for it epitomises for many the 'soteriological problem of evil':

> ...how could a just and loving God consign to eternal torment those whose *providential* circumstances prevented them from hearing? If there were an exegetically based position that would relieve this (perceived) problem of eternal injustice, it would be of great help in theodicy among both Christians and unbelieving critics.[52]

Again this is put in more emotive terms, "Can we really accept that the God revealed in Christ, a loving father of 'generous, unlimited Divine love,' has denied so many millions the means to salvation - through no fault of their own?"[53] However, if we say that those who never hear the gospel can be saved apart from hearing about Christ, then this must in some way qualify or even compromise any definition of the *solus Christus*. There appears to be no way to mediate this tension without moving into the inclusivist or pluralist paradigms.

This question is not a piece of irrelevant theological abstraction or obscurantism, for when we speak of 'those who have never heard the Gospel,' we are not simply debating a hypothetical indigenous tribe, but a substantial group of human beings. It can be argued that we are talking about the majority of the human race. Such a large number of people would seem to demand a response as regards the possibility of their salvation and an explanation of what such a response means for our understanding of God, His love, justice and mercy. As John Hick says:

> We say as Christians that God is the God of universal love, but we also say, traditionally that the only way to salvation is the Christian way. And yet we know, when we stop to think about it, the large majority of the human race who have lived and died up to this present moment have lived either before Christ or outside the borders of Christendom. Can we then accept the conclusion that the God of love who seeks to save all mankind has nevertheless ordained that men must be saved in such a way that only a small minority can in fact receive this salvation? It is the weight of this

---

[52] W. Gary Phillips, 'Evangelicals and Pluralism: Current Options' in *Proceedings of the Wheaton Theological Conference Vol. 1* (Wheaton, 1992), p. 175.
[53] Gavin D'Costa, *Theology and Religious Pluralism* (Oxford, 1986), p. 67.

moral contradiction that has driven Christian thinkers in modern times to explore other ways of understanding the human religious situation.[54]

It is well documented that for Hick and other like-minded individuals, the tension in affirming both an axiom of particularity and one of universality has been unbearable, and that they have found release only in the rejection of the very foundation of particularity, the *solus Christus*. Hence his call for a "Copernican revolution"[55]; a paradigmatic shift out of "Ptolomaic" exclusivism with its imperialistic notions of Christocentricity, and into pluralism with its inclusive affirmation of "Reality-centricism."[56] Somewhat polemically it could be said that for Hick and those like him, the Herculean task has proved too difficult and that faced with twin perils, the dangers of the whirlpool have been less fearsome than that of the monster.
Moving this question of the unevangelised into the evangelical community only heightens the tension. Before I concern myself with issues of systematic theology, though, it seems appropriate to briefly sketch the recent history of this issue in the evangelical community. This will provide the context in which the debate revolves.

AN ORTHODOX EVANGELICAL 'POSITION'?

There seems to be no consensus on what represents an 'historic orthodox' evangelical position on the question of the unevangelised. Lindsell has written, "evangelicals have insisted and continue to insist that in order for men to be converted they must hear of Jesus Christ and respond to his invitation in faith. If they die without the knowledge of faith, they perish."[57] However, this historical interpretation has been recently challenged by John Sanders in his book *No Other Name*[58] which remains the most comprehensive survey of the question of the unevangelised within evangelicalism. He refers back to James Hunter's survey[59] and notes the views of a cross-section of evangelical students. One third of those interviewed held the view that "the only hope for heaven is through personal faith in Jesus Christ *except for those who have not had an opportunity to hear of Jesus Christ.*"[60] Sanders does not see this as a recent trend but argues that there has always been a

---

54 John Hick, *God and the Universe of Faiths* (Oxford, 1993), p. 122f.
55 Ibid., pp. 120-133.
56 For a brief description and critique of Hick's position and its relation to other positions in the theology of religions see Gavin D'Costa, 'Theology of Religions' in ed. David F. Ford, *The Modern Theologians* Vol. II (Oxford, 1993), pp. 274-291.
57 Harold Lindsell, 'Missionary Imperatives: A Conservative Evangelical Exposition,' in ed. Norman Horner *Protestant Crosscurrents in Mission* (Nashville, 1968), p. 57, quoted from Sanders, op. cit., p. 21.
58 op. cit.
59 Referred to above, p. 12.
60 Hunter, op. cit. p. 35.

plethora of views when discussing those people who have never heard of Christ, stretching back through Christian history. He argues that the reason for the perceived unanimity on the subject is due to political circumstances and distinguishes between those who have hope for the unevangelised, "progressive evangelicals," and those who do not, "establishment evangelicals."[61] He states: "Establishment evangelicals have traditionally had a greater degree of control over evangelical publishing and educational institutions than have progressive evangelicals and concerns about reactions to their views...have kept many progressive leaders from speaking their mind on the issue."[62]

Harold Netland concurs with this view, but from a slightly different perspective. He comments that there is a perception from those outside the evangelical community that evangelicals are agreed on all matters of doctrine and that there is no ambiguity or uncertainty on any issue. This, Netland disagrees with: "It is becoming increasingly evident that one issue on which there is considerable disagreement among evangelicals is the question of the fate of those who never hear the gospel of Jesus Christ. And there are strong indications that this will be an even more controversial and divisive issue among evangelicals in the years to come."[63]

How is one to interpret these conflicting views on the state of the question within evangelicalism? That there is a debate, highlights I think the ongoing problems of defining evangelicalism. Are we to define the 'historic' position by looking to the 'establishment' or to the 'progressive camp'? It would be fair to say that Sanders does not represent the 'establishment' and his use of the term is slightly emotive, he being firmly part of the 'progressive camp.' There may be strategic reasons why Sanders wishes to produce evidence that there has been no firm consensus on the fate of the unevangelised, for he wishes to see his own position (he holds to a form of inclusivism) as not being so unorthodox as it might at first sound. Having said this, the evidence he gleans from Hunter's survey is quite persuasive. Sanders is perhaps nearer to the mark when he says:

> Even though the belief that no unevangelised person can be saved is not in the doctrinal statements of many evangelical institutions, it can be safely said that it is for many an unwritten article of faith, and those who disagree with it can expect the same response as if they denied the deity of Jesus Christ. Nevertheless, I have found that many laypeople have hopes for the unevangelised but do not know how to articulate and defend

---

[61] John Sanders, *No Other Name*, p. 22.
[62] Ibid.
[63] Netland, op. cit., p. 264.

such hopes. Within evangelicalism, the wider hope is more popular in the pews than in the pulpits.[64]

We will return to another aspect of this quotation shortly. Certainly there does seem to have been an implicitly held belief amongst the majority of evangelicals that the unevangelised are not saved, but this has not been a dogmatic assertion because until recently it has not been explicitly discussed and has remained in the background of debate. While some of the major evangelical missionary statements have stressed the exclusivity of Christ, the majority have avoided the question of those who never hear about him.[65]

However one interprets this historical data, there can be no denying that the last ten years have seen a dramatic increase in the amount of literature

---

[64] Sanders, *No Other Name*, p. 23.

[65] One example of this is the way major evangelical conventions have dealt with the question. Both the Keele statement of 1967 and the Lausanne Conference of 1974 speak in strongly exclusivist language but do not explicitly deal with the fate of those who never hear the Gospel. Whether this can be assumed or not remains a matter of interpretation. For example paragraph 3 of the Lausanne Covenant (1974) reads: "We affirm that there is only one Saviour and only one Gospel, ...There is no other name by which we must be saved ...Yet those who reject Christ repudiate the joy of salvation and condemn themselves to eternal separation from God." However, as Okholm and Phillips, op. cit., note, after hearing Harold Lindsell's address on the subject that offered no hope as the salvation of the unevangelised, "the universalism study group remained unconvinced. They responded with questions regarding infants, the mentally retarded, and 'those who have never heard of Christ in their lifetime.' They diplomatically concluded, 'We feel that some of these questions are covered under...this report.' J.D. Douglas, ed., *Let the Earth Hear His Voice: International Congress on World Evangelism, Lausanne, Switzerland* (Minneapolis: World Wide Publications, 1975), 1206-15 (p. 22 n.29). The Congress statement of Keele (1967) states, "A persistent and deliberate rejection of Jesus Christ condemns men to hell" (I.11). Again this statement does not mention those who have never had the opportunity to accept or reject Christ. See David Edwards and John Stott, *Essentials* (London, 1988), p. 320. There are two statements that are more explicit on the subject. The 'Frankfurt Declaration' (1970) was produced by Peter Beyerhaus and approved by a number of German Evangelicals. It reads: "we therefore oppose the false teaching...that Christ himself is anonymously so evident in world religions, historical changes and revolutions that man can encounter him and find salvation in him without the direct news of the Gospel... The adherents to the nonchristian religions and world views can receive this salvation only through participation in faith" quoted from Sanders, *No Other Name*, p. 49. Similarly one of the messages delivered in Chicago at the 1960 Congress on World Mission stated: "In the years since the war, more than one billion souls have passed into eternity and more than half of these went to the torment of hell fire without even hearing about Jesus Christ, who he was, or why He died on the cross of Calvary" in *Facing the Task Unfinished: Messages Delivered at the Congress of World Mission, Chicago, Ill., 1960* ed. J. O. Percy (Grand Rapids, 1961), p. 9, quoted from John Hick, op. cit., p. 121.

published on this topic. The issue is subject to much discussion at evangelical conferences and a new vocabulary has been developed to describe the positions evangelicals can take on the question. Most importantly, a number of articles and books have been written, all of which deal with the subject to a greater or lesser extent and which have had wide circulation in the evangelical community.[66] The issues raised by them are still being discussed in all areas of the community and in this respect the territory feels new and unexplored for evangelicals. What should be noted is that this whole debate appears to be centred around the evangelical community in North America. Certainly the main figures in the debate either come from North America or teach in North American evangelical seminaries.[67] This is not to say that non-American evangelicals have had nothing to contribute to the debate, but that the lead appears to have been taken from the academic scene in North America. Again this is a statement as to the definition and nature of evangelicalism more than anything else.[68]

---

[66] Some of the more important treatments of the issue are: John Sanders, 'Is Belief in Christ Necessary for Salvation?' in *Evangelical Quarterly* 60 (1988), pp. 241-259; John Sanders, *No Other Name. Can Only Christians Be Saved?* (London, 1994); John Sanders, 'Evangelical Responses to Salvation Outside the Church' in *Christian Scholars Review* 24/1 (1994), pp. 45-58; Clark H. Pinnock, *A Wideness in God's Mercy. The Finality of Jesus Christ in a World of Religions* (Grand Rapids, 1992); eds. William Crockett and James Sigountos *Through No Fault of Their Own ? The Fate of Those Who have Never Heard* (Grand Rapids, 1991); eds. Andrew Clarke and Bruce Winter, *One God, One Lord. Christianity in a World of Religious Pluralism* (Grand Rapids, 1992); *Proceedings of the Wheaton Theological Conference. The Challenge of Religious Pluralism: An Evangelical Analysis and Response*, (Wheaton, 1992); ed. John Sanders, *What About Those Who Have Never Heard? Three Views on the Destiny of the Unevangelised.* (Downers Grove, 1995); Ramesh P. Richard, *The Population of Heaven. A Biblical Response to the Inclusivist Position on Who Will be Saved* (Chicago, 1994); Millard Erickson, 'The Destiny of the Unevangelised' in *Bibliotheca Sacra* published in 3 parts: Pt.1. Vol. 152 (Jan.-Mar. 1995), pp. 3-15; Pt. 2 Vol. 152 (Ap.-Jun. 1995), pp. 113-144; Pt. 3. Vol. 152 (Jul.-Sep. 1995), pp. 259-272.

[67] Sanders teaches at Oak Hills College, Minnesota, Pinnock at McMaster Divinity College, Ontario. The conferences where the question has been discussed have all been in America e.g. The Wheaton Theological Conference 1992, The Evangelical Theological Society which discussed the question at its Annual meetings in 1989, 90 and 91; The Evangelical Affirmations Conference held at Trinity Evangelical College in 1989.

[68] The book edited by Clarke and Winter, op. cit. is a contribution by British evangelicals and originates from a Tyndale Fellowship Conference held in Cambridge 1991. For other British contributions see Hywel R. Jones, *Only One Way. Do You Have to Believe in Christ to be Saved?* (Kent, 1996); Norman Anderson, *Christianity and World Religions: The Challenge of Pluralism* (Downers Grove, 1984); Alister McGrath, *A Passion for Truth. The Intellectual Coherence of Evangelicalism* (Leicester, 1996), pp. 201-240; 'A Particularist View: A Post-Enlightenment Approach' in eds. Okholm and Phillips, *More Than One Way?*, pp. 149-181. For an Indian evangelical response see Ivan Sat-

The Organic Nature of Doctrine

Having briefly shown the question's recent history in evangelicalism, I now wish to return to the reasons why this particular question has become an issue of great debate to evangelicals. The tension caused by the 'soteriological problem of evil' has already been mentioned above. For evangelicals who stress biblical authority, this tension is more acute because it represents a biblical tension founded on two axioms. Firstly, evangelicals wish to maintain Jesus as the Only Saviour (e.g.. Heb. 1:1-3; Jn. 14:9; Acts. 4:12, Jn. 14:6) but secondly they also have to take seriously biblical passages which emphasise the scope of salvation, "God our Saviour, who desires all men to be saved and to come to a knowledge of the truth," (1Tim. 2:4). Both these axioms have been interpreted to justify what are perceived to be the extremes, on the one hand what John Sanders calls "restrictivism," (Christ can *only* be known through explicit preaching of the gospel in this life: therefore the unevangelised are not saved),[69] and on the other hand classical universalism (*all* will eventually be saved through Christ). Indeed one of the main reasons why the topic has surfaced and is being debated, is because theologians like John Sanders and Clark Pinnock see these two extremes as unsatisfactory biblically, theologically and emotionally, and so seek new ways to relieve the tension while still upholding the two biblical axioms

Another reason for evangelical interest in this issue is the implications it has for missions, a fundamental tenet of the evangelical movement and one of the key beliefs noted in the previous chapter. Although modern missiolology is a much debated discipline in terms of its definition, aims and objectives,[70] it would be fair to say that traditionally the motivation for mission has been the conviction that, "all must be reached with the good news of the gospel, because all are lost and are under God's condemnation for their sins."[71] Therefore, any position that posits the idea that salvation can come about other than through the missionary, is seen as a serious threat to

---

yavrata, 'God has not left Himself without a Witness.' in *AETEI Journal* (5th Dec. 1992), pp. 2-5.

[69] Sanders, *No Other Name*, p 37.

[70] See Netland op. cit., Ch. 8; Pinnock, op. cit., pp. 176-180; John Piper, *Let the Nations Be Glad: The Supremacy of God in Missions* (Leicester, 1993), pp. 7-71; Ken Gnanakan, *Kingdom Concerns: A Theology of Mission Today* (Leicester, 1989).

[71] Milliard Erickson, 'The Fate of those who never Hear' in *Bibliotheca Sacra* 152 (Jan-March 1995), p.3-15. On the importance of mission to evangelicalism see J. Herbert Kane, *Understanding Christian Missions* (Grand Rapids, 1988); Alister McGrath, *Evangelicalism and the Future of Christianity* (London, 1994), pp. 70-73; Netland, op. cit., pp. 278-314; Nash, op. cit., pp. 165-169. David Bebbington in his book, *Evangelicalism in Modern Britain* (Grand Rapids, 1992), pp. 2-3, lists "conversionism" as being one of the four distinguishing features of evangelicalism.

missionary activity.[72] Pinnock sees the dilemma: "It pits access against urgency. If we say there is equal access to salvation for all, including the unevangelised, we will be charged with eliminating the urgency of mission. But if we preserve the urgency, people will protest that this means millions will go to hell without any chance to avoid it."[73] Both these issues of biblical tension and missionary activity are important reasons why debate on this issue has been so fierce within evangelicalism in recent years. However, I think they are only examples of a wider issue which is the real reason fuelling the discussion on the unevangelised.

This wider issue concerns the organic nature of doctrine. Erickson expounds this idea: "Doctrine is organic, so that the position taken on one doctrine influences conclusions in other areas as well. Even when this is not done, and a doctrinal scheme is internally inconsistent, sooner or later the logic of the matter prevails, producing a modification in other beliefs."[74] From the perspective of the discipline of 'systematic' theology, this may seem an obvious statement to make, but is worth special consideration in this debate. The issue of the unevangelised in itself may seem to be a minor doctrinal issue, but in formulating a position, the theologian has need to refer to more fundamental doctrines. In this case, these more basic issues form the core of evangelical doctrine and identity. Therefore, the answer one may reach on the unevangelised is in some ways less important than *how* the answer has been reached. Any position one comes to is founded on certain issues of soteriology including the nature and extent of saving faith, the nature of revelation and the doctrines of grace. In turn, these doctrines are founded on the certain understandings of the nature of God, most importantly the long disputed tension revolving around the sovereignty of God and human responsibility. Underlying all this, are issues concerning biblical authority and hermeneutics. As I shall demonstrate, evangelicals who disagree on the issue of the unevangelised are more than likely to disagree on these other more fundamental doctrines as well.

It is for this reason then, that the question surrounding the unevangelised has become so controversial in recent evangelical theology. It has become the gateway to discuss older and more basic doctrinal issues that form the 'fundamentals of the faith,' and this is where I feel the real debate and disagreement takes place. It is on the issue of the organic nature of doctrine that I wish to return to the point made by John Sanders where he appears to take a critical stance towards evangelicals who deem those holding to 'wider hope' views on the unevangelised as being 'heretical' despite the fact they hold to all the orthodox tenets of the faith. Sanders notes:

---

[72] See, for example, John K. Barrett, 'Does Inclusivist Theology Undermine Evangelism' in *Evangelical Quarterly* 70:3 (1998), pp. 219-245.
[73] Pinnock, op. cit., p 150.
[74] Erickson, op. cit., p. 4.

The reason for this, as George Marsden astutely observes, is that evangelicals have no creeds or ecclesiastical courts to settle disputes, and so "theological minutiae" - the doctrine of the rapture, for example - are called upon to play that role" (*Reforming Fundamentalism* [Grand Rapids, 1988], p. 153). In the process, it becomes increasingly difficult to distinguish the truly fundamental doctrines from the peripheral. The topic of the salvation of the unevangelised is certainly one area in evangelical theology where the peripherals are often confused with the truly fundamental.[75]

While I agree that there is a need to discern the fundamental from the peripheral, I also believe that if doctrine is to be a coherent system, then believing in one doctrine implies another and so on. As I stated in the introduction, one of the aims of this study is to demonstrate that if one is to be consistent, there are strong and necessary theological links between one's position on the unevangelised and other so-called 'fundamental areas' of doctrine; the positions of Sanders and Pinnock being prime examples of this. In this respect, and on closer inspection, I do not believe the question of the unevangelised to be a matter of "theological minutiae." It may well be true, as Sanders notes, that many laypeople have hopes for the unevangelised. However while not wanting to be condescending to 'laypeople,' whoever they might be, could it not be argued that they might have hopes about the unevangelised because they have thought about the issue of the unevangelised in an isolated way and have not made the systematic doctrinal connections? Such people might well revise their stance *if* it were proved that to hold to a certain belief on the unevangelised compromised, for example, the *solus Christus*. Surely one of the main tasks of a professional theologian is to highlight the connectedness of doctrine. Article 1.6 of the Westminster Confession of Faith famously states, "The whole counsel of God concerning all things necessary for his own glory, man's salvation, faith and life, is either expressly set down in Scripture, or by good and necessary consequence may be deduced from Scripture." As the Bible appears somewhat opaque concerning a group of people called the 'unevangelised,' one of the aims of this study is trying to discern whether a position on the salvation of the unevangelised can be established by good and necessary consequence.[76]

---

[75] Sanders, *No Other Name*, p. 23 n.25.
[76] To be fair to Sanders, he does make the point I have just made. In ed. Sanders, *What About Those Who Have Never Heard?*, he writes, "What *is* significant for determining one's position on the unevangelised is one's particular view of the nature of God, ...the nature of the church, the significance of physical death, the value of God's

Evangelical Parameters of Study on the Question of the Unevangelised

Earlier in this chapter, I stated that I was taking quite an inclusive working definition of evangelicalism but one not so inclusive as to make the term 'evangelical theology' so elastic as to be meaningless. Whilst I agree that opposite ends of this evangelical spectrum I have delineated build theological frameworks which are sharply in disagreement with one another, I would maintain that even these frameworks are still constructed within certain parameters which make them 'evangelical' over and against 'Protestant Liberal,' 'post-liberal,' Roman Catholic or Eastern Orthodox traditions. In view of the debate on the unevangelised, I would like to note five theological criteria that form the parameters within which all the positions are located.[77] Here I am expanding on Sanders' introduction in *What About Those Who Have Never Heard?*,[78] where he notes that the positions on the unevangelised mentioned in his book are all marked by certain characteristics. He lists three characteristics, I have expanded the list to five.[79]

Firstly, all those taking positions on the unevangelised, affirm the *solus Christus*: Jesus Christ as the ontological basis of salvation both in particularity and finality. Sanders states:

> The term 'finality' refers to the unsurpassibility and normativity of both the work (e.g. atonement) and the revelation of Jesus. The term 'particularity' refers to the fact that the salvation provided by God is available *only* through Jesus. Jesus as the Son of God, is the highest, clearest, and absolutely normative expression of the character of God. Furthermore Jesus is *the* Savior. There are no others.[80]

Another word that could be used is that Jesus is the 'constitutive' mediator of salvation. The Roman Catholic theologian J. Peter Schineller defines this as follows: "To say that Jesus is the constitutive mediator of salvation is to say that he is not only normative but the indispensable one. Without him there would be no salvation. He is the efficient cause or the condition apart from which there would be no saving grace in the world..."constitutive," therefore, means that without this historical incarnation, life, death and res-

---

revelation in creation, the nature of saving faith, the means of grace, and what is the best method for doing theology"(p.17) These are hardly matters of "minutiae."

[77] I outline these positions in Appendix 1, pp. 294-331.
[78] op. cit., p.15.
[79] Of course a large part of the debate revolves around whether certain positions conform to these specifically evangelical parameters, or whether they move so far away from these moorings that they can no longer be called 'evangelical' at all. This notwithstanding, I think that all those taking positions on the unevangelised would *claim* that they were still tethered to these basic areas.
[80] Sanders, *No Other Name*, p. 26.

urrection, no person would be saved."[81] This belief is not negotiable for evangelicals although, as we shall see, the outworking of such a belief can be construed very differently and may prompt one to reconsider what one means by terms such as 'particularity' and 'finality.'

Secondly, all those taking positions on the unevangelised, claim to base their arguments on the biblical narrative and view the Bible as the ultimate authority concerning any matter of doctrine: *sola Scriptura*. Although this criterion will be elaborated in the introduction to Part 3, I will make a few observations here. As I have already indicated, the Bible does not explicitly refer to any people or group called 'the unevangelised' and so all evangelicals rely on a cumulative case for coming to a conclusion on the subject. Phillips notes a word of caution on this method, "When Scripture is not explicit, then putative implicit speculations which have such broad ranging implications should be approached with great caution."[82] However in spite of this caution, all the positions claim to be more 'biblical' than the others in terms of their exegesis and hermeneutical method. What is clear is that the way a biblical passage is interpreted and used depends on the broader theological framework being employed. As we shall see, key passages of Scripture are interpreted very differently by the various theologians because of the very different frameworks being employed.[83] Whatever theological frameworks are employed, all serious evangelical scholars believe that "genuine appeal to the authority of Scripture does not consist in merely citing a list of verses and then concluding that one's position has been proved."[84] Any person involved in a sensitive reading of the biblical narrative will realise the importance of contextual horizons.[85] This will involve using the 'analogy of faith': using Scripture to interpret Scripture and see-

---

[81] J. Peter Schineller, 'Christ and the Church: A Spectrum of Views' in *Theological Studies* 37 (1976), p. 553.

[82] Gary Phillips, 'Evangelicals and Pluralism: Current Options' in *Proceedings of the Wheaton Theological Conference*, p. 187.

[83] One example of this is the way the word 'all' is interpreted in a passage such as 1Tim. 2:4: 'God our Saviour who desires all men to be saved and to come to the knowledge of the truth.' As I shall show, the interpretation of this verse depends on and is itself evidence of, whether one holds to the doctrine of unlimited atonement (God desires to save all men) or limited atonement (God desires to save only the elect). For a more detailed analysis of this issue see Ch. 9.

[84] Sanders, *No Other Name*, p. 33.

[85] Like Sanders I agree that "evangelicals need to become more cognizant of their own interpretative "horizon" in handling the biblical text." *No Other Name*, p. 32 n.38. On the issue of hermeneutics, pluralism and authority, see Carson, op. cit., pp. 57-193; ed. Moisés Silva, *Foundations of Contemporary Interpretation* (Leicester, 1996); Richard Lints, *The Fabric of Theology: A Prolegomenon to Evangelical Theology* (Grand Rapids, 1993), pp. 191-310; Grant R. Osbourne, *The Hermeneutical Spiral: A Comprehensive Introduction to Biblical Interpretation* (Downers Grove, 1991).

ing every passage in its canonical context. Of course whether or not this is done by the various positions is to pre-empt our discussion and to validate one position over another.

Thirdly all these evangelicals[86] agree that an 'act of faith' is necessary for appropriating salvation in a person's life: *sola fide*. To define 'faith' here in terms of its content and object would again be to pre-empt the discussion, as this is a matter of debate concerning the unevangelised. However it can be said that any evangelical view of faith would deny that it is a simple bare propositionalism but contains the traditional threefold distinction of, *notitia* - knowledge by our minds; *assensus* - the assent of our wills; and *fiducia* - the trust of our hearts.[87] This holistic view affects the entire person and instigates a change in the person's being and life. The role of this 'act of faith' is important because it ties all the theologians to their Reformation Protestant heritage centred around Luther and Calvin.

Fourthly, all those taking positions see themselves as having an historical precedent that helps give validation to their arguments. The work of Sanders here has been especially valuable in this respect, for he remains the only evangelical theologian to give comprehensive historical bibliographies for all the positions pertaining to the unevangelised.[88] Sanders sees the historical side of this debate as important for two reasons, "First, it corrects the historical amnesia whereby we often discredit one another's views as being either "new" or "old," depending on our biases... Second, it shows that Christians have never reached a consensus on this important but difficult subject."[89] Although this study is concerned with 'recent' evangelical theology and is more of an exercise in systematic theology than historical theology, at times it will have recourse to refer to the particular history of a position in the light of the Church.

Fifthly, all deny classical 'universalism,' either in its Augustinian form, which emphasises God's sovereign love and God's election of all man-

---

[86] Except the position which uses 'middle knowledge' to answer the question of the unevangelised, although it could be said that potentially faith plays a role in the salvation of the individual. For a discussion on this 'middle knowledge' position see Appendix 1, pp. 325-329.

[87] I have adapted these distinctions from Fackre's response to Sanders in ed. Sanders, *Four Views*, p. 57 by removing the object of faith which Fackre insists must be Christ. As I will outline, certain positions on the unevangelised believe that 'God' can be the object of faith.

[88] See Sanders, *No Other Name*, pp. 20-25 and the historical bibliographies at the end of each chapter. Sanders divides these bibliographies into three sections: 1. Early Church through to the Eighteenth Century; 2. The Nineteenth Century; 3. The Twentieth Century. The only other book length treatment on the destiny of the unevangelised is J. Oswald Sanders, *What of the Unevangelised?* (Crowborough, 1966).

[89] Sanders, *Four Views*, p. 15.

kind,[90] or the non-Augustinian form which emphasises God's infinite patience, giving people (even in hell) infinite chances to turn back to God.[91] Although there will be reference made to the universalist argument as it is relevant to the unevangelised, it is mentioned here as a point which unites in opposition all the diverse evangelical positions, simply because I do not believe that 'universalism' can be a credible option for evangelicals of whatever background. The reason for this is methodological rather than theological, for although classical universalism, "meets the test of evangelical orthodoxy to the extent that it characterises sin as rebellion against God, asserts that grace is necessary for salvation and holds Jesus as the highest expression of that grace,"[92] any serious evangelical theologian whose ultimate authority is Scripture, cannot ignore the clear passages which refer to the reality of judgement and hell and the prophetic element which declares that some will never believe and repent.[93] To hold a high view of Scripture and then attempt to interpret these passages in such a way as to embrace universalism would require an extraordinary hermeneutic and I know of no published evangelical who holds to the doctrine of universalism. As I shall demonstrate, even those evangelicals who are very optimistic about the numbers of people who will be eventually saved still do not believe in universalism; for it is not a matter of degree to move from the belief that the majority of humanity will be saved to a belief that all will be saved, but a matter of kind, for it raises serious questions concerning biblical methodology.[94]

Perhaps it would be appropriate here to mention the Reformed 'quasi-universalism' of Karl Barth.[95] I have already noted the uneasy relationship

---

[90] Sanders calls this a 'deterministic universalism' and lists Schleiermacher (1768-1834) as being its leading defender. See Schleiermacher, *The Christian Faith* 2 Vols. (New York, 1963), 2:539-60, 720-722.

[91] Sanders calls these 'freewill' universalists because God does not override the human decision to accept Christ. There are many advocates of this position, one example being J.A.T. Robinson in his book *In the End God* (London, 1950). See also Sanders, *No Other Name*, op cit., pp. 104-106; Trevor Hart, 'Universalism: Two Distinct Types' in ed. Nigel M. de S. Cameron, *Universalism and the Doctrine of Hell*, pp. 15-35.

[92] Sanders, *No Other Name*, p. 106.

[93] This cannot be the place to go into detail in criticising the universalist position. Over the last ten years there have been a great many evangelical works that do this adequately. See for example, ed de Cameron, *Universalism and the Doctrine of Hell* (Edinburgh, 1991); ed. Crockett and Sigountos, *Through No Fault of their Own*, Chs. 1,3,5,12,13,15; Sanders, *No Other Name*, Ch. 3.

[94] See Pinnock, op. cit., pp. 155,156; Sanders, *No Other Name*, Ch.3.

[95] For Barth's views on universalism see Karl Barth, *Church Dogmatics* 4 Vols. (Edinburgh, 1936-1969), 2/2: pp. 145-181;4/3: pp. 461-478. See also John Colwell, 'The Contemporaneity of the Divine Decision: Reflections on Barth's Denial of 'Universalism' in ed. de Cameron, *Universalism and the Doctrine of Hell*, pp. 139-161.

between Barth and evangelicalism. In Barth's theology, all people have been elected in Jesus Christ, the Elected One and all are reconciled although they may not be aware of it. Despite this, Barth recognises the possibility of unbelief, although "for Barth, the possibility that some might finally be condemned does not rest on their perverse freedom to reject what God has provided but on *God's* freedom."[96] Barth never holds to a dogmatic universalism, for this would impinge on God's sovereignty. However his views on election and on the 'triumph of grace' strongly point towards an eschatological universalism where no one will resist God's overwhelming grace. Even an evangelical like Donald Bloesch who relies heavily on Barth in his formulation of the doctrine of election, cannot accept the quasi-universalistic implications of Barth's position:

> We also uphold a universalism of hope in which no person is given up as lost, in which even the most depraved can be reclaimed by sovereign grace; yet at the same time we cannot close our eyes to the biblical testimony that only some will persevere to the end, that some will finally be cut off from the promises of the Kingdom.[97]

Again I return to the methodological issues surrounding any doctrine of universalism or quasi-universalism that strongly 'hopes' that all will be saved. To believe this goes against too much biblical evidence to the contrary.

Towards a Working Definition of the Unevangelised and Inclusivism

The purpose of the above sections has been to sketch the background to the question of the unevangelised within evangelicalism before concentrating on one particular response, that of Clark Pinnock. Before I start this analysis I wish to finish this preparatory chapter by defining two crucial terms that will help to understand the context of this study.

Delineating 'the Unevangelised'

So far this study has been using phrases such as the 'unevangelised,' or 'those who have never heard the Gospel through no fault of their own,' without defining what groups are meant when using such terms. Other terms that have been used in the relevant literature are 'the invincibly igno-

---

[96] Carson, op. cit., p. 143.
[97] Donald Bloesch, *Essentials of Evangelical Theology Vol. 1* (New York, 1978), pp. 166-169. For other evangelicals who show a Barthian influence see Bernard Ramm, *After Fundamentalism: The Future of Evangelical Theology* (New York, 1983); and Richard Quebedeaux, *The Worldly Evangelicals* (New York, 1978), p. 152.

rant,'[98] the 'unreached' or more pejoratively the 'heathen' and the 'pagan.'[99]

Let us take our definition of 'evangelism' from the Lausanne Covenant (1974), "..evangelism is itself the proclamation of the historical biblical Christ as Saviour and Lord, with a view to persuading people to come to him personally and so be reconciled to God."[100] At its most basic, the Greek *euangelizomai* means to bring or announce the *euangelion*. Traditionally, the way this has been understood to be achieved, is primarily through the human messenger speaking/preaching, and the recipient of the message hearing and responding. This is what is meant by *fides ex auditu* (faith by hearing). Therefore on this definition, it would appear that the *un*evangelised refers to anyone who has not heard or responded to the gospel because it has not been presented to them.

In the discussion on the unevangelised, this definition has referred to four different categories of people:

1. Those since the time of Christ, who have lived and died without receiving the gospel *ex auditu*. This may be because they have lived in remote geographical regions where the gospel has never been preached.

2. Those who lived prior to the coming of Christ and so before the formulation known as 'the gospel.' This includes both Jew and Gentile from the time of Adam to the birth of Christ.

3. Those who are in hearing range of the gospel and are able to hear the gospel in the 'biological' sense of the word 'hearing' but are unable to understand the words that are being spoken. This group is seen to be children who die in infancy, those who have special needs and are considered to be

---

[98] For example, Gavin D'Costa, 'Theology of Religions' in ed. David F. Ford, *The Modern Theologians* Vol. 2 (Oxford, 1989), p. 275. This appears to be the Roman Catholic term for the unevangelised.

[99] For an example of a theologian who uses both of these latter terms see Carl Henry, 'Is it Fair' in ed. William Crockett and James Sigountos, *Through No Fault of Their Own?* (Grand Rapids, 1992), p. 245f. As Henry points out the term 'heathen' [and 'pagan' for that matter] has multiple meanings. For him it refers to "those who have never heard the good news that God offers sinful humanity divine forgiveness on the ground of the substitutionary death of Jesus Christ." (p. 246); See also Lorraine Boettner, *The Reformed Doctrine of Predestination* (Grand Rapids, 1954), p. 117.

[100] ed. J. D. Douglas *Let the Earth Hear His Voice: International Conference on World Evangelisation, Lausanne, Switzerland* (Minneapolis, 1975), p. 4. quoted in Harold Netland, *Dissonant Voices* (Leicester, 1991), p. 280.

unable mentally to understand the gospel message, and those who have been presented 'historically' with the Gospel, but not existentially.[101]

4. Those who have not been presented with a full and adequate presentation of the Gospel and have received only a perverted or incomplete gospel. Sanders defines these people as, "those who have been driven away from Christ not by the gospel, but by poor testimony or lifestyle of professing Christians. Our bigotry and greed...may prevent others from genuinely perceiving God's grace."[102] This group could also include those who live in a society (like our own) where Christianity is known and practised, but who still never come into contact with the gospel message and remain ignorant of Christianity. It is conceded that only God knows who has heard a full and adequate presentation of the gospel.

In the discussion on the possibility of the salvation of the unevangelised, different positions vary on which of the four groups they include in their definition. So for example, inclusivists (who hold that the unevangelised can be saved), accuse restrictivists (who maintain that salvation can only come through *fides ex auditu*) of inconsistency when they maintain that infants can be saved but not adults, "if God's salvific will encompasses babies and the mentally incompetent who die unevangelised, why should his saving will not also include all those who have never heard of Christ?"[103] We should be aware of the ways theologians define 'the unevangelised.' For some theologians, an important part of their argument rests on linking all these groups together as one and using analogy to demonstrate a particular argument.[104] Others see distinct differences between the groups that leads them to conclude that God deals with them in a different manner. In this latter case, the way the groups are distinguished is through showing how some groups are more 'accountable' than others, or that some groups come under different 'covenants' and so are dealt with in a different manner.

Although this is not the place to judge which view is correct (this will become clearer later on), many of the theologians who are involved in the debate, use the phrase 'unevangelised' without clearly delineating the referent. When this is done, without reference to a community, it almost always refers to the first and (to a qualified extent) fourth groups I defined, that are

---

[101] For example missionaries who have taken the Gospel to an unreached people and have proceeded to preach the Gospel in the missionaries' own language. Technically they have preached the Gospel but of course no-one has understood it.

[102] John Sanders, *No Other Name?*, p. 15 n.2.

[103] Ronald Nash, *Is Jesus the Only Savior* (Grand Rapids, 1994), p. 135.

[104] For example inclusivists who draw an analogy between premessianic salvation and those people after Christ who are classed as being 'informationally premessianic.' See Ch. 5 for a detailed exposition of this view.

those who are in a position to *potentially* both hear and comprehend the gospel, but *actually* never hear it.[105]

In order to encompass all evangelical positions on the unevangelised I will deal with the four different classifications of people and their relationships to one another as the study progresses, and define the 'unevangelised' simply as: *any person in history who has lived and died without hearing and understanding the Gospel of Jesus Christ from a human messenger.*[106]

Defining Inclusivism

The focus of this study, is the 'inclusivism' of Clark H. Pinnock. In Appendix 1, I outline a particular typology for describing the various positions evangelicals have taken regarding the possibility of salvation among the unevangelised, and then describe these positions. The purpose of my typology is to give an indication as to some of the wider doctrinal issues involved in coming to a particular position on the question of the unevangelised. As such this typology is not concerned exclusively with the fate of the unevangelised but how this question fits into the whole area of soteriology. I argue that all evangelical positions on the unevangelised comprise a number of beliefs selected from six categories:

---

[105] I have purposely not referred to the spiritual state of these people groups because the various positions view the condition of these people differently. Indeed positions like Carl Henry's Reformed 'hard' restrictivism (as described in Appendix 1, pp. 382-386) question whether the term 'unreached' can be applied to any person and consequently whether there is a class of people who are 'unevangelised,' Carl Henry, 'Is it Fair?' in ed. William Crockett and James Sigountos, *Through No Fault of Their Own?* (Grand Rapids, 1991), pp. 245-255. On this same line of thinking, any evangelical position which stresses God's total sovereignty in election and calling would appear to have difficulty with the fourth group we defined, for what does a 'full and adequate' presentation of the gospel mean if salvation is totally an act of grace which does not ultimately depend on the person who presents the message? However these same evangelicals believe in the responsibility of the hearer to accept the message and still agree with biblical passages which stress increased and diminished levels of responsibility. The Reformed position with regard to the unevangelised, will be discussed in greater detail later in the study.

[106] Such a broad definition allows positions like Henry's to be included, for while a position like Henry's may question whether any person is ever unreached by God's revelation and therefore can ever be *un*evangelised, he would concede that many have not encountered the gospel through the means of a human proclamation.

Divine Salvific Will	EVANGELICAL PRESUPPOSITION: THE FINALITY PARTICULARITY and SALVIFIC NECESSITY OF JESUS CHRIST
B1: Particular	
B2: Universal	
Divine Salvific Provision	
B3: Particular	
B4: Universal	
Salvific Hope	
B5: Heilspessimismus	
B6: Heiloptimismus	

SALVIFIC ACCESSIBILITY
B7: PARTICULAR
B8: UNIVERSAL

SALVIFIC MEANS	
B9: Christ Epistemologically Necessary Means: Special Revelation	**B10**: Christ Not Epistemologically Necessary Means: Special and General Revelation

SALVIFIC ESCHATOLOGICAL OPPORTUNITY	
B11: Determined by Acceptance / Rejection of Christ in this life	**B12**: Not Necessarily Based on Acceptance / Rejection of Christ in this life

Given that all evangelical theologians affirm the finality, particularity and salvific necessity of Christ, in this typology I distinguish two main theological groupings, (which themselves are generated prior presuppositions): those who believe that salvation is universally accessible in terms of a universal opportunity, and those who believe that salvation is only accessible to a particular group of people. I then make a number of further distinctions concerning the means of salvation, the eschatological opportunity of salvation and the hope of salvation.

When defining a theologian as being an 'inclusivist,' I am not only saying that (based on the presuppositions that God *includes* everyone in His salvific will (**B2**), and that Jesus' salvific provision *includes* everyone in its scope (**B4**)), salvation is universally accessible (**B8**), that is, it *includes* everyone, and that from this belief one can be inclusive concerning the final number of people saved (**B6**) for as William Lane Craig points out, "salvation is *available* to more people under inclusivism...does not imply that more people actually *avail* themselves of salvation... It seems perverse to call a view inclusivistic if it does not actually include any more people in salvation."[107] It is my contention that there are other theologians who hold the above beliefs but who are not inclusivist, for my definition includes all the above beliefs but most importantly adds another belief by stating that in terms of salvific means, the saving boundaries of revelation are widened as to *include* God's universal general revelation (**B8**) as opposed to a theologian who believes that salvation is confined to God's special revelation (**B7**). Therefore it is the combination of **B2**, **B4**, **B6**, **B8**, and **B10** that form inclusivism.[108]

In this study, I am dealing with an example of one such position.[109] Firstly, I will be describing and critiquing a form of inclusivism that has become widely accepted as *the* most sophisticated inclusivist position within the evangelical community, this is the inclusivism of Clark H. Pin-

---

[107] William Lane Craig, 'Politically Incorrect Salvation,' in eds. Timothy R. Phillips and Dennis Okholm, *Christian Apologetics in the Postmodern World* (Downers Grove, 1995), p. 84, quoted in eds. Timothy R. Phillips and Dennis Okholm, *More than One Way? Four Views on Salvation in a Pluralistic World* (Downers Grove, 1995), p. 16.

[108] Although it will be mentioned in Appendix 1, I believe that there are important similarities and dissimilarities between my use of the term inclusivism and the mainstream theological definition of inclusivism given by Alan Race, *Christians and Religious Pluralism* (Maryknoll, 1982); and Gavin D'Costa, *Theology and Religious Pluralism*, op. cit. They are similar in that both my definition of inclusivism and that of Race/D'Costa affirm the universal salvific will of God and the universal accessibility of salvation. They differ in that the focus of the Race/D'Costa's typology is the status and salvific value of other religions, as corporate structures, and their relationship to Christianity. The focus of my typology is the possibility of salvation *extra ecclesium* or without the *fides ex auditu* and which *may or may not* include discussion on the role of other religions as mediating salvation. A better comparison is between my definition of inclusivism and the second position of the Catholic theologian J. Peter Schineller's four-fold typology on the relationship between Christology and ecclesiology, outlined in 'Christ and Church: A Spectrum of Views' in *Theological Studies* 37 (1976), pp. 545-566. Schineller calls this second position 'Christocentric universe, inclusive Christology' and says of it: "It is more optimistic about the possibility of salvation. While persons can only be saved by the grace of Christ, that grace is offered and available to all, even to those who have never heard of Jesus of Nazareth" (p.552).

[109] The other evangelical inclusivist who fits into my own definition of inclusivism is John Sanders. See ed. Sanders, *What About Those Who Have Never Heard?*, pp. 21-56.

nock. What will become apparent is that while my analysis and critique concentrates exclusively on Pinnock's own particular construal of inclusivism, based on his firm acceptance of **B2**, **B4**, **B6**, **B8** and **B10**, and what this says about the nature of God, christology and soteriology, I hope, through this particular critique, to raise questions concerning other versions of evangelical inclusivism.

In defining inclusivism in this way I think I am in line with the definition given by Okholm and Phillips, of which Pinnock represents 'An Inclusivist View.' They define inclusivism as follows:

> The salvation offered in Jesus Christ is available not only for those who hear his name; saving grace *must be* universally available in all cultures, without regard to geography or age. The old qualititative distinctions between general and special revelation - between God's universal presence and his personal action in Jesus Christ - are undercut. However the final expression and norm for this immanent revelation is still Jesus Christ. Inclusivists demonstrate the coherence of these two principles - the universal accessibility of saving grace and the finality of Jesus Christ - by their explanations of how God's saving grace is operative in every culture, place and time...there is no one definitive shape to the inclusivist proposal.[110]

My definition of inclusivism includes the definition of inclusivism given by other evangelicals that Christ is *ontologically* necessary for salvation but

---

[110] Okholm and Phillips, p. 24. In this book John Hick represents pluralism; Pinnock inclusivism, and Alister McGrath and Geivett/Phillips two version of evangelical particularism.

not *epistemologically* necessary.[111] However, as I have already stated, my definition includes more than this and says something about salvific accessibility and salvific hope. It is to Clark H. Pinnock's version of inclusivism that I now turn.

---

[111] See, for example, Carson, op. cit., p. 279; Phillips, op. cit., p. 181; David K. Clark 'Is Special Revelation Necessary for Salvation?' in ed. William Crockett and James Sigountos, *Through No Fault of Their Own?* (Grand Rapids, 1991), pp. 41f.

PART 2
The 'Pneumatological Inclusivism' of Clark H. Pinnock

CHAPTER 2

An Introduction to the Thought of Clark H. Pinnock

Introduction

Reasons for Study

In the next four chapters I wish to describe in detail the inclusivism of the Canadian Baptist theologian Clark H. Pinnock.[1] There are several reasons for choosing Pinnock as a representative of this particular position on the unevangelised in recent evangelical theology. Firstly, and compared to other forms of evangelical inclusivism, Pinnock's argument is the most fully developed and systematic, and as a position has matured and become more nuanced over two decades. Although it is probably the most radical form of evangelical inclusivism, there is much to interact with, and all the important issues concerning the unevangelised that have been discussed in the previous chapter are brought out in a discussion of Pinnock's work.

Secondly, in the evangelical community, and especially in North America, Pinnock is one of the most stimulating, controversial and influential evangelical theologians, and is not afraid to admit that he struggles with certain aspects of the evangelical tradition in search of non-deterministic theology.[2] Alister McGrath states that Pinnock, "has been the catalyst for much re-thinking in the evangelical movement,"[3] and Robert Rakestraw comments on the impact of Pinnock: "as a creative theologian and risktaker, his influence on the content of evangelical theology at the end of the

---

[1] Pinnock (b. 1937) is currently professor of theology at McMaster Divinity College, Hamilton, Ontario, Canada. Biographical and bibliographical details can be found in Robert M. Price, 'Clark H. Pinnock: Conservative and Contemporary' in *Evangelical Quarterly* 88.2 (1988), pp. 157-183; Robert V. Rakestraw, 'Clark H. Pinnock: A Theological Odyssey' in *Christian Scholars Review* 3 (1990), pp. 252-270; Ray C.W Roennfeldt, *Clark H. Pinnock on Biblical Authority: An Evolving Position* (Michigan, 1993), pp. 71-79; Daniel Strange, 'Biographical Essay: Clark H. Pinnock: The Evolution of an Evangelical' in eds. Tony Gray and Christopher Sinkinson, *Reconstructing Theology: A Critical Assessment of the Theology of Clark Pinnock*. (Carlisle, 2000), pp. 1-18.
[2] See Clark H. Pinnock, *Flame of Love: A Theology of the Holy Spirit*. (Downers Grove, 1996), p. 18.
[3] Alister E. McGrath, 'Response to Clark H. Pinnock' in eds. Dennis L. Okholm and Timothy R. Phillips, *More Than One Way? Four Views on Salvation in a Pluralistic World*. (Grand Rapids, 1995), p. 129.

twentieth century will be more in forging new patterns of thought than in honing and defending established evangelical doctrines."[4]

In the previous chapter it was established that the question of the unevangelised pulls on the resources of a wide-range of fundamental doctrine and this is why it is such a crucial area for study. Much of Pinnock's recent writing has been concerned with questioning these areas of doctrine, most importantly the doctrines of God (in his espousal of 'trinitarian openness'), and salvation (as one of the main defenders of contemporary Arminianism).[5] In analysing his inclusivism then, it will become necessary to refer to Pinnock's wider theological framework, a framework that questions the nature and identity of contemporary evangelicalism.

Finally, in placing evangelical responses to the question of the unevangelised in the broader context of the mainstream debate on the theology of religions, the work of Pinnock is apposite, as his inclusivism is influenced more by traditions and communities *outside* evangelicalism than from within it (most noticeably the Roman Catholic statements of Vatican II, the Eastern Orthodox understanding of the Spirit and the theology of the early Greek Fathers). Again it is such influences that make Pinnock controversial and provocative as an evangelical theologian, but nevertheless important in that he still wishes to retain the label 'evangelical' while being catholic in drawing from very different traditions; traditions which have been seen in the past to be the antithesis of evangelical theology and methodology. In this sense, whether one agrees with him or not, Pinnock's inclusivism can be seen as a gateway for evangelicals to explore mainstream theology with less suspicion, and for mainstream theologians to look at evangelicalism as a credible theological alternative. All the above points make Pinnock a suitable theologian on whom to base discussion.

Having said this, I should note two characteristics of Pinnock's theology that make him problematical as a focus for study. Firstly, Pinnock openly professes that he has changed his mind on various theological issues. He writes that "some theologians are idealogues, so cocksure about the truth that they are willing to force reality to fit into their own system; others are not so sure and permit reality to change them and their systems instead. I

---

[4] Rakestraw, op. cit., p. 269.

[5] These two areas will be briefly discussed below. For an overview of Pinnock's model of God he calls 'trinitarian openness,' see Clark H. Pinnock, 'God Limits His Knowledge' in Randall Basinger and David Basinger, *Four Views on Predestination and Freewill*. (Downers Grove, 1986), p. 143-162; 'Between Classical and Process Theism' in ed. Ronald Nash, *Process Theology*. (Grand Rapids, 1987), pp. 309-329; 'Systematic Theology' in ed. Clark H. Pinnock, *The Openness of God. A Biblical Challenge to the Traditional Understanding of God*. (Downers Grove, 1994), pp. 101-126. For more detail on Pinnock's Arminianism see Clark H. Pinnock, 'Responsible Freedom and the Flow of Biblical History' in ed. Clark H. Pinnock, *Grace Unlimited*. (Minneapolis, 1977), pp. 95-109; 'From Augustine to Arminius: A Pilgrimage in Theology' in ed. Clark H. Pinnock, *The Grace of God and Will of Man*. (Minneapolis, 1995), pp. 15-31.

am a theologian of the latter type."[6] A positive perspective of this, is that rather than this being a sign of theological instability, one could argue that this 'changing' is a sign of thoroughness and a striving to work through the full implications of earlier presuppositions. It is more like an evolution of thought moving in one direction, than a regression that is unstable and whimsical.[7]

Secondly and more importantly, Pinnock does not concentrate his work in one area of systematics but writes and has written on a wide range of theological topics.[8] He calls himself "serendipitous" in this respect,[9] and realises that a disadvantage to working in this manner is that no one area is given comprehensive treatment, but is often left without detailed explanation. There is an almost 'impressionistic' feel to his theology as he paints with broad brushstrokes. This is evident in many of the areas that will be discussed in the next two chapters. This may give rise to the accusation of superficiality and crudeness in explaining certain ideas, and as will be seen in Part 3 of this study, one of my criticisms of Pinnock's position is that key areas in his theological argument remain worryingly ambiguous and underdeveloped. However, a benefit of this approach is that it is easier to see how one area of systematics fits into Pinnock's wider theological concerns as he has written on so many areas.

Therefore in spite of the above weaknesses, using Pinnock's theology as a focus for study seems entirely appropriate; strategically, because of his historical contextual place in contemporary evangelicalism, and substantially, because Pinnock's inclusivism is an excellent facilitative vehicle to highlight and explore the range of theological, biblical and philosophical issues raised by the problem of the unevangelised.

---

[6] Roennfeldt, op. cit., p. xv.
[7] From Pinnock's 'conversion' to Arminianism in the 1970's, his theology could be summarised as an attempt to work out the full philosophical, theological and biblical implications of this initial change. See below for further exposition of this point.
[8] They include such areas as cultural apologetics, soteriology, doctrine of God, theology of religions, political theology and the New Pentecostalism. For details on Pinnock's theological career see Price, 'Clark H. Pinnock: Conservative and Contemporary,' Rakestraw, 'Clark H. Pinnock. A Theological Odyssey,' Roennfeldt, op. cit., Ch. 2.
[9] Quoted in an interview between Daniel Strange and Clark H. Pinnock at McMaster Divinity College, Aug. 1997. On his approach to theology Pinnock refers to Moltmann's statement that theology must always be seen as an adventure and a matter of curiosity, not knowing where he (Moltmann) is going or how he will get back. It is this 'playfulness' concerning theological study that is Pinnock's *modus operandi*. Such a philosophy has obvious strengths and weaknesses.

Methodology

I would like to indicate several methodological assumptions characteristic in my description of Pinnock. Firstly, and as already alluded to above, Pinnock's thinking on the subject of pluralism and the unevangelised has significantly developed from his first main essay, 'Why is Jesus the Only Way'(1976),[10] to his latest work, *Flame of Love: A Theology of the Holy Spirit* (1996).[11] What are seeds of thought and tentative suggestions in the early works have become definite proposals in subsequent writings. Some ideas have been discarded in favour of more suitable ones, and although one can see the foundations of his inclusivism in earlier works, it is only in the last ten years 1986-1996, that Pinnock has put forward a positive inclusivist paradigm. Therefore I will primarily focus my description on the more developed position, concentrating on three main works of the inclusivist period: *A Wideness in God's Mercy: The Finality of Jesus Christ in a World of Religions* (1992);[12] 'An Inclusivist View' in eds. Okholm and Phillips, *More Than One Way? Four Views On Salvation in a Pluralistic World* (1995);[13] and *Flame of Love: A Theology of the Holy Spirit* (1996).[14]

Secondly, though, I still wish to trace chronologically Pinnock's development in his thinking on the unevangelised, not wanting to focus on the content of earlier treatments of this issue, but wanting to highlight where Pinnock has significantly changed his position on certain issues pertaining to the unevangelised. The reason for including this chronological development, is that one of my aims in this study is to not only to describe *what* Pinnock's position is on the question of the unevangelised, but *how* and *why* he comes to his particular position. I intend to argue that that there is a direct correlation and parallel between the development of Pinnock's doctrine of the unevangelised which he started exploring in the 1970's, and the development of his theistic framework he calls the "trinitarian openness of God"[15] (from now on 'trinitarian openness'), which also can be seen in embryonic form in the 1970's. The point I wish to stress here, is that the ques-

---

[10] Clark H. Pinnock, 'Why is Jesus the Only Way?' in *Eternity* Dec. 1976, pp. 13-15.
[11] op. cit.
[12] Clark H. Pinnock, *A Wideness in God's Mercy. The Finality of Jesus Christ in a World of Religions.* (Grand Rapids, 1992).
[13] Clark H. Pinnock, 'An Inclusivist View' in eds. Okholm and Phillips, *More Than One Way?*, pp. 93-149.
[14] Pinnock, *Flame of Love.*, op. cit.
[15] This title is used by Pinnock in his paper 'Evangelical Theologians Facing the Future: An Ancient and a Future Paradigm' in *Wesleyan Theological Journal* 33 (Fall, 1998), pp. 7-28. I will use this title rather than others that have been given to this proposal (see p. 47) because it is the title which Pinnock himself seems to prefer. He believes that the title 'free-will theism' gives the mistaken impression that the paradigm is primarily driven by philosophical considerations on freewill, rather than the biblical picture of God.

tion of the unevangelised is one small area of doctrine which rests upon other doctrine which in turn rests upon others and so on. That this is the implication of any 'systematic' study in theology may appear obvious. However, in discussing the doctrine of the unevangelised in evangelical theology, the interconnectedness of doctrine appears at times to be overlooked as if the unevangelised can be discussed apart from other areas. By contextualising Pinnock's inclusivism with his wider theological concerns, this study will restate the 'organic' nature of theological study.

Thirdly, and following on from the above points, I will have recourse to refer to a corpus of material by Pinnock which does not explicitly deal with the question of the unevangelised but which is absolutely relevant in that it provides the theological presuppositions on which the doctrine of the unevangelised rests. This, therefore, is the justification for the detailed treatment of the divine sovereignty/human freedom problem, the exposition of Pinnock's Christology, and his model of atonement, before coming to his actual inclusivist position on the unevangelised.

Fourthly, it should be noted here, that in these three chapters and in terms of Pinnock's biblical and historical exposition of certain themes, movements and individuals, I will not *at this juncture* question Pinnock's interpretation, taking it at face value. However, in the critical chapters I will explicitly focus on some difficulties concerning the superficiality of Pinnock's hermeneutic of certain traditions and ideas.

Finally, in these chapters it will become apparent that important areas of Pinnock's theology are in part a reaction against certain doctrine held by the Calvinist/Reformed wing of the evangelical community, most importantly: the nature of divine sovereignty and human freedom; the nature and extent of the atonement; and the nature of saving grace. Where Pinnock reacts against this view, I will try to outline what the Calvinist/Reformed position is. Such descriptions will also be important for Part 3 that will contain a critique of Pinnock mainly from the perspective of the Calvinist/Reformed position.

A Synopsis of Part 2

The structure of the next three chapters will reflect the stated methodological assumptions. The second half of this chapter will build up a picture of Pinnock's theology starting with a description of some of his theological and philosophical presuppositions on the doctrine of God and the nature of human beings: i.e. his reconciliation of the divine sovereignty/human responsibility tension which is integral to the theistic framework he calls 'trinitarian openness.' Building on this, Ch. 3 will then outline the two foundational theological and biblical axioms around which Pinnock believes any discussion of the unevangelised should revolve. These are:

An Introduction to the Thought of Clark H. Pinnock 47

1) God's universal salvific will, and 2) the finality and particularity of Jesus Christ.

In Chs. 4 and 5, I will describe Pinnock's attempt to mediate the tension that the question of the unevangelised poses for the upholding of these axioms. This is Pinnock's actual doctrine of the unevangelised. I have called this section the 'cosmic covenant' as it deals with the two main parts of Pinnock's theology of the unevangelised: the universal access and offer of salvation by the Spirit (Ch. 4); and Man's free response to prevenient grace through the 'faith principle' (Ch. 5). In the final part of Ch. 5, I will deal with a number of issues that arise from the previous section, namely the role and importance of mission for Pinnock, and his espousal of a post-mortem encounter with Christ, which he holds in tandem with his inclusivism.

Theological Presuppositions: Pinnock on the Nature of Freedom and 'Trinitarian Openness'

In this second half of the chapter, I wish to look at certain aspects of Pinnock's model of God that he calls at various times, "free-will theism,"[16] "creative love theism,"[17] and the "trinitarian openness of God."[18] I will do this by focusing on Pinnock's reconciliation of the tension between divine sovereignty and human freedom/responsibility that lies at the heart of this theistic model.[19] The ramifications of this discussion filter down through every area of Pinnock's theology and are crucial if Pinnock's position on the unevangelised is to be properly understood.

---

[16] Pinnock first uses this title in 'From Augustine to Arminius,' p. 26.

[17] This title is used in the book Pinnock has edited with Robert Brow, *Unbounded Love: A Good News Theology for the 21st Century* (Downers Grove, 1994), p. 8.

[18] *The Openness of God* was the title of the book Pinnock has edited with Richard Rice, John Sanders, William Hasker and David Basinger. Pinnock refers to this title in his chapter, 'Systematic Theology,' p. 103. By 'Evangelical Theologians Facing the Future,' Pinnock had added the 'trinitarian' prefix. I will use this title as it describes Pinnock's position well.

[19] For a description of this tension and attempts to resolve it, see D.A. Carson, *Divine Sovereignty and Human Responsibility: Biblical Themes in Tension* (Grand Rapids, 1994); eds. David Basinger and Randall Basinger, *Predestination and Free Will: Four Views of Divine Sovereignty and Human Freedom* (Downers Grove, 1986); David M. Ciocchi, 'Reconciling Divine Sovereignty and Human Freedom' in *Journal of the Evangelical Theological Society* 37/3 (September 1994), pp. 395-412; Paul Helm, *The Providence of God* (Leicester, 1994).

Pinnock's Pilgrimage Concerning the Nature of Freedom

Pinnock tells the story of his pilgrimage in theology "From Augustine to Arminius."[20] Theologically educated in a Calvinist environment, he had sometimes understood the divine sovereignty/human freedom question either as a divine mystery or antinomy which simply accepted that human actions are determined yet free, or he had attempted to reconcile the two concepts by defining freedom compatibilistically, that is a version of freedom compatible with divine determinism. However he says that around 1970 while teaching on the book of Hebrews, he began to have doubts about the whole Calvinist system because he could not square the doctrine of the perseverance of the saints[21] with the biblical passages about falling away from Christ (Heb. 3:12, 10:26). He writes:

> The exhortations and the warnings could only signify that continuing in the grace of God was something that depended at least on the human partner. And once I saw that, the logic of Calvinism was broken in principle, and it was only a matter of time before the larger implications of its breaking would dawn on me. The thread was pulled, and the garment must begin to unravel, as indeed it did.[22]

Philosophically basic to this change was Pinnock's definition of human freedom, "I began to doubt the existence of an all-determining fatalistic blueprint for history and to think of God's having made us significantly free creatures able to accept or reject His purposes for us."[23] Pinnock believes that moral responsibility requires us to believe that human actions are not determined either internally or externally. This is variously described by philosophers as categorical, indeterministic, contracausal or libertarian freedom.[24] It can be summarised as this: "an agent is free with respect to a given

---

[20] This is the title of Pinnock's essay in *The Grace of God, the Will of Man*.

[21] This is the belief that those who are saved will be kept by the grace of God and will persevere until they are glorified. See John Murray, *Redemption Accomplished and Applied* (Grand Rapids, 1955), pp. 151-161; Wayne Grudem, *Systematic Theology* (Grand Rapids, 1994), Ch. 40, pp. 788-809.

[22] Pinnock, 'From Augustine to Arminius,' p. 17. Pinnock claims that it was I. Howard Marshall who called his attention to this tension in the entire New Testament in his influential book, *Kept by the Power of God: A Study of Perseverance and Falling Away* (London, 1969). Pinnock is keen to stress that it was primarily biblical considerations not philosophical ones that prompted this change in his theology.

[23] Ibid., p. 18.

[24] See, for example, David Ciocchi, 'Reconciling Divine Sovereignty and Human Freedom,' pp. 402-404; *idem* 'Understanding Our Ability to Endure Temptation: A Theological Watershed' in *Journal of the Evangelical Theological Society* 35/4 (December, 1992), pp. 463-479; William Hasker, 'A Philosophical Perspective' in ed. Clark H. Pinnock *et al.*, *The Openness of God*, pp. 136-138; John S. Feinberg, 'God, Freedom and Evil in Calvinist Thinking' in eds. Thomas R. Schreiner and Bruce A. Ware, *The Grace*

action at a given time if at that time it is within the agent's power to perform the action and also in the agent's power to refrain from the action."[25] So while reasons and causes can always affect our decisions, they cannot determine them and the agent can always categorically do otherwise than what she did.

Pinnock believes that in creating human beings in the *imago Dei*, God gave humanity this relative autonomy of self-determination and it is only this definition of freedom that can account, firstly, for the mutuality and relationality we see between God and His creatures; and secondly, which does not make God responsible for our sin. Significant freedom shows itself in the fact that we are sinners who have rejected God's plans, "our rebellion is proof that our actions are not determined but are free - God's plan can be frustrated and ruined."[26] Pinnock believes this not only to be a rational and biblical truth, but also existentially true on an intuitional level, "Universal man almost without exception talks and feels as if he was free...this fundamental self perception, I believe, is an important clue to the nature of reality."[27]

So far this debate on the nature of freedom will be a very familiar one to those acquainted with the theological positions known as Calvinism and Arminianism. In light of this revelation on Hebrews and the subsequent shift to libertarian freedom, Pinnock realised that he had to reformulate certain areas of his theology,[28] especially his soteriology. Some of these changes will be encountered later in the chapter as they are extremely pertinent to a discussion on the unevangelised. For now they can be summarised as follows: contrary to Calvinism, human beings were never so depraved (either in their natural state or because of a restoring grace) that they could not freely respond to grace; election was conditional and based on the hu-

---

of God, The Bondage of the Will Vol. 2 Historical and Theological Perspectives on Calvinism (Grand Rapids, 1995), pp. 462-465.

[25] William Hasker, 'A Philosophical Perspective' in ed. Clark H. Pinnock, *The Openness of God*, p. 136.

[26] Pinnock, 'God Limits His Knowledge,' p.147.

[27] Pinnock, 'Responsible Freedom and the Flow of Biblical History,' p. 95.

[28] This paradigm shift in the nature of sovereignty/freedom has also affected Pinnock's doctrine of Scripture, an area of theology on which he has written extensively. To see how Pinnock's theological development relates to his perspective on biblical reliability and authority, see Ray C.W. Roennfeldt's Ph.D. study, *Clark H. Pinnock on Biblical Authority: An Evolving Position*. Roennfeldt critically compares and contrasts Pinnock's two major works on biblical authority and inspiration, *Biblical Revelation: The Foundation of Christian Theology* (Chicago, 1971) and *The Scripture Principle* (San Francisco, 1984). Pinnock himself admits that this later work represents a more Arminian way of approaching biblical authority and reliability (foreword p. xxi) which surrenders the Calvinistic model of absolute divine control over the text of the Bible in inspiration, because of the way he thinks about divine power, preferring as he does a model of partnership to one of coercion (p. xxii).

man response of faith; the atonement was unlimited and included everyone in its provision; grace was resistible and could be accepted or rejected; and believers could fall away and lose their salvation.[29] All these tenets must be held together if the two elements of libertarian freedom are upheld, namely not only the ability to choose, but the ability to choose otherwise; and that ability limits obligation; that is, human beings *ought* to turn to God because they *can* turn to Him.

So far I have analysed Pinnock's change from Calvinism to Arminianism philosophically, arguing that the concept of freedom was the driving force behind such a change. However, Pinnock believes that the philosophical aspect of this change was only one small part of a larger change. Pinnock's crisis over the perseverance of the saints had made him rethink what he calls his "root metaphors" for God.[30] He defines these metaphors as, "basic portrayals of God which affect how we view and relate to him."[31] Rather than having a root metaphor of God which stressed absolute sovereignty and power, Pinnock's metaphors of God now revolved around the ideas of a loving parent and a personal, relational God who was involved in reciprocal relationships with His creatures. For him, an integral presupposition in adopting this second view of God, is construing human freedom as libertarian and indeterministic.

Pinnock's Espousal of 'Trinitarian Openness' and his New Understanding of Divine Sovereignty

In the last ten years, Pinnock has realised that there are further implications of adopting a root metaphor of a personal God and a libertarian view of freedom, if one is to remain internally consistent. This has led him in more detail into the territory of the doctrine of God, a journey in which he has been accompanied by like-minded evangelicals, namely Richard Rice, David Basinger, William Hasker and John Sanders.[32] The outcome of this

---

[29] These are commonly known as the 'five points of Arminianism.' For a more detailed look at Arminianism see essays in ed. Pinnock, *Grace Unlimited*, and ed. Pinnock, *The Grace of God, the Will of Man: A Case for Arminianism*, op. cit. For a more critical account of Arminianism see J.I. Packer, 'Introductory Essay' to John Owen's, *Death of Death in the Death of Christ*. (London, 1959), pp. 1-25; idem 'Arminianisms' in eds. Godfrey and Boyd, *Through Christ's Word: A Festschrift for P.E. Hughes*, (New York, 1985), pp. 121-148; Richard A. Muller, 'Grace, Election, and Contingent Choice: Arminius' Gambit and the Reformed Response' in eds. Schreiner and Ware, *The Grace of God, The Bondage of the Will. Vol. 2: Historical and Theological Perspectives on Calvinism*, pp. 251-279.

[30] Clark H. Pinnock, *Theological Crossfire. An Evangelical/Liberal Dialogue* (Michigan, 1990), p. 66.

[31] Ibid.

[32] All these evangelicals co-ed., *The Openness of God*, op, cit. which could be called the manifesto for the 'trinitarian openness of God.'

has been the proposal of a new theistic paradigm that Pinnock calls the "trinitarian openness of God." This places itself between the "biblical-classical synthesis"[33] model of God (which is accused of being heavily influenced by Neo-Platonism and which exaggerates God's transcendence), and process theology (which stresses a radical immanence). Pinnock summarises his model as such:

> Our understanding of Scripture leads us to depict God, the sovereign Creator, as voluntarily bringing into existence a world with significantly free personal agents in it... In line with his decision to make this kind of world, God rules in such a way as to uphold the created structures and, because he gives liberty to his creatures, is happy to accept the future as open, not closed and a relationship with the world that is dynamic and not static... Our lives make a difference to God - they are truly significant.[34]

There are three particular doctrines which form the basis of this model of God: the 'social analogy' of the Trinity; God's transcendence and immanence in creation; and a reformulation of the divine attributes. I will deal with the first two areas in subsequent chapters because they form part of Pinnock's foundations for his inclusivism. For now I will concentrate on the third area.

In order to maintain a belief in a mutuality between God and his creatures, Pinnock has had to rethink the nature of divine sovereignty. God is sovereign in that He created the world *ex nihilo* and does not rely on anything for His existence (which according to Pinnock is *contra* process theism). Indeed God could have created a world in which He determined everything, but He has not done this. In fact He has created creatures with genuine autonomy and so has accepted limitation on His divine power. Therefore God's sovereignty is not in the form of dominion but in God's ability to anticipate obstructions to His will and deal with them. In this way God's ultimate goals will finally be realised. Omnipotence is not the power to determine everything, but the power to deal with every circumstance that can arise, it is an omnicompetence, "the idea that it [omnipotence] means a divine decree and total control is an alarming concept and contrary to Scriptures. Total control is not a higher view of God's power but a diminution of it."[35]

There have been similar questions raised and revisions made to the doctrines of divine impassibility and immutability, God's eternity and divine

---

[33] See John Sanders, 'Historical Consideration' in *The Openness of God*, pp. 59-101, p. 60. Sanders claims that this model that imported Greek metaphysics to interpret Scriptural descriptions of God, is assumed as correct by the majority of conservative theologians today and not questioned.
[34] Pinnock, 'Systematic Theology,' p. 104.
[35] Ibid., p. 114.

omniscience.³⁶ I will very briefly describe these revisions. Suggesting that the doctrine of impassibility arises more from Plato than the Bible, Pinnock notes that the suffering or pathos of God is a prominent biblical theme. Although God does not suffer in the same way as creation, God 'sympathises' in his relationship with us: "God risked suffering when he opened himself up to the world, when he made it possible for the creature to have an impact on him. God risked suffering when he decided to love and be loved by the creature."³⁷

Although Pinnock is quick to affirm the unchangeability of the Trinity and the complete faithfulness of God, Pinnock believes that classical theism has taken immutability to mean immobility and inertness. Pinnock believes that such a view is very different from the biblical portrait of God, a God who changes in his response to events in history. Pinnock writes: "God is changeless in nature, but his nature is that of a creative person who interacts. God's immutability does not rule out God's responsiveness, that quality that enables God to deal with every new happening and to bend it toward his objectives without violating its integrity."³⁸

Pinnock now asks whether we should say that God is temporally everlasting or timelessly eternal. Although he recognizes that classical theism has made the claim that God is timeless (and that such a view implies transcendence, immutability and impassibility), Pinnock sees four theological difficulties in accepting such a view. Firstly, we cannot form an idea of a God outside of time, since all our thinking is temporally conditioned. Secondly, the biblical history presents a God "who projects plans, experiences the flow of temporal passage and faces the future as not completely settled."³⁹ Thirdly, our worship is undermined because we praise God not because he is beyond time but because he works redemptively within time. Finally Pinnock notes that "if God did not experience events as they transpire, he would not experience or know the world as it actually is… Experiencing temporal passage, God confronts a future that is open. The distinction between what is possible and what is actual is valid for God as well as for us. The past is actual, the present is becoming, and the future is possible."⁴⁰

This leads us on finally to by far the most controversial aspect of this proposal that is Pinnock's redefinition of divine omniscience. Pinnock questions not only the traditional Calvinist belief in foreordination⁴¹ but

---

³⁶ See Pinnock, 'Systematic Theology,' pp. 117-121 where he outlines the reformulations of these attributes.
³⁷ Ibid., p. 119.
³⁸ Ibid., p. 118.
³⁹ Ibid., p. 120.
⁴⁰ Ibid.
⁴¹ This is defined by Helm as A-foreknowledge, "If X A-foreknows that p then he knows that p as a result of ordaining or effectively willing or otherwise ensuring that p is

also the classical Arminian belief in foreknowledge[42] because he believes that if future decisions are known, then our choices would not be truly significant. This is not only a rejection of simple foreknowledge but also the other 'solutions' which Arminians have put forward to reconcile libertarian freedom and exhaustive foreknowledge, namely the 'timeless eternity' solution and the appeal to 'middle-knowledge.'[43] Therefore Pinnock points the way forward to a more consistent 'neo-Arminian' position that attempts to uphold full libertarian freedom and a doctrine of omniscience.

Pinnock defines an omniscient being as one that knows everything logically knowable. If, as Pinnock maintains, human decisions are genuinely creative, then there is no deficiency in the divine knowledge if God does not know about them until they occur. God does know directly what will happen as a result of factors that already exist and He also knows His general strategies for the world will finally prevail. All He does not know is future human decisions although He can predict many human decisions based on His exhaustive knowledge of past and present.

Pinnock sees many benefits from adopting this view of omniscience. God is said to be pictured in more dynamic terms. He takes risks and opens Himself to genuine rejection and failure. This is the stuff of genuine personal relationships where one partner not only acts but also reacts to the other. Such a view also means that so-called 'anthropomorphic' or 'anthropochronic' metaphorical descriptions of God which refer to Him rejoicing, repenting, grieving, changing His mind, being frustrated etc., can be interpreted as bearing a closer resemblance to the divine reality:

> What does the Bible say about God's knowledge? Many believe that the Bible says that God has exhaustive foreknowledge, but it does not. It says, for example that God tested Abraham to see what he would do and after the test he says through the angel: "Now I know that you fear God" (Gen. 22:12). This was a piece of information that God was eager to secure. In another place Moses said that God was testing the people in order to know whether they actually love him or not (Deut. 13:3). Total foreknowledge would jeopardize the genuineness of the divine-human relationship. What kind of dialogue is it where one party already knows what the other will say and do? I would not call this personal relationship.

---

true. At the very least X's A-foreknowledge that p is causally necessary for the truth of p and perhaps it is causally sufficient as well." Paul Helm, *Eternal God. A Study of God Without Time.* (Oxford, 1988), p. 129.

[42] This is defined by Helm as O-foreknowledge, "If X O-foreknows that p then X knows that p but not as a result of bringing it about that p is true. There is a contingent connection between the foreknowledge of p and the making of p true." Helm, op. cit., ibid.

[43] For details of this rejection see, Richard Rice, 'Divine Foreknowledge and Free-will Theism' in ed. Pinnock, *The Grace of God, the Will of Man*, pp. 121-140; Hasker, 'A Philosophical Perspective,' pp. 126-155.

Commenting on Israel's wickedness, God expresses frustration: "nor did it enter my mind that they should do this abomination" (Jer. 32:35 NRSV). God had not anticipated it. In the book of Jonah, God threatens Nineveh with destruction and then calls it off (much to Jonah's chagrin) when the people repent (Jon. 3:10). Their repenting was not something God knew in advance would happen. He was planning to destroy them but changed his mind when they converted.[44]

Finally, such a definition of omniscience provides a powerful theodicy, for although God knows that evil will occur, He does not know what specific instances will arise from free human decisions, "rather God governs the world according to general strategies which are, as a whole, ordered for the good of creation but whose detailed consequences are not foreseen or intended by God prior to the decision to adopt them."[45] Although God will ultimately be victorious, history is the scene of a real battle between God and evil, and God is not orchestrating both sides.

Summarising this theological paradigm, Pinnock states:

> The picture of God that I receive from the Bible is of One who takes risks and jeopardizes his own sovereignty in order to engage in historical interactions with created reality. The triune God pursues this path out of love that is fundamental to his very being. This does not make history the author of God. It portrays God as the author of history who delights in meaningful interaction with creatures as his purposes for the world are realised.[46]

This new 'trinitarian openness' of God with its espousal of mutuality and libertarian freedom, has resulted in a paradigm shift in Pinnock's biblical hermeneutics. He writes, "I am in the process of learning to read the Bible from a new point of view, one that I believe is more evangelical and less rationalistic... I find that many new verses leap up from the page, while

---

[44] Pinnock, 'Systematic Theology,' p. 122.
[45] Hasker, 'A Philosophical Perspective,' p. 152.
[46] Pinnock, 'Systematic Theology,' p. 125.

many old familiar ones take on new meaning."[47] It is from within this new paradigm that we move on to a description of the two fundamental axioms that ground Pinnock's doctrine of religious pluralism and the unevangelised.

---

[47] Pinnock, 'From Augustine to Arminius,' p. 21.

CHAPTER 3

Two Foundational Axioms: Universality and Particularity

Introduction

A common thread that can be seen in all of Pinnock's work concerning the unevangelised, is his desire to uphold two fundamental axioms that he believes to be non-negotiable for any responsible Christian understanding of religious pluralism. The first can be called the 'universality axiom' and consists of: firstly, a belief in God's love for all humanity; secondly, His universal salvific will; and thirdly, an optimism in the numbers that will eventually be saved. The second axiom can be called the 'particularity axiom' and stresses the finality of Jesus Christ, retains the language of a 'high Christology,' and emphasises that any and everyone saved is saved through the person and work of Christ.[1] Pinnock comments on the relationship between these two axioms:

> The two axioms are inseparable, and both are primary in their own way. The universality axiom is theologically first but grounded in the other; the particularity axiom is epistemologically and redemptively first but intelligible because of the other. They belong together and enjoy an interchangeability in terms of the order.[2]

Therefore far from viewing them as mutually opposing axioms in which mediation is impossible, as for traditional restrictivism that denies univer-

---

[1] Pinnock establishes these two axioms in Clark H. Pinnock, 'Toward an Evangelical Theology of Religions' in *Journal of the Evangelical Theological Society* 33/3 (Sep. 1990), pp. 359-368; idem *A Wideness in God's Mercy: The Finality of Jesus Christ in a World of Religions* (Grand Rapids, 1992), Chs. 1 and 2; idem *Flame of Love: A Theology of the Holy Spirit* (Downers Grove, 1996), Ch. 6. Karl Rahner also lays the foundation for his 'theology of religions' by affirming both the *solus Christus* and the universal salvific will of God. See 'Christianity and the Non-Christian Religions' in *Theological Investigations* Vol. 5. (London, 1966), pp. 115-134. See also the discussion comparing Rahner and Pinnock in Chs. 4 and 5 of this study.

[2] Pinnock, 'Toward an Evangelical Theology of Religions,' p. 360.

sality, or pluralism that denies particularity, Pinnock sees the two axioms as complementary truths that are present throughout the biblical narrative. Universality must be Christologically defined, and particularity does not entail a narrowness in the scope of God's salvific will.

However, I would like to note that such a mediation is only possible if one clearly defines what Pinnock means by these two axioms. As I shall demonstrate, it is Pinnock's own particular construal and interpretation of these axioms that makes the mediation of them theologically coherent. Therefore a description of these axioms is warranted as they lay the foundation for Pinnock's inclusive position concerning the salvation of the unevangelised.

The Scope of God's Salvific Will and an Optimism in Salvation

Pinnock believes that all theology must speak of universality and inclusion as opposed to views that are narrow and restrictive. He notes that such a belief stems from his understanding of God as seen in the biblical narrative, "my reading of the gospel of Jesus Christ causes me to celebrate a wideness in God's mercy and a boundlessness in his generosity toward humanity as a whole."[3] Biblical statements such as, "God wants all men to be saved and to come to a knowledge of the truth," (1Tim. 2:4) and "For the grace of God that brings salvation has appeared to all men" (Titus 2:11), are interpreted by Pinnock as meaning that God seriously desires every person who has ever lived to be saved. Here he wants evangelicals to move from positions of pessimism concerning the salvation of humanity, to positions of hopefulness, understanding the true scope of God's love. Pinnock grounds such optimism and universality not in wishful thinking, but in three areas, the first being biblical, the second being historical, and the third being theological. I will outline all three areas.

Universality and Biblical Revelation

Pinnock believes that the tenor of the biblical narrative from Genesis to Revelation demonstrates universality and an optimism in salvation. This he calls his "hermeneutic of hopefulness."[4] There is a recurring theme throughout Scripture which shows how universality and particularity can be associated together: "it seems to be God's way to choose a single representative of the group to deal with the whole group."[5] This is seen in the calling of Abraham and more specifically the cosmic covenant that God establishes with Noah in Gen. 8-9: "by this pledge we understand that God is

---

[3] Pinnock, *Wideness*, p. 18.
[4] Ibid., p. 20.
[5] Ibid.

concerned not with a single strand of history, but with the entire historical tapestry, including all the earth's people."⁶ In the Noahic covenant God announces His love for humanity and decrees that He will be salvifically working among all people who share a common ancestry with Noah. Therefore God's calling of Abraham must be seen in the context of the earlier creational and cosmic covenants, it is the beginning of the implementation of the Noahic covenant, the demonstration of His universal love for the world. Pinnock writes:

> It needs to be said emphatically that the choosing of Abraham has nothing to do with choosing one man to be saved and leaving the rest to perish. God's purpose in calling Abraham is to prepare a people that would serve to bless the whole earth. It is a central aspect of God's strategy to implement his universal saving will. This choice was not for Abraham's benefit alone, but beyond him to Israel and finally to all nations. God does not have a secret plan according to which he only desires to save some.⁷

Abraham was chosen by God because he was faithful and heeded the divine call. God uses him to achieve His goals for human history: "the decision to call Abram designates the path God has chosen to bring about the salvation of the many through the faith of the one, the principle of representation."⁸ For Pinnock the category of 'election' is not to be understood in terms of special redemptive privilege as in the Augustinian paradigm, but rather it is a corporate category for service and witness.⁹ This is seen in the calling of Israel:

> This is the election of a people to a ministry of redemptive servanthood. Election does bring privileges, but primarily it carries responsibilities. God chose Israel because he had a special task for the Jews to perform, not because he loved them as opposed to loving others, or because they were better that the rest. It is a calling that can succeed or fail.¹⁰

As well as God revealing Himself to all through the ministry of the one, Pinnock argues that a neglected theme is one of God in dialogue with Gentiles independent of Israel's election. Figures like Job and Melchizedek lived outside the Abrahamic covenant and yet had a relationship founded on

---

⁶ Ibid., p. 21.
⁷ Pinnock, 'Responsible Freedom and the Flow of Biblical History,' in ed. Clark H. Pinnock, *Grace Unlimited* (Minneapolis, 1975), p. 105.
⁸ Ibid., p. 23.
⁹ Pinnock's view on election has been influenced by Robert Shank, *Elect in the Son: A Study of the Doctrine of Election* (Springfield, 1970); William W. Klein, *A New Chosen People: A Corporate View of Election* (Grand Rapids, 1990).
¹⁰ Pinnock, *Wideness*, p. 24.

the cosmic covenant of Noah, "these examples prove...that God is prepared to be the God of pagan peoples who believe and that he is present in the religious spheres of their lives."[11] In citing this biblical theme, Pinnock wishes to emphasise that there is not a disjunction between salvation history and world history but that both are co-extensive. As revealed in the universal covenants, God reaches out into all the world and reveals Himself to both Jews and Gentiles. Such universality is the whole tenor of the Old Testament revelation.[12]

Moving into the New Testament, Jesus' own mission speaks of the generosity of the grace of God, "God's grace will issue in the eschatological pilgrimage of the nations, a theme drawn from the prophets of the Old Testament."[13] Here one should not confuse penultimate means with ultimate ends, "although God had a special arrangement with Israel which Jesus had to pursue, the overarching goal was the inclusion of Jew and Gentile alike in the kingdom of God."[14] For Pinnock, the writings of Luke are particularly strong on the theme of God's love for all humanity.[15] The theme of his Gospel and Acts are epitomised by Peter in his dealings with Cornelius in Acts.10-11. Peter states after this incident, "I now realise that God does not show favouritism but accepts men from every nation who fear him and do what is right" (Acts. 10:34-35). As we shall see, this verse is seminal to Pinnock's whole position on the unevangelised.

In the New Testament Epistles, Pinnock's hermeneutic of hopefulness is concentrated on the person and work of Christ. Although I will be discussing this area in more detail shortly, one can summarise the sentiment of Pinnock when he says, "truly, Jesus is the Saviour of the world (1 Tim. 2:4-6) and the one through whom God has reconciled the whole world (2 Cor. 5:18-21). This is a most universal vision."[16]

Finally, Pinnock sees this universal scope of God's love clearly present in the book of Revelation. God will win a victory over the nations not by

---

[11] Ibid, p. 27.
[12] For more examples, see Pinnock, *Wideness*, pp. 20-28.
[13] Ibid., p. 31.
[14] Ibid.
[15] Pinnock's hermeneutic does not solely concentrate on those passages which speak of God's love for humanity. He also turns his hermeneutic to a traditional restrictivist text like Acts 4:12, "Salvation is found in no one else, for there is no other name under heaven given to men by which we must be saved." See Clark. H. Pinnock, 'Acts 4:12 - No Other Name Under Heaven' in eds. William V. Crockett and James G. Sigountos, *Through No Fault Of Their Own? The Fate of Those Who Have Never Heard* (Grand Rapids, 1991), pp. 107-115. In this article, Pinnock argues that restrictivists come to this text with a restrictive presuppositional framework and do not take into account the context of the passage. For Pinnock this verse speaks about the holistic messianic salvation found in Christ that is unique and normative for all humanity. However he says that this text says nothing about the unevangelised or the status of other religions.
[16] Ibid., p. 34.

destruction, but by healing (Rev. 22:2). In Revelation one is introduced to the third element of the universality axiom, for not only must Christians emphasise the universal salvific will of God, and Christ's universal provision, but they can also be optimistic about the number of people that will be eventually saved (the so-called *Heilsoptimismus*) while still upholding Man's freedom to accept or reject God's grace. This is a separate element from God's universal salvific will as it would be quite possible to hold together both a belief that God desires everyone to be saved and also a *Heilspessimismus* - that is only a few will eventually be saved. Pinnock believes there should be cause for optimism in God's victory:

> How could the One who is 'king of the ages,' who created the whole world, and whose throne is surrounded by Noah's rainbow, not have a purpose for the whole of creation or be content to rescue a pathetic remnant (Rev. 15:3; 10:6; 4:3)... Salvation is going to be extensive in number and comprehensive in scope.[17]

Again Pinnock believes that this optimism pervades the biblical narrative. Luke says, "People will come from east and west and from north and south, and will take their places at the feast in the Kingdom of God" (Lk. 13:29). This is echoed in John's vision, "After this I looked out and there before me was a great multitude that no-one could count, from every nation, tribe, people and language, standing before the throne and in front of the Lamb"(Rev. 7:9). Pinnock believes that evangelicals have looked at the biblical narrative through the lens of Western individualism which puts emphasis on the judgment of individuals rather than on the truly biblical emphasis of corporate judgement and restitution where, on a universal scale, those who have been victimised on earth will be vindicated and where the oppressors will be judged. Passages like Mt. 6:10, 1 Cor. 15:20-28 and Rev. 21:24 suggest to Pinnock, "that the Bible is more concerned about structural redemption than the fate of individuals in contrast to ourselves."[18] Seen in this light, Pinnock believes there is a much broader hope for the future as God's primary concern is with the healing of the nations.[19] He states:

> God allows us a generous hope, however we explain it, however the mechanics work. God boosts our morale by sharing with us the information that salvation will be large and generous in the end. This hope coheres well with the picture of God's love for the whole world and the universal covenant he made with all flesh.[20]

---

[17] Ibid., p. 35.
[18] Ibid., p. 152.
[19] For more on this see *Wideness*, pp. 151-153.
[20] Ibid., p. 154.

In light of my earlier description of Pinnock's 'trinitarian openness,' one question Pinnock must face is this: Given his denial of exhaustive divine foreknowledge, how can he be sure that such a large number of people will be saved? Is it not possible that the majority will reject God in this life? Pinnock anticipates this question and answers, "It must be that God knows us well, and he knows that what he has done to save us will produce a large result. The delay of the Parousia would suggest that God is patiently waiting for more to repent (2 Pet. 3:9)."[21] From what God has done in the past and what He continues to do now, we can be hopeful that many will be saved on the last day.

Universality and Western Theology

Having given a broad sweep of the biblical material, Pinnock now focuses his hermeneutic on the history of Western theology. He claims that evangelicalism, as heir to the Augustinian tradition, has not held to a hermeneutic of hopefulness but has narrowed the scope of God's love and been pessimistic concerning the numbers who will be saved. Conversely, Pinnock believes that the early Greek Fathers held to an optimism of salvation and a wideness in the mercy of God and that this theologically manifested itself in various formulations, for example the motif of recapitulation in Irenaeus, and the doctrine of the *Logos* developed by Justin Martyr, Clement, Origen, Theophilus and Athenagoras.[22] Pinnock comments, "it is clear that Christian theology began with a conviction that God was concerned about all people and was at work among them all."[23]

In spite of this optimistic and inclusive theological framework that the early Fathers employed, Pinnock states that such a framework was largely superseded by the exclusive theology of Augustine, finally summarised in Cyprian's axiom: *extra ecclesiam nulla salus* (no salvation outside the church). Pinnock believes that the reason Augustine adopted such a pessimistic framework was because of the Pelagian controversy and the resulting emphasis on the total sovereignty of God and the gratuity of grace with no human contribution. This restrictive paradigm became the dominant model of the Western Church:

> I have to suppose that it was the bitter controversy with Pelagius that drove him to place such a strong emphasis on divine sovereignty in grace and to accept harsh notions which accompany it, including soteriological

---

[21] Ibid., p. 175f.
[22] Ibid., p. 36. For a similar optimistic assessment regarding this period of history, see Richard Henry Drummond, *Toward a New Age in Christian Theology* (New York, 1985), pp. 25-33.
[23] Ibid.

predestination, total depravity, everlasting conscious torment in hell, strict limitations on who can be saved, forbiddingly high ecclesiastical walls...and pessimism for anyone living beyond its borders.[24]

Such doctrines were re-emphasised by the Magisterial Reformers, especially Luther and Calvin, and have continued to be held as orthodox evangelical doctrines to this day.

Pinnock makes three remarks concerning this development. Firstly, he wants us to remember that the Augustinian model has not always been dominant and that "it was once a novelty in the history of doctrine, being the view neither of Scripture nor the first theologians. We are free to deny that God is glorified by saving as few as possible, or by excluding the majority from salvation."[25] Secondly, he believes it to be ironic that evangelicalism has been associated with the Augustinian model because it does not seem to contain the 'good news' of the *euangelion*, but is more like 'bad news.'[26]

Thirdly, Pinnock believes that an Augustinian exclusivity propagates radical pluralism:

> It incites some to forsake orthodox traditions entirely, and to fall into vague unitarianism to escape them. The irony of this is that trinitarian orthodoxy was created, not by Augustine who inherited it, but by theologians like Irenaeus who rejected the sort of harsh views that were introduced later by the Bishop of Hippo.[27]

Despite the predominance of the Augustinian model in evangelicalism, Pinnock believes that there has recently been a change to a more 'lenient' model throughout the Christian world and a move back to a more inclusive and generous stance towards humanity. For Pinnock, the Second Vatican Council was a major event that moved towards adopting this new position, Greek Orthodoxy has always emphasised the universality axiom, and mainline Protestants and even some evangelicals are now turning to this new model.[28] Why is this? Pinnock's answer is based on the work of God

---

[24] Ibid., p. 39.
[25] Ibid., p. 41.
[26] Ibid.
[27] Ibid.
[28] Pinnock here refers to chapter 5 'The Long Way Up Out And Up' in Drummond, op. cit., pp. 46-86. In this chapter Drummond charts the "process of liberation"(p. 46) of Christian faith from the Augustinian paradigm. In the second half of the chapter he looks at the statements of the W.C.C. from Galyato, Hungary in 1956 to Nairobi in 1975 that are progressively inclusive in their pronouncements. In terms of evangelical theology, he mentions the presence of Stott and Hubbard at the W.C.C. meeting in Uppsala in 1966 and the sophistication with which evangelicals now look at issues of pluralism. He mentions the theology of Donald Bloesch, and the impact of C.S. Lewis as being two exam-

in the current theological climate: "God is correcting a mistake in historical theology by means of historical factors, combined with a fresh reading of Scripture... Believers everywhere are coming to appreciate more adequately the grand scope of God's generosity in Jesus Christ."[29]

Pinnock believes that for many Christians, the belief in the universal salvific will of God has become a "primary truth that cannot be compromised."[30] In affirming (or re-affirming) the universal salvific will of God, Pinnock is quick to deny relativism, universalism and unitarianism as being necessary corollaries of such an axiom. Simply because God is generous in His salvation does not lead us to conclude that all truth claims are equally valid. Similarly, one cannot conclude that everyone will be saved because there are too many biblical affirmations to the contrary and people have always had the freedom to reject the grace of God. Finally, one cannot conclude a unitarian Christology because, "far from helping us solve the problem of religious pluralism, denying the incarnation undercuts any hope of salvation of the nations since it is from the Gospel that people discover how loving God is."[31]

Against the theocentric proposals of theologians like John Hick and Paul Knitter, Pinnock believes that theocentricity can only be properly understood by the Incarnation where God is seen most clearly in the person and work of Christ, "focusing on Christ is not different from being God-centered - it is a way of being God-centered...the paradox lies in the fact that the universality of God's love is known through the particular event of the Incarnation."[32]

---

ples of how evangelicals have moved away from fundamentalism towards adopting a more inclusive outlook. With regard to Eastern Orthodoxy, Drummond writes, "the vision of the cosmic Christ in the theology of the early Greek Fathers was never lost in the Eastern Orthodox Churches" (p. 83). He refers to the work of Georges Khodr, a theologian whom Pinnock mentions in his understanding of pneumatology, see Georges Khodr, 'Christianity in a Pluralistic World - The Economy of the Holy Spirit' in *Ecumenical Review* 23 (1971), pp. 118-128. On Vatican II see ed. Walter M. Abbott *The Documents of Vatican II* (New York: 1966).

[29] Pinnock, *Wideness*, p. 42. In 'An Inclusivist View,' op.cit., Pinnock defines this work of God more specifically in terms of the influence of the Holy Spirit: "Theological interpretation ought to be both faithful and *timely*: true to divine revelation and discerning the ways of the Spirit. The awareness of religious pluralism is a characteristic of the present moment, and we must ponder what the Spirit is saying to us about it. It is not enough to get information of past revelation right if, at the same time, we are not discerning as to what God is doing right now (Luke 12:56)" p.96.

[30] Pinnock, 'An Inclusivist View,' p. 97.

[31] Pinnock, *Wideness*, p. 45.

[32] Ibid.

Universality and the Doctrine of the Trinity

Strangely, it is only in recent years that Pinnock has turned his attention to what is perhaps the primary evidence for his universality axiom - that is his belief in the Trinitarian relations between Father, Son and Spirit, both in the nature of the Godhead itself (the immanent Trinity) and in the economy of salvation where all three Persons play a role. Pinnock's development of 'trinitarian openness' has made him look closely at the nature of God, and the doctrine of the Trinity has been given new prominence.[33] Pinnock realises that God's triune identity underlies his entire theological enterprise, "The Christian understanding of God as pure relationality is such a stunning contribution to human understanding about ultimate matters that it must come first."[34] Pinnock regards the Trinity as a divine mystery but a truth communicated to us through the New Testament which speaks of Father, Son and Spirit working in relational pattern to bring salvation to the world. Although it is mysterious, Pinnock believes it to be a rational doctrine, because "once we think of God as loving, personal and communicative, we are on our way to thinking of God in social terms."[35]

Pinnock holds to the 'social analogy' of the Trinity,[36] a relational ontology concerning three Persons in loving communion. He writes, "the picture is of a transcendent society or community of three personal entities. Father, Son and Holy Spirit are members of a divine community, unified by a common divinity and a singleness of purpose. The Trinity portrays God as a community of love and mutuality."[37] The very essence of this community is stated in 1 John 4:8, "God is love." This is a primary Christian truth, not only referring to how God relates to His creation but referring to the inner-life of the triune God. In fact God's love for humankind is based on the Father's love for Son and Spirit, "as the Father has loved me, so I have loved you" (John 15:19).[38] Therefore Pinnock speaks of God not as an egocentric solitary potentate, but as an "event of loving communion,"[39] and of God existing, "in a dynamic of love, an economy of giving and receiving."[40]

---

[33] See Clark H. Pinnock and Delwin Brown, *Theological Crossfire. An Evangelical/Liberal Debate* (Grand Rapids 1990), pp. 61-73; Clark H. Pinnock and Robert C. Brow, *Unbounded Love. A Good News Theology for the 21st Century* (Downers Grove, 1994), Ch. 4; ed. Pinnock, *Openness*, pp. 107-109; Pinnock, *Flame of Love*, Ch. 1.
[34] Pinnock, *Flame of Love*, p. 22.
[35] Pinnock and Brown, *Theological Crossfire*, p. 64.
[36] For an overview of the 'social analogy' of the Trinity and its place in modern trinitarian thought see Thomas R. Thompson, 'Trinitarianism Today: Doctrinal Renaissance, Ethical Relevance, Social Redolence' in *Calvin Theological Journal* 32 (1997), pp. 9-42.
[37] Pinnock, *Flame of Love*, p. 29.
[38] Quoted in Pinnock, *Flame of Love*, p. 30.
[39] Pinnock, 'An Inclusivist View,' p. 103.
[40] Pinnock, *Flame of Love*, p. 30.

Pinnock believes we can know something of the inner-life of God, because God has revealed Himself not through philosophical speculation, which was the method of classical theism seen for example in Aquinas' "Greek thinking,"[41] but through revelation in history and the biblical text. Pinnock believes that the economic Trinity is the immanent Trinity, although the former does not exhaust the latter, there being much in the inner-life of God that remains a mystery: "What we see happening in the Gospel narrative between the Persons we understand also to take place in the life of God. Thus the self-giving love that we see in the Gospels has roots in what transpires within God the Trinity. We joyfully name God Father, Son and Spirit even while remaining well aware that our knowledge in these matters is very limited."[42]

Historically, Pinnock believes that the Cappadocian Fathers held to a more social analogy of the Trinity, but that with Augustine, the psychological analogy superseded the social, and so the idea of relationality in God was lost. Agreeing with William J. Hill, Pinnock calls both Karl Barth and Karl Rahner "neomodalist"[43] in their doctrine of the Trinity because they stressed unity over diversity by speaking of three modes and three 'ways of existing' rather than three distinct Persons.[44] However Pinnock sees in some currents of modern theology something of a return to the social analogy in the work of theologians like Moltmann, Pannenberg and Gunton.[45] Pinnock believes he can guard against tritheism by saying that the Trinity, "is a society of persons united by a common divinity. There is one God,

---

[41] Ibid., p. 31.

[42] Ibid., p. 32. In a footnote, and as if to confirm his own position Pinnock writes, "Karl Rahner equates the immanent and the economic Trinity"(p. 253) and refers to Rahner's, *Foundations of the Christian Faith* (New York, 1978), p. 136. Pinnock makes no reference here to Rahner's main statement on the matter, *The Trinity* tr. Joseph Donceel (London, 1970). Pinnock also does not comment on Rahner's belief that the economic is the immanent, *and the immanent is the economic* (*The Trinity*, p. 22) that would appear to be a different position from the one Pinnock is advocating. As Thompson, op. cit., writes "Rahner's formula has become all but axiomatic in today's "Trinity talk" (Peters), though its precise application and meaning remains variable, subject to the particular trinitarian theology within which it is employed. Its evaluation, therefore, is theologian-specific"(p. 21). As I shall outline in more detail in Ch. 8, Pinnock's use of Rahner's axiom of economic and immanent equivalence seems to me to be more 'analogical' than 'literal.' See Gary Badcock, *Light of Truth and Fire of Love: A Theology of the Holy Spirit* (Cambridge, 1997), pp. 223-225.

[43] Here Pinnock is referring to William J. Hill, *Three-Personed God: The Trinity as Mystery of Salvation* (Washington, 1982), Ch. 5 'Neo-modal Trinitarianism: The Unipersonal God of Three Eternal Modes of Being.'

[44] Ibid., p. 34. Pinnock refers to Barth's *Church Dogmatics* 1/1, trans. G.T. Thompson (Edinburgh, 1936), p. 400, but gives no reference to Rahner.

[45] See Jürgen Moltmann, *The Trinity and the Kingdom of God* (San Francisco, 1991); Wolfhart Pannenberg, *Systematic Theology* Vol. 1 (Grand Rapids, 1991); Colin Gunton, *The Promise of Trinitarian Theology* (Edinburgh, 1991).

eternal, uncreated, incomprehensible, and there is no other."[46] However Pinnock believes that it is God's essence to be relational, this is what defines God, "God is a triadic community, not a single undifferentiated unity."[47]

In defending a social Trinity based on love between the Persons, Pinnock believes he can say something of the universality of the love of God for His creatures. God did not have to create the world, He is self-sufficient in His fullness, but He chose freely to do so, and both creation and redemption are grounded in God's love:

> Out of the fullness of shared life, God calls forth a world to mirror his own loving mutuality, inviting everyone to participate in the fullness of triune life, in a community of love that constitutes tripersonal being. Inclusivism responds to the boundless love that God is by nature and brings its model forward to respond to the challenge of religious pluralism.[48]

In this understanding of the Trinity, Pinnock appears to be trying to give more theological substance to his universality axiom. Christians can be optimistic about salvation because they know that God loves every single human being, indeed the whole of creation is loved by God and was made to echo the Trinitarian life: "the loving communion between the Persons is diffusive - it tends to radiate out from the centre. Its diffusiveness manifests itself in our existence as loving and lovable creatures and alerts us to our destiny, which is to participate in God's love."[49] We can be sure of God's love because we see from the Bible that love is not merely an attribute of God but that God is love and this love overflows into all the world. The characteristic of this love is that it is not like the benevolence of a distant king but rather like, "the tender love of a nursing mother (Is. 49:15)."[50] No group of people nor institution can have a monopoly on this love, it is a gift to the whole of the created order. Here again Pinnock refers to the idea of our root metaphors or basic models of God: "Loving mutuality and relationship belong to the essence of God. In recognising this, theology makes explicit what the heart has always known. Let God not be defined so much

---

[46] Pinnock, *Flame of Love*, p. 35. He says nothing more on defending himself from the accusation of tritheism. However, fellow evangelicals like Henri Blocher are worried that those who follow the Cappadocian Fathers and adopt a social analogy could be open to this accusation, "Did not even the great Basil slip into embarrassing turn of phrases that could suggest a merely *generic* unity of the Three?" See Blocher, 'Immanence and Transcendence in Trinitarian Theology' in ed. Kevin J. Vanhoozer, *The Trinity in a Pluralistic Age* (Cambridge, 1997), p. 106. I return to this later on in Ch. 8.
[47] Ibid.
[48] Pinnock, 'An Inclusivist View,' p. 103.
[49] Pinnock, *Flame of Love*, p. 47.
[50] Pinnock, 'Systematic Theology,' p. 108.

by holiness and sovereignty in which loving relatedness is incidental, but by the dance of the Trinitarian life."[51]

Pinnock believes that this concept of the Trinity indwells the Gospel narratives in the New Testament and is the source of later dogmatic development. This self-revelation of God shows the threefold nature of God. In saying this Pinnock can assert that the Trinity that most fundamentally demonstrates the universality axiom, underpins the particularity axiom, that is the revelation of Jesus Christ. It is to this axiom that we now turn.

The Finality of Jesus Christ: Universality Through a Particular Act of Representation

Although the following section on particularity may appear to have nothing explicitly to do with the question of the unevangelised, it forms an integral part of Pinnock's inclusivist paradigm. As I have already stated, Pinnock's project is to mediate both the universality axiom and particularity axiom. I have already outlined Pinnock's defence of universality and it now remains to see how he deals with particularity in such a way that universality is not compromised. In this section I want to show how, in earlier work (especially 'The Finality of Jesus Christ in a World of Religions'(1988);[52] *Theological Crossfire* (1990);[53] *A Wideness in God's Mercy* (1992)),[54] Pinnock has struggled with this problem of mediating universality and particularity, in his Christological formulation and his model of atonement, and how in his most recent work *Flame of Love* (1996),[55] he has claimed to have found a mediation by emphasising the work of the Spirit in incarnation and atonement. It is the prominence of the Spirit that makes it possible for the axioms to be drawn together. Understanding Pinnock's argument on this point is vital if we are to understand his inclusivism concerning the unevangelised because, as we shall see in the next chapter, Pinnock claims that it is the Spirit who provides the means by which they can be saved, hence my decision to call Pinnock's inclusivism 'pneumatological.' Therefore it would appear fundamental to understand the relational dynamics between: Christ and the Spirit; the unevangelised and the Spirit; and Christ and the unevangelised, remembering our broad definition of inclusivism that the unevangelised are ontologically saved by Christ whilst being epistemologically unaware of him.

---

[51] Ibid.
[52] Clark H. Pinnock, 'The Finality of Jesus Christ in a World of Religions' in eds. Mark A. Noll and David F. Wells, *Christian Faith and Practice in the Modern World* (Grand Rapids, 1988), pp. 152-171.
[53] op. cit.
[54] op. cit.
[55] op. cit.

Pinnock's Christological formulation is one that retains the language of a high Christology while rejecting any narrowness or restrictivness that may have been associated with such a formulation. In the last ten years, Pinnock's interpretation of the finality of Christ has undergone development, and the reason for this seems to be the need to stress the universality of the person and work of Christ. In this way, Pinnock wishes to draw the two axioms of universality and particularity closer together, re-emphasizing their complementary nature. This section consists of two parts: the first part will trace the development of Pinnock's Christological formulation, arguing that the main reason for this development is the need to find an appropriate Christological base to ground Pinnock's inclusive model of the atonement which has also undergone recent development; the second part will look specifically at Pinnock's doctrine of the atonement.

The Person of Christ

MODELS OF INCARNATION AND *KENOSIS*.

In his essay 'The Finality of Jesus Christ in a World of Religions' (1988), Pinnock says that Peter's phrase in Acts 10:36, "Jesus Christ is Lord of All" is, "a basic rule of Christian speech... When we confess Christ as Lord we intend to make a first-order claim about reality as it ultimately is."[56] In making such a claim, Pinnock does not require the believer to hold to Chalcedonian orthodoxy (although, importantly, he says that he does), rather all he wishes to claim is that, "Christians ought to confess that Jesus was and is the unique vehicle and means of God's saving love in the world and its definitive Savior."[57]

This description of the person of Christ receives greater detail in *Theological Crossfire* (1990).[58] In an attempt to enrich evangelical Christology, which he thinks has belaboured the deity of Christ to the detriment of his humanity, Pinnock thinks it useful to distinguish between functional and ontological categories, and the human and divine sides of Christology. Pinnock believes that we must first make sense of Christ from the context of his own people, "The Christ event occurs on a horizontal line of divine activity in history... Jesus was revealed to be God's Son in the Old Testament redemptive-historical and nonmetaphysical sense."[59] Christ was God's covenant partner and the archetype of humanity and Israel. In his life we see the supreme example of what sonship means, "sonship denotes the messianic likeness which will be ours in the end."[60] However, having stressed

---

[56] Pinnock, 'Finality of Christ...' p. 155.
[57] Ibid.
[58] Clark H. Pinnock and Delwin Brown, *Theological Crossfire*, op. cit.
[59] Ibid., p. 142.
[60] Ibid., p. 143.

the human side of Christology, Pinnock then goes on to speak of the title 'God's Son' in an ontological sense:

> Jesus is more than mere man. He is God's Son in a more exalted and ontological sense. He is also the eternal Son who was with the Father before all ages and became flesh. Sonship in this ontological sense should not be seen as an idea that evolved out of a simpler functional usage but rather as an idea that has always been there alongside and implicit with it.[61]

Pinnock claims that the language of incarnation describes this best and that St. John's language of the pre-existent *Logos* has become the preferred way of speaking of Christ, especially in orthodox and evangelical theology. Pinnock falls within this grouping himself by affirming both the full humanity and divinity of Jesus, "for us Jesus not only assumes humanity; Jesus is truly human. Jesus not only reveals God; Jesus is truly God. Humanity and divinity are objectively and ontologically present in Christ."[62]

Although Pinnock affirms a 'classical' or 'high' Christology, we do see some signs of uneasiness in the exact formulation of the two-natures. Pinnock asks why liberal Christianity wishes to reject the ontological and metaphysical claims of Chalcedon and find a functional equivalent.[63] He believes that one of the stronger reasons is that it does not make sense to claim that Jesus is both God and man: it is a logical contradiction. To answer this claim, Pinnock introduces a further development, "I believe that a *kenotic* Christology raises the intelligibility of orthodoxy and robs its critics of much of their ammunition against the doctrine of the incarnation."[64] Pinnock only briefly explains what he means by employing the category of *kenosis*:

> The eternal Son in his incarnation by a voluntary act limited himself to a historical human consciousness and to human faculties of knowledge and action. Kenotic theory is, I think, the most important fresh contribution to Christology since the early centuries. It helps explain how Jesus could be

---

[61] Ibid.
[62] Ibid., p. 144.
[63] Ibid., p. 145. Here he mentions Schleiermacher who reduced Jesus' divinity to 'God consciousness'; Ritschl who speaks of Jesus revealing the will and character of God; Tillich's Christ who overcomes estrangement; Niehbuhr who sees Jesus as the perfect symbol of Love; Baillie who argues that God is fully present in Jesus' life and process theologians who claim that Jesus was the normative revelation when he fully actualised the special aim that God had placed before him.
[64] Ibid., p. 147.

a human like us, one who grew in wisdom and knowledge, was limited in time and place, and who depended on the Spirit for his effectiveness.[65]

For those who question the possibility of this, Pinnock remarks that many problems surrounding the rationality of the Incarnation originate in problems with the rationality of the divine attributes themselves, "if, after all, we say that God cannot change or suffer at all [immutability], then of course the *Logos* cannot become flesh and die. The difficulty would lie with our theism not with our Christology. So we would have to go back to our doctrine of God and clear up the difficulties with it first."[66] As mentioned above, Pinnock's 'trinitarian openness' is an attempt to do just this with revisions in our understanding of immutability and impassibility.[67] Pinnock makes no further reference to *kenosis* in *Theological Crossfire* (1990), but as I will demonstrate, its inclusion here lays the foundation for further development in subsequent thought where Pinnock uses the category of *kenosis* to re-emphasise the Spirit's role in incarnation, a role which is the basis of his inclusivism and his ideas of universality in particularity.[68]

A Wideness of God's Mercy (1992) further develops Pinnock's Christology in the context of religious pluralism. Pinnock again affirms the incarnation as the distinctive feature of Christianity although it must be seen in the context of the theocentric Bible: "Uniqueness belongs first of all to the God of the Bible; and if it should be said that Jesus is unique, it will only be because of the special relation to God he is thought to enjoy as God's Son. Uniqueness and finality belong to God. If they belong to Jesus, they belong to him only derivatively."[69]

---

[65] Ibid., p. 146. Because he says so little about it, it is difficult to place Pinnock on the spectrum in relation to *kenotic* theories offered by theologians. Compared to some of the theories offered, Pinnock's seems to be more like the less radical proposals of Thomasius and Delitzsch (where the second Person of the Trinity gives up his relative attributes and retains his immanent attributes), than the *kenotic* theologies of Gess and Godet (which stress that the *Logos* gave up all his divine attributes and depotentiated himself into the form of a man). Possibly Pinnock's position comes closest to Charles Gore (1853-1932) who in *Incarnation and the Son of God* (London, 2nd ed. 1898), outlines his belief that the Son gave up all use of his divine attributes, especially omnipotence and omniscience, and relied on the power of the Spirit to work the miracles he did. For a useful summary of *kenotic* theologies see Donald Macleod, *The Person of Christ* (Leicester, 1998), pp. 205-221; Gordon R. Lewis and Bruce A. Demarest, *Integrative Theology* Vol. 2. (Grand Rapids, 1992), pp. 252-254, 283-286; Alister E. McGrath, *Christian Theology. An Introduction* (Oxford, 1994), pp. 225-226, 306-308.

[66] Ibid.

[67] For the view of immutability and mutability from the perspective of 'trinitarian openness' see ed. Pinnock, *The Openness of God*, pp. 118-119.

[68] See below for further exposition of this point.

[69] Pinnock, *Wideness*, p. 53.

The main emphasis in sections on Christology in *Wideness* is apologetic in defending the incarnation against any reductionism or 'watering-down' by pluralists and relativists who believe that a 'high' Christology entails narrowness and so seek to revise Christology downwards. In this way Pinnock places himself firmly in the tradition of evangelical apologetics that has sought to defend a 'high' Christology. However, in this defence he makes some interesting and revealing comments. Firstly, in discussing what Jesus claimed about himself and what the Gospel writers claimed about Jesus, Pinnock again makes the distinction between ontological and functional categories of Christology. He claims that those who wish to jettison any ontological claims of 'God in flesh' and retain Jesus as 'God in action,' still would not solve the problem of normativity or universal relevance when considering Christ, because the Christ event would still be seen as the decisive disclosure of God in any and every cultural setting. Pinnock speculates on what would happen if a person were to confess Christ on the basis of the functional understanding derived from the Synoptic Gospels (this is the horizontal redemptive-historical plane emphasised in *Theological Crossfire* (1990)), rather than the metaphysical claims made in John. He believes that such a person could be saved although they would not be 'Christian' in the orthodox sense. He says, "It would not be a question of them denying the doctrine of the Incarnation in the metaphysical sense, but of preferring the dynamic biblical language as more understandable than later formulations."[70]

Secondly, in discussing the category of incarnation itself, Pinnock admits that it is only John who claims Jesus to be the Word of God incarnate and that historically Johannine Christology provides the main framework for all subsequent discussion on the person of Christ. For Pinnock then, 'incarnation' is not the normative category for the New Testament, and while it is true and carries with it the strongest claims for finality, it should not be the only line of interpretation in Christological reflection. It should complement other models and be seen as one piece of a larger picture.[71]

As in *Theological Crossfire*, Pinnock wishes to remain 'orthodox' in his espousal of Chalcedonian and ontological categories of incarnation, while at the same time giving greater emphasis to the humanity of Jesus and the functional side of the Christ's person. The question to be asked is whether he can find a mediation between both evangelical and liberal camps by affirming both evangelical orthodoxy and by also dealing with the fears and criticisms that liberals have with a high Christology. In *Theological Cross-*

---

[70] Ibid., p. 60. Such a view has wide ramifications for Pinnock's theology of religions that he himself realises, "This is not an idle question, since it would be easier for Jews and Muslims to accept Jesus in those terms [functional] rather than under the incarnational category." (p. 60) However he does not develop this point apart from his general position on other religions.

[71] Ibid., p. 62.

fire, we saw the beginnings of an attempt to do this in the espousal of a *kenotic* Christology that answered liberal claims of incarnation being irrational and logically contradictory. In *Wideness*, Pinnock highlights another reason why certain theologians feel the need to revise Christology downwards making it non-normative, "what disturbs people most is not high Christology itself but the thought that such a belief entails a narrowness in divine salvation and what this belief may say about our attitude to other people."[72] Here we see an apparent tension in affirming both universality and particularity. Pinnock's critique is that evangelicals have often stressed particularity to the detriment of universality and that pluralists have done the opposite. Pinnock, though, sees not an 'either/or' here, but a 'both/and':

> What has to be said here forthrightly is that a biblically based Christology does not entail a narrowness of outlook toward other people. The church's confession about Jesus is compatible with an open spirit, with an optimism of salvation, and with a wider hope... God's decision to deal with humanity through the agency of Jesus does not mean or imply that his plan is lacking universal implications. According to the New Testament, the work of redemption, which spans all ages and continents and comes to fullest expression at a particular point in history, also issues out again into universality.[73]

A 'SPIRIT ENRICHED' CHRISTOLOGY

Pinnock's attempt in mediating universality and particularity is theologically developed in his book *Flame of Love* (1996). This work is a theology of the Holy Spirit and Pinnock's *modus operandi* behind it was to enrich evangelicalism by emphasising aspects of theology that Pinnock thinks have been neglected.[74] In a chapter entitled 'Spirit and Christology,' Pinnock suggests that instead of speaking solely in terms of '*Logos* Christology,' that is, an interpretation of the event if Jesus Christ "in terms of the divine *Logos* becoming flesh,"[75] we should look at another possibility, that of Spirit Christology, "Let us see what results from viewing Christ as an aspect of the Spirit's mission, instead of (as is more usual) viewing Spirit as a function of Christ's."[76] This is not to reject *Logos* Christology, but to balance it with another model of Christology: the work of the Holy Spirit in the life and ministry of the Son. Here I quote Pinnock in some detail:

---

[72] Ibid., p. 74.
[73] Ibid.
[74] Mentioned in interview between Clark H. Pinnock and Daniel Strange, McMaster Divinity College, Aug. 1997.
[75] Pinnock, *Flame of Love*, p. 80.
[76] Ibid.

Two Foundational Axioms: Universality and Particularity

> It is not right to emphasise the descent of the *Logos* and ignore the work of the Spirit in the Son... It was anointing by the Spirit that made Jesus "Christ," not the hypostatic union, and it was anointing that made him effective in history as the absolute Savior. Jesus was ontologically Son of God from the moment of conception, but he became Christ by the power of the Spirit... We emphasise God's sending the Son and must not lose the balance of a double sending. God sends both Son and Spirit. Irenaeus spoke of them as God's two hands, implying a joint mission (*Against Heresies* 4.20.1). The relationship is dialectical. The Son is sent in the power of the Spirit, and the Spirit is poured out by the Risen Lord. The missions are intertwined and equal... It is not right to be Christocentric if being Christocentric means subordinating the Spirit to the Son. The two are partners in the work of redemption.[77]

By stressing the work of the Spirit in Christ, Pinnock believes that he can overcome the problem of exclusivity when affirming a high Christology. The details of the Spirit's activity and the idea of a 'double-sending' will be expounded below as it is an integral part of Pinnock's argument that the unevangelised can be saved. However in summary, Pinnock believes there to be a history of the Spirit that preceded Jesus, that started in creation and which offers grace to all men and women. Jesus represents the ultimate manifestation of this offer of grace, "there is a history of grace that has now reached its climax in Jesus Christ, the sacrament of salvation, the revelation of God's unambiguous love for the world."[78] Pinnock claims that Jesus is not merely a symbol of this love, but his whole ministry makes this love possible (as we shall see in describing Pinnock's view of atonement):

> In Jesus the Spirit experienced an undistorted acceptance of God's love and found the ideal receptacle for God's self-communication as the Son. Thus all the creating and redeeming activities of the Spirit reached their goal in him. The kingdom was inaugurated, the new order had begun, the power could be poured out.[79]

In describing how the Spirit was manifest in Jesus' life, Pinnock returns to the idea of some form of *kenosis*, "The Gospels...reveal Jesus as a gift of the Spirit. He was the Son of God who nevertheless emptied himself to live in solidarity with others, as dependent on the Spirit as any of them."[80] For Pinnock, all Christ's divine attributes are the work of the Spirit in his life, "his sinlessness was really due to his relation with the Spirit, not his own

---

[77] Ibid., pp. 80-82.
[78] Ibid., p. 83.
[79] Ibid., p. 91.
[80] Ibid., p. 85.

deity... He conquered in the power of the Spirit."[81] Pinnock describes this *kenotic* element in more detail:

> In becoming dependent, the Son surrendered the independent use of his divine attributes in incarnation. The Word became flesh and exercised power through the Spirit, not on its own. The Son's self-emptying meant that Jesus was compelled to rely on the Spirit... Self-emptying is characteristic of God, who is self-giving love itself. Spirit is important for understanding the *kenosis*. Spirit enabled Jesus to live within the limits of human nature in this life. The Son decided not to make use of divine attributes independently but experience what it would mean to be truly human. Therefore he depended on the Spirit to live his life and pursue his mission.[82]

Before moving on to a discussion of what this Spirit Christology signifies for Christ's mission and work, we must be clear on what Pinnock is advocating here, although critical interaction with this area of Pinnock's theology will be left for a later chapter.

Pinnock stresses throughout this chapter that he does not wish to replace *Logos* Christology with Spirit Christology. Rather his aim is to enrich our understanding of Christ by re-emphasising a neglected area of theology - that is the work of the third person of the Trinity in the life of Christ. To the claim that this is a form of adoptionism, Pinnock states that his position is very different from the christologies of theologians such as G. W. H. Lampe and Paul W. Newman that Pinnock calls inspirational rather than incarnational.[83] Indeed Pinnock notes that to call his formulation a 'Spirit Christology' might be misleading, "when I refer to Spirit Christology, I do so in an orthodox way that preserves the trinitarian distinctions."[84] Perhaps a more suitable title might be that of a 'Spirit-enriched Christology.' Pinnock also refers to his indebtedness to Eastern Orthodox theology, which he believes has always claimed that Western theology diminishes the role of the Spirit by giving the Son an ontic role and the Spirit only a noetic one.[85]

---

[81] Ibid., p. 88.
[82] Ibid.
[83] See G. W. H. Lampe, "The Holy Spirit and the Person of Christ" in *Christ, Faith and History* eds. S. W. Sykes and J. P. Clayton (Cambridge, 1972), pp. 111-131; and Paul W. Newman, *A Spirit Christology: Recovering the Biblical Paradigm of Christian Faith* (Maryland, 1987).
[84] Ibid., p. 92.
[85] Ibid. Pinnock refers to two works which describe the Eastern Orthodox position: Ralph Del Colle, 'Pneumatological Christology in the Orthodox Tradition,' chap. 1 in *Christ and the Spirit: Spirit Christology in Trinitarian Perspective*. (New York, 1994); and Yves Congar, *I Believe in the Holy Spirit* 3 Vols. (New York, 1983), 3:165-173. It is unclear as to whether Pinnock has referred to any Eastern Orthodox theologians them-

The question to be asked is whether this development is one merely of emphasis or whether it constitutes a real change in orthodox Christology. This is difficult to answer, for while Pinnock explicitly states that he still holds to Chalcedon and still affirms the truth of the *Logos* Christology,[86] implicitly, statements such as, "the deity of Christ is seen only in his humanity as filled by the Spirit,"[87] and that "the Spirit facilitated the Incarnation"[88] may compromise, not complement orthodox evangelical Christological formulation especially when the idea of *kenosis* is mentioned.[89] Roger Haight writes that Spirit Christology has become attractive because it appeals to our historical consciousness by emphasising the humanity of Jesus while still having the resources to formulate expressions referring to Jesus' divinity without reliance on *Logos* language.[90] Whether this is possible is a matter of contention. More pointedly we must ask whether Pinnock can have all the benefits of a Spirit Christology and affirm a *Logos* Christology without falling into incoherence. We will deal with more detailed criticisms of Pinnock's idea of Spirit Christology and *kenosis* in Ch. 7.

---

selves or whether he is relying entirely on Western interpretations of Eastern Orthodox theology. This methodological point will be brought up in the following chapter.

[86] Interestingly, in a recent short essay that claims to be an evangelical response to Paul Knitter's 'five theses' regarding the uniqueness of Christ, Pinnock, in what I think for him is quite a conservative and orthodox statement, re-affirms his strong belief in incarnation and makes no reference to the Spirit's role. He writes, "More than an ethical norm, more that God's love in action, Jesus is God's presence in history according to our canon and tradition. Arguing in this manner, I am making an assumption about theological method. I am assuming that Christian theology ought to be a faithful rendition of the canonical symbols and not free-wheeling doctrinal construction. While there is room under this method to reenvisage categories like the uniqueness of Jesus, our freedom does not extend to straying beyond limits or ignoring central canonical emphases... The center of New Testament christology is the crucified Jesus, now risen and exalted as Lord." Clark H. Pinnock 'An Evangelical Response to Knitter's Five Theses' in eds. Leonard Swidler and Paul Mojzes, *The Uniqueness of Jesus: A Dialogue with Paul F. Knitter* (Maryknoll, 1997), pp. 117f.

[87] Ibid., p. 91.

[88] Comment made in interview between Clark H. Pinnock and Daniel Strange, McMaster Divinity College, Aug. 1997.

[89] Such criticisms are founded not so much on Christology but on Pinnock's view of God, especially his denial of immutability.

[90] Roger Haight, 'The Case For Spirit Christology' in *Theology* 53 (1992), pp. 257-287.

The Work of Christ

THE REJECTION OF PENAL SUBSTITUTION AND THE SEARCH FOR A NEW MODEL OF ATONEMENT

This discussion on the person of Christ is a prelude to what Pinnock says about the work of Christ. Before picking up Pinnock's thought on the atonement in *Flame of Love*, we must briefly describe Pinnock's development of this doctrine up to this point. One of the defining marks of evangelicalism is its doctrine of the atonement. Orthodox evangelical theology has held to the 'penal substitution' model of atonement.[91] To summarise the elements of this model, and because of its lucidity and brevity, I will use J.I. Packer's threefold typology of ways Christ's death has been understood in the Church.[92] The first account is subjective and sees the cross having its effect entirely on men and women, by revealing God's love to us or setting an example for us.[93] A second account sees the cross as having an effect on the external hostile forces that have imprisoned humanity. Christ's death secures our release from these.[94] The final account includes both the first and second accounts but says that there is more than this: that humanity stands under God's judgement and that Christ's death has its effect first on God who propitiates Himself and receives satisfaction for humanity's sin.[95] The penal substitution model comes under this third category. It can be summarised like this: "...Jesus Christ our Lord, moved by a love that was determined to do everything necessary to save us, endured

---

[91] For some typical evangelical treatments of the atonement and of penal substitution see Leon Morris, *The Atonement: Its Meaning and Significance* (Leicester, 1983); Robert Letham, *The Work of Christ* (Leicester, 1993); Wayne Grudem, *Systematic Theology* (Leicester, 1994), Ch. 27 'The Atonement.' In the bibliographical section at the end of this chapter, Grudem refers to sections on the atonement in all major evangelical systematic theologies, pp. 605-607; John Murray, *Redemption Accomplished and Applied* (Grand Rapids, 1955), Part 1; J.I. Packer, 'What did the Cross achieve? The Logic of Penal Substitution' in *Tyndale Bulletin* 25, 1974, pp. 3-46.

[92] Packer, 'What did the Cross achieve?' op. cit. It may seem slightly strange to base an exposition of such an important doctrine on a brief journal article written nearly 25 years ago. However, I have chosen this exposition of Packer because it clearly sets out the important issues in discussing the work of Christ. Pinnock also refers to this work when referring to the penal substitution model. See *Flame of Love*, p. 263 n.61.

[93] Ibid., p. 19. One might include in this, Peter Abelard's 'Moral Influence' theory and Faustus Socinius' 'Example' theory. For summaries of these two models see Lewis and Demarest, *Integrative Theology*, p. 373f; McGrath, op. cit., pp. 355-357.

[94] Packer, op. cit., p. 19. Origen was the earliest proponent of this idea. In the 20th century, Gustaf Aulen has championed this idea. See his *Christus Victor* (London, 1931). For more details see Letham, op. cit., p. 161f.

[95] Packer, op. cit., p. 19. Letham writes that the classical documents of Protestantism all follow this line, *The Formula of Concord* (1576) (V: iv), *The Thirty - Nine Articles of the Church of England* (1563, 1571) (Art. XXXI); *The Westminster Confession of Faith* (1647) (VIII: v). See Letham, op. cit., pp. 163-166.

and exhausted the destructive divine judgement for which we were otherwise inescapably destined, and so won us forgiveness, adoption and glory."[96]

This model is complex, and it is when one goes into the details of it that certain divisions between evangelicals begin to surface. The most debated area surrounds the scope or intent of the atonement and the question 'For whom did Christ die?' The problem surrounds the precise nature of substitution. Packer asks: "...if Christ specifically took and discharged my penal obligation as a sinner, does it not follow that the cross was decisive for my salvation not only as its sole meritorious grounds, but also as guaranteeing that I should be brought to faith and through faith to eternal life?"[97] If this is true then there is a choice of two options: either Christ's death secured salvation for everyone (universalism) or Christ died to save only part of the human race (particular redemption). Reformed/Calvinist theologians have held to a doctrine of particular redemption by saying that Christ died only for those whom God has predestined: the elect.[98] Such a position fits into the Calvinist worldview alluded to earlier in the chapter. However, Arminians have not been satisfied with these alternatives and have subsequently re-thought the nature of Christ's substitution.[99]

Here one comes to Pinnock's understanding of the problem. It was mentioned in Ch. 2, that Pinnock's view of libertarian freedom that he had come to in the 1970's, meant that he had had to re-think all areas of doctrine. The work of Christ was one such area:

> I also found I had to think about the atoning work of Christ. The easy part was accepting the obvious fact that contrary to Calvinian logic Jesus died for the sins of the whole world according to the New Testament... I had

---

[96] Packer, op. cit., p. 25.
[97] Ibid., p. 36.
[98] For expositions of limited atonement or particular redemption see Letham, op. cit., pp. 245-247. Still a standard source which argues for limited atonement from the biblical text is John Owen's, *The Death of Death in the Death of Christ: A Treatise in Which the Whole Controversy About Universal Redemption is Fully Discussed (1648)* (London, 1959); Murray, op. cit., Part 1 - this is another classic exposition of limited atonement; Grudem, op. cit., pp. 594-603. For historical studies see Stephen Strehle, 'The Extent of the Atonement and the Synod of Dort' in *Westminster Theological Journal* 51 (1989), pp. 1-23 and 'Universal Grace and Amyraldianism' in *Westminster Theological Journal* 51 (1989), pp. 345-357; Paul Helm, *Calvin and the Calvinists* (Edinburgh, 1982); Roger Nicole, 'Covenant, Universal Call and Definite Atonement' in *Journal of the Evangelical Theological Society* 38/3 (Sept. 1995), pp. 403-412; G. Michael Thomas, *The Extent of the Atonement: A Dilemma for Reformed Theology from Calvin to the Consensus* (Carlisle, 1997).
[99] See Lewis and Demarest, op. cit., p 375f. For a defence of unlimited atonement against limited atonement see Terry L. Miethe, 'The Universal Power of the Atonement' in ed. Pinnock, *The Grace of God and the Will of Man*, pp. 71-96.

no difficulty with the verses that asserted Christ's death on behalf of the whole race because they fitted so obviously into the doctrine of God's universal salvific will, which I had already come to accept.[100]

The problem for Pinnock was finding a theory of atonement which would explain a universal atonement but which would not lead to universalism, "What kind of substitution, if unlimited in scope, does not entail absolute universalism in salvation?"[101] Pinnock realised that he was being led to revise his understanding of Christ's substitution, "Obviously it required me to reduce the precision in which I understood the substitution to take place. Christ's death on behalf of the race did not automatically secure for anyone an actual reconciled relationship with God, but made it possible for people to enter into such a relationship by faith."[102] This made Pinnock look at other models of atonement like those of Anselm and Grotius who view the atonement as an act of judicial demonstration rather than a quantative substitution.[103] Pinnock was also impressed by Barth's version of substitution although he thought Barth was too objective and veered toward universalism, not placing enough emphasis on the human appropriation of Christ's saving act.[104]

Pinnock is critical of the 'penal substitution' model because he believes it to be based on a rationalistic Latin judicial framework that is an alien context from the biblical interpretation of the atonement. Here, God is the angry judge who requires retribution and satisfaction, "In dying, Jesus addressed a tension in God's nature and resolved it. God was made favourable toward sinners by Christ dying for them."[105] What he is searching for is a model of the atonement that fits into his framework of 'trinitarian openness.' This would be a more relational model "in which we frame the problem as broken relationships, not divine anger and honor."[106] As in his understanding of the person of Christ, what Pinnock wants to do is *enrich* the way evangelicals view the atonement. Firstly, with regard to the purpose of the atonement, he wants evangelicals to highlight more than the removal of

---

[100] Pinnock, 'From Augustine to Arminius...,' p. 22.
[101] Ibid.
[102] Ibid., p. 23. Saying this of course leads onto a discussion of the nature of faith and the conditionality of salvation. The question revolves around the nature of election: is it conditional on an act of faith (Arminianism) or is it unconditional and an act of divine monergism (Calvinism)?
[103] Ibid. For details on Grotius' and Anselm's theories see Letham, op. cit., pp. 163-169; Gordon R. Lewis and Bruce A. Demarest, *Integrative Theology Vol. 2* (Grand Rapids, 1990), pp. 374-377.
[104] Ibid. See Karl Barth, *Church Dogmatics* 4/1, trans. G. W. Bromiley (Edinburgh, 1956), pp. 157-210.
[105] Clark H. Pinnock and Robert C. Brow, *Unbounded Love* (Downers Grove, 1994), p. 102.
[106] Ibid., p. 103.

guilt through justification. Secondly, he wants evangelicals to enrich their perspective on the extent of the atonement. Christ died for everyone and everyone has the opportunity to benefit from his mission, "surely it would be better to say that God is love, everywhere and always, and that what we needed from Christ was a decisive presentation of it in history."[107]

RECAPITULATION AND THE ROLE OF THE SPIRIT IN ATONEMENT

The first thoughts of such a model can be seen in Pinnock's paper 'Salvation by Resurrection'(1993).[108] Stressing the soteriological significance of the resurrection which he believes has been largely forgotten due to the overemphasis of law and propitiation in the penal model, Pinnock wishes to focus on the whole of the incarnation as being a salvific event, "Somehow by his life, death and resurrection then, the divine Son rescued us from wrath and delivered us from this present evil age... Humanity which is subject to the powers of darkness needs deliverance from sin, death and Satan, and Christ has set us free from them by his triumph in life, death and resurrection."[109] This seems to resemble the *Christus Victor* model of atonement and Pinnock draws on Irenaeus and the early Greek theologians to support his argument. Jesus' life was one of conflict with the powers of evil and on the cross, "God absorbs all that sinners can do without striking back at them."[110] The resurrection delivers us from the power of death.

As to how this is achieved, Pinnock focuses on the idea of Christ's solidarity with humanity as the last Adam, "He became a universal person... Salvation was completed in his representative human nature before it could be completed in ours."[111] Pinnock argues that Paul portrays Christ as a corporate being. Since humanity had failed, God sends Christ to mediate salvation:

> God therefore involved us in his dying and rising, as we had been involved in Adam's living and dying. Christ is the representative of humanity and having been raised to life has entered a new mode of existence. He has become both the pattern and the life giving source of our resurrection.[112]

Pinnock develops this further in *Flame of Love* (1996). Just as the Holy Spirit figured in Pinnock's understanding of *kenosis*, so the Spirit plays a prominent role in Pinnock's view of atonement. Pinnock asks what it was

---

[107] Pinnock, *Theological Crossfire*, p. 149.
[108] Clark H. Pinnock, 'Salvation by Resurrection' in *Ex Auditu* 9 (1993), pp. 1-11.
[109] Ibid., p. 3.
[110] Ibid., p. 4.
[111] Ibid.
[112] Ibid., p. 5.

about Christ's life and death that made them a turning point in the history of redemption. He says that having restored the role of the Spirit in the person of Christ, he can now put forward an interpretation of the work of Christ: "the heart of it is that the Spirit facilitated the Christ event in order to save humanity by *recapitulation*. This is what atonement looks like when Christology is placed within the mission of the Spirit."[113] Pinnock calls his model participatory: Jesus' life, death and resurrection created a new state of affairs and "triggered the end times,"[114] where humanity is released from the bondage of sin and death by the power of the Spirit: "the point is that there had to be a representation before Pentecost could happen. There had to be a participatory journey to realize God's purpose for creation and bring about reconciliation. This would be the means of grace which the Spirit could then apply to sinners and transform them."[115] The Spirit leads Jesus through an act of representation and this culminates in the annihilation of death and sin. This theme of recapitulation, Pinnock borrows from Irenaeus.[116] In the language of classical Greek rhetoric, 'recapitulation' was a technical word literally meaning 'to sum up' or to go over the main points.[117] Paul used this language when speaking of the Father summing up (ανακεφαλαιοω) all things in Christ (Eph. 1:10). Irenaeus believed that there was a mutual union between God and humanity. In the incarnation, the seminal first union, God was united to humanity, and so humanity attaches itself to God. The second moment of union is when the Holy Spirit enters into the life of the believer. Hart comments that there are two aspects to Irenaeus' understanding of recapitulation in Christ. Firstly, Christ reiterates and goes back over the history of mankind's relationship with God. Christ is the new Adam who reverses the destructive path followed by Adam. Minns comments, "He [Christ] recapitulated Adam...by retracing Adam's temptation and defeat in the victory of his own obedience. In this sense the recapitulation of Adam, is Adam's renewal, his restoration to the glory God intended for him from the beginning."[118] This becomes a new beginning for humanity as Christ, "remoulds human nature and puts it on a new footing with God."[119] The second aspect of recapitulation in Irenaeus is the idea that Christ's humanity is not only reiterative but inclusive:

---

[113] Pinnock, *Flame of Love.*, p. 93.
[114] Ibid., p. 94.
[115] Ibid.
[116] See Irenaeus, *Against Heresies* Bk. V. For detailed exposition of this theory of recapitulation see Jean Danielou, *Gospel Message and Hellenistic Culture* (London, 1973), pp. 166-183; Trevor A. Hart, 'Irenaeus, Recapitulation and Physical Redemption' in eds. Trevor Hart and Daniel Thimell, *Christ in Our Place. The Humanity of God in Christ for the Reconciliation of the World* (Exeter, 1989), pp. 152-181; Denis Minns, *Irenaeus* (London, 1994), pp. 92-94.
[117] See Minns, op. cit., p. 92; Danielou, op. cit., p. 172f.
[118] Minns, op. cit., p. 93.
[119] Hart, op. cit., p. 172.

He is the 'firstfruits' of the new humanity, the part that represents the whole, and in which the whole is in some sense included... The point is clearly made that there is an ontological solidarity between this one man and all others whereby all that he does, and indeed all that he is, may be predicated of them too.[120]

Pinnock adapts this idea in his own understanding of the atonement. The role of the Spirit is crucial in understanding the link between Christ's representation and our own personal union with God, "the idea is that what took place in Christ paradigmatically will be applied to and realised in us."[121] There is thus an objective and subjective side to Christ and the salvation he offers:

In his death and resurrection, humanity *de jure* passed from death to life, because God had included it in the event. Its destiny has been objectively realised in Christ - what remains to be done is a human response and salvation *de facto*...we only have to accept what has been done and allow the Spirit to conform our lives to Christ.[122]

As in 'Salvation by Resurrection'(1993), Pinnock argues that the resurrection must be seen as a soteriological act, "death must be dealt with if we are to be saved; therefore God saves us through the resurrection. Humanity is taken through death into resurrection by the representative act of Jesus Christ."[123] In his resurrection we see a glimpse of what is to come, "The Risen One is the vanguard and embodiment of the new order. Jesus prefigures what will be true for us also in the new creation. It is the seminal event, the seed from which the reality grows."[124] Pinnock stresses that this act of representation includes all humanity and does not exclude anyone. The act of atonement is unlimited, "All humanity has the potential to be children of God, because all were included in his representation. What remains is for everyone to be reconciled to God personally and subjectively."[125]

This is not to say that Pinnock neglects the centrality of the cross, but that we have to see the cross as part of Christ's representative journey:

In order to confront the world with the rule of God, Jesus walked into the eye of the storm... The Spirit led him along a path in which wrath, pain

---

[120] Ibid., p. 175.
[121] Pinnock, *Flame of Love*, p. 95.
[122] Ibid. p. 96.
[123] Ibid., p. 99. For more detail on Pinnock's view of the resurrection in the economy of salvation see his article, 'Salvation by Resurrection' in *Ex Auditu* 9 (1993), pp. 1-11.
[124] Ibid., p. 101.
[125] Ibid., p. 100.

and evil became absorbed by the heart of the suffering Servant King. The incarnate God, anointed by the Spirit, defeated the enemy by an act of defenceless love and by the same Spirit enabled us all to be involved in his dying and rising.[126]

What we see in the cross is the true nature of love that is characterised by giving and receiving. Pinnock calls it an "intratrinitarian drama"[127] where the Son offers himself to the Father through the Spirit and where forgiving love and suffering love are brought together by the Spirit.

Pinnock still wishes to say that Christ dies in our place as a substitute, but rather than the cross being the place of appeasement, it is the surrender of a life where Christ takes on the sin of the world and defeats the powers of darkness. From here the Spirit implements the reconciliation between humanity and God, "by the Spirit we enter into union with Christ and begin the journey towards transformation. The Spirit deals with the powers of sin in us until we share the glory of the risen Lord."[128] The Spirit's role is central in this act of atonement, the Spirit led Jesus to death, the Spirit raised Jesus from the dead and the Spirit now forms Christ in us gradually making us like him:[129]

> The cross reflects not God's thirst for retribution but his determination to overcome alienation and enslavement. The means to do this is the participatory journey of Jesus into which the Spirit draws us. Christ's death expressed obedience to the Father that, in representing us, frees us from sin and alienation. As the Risen One he is present with us, making his journey our own. By the Spirit we begin this journey ourselves and experience transformation.[130]

But does Pinnock find any truth in the penal substitution model? He is critical of this model because it gives the impression that the Father hated sinners and needed to be placated before He could love them. So Christ is punished instead of us and grace is made possible. Pinnock states, "God was *not* disinclined to be favorable until his wrath was appeased. He is not humanity's enemy...our Lord's self-sacrifice bespeaks a gracious God, not an angry God."[131] The cross puts us right with God but Pinnock cannot find a completely rational explanation of how this happens. He does believe that sin is a problem, and there is the concept of punishment that he wishes to retain in his model. He attempts to formulate an explanation of this. He asks

---

[126] Ibid., p. 103.
[127] Ibid., p. 104.
[128] Ibid., p. 105.
[129] Ibid., pp. 105f.
[130] Ibid., p. 109.
[131] Ibid., p. 107.

what it means to say that God abandoned Jesus on the cross. Here Pinnock believes that God thought it appropriate not to dismiss sin but to demonstrate the seriousness of it. The cross shows the wrath of God. But what is important to understand is *to whom* this wrath is directed, "it blazed against the old humanity represented there. It did not fall on Jesus as a third party, not as a victim in isolation, but on Jesus as humanity's representative. God's wrath flashed out against the old Adamic solidarity."[132] So as in the penal model, there is an idea of judgement in the cross where God judges the Old Adam in the death of the New Adam. God does not punish the Son, but punishes the representative of humanity. Sin is therefore defeated, "Calvary is something like a black hole into which is sucked all the power of death and law, wrath and alienation, to be annihilated."[133]

The above description raises important questions to which we will return in later chapters. These questions concern the rationality and coherence of Pinnock's model, the relationship between the objective and subjective efficacy of the cross and whether Pinnock's model of atonement is representative or constitutive. For the moment we should say that there appears to be a degree of hesitancy and ambiguity over these questions. On the one hand, Pinnock does not want to say that something in God needs reconciling before grace can abound. However on the other hand, he seems to want to say that the cross is necessary for the human situation and that there is a new state of affairs in its wake. As we shall see, the category of people known as the unevangelised heighten the acuteness of these questions on the atonement, and it is only in Pinnock's treatment of *these* people that we can see him implicitly answering these questions.

Summary

Pinnock summarises his thinking on Christology:

> The work of Jesus can be understood within the history of the Holy Spirit. To do so does not negate but enriches Christology by exalting Christ as the anointed representative of the new humanity. The Spirit enabled the conception of Jesus, the union of the *Logos* with flesh and the completion of the participatory journey. The incarnation depended on the work of the Spirit and unfolded as a Spirit-empowered representation on behalf of humanity, fulfilling the purpose of creation and healing humanity through a recapitulation of the human journey.[134]

---

[132] Ibid., p. 108.
[133] Ibid., p. 109.
[134] Ibid., p. 111.

As in his understanding of the person of Christ, Pinnock's aim in his theory on atonement is to enrich evangelical understanding that has overemphasised the penal model. He believes that his participatory model restores the balance and can still include a legal dimension ("family room cannot altogether displace courtroom in our theological analogies,")[135] while not casting the atonement entirely in a legalistic framework.

Pinnock's Christological formulation becomes relevant for this study when we view it in a wider context, for both his views on the person and work of Christ appear to be attempts to give internal coherence to his theological project which he calls 'trinitarian openness.' For him emphasising the Spirit's role in incarnation and atonement coheres well with his presuppositions of a loving, relational and personal God. But how is this relevant to the doctrine of the unevangelised? Pinnock believes that by stressing the Spirit's role, he can still claim the finality of Christ while at the same time not making the incarnation a limiting principle. The focus of Ch. 4 will be to see how Pinnock relates Christ and the Spirit to the unevangelised.

---

[135] Ibid.

CHAPTER 4

The 'Cosmic Covenant': God's Universal Saving Presence

From Universality to the Principle of Universal Accessibility

Having established both exegetically and systematically the two foundational axioms of universality and particularity, Pinnock now takes the next step that creates the tension from which the question of the unevangelised is generated and cradled. As outlined in the universality axiom, God seriously desires everyone to be saved and not just a remnant called the elect. There is a wideness in the mercy of God and Christians should be optimistic about the eventual numbers of those saved. But this 'desire' is not an impotent wish because, as the particularity axiom established, salvation has been provided for in the life, death and resurrection of Christ in an act of representation that was a provision for all humanity and not just some.

Pinnock takes an important logical step here, for he claims that given the truth of the above axioms, salvation must be universally accessible, "the opportunity must be given for all to register a decision about what was done for them."[1] Here he concurs with the evangelical apologist Stuart Hackett:

> If every human being in all times and ages has been objectively provided for through the unique redemption in Jesus, and if this provision is in fact intended by God for every such human being, then it must be possible for every human individual to become personally eligible to receive that provision - regardless of his historical, cultural, or personal circumstances and situation, and quite apart from any particular historical information or even historically formulated theological conceptualisation - since a universally intended redemptive provision is not genuinely universal unless it is also and for that reason universally accessible.[2]

---

[1] Clark H. Pinnock, *A Wideness in God's Mercy: The Finality of Jesus Christ in a World of Religions* (Grand Rapids, 1992), p. 157.
[2] Stuart Hackett, *The Reconstruction of the Christian Revelation Claim.* (Grand Rapids, 1984), p. 244.

There also seems to be the issue of justice that is seen to be an attribute of God's character. As Clarke writes, "God need not save everyone to be just, but the moral principle of distributive justice (that is justice as fairness) does seem to require that each one have a genuine opportunity to be saved."[3]

Now we come to the crux of the discussion, for Pinnock admits that despite this universal provision, the majority of the human race has never heard of Christ through no fault of their own, because they have not had access to the preaching of the gospel through human messengers, and so have been unable to explicitly accept or reject the love of God. Given that Pinnock believes in the principle of universal accessibility and that many will eventually be saved (*Heilsoptimismus*), he concludes that many will be saved from among the unevangelised. How is this possible if they have never heard of Christ? He admits, "the idea of universal accessibility, though not a novel theory, needs to be proven. It is far from self evident, at least biblically speaking. How can it best be defended?"[4]

The question that Pinnock now has to tackle is one of access to salvation, to present a coherent and plausible, biblical and theological argument, which shows the *ways* and *means* through which grace is mediated. Pinnock needs a theory of universal accessibility. The remaining part of this chapter and the following chapter will be devoted to Pinnock's theory of universal accessibility which I have labelled the 'cosmic covenant' because it involves two movements, the first by the trinitarian God who makes Himself universally present through the Spirit, and the second by human beings who accept a relationship with God through faith.

Trinitarian Foundations: The Cosmic Breadth of the Spirit

One could outline Pinnock's position like this: God is present in the whole world; where God is, so there is saving grace because all grace is potentially salvific and can be accepted or rejected by what Pinnock calls the 'faith principle.' Therefore God reveals Himself in a multiplicity of ways to all people giving them an opportunity to respond to His love. I will deal

---

[3] David K. Clarke, 'Is Special Revelation Necessary for Salvation?' in Crockett and Sigountos, *Through No Fault Of Their Own*, p. 41. For more on the concept of distributive justice see Bruce R. Reichenbach, 'Freedom, Justice, and Moral Responsibility' in ed. Pinnock, *The Grace of God and the Will of Man*, (Minneapolis, 1995), pp. 277-305.

[4] Pinnock, *Wideness*, p. 157. Karl Rahner also believed in the principle of universal accessibility, "...the individual ought to and must have the possibility in this life of partaking in a genuine relationship with God, and this at all times and in all situations of the history of the human race. Otherwise there could be no question of a serious and also actually effective salvific design of God for all men, in all ages and places" in 'Christianity and the Non-Christian Religions' in *Theological Investigations* Vol. 5 (London, 1966), p.128.

with the 'faith principle' separately as this forms humanity's part of the cosmic covenant. For the moment I wish to concentrate on Pinnock's argument as to the way every person in every age, in every position, can be confronted with the saving grace of God. In order to understand Pinnock's position it will be necessary to move outside the confines of evangelicalism and look at the non-evangelical sources Pinnock relies on in formulating his inclusivism.

On the issue of trinitarian appropriation in the economy of the universality of salvation, Pinnock has significantly developed his position in recent years. In *Wideness* (1992), he speaks generally about all three Persons of the Trinity being present in the world and involved in revelation and salvation: "The triune God is a missionary God. The Father sends the Son and the Spirit in to the world (Gal 4:4-6)."[5] In spite of our earlier discussion on Christology, Pinnock in *Wideness* wishes to speak of the mission of the Son apart from the work of the Spirit. This is not so much a discussion of the work of Christ and its universal significance, but the universal presence of the pre-existent *Logos* as hinted at in John 1:9, Christ, "the true light that gives light to every man was coming into the world." Pinnock refers favourably to early theologians like Justin Martyr, who spoke of the *Logos* as being the incarnate Christ and who believed that those who lived before Christ but who had lived by the seeds of the *Logos* or reason were Christians.[6] Here again the most important idea is one of universality:

---

[5] See Pinnock, *Wideness*, p.78. Having said this, Pinnock does appear to speak of the Father as doing more than merely 'sending' the Son and Spirit. Taking the structure of the Nicene Creed, Pinnock says of God the Father: "God is within and God is beyond all human structures and institutions. God is the unity in the midst of all the diversity. He is the gracious God, the God who loves the world so much that he sent His Son to be redeemer of the world... God the Father is present everywhere in His graciousness, not only where Jesus of Nazareth is named. God is present and at work in every sphere of human life, secular as well as sacred... There is no other source from which anyone draws life, and the mystery which surrounds us is the God who loves us in Jesus Christ." (p. 76). The problem with this statement is that it is difficult to know whether Pinnock, when referring to 'God,' means the triune God or specifically the person of the Father, the first Person of the Trinity. Pinnock gives no further elaboration here. I think it is safe to say on the basis of later development concerning the role of Son and Spirit that for Pinnock, the Father demonstrates boundless grace and generosity even though this is implemented in the world not by Him but by the other two Persons.

[6] See Pinnock, *Wideness*, p. 36. Justin writes, "We have been taught that Christ is the first-begotten of God, and we have declared him to be the first-begotten of God, and we have declared him to be the *Logos* of which all mankind partakes. Those, therefore, who lived according to reason (*Logos*) were really Christians, even though they were thought to be atheists, such as, among the Greeks, Socrates, Heraclitus and others like them." *First Apology* 46 in *The Fathers of the Church* (Washington), 6, pp. 83-84. Pinnock refers to an article by J. Dupuis, 'The Cosmic Christ in the Early Fathers' in *Indian Journal of Theology* 15 (1966) pp. 106-120. For more detail on Justin's exposition of the

...though Jesus Christ is Lord, we confess at the same time that the *Logos* is not confined to one segment of human history or one piece of world geography. The second Person of the Trinity was incarnate in Jesus, but is not totally limited to Palestine. In a real sense, when missionaries take testimony about Jesus to the world, they take the gospel to places where the *Logos* has already been active.[7]

This idea of the 'cosmic Christ' means that we can be optimistic about salvation and not be unitarians when it comes to the second person of the Trinity (a criticism he makes of evangelicals),[8] "God the *Logos* has more going on by way of redemption than what happened in first-century Palestine, decisive though that was for the salvation of the world."[9] Those who respond positively to the work of the *Logos* belong to God and so, "the *Logos* connects Jesus of Nazareth to the whole world and guards the Incarnation from becoming a limiting principle."[10] With statements such as these, one is left asking for more detail and explanation.[11] However no more is forthcoming in *Wideness*, there is no mention of the *Logos* in 'An Inclusivist View'(1995),[12] and *Flame of Love* (1996)[13] only refers to it in dealing with

---

Logos see his *First Apology* 10, 14 and 46, and his *Second Apology* 10 and 13. See also Francis A. Sullivan, *Salvation Outside the Church? Tracing the History of the Catholic Response* (London, 1992), pp. 14-18; Danielou, op. cit., pp. 160-166. For a more detailed exposition of Pinnock's position on the *Logos* see James E. Bradley, '*Logos* Christology and Religious Pluralism: A New Evangelical Proposal' in *Proceedings of the Wheaton Theology Conference. The Challenge of Religious Pluralism: An Evangelical Analysis and Response* (Wheaton, 1992), pp. 190-208. It is interesting that Pinnock makes no reference to so-called Christophanies in the Old Testament, for example the figure walking in the fiery furnace in Daniel 3.

[7] Ibid., p. 77.
[8] Ibid.
[9] Ibid.
[10] Ibid., p. 104.
[11] For example, in his critique of Pinnock's idea of the *Logos*, Bradley, op. cit., wonders what Pinnock is talking about when he refers to the *Logos*. Pinnock accuses evangelicals of exhausting or confining God to Christ. As Bradley notes though, "it is not traditional to think of the Incarnation as containing the second person of the Trinity as if God were circumscribed by the physical body of Christ. The doctrine that came to be known as 'the extra doctrine that Calvin taught' (the *extra Calvinisticum*) was taught long before Calvin and is not to be equated with the *Logos* Christology of the Apologists. Pinnock, however, makes no distinction between the two" (p. 199).
[12] Clark H. Pinnock, 'An Inclusivist View' in eds. Dennis L. Okholm and Timothy R. Phillips, *More Than One Way? Fours Views of Salvation in a Pluralistic World* (Grand Rapids, 1995), pp. 93-124.
[13] Clark H. Pinnock, *Flame of Love: A Theology of the Holy Spirit* (Downers Grove, 1996).

creation.[14] Pinnock seemingly abandons this explanation for universal accessibility to concentrate his attention solely on the work of the Spirit.[15]

In *Flame of Love* (1996), Pinnock gives greater emphasis to the Spirit's role in the economy of salvation and looks at the work of the Father and the Son through the perspective of the Spirit (as we saw in his Christology). This later idea of universal accessibility through the Spirit seems a logical development in Pinnock's thinking and is a much more substantial argument than his argument in *Wideness* (1992). I wish to outline this development in Pinnock's theology, concentrating on the role of the Spirit in reaching the unevangelised.

I shall call Pinnock's overall position on the unevangelised, 'pneumatological inclusivism' because of the great emphasis on the work of the Spirit, the third Person of the Trinity, who makes grace and salvation universally accessible even to those who have never come into contact with the gospel of Christ. The initial exploration into the work of the Spirit can be seen in *Wideness* (1992): "The Spirit is the mysterious presence, the breath and vitality of God in the world...God is active, by his spirit in the structures of creation, in the world of history, even in the sphere of the religions. The breath of God is free to blow wherever it wills (Jn. 3:8). The economy of the Spirit is not under our control, and certainly is not limited to the church."[16] The work of the Spirit is developed fully in 'An Inclusivist View'(1995) and *Flame of Love* (1996). Pinnock builds a picture of the Spirit's mission in three stages.

Spirit and Creation

Pinnock wants to remind us that the omnipresent Spirit was and is involved in creation as well as redemption, indeed, "there could not be redemptive actions unless first there had been creative actions... The Spirit who brings salvation first brooded over the deep to bring order out of chaos."[17] There is a unity to the work of God in creation and redemption and not a dualism, "It is not as if creation before the Fall was graceless. Spirit is moving the entire process toward participation in the love of God, and the whole creation is caught up in it."[18] In my brief examination above of Pinnock's understanding of the Trinity, I mentioned that all of creation is an overflowing and outpouring of God's intrapersonal love that has always existed between the

---

[14] Pinnock writes, "the Son is the *Logos* of creation, the origin and epitome of its order, while the Spirit is the artisan who by skillful ingenuity sees to it that creaturely forms arise and move toward fulfilment." Pinnock, *Flame of Love*, p. 60.

[15] This is a common pattern in Pinnock's theology where he develops a number of possible lines of enquiry only to pursue and develop one at a later juncture.

[16] Pinnock, *Wideness*, p. 78.

[17] Pinnock, *Flame of Love*, op. cit., p. 50.

[18] Ibid., p. 52.

three Persons.[19] Creation, then, is a fruit of God's love, "being love, God ever seeks to share being and communicate presence with it. As a bond of love, as one who fosters fellowship, the Spirit opens up the relationship between God and the world."[20] God created the world for His own pleasure and wants a relationship with it. This involves risk, as part of being in a significant relationship is that love cannot be coerced but must be freely given. God is looking for the echo of Trinitarian life in His creation, this is what brings Him delight.[21] The Spirit's role is to mediate God's presence in creation, making it possible for the creature to participate in God, "as the Spirit mediates the relationship between Father and Son, he also mediates the relationship between creatures and God. The goal is that we may enjoy the responsive relationship the Son enjoys with the Father...bringing creation to its goal is the main task of the Spirit."[22] Pinnock believes there to be some important implications of seeing the Spirit in creation.

The omnipresence of the Spirit means that, "God is present to us in creation, and the world is a natural sacrament."[23] This involves a struggle as the Spirit has to break down the human negation of God that is often seen in the world. However, "...when sin abounds, the Spirit's grace does much more abound."[24] The Spirit cannot be restricted by ecclesiastical boundaries, and because of the Spirit, God is close to every person and can relate to every person through creation. Psalm 139:7 sums up this idea, "Where can I go from your spirit, Where can I flee from your presence," as does Paul in Acts 17:27, "God did this so that men would seek him and perhaps find him, though he is not far from each one of us." Pinnock states:

> The cosmic breadth of Spirit activities can help us conceptualise the universality of God's grace. The Creator's love for the world, central to the Christian message, is implemented by the Spirit... There is no general revelation or natural knowledge of God that is not at the same time gracious revelation and a potentially saving knowledge. All revealing and reaching out are rooted in God's grace and are aimed at bringing sinners home.[25]

A primary truth for Pinnock is that grace is present wherever the Spirit is, for the Spirit is the love of God in the world. Therefore instead of the axiom *extra ecclesiam nulla salus*, (outside the church there is no salva-

---

[19] pp. 64-67.
[20] Pinnock, *Flame of Love*, p. 56.
[21] Ibid., p. 57.
[22] Ibid., p. 60.
[23] Ibid., p. 62.
[24] Ibid.
[25] Ibid., p. 187.

God's Universal Saving Presence 91

tion), Pinnock wishes to hold to the axiom *extra gratiam nulla salus* (outside grace there is no salvation).[26]

An important point I want to note is the strong relationship between the Spirit and the doctrines of providence and divine immanence. On providence Pinnock writes: "*Providence* refers to God's sustaining and governing all things, and therefore indirectly to Spirit's moving in continuing creation."[27] Pinnock's references to divine immanence are important in understanding the trajectory of his theology because as I noted in Ch. 2, Pinnock's paradigm of trinitarian openness seeks to restore a balance in theology by re-affirming the immanence of God. Expounding this further he writes:

> By divine immanence I mean that God is everywhere present in all that exists. The world and God are not radically separated realities - God is present within every created being. As Paul said, quoting a Greek poet, "In him we live and move and have our being" (Acts 17:28). Today we understand the world as an interconnected ecosystem, a dynamic and developing whole, which has made this idea of God's immanence even more meaningful. It has become easier for us to imagine God the Spirit everywhere working as creativity in the whole cosmic situation... Social trinitarian metaphysics (a relational ontology) gives us a God who is ontologically other but at the same time is ceaselessly relating and responsive.[28]

Although Pinnock affirms that God created the world *ex nihilo*[29] and is very careful to distinguish an ontological difference between God and the world,[30] he is not afraid to speak in language that without further explanation could well be interpreted as gravitating towards the boundaries of the 'panentheistic': "God is not a being who dwells at a distance from the world, nor is God a tyrant exercising all-controlling power. Of course God is not the world and the world is not God, *yet God is in the world and the world is in him*. Because he is at the heart of things, it is possible to encoun-

---

[26] Ibid., p. 194. The characteristics and concrete mediation of this grace will be described shortly.
[27] Ibid., p. 53.
[28] Pinnock, 'Systematic Theology,' p. 111f.
[29] Ibid., p. 109.
[30] For example in 'Systematic Theology,' he contrasts his position with that of process theology: "Process theology denies ontological independence, maintaining that God needs the world as much as the world needs God. This drops out the crucial distinction between God and the world so central to the scriptural portrayal. It makes God too passive, able only to experience the world and to organise the elements that present himself to him... The relation of God and creation is asymmetrical" (p. 112).

ter God in, with and beneath life's experiences."[31] Although I will return to the immanence of the Spirit in creation shortly, I want to note that in Pinnock's understanding of God's salvific relation to the world and of the divine presence in creation, there is what might be called a "uniformity of presence," that is to say that Pinnock does not indicate different ways in which God is present to His creation: "The Spirit is present in all human experience and beyond it. There is no special sacred realm, no sacred-secular split - practically anything in the created order can be sacramental of God's presence."[32]

---

[31] Pinnock, *Flame of Love*, p. 61 (my emphasis). Note also this statement: "The Spirit of God indwells creation and works on the inside of it by means of subtle operations... Theology tells us of the power of love within the world that is pushing things forward... Theology can illumine what science discovers by naming the bias toward order within the world. It identifies Spirit as working within nature, unfolding God's purposes by immanent operations. It can point to grace at work within the structures of the world, facilitating the self-transcendence of the creature and bringing a groaning creation to birth." (p. 66). Compare these statements with Kevin Vanhoozer's definition of panentheism: "Panentheism holds that the world is in some sense *in* God, though God exceeds the world... To speak of God the Creator implies not a hard and fast distinction between God and the world but rather a recognition of 'the presence of God *in* the world and the presence of the world *in* God.' [Moltmann, *God in Creation* (San Francisco, 1985), p. 13] Panentheism sits nicely with the notion of continuous creation - the idea that God has established processes in nature that bring about God's purposes over time. It is not as though God has to intervene in the world 'from outside' the world then, but rather that the 'processes revealed by the sciences are themselves God acting as Creator' [A. Peacocke, *Theology for a Scientific Age* (Minneapolis, 1993), p. 176]." in Kevin J. Vanhoozer, 'Effectual Call or Causal Effect? Summons, Sovereignty and Supervenient Grace' in *Tyndale Bulletin* 49.2 (1998), p. 226. Norman Geisler in his book *Creating God in the Image of Man? The New 'Open' View of God - Neotheism's Dangerous Drift* (Minneapolis, 1997) gives a detailed comparison and contrast between classical theism, panentheism and 'trinitarian openness' (what he calls "neotheism"(p. 11)). He notes that while neotheistic positions like Pinnock's cannot be *totally* equated with the panentheism as represented by figures like Alfred North Whitehead, Charles Hartshorne, Schubert Ogden, John Cobb, and Lewis Ford, Pinnock does agree significantly in many areas, for example, the radical reformulation of divine immutability, eternality, simplicity and actuality. His overall conclusion is bluntly negative: "Neotheism finds itself in a theological no-man's-land. For confessedly it fits neither into the categories of classical theism nor contemporary panentheism - deserving a category of its own. Nonetheless, it desires to partake of mutually exclusive attributes, some from classical theism and others from contemporary panentheism. But since these are internally consistent but mutually exclusive systems, one cannot pick and choose among God's essential attributes. This leaves neotheism with an internal incoherence and makes it logically self-destructive and predictability short-lived" (p. 126).

[32] Pinnock, *Flame of Love*, p. 62.

The Spirit and Prevenient Grace

Having noted the universal presence of the Spirit, Pinnock states:

> The Spirit embodies the Prevenient grace of God and puts into effect that universal drawing presence of Jesus Christ. The world is the arena of God's presence, and the Spirit knocks on every human heart, preparing people for the coming of Christ; the Spirit is ever working to realise the saving thrust of God's promise to the world. From the Spirit flows that universal gracing that seeks to lead people into fuller light and love.[33]

It is important to understand Pinnock's use and understanding of 'prevenient grace.' In evangelicalism, the term has been associated with Wesleyan theology,[34] and initially it will be useful to review John Wesley's understanding of the term before coming to Pinnock's use of it.

A WESLYAN UNDERSTANDING OF PREVENIENT GRACE

Wesley's anthropology retains the doctrine of 'total depravity' in line with Calvinist theology. This is the belief not that human beings are as sinful as they can possibly be, but that in their corrupted nature inherited from Adam, every faculty of their being is affected by sin and they are unable to make any move towards God by themselves. Human beings are 'free' according to their nature but in their nature they always choose to reject God: they are slaves to sin.[35] Within Western theology, Reformed Protestants have drawn logical conclusions that such a doctrine leads ultimately to the doctrines of unconditional election and limited atonement.[36] Roman Catholicism on the other hand has generally denied that human beings are totally depraved, and that they are free (albeit through an act of grace in creation) to turn to God in their natural state. Wesley was not satisfied with ei-

---

[33] Pinnock, 'An Inclusivist View,' p. 104.

[34] See ed. T. Jackson, *The Works of John Wesley* 14 Vols. (1832; reprint, Grand Rapids, 1979) 5: 141; 6: 508-512; 7: 373-374, 382; 9: 103; 10: 229-232; 12: 157; 14:356. Pinnock refers to two main works on Wesley, Randy L. Maddox, *Responsible Grace: John Wesley's Practical Theology* (Nashville, 1994); pp. 83-93; H. Ray Dunning, *Grace, Faith and Holiness: A Wesleyan Systematic Theology* (Kansas City, 1988), pp. 158, 338, 431-436. For a more detailed critical interaction with Wesley's doctrine of prevenient grace see Thomas S. Schreiner, 'Does Scripture Teach Prevenient Grace in the Wesleyan Sense?' in eds. T. Schreiner and B. Ware, *The Grace of God, the Bondage of the Will. Vol. 2. Historical and Theological Perspectives on Calvinism* (Grand Rapids, 1995), pp. 365-383. For my exposition of prevenient grace, I have relied heavily on Maddox. He presents a nuanced interpretation of Wesley as well as outlining the main interpretations given in contemporary Wesleyan theology.

[35] I will discuss this concept further in Ch. 9.

[36] This is because the gift of faith is given only to those who are elected and for whom Christ died.

ther of these options. Maddox writes that Wesley felt that the Protestant position limited the scope of grace whereas the Catholic position underestimated the depth of the Fall:

> Thus his orienting concern drove Wesley to search for a way to affirm that *all* possibility of our restored spiritual health - including the earliest inclination and ability to respond to God's saving action - is dependent upon a renewing work of God's grace, *without* rendering our participation in this process automatic. In this search he turned to an emphasis on "prevenience;" i.e. that God's grace always pre-vents (comes before) and makes possible human response.[37]

The idea is that one of the universal benefits of Christ's death is that inherited guilt and total depravity are cancelled.[38] Prevenient grace restores to our nature the ability to respond positively to God's offer of salvation. This restoration is the ability to discern some rudimentary truths about God as well as the ability to discern between good and evil i.e. a conscience. As well as this we are able to respond freely to God: our liberty has been restored. This liberty is the power to accept or reject God's overtures to us: grace is therefore resistible.[39] Here Maddox points to a crucial distinction in Wesley, for prevenient grace is not only the partial restoration of faculties in mankind, but is also God's initial overture to individuals. If a person keeps on rejecting God's overtures, then they may harden their hearts, "the restored potential of our faculties to perceive and respond would theoreti-

---

[37] Maddox, op. cit., p. 83.

[38] Texts cited for this are Tit. 2:11; Jn. 1:9 and Jn. 12:32. In the contemporary analyses consulted concerning Wesley's understanding of prevenient grace, there is no detailed treatment as to the root of this grace. Where does it originate? It is almost assumed that it originates in the death of Christ because of its soteriological function. If this is true then one must ask how (if at all) it operated before the time of Christ. Presumably one answer given is that the benefits of the cross must be seen eternally as God is outside time.

[39] On the basis of prevenient grace, Maddox, op. cit. discusses very briefly Wesley's own position on the unevangelised. He notes that "His conviction of the unfailing justice and universal love of God made it impossible for him to believe that people who lacked knowledge of Christ through no fault of their own (invincible ignorance) would be automatically excluded from heaven" (p. 33). Maddox notes that the later thought of Wesley indicated that the unevangelised could be saved on the basis of the response (made possible through prevenient grace) to the revelation they had received: "while such salvation might be possible without explicit acquaintance with Christ, Wesley would always maintain that it too was 'through Christ,' since any human response to God was possible because of the universal Prevenient Grace of God, which is rooted in the atoning work of Christ" (p. 34).

cally remain upheld, but would be fruitless because unaddressed."⁴⁰ Such a person would need future overtures to be 'awoken.'

Maddox notes that there is much variation in Wesleyan scholarship as to the exact status of prevenient grace. He refers to Thomas Langford's fourfold typology.⁴¹ At one end of the spectrum is the idea that the benefits of prevenient grace are part of the nature of humanity, "this position verges on dismissing total depravity and attributing prevenient grace to creation rather than merciful restoration; i.e. humans are accountable determinators of their destiny simply by the virtue of being human."⁴² The opposite to this reading is the idea that prevenient grace awakens ourselves to our inability and drives us to despair. We realise we can do nothing and can raise no resistance to God's saving grace.⁴³ Maddox comments that Langford believes a truer reading to lie between these extremes, here the difference being one of emphasis: "some scholars stress the possibility of human participation in salvation that prevenient grace restores... Other scholars shy away from any language of human initiative. They argue that the provisions of prevenient grace are simply preparatory to God's further initiative in salvation."⁴⁴

Maddox notes one more characteristic of prevenient grace that needs mentioning, as it is relevant for understanding Pinnock inclusivism. Wesley often equates God's grace with God's love, "since love is inherently a relationship between two persons, this identification suggests that Wesley's conception of grace...is fundamentally relational in nature."⁴⁵ The question now is whether Wesley understands prevenient grace to be 'created' or 'uncreated.' Maddox states that Western theology has generally seen grace as 'created,' that is "a divinely-originated *product* bestowed on humanity,"⁴⁶ and then debated over whether it is the imputation of an alien righteousness (a Conservative Protestant position), or the infusion of an actual character in us (Roman Catholicism). However Eastern theologians have understood grace to be uncreated, it is not a product or possession given to humanity but "the Divine energies *per se* present within us" through the Holy Spirit.⁴⁷ Both Maddox and Langford interpret Wesley's notion to be on the uncreated side, "prevenient grace should not be considered *from* God, but the gift

---

⁴⁰ Ibid., p. 88.
⁴¹ Ibid. See Thomas Langford, 'John Wesley's Doctrine of Justification by Faith' in *Bulletin of the United Church of Canada Committee on Archives and History* 29 (1980), pp. 55-58.
⁴² Ibid., p. 89.
⁴³ Ibid.
⁴⁴ Ibid.
⁴⁵ Ibid., p. 85f.
⁴⁶ Ibid.
⁴⁷ Ibid.

of God's activity in our lives, sensitizing and inviting us."[48] They therefore state that Wesley's consonance is with the Eastern Orthodox position.

PINNOCK'S UNDERSTANDING OF PREVENIENT GRACE

Coming to Pinnock's understanding of prevenient grace, one notices, as with many of the areas mentioned above, that his position has gradually developed over the last twenty years and in this case must be seen in tandem with his development of his anthropology. In his essay 'Responsible Freedom and the Flow of Biblical History' (1975),[49] he refers to sin as being 'inherited' not in a biological or legal sense but historically, we are born into a sinful world and are affected by our surroundings. The misuse of our freedom is the basis of our responsibility before God. The Fall did not take away our ability to choose, rather "it initiated a historical process in which man uses his freedom in morally perverted ways. It did not nullify the fact of man's freedom; it only altered the moral direction of it."[50]

In 'From Augustine to Arminius' (1989), this is given more detail.[51] As already mentioned in Ch. 3, Pinnock's belief in a reciprocity between God and human beings and his espousal of libertarian freedom led him to revise other aspects of his theology, and one area was the depth of human sinfulness. He states that he had two paths to follow: either opt for a doctrine of prevenient grace or question the category of total depravity. Believing that the Bible had no developed doctrine of prevenient grace, Pinnock concentrated on the second path, "...what became decisive for me was the simple fact that Scripture appeals to people as those who are able and responsible to answer to God (however we explain it) and not as those incapable of doing so, as Calvinian logic would suggest."[52] *Theological Crossfire* (1990) continues to deny total depravity while at the same time exploring the possibility of a Wesleyan notion of prevenient grace, "Wesley began to move in a better direction...he taught that the natural propensity to sin can be conquered by God's grace, which is at hand."[53]

Wideness (1992) contains the most unambiguous espousal of a Wesleyan form of prevenient grace. Referring to Romans 3:11, Pinnock states:

---

[48] Ibid., p. 89.

[49] Clark Pinnock, 'Responsible Freedom and the Flow of Biblical History' in ed. Clark Pinnock, *Grace Unlimited* (Minneapolis, 1975), pp. 95-110.

[50] Ibid., p. 104f.

[51] Although Pinnock deals with the issue of freedom, he seems not to have dealt explicitly with this issue of prevenient grace after 1975 until his next work on Arminianism 'From Augustine to Arminius,' op. cit. in 1989.

[52] Pinnock, 'From Augustine to Arminius,' in *The Grace of God and the Will of Man*, p. 22.

[53] Pinnock, *Theological Crossfire*, p. 127f.

Paul is saying that sinners left entirely on their own without the prevenient grace of God do not naturally seek God... Apart from divine grace sinners do not have the inclination to seek God, but under the influence of prevenient grace they may choose to do so...the grace of God mitigates the effects of sinful human life and preserves the creature from self-destruction.[54]

I think that what Pinnock is attempting to do here is to deny total depravity (*contra* Wesley) because this would impinge on libertarian freedom and absolve us of responsibility before God, *and* adopt a notion of prevenient grace in the second sense that Wesley used it, that is referring to God's overtures to the human being.

Pinnock attempts an explanation of this in his latest works and yet again the key to understanding his position is the work of the Spirit. With reference to whether prevenient grace is created or uncreated, Pinnock does not explicitly mention the distinction or which side he favours. However a few statements he makes suggests (albeit quite cryptically) that he comes down on the uncreated side. For example, in 'An Inclusivist View'(1995) he writes, "The Spirit *embodies* the prevenient grace of God and puts into effect that universal drawing action of Jesus Christ."[55] *Flame of Love* (1996) continues this idea, "Spirit challenges everyone to relate to God by means of his self-disclosure... God is revealed in the beauty and order of the natural world and *is* the prevenient grace that benefits every person,"[56] and "Spirit prepares the way for Christ by gracing humanity everywhere. Spirit supplies the prevenient grace that benefits every person."[57]

But is this prevenient grace solely an external overture that can be accepted or rejected by humanity in its natural state? Although Pinnock mainly sees prevenient grace as an offer to the human, he still does refer to an internal working of this grace, "Spirit prepares the sinner to be disposed for relationship, but the outcome is not assured. People may resist God's overtures...grace works within us, but we may stifle the invitation and shut ourselves off."[58] For Pinnock part of being made in the *imago Dei*, means that we can always respond to or resist the Spirit's overtures, this is part of what it means to be human, and has not been destroyed by the Fall: "There is an ember of the image still in us, and the Spirit blows upon it. People have capacity for the faith God looks for. The Spirit woos us but does not impose on us... Salvation requires both the operation of grace and the hu-

---

[54] Pinnock, *Wideness*, p. 103.
[55] Pinnock, 'An Inclusivist View,' p. 104 (my emphasis).
[56] Pinnock, *Flame of Love*, p. 61 (my emphasis).
[57] Ibid., p. 63.
[58] Ibid., p. 158f.

man will."⁵⁹ On what it means to be made in the *imago Dei*, Pinnock likes the distinction Orthodox theologians make between the image and likeness of God. He says that the Fall threatened our likeness to God, but we remain in the image of God and part of this image is not a radical loss of dignity and freedom. He writes, "Orthodoxy's recognition of the distinction between image and likeness explains in part why the doctrine of original sin did not take hold in Orthodox circles as strongly as it did in the West."⁶⁰

How are we to understand these statements? Clearly in holding together both prevenient grace and a denial of total depravity, there is an ambiguity in a statement like, "God invites us to turn because we *can* turn."⁶¹ Does this mean that we can turn to God in our natural state without prevenient grace? Or does it mean that we need God's prevenient grace to be able to turn to God? Is our ability to respond to God grounded in creation (being made in the image of God) or grounded in restoration (the work of prevenient grace after the Fall)? Pinnock definitely believes that prevenient grace co-operates with the human will: "Apart from grace there cannot be faith, but faith is authentically a human response and act of cooperation. Faith does not make grace unnecessary, and grace does not make faith automatic."⁶²

Within the context of Wesleyan theology, Pinnock seems closest to Langford's first interpretation that says that the benefits of prevenient grace are part of what it means to be human. What all humans witness throughout their lives is the overtures of the Spirit - that is prevenient grace. What is interesting here, is that Langford refers to this position being implied in Umphrey Lee's claim that for Wesley, the 'natural man' is a logical abstraction.⁶³ Language like this suggests that discussing Pinnock's concept of prevenient grace in the context of Wesley's soteriology may be in fact the wrong context in which to understand Pinnock, and may be the cause of confusion over what exactly he is saying. This feeling is heightened as Pinnock contrasts his version of prevenient grace with the Calvinist/Reformed doctrine of 'common grace' that too is a universal grace. Berkhof defines 'common grace' as follows:

> ...those general operations of the Holy Spirit whereby, He, without renewing the heart, exercises such a moral influence on man through His general or special revelation, that sin is restrained, order is maintained in so-

---

⁵⁹ Ibid., p. 160.
⁶⁰ Ibid., p. 175. On the Orthodox distinction between image and likeness, Pinnock refers to Vladimir Lossky, *Orthodox Theology: An Introduction* (Crestwood, 1978), pp. 119-137, and idem *In the Image and Likeness of God* (London, 1975).
⁶¹ Ibid.
⁶² Ibid., p. 161.
⁶³ Maddox, op. cit., p. 89, n. 173. Langford is commenting on Umphrey Lee, *John Wesley and Modern Religion* (Nashville, 1936), pp. 124-125, 315.

cial life, and civil righteousness is promoted; or, those general blessings, such as rain and sunshine, food and drink...which God imparts to all men indiscriminately where and in what measure seems good to him.[64]

The crucial distinction to be made here, is that although common grace is universal and indiscriminate, it is not saving grace and special grace is needed to remove the penalty and guilt of sin. Special grace is irresistible and discriminate; it comes only to the elect.[65] For Pinnock such a distinction between common grace and special grace is dualistic, as for him it implies two Spirits at work in the world.[66] For him where there is the Spirit, there is grace, for the Spirit embodies grace. All grace is an overflow of God's trinitarian love. So there can be no distinction between common and special grace because Pinnock's definition of grace is not so much God's unmerited and undeserved favour (although it includes this), but rather it is God's providential presence in all humanity that has the potential to lead to salvation. Again it should be added that as just as I noted a 'uniformity' in Pinnock's theology with regards to God's relationship to the world and the divine presence, so the same can be said about Pinnock's conception of grace: all grace is saving grace, wherever God is present so saving grace is present.[67] By Pinnock positing one type of universal potentially saving grace, the context for discussion appears to have moved out of the doctrine of soteriology which in evangelical theology has been the traditional location in which to discuss grace, and moved into the doctrine of creation.

Putting together the above insight on the location of grace, I want to suggest that a more suitable context in which to understand Langford's first interpretation, and therefore Pinnock's view of prevenient grace which I have aligned to it, is a particular understanding of the traditional nature/grace debate as evident in much modern theology. If one adds to this what I have said about the Spirit's immanence in creation, then I think one can begin to see more clearly the theological context and genesis of his position. Kevin Vanhoozer talks about prevenient grace but not in the Wesleyan sense. Referring to those like Pinnock who hold an 'open view' of God, he writes:

For these theologians, there is only one kind of grace, one kind of call, and one kind of way in which God is related to the world. God exerts a

---

[64] Louis Berkhof, *Systematic Theology* (Edinburgh, 1958), p. 436.
[65] For a useful summary of common grace see Grudem, op. cit., pp. 657-667. Again at the end of this section, Grudem lists treatments of common grace in the major evangelical systematic theologies, pp. 666f.
[66] See *Wideness*, p. 103; *Flame of Love*, p. 200.
[67] Shortly, I will note the same feature concerning Pinnock's doctrine of revelation, i.e. all revelation is saving revelation.

constant attractive force on the soul - a kind of divine gravity. This universal call comes through a variety of media: the creation itself, conscience, as well as proclamation about Christ. Grace is therefore 'prevenient': that which 'comes before' a person's ability to repent and believe.[68]

This returns us to Pinnock's notion of divine immanence through the cosmic presence of the Spirit. Compare Pinnock's version of prevenient grace with another insight of Vanhoozer:

> Tillich, Schleiermacher and many other modern theologians agree that God is the one to whom we are always/already related... God is not a being alongside other beings, but an energy that is constantly being experienced to sustain us on our way, whether or not we are conscious of the fact: 'all divine grace is always prevenient.' [Schleiermacher, *The Christian Faith* (Edinburgh, 1928), p. 485, n. 2] For much modern theology, then, prevenient grace has become a matter of *ontology*.[69]

Rather than seeing nature and grace as distinct and separate concepts, Pinnock appears to be advocating the infusion of the two with saving grace being present within the natural realm from creation: "We refuse to allow the disjunction between nature and grace...on the supposition that, if the triune God is present, grace must be present too."[70]

At this point and in order to further understand Pinnock's notion of prevenient grace, I want to place Pinnock's argument on the Spirit's immanence and embodiment of grace within the context of the Roman Catholic understanding of nature and grace and more specifically within the context of Vatican II and Karl Rahner's notion of the 'supernatural existential,' his solution to the nature/grace debate and what Duffy calls "the single most significant Catholic contribution to an understanding of the nature-grace dialectic in the twentieth century."[71] This move into the realm of Catholic theology is prompted by Pinnock himself: "I make no apology as an evangelical in admitting an enormous debt of gratitude to the Council for its guidance on this topic."[72]

---

[68] Vanhoozer, op. cit., p. 223.

[69] Ibid., p. 224f. Vanhoozer notes that such a conception of grace has implications as regards grace's efficacy: "God is not the ruler of the universe but its wooer, working not with causal power but with the power of love and persuasion...God and the world come together to converse, to 'enjoy' one another." (p. 225). This language is very similar to that of Pinnock.

[70] Pinnock, 'An Inclusivist View,' p. 98.

[71] Stephen J. Duffy, *The Graced Horizon: Nature and Grace in Modern Catholic Thought* (Minnesota, 1992), p. 206.

[72] Pinnock, 'An Inclusivist View,' p. 97. Further on in this essay he notes: "As an inclusivist, I acknowledge my debt to the Catholic Church for its leadership in this regard,

PREVENIENT GRACE AND THE 'SUPERNATURAL EXISTENTIAL'

Noting the classical Thomist distinction between *gratia creata sive communis* (the gracious providence of the Creator of all beings), and *gratia increata sive supernaturalis* (salvific Christological grace and the participation in the properties of the triune God), Miikka Ruokanen notes that through development, the standard dogmatic position on the possibility of salvation *extra Ecclesiam* by Vatican II was that by natural grace

> all rational beings... are able to recognise the existence of their Creator through analogy with nature, and to understand basic moral truths on the basis of natural moral law engraved on their consciences. God may offer a special kind of grace for achieving eternal blessedness to such a man of 'good will' who reveres God, seeks his truths, and is obedient to his voice heard on conscience.[73]

Already, this brief definition has affinities with what I will say in the next chapter concerning Pinnock's construction of the 'faith principle.' However, given what I have already noted about the immanence of the Spirit in creation, I think there is an even stronger affinity between Pinnock's version of prevenient grace and the *"nouvelle théologie"*[74] which attempted to merge the distinction between *gratia creata sive communis* and *gratia increata sive supernaturalis*. Ruokanen writes:

> New theology emphasised that man is never 'pure nature,' but his nature is by definition graced nature; all human existence is influenced by the supernatural finality inherent in it. *Gratia universalis* is not just an offer of salvific christological grace, but consists of the reality of supernatural, christological grace already existing within all humanity; this grace is unconditionally poured out upon all humanity everywhere. All human beings, created in God's image, are, by virtue of creation and incarnation, already partakers in supernatural divine light of revelation, and in the superadditional grace of the Triune God; innate *gratia creata sive communis* is supernatural christological and pneumatological grace as such. In the modern concept of grace, the independent theology as focused on nature

---

and, as an evangelical, I am concerned that the model be shown to be congruent with the Scriptures. In agreement with the Scriptures, I want the model to be not only theologically coherent but also exegetically well founded" (p. 109).

[73] Miikka Ruokanen, *The Catholic Doctrine of Non-Christian Religions According to the Second Vatican Council* (Leiden, 1992), p. 13.

[74] Ibid., p. 25.

as well as the concept of natural moral law are weakened in favor of the theologies of redemption and sanctification.[75]

In *Flame of Love* (1996), Pinnock claims that Karl Rahner's "supernatural existential" defends the doctrine of prevenient grace and the universality of the Spirit's operations albeit in existential neo-Thomistic language.[76] Rahner too seeks to mediate universality and particularity and the 'supernatural existential' opens up the possibility to accept or reject God's grace. Departing from the classical distinction between nature and grace, Rahner does not view grace as an external 'add on' to human nature, but rather sees nature as being infused with grace, so blurring the traditional distinctions between the two concepts: "This 'supernatural existential,' considered as God's act of self-bestowal which he offers to men, is universally grafted into the very roots of human existence."[77] This grace is uncreated. As Badcock notes, "What is communicated, as Rahner puts it, is not information about God, or some non-divine creaturely reality that mediates grace, but rather grace as the gift of God himself: 'God in his own proper reality makes himself the innermost constitutive element of man.'"[78] Both Duffy and Ruokanen echo this point:

> Thus the supernatural existential that marks historical humanity's situation is seen to be God's ever-present offer of God's own Self. So it is that grace, transcendental revelation, and supernatural existential express one and the same reality. The supernatural existential refers to the abiding di-

---

[75] Ibid. Ruokanen includes in this category, Henri de Lubac, Jean Daniélou, Karl Rahner, Heinz Robert Schlette and Hans Küng.

[76] See Pinnock *Flame of Love*, p. 199. Here Pinnock refers to Karl Rahner's *Foundations of the Christian Faith* (New York, 1978), pp. 126-137, 147, 176. See also Karl Rahner *Theological Investigations* Vol. 1. (London, 1961), 'Concerning the Relationship Between Nature and Grace' pp. 287-317; 'Some Implications of the Scholastic Concept of Uncreated Grace,' pp. 319-346; *Theological Investigations* Vol. 4 (London, 1966), Ch. 7: 'Nature and Grace.'

[77] Karl Rahner, 'Church, Churches and Religions,' in *Theological Investigations* Vol. 10, (New York, 1974), p. 36.

[78] Gary Badcock, 'Karl Rahner, the Trinity and Religious Pluralism' in ed. Vanhoozer, *The Trinity in a Pluralistic Age*, p. 145. Badcock is quoting Rahner from, 'The Christian Understanding of Redemption,' in *Theological Investigations* Vol. 21 (London, 1988), p. 116. Rahner makes the same point in his essay 'Nature and Grace,' op. cit., "With a more exact concept of 'uncreated grace' in mind, we can see more clearly how the Catholic theology of grace, on its own proper principles (grace is not just pardon for the poor sinner but 'participation in the divine nature'), can go beyond the notion of a *merely* entitative, created state and merely 'ontic' and non-existential element of a 'physical accident.' Grace is God himself, the communication in which he gives himself to man as the divinizing favour that he is himself. Here is work is really *himself*, since it is he who is imparted" (p. 177).

vine immanence in which God offers to humanity Godself and the possibility of the free response of faith.[79]

From the ontological point of view, God is the "innermost substance" (entelekheia) of the world. Because of the essential presence of God in being, the human world has become habitually saturated with the grace of God. Consequently, ontologically every man exists under the influence of divine supernatural grace.[80]

Human existence then is 'supernatural' as there is a transcendental revelation infused into our nature. Therefore like Lee's claim, the 'natural man' is a logical abstraction because he cannot be separated from the graced Man. As Demarest notes:

> Grace, in fact, interpenetrates nature and divinizes it; i.e., supernaturally imparts to it divine life and power. Man thus finds grace where he finds himself - in the everyday life of his finite spirit. Man as transcendental consciousness, discovers that he is energised by the *élan* of grace, as the inescapable condition of his existence. On this showing, the existence even on the unbeliever is constantly being shaped by the supernatural grace that inexorably is being offered to it. Even secular experience in a profound sense is an experience of grace.[81]

This divine-self communication can be accepted and said to be 'salvific:'

> When a person in theoretical or practical knowledge or in subjective activity confronts the abyss of his existence...and when this person has the courage to look into himself and to find in these depths his ultimate truth, there he can also have the experience that this abyss accepts him as his true and forgiving security.[82]

This is a transcending of the ego and a grasping for God, even though it may be unreflexive and unthematic: it is a real act of faith prompted and

---

[79] Duffy, op. cit., p. 210. In his book, *A Rahner Reader* (London, 1975), G. McCool, in his introduction to a selection of Rahner's essays on 'Nature and Grace,' writes: "God's offer of grace is an offer of himself. Justifying grace is primordially Uncreated Grace, the indwelling of the economical Trinity within the justified soul. Because of the inseparable connection between God's decrees of creation and of the Incarnation, Uncreated Grace has been offered to man since the beginning of human history as the grace of Christ" (p. 174).
[80] Ruokanen, op. cit., p. 32.
[81] Bruce Demarest, *General Revelation: Historical Views and Contemporary Issues* (Grand Rapids, 1982), p. 190.
[82] Rahner, *Foundations of the Christian Faith*, p. 132.

made possible by grace. It is a universal possibility and takes place, "wherever we are living out our existence."[83] More will be said about this act of faith when we come to discuss Pinnock's 'ethical faith principle.'[84]

Can Pinnock's understanding of prevenient grace be compared to Rahner's 'supernatural existential'? Clearly there are significant differences, in that Rahner's framework for his theological anthropology is transcendental Thomism.[85] However both Pinnock and Rahner wish to affirm: God's universal salvific will; the universal accessibility of saving grace (grace being the self-communication of God Himself); the notion that creation is in some way graced and can be sacramental of God's presence; and the idea that if one opens oneself up to the 'divine mystery,' one can have a relationship with God. Pinnock appears to be striving for an evangelical Protestant version of Rahner's 'supernatural existential' using the language of the Spirit: "Because he is at the heart of things, it is possible to encounter God in, with and beneath life's experiences. By the Spirit, power of creation, God is closer to us than we are to ourselves."[86] It is interesting to note that Paul Knitter calls Rahner's 'supernatural existential,' "the Catholic version of the mainline Protestant affirmation of general revelation."[87] From what I will say shortly about general revelation, I do not think this comparison would normally be correct as orthodox evangelicalism has maintained that general revelation is not a salvific revelation. However, again as I will show below, for Pinnock this revelation can be salvific and so Knitter's comparison is a legitimate one.

Using this concept of prevenient grace, Pinnock can now demonstrate clearly the principle of universal accessibility:

---

[83] Ibid.
[84] See below pp. 116-125.
[85] D'Costa defines this as, "interpreting Aquinas in the light of Kant, understood through the filter of the early Heidegger and Maréchal." in 'Theology of Religions' in ed. David F. Ford, *The Modern Theologians. An Introduction to Christian Theology in the Twentieth Century* Vol. II (Oxford, 1993), p. 278.
[86] Pinnock, *Flame of Love*, p. 61.
[87] *No Other Name? A Critical Survey of Christian Attitudes Toward the World Religions* (New York, 1994), p. 125. This parallel is seen to be even more explicit if one equates the 'supernatural existential' with one's conscience, as in Protestant theology the conscience has traditionally been seen as a fruit of general revelation. Bruce Demarest in his critique of Pinnock, notices the similarities between his view of grace and Rahner's: "[Pinnock's] exposition of grace reminds us of Karl Rahner's concept of the 'supernatural existential,' which the neo-Scholastic, Catholic theologian developed within a panentheistic world-view"(p. 202). See Bruce Demarest, 'General and Special Revelation. Epistemological Foundations of Religious Pluralism' in eds. Andrew D. Clarke and Bruce W. Winter, *One God, One Lord, Christianity in a World of Religious Pluralism* (Grand Rapids, 1992).

God wants a relationship with sinners, and if we accept the category of prevenient grace, we acknowledge that God offers himself to creatures. Spirit speaks to everyone in the depths of their being, urging them not to close themselves off to God but to open themselves up. Because of Spirit, everyone has the possibility of encountering him - *even those who have not heard of Christ may establish a relationship with God through prevenient grace.*[88]

But if grace is to be located in the Spirit's presence in creation, then how is grace related to re-creation in Christ?

The Spirit and Christ

CHRISTOLOGY FROM THE PERSPECTIVE OF PNEUMATOLOGY

Pinnock believes that recognising the Spirit in creation means that there will not be a disjunction between the *opera ad extra* in creation and redemption. As outlined in Pinnock's Christology, we must look at redemption from the perspective of the Spirit: "Spirit prepares the way for Christ by gracing humanity everywhere...what one encounters in Jesus is the fulfilment of previous invitations of the Spirit."[89] Here one must be careful not to misunderstand Pinnock. He understands the tension caused by affirming universality (God loves the whole world) and particularity (Jesus is the only way to God). To mediate this we must understand the twin missions of Son and Spirit which are complementary not contradictory:

> The truth of the incarnation does not eclipse the truth about the Spirit, who was at work in the world before Christ and is present now where Christ is not named... On the one hand, the Son's mission presupposes the Spirit's - Jesus was conceived and empowered by the Spirit. On the other hand, the mission of the Spirit is orientated to the goals of incarnation. The Spirit's mission is to bring history to completion and fulfilment in Christ.[90]

For Pinnock the idea of the "two hands of God"[91] answers the question of access to grace: "Access to grace is less of a problem for theology when we consider it from the perspective of the Spirit, because whereas Jesus be-

---

[88] Pinnock, *Flame of Love*, p. 199 (my emphasis).
[89] Ibid., p. 63.
[90] Ibid., p. 194.
[91] Ibid., p. 58. Pinnock borrows this phrase from Irenaeus. See Irenaeus' *Against Heresies* V, 6, I.

speaks particularity, Spirit bespeaks universality. The incarnation occurred in a thin slice of Palestine, but its implications touch the farthest star."[92]

The incarnation must be seen as the apex of the Spirit's mission begun at creation. Jesus is the clearest and most explicit demonstration of God's love, but was not the first demonstration of this love. We will return to this point in the next chapter for it raises the crucial question as to whether the incarnation for Pinnock is representative or constitutive.

THE REJECTION OF THE *FILIOQUE*

One important trinitarian point in Pinnock's understanding of the twin missions of the Son and Spirit is his denial of the *filioque* in line with Eastern Orthodox thinking.[93] Far from being a "futile and useless question,"[94] Pinnock thinks that a denial of the *filioque* is crucial to the universality axiom. For him, the *filioque* can promote Christomonism because it "could give the impression"[95] that the work of the Spirit is restricted to the sphere of the Son and the boundary of the Church, rather than a gift of the Father to creation universally. It encourages the subordination of the Spirit and diminishes his own special, separate role in the economy of salvation. He says that the *filioque*

> ...does not encourage us to view the divine mission [of the Spirit] as being prior to and geographically larger than the Son's. It could seem to limit Spirit to having a noetic function in relation to Christ, as if the Spirit fostered faith in him and nothing more... The creed was better before this term was added to it, because it recognised Spirit as the power permeating the cosmos and energizing all of history. The mission of the Spirit is not subordinate to the Son's but equal and complementary. The *filioque* was introduced into the creed in an irregular way and adversely affects our understanding of salvation.[96]

---

[92] Ibid., p. 188.

[93] Ibid., p. 196f. Pinnock appears to have been influenced by an article by Georges Khodr, 'Christianity in a Pluralistic World - The Economy of the Holy Spirit' in *Ecumenical Review* 23 (1971), pp. 118-128; Yves Congar, 'Christomonism and the *Filioque*' chapter 7 in *The Word and the Spirit* (London, 1986); Ernst Benz, *The Eastern Orthodox Church* (New York, 1963); and Timothy Ware, *The Orthodox Church* (London, 1963), p. 222. At this point, Pinnock makes no reference to the symposium ed. Lukas Vischer, *Spirit of God, Spirit of Christ: Ecumenical Reflections on the Filioque Controversy* (London, 1981); nor Vladimir Lossky, 'The Procession of the Holy Spirit in Orthodox Trinitarian Theology' in, *In the Image and Likeness of God* (New York, 1974), pp. 71-96. Pinnock is familiar with this latter work (see p. 98 n. 50). However he does not mention it in connection with the discussion on the *filioque*.

[94] Pinnock, *Wideness*, p. 78.

[95] Pinnock, *Flame of Love*, p. 196.

[96] Ibid, p. 196f.

Limiting the activity of the Spirit is one criticism Pinnock has of Barth. He claims that Barth was not open to general revelation or other religions because he was a strong defender of the *filioque* and so became a Christomonist: "Barth is proof that a high Christology can be used to entail narrowness and justify pluralist fears in that regard."[97]

Summary

To summarise this section the following may be said: From the foundation of the relational ontology of the Trinity, God through the interdependent twin-missions of Son and Spirit pours out His love into the world thus demonstrating His universal salvific will. The Spirit is omnipresent in every part of the world offering to every man and woman prevenient grace; a grace that is fulfilled in the universal act of representation made by Christ through his life, death and resurrection. Therefore salvation is universally accessible even for those who never come into contact with the Gospel and we can be optimistic about the number of people accepting this offer of grace.

In this chapter I have described Pinnock's position of universal accessibility through the work of the Spirit. However, this is only half the story: one half of the 'cosmic covenant.' Having established the universality of Christ's work and the offer of prevenient grace through the omnipresence of the Spirit, two questions remain with respect to the unevangelised: How can the unevangelised accept the offer of prevenient grace? Through what channels is this prevenient grace mediated to the unevangelised? The answers to one question necessarily impinges on the other and together they form humanity's response to the 'cosmic covenant.' This Pinnock calls the 'faith principle.'

---

[97] Pinnock, *Wideness*, p. 79. Pinnock makes no references to where Barth defends the *filioque*. For Barth's defence see *Church Dogmatics* 1.1: 'The Doctrine of the Word of God' (Edinburgh, 1975), pp. 473-487.

CHAPTER 5

'The Cosmic Covenant': Humanity's Free Response to God through the 'Faith Principle'

Introduction

God offers Himself to every person in the world through the prevenient grace of the Spirit whether they have heard of Christ or not. Pinnock believes that the unevangelised can be saved by the "faith principle"[1]: "By faith, one receives the prevenient grace of God on the basis of an honest search for God and obedience to God's word as heard in heart and conscience... There is no time or space where he [Spirit] is not free to move or where a person cannot call on God for mercy."[2]

The idea of the 'faith principle' first appears in embryonic form in 'The Finality of Jesus Christ in a World of Religions'(1988). Speaking on the problem of accessibility of salvation to the marginalised, Pinnock states that God has regard for faith even when it is incomplete propositionally speaking. This is how Old Testament believers were saved, and so, "in the same way today, people who are spiritually "before Christ" even though they are chronologically "Anno Domini" can trust God on the basis of the light they have."[3] In 'Toward an Evangelical Theology of Religions' (1989) Pinnock re-enforces this idea: "surely God judges the heathen in relation to the light

---

[1] Pinnock's first use of this term is in *A Wideness in God's Mercy: The Finality of Jesus Christ in a World Of Religions* (Grand Rapids, 1992), p. 96.

[2] Clark H. Pinnock, 'An Inclusivist View,' in eds. Dennis L. Okholm and Timothy R. Phillips, *More Than One Way? Four Views of Salvation in a Pluralistic World* (Grand Rapids, 1995), p. 117.

[3] Clark H. Pinnock, 'The Finality of Jesus Christ in a World of Religions' in eds. Mark A. Noll and David F. Wells, *Christian Faith and Practice in the Modern World* (Grand Rapids, 1988), pp. 152-171. On this point Pinnock appears to align himself with Norman Anderson's argument in his seminal *Christianity and World Religions: The Challenge of Pluralism* (Leicester, 1984). For more on this book and its influence on Pinnock see below p. 111 n. 11; p. 135 n. 108.

they have, not according to the light that did not reach them."[4] It is also worth noting that even at this early stage Pinnock states that one cannot deny the "essential truth"[5] of Vatican II's *Dogmatic Constitution of the Church* 16.[6]

These ideas start to receive more detailed treatment in *Wideness* (1992) where Pinnock actually first uses the term 'the faith principle.' Pinnock believes this principle to be enshrined in Heb. 11:6, "Without faith it is impossible to please God, because anyone who comes to him must believe that he exists and that he rewards those who earnestly seek him." For Pinnock it is not a certain amount of theological information that saves, but the direction of the heart and the way people respond to the light of revelation they do have through the witness of creation and providence which are gifts of God and potentially salvific. God has not left himself without a witness (Acts 4:17).

But what is the specific content of Pinnock's definition of faith, and to whom is it directed? Pinnock writes that the 'faith principle' is epitomised in Peter's statement directed towards Cornelius in Acts 10:34, "I now realise how true it is that God does not show favouritism but accepts men from every nation who fear him and do what is right." In this statement there are two criteria that comprise the 'faith principle,' the cognitive (fearing God), and the ethical (doing what is right). Pinnock admits that Peter puts both criteria together in association.[7] However in 'An Inclusivist View'(1995) and *Flame of Love* (1996),[8] Pinnock appears to treat both criteria separately as if both can independently fulfill the condition of faith to enter into a saving relationship with God. I will deal therefore with both 'versions' of the faith principle: the cognitive, propositional or explicit 'faith principle' which is an extension of (but in line with) more orthodox evangelical positions on the unevangelised,[9] and the ethical, behavioural or implicit version which is far more controversial for evangelicals and which bears closer resemblance to certain mainstream inclusivist positions.[10]

---

[4] Clark H. Pinnock, 'Toward an Evangelical Theology of Religions' *Journal of the Evangelical Theological Society* 33 (September 1990), p. 367.
[5] Ibid.
[6] Pinnock refers to this again in later writings, see below p. 117.
[7] Pinnock, *Wideness*, p. 98.
[8] Clark H. Pinnock, *Flame of Love: A Theology of the Holy Spirit* (Downers Grove, 1996).
[9] See Appendix 1 for a list of evangelicals who with regard to the salvation of the unevangelised hold to some form of 'implicit faith.'
[10] For example the statements of the Second Vatican Council on other religions, and Karl Rahner's position on the anonymous Christians.

The Cognitive 'Faith Principle'

The Analogy with Premessianic Believers

Firstly, Pinnock draws our attention to the "holy pagans" of the Old Testament, figures including Enoch, Melchizedek, Abimelech, Jethro and Job.[11] Such figures fell outside the stream of revealed religion given to Abraham and then Israel, but were saved because they cast themselves on the mercy of God despite having an inadequate theology. They did have faith in God and trusted in Him, and God took account of this. Pinnock says that no evangelical today would doubt the salvific status of these figures despite the fact that epistemologically they knew nothing about Christ. Pinnock now asks whether it would make any difference if Job had been born in A.D. 1900 in Outer Mongolia? He believes God would deal with a person in the same way, for the unevangelised are informationally premessianic and in the same spiritual state. They can be saved by faith like these chronologically premessianic figures:[12]

> Like Job and Abimelech, there are those who, due to an inner voice, come to a fork in the road and come to God in faith. There is always a way, whatever the path, to come to God. It is always possible to move closer to God than farther away. Those who desire God will be led by his Spirit to closer communion with him.[13]

Pinnock believes that this is a valid analogy because the unevangelised and the 'holy pagans' of the Old Testament both fall under the universal covenant that God established with Noah (Gen. 8). If salvation denotes a relationship with God, then people can be saved under the Noahic covenant, the Old covenant established with Abraham, and the New covenant established in Christ. He admits that there is more complete knowledge and assurance in the later covenants, but that God can relate to people in all three covenants, "In all three, God justifies Jews and Gentiles on the ground of faith, the condition for salvation in all dispensations."[14]

It is not only 'holy pagans' who were saved by the 'faith principle.' Premessianic Jews, although living in a specific covenant, were still saved by faith as the story of Abraham shows, "Abraham believed in the Lord, and he credited it to him as righteousness." (Gen. 15:6); "All who have faith are sons of Abraham and are blessed with him" (Gal. 3:7). They too

---

[11] Pinnock, *Wideness*, p. 161; Pinnock, *Flame of Love*, p. 198. Pinnock derives the expression 'holy pagan' from Jean Danielou, *Holy Pagans of the Old Testament* (London, 1957).
[12] See Pinnock, *Wideness*, p. 161.
[13] Ibid., p. 161f.
[14] Ibid., p. 105.

had no knowledge of Christ although they were saved by his life, death and resurrection. The sacrificial system did not save in itself but foreshadowed the greatest sacrifice, the Lamb of God who took away the sins of the world.[15]

The Nature and Efficacy of General Revelation

Pinnock's argument seems to aim at widening the boundaries of propositional knowledge required in order to be saved. Rather than having a restrictive definition of faith that includes knowledge of Christ and his work that is only available through the Gospel proclamation and 'special revelation,' Pinnock's looser definition means that the knowledge available through 'general revelation' is sufficient to be saved if it is believed. So instead of the classical definition of Christian faith as *notitia* - the knowledge by our minds of Jesus Christ; *assensus* - the assent of our wills to Jesus Christ; and *fiducia* - the trust of our hearts in Jesus Christ,[16] Pinnock's definition of faith could be defined as follows: *notitia* - the knowledge of our minds of God; *assensus* - the assent of our wills to God; and *fiducia* - the trust of our hearts in God. This is still a holistic definition of faith and not a bare propositionalism but the object of knowledge has changed. Salvation can therefore be universal because 'general revelation' is universal.

But what precisely is 'general revelation' and what is its efficacy? Pinnock's definition of general revelation is in line with evangelical orthodoxy, it being the witness of God in creation, providence and the *imago Dei*. Pinnock states that although conservative evangelical theology as the heir of Augustinianism has not followed the Christomonistic tendency of Barth and denied that general revelation exists, these same evangelicals have been pessimistic about the salvific ability of general revelation.[17] Demarest's

---

[15] Ibid., p. 163. Here Pinnock refers to Norman Anderson, *Christianity and World Religions* (Downers Grove, 1984), p. 144. Anderson's book originally entitled 'Christianity and Comparative Religion' (1970) but revised and re-titled *Christianity and World Religions* (1984) has become somewhat of an evangelical *locus classicus* on exclusivism and religious pluralism and was one of the first evangelical works to draw the analogy between pre-messianic believers and the unevangelised. Pinnock comments that the work of Anderson helped him as a student, "avoid the narrow outlook toward other faiths that was otherwise characteristic of evangelicalism" in 'An Inclusivist View,' p. 107.

[16] Quoted from Gabriel Fackre, 'Response to Sanders' in ed. J. Sanders, *What About Those Who Have Never Heard? Three Views on the Destiny of the Unevangelised* (Downers Grove, 1995), p. 57.

[17] To whom is Pinnock referring to here? This is difficult to specify but I think he means the Reformation tradition beginning with Luther and Calvin (Calvin in the *Institutes* I (vi) distinguishes between the knowledge of God as Creator and the knowledge of God as Redeemer), the Reformed Confessions of faith (e.g. Article II of the Belgic

summary of this position on general revelation is useful and I will mention some of the main points he makes.[18]

Evangelicals have maintained that there is genuine knowledge of God to be found in creation and the *imago Dei*, most importantly the conscience which is the "law written on their [the Gentiles] hearts" (Rom. 2:15). Some of the classical texts for general revelation are Rom. 1: 18-32; 2: 12-16; Psalm. 19:4; Acts. 14:17; 17:26-27; Deut. 4:19. Interpreting these passages, Demarest notes six points concerning general revelation:

1. All people everywhere know God and His defining characteristics. This is theism defined in H.P. Owen's words as "belief in one God who is personal, worthy of adoration, separate from the world but consciously active in it."[19]

2. Knowledge of God is an *a priori* intuition, the supreme first truth, "they know God's righteous decree" (Rom. 1:32).

3. Knowledge of God is also *a posteriori* by reflection on the created world.

4. Mankind consistently suppresses this intuitive and inferred knowledge of God and turns to idolatry. By nature pre-Christians do not know God in a redemptive sense.

5. The result of this universal rebellion is that God gives human beings over to their sin and permits its consequences to take its course.

6. This rebellion establishes Man's guilt before God. They are without excuse and accountable. Demarest writes, "In practice, then, general revela-

---

Confession (1561/1619) and Art. I.1 of the Westminster Confession of Faith) and the work of contemporary 'Reformed' evangelicals like Carl Henry, *God, Revelation and Authority*, 6 Vols. (Waco, 1976-1983), 1:399-402; 2:69-76, 83-90. Milliard Erickson, *Christian Theology* 3 Vols. (Grand Rapids, 1981), pp. 57-77, 276-277; and Bruce Demarest, *General Revelation: Historical Views and Contemporary Issues* (Grand Rapids, 1982); *idem* 'General and Special Revelation: Epistemological Foundations of Religious Pluralism' in eds. Andrew D. Clarke and Bruce W. Winter, *One God, One Lord, Christianity in a World of Religious Pluralism* (Grand Rapids, 1992); Gordon R. Lewis and Bruce Demarest, *Integrative Theology* 3 Vols. (Grand Rapids, 1987), 1: 59-93. For some nuances on general revelation between three different Reformed theologians, see N. H. Gootjes, 'General Revelation in its Relation to Special Revelation' in *Westminster Theological Journal* 51 (1989), pp. 359-368.

[18] See 'General and Special Revelation,' op. cit.

[19] H. P. Owen, 'Theism' in *Encyclopedia of Philosophy* (New York, 1967), Vol. 8:97. Quoted from Lewis and Demarest, *Integrative Theology*, 1: 72.

tion becomes not an instrument of universal judgment...the *effect* of general revelation, not God's *purpose* in it, is to render sinners judicially guilty."[20]

Therefore general revelation is not sufficient to save, it can only condemn. This is because firstly, it is epistemologically deficient and contains no redemptive truths.[21] The most it can do is reveal our guilt before God. What is needed is a more effectual revelation, and this comes through the stream of redemptive history culminating in the incarnation: "this fuller knowledge of God's nature and redemptive purposes provides the objective basis for faith's informed decision."[22] Secondly, even if this revelation could save, no-one would ever respond to it. Sin is so entrenched in the human race that everyone suppresses the truth they have about God. General revelation is sufficient to condemn but lacks the sufficient grace of enablement which makes faith possible, even faith which involves honouring God, giving Him thanks or casting oneself on God's mercy.

Pinnock strongly disagrees with this view of general revelation, as he believes that all revelation has salvific potential. As seen earlier, Pinnock sees a unity in God's work, the Spirit being active in creation and redemption, "Creation and redemption, then, are continuous, not discontinuous. Creation is not a work lacking in grace but the gift of divine love."[23] The revelation in creation is capable of mediating knowledge about God, "God, the compassionate Father of our Lord Jesus Christ, is always and everywhere seeking lost sheep."[24] Pinnock accuses those who hold to a disjunction between general and special revelation as being 'neo-Marcionites' because they deny that creation is an act of grace.[25] Pinnock agrees with the rhetorical question of Dale Moody: "What kind of God is he who gives enough knowledge to damn him but not enough to save him?"[26]

---

[20] Demarest, 'General and Special Revelation,' p. 197.

[21] Demarest's exposition is possibly the most detailed, nuanced and sophisticated treatment on general revelation in recent years, and although he notes the value of general revelation, his conclusion is that general revelation is not a 'salvific revelation.' See *General Revelation*, pp. 227-262. For critical interaction with Demarest see N. H. Gootjes, 'The Sense of Divinity: A Critical Examination of the Views of Calvin and Demarest' in *Westminster Theological Journal* 48 (1986), pp. 337-350; 'General Revelation in its Relation to Special Revelation' in *Westminster Theological Journal* 51 (1989), pp. 359-368; Ivan Satyavrata, 'God has not left Himself without a Witness,' in *AETEI Journal* 5 (1992), pp. 2-9.

[22] Ibid., p. 199.

[23] Pinnock, *Flame of Love*, p. 198.

[24] Pinnock, 'An Inclusivist View,' p. 118.

[25] Pinnock, *Flame of Love*, p. 198.

[26] Dale Moody, *The Word of Truth* (Grand Rapids, 1981), p. 59. Quoted in Pinnock, *Wideness*, p. 104.

Pinnock rejects both reasons why general revelation has been thought to be insufficient for salvation. Firstly, there is enough propositional content in general revelation to fulfill the 'faith principle.' Humans can know God exists, realise their inadequacy, and throw themselves on the mercy of God, hoping God will answer their plea. Secondly, in response to the claim that even *if* the 'faith principle' was propositionally sufficient, no-one would ever throw themselves on the mercy of God because of the depravity of their sin, Pinnock responds by saying that although sin is entrenched, part of being in God's image means we are able to respond to the Spirit's prevenient grace in creation. Far from being a hypothetical possibility we know that people can and do respond to the light they have been given because there are many examples in the biblical narrative. The 'holy pagans' of the Old Testament were saved in this way by realising their own sin and throwing themselves on the mercy of God. Indeed God ordained that this could be a way to salvation in his covenant with Noah. Pinnock does not claim any originality in this position on general revelation. He states that this view was present in the writings of the Early Fathers who did not draw the later distinction between general and special revelation.[27]

The Nature of Faith in the 'Faith Principle'

It is important that Pinnock's concept of the 'faith principle' be seen in the wider context of his soteriology. Pinnock claims that evangelicals have placed undue emphasis on justification and the change of status of the sinner from guilty to not guilty rather than on the more relational side of salvation:

> Salvation is the Spirit, who indwells us, drawing us toward participation in the life of the triune God... The Spirit summons us to a transforming friendship with God that leads to sharing in the triune life... To think of salvation in this way is to recover what early theologians called *theosis*.[28]

---

[27] Pinnock, 'An Inclusivist View,' p. 118. He refers to Irenaeus who in opposition to the Gnostics stressed the work of the Spirit in both creation and new creation. See Irenaeus, *Against Heresies* 5.18.2.

[28] Pinnock, *Flame of Love*, p. 150. I will say more about the concept of union with Christ and *theosis* in Ch. 8. Pinnock believes that the idea of salvation as union with God can open up the possibility of dialogue with a religion like Hinduism. Noting that the union he conceives is not an ontological union but a personal union, he writes: "Even Hinduism, which sounds monistic and nondualistic, speaks dialectically. It is not always clear that nonduality is meant. Sankara, who understands God to be beyond conceptual reach and salvation as union, can sound rather Christian at times... It may be that when we celebrate union with God as the goal of salvation, we have something in common not only with the Eastern churches but also with non-Christian Eastern religions... Believing in the prevenient grace of God as we do, we would find this cause for

> Being saved is more like falling in love with God... Salvation, then, is more than relief at not being condemned; it sweeps us up into the love of God for participation in the divine nature. The key thing is that salvation involves transformation. It is not cheap grace, based on bare assent to propositions, or merely a change of status.[29]

The Spirit's offer of prevenient grace is an 'offer' of relationship. Human beings can freely respond to this offer through faith, or reject it. As Vanhoozer notes:

> On this view, God's call offers the possibility of salvation (salvation potential) to every human being. Sufficient grace becomes efficient, that is, only when the sinner cooperates with and improves it. As one cooperates, the potential of salvation is actualised and becomes, for that person a reality. In short, it is human response - an exercise of free will - that makes the sufficient grace of God common to all efficient in the case of the individual.[30]

Unlike Reformed evangelicals, Pinnock does not believe that saving grace is irresistible, one can always reject the Spirit's overtures. This has implications for the exact status of faith. Rather than faith being a gift of God in regeneration and its status being simply the instrumental cause through which the sinner is justified (the material cause of justification being the imputed righteousness of Christ) as in Reformed theology,[31] for Pinnock the act of faith is more the ground of justification and all humanity can display it as it is part of our relational nature. He writes, "faith pleases God, and he rewards those who seek him (Heb. 11:6). God took the initiative, but Abram responded. Pleased by his response, God made him a partner in the work of redemption."[32] According to Pinnock we are co-workers in our salvation. The slogan *sola gratia* does not mean a work of divine monergism as the Reformers concluded, rather, "salvation requires the operation

---

thankfulness, because it could open up more fruitful dialogue and enhance our witness among the peoples of India" (p. 155).

[29] Ibid., p.156.

[30] Vanhoozer, op. cit., p. 223. Vanhoozer calls the grace involved in this offer of salvation, *convenient* grace: "God is not the ruler of the universe but its wooer, working not with causal power but with the power of love and persuasion... The way God works with the world, that is, is by *convening* a cosmic conversation. Grace, we may say, is therefore *convenient*, achieving its effects not causally, but as it were, conversationally"(p. 225).

[31] For a good survey on the Reformed position on 'forensic justification' see, Lewis and Demarest, *Integrative Theology*, op cit. 3:133-137, 147-157.

[32] Pinnock, *Flame of Love*, p. 157.

of both grace and the human will."³³ Only such a view can make a person fully responsible for rejecting God. Faith is a free human response, a 'yes' to Jesus' act of representation and recapitulation against Adamic solidarity. Pinnock states:

> What I want to focus on is God's desire to be loved in a non-programmed way. He asks us, "Do you love me?" Our whole life is our answer to that question. At every point in the journey is an opportunity to say yes or no. God treats us as significant agents - that is why the human response is integral to salvation. The proof of this is hell: the only reason for it is the fact that God honors our freedom that much. He refuses to override a no even though he would dearly love to.[34]

As this stands, Pinnock's position on general revelation, and the analogy with Old Testament believers is not a radical departure for evangelicals and has been argued by other scholars albeit in a much more diluted form.[35] However Pinnock does not leave the 'faith principle' here, but develops it one stage further to enter into new territory for an evangelical theologian.

The Ethical 'Faith Principle'

This is another of Pinnock's concepts that has seen dramatic development in recent years. I will give an exegetical example to illustrate this point. In showing how salvation may be accessible to the unevangelised, Pinnock in 'The Finality of Jesus Christ in a World of Religions' (1988), comments on the 'sheep and goats' discourse in Mt. 25: 31-46, a text he says liberation theologians use to demonstrate how salvation can come from acts of morality without being explicitly 'Christian.' Pinnock at this time demonstrates that he thinks this is an unlikely interpretation because the 'least of these brothers' (v.40) referred to are Christian missionaries, and so the Gospel message would accompany them explicitly.[36] However in *Wideness* (1992), Pinnock refers to this text as evidence that the unevangelised can be saved.

---

[33] Ibid., p. 160.
[34] Ibid., p. 162.
[35] See for example Bruce A. Demarest, *General Revelation* (Grand Rapids, 1982), p. 260; J. I. Packer, 'Good Pagans and God's Kingdom' in *Christianity Today* 30/1 (17 Jan. 1986), pp. 22-25; Milliard J. Erickson, 'Hope for those who haven't heard? Yes, but...' in *Evangelical Missions Quarterly* 11 (Apr. 1975), pp. 122-126. In Appendix 1, I call these 'implicit-faith' positions.
[36] See Pinnock, 'Finality of Jesus Christ...' p. 116. Pinnock does not refer to any commentaries that would support him on this although he does cross reference Mt. 10:42 as being evidence that it is missionaries that are being referred to, "And if anyone gives even a cup of cold water to one of these little ones because he is my disciple, I tell you the truth, he will certainly not lose his reward."

He mentions the possibility that the reference to 'the least of these brothers' could be Christian missionaries, but then says he thinks this is unlikely and unjustified. Rather what the passage is saying is that acts of love done in the spirit of the Noahic covenant will be judged favourably by God because they have been done to Christ. Pinnock states, "Such a reading coheres well with the principle in his [Jesus'] teaching that noncognitive responses to God count as much as cognitive responses do... Serving the poor embodies what the love of God himself is, and is accepted as the equivalent of faith."[37]

Another passage which Pinnock comments on, is Acts 10:34 which was referred to earlier, and which states that God accepts men who fear God and do what is right. Pinnock comments that any propositional confession of God must accompany a heart response as Mt. 7:21 demonstrates,[38] and that the ethical criterion should be taken seriously. He then asks what would happen if *only* the ethical criterion were present in a person's life. He refers to the Vatican II's *Dogmatic Constitution of the Church* Ch. 16, which speaks of those people moved by grace who strive to live a good life, as being prepared for the Gospel.[39] Pinnock states that Vatican II, "went out on a limb"[40] by saying that the atheist could be saved because although he rejects 'God' (as he understands God), he implicitly accepts Him through his actions.[41] Although Pinnock believes this goes further than anything Peter says in the Cornelius narrative, he does entertain the possibility that a person may know God without coming to verbal expression. By the time of writing 'An Inclusivist View' (1995), Pinnock seems more certain and states that there is more to faith than the intellectual, "Someone might be an atheist because he or she does not understand who God is, and still have faith."[42]

Excursus: An Outline of Pinnock's 'Theology of Religions'

I think at this point in my exposition it will be helpful to outline the reason *why* Pinnock has taken the major step of separating the cognitive/explicit from the ethical/implicit. It is no coincidence that the ethical faith principle has developed in parallel with Pinnock's 'theology of religions' as I would argue that both areas are inextricably linked. Bringing into my exposition Pinnock's 'theology of religions' does add to the complexity of the discus-

---

[37] Pinnock, *Wideness*, p. 165.
[38] "Not everyone who says to me, 'Lord, Lord,' will enter the kingdom of heaven but only he who does the will of my Father who is in heaven."
[39] See ed. Abbott, *The Documents of Vatican II*, op. cit.
[40] Pinnock, *Wideness*, p. 98.
[41] Ibid.
[42] Pinnock, 'An Inclusivist View,' p. 118.

sion. However, I believe that one can only understand the content and motives behind the establishment of the ethical faith principle if one understands Pinnock's 'theology of religions.'

Before Pinnock's position on the status of religions is outlined, it should be noted that the question of the unevangelised and the theology of religions have different emphases. The doctrine of the unevangelised deals with those people who have never 'heard' the Gospel whether they belong to another religion, or belong to no religion at all. Such a study tends to focus more on individuals. The 'theology of religions' is exploring the relationship between Christianity and other religions as belief systems and cultures. This area tends to be more corporate in its thinking, focusing on the religions themselves. This difference means that someone could be an adherent of another religion and not be unevangelised. Conversely a person can be unevangelised and not belong to another religion.[43] Where the two areas mix, is when an unevangelised person *is* part of another religious culture. Pinnock has already established, through the cognitive faith principle, that prevenient grace is offered through the general revelation of creation. But can God reveal Himself through the structures of religion to reach the unevangelised? Pinnock realises that the unevangelised do not exist in a vacuum, but that they do live in diverse cultures and possess other religious beliefs, some of which are in opposition to Christianity both at a propositional level and a political level. This generates new questions in dealing with the unevangelised.

Pinnock calls his position on other religions "modal inclusivism."[44] In the spectrum of different types of inclusivism within Race's and D'Costa's threefold typology of pluralism, inclusivism and exclusivism,[45] Pinnock sees his position as being 'cautious,' resembling the statements found in Vatican II.[46] He does not say that other religions are vehicles of salvation or that God must or does use religion to convey grace:

---

[43] These are important differences and the tensions brought out in exploring these differences will become apparent below.

[44] Pinnock, 'An Inclusivist View,' p. 100. Pinnock adopts this term from Paul J. Griffiths, 'Modalizing the Theology of Religions' in *Journal of Religion* 73 (1993), pp. 382-389.

[45] Alan Race, *Christians and Religious Pluralism* (Maryknoll, 1982); Gavin D'Costa, *Theology and Religious Pluralism* (Oxford, 1986).

[46] See *The Documents of Vatican II* ed., Walter M. Abbott. (New York, 1966) especially, 'Dogmatic Constitution of the Church' (*Lumen Gentium*); 'Pastoral Constitution On the Church in the Modern World' (*Gaudium et Spes*); 'Decree on the Church's Missionary Activity' (*Ad Gentes*); and 'Declaration on the Relationship of the Church to Non-Christian Religions' (*Nostra Aetate*). More precisely (although in Wideness (1992), Pinnock tends to treat the statements of the Council as if there were a unified consensus of interpretation as to their meaning and significance), Pinnock, on the status of other religions, follows the more conservative interpretations of Vatican II, particularly

It seems wiser to say that God *may* use religion as a way of gracing people's lives and that it is one of God's options for evoking faith and communicating grace. This avoids a priori judgments concerning God's use or nonuse of religion. Whether God makes use of religion is a contingent matter to be explored case by case by discernment.[47]

Such a view is part of Pinnock's doctrine of the Spirit and of prevenient grace. If God can use the moral dimension of the *imago Dei*, and the witness of creation to reveal Himself and engender faith, if the Spirit is present in every sphere of existence offering prevenient grace to every creature, why should the Spirit be excluded from that area of life called religion? For Pinnock, religions are an important part of the human social search of meaning, a part of what it means to be in the image of God. It is therefore

---

Miikka Ruokanen, *The Catholic Doctrine of Non-Christian Religions* (Leiden, 1992). Ruokanen's analysis is based on the idea that Vatican II was still working under the classical distinction between nature and grace and concludes his study by saying, "A sincere seeker of truth and doer of good may be an adherent of any religion or of none. Non-Christian religions are neither demonized nor divinized; they are seen as nautili good. They are, however, neutralized and relativised: religions are a part of human life and culture - neither any particular hindrance nor any special advantage in a non-Christian's relation to his Creator. To varying degrees, religions express the cognition of and celebrate rituals of the one Creator of all: in any case they are manifestations of man's sincere search for God, and in any case they contain moral truths common to all human beings" (p.117). I should note that a theologian like Paul Knitter interprets the data differently: "I admit that the documents of the Second Vatican Council are silent about the issue of whether religious traditions can be *viae salutis* or ways to salvation... Within [the] broader context of Catholic experience and tradition, there are, I suggest, even clearer and more persuasive reasons to interpret the Council's silence in a *positive* sense to conclude, with the majority (not just "many") of contemporary Roman Catholic theologians that Vatican II implicitly affirms the salvific potential of other religions." 'Appendix B - Discussion in the International Bulletin of Missionary Research' in Ruokanen, op. cit., pp. 144f; and Paul Knitter, *No Other Name? A Critical Survey of Christian Attitudes Toward the World Religions* (New York, 1994), pp. 121-125. For an evangelical perspective on Catholic interpretations of Vatican II see, David Wright, 'The Watershed of Vatican II' in eds. Andrew D. Clarke and Bruce W. Winter, *One Lord, One God: Christianity in a World of Religious Pluralism* (Grand Rapids, 1992), pp. 207-226.

[47] Pinnock, 'An Inclusivist View,' p. 100. Pinnock's position on other religions has some similarities with that of the Roman Catholic theologian Gavin D'Costa although D'Costa's position is far more nuanced. See his 'Christ, the Trinity and Religious Plurality' in ed. Gavin D'Costa, *Christian Uniqueness Reconsidered* (New York, 1990), pp. 16-30; and 'Revelation and Revelations: Discerning God in Other Religions - Beyond a Static Valuation' in *Modern Theology* 10:2 April 1994, pp. 165-183; *The Trinity and the Religions* (New York, 2000).

another facet of general revelation just as "family, guilds, governments, and the like,"[48] are social bearers too. Pinnock asks: "Does prevenient grace bear fruit in the religious life and traditions of humankind? If the Spirit is gracing the world, does he grace it in the area of religions? Does God's offer ever get thematised in the myth, doctrine or ritual of non-Christian religions?"[49] Pinnock is open to seeing both truth and falsity in other religions and admits that other religions can suppress truth as well as reveal it. He states that some religions are under Satanic influence leading to hell rather than being under the influence of the Spirit. Often there is a great deal of resistance to God in other religions, and that, "this is of such magnitude that pursuing this avenue is even futile for God, who does not always get his way."[50] He calls Rahner's theory of 'lawful religion,'[51] "naïve speculation"[52] because it is not realistic: "there are so many evil sides to religion that the fulfilment paradigm (the idea that religions point people to Christ) is out of the question. Religions are not ordinarily stepping stones to Christ."[53] He also notes that Rahner's position on other religions, "arises out of the sacramental orientation of his Catholic theology, which reasons in this manner: If grace is communicated to people outside the church, the sacramental means by which it is mediated must be the religions available to them."[54]

Pinnock wishes to stress the difference between being attentive to the Spirit at work in a religion and claiming that a religion is a vehicle of grace. Pinnock's attitude is a flexible one, to say yes and no to other religious traditions. So for example he welcomes the Saiva Siddhanta literature of Hinduism, which celebrates a personal God of love but believes Christians must confront, "the circular character of Eastern thinking and the meaninglessness of the world that arises from it."[55] Here again Pinnock believes that the biblical witness testifies to this flexibility. God constantly calls humanity to turn away from idolatry as it is an abomination to Him (Amos 5:21). However, Abram's encounter with Melchizedek in Gen. 14, reveals that God had been working in Cannaanite culture before their encounter and

---

[48] Ibid., p. 99.
[49] Pinnock, *Flame of Love*, p. 200.
[50] Pinnock, 'An Inclusivist View,' p. 116.
[51] Karl Rahner, *Theological Investigations*, Vol. 5, pp. 121-131.
[52] Pinnock, *Wideness*, p. 91.
[53] Ibid.
[54] Pinnock, 'An Inclusivist View,' p. 99. This seems to be Knitter's point in his book *No Other Name*, op. cit. when commenting on the Catholic position on salvation *extra ecclesium* leading up to Vatican II. He writes: "Theologians, even quite recently, spoke of the universal offer of grace as if it were some free-floating agent that touched individuals privately, through some form of mystical communication. No one ventured the suggestion that such grace might be operating through pagan religions."(p. 123).
[55] Ibid., p. 145.

Abram accepted that the king of Salem was worshipping the true God they called *El Elyon*. Cornelius' testimony in Acts 10 shows that the Spirit was working in his life before the Gospel was preached to him,[56] and Paul's speech to the Athenians (Acts 17:22-31) connected Greek worship with knowledge of God. Pinnock comments on this text, "Of course the Athenians' theology was distorted and incomplete. But it did contain certain insights into God's purpose."[57]

In summary one may say this: The world religions are Man's search for God and Man's response to general revelation in creation and conscience. Some reject this general revelation and their religion becomes one of idolatry. The Spirit has to work independently and against such religions to offer prevenient grace to a person. However many religions are a patchwork of truth and untruth. Humans have grasped some truths of general revelation and in time they become thematised in various rituals and traditions. The Spirit may work through these positive aspects to confront a person with prevenient grace. Alongside these positive aspects may be distorted or perverted truths. Again the Spirit may have to lead a person away from these negative areas or begin a complete transformation in these areas.[58]

---

[56] One evangelical who has written concerning the presence of God in other religions is the missiologist Don Richardson. See his book, *Eternity in Their Hearts* (Ventura, 1981). Richardson notes that pre-Abrahamic peoples (Noah, Melchizedek) possessed only general revelation but were redemptively related to God. He calls this the "Melchizedek Factor" (p. 156). He says that where general revelation is not perverted, we should expect to find unevangelised peoples saved by the 'Melchizedek Factor.' As a missionary, Richardson believes he has empirical evidence to support this truth in African communities he has met whose tribal beliefs are very similar to the Gospel. On this same point see Evert Osburn, 'Those who have never heard: Have they no hope?' in *Journal of the Evangelical Theological Society* 32 Sept. 1989, pp. 370-379.

[57] Pinnock, *Flame of Love*, p. 201.

[58] A very interesting aspect of Pinnock's 'theology of religions' outlined in Ch. 4 of *Wideness*, pp. 115-149, is his doctrine of the 'powers.' Pinnock talks about history being a battleground between the Divine and the demonic in which the religions play a part, "God's plan to make all things new, to bring the powers of oppression under Christ, to transform history and culture, necessarily includes in its scope the religious."(p. 119) Although Paul makes no comment on their metaphysical status, these 'powers' were created by God to implement His will (Col. 1:16) but became sinful and destructive (Eph. 2:1-1) and manifest themselves in all areas of human life including religion. But Christ won the victory over them, "and is now in a position to impact them as far as their functioning in history is concerned (1 Cor. 15:24-26; Eph. 1:20-22; Col. 2:15)."(p. 120) One of the battlegrounds of this cosmic struggle is the area of religion. Christ challenges the powers in other religions to submit to him. Pinnock comments on religions with incompatible belief systems to Christianity, "...as God calls people and as the kingdom impacts them, these doctrines and practices can be loosened, as it were, from their original complexes and be refashioned to express something different."(p. 123) Pinnock

Pinnock's 'Theology of Religions' and the Ethical 'Faith Principle'

How does Pinnock's theology of religions relate to the ethical faith principle in the doctrine of the unevangelised? In *Wideness* (1992), Pinnock makes a distinction between "subjective religion" which he defines as the "heart response to God" being existential faith or piety, and "objective religion" which is, "the cumulative traditions such as Christianity and Buddhism, insofar as they are institutions and cultural movements."[59] Pinnock believes that God is concerned more about our subjective religious responses than our objective ones even though from within objective religion one might exercise faith in God in a more explicit way. Having made this distinction Pinnock can say that although, for example, if someone is a Buddhist we cannot conclude that this person is not seeking God in their heart. Pinnock realises the danger of this in that one could ignore the objective aspects of religion entirely and concentrate solely on the subjective aspects. He writes: "This would be ill-advised because religion as a framework influences religion as faith and trust. It would be wrong to drive a wedge between them... Religious tradition will colour a person's outlook and as such it can help them. But it can also hinder."[60]

But how can the Spirit offer prevenient grace to an unevangelised person who has been brought up in a culture that espouses false beliefs, that is beliefs that are contradictory to the truths of the Christian revelation? In 'An Inclusivist View' and *Flame of Love*, he appears to further separate the propositional from the ethical, "While it is true that incorrect beliefs do not lead people to faith that is not the whole story about religion... The act of faith is more than cognitive. Authentic faith and holy action may flow from persons inhabiting an uncompromising religious and doctrinal culture."[61]

Pinnock links the idea he is developing with the Catholic concept of the 'baptism of desire' an idea first propounded in the Middle Ages,[62] given formal ecclesiastical expression by Pius XII in 1949,[63] and picked up again

---

notes how many religions have vanished because they were defeated by God (e.g. the gods of the Ancient Near East) and how many religions have changed when confronted with the Gospel. They are not static or monolithic but diverse internally, constantly changing and vulnerable to being transformed by Jesus Christ. Pinnock writes in *Flame of Love*, "The history of Israel, for example, led to the coming of Jesus. Here God was at work apart from Jesus Christ but leading up to him. By analogy with Israel, we watch for anticipations in other faiths to be fulfilled in Christ."(p. 208).

[59] Pinnock, *Wideness*, p. 84.
[60] Ibid., p. 112.
[61] Pinnock, 'An Inclusivist View,' p. 118.
[62] See 'Baptism of Desire' in *Sacramentum Mundi: An Encyclopedia of Theology* (New York, 1968), pp. 144-146.
[63] Ibid. See also Ruokanen, op. cit p. 18f. Ruokanen writes: "when a person does not know the truths of Catholicism but, by his natural yearning for God, becomes a latent member of the church through desire (*voto et desiderio*) and thus has an implicit desire

at Vatican II.[64] Here, acts of love and charity demonstrate a desire for Christ that would be sufficient to be saved. Pinnock uses this idea, putting it into the language of the Spirit: "One can avoid the one-sided Christic view by referring to the Holy Spirit who renders effective the mission of Christ and makes God's reign present everywhere."[65] God who is omnipresent through the Spirit knows how to recognise inclinations toward Him even where the Gospel is not known:

> Such a desire for God does not give people everything they will ultimately need - it is a weak initiation and lacks the nurturing context of church. But it allows a decision to turn from self-centredness and to give oneself to God and neighbour. It involves a kind of dying to self and rising to life. It is...a work of grace. It involves being gifted and enriched by God.[66]

This is not salvation by works, but rather that good works may signal a positive response to the promptings of the Spirit and prevenient grace. These are the fruit of the Spirit as outlined in Gal. 5:22-23. Such a response may be non-cognitive and implicit and may even accompany, at an explicit propositional level, false beliefs or a mixture of true and false beliefs. One should look past the propositional to the direction of a person's heart:

> They called Socrates an atheist because he did not believe in the unworthy gods of the Athens, but we assume that he had more faith that the general populace of that city. Did Jesus not tell us that giving the thirsty a drink of cold water is an act of participation in the selfless love of God

---

or intention, *implicitum votum*, to conform to the will of God. Such a desire is man's free response to experiencing the presence of the grace-bearing Triune God in life and creation. According to Pius, God effects salvation by presenting supernatural faith (*fides supernaturalis*) to man on the basis of man's inherent desires. Such a person is associated with the Church and the realm of salvation - yet *solo voto implicito*"(p. 18).

[64] See for example *The Documents of Vatican II*, *Lumen Gentium* no. 16 which says, "Nor is God remote from those who in the shadows and images seek the unknown God, since he gives to all men life and breath and all things (Acts 17:25-28), and since the Saviour wills all men to be saved (1 Tim. 2:4). Those also can attain to everlasting salvation who through no fault of their own do not know the gospel of Christ, yet sincerely seek God and, moved by grace, strive by their deeds to do his will as it is known to them through the dictates of conscience - those too may achieve eternal salvation. Nor shall divine providence deny the assistance necessary for salvation to those who, through no fault of their own, have not yet arrived at an explicit knowledge of God, and who, not without grace, strive to lead a good life... Whatever goodness or truth is found among them is looked upon by the Church as preparation for the Gospel."

[65] Pinnock, *Flame of Love*, p. 206.
[66] Ibid.

revealed in the gospel and makes one his sheep (Matt. 25:31-40)? *Created in God's image, a person can decide to accept the mystery of one's being, which is the goal of his or her life.*[67]

Though Jesus is not known to the unevangelised, the Spirit is present and may be experienced implicitly through acts of love. For Pinnock, this seems to be another way of saying 'yes' to Jesus' act of representation, be it subconscious and unthematised. At this point I would like to suggest that on this idea of the ethical faith principle (not on the status of other religions), Pinnock appears closer to Rahner's 'supernatural existential' than to the statements of Vatican II, particularly if Pinnock has relied on Ruokanen's analysis of the Council. Although Ruokanen notes that "Rahner's concept of anonymous Christians is a logical continuation of the principle expressed by Pius XII of the "implicit desire" of a non-Christian to conform to God's will,"[68] he still interprets the statements of the Council through the traditional nature/grace distinction, whereas Pinnock, I think, sees far less a distinction between a natural grace and supernatural grace. For him all grace is saving grace because it is the same omnipresent and immanent Spirit who embodies grace. Compare Pinnock's statement about 'accepting the mystery of one's being' with Rahner's idea that "in order to have a relationship with God, man does not need first to find some "object" in which to trust or to believe. To know God is inseparable from being aware of one's own existence."[69] Rahner writes:

> Our whole spiritual life is lived in the realm of the salvific will of God, of his prevenient grace, of his call as it becomes efficacious: all of which is an element within the region of our consciousness, though one which remains anonymous as long it is not interpreted from without by the message of faith. Even when he does not 'know' it and does not believe it, that is, even when he cannot make it an individual object of knowledge by merely inward reflection, man always lives consciously in the presence of the triune God of eternal life... The preaching is the express wakening of what is already present in the depth's of man's being, not by nature, but by grace. But it is a grace which always surrounds man, even the sinner and unbeliever, as the inescapable setting of his existence.[70]

In his own analysis of Rahner, Bruce Demarest rightly says that in Rahner's theology the "traditional concept of revelation as an intrusion *ab ex-*

---

[67] Pinnock, 'An Inclusivist View,' p. 119 (my emphasis).
[68] Ruokanen, op. cit., p. 31.
[69] Ibid.
[70] Rahner, 'Nature and Grace,' p. 180f.

tra, which conveys truths in the form of propositions, must be abandoned"[71] in favour of a transcendental revelation (the 'supernatural existential' which replaces general revelation), and a predicamental historical revelation (the conceptual thematization or objectification of the transcendental revelation which replaces special revelation). In the final chapter of *Flame of Love*, Pinnock deals briefly with the doctrine of revelation. Noting that God reveals Himself through creation and history as well as Israel and Christ, and rejecting both liberal theology which defines revelation in terms of human experience, and traditional evangelical theology which is too cognitive in its view of revelation, Pinnock propounds his own definition of revelation:

> Revelation is neither contentless experience (liberalism) nor timeless propositions (conservatism). It is the dynamic self-disclosure of God, who makes his goodness known in the history of salvation, in a process of disclosure culminating in Jesus Christ. Revelation is not primarily existential impact or infallible truths but divine self-revelation that both impacts and instructs. The mode of revelation is self-disclosure and interpersonal communication.[72]

While Pinnock's idea of the cognitive faith principle may keep together both a cognitive content of revelation together with the experience of grace through the Spirit, the whole *raison d'être* of the ethical 'faith principle' is the separation of the cognitive and the ethical, the idea being that a positive acceptance of prevenient grace can take place even though at a cognitive level God may have been rejected. Again, compare this idea to Rahner:

> The grace of Christ is at work in a man who never expressly asked for it, but who already desired it in the unspeaking, nameless longings of his heart. Here is a man in whom the unspeaking sighings of the Spirit has invoked and petitioned for that silent but all pervading mystery of existence which we Christians know as the Father of our Lord Jesus Christ.[73]

While one must take account of their different theological backgrounds, and while Pinnock is more cautious than Rahner on other religions being vehicles of grace, one cannot but notice the similarities between Rahner's concept of 'anonymous faith'[74] and Pinnock's 'ethical faith principle.'

---

[71] Demarest, *General Revelation*, p. 190.
[72] Pinnock, *Flame of Love*, op. cit., p. 226.
[73] Karl Rahner, *The Church After the Council* (New York, 1966), p. 62, quoted from Demarest, *General Revelation*, p. 191.
[74] Molly Marshall comments that when Rahner speaks about 'anonymous faith' he means a faith that presupposes salvation. It is hope and love of God and Neighbour, yet [as Rahner says], "without any explicit and conscious relationship...to the revelation of Jesus Christ contained in the Old and /or New Testament and without any explicit refer-

Discerning the Spirit

The key area for Pinnock now becomes one of discernment: how can we recognise the Spirit moving in other religions and among the unevangelised? Although he affirms the universal presence of Spirit he recognises that the Spirit is not identical with everything in the world. To discern the Spirit we must once again focus on universality and particularity and the twin mission of Son and Spirit, "Christians find the criterion in Jesus Christ, the Saviour of the world, in whom God has been revealed decisively."[75] The Spirit cannot contradict truth incarnate and so to identify a response to prevenient grace we must look to Christ. Where we see acts of love and peace, longings for justice, beauty and generosity, "we know the Spirit of Jesus is present. Other spirits do not promote broken and contrite hearts. Such things tell us where the brothers and sisters of Jesus indwelt by the Spirit are."[76] These fruits of the Spirit do not have to be cognitive to be a sign of opening up for a relationship with God. Jesus Christ is the "interpretative lens"[77] through which we discern the Spirit's movement. Pinnock notes that this is one way in which we can affirm the *filioque*, "the truth of it is precisely the point about Christ's being the criterion of Spirit activity."[78]

What should we call those unevangelised people who respond positively to prevenient grace either through the cognitive or ethical faith principles? Pinnock dislikes the term 'anonymous Christian' because it obscures the difference that the explicit gospel makes in a person's life (see below). Also the 'holy pagans' of the Old Testament were not Christians but premessianic believers awaiting the Messiah. He prefers to refer to the unevangelised who respond to grace as 'believers' or "not-yet- Christians"[79]: they are, "latently a member of Christ's body and destined to receive the grace of conversion and explicit knowledge of Jesus Christ at a later date, whether in this life or after death."[80]

---

ence to God through an objective idea of God." See Molly Marshall, *No Salvation Outside the Church? A Critical Inquiry* (Lampeter, 1993), p. 132. For Rahner's position on implicit faith see 'Membership of the Church According to the Teaching of Pius XII's Encyclical *Mystici Corporis Christi*' in *Theological Investigations* Vol. 2 (London, 1963), pp. 1-89.

[75] Pinnock, 'An Inclusivist View,' p. 114.
[76] Pinnock, *Flame of Love*, p. 210.
[77] Pinnock, 'An Inclusivist View,' p. 114.
[78] Pinnock, *Flame of Love*, p. 211.
[79] Ibid., p. 213.
[80] Pinnock, 'An Inclusivist View,' op. cit., p. 117. The implications of this statement will be discussed shortly.

Summary

Before dealing with a number of related issues, I wish to conclude this section with a statement of Pinnock that draws together the description above and that succinctly summarises his position on the unevangelised:

> God's universal salvific will is broad and generous, but how can those who have not heard the gospel in any clear or empowered sense gain access to it? Spirit is the key to the universality through particularity. Grace is always present by the Spirit. Though one is free to accept or refuse the offer, the possibility of salvation exists for everyone, grounded in the generous and reckless love of God. Life is filled with opportunities to say yes or no to God.[81]

Motivation for Missions, The Post-Mortem Encounter with Christ and Related Issues

Motivation for Missions

Pinnock understands one of the main objections to his position from evangelicals: does not universal access to salvation take away the urgency for mission, one of the primary characteristics of the evangelical community? Pinnock believes that his position does not lessen the urgency for three reasons.

Firstly, one must see evangelism for what it really is. For Pinnock the main motive in evangelism is not to warn people that they are under eschatological wrath and are damned unless they believe the gospel. Rather evangelism should be proclaiming the kingdom of God, telling people about Jesus and calling them to enter into relationship through Spirit. Through mission, Christians can powerfully transform the world and change history. The goal is quantitative in the formation of new Christian communities, and qualitative, "to change life's atmosphere, to infect people with hope, love, and responsibility for the world."[82] To hold that the Spirit has gone before human mission, preparing hearts for the Gospel is, for Pinnock, a great incentive to evangelism.

Secondly, another incentive for mission is the spiritual state of these 'not-yet Christians.' For although their salvific status is secured in their acceptance of prevenient grace by faith, their relationship with God is at a superficial level and they need to experience full salvation that only the Gospel can bring. This brings with it propositional knowledge, forgiveness, assurance, community and love. In Paul's words, what they saw as a poor reflection, they now see face to face in the Gospel story (Rom. 13:12). It is

---

[81] Pinnock, *Flame of Love*, p. 212.
[82] Pinnock, *Wideness*, p. 178.

a fulfilment and enrichment. Pinnock talks about these people needing to experience salvation, "in the dimension of Pentecost" and to be "caught up in the kingdom surge."[83] This is the holistic messianic salvation that Peter was referring to in Acts 4:12. This is why Pinnock does not want to call unevangelised believers 'Christians,' anonymous or otherwise, because being a Christian is so much more than deliverance from wrath. The Spirit's mission anticipates the message of the Gospel, it is preparatory and not complete in itself although it is salvific: "To the one who has already reached out to God in the premessianic situation, we call them to come higher up and deeper in, to know God better and to love God more."[84] Although I noted earlier that in Pinnock's argument there was a uniformity of the way God is present in creation and redemption, Pinnock does seem to distinguish differences in the way God is present in the world as he is in the church:

> Scripture encourages us to see the church not so much as the ark, outside of which there is no hope of salvation, but as the vanguard of those who have experienced the fullness of God's grace made available to all people in Jesus Christ. The Spirit is universally present in the world as well as uniquely present in the fellowship of the church.[85]

On this point of fulfilment and enriching within the Christian community, Pinnock refers to Vatican II's, 'Decree on the Missionary Activity of the Church,' Ch.1, which says, "Whatever truth and grace are found among the nations, as a sort of secret presence of God, this missionary activity frees from all taint of evil and restores to Christ its maker...whatever good is found to be sown in the hearts and minds of men...is healed, ennobled, and perfected for the glory of God..."

Having noted Pinnock's reference to Vatican II, I think there is an important distinction to be made between what Pinnock is saying here and, for example, Miikka Ruokanen's 'conservative' reading of Vatican II. Ruokanen appears to be far more cautious and reticent over the precise nature and details of salvation *extra ecclesiam*. On the one hand he states that:

> If a non-Christian is saved, he is saved on the basis of his honest search for truth and his obedience to the voice of his Creator which he hears in his conscience. Such a non-Christian person, being taken into the realm of the salvific *gratia praeveiens*, receives the hidden grace of God in a pro-

---

[83] Ibid.
[84] Pinnock, 'An Inclusivist View,' p. 120.
[85] Ibid., p. 110.

leptic manner. He is a latent member of Christ's body, and he has *fides implicita*, the salvific faith accepted by God.[86]

On the other hand he speaks of the need to receive the gift of *gratia increata sive supernaturalis* administered through the Church "in order to fully participate in the creative, redemptive, and sanctifying grace of the Triune God... This is the superabundant gift of God's grace which cannot be obtained unless through conversion and Christian baptism."[87] In this sense salvation *extra ecclesium* is seen as *preparatio evangelica*: "In a way not plain to us, God's grace perfects and strengthens what is already given in human life and in the natural moral law, inherent in human life. These non-Christians may become saved and attain eternal life in a way hidden to us."[88] What Ruokanen appears to be saying is that even the loftiest form of natural revelation and grace can at best be seen as *preparatio* and shows at most a readiness to accept the Gospel in this life or the next. In other words, while it may prepare one for the Gospel it is not in itself salvific.

One might discern that this *is* Pinnock's position with his espousal of the post-mortem encounter (which I will outline shortly) that is entirely in line with the concept of the *preparatio evangelica*. Pinnock's language at times speaks in terms of *preparatio*: "Inclusivism can improve our motivation and enhance our hope as we go forth to testify to Christ, since we are entitled to believe that God has gone before us, preparing the way for the Gospel."[89] However elsewhere, it appears that Pinnock is going further than the conservative reading of Vatican II because in his pneumatology and his 'ethical faith principle,' the Spirit has a far more dramatic role and undertakes more than mere *preparatio*. Rather, the Spirit conveys saving grace and in doing this the unevangelised believer accepts the Gospel of Christ, albeit implicitly. Such a person is saved there and then and becomes part of the kingdom of God. This is even more acute when Pinnock posits that God *may* use elements of another religion to evoke faith and communicate grace, i.e. elements of other religions become part of the salvific process. It is not surprising that despite Pinnock's protestations to the contrary, certain critics have aligned Pinnock's inclusivism with Rahner's theory of 'anonymous Christians.'[90] Returning to Ruokanen's analysis, it is interesting to note that

---

[86] Ruokanen, op. cit., p. 120.
[87] Ibid.
[88] Ibid., p. 142. When talking of the idea of *gratia creata sive communis* he notes that "the merciful God, willing the salvation of all people, does not deny his grace to them, but they live under the influence of his mercy. *The final result of this* is eternal salvation (aeterna salus)"(p. 99, my emphasis).
[89] Ibid., p. 120.
[90] See Carson, *The Gagging of God: Christianity Confronts Pluralism* (Leicester, 1996), p. 279; Richard, op. cit., p. 128.

he does note the possibility of interpreting Vatican II in a more progressive way:

> The Council itself proceeded very much along the lines of traditional Catholic theology. But it is significant that the new ideas of supernatural universal grace, promoted above all by Henri de Lubac and Karl Rahner even before the Council, were by no means reprobated... In regard to the question of God's common saving grace, the Conciliar documents use precautious and minimalistic statements. This can be understood as a compromise which can be accepted by more conservative as well as by more progressive Catholic theologians.[91]

I think it is safe to say that in some areas Pinnock aligns himself with more conservative readings of the Council, and in others he definitely takes a more liberal reading.

Leading on from the above two points, and the final reason why the urgency of mission is not lessened by inclusivism, is that Pinnock implies that it always must be 'better' to hear the Gospel *ex auditu* through evangelism, than through general revelation. The proclamation of the Gospel comes to 'not-yet-Christians' and unbelievers and challenges them explicitly to accept Christ's act of representation. Although God can be salvifically known through general revelation, "it is not the same high wattage as the light which shines from the face of Jesus Christ."[92] The Spirit's activity is most clearly focused and unambiguous in the incarnation and no-one should be denied access to this unique revelation. Certainly there is a greater responsibility to respond to God through the Gospel than through general revelation.[93] This discussion leads to two important questions: firstly, what happens if an unevangelised believer rejects the Gospel when presented with it? Secondly, what happens if an unevangelised believer never comes into contact with the Gospel? Pinnock answers both questions.

The Rejection of the Gospel by 'Not-yet Christians'

In *Wideness* (1992) Pinnock is quite unequivocal. Jesus is the fulfilment of the Spirit's work and of God's revelation. Therefore premessianic believers would see Jesus as being the fulfilment of what they have gleaned from creation, the *imago Dei* and truths in other religions. He writes:

---

[91] Ruokanen, op. cit., p. 119.
[92] Ibid., p. 180.
[93] Rahner makes the same point, "the individual who grasps Christianity in a...more reflexive way has...a still greater chance of salvation than someone who is merely an anonymous Christian." 'Christianity and the Non-Christian Religions,' p. 132.

Pre-Christian faith is valid up until that moment when Christ is preached not afterwards. When Christ is known, the obligation comes in force to believe in him. The unevangelised are expected to receive the Good News when it reaches them. God's offer becomes an objective obligation at that time, and refusal to accept that offer would be fatal. No hope can be offered to those declining God's offer to them in Christ.[94]

However, in 'An Inclusivist View'(1995) and *Flame of Love* (1996) Pinnock is more cautious. He says this is an area that needs more attention by inclusivists. He gives the example of a Muslim who has been drawn by the Spirit but who cannot break with his people. Coming from a country where one is free to profess any religion, Pinnock says that his immediate feeling is to leave this matter with the grace of God: "Do we have any notion how hard it must be for not-yet-Christians to extricate themselves from their own cultural-linguistic communities and become baptised Christians?"[95] This said, he does note that, "it is no small matter to turn away from the grace of God (Heb. 2:1-3)."[96]

This 'softening' in Pinnock's position has arisen because of his struggle to deal with one of the most fundamental questions concerning the unevangelised: when does an unevangelised person become evangelised? When is an adequate proclamation of the Gospel heard? What do we say about the Muslim who has responded to prevenient grace but who believes Christianity to be inextricably linked with Western cultural values and imperialistic in nature, Jesus being a conqueror? Has this person heard the Gospel or not? Pinnock believes that all 'not-yet Christians' are drawn to Christ and that theoretically if they hear the true Word then they must receive it, or else it would not be pre-Christian faith. However Pinnock is far more sensitive historically to the enormous barriers put in the way of hearing the 'true Word.' Only God can know who is a 'not-yet Christian' or not and who has heard the Gospel in an existentially real way or not.

The Post-Mortem Encounter with Christ

Linked to the previous discussion, is Pinnock's answer to the second question: what if a 'not-yet Christian' never hears an adequate presentation of the Gospel in this life? Here Pinnock posits a post-mortem encounter in combination with his belief in universal accessibility by the 'faith principle.' Pinnock believes there is much theological sense in believing in a post-mortem encounter with Christ. He claims that all evangelicals believe that at the Parousia, all humanity will come before Christ and give an ac-

---

[94] Ibid., p. 168.
[95] Pinnock, *Flame of Love*, p. 214.
[96] Pinnock, 'An Inclusivist View,' p. 120.

count of themselves (Rom. 14:7-12). But does believing in such an encounter negate the 'faith principle' so carefully argued for above? If everyone will encounter Christ anyway, why bother with an argument of universal accessibility in this life? Pinnock believes that both positions complement each other because this encounter is not evangelism in the sense that people will have a 'second chance' to believe in the Gospel. Pinnock believes that such a position disregards our life lived on earth, and makes only one decision important, namely whether we accept or reject Christ post-mortem. Pinnock firmly believes that our decision for or against God is fixed in this life and that the post-mortem encounter is merely a confirmation of pre-mortem decisions.[97] It is important to understand the nature of this 'fixity.'

At the Eschaton everyone will stand before God in the presence of His grace and will be able to ask for mercy. However, "the question is whether sinners would respond on that occasion any differently than they have already responded in life on earth."[98] Pinnock believes that they would not, "the opportunity would be there for all to repent after death but not the desire. At Judgment, believers from every age will love God more, while the wicked will love him less."[99] Pinnock here is back to commenting on the nature of freedom. Although he espouses a strong definition of libertarian freedom, he still admits that this is still a creaturely freedom. He says that for a person living enough years in a certain way, choices become fixed, that is who you are. One is not born habitually choosing one way of living (as Calvinism states), but that choices can *become* habitual by a constant choice in one direction.[100] Steven Travis echoes the same point: "Is it not psychologically and spiritually true that persistent refusal to respond to love makes love harder rather than easier? The more often we are moved to

---

[97] This goes against Nash and Carson's understanding of Pinnock's synthesis of inclusivism and a post-mortem encounter. Calling this encounter 'evangelism,' they believe that the unevangelised will receive a 'second chance' to accept Christ. Carson writes: "...it is very hard to see why anyone would want to hold both views simultaneously. If faith that is consciously focused on Jesus is not necessary for salvation, why should people be offered a further chance beyond death. Alternatively, if a further chance is offered beyond death, with the structure of the gospel clearly presented, why should people be thought disadvantaged if they do not hear the gospel in this life?" *The Gagging of God. Christianity Confronts Pluralism.* (Leicester, 1996), p. 300. See also Ronald Nash, *Is Jesus the Only Savior?* (Grand Rapids, 1994), pp. 149f. However, Pinnock is not saying that anyone receives a second chance. The post-mortem encounter ratifies and fulfills the decisions made on earth, either by explicit evangelism, the 'cognitive faith principle' or 'ethical faith principle.' On these terms the combination of inclusivism and a post-mortem encounter seem logical and necessary.

[98] Pinnock, *Wideness*, p. 170.

[99] Ibid.

[100] This argument came out in the interview I had with Pinnock, at McMaster Divinity College, Aug. 1997.

do something and fail to do it, the less likely it is that we will ever do it."[101] Pinnock sees heaven not as an extrinsic reward, but an intrinsic reward, where the consequences are homogeneous with the actions rewarded. So he strongly believes that someone like Hitler will not change his mind when he comes into the glory of the Lord, "Heaven would be the worst place he could imagine."[102]

Christians will receive a new clarity of understanding in the post-mortem encounter as all Christians are conceptually inadequate. However for those 'not-yet Christians' who never received the full Gospel message, a post-mortem encounter will be even more of a blessed event because they will for the first time meet Christ the source of their salvation and the fulfilment of their search for God. The direction of their hearts will be confirmed when they meet Christ and God will honour the faith they showed in this life. This will include the 'holy pagans' of the Old Testament, those Jews who lived before Christ, and those who were informationally premessianic but who responded to prevenient grace through the 'faith principle'.

But what about that group of people already touched on, namely those who historically may be called 'evangelised' but who have only been exposed to a perverted or incomplete Gospel? Will they be able to decide for or against Christ for the first time when they meet him after death? Pinnock believes that the category of an 'ethical faith principle' means that such people would have ample opportunity to respond positively or negatively to God in this life. They might have responded negatively to Christianity as they understood it and even hated the God who had been presented to them, but in other ways they could demonstrate their heart for God through implicit faith. In this sense they have been 'evangelised' by the Spirit's overtures and so for them again the post-mortem encounter would be merely confirmation of how they responded to Spirit through the 'ethical faith principle.' Their destinies had been fixed by the lives they lived on earth. Pinnock is agnostic as to how large or small this group may be. He does say though: "Those who will suffer everlasting destruction will not be the unevangelised but those who neither obey the Gospel nor any other form of revelation they have been given. In the last judgment, God's enemies and not the inculpably ignorant are rejected."[103]

---

[101] Steven Travis, *Christian Hope and the Future of Man* (Leicester, 1980), p. 130. Quoted from R.R. Cook, 'Is Universalism an Implication of the notion of Post-Mortem Evangelism?' in *Tyndale Bulletin* 45.2 (1994), pp. 395-409. This essay explores in more detail Pinnock's idea that people will not change their mind in a post-mortem encounter.
[102] Pinnock, *Wideness*, p. 172.
[103] Ibid., p. 174.

The Analogy of Children who Die in Infancy and the Mentally Incompetent

I mention this topic here almost as an appendix to Pinnock's inclusivism. Its role in Pinnock's argument is to critique restrictivism as well as being another piece of cumulative evidence that the unevangelised can be saved. Pinnock classes those who die in infancy as being 'unevangelised.' He argues thus:

> Since most Christians today grant that these people will be saved, they constitute a prime example of the unevangelised being saved apart from faith in Christ, apart even from faith in God in most cases. They are a practically uncontested example of unevangelised people being saved.[104]

Pinnock questions the consistency of Calvinist theologians like B.B. Warfield who argued that all infants who die are elected by God and therefore saved.[105] For Pinnock this belief is inconsistent with the rest of the Reformed system: "Logically, as a high Calvinist, Warfield should say there are elect and non-elect among even the babies who die, just as there are among the rest of the race...[but] He is a universalist when it comes to babies... Why so great a compassion for infants who cannot believe, and so little for large numbers of others perishing without lifting a finger to save them?"[106] The assumption made in Pinnock's argument is that there is a valid analogy to make between the 'unevangelised' who die in infancy or are mentally incompetent, and the 'unevangelised' who do not hear the Gospel due to historic or geographic circumstances.

On the salvation of those who die in infancy, Pinnock questions whether he can be a universalist to remain internally consistent. He believes that they were included in Christ's act of representation. Normally this would need to be ratified by the person in this life but obviously this cannot happen. He writes, "In the case of babies...the decision can come after death... This in turn may suggest that they are given time to grow up and mature, so

---

[104] Ibid., p. 166f.
[105] B.B. Warfield, *Studies in Theology* (New York, 1932), pp. 411-444.
[106] Pinnock, *Wideness*, p. 167. For a more detailed critique of the apparent inconsistency in Warfield's position see David K. Clarke, 'Warfield, Infant Salvation, and the Logic of Calvinism' in *Journal of the Evangelical Theological Society*, 27/4 (Dec. 1984), pp. 459-464. Clarke says that to the charge of inconsistency of God's action with respect to infants and adults, "...classical Calvinism does not feel the need to justify apparently contradictory actions of God. Writes Calvin. 'If...we cannot determine a reason why he vouchsafes mercy to his own, except that it so pleases him, neither shall we have any reason for rejecting others, other than his will.' (*Institutes of the Christian Religion* 3.22.11)" (p. 463).

then a decision could be made. In this case the salvation of all the unevangelised would not be certain."[107]

Conclusion

I have now described Pinnock's inclusivist position on the unevangelised, a position which for Pinnock steers the best course through the Scylla of restrictivism and the Charybidis of pluralism. Far from straying from the biblical narrative or forcing the narrative into a foreign matrix to make this mediation possible, Pinnock believes that his hermeneutic is one demanded by the narrative, for time and again he sees both God's desire to save all humanity satisfactorily coupled with the finality and particularity of the Incarnation. Christians need to stress the truth of both statements and when this is done they will see that God is at work outside His external church, working among the unevangelised, offering to them the opportunity to respond to Him, and preparing them for ultimate fulfilment in Christ.

As an evangelical theologian Pinnock is not afraid to criticise his own community for over-emphasising exclusivity, neither is he afraid to look outside evangelicalism to find elements of other traditions which for him do more justice to the biblical truths of universality and particularity. As we have seen, Pinnock is far more influenced by certain elements of Eastern Orthodoxy, Vatican II Roman Catholicism and the teachings of the Early Fathers, than he is by contemporary evangelical theologians.[108] Commenting on this influence, I would concur with the assessment of Chester Gillis on evangelical inclusivists like Pinnock:

> While Pinnock heralds Vatican II and cites several recent Catholic theologians approvingly…at times sounding more Roman Catholic than evangelical Protestant, still he refutes certain theories arising from Catholic thinkers… It is a particular brand of inclusivism they espouse, accepting some elements of the main-line versions and rejecting others. Sometimes they seem as if they are attempting to carve out an 'evangelical inclusivism' that will both distinguish them from main-line Catholics and Protestants and continue to endear them to evangelicalism.[109]

---

[107] Ibid., p. 168. On some of the difficulties with this view see Appendix 1 of this study, p. 324 n. 99.
[108] Having said this, Pinnock does mention the influences of C.S. Lewis and Norman Anderson on him during his formative years. See Pinnock, 'An Inclusivist View,' p. 123.
[109] Chester Gillis, 'Evangelical Inclusivism: Progress or Betrayal?' in *Evangelical Quarterly* 68/2 (April 1996), p. 148.

Pinnock offers his model on the unevangelised and other religions as a serious option for evangelicals. As he says, "I think that if we were to reform theology in the direction of inclusivism, we might enhance the credibility of our faith and render more radical options unnecessary."[110] It remains for us to see whether evangelicals can adopt this model exegetically and systematically.

---

[110] Pinnock, 'An Inclusivist View,' p. 123.

PART 3
An Analysis and Critique of Clark H. Pinnock's 'Pneumatological Inclusivism'

CHAPTER 6

The Covenant, Christ and Confession of Christ: A Redemptive-Historical Critique of Pinnock's Inclusivism

Introduction: Aims and Objectives

In the following four chapters, I wish to analyse and critique Pinnock's pneumatological inclusivism with a number of specific aims and objectives in mind. Firstly, I wish to demonstrate that in spite of its theological broadness as a community, Pinnock cannot legitimately claim his inclusivism to be a viable 'evangelical' position because his argument is at variance with several fundamental evangelical beliefs.[1] However, given the problems of theological diversity within the evangelical community and the diversity over its definition as a community, at a second level I wish to focus my critique of Pinnock from an explicitly 'Reformed' perspective[2] (which is a more unified community within evangelicalism, but of course, far from being uniform), remembering that the Reformation tradition is one of the foundational historical pillars of contemporary evangelicalism. Here I will argue that a Reformed understanding of key themes is to be preferred both hermeneutically and theologically. From this critical standpoint, a final objective emerges, which is my intention not only to critique Pinnock's inclusivism *per se*, but to ask serious questions of the genesis of Pinnock's inclusivism which I believe can be ultimately traced back to within the bounda-

---

[1] However, given the controversy over defining 'evangelicalism' and because of its plasticity as a label, alluded to in Ch. 1, the force of my conclusion here can only be modest. Certainly Pinnock's definition of evangelicalism would encompass his inclusivism, see Clark H. Pinnock, 'Evangelical Thelogians Facing the Future: An Ancient and a Future Paradigm' in *Wesleyan Theological Journal* 33 (Fall 1998), pp. 7-28. It must be remembered though, that this study is not primarily about the definition of evangelicalism as a semantic label, but the truth/falsity of the possibility of salvation among the unevangelised.

[2] For a basic definition of this perspective see Ch. 1, p. 8ff.

ries of non-Reformed evangelicalism.[3] Therefore, through explicitly discussing and critiquing Pinnock, I will be implicitly discussing and critiquing non-Reformed evangelicalism of which Pinnock's position is but a logical extension, a point I have attempted to demonstrate throughout this study. So even if 'evangelicalism' as a unity can refute Pinnock's inclusivism for straying outside its parameters, there is still an internal debate between Reformed and non-Reformed evangelicalism over the question of the universality axiom which impinges directly on the problem of the unevangelised. While the root of this internal conflict ultimately lies in more basic areas of systematics not covered in this study, the question of the unevangelised provides a suitable forum to highlight this conflict as it draws on many of these basic areas.

Setting out an Evangelical Theological Framework

In the remaining part of this introduction I which to focus on methodological issues, and in particular the construction of an evangelical methodology. Far from straying away from the focus of this study, it is the adoption of the following evangelical theological framework that forms the 'scaffold' around which I build my critique in subsequent chapters.

Sola Scriptura

The scope of inquiry in this study has been focused within the boundaries of the evangelical community. In the 'Introduction' to this study, the difficulty of defining evangelicalism was outlined, but a working definition was adopted. In evaluating Pinnock's inclusivism, I propose to use a particular evangelical hermeneutical and theological framework that draws from the insights of exegetical, biblical and systematic theology.[4] At the most foundational level, any theological argument that claims to be 'evangelical' must be tested against *the* evangelical means of authority: the biblical text. That is to affirm, that for evangelical theology, the *principium cognoscendi theologiae* is *sola Scriptura*. Here, in order to incorporate the full spectrum

---

[3] I briefly charted the development of Pinnock's theology in Ch. 2.

[4] It should be noted that Pinnock briefly sets out his own evangelical theological methodology in Clark H. Pinnock, 'How I Use the Bible in Doing Theology' in ed. Robert K. Johnston, *The Use of the Bible in Theology: Evangelical Options* (Atlanta, 1985), pp. 18-34; Clark H. Pinnock and Delwin Brown, *Theological Crossfire: An Evangelical/Liberal Dialogue* (Grand Rapids, 1990), pp. 37-57; and in Clark H. Pinnock, *Flame of Love: A Theology of the Holy Spirit* (Downers Grove, 1996), pp. 215-247. Pinnock is not afraid to speak about the quadrilateral sources of authority: Scripture, tradition, experience and reason. He writes about these four: "there are multiple sources to help us and not only one. Scripture though eminent, is not the only source we have to invoke." Pinnock, *Theological Crossfire*, p. 47.

of 'evangelical' theologies, we must adopt a generalized working definition which affirms the biblical text as the inspired[5] and authoritative Word of God and normative in matters of spirituality, doctrine and ethics. As the Westminster Confession of Faith (I vi) states:

> The whole counsel of God, concerning all things necessary for his own glory, man's salvation, faith and life, is either expressly set down in Scripture, or by good and necessary consequence may be deduced from Scripture; to which nothing at any time is to be added, whether by new revelations of the Spirit, or traditions of men.

Alister McGrath says, "In part, the evangelical commitment to the authority of Scripture represents a careful and critical assessment of rival approaches to authority, and an affirmation that Scripture must be regarded as carrying

---

[5] There still seems to be considerable debate between evangelical theologians over the nature of issues such as inspiration, infallibility and inerrancy, and what constitutes a truly 'evangelical' position regarding these terms. See Gordon R. Lewis and Bruce A. Demarest, *Integrative Theology* Vol.1 (Grand Rapids, 1987), pp. 129-175; Wayne Grudem, *Systematic Theology* (Leicester, 1994), pp. 73-105. For some contemporary and sophisticated traditional evangelical treatments which uphold full inspiration, infallibility and inerrancy of Scripture, see the following works: two symposia edited by D.A. Carson and John D. Woodbridge, *Scripture and Truth* (Grand Rapids, 1983); idem *Hermeneutics Authority and Canon* (Grand Rapids, 1986); Ronald H. Nash, *The Word of God and the Mind of Man: The Crisis of Revealed Truth in Contemporary Theology* (Phillipsburg, 1982); Paul D. Feinberg, 'The Meaning of Inerrancy' in ed. Norman L. Geisler *Inerrancy* (Grand Rapids, 1979), pp. 267-304. I adopt a 'concursive' theory of inspiration which sees God "so superintending and preserving the human authors that what they wrote, while being precisely what they intended should be written, is nothing less than what God intended should be written." Don Carson, *The Gagging of God* (Leicester, 1996), p. 152. Of course, such a view presupposes a certain view of God's sovereignty and human freedom that not all evangelicals accept. For a noninerrancy position see, Jack Rogers and Donald McKim, *The Authority and Interpretation of the Bible: An Historical Approach* (San Francisco, 1979). Clark Pinnock himself has written extensively on the nature and authority of Scripture and has moved from an inerrantist position to a noninerrantist one. See Ray C.W Roennfeldt's PhD study, *Clark H. Pinnock on Biblical Authority: An Evolving Position* (Michigan, 1993) especially, pp. 140-294. I will say more on Pinnock's view of the Bible in Ch. 8.

greater theological and spiritual weight than them."[6] As Lints notes: "The biblical revelation is the final court of appeals for the theologian."[7]

Towards an Evangelical Framework

Having briefly summarised the principle of *sola Scriptura*, I now intend to describe a particular evangelical methodology/framework that will help verify and validate the biblical veracity of a theological position. Here I intend to draw upon and integrate the work of two differing evangelical approaches to the theological task, the more traditional 'systematic' ap-

---

[6] Alister McGrath, *A Passion for Truth. The Intellectual Coherence of Evangelicalism.* (Leicester, 1996), p. 66. On the relationship between Scripture and other sources of authority such as tradition, community, experience and philosophy, see McGrath, op. cit., pp. 66-102; Grant R. Osbourne, *The Hermeneutical Spiral: A Comprehensive Introduction to Biblical Interpretation* (Downers Grove, 1991), pp. 286-299.

[7] Richard Lints, *The Fabric of Theology: A Prolegomenon to Evangelical Theology.* (Grand Rapids, 1993), p. 66. Before going into more detail concerning *sola Scriptura*, it must be noted that evangelical theology is aware and has reacted (albeit belatedly) to the contemporary challenges of postmodernism and deconstructionism and the concerns of the influence of pre-understanding and the nature of meaning in hermeneutics. Richard Lints represents a typical evangelical position on these issues: "The Scriptures in their fullness are the divine witness to and interpretation of God's redemptive activity in history. God both speaks and acts to save his people, but he does not remove them from either their culture or their history. God saves his people *in* history, not *from* history. Awareness of this fact should force the theological vision to take into account the "filters" of that history: tradition, culture and reason. The biblical revelation stands in an authoritative position relative to these filters, but inevitably they influence the interpretation of that authority. The goal of theology is consciously to bring the biblical revelation into a position of judgment on all of life, including the filters, and thereby to bring the cleansing power of God's redemption into all of life"(p. 82); and "...we hear the divine conversation only after it has passed through several filters- our culture, our religious tradition, our personal history, and so on. If we take these filters seriously, we may be able to decrease the distortion with which we hear the conversation. In the words of modern discourse, the biblical text has a trajectory... In calling attention to the filters through which we hear conversation with God, I am calling attention to an emphasis that for the most part has been lost in evangelical discussions of theology. And yet I want to retain the fundamental point of the evangelical tradition - namely, that theology begins with the speech of God. The Christian theological framework originates with the text of Scripture, and the interpreter enters the process only derivatively"(p. 61). For more detailed evangelical treatments on these issues see the following: Lints, op. cit., pp. 57-132; Grant R. Osbourne, op. cit., pp. 286-314, 366-411; eds. D. A. Carson and John D. Woodbridge, *Scripture and Truth* (Grand Rapids, 1983); eds. D. A. Carson and John D. Woodbridge, *Hermeneutics, Authority and Canon* (Grand Rapids, 1986); D. A. Carson, *The Gagging of God: Christianity Confronts Pluralism* (Leicester, 1996), pp. 57-193; Anthony Thiselton *New Horizons in Hermeneutics* (London, 1992); ed. Moisés Silva, *Foundations of Contemporary Interpretation* (Leicester, 1997).

proach of Grant Osbourne and the approach of Richard Lints that seeks to bring the structure of biblical theology[8] to systematic theology.[9]

Osbourne's method for verification is a 'critical realist' approach: that theological assertions are 'real' in the sense that they "are valid representations of the 'way things are,'"[10] but "'critical' because it never assumes that

---

[8] John Frame states that the term 'biblical theology' is something of a misnomer. He describes it as the study of the history of God's dealings with creation and variously calls it 'the history of redemption' or 'the history of the covenant'. Such a discipline has been developed by Reformed figures such as Geerhardus Vos, H. N. Ridderbos, Richard B. Gaffin, and Meredith Kline. For a more detailed description of this discipline see Frame, *The Doctrine of the Knowledge of God* (Phillipsburg, 1987), pp. 207-212; Geerhardus Vos, *Biblical Theology* (Edinburgh, 1975), pp. 3-19; Grant R. Osbourne *The Hermeneutical Spiral: A Comprehensive Introduction to Biblical Interpretation* (Downers Grove, 1991), pp. 263-284; Willem van Gemeren, *The Progress of Redemption: From Creation to New Jerusalem* (Carlilse, 1988), pp. 17-42.

[9] Grant R. Osbourne, op. cit.; Richard Lints, *The Fabric of Theology: A Prolegomenon to Evangelical Theology* (Grand Rapids, 1993). I have chosen these two figures because they represent different approaches (both methodologically and confessionally) and so I, hopefully, avoid bias towards one method. Another recent 'evangelical' approach which attempts to combine the insights of systematic, biblical, historical, apologetic and practical fields, is that of Gordon R. Lewis and Bruce Demarest, *Integrative Theology* Vol. 1 (Grand Rapids, 1987-1994), p. 8; Lewis/Demarest propose three interrelated test criteria of truth : 1) logical consistency 2) agreement with the data of revelation 3) existential viability. One reservation with this schema, is the compartmentalization of these three criteria, rather than seeing both logical coherence and existential viability being part of what it means to agree with the biblical data. As Frame points out: "It is not that 'coherence' or 'logical consistency' is a kind of neutral principle by which all religious claims can be tested. The meaning of 'theological coherence' must itself arise from Scripture. Otherwise, it is difficult to escape the objection against the coherence theory that there may be possibly more than one fully coherent system. But if we develop our concept of coherence from Scripture, then we presuppose that competing systems will not, in the final analysis, be proved coherent, that they are unstable in themselves, and that they depend on Christian concepts - 'borrowed capital' - for their apparent plausibility. We value coherence because we have been overwhelmed by the divine wisdom displayed in Scripture, not the other way round." John Frame, op. cit., p. 134. In my critique I hope to show that there are major lacunas and ambiguities in Pinnock's position on the unevangelised that lead to concerns over his internal coherence and consistency. This part of my argument, though, is not divorced from his adherence/non-adherence to Scripture but is part of it. The criteria of 'existential viability' is even more problematical and can mean nothing other than the fact that there has to be question as to whether the biblical lens makes sense of what we see and experience in the world. For a community which holds to the principle of *sola Scriptura*, holding to such a criterion seems strange because it would seem that all reality is existentially viable because the Bible determines how one interprets reality and to interpret reality differently must mean an erroneous interpretation. Such a view can never be falsified *a posteriori* and is always *a priori*.

[10] Osbourne, op. cit., p. 310. See also Lints, op. cit., pp. 19-28.

theological constructions are *exact* depictions of revealed truth (unlike "naive realism")."[11] Similarly, Lints states the two philosophical assumptions employed in his work are the "realism principle: Individuals normally know the world pretty much as it really is"[12] and the "bias principle: Individuals never know the world apart from biases that influence their view of what is really the case."[13]

Osbourne lists six criteria to test the validity of a theological construction[14]:

1. Coherence - Does it accurately portray Scriptural teaching?
2. Comprehensiveness - Does it account for all the statements of Scripture?
3. Adequacy - Does the formulation provide a better description of doctrine than competing schools?
4. Consistency - Is the system consistent?
5. Continuation - is the theological construction durable?
6. Cross-fertilization - Have differing schools of thought accepted the viability of the assertion?

On these criteria, Osbourne notes:

In the final analysis these criteria do not 'prove' a doctrine or theological construction. Rather they help both the individual and the community to keep returning to Scripture in order to ascertain the actual teaching of the Word of God *as a whole* and the extent to which the modern redescription of the biblical teaching coheres with it. In addition a critical-realist approach will suggest ways in which the modern statement can be reworked so as to conform more closely to the biblical teaching.[15]

---

[11] Ibid. As he notes: "...dogma is an analogical model that approximates or *re*-presents truth. Thus critical realists never assume that they have achieved the 'final' statement of theological truth, ...though of course one can verify that a particular statement is an accurate depiction of the biblical norm. The process of validation within a critical realist approach is at once simple and complex. It is simple because verification comes via criteria of coherence, comprehensiveness, adequacy and consistency. It is complex because each criterion must be applied hermeneutically to many interpretations and organising patterns of the competing systems"(p. 310).

[12] Lints, op. cit., p. 20.

[13] Ibid. For more detail see: idem pp. 19-28; Lewis and Demarest, op. cit., pp. 36f.

[14] Osbourne, op. cit., p. 311.

[15] Ibid.

I wish to expound the first four of these criteria by integrating them into an evangelical theological framework.[16]

A Redemptive-Historical Approach

In this section I wish to outline Richard Lint's "redemptive historical"[17] approach which builds on the work of theologians such as Jonathan Edwards and Geerhardus Vos.[18] Before outlining Lints' proposal I wish to note two caveats on the framework I am about to describe. Firstly, like Frame, I view the traditional divisions of theology (i.e. exegetical, systematic), not as competing disciplines but as being "perspectivally related - each embracing the whole of theology and therefore embracing the others...they differ from one another in focus and emphasis and in the way they organise their material, but each is permitted (and obligated) to use the methods characteristic of the others."[19] I wish to use the 'redemptive historical' approach of Lints because I believe it is relevant in my assessment of Pinnock's inclusivism. In view of this, I also note Frame's second quali-

---

[16] Osbourne's final two criteria of continuation and cross-fertilization, deserve a brief mention here. Osbourne is right to say that an equation of tradition with 'magesterium' is simplistic and neglects the importance of tradition for the evangelical community (p. 290). As McGrath, op. cit. states: "Evangelicals have always been prone to read Scripture as if they were the first to do so. We need to be reminded that others have been there before us, and have read it before us. This process of receiving the scriptural revelation is 'tradition' - not a source of revelation in addition to Scripture, but a particular way of understanding Scripture that the Christian church has recognised as responsible and reliable. Scripture and tradition are thus not seen as two sources of revelation; rather they are coinherent"(p. 95). What is important to recognise is that tradition possesses no intrinsic authority and is not the ultimate norm for evangelicals. Linked to this is the importance of community. Certainly "community exegesis"(p. 243) ("dialogue with the past community via commentaries and so forth and with present communities via constant interaction") serves the necessary check to an "ecclesiastical aristocracy or an academic elite to reign supreme over matters pertaining to the Bible" (Lints, op. cit., p. 286). It also avoids the individualistic reading of Scripture: "The work of theology is not the work of one individual seeking to gain a complete knowledge of God on his own but the corporate work of the church in which Christians together seek a common mind on the things of God" (Frame, op. cit., p. 304). The same comments apply to the creeds that must be seen as being ruled by Scripture (*norma normata*) and not rules that rule Scripture (*norma normans*). See Frame, op. cit., pp. 304-306.

[17] Lints, op. cit., p. 262.

[18] In a chapter entitled, 'The Theological Past' Lints notes the work of Edwards and Vos as best anticipating his own methodological conclusions (p. 141). In particular he concentrates on Edwards' 'A History of Redemption' in vol. 9 of the Yale Edition of the *Works of Jonathan Edwards* (New Haven, 1989), and Geerhardus Vos' *Biblical Theology*. See Lints, op. cit., pp. 171-190.

[19] Frame, op. cit., p. 206.

fication that Scripture is a redemptive history but not exclusively redemptive history: "Theology...must take account of redemptive history but not of redemptive history only. It must also be concerned to do justice to Scripture as law, poetry, wisdom, gospel - all the authoritative aspects of the Word of God. Theology is not, therefore, to be controlled exclusively by redemptive history, in opposition to other aspects or perspectives."[20]

Lints states that not only should we be concerned as to the content of our theological framework, but also the 'shape' of such a framework: "It is important to ask seriously whether the conception of doing theology by stringing together doctrines like that of a pearl necklace might not be undermining the essential unity of the biblical message."[21] Rather than viewing the Bible as an ancient theological textbook where the truth of an issue can be ascertained inductively by finding the most biblical references on that issue, and ordering the results around an abstract category, he reminds us that the Bible is a text with a developing story. The theme of this story is the story of redemption and as redemption progresses so does revelation. He writes:

> We must remember that Scripture not only witnesses to God's redemption but is an effective agent of that redemption. Biblical revelation progresses because it mirrors the progressive nature of redemption. The 'story' of God's involvement with and redemption of his people is acted out on the stage of history with many distinct but related parts... The covenantal relation between God and his people has a history to it, and in order to understand the relationship between God and his people, one must understand their history together. Redemption does not happen all at once, nor does it evolve uniformly. Rather it develops with strange twists and turns in separate but related epochs. These epochs are demarcated largely by God's acts and redemptive covenants.[22]

Not only are the divine acts recorded in Scripture but they are given divine interpretations as well, so re-enforcing the idea that Scripture is part of the redemptive history. As Vos notes, "We must place act-revelation by the side of word-revelation...such act-revelations are never left to speak for themselves; they are preceded and followed by word-revelation."[23] Act and word are inextricably linked and cannot be separated.[24]

The epochs of redemptive history are linked together (or perhaps better 'woven together') because the same God holds the redemptive history to-

---

[20] Ibid., p. 210.
[21] Lints, op. cit., p. 261.
[22] Ibid., p. 263.
[23] Vos, op. cit., p. 6f.
[24] I will make more of this in Ch. 8, where I speak about the Holy Spirit's interpretation of history in the inspiration of Scripture.

gether. As Lints points out, Jesus relies on the 'story' of the Old Testament to explain his person and mission: "It is the connection with the past that makes the present and future explicable."[25] Lints now moves from the notion of redemptive revelation to the idea of redemptive theology. If the essence of theology is the interpretation of the history of redemption, then no point in the history can be understood until it is related to its past and future history, that is to say, that a theological framework has a definite teleology. What is significant is that all of history is part of this redemptive history, there can be no sacred/secular split because all history has this same teleological function.[26] He continues:

> Many evangelical theologians have supposed that the task of systematic theology consists in the search for doctrinal models and keys that fit the Bible's complex locks and opens them up to the reader... But this model of the theological framework betrays in significant ways the central insight of the Protestant reformers - *sola Scriptura*. If we fail to link the structure of theology to the structure of Scripture carefully, we undermine the normative role of Scripture. This is not to say that a theological framework ought simply to repeat the Scriptural text, but it is to urge that great care be taken to ensure that the conceptual categories of the theological framework adequately reflect the phenomena of Scripture.[27]

Such an approach seeks to integrate exegetical, biblical and systematic theology so that the three disciplines do not operate in isolation from one another but rely on each other. In essence this approach seeks to inject what can sometimes seem like 'static' systematics, with the historical movement of biblical theology: "The sense of movement so critical to the biblical text ought to be part and parcel of the theological framework. The organic relations between the various episodes (or epochs) of Scripture ought to be de-

---

[25] Lints, op. cit., p. 267.

[26] Ibid. "The Scriptures provide the interpretive matrix that explains human history in global terms and enables us to understand our own role in that history - which, for those with eyes to see and ears to hear, is ultimately purposeful. Our interpretive matrix should be the interpretive matrix of the Scriptures" (p. 269).

[27] Ibid., p. 269f. Lints explicitly refers to Pinnock as being an example of a theologian who searches for a doctrinal model to open up Scripture. Here he refers to Pinnock's essay, 'How I Use the Bible in Doing Theology,' op. cit. John Frame, op. cit., is less worried over a structural departure from the text: "the work of theology is not to mimic the Scriptural vocabulary or its order and structure but to *apply* the Bible. And to do this, theology may (indeed must) *depart* somewhat from the structure of Scripture itself, for otherwise it could only repeat the exact words of Scripture from Genesis to Revelation... The resemblance between Scripture and the biblical theologies is somewhat overstated. There is a great deal of difference between Vos's *Biblical Theology* and the Pauline Epistles for example!"(p. 211).

veloped in such a manner as to envelop the modern epoch and thereby bring the entirety of history under the interpretive umbrella of history."[28] The Bible itself provides its own theological structure and it is this structure that should be the context for all theology: "All biblical texts are related to one another by the redemptive purposes that underlie the canon as a whole. The canon in its entirety gives the meaning of those redemptive purposes."[29]

Once this principle is established then some further insights follow. Firstly, the theological narrative or 'story-like' character of the Bible will be important structurally. There is a 'plot-line' to this story with central characters involved.[30] Secondly, (and a point that will be crucial in evaluating Pinnock's inclusivism), Lints says that we note the organic unity of the Scripture. This means focusing on our "redemptive historical index,"[31] that is, our place in the history of redemption. If we do not understand our relationship between the preceding and subsequent epochs, "we will retain a hopelessly fragmented conception of ourselves and our culture... Our sense of place is dependent on the coherence of redemptive history, and this begins with the unity of redemptive history as recorded and interpreted in Scripture."[32]

Lints acknowledges that the idea of unity in salvation has been disputed by much of contemporary theology. However, he believes that understanding this unity is vital: "I would suggest that the working assumption of an evangelical theological framework ought to be the unity-in-diversity of the Testaments with unity being prior to diversity since it is one God who manifests himself in the diversity of historical epochs."[33] There is, therefore, a need to understand the 'flow' and 'organic unity' of redemptive history which balances both continuity and diversity between the epochs: "This need not result in a bland uniformity or essential contradictions of principles across epochs; rather, it should help the reader to see overarching purpose progressively revealed through the different epochs of the Scriptures."[34] Vos comments that the progress is akin to that of seed to tree, not-

---

[28] Ibid., p. 271.

[29] Ibid., p. 274.

[30] Ibid. He writes: "The Scriptures have many authors, and yet they have one author. Careful attention reveals Scripture to be a masterpiece, complex beyond imagination and yet, paradoxically, simple enough for a child to read"(p. 275).

[31] Ibid., p. 276.

[32] Ibid., p. 276f.

[33] Ibid. p. 278. Lints claims that overstressing the diversity between the epochs leads one to some form of dispensationalism and overstressing the continuity leads to some form of theonomy. In the next chapter, I will outline the basis of a dispensational critique of Pinnock, but opt for a position of covenantal continuity for precisely the same reason as Lints.

[34] Ibid., p. 278.

ing that the seed is no less perfect than the tree.[35] If we are to see a unity-in-diversity, then we should be aware of certain patterns and themes that occur throughout the text. These are intrinsic to the text and not a creation of the interpreter, "The significance lies in the reality of the redemptive (and therefore purposeful) activity of God to which the Scriptures are providing witness."[36]

Once it is recognised that a theological framework must mirror the structure of Scripture then there must be some parameters to move from text to framework. Lints notes that while evangelicals have retained the principle of *sola Scriptura*, they have failed to realise the hermeneutical parameters which come with such an affirmation: "If Scripture is a final authority, then in some important sense Scripture must be allowed to interpret Scripture...the *analogia fidei* (the analogy of faith). The faith defined in any given scriptural passage is to be interpreted by the faith defined in the whole of Scripture."[37] Lints proposes that the biblical text has "three horizons" of redemptive interpretation, the textual, the epochal and the canonical[38]

In summary, the textual horizon will continue the 'grammatical-historical' tradition favoured by the Reformers, but will realise the diversity

---

[35] Vos, op. cit., p. 7. This illustration highlights another aspect which I will make use of later on: "The feature in question explains further how the soteric sufficiency of the truth could belong to its first state of emergence: in the seed-form the minimum of indispensable knowledge was already present"(p. 7).

[36] Lints, op. cit., p. 284. Osbourne, op. cit., p. 273, warns that one should not lapse into the error of 'parallelomania' which tends to apply any analogous passage to define the meaning of a biblical idea, or "what Carson calls an 'artificial conformity' that ignores the diversity of expression and emphasis between divergent statements in the Bible." See Don Carson 'Unity and Diversity in the New Testament: The Possibility of Systematic Theology' in eds. Don Carson and John D. Woodbridge, *Scripture and Truth* (Leicester, 1983), pp. 65-101.

[37] Ibid., p. 291. Osbourne, op. cit. prefers the term *analogia scriptura* because the term *fidei* suggests that that the system of dogma still has a certain predominance. Osbourne states that the basic principles involved in the *analogia scriptura* are that no single statement can set aside a doctrine established in several passages, and that no doctrine can be established on the basis of just one passage alone, but must be built upon the tenor of a number of passages in order to gain an authoritative status as dogma (p. 11). Moreover, he notes, "all such doctrinal statements should be made on the basis of all the texts that speak on the issue rather than on the basis of proof-texts or 'favorite' passages (p. 11).

[38] Ibid., p. 293. VanGemeren, op. cit. p. 30-32, uses the same 'trifocal' strategy calling them the 'literary form' the 'canonical place' and the 'redemptive-historical significance'.

of biblical genre.[39] The epochal horizon will recognise the progress of revelation and redemptive purposes of God and understand a passage, book, character, era, or place in the 'redemptive historical index': "Each of the biblical epochs must be understood in its own right as well as in relationship to the others."[40] Lints notes that essential to the canonical horizon is a "promise-fulfillment"[41] model present throughout Scripture: God who had been faithful in the past would be faithful in the future. This is the 'glue' holding the various epochs together. Central to this horizon is the notion of 'typology,' where an earlier event, character or institution is called the 'type,' and the later one is called the 'antitype.' Lints notes two characteristics of this pattern, firstly the repetition of the promise-fulfilment pattern, the second that there is a different degree between the former acts of God and the new ones. As he notes:

> Theological construction must begin to wrestle with the fact that this progressive fulfillment lies at the heart of a theological framework. The meaning of the past epochs is invested into later epochs in the Scriptures,

---

[39] Ibid. He comments: "It is imperative, then, that the theological interpreter of the biblical text understands the multifaceted character of the sentences in Scripture as well as the multitude of different forms of sentences in the Scriptures" (p. 298).

[40] Ibid., p. 301. This horizon will form an important part of my analysis in the next chapter.

[41] Ibid., p. 303. I must note the various problems in defining a 'theological centre of Scripture' or a 'master context'. VanGemeren, op. cit. p. 26, notes that within evangelical theology there is much disagreement as to what this centre is: "Theological centers such as promise (Kaiser), covenant (Robertson; McComiskey), and kingdom (Van Ruler) have the advantage of serving as organising principles from which the biblical revelation may be approached. The recognition of a theological centre highlights one aspects of God's plan in distinction from others." VanGemeren himself, opts for the focus being, "Jesus Christ is the revelation of the salvation of God." Osbourne, op. cit. pp. 280-285, also notes the problem of defining a unifying centre. A possible solution to this problem is to adopt the 'perspectival' approach of Frame once again. He notes that although he believes that Christ is the central message of the Scriptures, that to understand Christ we need the whole biblical canon and so there is a "'perspectival' reciprocity between the central message of Scripture and its detailed, particular messages" (p. 192). For Frame there can be many themes that are central to Scripture, "if these concepts are perspectivally related, then they do not exclude one another; we do not have to choose among them. Rather, we can find in each an aspect of the precious diversity, the precious richness that God has written into His Word."(p. 193). As will be seen in the next chapter, my critique against Pinnock concentrates on the perspective of 'covenant.'

and the meaning of those epochs is in turn invested into future epochs. This might be referred to as the 'epochal' reach of typology.[42]

On the relationship between these three horizons, Lints notes that no one horizon must take precedence over the other but that "the theological interpreter of Scripture must allow the three horizons to dialogue with one another, helping to explain and clarify the meaning of the others."[43] Only when all three horizons are taken into account will the interpreter be able to discover the questions, the Bible considers important and the necessary framework to answer those questions.

An Outline for Chapters 6-9

It will be noted in what follows that Pinnock's inclusivism has already been criticised elsewhere by a number of evangelical theologians. However these critiques have only focused on one area of Pinnock's argument or have been somewhat 'superficial' in depth. The overall result has been fragmented in that each critique has failed to tackle the whole of Pinnock's inclusivism, including not just his actual theory of the 'faith principle' but the presuppositions on which this theory rests. In the next four chapters I wish to synthesise all these various strands of criticism to mount a detailed, sustained, and comprehensive critique of Pinnock's inclusivism. This will involve the significant amplification of existing lines of criticism as well as the adding of new ones.

The essence of Pinnock's inclusivism in support of the salvation of the unevangelised, is his separation of epistemology and ontology, that is one can be ontologically saved by Christ whilst being epistemologically unaware of him. It is to this argument that my critique will be directed in the remaining part of this chapter and in Chs. 7 and 8. In these chapters I not only want to show that there is no salvation without a confession of Christ, but *why* there can be no salvation without a confession of Christ. In this chapter, I concentrate on exegetical and hermeneutical issues, focusing particularly on the analogy Pinnock draws between the chronologically pre-messianic and the epistemologically pre-messianic. Building on these findings, Chs. 7 and 8 analyse Pinnock's argument from a more systematic theological perspective. Ch. 7 focuses on the implications of Pinnock's inclusivism for his doctrines of the person and work of Christ; Ch. 8 concentrates on certain Trinitarian issues, particularly the relationship between the Second and Third Persons of the Trinity. Finally, Ch. 9 critically focuses on

---

[42] Ibid., p. 305. On the use of typology in evangelical theology see W. Edward Glenny, 'Typology: A Summary of the Present Evangelical Discussion' in *Journal of the Evangelical Theological Society* 40/4 (Dec. 1997), pp. 627-638.
[43] Ibid., p. 293.

the foundation of Pinnock's inclusivism which generates his position on the unevangelised: the 'universality axiom,' and asks whether this axiom is present within the biblical text.

In the previous chapter, I traced the gradual development of Pinnock's inclusivism from his first essay 'Why is Jesus the Only Way?'(1976),[44] to *Flame of Love* (1996).[45] In the following chapters, I will focus my critique on the most developed form of Pinnock's inclusivism, that is his 'pneumatological' form, concentrating on *A Wideness in God's Mercy* (1992)[46] which establishes the biblical and theological framework for an inclusivist position, and 'An Inclusivist View' (1995)[47] and *Flame of Love* (1996) which develop the pneumatological perspective of Pinnock's inclusivism.[48]

Introduction: Approaching the Biblical Texts on these Issues

One of the central biblical and theological tenets of Pinnock's inclusivism is the analogy he draws between chronologically pre-messianic believers and epistemologically pre-messianic believers. The theme of 'covenant' is central to Pinnock's argument as he grounds any relationship to God through a covenant:

> According to the Bible, persons can relate to God in three ways and covenants: through the cosmic covenant established with Noah, through the Old covenant made with Abraham, and through the New covenant ratified by Jesus. One may even speak of salvation in the broad sense in all three covenants... In all three, God justifies Jews and Gentiles on the ground of faith, the condition for salvation in all dispensations.[49]

---

[44] Clark H. Pinnock, 'Why is Jesus the Only Way?' in *Eternity* (Dec. 1976), pp. 13-15.
[45] Pinnock, *Flame of Love*, op. cit.
[46] Clark H. Pinnock, *A Wideness in God's Mercy: The Finality of Jesus Christ in a World of Religions* (Grand Rapids, 1992).
[47] Clark H. Pinnock, 'An Inclusivist View' in eds. Dennis L. Okholm and Timothy R. Phillips, *More Than One Way? Four Views on Salvation in a Pluralistic World* (Grand Rapids, 1996), pp. 93-124.
[48] I have purposely left out of this critique any reference to a *Logos* theology that Pinnock mentions in *Wideness* for two reasons: 1) Although this is an important theme in *Wideness*, Pinnock does not develop the idea much in 'An Inclusivist View' (1995) or *Flame of Love* (1996), concentrating on the Spirit's role. 2) As a *Logos* theology was mentioned in *Wideness* (1992), other evangelicals have focused their critique on this aspect and so a re-iteration would not be profitable. See James E. Bradley, '*Logos* Christology and Religious Pluralism: A New Evangelical Proposal' in *Proceedings of the Wheaton Theological Conference* (Wheaton, 1992), pp. 190-208.
[49] Clark H. Pinnock, *A Wideness in God's Mercy* (Grand Rapids, 1992), p. 105. Note also that he speaks of a covenant prior to the Noahic covenant: "We can speak of a

To substantiate the 'faith principle' Pinnock uses both the Noahic covenant and Abrahamic covenant to show how believers were saved, although their faith was propositionally deficient. However, the unevangelised actually fall under God's cosmic covenant made with Noah and because of this, I labelled Pinnock's inclusivist theory of universal accessibility the 'cosmic covenant' because it involved two definite parts or movements, the first by the trinitarian God who makes Himself universally present through the Spirit, and the second by human beings who freely accept a relationship with God through the 'faith principle'.

In this chapter I want to argue that Pinnock's analogy between pre-messianic believers and the unevangelised de-contextualises both parties' position in the history of revelation. Pre-messianic believers were not responding to an abstract and generalised faith principle, but were in direct contact with God Himself: this was a special revelation and cannot be compared to the unevangelised who can learn something of God through general revelation. I wish to demonstrate this point from the perspective of 'covenant theology'. However I will mention briefly another viable evangelical position that comes to the same conclusion as 'covenant theology' but from a different perspective.[50]

Dispensationalism

Realising that dispensationalism,[51] as a sub-species of evangelical theology, is not a unified movement but contains a wide spectrum of positions, there

---

covenant of creation such that the whole world and its people belong to God who created humanity to relate to him." (p. 20).

[50] I have already noted on p. 148 why I do not agree with the dispensational position.

[51] Dispensationalism is a theological grouping within evangelical theology. Grudem in his *Systematic Theology* (Grand Rapids, 1994), p. 859 n. 14, defines dispensationalism as follows: "Although there are several distinctives that usually characterize dispensationalists, the distinction between Israel and the church as two groups in God's overall plan is probably the most important. Other doctrines held by dispensationalists include a pretribulational rapture of the church into heaven, a future literal fulfilment of Old Testament prophecies concerning Israel, the dividing of biblical history into seven periods or 'dispensations' of God's ways of relating to his people, and an understanding of the church age as parenthesis in God's plan for the ages, a parenthesis instituted when the Jews largely rejected Jesus as their Messiah. However, many present-day dispensationalists would qualify or reject several of these other distinctives. Dispensationalism as a system began with the writings of J. N. Darby (1800-1882) in Great Britain, but was popularized in the USA through the Scofield Reference Bible." This system of thought has been defined and developed over the years and some of the leading 'progressive' dispensationalists include Robert L. Saucy, Craig Blaising and Darrell L. Bock. For a brief historical and theological overview of dispensationalism see Gordon Lewis and Bruce Demarest, *Integrative Theology* 3 Vols. (Grand Rapids, 1988-1994) Vol. 3, pp. 312-316; Vern Poythress, *Understanding Dispensationalists* (Phillipsburg, 1994); John

are potentially a number of forms that this position could take. As an example of such a form, I will briefly summarize the argument presented by Ramesh Richard in his critique of Pinnock entitled *The Population of Heaven* (1994).[52] Richard refers to 'dispensationalism' "in the moderate sense of a branch of evangelicalism that maintains distinctions between Israel and the church in the administration of God's program in history."[53] Specifically this administration is constituted by a number of 'dispensations'. Against Pinnock's inclusivism, Richard calls his position and those like it "epoch-related discontinuity."[54] He argues that there is a specific and exclusive content of faith in every dispensation/epoch, and that historical location is integrated with epistemological content:

> One of the distinctives of dispensationalism may well hover on this point that the specific content of saving faith defines, demarcates, and distinguishes a dispensation. Such a distinctive is important in relation to the inclusivist question. That is, it is possible for people to be saved without any explicit knowledge of Christ before Christ came, but not after He came. In this way we preserve the truth and the adequacy of Old Testament revelation for salvation, while emphasizing that in this age a personal relationship with God is mediated *exclusively* through the Son.[55]

Therefore in the present dispensation, confession of Christ is necessary for salvation whereas in previous dispensations it was not necessary. So one cannot compare the way Abraham was saved to how the unevangelised are saved. It is not comparing 'like with like' as Pinnock suggests.[56]

S. Feinberg, 'Systems of Discontinuity' in ed. John S. Feinberg, *Continuity and Discontinuity: Perspectives on the Relationship Between the Old and New Testaments* (Westchester, 1988), pp. 63-86. For a more detailed understanding of Dispensationalism as compared and contrasted to covenant theology, see the entire collection of essays written in honour of S. Lewis Johnson, Jr., ed. John S. Feinberg, *Continuity and Discontinuity: Perspectives on the Relationship Between the Old and New Testaments* (Westchester, 1988).

[52] Ramesh P. Richard, *The Population of Heaven. A Biblical Response to the Inclusivist Position on who will be Saved* (Chicago: 1994).

[53] Ibid., p. 140 n. 21.

[54] Richard, op. cit., p. 118 n. 8.

[55] Ibid., p. 123.

[56] For more details on Richard's argument see Richard, op. cit., pp. 115-143. I should note here Pinnock's references to dispensationalism with regards to his inclusivism. In *Wideness*, p. 162, Pinnock speaks favourably of Ryrie's statement that "The basis of salvation in every age is the death of Christ; the requirement for salvation in every age is faith; the object of faith in every age is God; the content of faith changes in the various dispensations," (taken from Charles C. Ryrie, *Dispensationalism Today* (Chicago, 1965), p. 123) as echoing his own position and being an influence on him at the beginning of his thinking on inclusivism. However he does not see contemporary dispensa-

Covenant theology[57]

Outlining 'covenant theology'[58]

In the first part of this chapter I outlined an evangelical framework that stressed the organic relations between the various epochs of redemptive history and the over-arching 'unity-in-diversity' of this history being careful to guide a careful path between continuity and discontinuity between the various historical epochs. Building around this methodological scaffolding, I wish to outline the approach known as 'covenant theology' that I believe best handles the concept of progressive revelation and the unity-in-diversity of Scripture.

The term 'covenant theology' encompasses a wide variety of positions that believe that the history of the world is demarcated by various covenants.[59] The Westminster Confession of Faith (1647) which perhaps remains the standard creedal affirmation of this type of theology, affirms the existence of two covenants, the so-called 'covenant of works'[60] made with

---

tionalism (he mentions Richard's book) following his lead. In 'An Inclusivist View,' he writes: "I keep hoping dispensational theology will progress in this direction too and that a dispensational inclusivist will come forward to help people burdened by restrictivism in his or her camp. It hasn't happened yet, and I'm not holding my breath"(p. 108).

[57] Sometimes 'covenant theology' is referred to as 'federal theology' from the Latin *foedus* meaning covenant.

[58] In this section, I can only summarise what is a complex theological framework. I have tried in the notes to point to the major areas of diversity and disagreement within this type of theology. A useful collection of essays on covenant theology and its relationship to dispensationalism historically, theologically and hermeneutically, can be found in ed. Feinberg, *Continuity and Discontinuity*.

[59] The emergence of 'covenant' theology can be traced back to the Reformation. Although the seeds of this theology can be seen in the work of Calvin, Zwingli and Bullinger, it is the so-called 'Heidelberg School' including Zacharias Ursinus (1534-1583), and Casper Olevianus (1536-1587) who are regarded as being the first main proponents of this covenantal schema. For historical development see Lewis and Demarest, op. cit., Vol. 3, pp. 308-312; G. Michael Thomas, *The Extent of the Atonement: A Dilemma for Reformed Theology from Calvin to the Consensus (1536-1675)* (Carlisle, 1997), pp. 104-119. I do not wish to restrict the term to only the fully developed positions of the seventeenth century, but wish to encompass those like Calvin and Zwingli.

[60] It must be noted here that there is much disagreement as to the exact status and nature of this covenant. Firstly there are those who have reservations that the covenant extends back to Adam: see W. J. Dumbrell, *Covenant and Creation: The Theology of Old Testament Covenants* (Carlisle, 1997), pp. 44-46. For the argument that the covenantal scheme does reach back to Adam, see O. Palmer Robertson, *The Christ of the Covenants* (Phillipsburg, 1984), pp. 17-27. Although I will be saying something on this covenant later in this chapter, especially concerning the validity of this covenant today, it is appropriate to outline the three main understandings of this covenant. The first

prelapsarian Adam and the 'covenant of grace' which extends from Gen. 3:15 to Revelation 22:21 and which is made through Christ with all believers.[61] As Poythress notes:

> The covenant of grace was administered differently in the different dispensations (Westminster Confession 7.4) but is substantially the same in all. Covenant theology has always allowed for a diversity of administration of the one covenant of grace. This diversity accounted for...the diversity of epochs in biblical history. But the emphasis was undeniably on the unity of the *one* covenant of grace.[62]

---

views this covenant as a conditional pact whereby after some unspecified 'probationary period', Adam would receive eternal life on the condition of obedience. Such a view seems to be implied in the Westminster Confession of Faith ("The first covenant made with Man was a covenant of works, wherein life was promised to Adam, and in him to his posterity, upon condition of perfect and personal obedience"), and is the view of Charles Hodge, *Systematic Theology* Vol. 2 (Grand Rapids, 1946), p. 117. However this position is criticised because (among other reasons) it firstly implies a certain conditionality between God and human beings such that God 's original plan was frustrated by Adam's Fall; secondly, it implies that Adam was not created in a covenant relation to God but that this was added after creation; and thirdly it suggests that Adam could 'earn' his salvation by works. A second view does not see this covenant as added onto creation, but as the act of creation itself. This 'creational bond' is an act of grace and therefore unmerited. Rather than focusing on works as the non-eating of the tree, the emphasis is on Adam's responsibility to his Creator. Rather than calling it a 'covenant of works', Robertson prefers the term 'covenant of creation.' See Robertson, op. cit., pp. 54-57, 67-87. Finally, there is the position that there is no 'covenant of works'/'covenant of grace' distinction, only a single covenant of grace. Here Adam was created in fellowship and harmony with God and this was by an act of grace alone. Adam's calling in this was a call to thankful obedience (not merit). However eternal life was not given to Adam here because on this view "it was not God's intention nor purpose to glorify Himself through Adam's perfect life in covenant fellowship. God had determined something better: the blessedness of covenant fellowship with Himself in Jesus Christ. See Herman Hanko, *God's Everlasting Covenant of Grace* (Grand Rapids, 1988), pp. 27-33; Herman Hoeksema, *Reformed Dogmatics* (Grand Rapids, 1966), pp. 214-227. Robertson, op. cit., p. 56, suggests that such a position forgets the role that works play in the covenant of grace: "Christ works for the salvation of his people. His accomplishment of righteousness for sinful men represents an essential aspect of redemption... While salvation is by faith, judgment is by works." In this sense, Berkhof, *Systematic Theology* (Edinburgh, 1958) can say that the covenant of works is not abrogated since its curses and promises continue for those in sin, but that in another sense it is abrogated for those under the covenant of grace because Christ as Mediator has met the obligations of the covenant for his people (p. 218).

[61] I have already noted that some do not extend the 'covenantal' scheme as far back as Adam.

[62] Poythress, op. cit., p. 40. A number of 'covenant' theologians (e.g. Louis Berkhof, op. cit. pp. 265-271) speak of a third covenant (although Berkhof sees it as another as-

Before I apply the insights of covenant theology to the question of the unevangelised and Pinnock's inclusivism, I wish briefly to outline the contours of 'covenant theology' noting its complexity and diversity as a movement. I will focus particularly on two areas, the definition of covenant, the unity/diversity of the covenantal epochs. All these will be important as we come to critique Pinnock's inclusivism.

Defining Covenant

How is one to define the biblical concept of covenant? Here there is debate over whether covenant is to be regarded as unilateral/unconditional or bilateral/conditional in its nature. While realising that there is a long tradition of interpreting covenant as a bilateral agreement,[63] I wish to adopt the unilateral/unconditional position: that the covenant is not a pact between equals but is rather an unchangeable sovereign imposition/dispensation by one party (God) on another (human beings) seen in the use of the Septuagint's use of *diatheke* as opposed to *syntheke*. This interpretation seems to be the consensus of opinion among covenant theologians.[64]

---

pect of the covenant of grace) variously known as the 'covenant of redemption', the *pactum salutis*, or the 'eternal covenant'. This covenant has been made eternally by the members of the Trinity where it is agreed that the Father would send the Son to represent His people and redeem them. Berkhof believes that this eternal covenant is the prototype of which the covenant of grace is but a faint ectype. Indeed it is the eternal covenant that gives the historical covenant its efficacy "for in it the means are provided for the establishment and execution of the latter."(p. 270). Wayne Grudem, *Systematic Theology* (Grand Rapids, 1996), p. 519, believes that the 'covenant of redemption' is a 'covenant' because it contains all the necessary elements of a covenant, and it also reminds us of the voluntary nature of God's redeeming work: it is not something He had to undertake by virtue of His nature. Hanko, op. cit., pp. 7-25, takes a slightly different approach. He defines a covenant as a 'bond of fellowship' and argues that God's perfect fellowship in triunity is the basis of his covenant life. For him the historical manifestation of the covenant of grace is the revelation of God's own covenant life to us and salvation is a matter of sharing in this perfect fellowship. He writes, "God takes his people into his own triune life... Peter is so bold as to say that we actually become partakers of the divine nature (2 Peter 1:4)"(p. 11). However the 'covenant of redemption' is not universally accepted. Robertson, op. cit., p. 54, believes that "a sense of artificiality flavours the effort to structure in covenantal terms the mysteries of God's eternal counsels," and that there is no Scriptural evidence for this pre-temporal covenant. I will briefly mention the idea of a *pactum salutis* in the next chapter.

[63] See John Murray, *The Covenant of Grace: A Biblico-Theological Study* (London, 1961), pp. 5-7.

[64] See Robertson, op. cit., p. 15; Dumbrell, op. cit., p. 15f; Robert Letham, *The Work of Christ* (Leicester, 1993), p. 39f; Berkhof, op. cit., pp. 262-264; Grudem, op. cit., p. 515; Geerhardus Vos, *Biblical Theology* (Edinburgh, 1985), pp. 23-26; Murray, op.

While noting the many nuances in definition, I wish to adopt Robertson's definition of the covenant that is "a bond-in-blood sovereignly administered"[65] This definition requires a little more explanation. Firstly, Robertson notes that although etymological studies regarding the word covenant are inconclusive, the contextual usage consistently points to a covenant being a bond or relationship which commits parties to one another and which is formalized by the binding of an oath: "This closeness of relationship between oath and covenant emphasises that a covenant in its essence is a bond."[66] The imagery of marriage is often used to illustrate the covenantal relationship, positively in the closeness and intimacy of fellowship, negatively in the 'adultery' that occurs when God's people break the covenantal bond for other loves.[67]

Secondly, the covenant is more than a bond, it is a 'bond in blood' or 'bond of life and death' because of the ultimacy of commitment between God and humanity. The phrase 'to make a covenant' literally means 'to cut a covenant' and this is reflected in the 'cutting' of animals seen in Gen. 15: "both biblical and extra-biblical evidence combine to confirm a specific significance of this ritual. The animal-division symbolizes a "pledge to death" at the point of the covenantal commitment. The dismembered animals represent the curse that the covenant - maker calls down on himself if he should violate the commitment which he has made."[68] The image of blood is an important part of this idea because blood represents life and the shedding of blood, a judgement on life:

---

cit., 1-32. There does appear to be a disagreement over the meaning of the term 'unilateral' in this context. Those theologians just mentioned seem to mean 'unilateral' in the sense that it is God who is entirely responsible for framing the terms of the covenant and that humanity can only accept or reject these stipulations. In this sense they still appear to be able to use the word 'agreement' in their definition of 'covenant', but there is no move into synergism (unlike Pinnock) because in their Reformed soteriology it is not human beings who fulfil their side of the agreement (they can do nothing) but Christ who does it on Man's behalf. Therefore Berkhof, op. cit., p. 280, can still talk about both unconditional and conditional aspects of the covenant: unconditional in that grace is never meritorious, conditional on the suretyship of Christ. This stance, though, is contrasted with the position of Hanko, op. cit., pp. 7-25, who rejects any notion of 'agreement' arguing that such language still implies a bilateral nature to the covenant that inevitably leads to synergism in salvation. He rejects the phrase 'agreement' because his definition of the covenant as a revelation of the everlasting bond of friendship within the Trinity takes away any reference to parties or conditions. For Hanko, God's covenant is everlasting and participation in it *is* salvation. To speak of a contract implies a means to an end which when fulfilled is finished and so becomes void.

[65] Robertson, op. cit., p. 4.
[66] Ibid., p. 7.
[67] See Jer. 2:1, 3:14; 31:31-34; Ezk. 16:1; Eph. 5:22-23, 29-32; Hos. 1,2.
[68] Ibid., p. 10.

This phrase 'bond in blood' accords ideally with the biblical emphasis that "apart from shedding of blood there is no remission" (Heb. 9:22)... The biblical imagery of blood-sacrifice emphasizes the interpretation of life and blood. The pouring out of life-blood signifies the only way of relief from covenant obligations once incurred. A covenant is a 'bond-in-blood,' committing the participants to loyalty on pain of death. Once the covenant relationship has been entered, nothing less than the shedding of blood may relieve the obligations incurred in the event of covenantal violation.[69]

Finally, and as already established, Robertson believes the covenant to be in a unilateral form and sovereignly administered. There is "no such thing as bargaining, bartering, or contracting characterizing the divine covenants of Scripture. The sovereign Lord of heaven and earth dictates the terms of his covenant."[70] More importantly, is the idea of sovereign administration, for even if one wants to speak of humanity's 'requirement' or 'condition' in fulfiling the covenant,[71] the point which cannot be overstressed is that it is God Himself who in His grace fulfils Man's side of the covenant on his behalf, whether this is seen in the accomplishment of salvation where Christ is obedient on our behalf, or in the application of salvation where God gives us the faith to believe:

We may say that faith is the *condition sine qua non* of justification, but the reception of faith itself in regeneration is not dependent on any condition, but only on the operation of the grace of God in Christ... Again, it may be said that the covenant is conditional as far as the first conscious entrance into the covenant as a real communion of life is concerned. This entrance is contingent on faith, a faith, however, which is itself a gift of God.[72]

For Robertson such a definition also answers another question surrounding the nature of the covenant as to whether promise or law is paramount. Robertson notes that successive covenants may emphasise either promissory or legal aspects, but that the basic character of administration remains the same. The same conclusion is reached by Letham who argues that both promise and law coexist by the law serving the promise: "In this sense grace is constitutive of the covenant relation, while law is regulative. It is by pure grace that God establishes his covenant... It is the law, however

---

[69] Ibid., p. 10f.
[70] Ibid., p. 15.
[71] I have already noted, that some do not. See p. 155 n. 60.
[72] Berkhof, op. cit., p. 280. The idea that it is Christ's response, not ours, that fulfils the covenant is an idea that I will more fully develop in the next chapter.

that defines both what sin is and also in what our obedience consists. It maps the path we are to follow in fulfilling our covenantal obligations."[73]

Unity and Diversity within the Covenantal Structure

While there is one covenant of grace, there are different manifestations/ epochs of this covenant. These display both elements of continuity and discontinuity, that is the unity-in-diversity mentioned earlier in this chapter.

CONTINUITY

On the continuity side there are two points I wish to make. Firstly, there is both a structural and a thematic organic unity between the epochs. Structurally, there is firstly a unity in historical experience in the covenantal inauguration, "each successive manifestation of the covenant builds upon what has gone before."[74] The Mosaic is based on the Abrahamic, the Davidic on the Mosaic, and at each stage, God's promise becomes clearer. This does not mean that with the institution of a new dispensation, the old becomes invalid. The history of Israel supposes both the Mosaic and Abrahamic administrations: "The Abrahamic covenant continued to function actively after the institution of the Mosaic covenant. In the context of the history of the Mosaic covenant, The Abrahamic covenant found a basic fulfillment."[75] This characteristic is what was called the 'epochal reach of typology' mentioned in the introduction of Part 3. As Lints says, "The promises of God often have two or more fulfillment horizons, one relatively immediate and the other some distance in the future."[76] This unity is further re-enforced by a unity in genealogical administration. As Letham notes: "Because of the principle of corporate solidarity, God is seen as making his covenant not only with those alive or physically present at the time but also with an endless succession of generations thereafter."[77] This genealogical dimension is not merely concerned with the biological or physical, for in the 'new' covenant, the gift of the Holy Spirit is seen as part of the promise and believers are the spiritual descendants of Abraham (Gal. 3:14). The concept of 'ep-

---

[73] Letham, op. cit., p. 41.
[74] Ibid., p. 42.
[75] Robertson, op. cit., p. 33.
[76] Lints, *The Fabric of Theology* (Grand Rapids, 1993), p. 305. He gives the example of God's promise to Abraham regarding descendants. On one level this was fulfilled in the birth of Isaac. On a second level it was fulfilled in the next epoch when Israel became a great nation. On a third level it was fulfilled in the group who came to faith following the death of Jesus. Finally the promise will receive final fulfilment in the new heavens and new earth. Lints notes: "The original promise given to Abraham can thus be said to have four fulfilment horizons, all of which are clearly identified in the Scriptures (Gen. 12; 17; Ex. 3; 33; Jn. 8; Acts 7; Gal. 3; Rev. 21-22)" (p. 306).
[77] Letham, op. cit., p. 43.

ochal reach' also illustrates the thematic unity between the epochs. The various dispensations of the covenant are united in God's promise "I will be your God, you shall be my people" repeatedly affirmed throughout the epochs.[78]

Secondly, and more importantly however, it is the way that this promise receives its fullest and definitive consummation that draws together and unites all the epochs. Here I am referring to the inauguration of the 'new' covenant in Christ that is the 'flowering' of the promise and the final fulfilment horizon. The various dispensations of the covenant are united in their Christocentric focus.[79] As Letham writes:

> From within an analysis of the covenant, Christ assumes a central and dominant role. In each redemptive covenant there are common features. Each contains certain promises, indicates the need for a mediator between God and his people, and places on the latter obligations that they are required to fulfill as partners of God in the fellowship of his covenant. Ultimately all these features find their realisation in Christ. Christ is the final fulfillment of the promises of God's redemptive covenant.[80]

> ...the covenant directs us to Christ. He is Lord of the covenant. The covenant exists to make him known. He is the constant theme, at first hidden and obscure but then with increasing clarity disclosed as the new covenant is introduced.[81]

Remembering the hermeneutic of the 'canonical horizon' re-enforces this fact. These manifestations of the covenant before the coming of Christ are typological and shadowy and all point towards the antitype and fulfilment of these promises. Hanko notes that all the dispensations before Christ, the law, the tabernacle, the temple, the religious and political life of Israel all reveal in some way the truth of Christ: "God revealed the truth of salvation typically and symbolically through the history that the church lives and by means of that history which that church experienced. All of *sacred* history is sacred exactly because it revealed the truth of God."[82] Christ is at the

---

[78] Gen. 17:7; Ex. 19:5, 20:1; Deut. 29:13; 2 Sam. 7:14, Jer. 31:33; Heb. 8:10.
[79] See also Edmund P. Clowney, *The Unfolding Mystery: Discovering Christ in the Old Testament* (Leicester, 1990); and Alec Motyer, *Look to the Rock: An Old Testament Background to our Understanding of Christ* (Leicester, 1996).
[80] Letham, op. cit., p. 46.
[81] Ibid., p. 49. Glenny, op. cit. in his survey of evangelical uses of typology, defines covenant theology in terms of its Christocentric approach to typology: "Basic to the understanding of typology in the covenant tradition is the conviction that history is salvation history or redemptive history. All biblical history moves forward towards Christ and his work of redemption as is fulfilled in Christ and his Church" (p. 629).
[82] Hanko, op. cit., p. 44.

centre of all the previous covenantal administration and "is the head of God's kingdom and the embodiment of God's covenant. In this person "I shall be your God and you shall be my people" receives incarnated reality."[83]

DISCONTINUITY

Paradoxically it is at the apex of noting the unity of typological features of the previous manifestations of the covenant of grace that we also must come to the central point of discontinuity in the covenantal system. Although covenant theologians posit various distinctions between the pre-creation and post-creation covenants and between the covenant of works and the covenant of grace, the main distinction to be drawn and the fundamental point of discontinuity in the covenantal scheme comes between the shadows and the fulfilment, the type and antitype i.e. between the 'old covenant' which is the relationship between God and humanity before Christ, and the 'new covenant' which is the relationship between God and humanity after Christ. Robertson states that "the incarnation of Christ represents the most basic differentiation-point in this history"[84] He notes that this dichotomy lies behind Paul's argument in Galatians:

> The period 'before faith came' contrasts drastically with the time in which 'faith has come' (Gal. 3:23, 25). The coming of Christ, and his consequent position as the object of faith, has altered the entire course of history. God's dealings with men cannot return to the old pattern once the Christ has come. The Judaizers are in error because they have not taken into account adequately the radical difference Christ's coming has made for history... From one perspective an absolute antithesis may be drawn between the periods of history before and after the coming of Christ... But from another perspective a single way of salvation has always been present.[85]

We have here then, in the covenantal scheme, the idea of a Christocentricity that displays both a unity/continuity and a disunity/discontinuity. This aspect is the crux of my argument against Pinnock's inclusivism because in what follows I want to demonstrate that Pinnock's notion of the 'faith principle' and the analogy he draws between pre-messianic believers and those who are today epistemologically pre-messianic, does not adequately deal with either the continuity or diversity of the biblical covenant and the history of redemption approach. In questioning the validity of this analogy, I also wish to say something regarding the particularity and unconditionality

---

[83] Robertson, op. cit., p. 51.
[84] Robertson, op. cit., p. 57.
[85] Ibid., p. 58.

of the covenant in terms of saving revelation and saving grace. My argument will be structured in two sections, the first dealing with issues of continuity and the second with issues of discontinuity.

Pre-Messianic Believers and the Nature of Saving Faith: Issues of Unity/Continuity

The Israelite Confession of Christ

Against Pinnock's argument that Israelite believers were saved by confessing a generalised 'faith principle' and that this provides the template for how the unevangelised are saved, I wish to argue from the foundation established above, that Israelite believers actually *confessed Christ* albeit in an embryonic way. Richard calls this type of position "Christocentric continuity":

> ...there is materially no difference between the content of faith in the Old and New Testaments. A necessary postulate of their position during Old Testament times is an embryonic knowledge of Christ as the One to come. Many would hold that Old Testament saints knew enough about the Seed of Abraham, the Greater Moses, the Lion of Judah, the Son of David, or the servant of Isaiah to be saved. Messianic themes, shadows, allusions, prefigurements in typological prophecy, and other connections between the Old and New Testaments are strong testimony to this line of specific knowledge of Christ by the Old Testament believer.[86]

---

[86] Richard, op. cit., p. 118. The difference in specificity in terms of the content of Israelite faith is quite marked among covenant theologians. In his essay 'The Biblical Method of Salvation: Continuity' in ed. Feinberg, *Continuity and Discontinuity*, pp. 130-160, Fred H. Klooster outlines what I think is probably represents the most popular position among covenant theologians, that is a 'progressive revelation' view. Commenting on Adam and Eve he writes: "Could they understand the mother promise as a clear pointer to Jesus of Nazareth? Of course not, and I doubt that any covenant theologian ever meant that... The details of their personal knowledge are not revealed to us. Unless Scripture provides specific clues, we can never know how much understanding a particular believer of any period had. Perhaps we tend to underestimate what OT believers understood, however. One is amazed, for example, at Abraham's obedience in sacrificing Isaac; Heb. 11:19 provides a clue to what he was thinking in his heart... What we have to concentrate on is the intent and content of the revelation presented without being able to discern the precise measure of a contemporary's understanding of that revelation. God's revelation is always linked to and therefore limited by the particular stage of his redemptive-historical work... Gen. 3:15 does not identify the Redeemer by name, but it tells us something about the way of salvation and presents the gospel in summary. Its gracious character stands out; God himself promises to intervene decisively to break Satan's stranglehold on Adam and Eve. God establishes the antithesis by grace; he puts enmity between the serpent and the women, his seed and her seed. We now know that

This is echoed by Charles Hodge:

> It is no less clear that the Redeemer is the same under all dispensations... He, therefore, from the beginning has been held up as the hope of the world, the SALVATOR HOMINUM... As the same promise was made to those who lived before the advent which is now made to us in the gospel, as the same Redeemer was revealed to them who is presented as the object of faith to us, it of necessity follows that the condition, or terms of salvation, was the same then as is now. It was not mere faith or trust in

---

this one is Jesus Christ! Only the footpath beginnings of that revelation could have been known to Adam and Eve as they left the Garden, but that small path led all the way to Calvary's victory over Satan. Gen. 3:15 was the first announcement of the one gracious way of salvation, the way that leads to him who is 'the way, the truth and the life' (John 14:6)"(p. 141ff). Compare the above statement with an example of the 'non-progressive revelation' view of Paul Blackham. In his essay 'Did the NT Writers Misunderstand the OT,' *http://freespace.virgin.net/lizzy.blackham/Papers/NTwritersonOT.htm,* September 27th 2000, Blackham focuses on nine NT passages (Jn. 8:54-59; Lk. 20:41; Rom. 10:5-19; 1Cor. 10:1-10; Heb. 1; 2:10-14; 3:1-6; 11:26; 1Pet. 1:10-12), and argues that "the basic conviction of the NT writers is simple – the God of the NT Testament is the God of the OT. On the basis of this they get on with treating the OT as if it were entirely Christian and they treat the NT Church as if it were in the same basic position as the Church in the OT. They name the LORD who walks, talks, wrestles, eats, fights, etc. in the OT 'JESUS' – and they understand Jesus as the One who still acts as He did throughout the OT"(p. 7). Underlying Blackham's position are three underlying theological presuppositions: "1. There is no knowledge of God outside of Jesus Christ. Jesus is the mediator between God and humanity from the beginning of the world to the end of the world. 2. There is no partial knowledge of God that can be built up from any source other than Jesus Christ... 3. The actions of God are **always** from the Father through the Son and by the Holy Spirit. We cannot consider any activity of the Living God in abstract terms. It is impossible to conceive of the Living God acting in a Unitarian way. All His activities are from the Father through the Son and by the Holy Spirit"(p. 7). Although the way the gospel is *taught* is different in the OT than in the New, i.e. in illustrations and pictures in the OT but in reality in the NT, and is much *clearer* in the NT than OT i.e. shadows as opposed to the reality found in Christ, the core *content* of gospel knowledge is exactly the same and includes and understanding of incarnation, atonement, resurrection and the Trinity. Blackham believes that any view of progress in revelation is a "concept of religious evolution, the 19th century myth of progress applied to the Bible, that still exercises a baneful effect on that discipline"(p. 9). The important questions I raise about a position like Blackham's are: 1) whether he makes any distinction between the second Person of the Trinity, Christ/Messiah and Jesus of Nazareth, and if not; 2) In all the instances of Christophany, who are the OT saints meeting and eating with: a pre-incarnate Christ, Jesus of Nazareth, Jesus' bodily resurrection form?

God, or simple piety, which was required, but faith the promised Redeemer, or faith in the promise of redemption through the Messiah.[87]

The analogy to be drawn then is not between the unevangelised and Pre-messianic believers, but between Pre-messianic believers and those who explicitly confess Christ today. There is a continuity of special revelation to Israel that progresses and develops the truth of God's promises. There is one covenant of grace that reaches full manifestation in Christ.[88] Kuyper

---

[87] C. Hodge, *Systematic Theology* II (New York, 1873), p. 370ff. Concerning this statement, there appears to be range of interpretations as to what Hodge might have meant. Klooster, op.cit., notes: "I do not believe Hodge was referring to the revelation of the name of the Redeemer to Adam and Eve or to their knowledge of the identity of that Redeemer. Rather, I understand him to say that the Redeemer who from the beginning 'has been held up as the hope of the world' we now know to be Jesus of Nazareth, Jesus the Christ. Be that as it may, if Hodge thought Adam and Eve could or did know that the promised one was specifically Jesus of Nazareth, I would also disagree." In his essay, 'The Biblical Method of Salvation: Discontinuity' in ed. Feinberg, *Continuity and Discontinuity*, pp. 161-178, Ross notes that it is not exactly clear how Hodge is to be taken: "If [he] means by them that the person and work of Jesus Christ was literally revealed to OT believers as the content of saving faith, then [his] position is untenable... it is most improbable that everyone who believed unto salvation consciously believed in the substitutionary death of Jesus Christ, the Son of God." What should be noted (as I have done already in what I have called a 'non-progressive' view of revelation) is that there are some who *do* believe that the content of faith in the OT is exactly the same as that in the NT and use quotations like Hodge's to show the historical precedent of such a position. In an unpublished paper entitled 'The Faith of Israel – Did the OT Saints have Faith in Christ', Partridge and Morris state that the position "that the OT saints had faith in Christ was taught robustly by the Church Fathers, the Reformers, the Puritans and their successors" and then give a number of quotations from Eusebius, Augustine, Luther, Calvin, Owen and Whitefield that claim to support their argument. The difficult question to be answered is whether concerning OT believers these writers here are talking about merely an *ontological* reality (which from out NT perspective we see clearly), or an *ontological* and *epistemological* reality. Take, for example their quotation from Calvin: "Calvin speaks of the 'rascal Servetus and certain madmen of the Anabaptist sect, who regard the Israelites as nothing but a herd of swine... they babble of the Israelites as fattened by the Lord on this earth without any hope of heavenly immortality' Rather, they had by God's grace a heavenly hope, and *'they had and knew Christ as Mediator through whom they were joined to God and were to share in his promises... The Old Testament fathers (1) had Christ as the pledge of their covenant, and (2) out in Him all trust of future blessedness'* (Institutes II.x.23)." Like the Hodge quotation, I would argue that both a progressive and non-progressive view could agree with Calvin's statement, although note that: 1) none of the above quotes state that OT saints believed in *Jesus* Christ but in Christ or the Messiah; 2) Calvin elsewhere in II.x. seems quite explicitly to take a progressive line (see below).

[88] This argument appears to be evidenced by a number of New Testament texts which speak of the faith of Old Testament believers: Jesus says "If you believed Moses, you would believe me, for he wrote about me" (Jn. 5:46); and "Your father Abraham rejoiced at the thought of seeing my day; he saw it, and was glad" (Jn. 8:56). 1 Pet. 1:11-

summarises that God's revelation through prophecy and theophany "produced in their [the Old Testament believers'] minds such a fixed and tangible form of the Messiah that fellowship with Him, which alone is essential to salvation, was made possible to them by *anticipation* as to us by *memory*."[89]

We must be careful not to adopt some kind of 'theological hindsight' from our post-Christ position in the historical redemptive index although as I have already indicated, it is possible to argue with varying levels of specificity as to what exactly the Old Testament hearers understood. The organic progressive nature of God's special revelation, would have revealed more and more details as time went on and as epoch followed epoch. So, it is possible to argue that Abraham knew more than Adam, Moses than Abraham and David than Moses, with the various horizons of the 'epochal reach' of typology being fulfilled in the various epochs. However, this does not invalidate the claim that all Israelite believers had a 'forward looking' faith in God's promises and that they knew full well that they were saved not by their present 'type' of revelation but by the coming 'antitype' of which the 'type' was but a pre-figurement and shadow. Calvin poetically explains this progression in Book Two of *The Institutes*:

... For the method and economy which God observed in administering the covenant of his mercy was, that the nearer the period of its full exhibition approached, the greater the additions which were daily made to the light of revelation. Accordingly, at the beginning, when the first promise of salvation was given to Adam (Gen. iii. 15), only a few slender sparks beamed forth: additions being afterwards made, a greater degree of light began to be displayed and continued gradually to increase and shine with greater brightness, until at length, all the clouds being dispersed, Christ the Sun of righteousness arose, and with full refulgence illuminated all the earth (Mal. iv)[90]

12, says "Concerning this salvation, the prophets who spoke of the grace that was to come to you, searched intently and with greatest care, trying to find out the time and circumstances to which the Spirit of Christ in them was pointing when he predicted the sufferings of Christ and the glories that would follow." Finally Hebrews notes that believers like Abel, Enoch, Noah, and Abraham "were still living by faith when they died. They did not receive the things promised; they only saw them and welcomed them from a distance" (Heb. 11:13); and that Moses "regarded disgrace for the sake of Christ, as of greater value than the treasures of Egypt, because he was looking ahead for his reward" (Heb. 11:26).

[89] Abraham Kuyper, *The Work of the Holy Spirit* tr. H. De Vries (New York, 1900), p. 55.

[90] See John Calvin, *Institutes of the Christian Religion* tr. Henry Beveridge (London, 1949), Book 2, Ch. 10, Sec. 20.

The Analogy with 'Holy Pagans'

INTRODUCTION

Even if one shows the analogy between Israel and the unevangelised to be invalid, then what is one to make of Pinnock's analogy drawn between the 'holy pagans' of the Old Testament who supposedly fell outside the Abrahamic covenant but who were nevertheless saved by virtue of being included in the universal Noahic covenant: "no one can deny the fact that the Bible presents these holy pagans as saved by faith, even though they knew neither Israelite nor Christian revelation...[faith] can and does occur outside as well as inside the formal covenant communities."[91]

I wish to describe five linked arguments that substantiate the claim that the epithet 'holy pagan' is a contradiction either because, firstly, the examples Pinnock cites were pagans who *became* saints by virtue of being ingrafted into Israel, or, secondly they were never 'pagans,' but were recipients of a special revelation and so cannot be counted as pagans.

THE SALVATION OF ANTE-DILUVIAN SAINTS

Hwyel Jones notes that *contra* Pinnock, it is not possible that ante-diluvian believers were saved by the Noahic covenant for the simple reason that this covenant had not yet been established. How then, did ante-diluvian saints have a saving relationship with God? Pinnock does briefly mention a 'creational' covenant made with Adam, but in terms of the category of 'holy pagans,' the Noahic covenant is used to substantiate his argument. Jones writes: "Pinnock does not examine the first three chapters of Genesis at all and that is surely a serious omission. They are foundational and have relevance to all biblical subjects and particularly to the covenant or binding arrangement made with Adam, the representative head of the entire human race."[92] The Noahic covenant must be seen in the context of God's covenantal dealings with human beings before the Flood. When this is done, one begins to see a different shape to the biblical narrative from Pinnock's.

It is not appropriate at this juncture to digress into the precise nature of the Fall and its consequences for Adam and humanity. However, Pinnock in his 'hermeneutic of hopefulness' fails to even mention this event with the result that the universalisation of human sin is missed from his narrative.[93] Whether one believes that sin is inherited biologically[94] or historically[95] or

---

[91] Pinnock, *Wideness*, p. 162.
[92] Hwyel R. Jones, *Only One Way: Do you have to Believe in Christ to be Saved?* (Bromley, 1996), p. 68.
[93] I will make more of this in Ch. 9.
[94] As Augustine believed.
[95] Pinnock himself advocates this view in his essay, 'Responsible Freedom and the Flow of Biblical History' in ed. Pinnock, *Grace Unlimited*, (Minneapolis, 1975), pp. 95-

that it is federally imputed,[96] evangelicals have traditionally maintained that when Adam fell as our representative, so in some way humanity fell as well. Therefore when Adam became a covenant breaker, the whole of humanity become covenant breakers. Relevant to our discussion, and from within the context of the Fall, are God's words to Adam, Eve, and the serpent in Gen. 3:15-19[97] which contain the *protoevangelium*, the germ of everything pertaining to salvation that was to come in the future. God establishes both blessing and curse on humankind. Enmity is to occur on three levels: between Satan and the women, between Satan's seed and the women's seed, between 'him' and Satan. It is this second and third levels of enmity that I think is important because they establish even at this early stage two opposing lines of human history with a resultant particularity rather than a blanket universality on God's part. Robertson notes:

> The women's seed could be identified with the totality of humanity. However, the immediately succeeding section in Genesis narrates Cain's murder of his brother Abel. (Gen. 4). The New Testament explicitly determines the significance of these two persons in the cosmic struggle between God and Satan. Cain originates "from the evil one" (1 Jn. 3:12). Though descended from Eve just as his brother, he cannot be regarded as belonging to the 'seed' of the women as described in Genesis 3:15. Instead of being opposed to Satan, he is the seed of Satan. The 'seed' of the women cannot be identified simply with all physical descendants of womenkind.[98]

There are two 'seeds,' that of the women and that of Satan and these are in conflict with one another throughout history. The *protoevangelium* is the promise to Adam and Eve that although the heel of the women's seed will be bruised, the head of the serpent will be crushed. Clowney and Robertson note that the term 'seed' can refer either to descendants as a corporate group or to one individual. Both agree that this 'seed' ultimately refers to Christ who represents the seed of women. As Berkhof states:

---

110. He writes: "It is plain from the biblical account, as well as from our own experience, that all human history is deeply mired in the morass of sin, and that this history is the *context* in which human selves emerge, their communities are shaped, and their ideals are formed... Man is shaped by the warped social situation into which he is born and in which he grows up to maturity" (p. 104).

[96] This is the traditional Reformed position. For a representative treatment see Grudem, op. cit., pp. 490-514; Instead of using the traditional terms of original sin and imputation, Grudem prefers the terms 'inherited guilt' and 'inherited corruption.' See also John Murray, *The Imputation of Adam's Sin*. (Grand Rapids, 1962).

[97] "And I will put enmity between you and the woman, and between your offspring and hers; he will crush your head, and you will strike his heel."

[98] Robertson, op. cit., p. 98.

> The death of Christ, who is in a preeminent sense the seed of the women, will mean the defeat of Satan. The prophecy of redemption is still impersonal in the *protoevangel*, but it is nevertheless a Messianic prophecy. In the last analysis the seed of women is Christ, who assumes human nature, and, being put to death on a cross, gains the decisive victory over Satan. It goes without saying that our first parents did not understand all of this.[99]

Jones claims that the background of all the saving disclosures of God is to be found in the *protoevangelium* of Gen. 3:15. He argues that Adam confessed the truth of this revelation by renaming his wife, and Eve did the same by naming her sons, "Cain (4:1) which means 'obtained' is linked with 'the LORD' and expresses Eve's belief that the promised seed has already come."[100] Eve was mistaken, but God gives her another son to replace Abel, 'Seth' meaning 'appointed'. Jones' point is that the knowledge of God's promise informed the faith of Abel, Enoch and Lamech who were of the Adam-Seth line *and not* the Cain-Lamech line:

"They...were looking for the one who would undo what sin had done... Given this information, they should not therefore be classified as *'pagan'* saints at all, but as belonging to the line that was the precursor of Israel and the Church. They were saints who were not pagans because saving revelation had been made known to them."[101]

THE USE OF YAHWEH ('LORD') IN THE PATRIARCHAL NARRATIVES

From within the covenantal framework, my argument has been that all Old Testament believers confessed Christ in some embryonic way. Developing this idea somewhat, the second point I wish to make is that there is a close relationship between this confession of Christ and of God's revelation of His name 'Yahweh' with its emphasis on God as the Covenant-Redeemer.[102] By and through calling on this divinely revealed name, believers were confessing that a characteristic of God is that He delivers His people, and in doing this, they were anticipating the ultimate redemption and deliverance of Christ, who calls himself "I AM" (Jn. 8:58).

Gen. 4:26b illustrates the point that God revealed Himself to a particular people in a particular way and that calling on the name of the Lord, which contains a specific propositional content, is crucial for relationship with Him. As Richard points out:

---

[99] Berkhof, op. cit., p. 294.
[100] Jones, op. cit., p. 69.
[101] Ibid.
[102] For more on the significance of this name see VanGemeren, op. cit., pp. 116f, 148-155.

So this named and identified deity began early in human history. The faith principle in any God - without or with another name; unknown or unknowable - is unsustainable from these passages. The "calling upon the *name* of the Lord" is the pre-flood (Gen. 4:26); post-flood (Abraham, Gen. 12:8); Israelite (Jer. 33:3); Christian (Rom. 10:13); and eschatological (Joel 2:32) condition for deliverance. It is a necessary and epistemological condition for God's intervention in human history...the Lord on whom people called was the God with whom they walked. Salvation was through a "faith-in-YHWH principle" for all peoples.[103]

In contrast to the self-exaltation of Lamech, certain people began to call on the name of Yahweh from the revelation they had been given. This revelation continued through the line of generation through to Noah and from him through Shem where it narrows, finally coming to Abraham and his seed.

So far in this study, my evangelical presuppositions and methodology have meant that I have assumed a certain stance regarding issues of biblical literary criticism. At this point in my analysis, however, I think it is appropriate to briefly comment upon the major literary-critical debate, (which is present within evangelical biblical studies as well as without), as to whether 'Lord' has been anachronistically read back by editors into the patriarchal narratives, and that, on the basis of Exodus 6:2 and 3, the patriarchs did not know God as Yahweh but only as *El* (with several epithets). While it is not possible to comment on the wider issues concerning biblical criticism, the implications of the source of 'Lord' have an important bearing on the discussion of the importance of confessing the Name of God for salvation and of patriarchal attitudes to other religions.

Evangelical Old Testament scholars like Chris Wright and Gordon Wenham question whether the patriarchs did know God as Yahweh, although it was Yahweh Himself who revealed Himself to them.[104] Wright argues for an approach to the development of Israelite religion, by which God transcended and transformed existing religious forms (i.e. "the Mesopotamian and west Semitic high god, *El*") and infused it with new meaning and significance. He does not call this syncretism but rather accommodation and

---

[103] Richard, op. cit., p. 33. Although Richard is coming at this from a dispensational view, I think I can adopt a more covenantal perspective by stressing the continuity and equivalence between confessing Yahweh and confessing Christ.

[104] See Gordon Wenham, 'The Religion of the Patriarchs' in eds. A. R. Millard and D. J. Wiseman, *Essays on the Patriarchal Narratives* (Leicester, 1980), pp. 157-188; Christopher J. H. Wright, 'The Christian and Other Religions: The Biblical Evidence' in *Themelios* 9/2 (Jan. 1984), pp. 4-15; John E. Goldingay and Christopher J. H. Wright, '"Yahweh Our God Yahweh One": The Oneness of God in the Old Testament' in ed. Andrew D. Clarke and Bruce W. Winter, *One Lord, One God: Christianity in a World of Religious Pluralism* (Grand Rapids, 1992), pp. 43-62.

assimilation.[105] This view has a number of implications for this present discussion. Firstly, Wright asks "can we infer from the Genesis story that men may worship and relate personally to the true, living God but under the name or names of some 'local' deity and without knowledge of God's saving name and action in Christ?"[106] Wright comments that Abraham's relationship with God was not primarily based on the divine disclosure of divine names, but on God's grace. Jones argues against this position because he sees within it the following implication:

> To adopt such a view that says that the patriarchs did not know the name Yahweh means that it becomes possible to argue that just as the patriarchs knew (the true) God savingly, without knowing the name Yahweh, so may others today, without knowing of the name of Jesus Christ. Wright concedes this possibility and included in it those like Noah and Enosh, Adam and Eve, that is those who lived before Abraham. Here is the beginning of the contemporary divide among evangelicals between those who adopt only a Christocentric view of the way of salvation and those who also take an epistemological view. The former see salvation as being only in Christ, but the latter see faith as also necessary.[107]

Jones has overstated his case here, for Wright does note that God relating to men in terms of their existing concepts of deity is "preparatory to bringing them to a knowledge of his historic revelation and redemptive acts (which in our era, means knowledge of Christ)."[108] As I will show in the next section, the theme of discontinuity highlights the truth that even if people could be saved without confession of Christ in the Old Testament (although this is an argument which I have rejected) then this does not mean that this Old Testament way is still viable after the coming of Christ. The dispensational position takes the same line here.

A stronger argument, which would appear to go against Wright's study, is based on the Christocentric continuity from Adam to Christ that I have been advocating in this chapter. The point at issue here is where one wishes to see the start of God's redemptive activity in history. Wright begins in Genesis 12 and the call of Abram. I have attempted to show that God's redemptive activity does not start here but can be traced back to Genesis 3 and the *protoevangelium*. God's dealing with Abram may usher in a new and clearer epoch in God's redemptive activity, but it cannot be divorced from what has come before, and must be seen in the total organic develop-

---

[105] Wright, op. cit., p. 6.
[106] Ibid.
[107] Jones, op. cit., p. 75.
[108] Wright, op. cit., p. 7.

ment of God's covenant of grace. From this wider perspective, I would like to make some observations.

Firstly, it is clear that in the patriarchal narratives the name *El* is the most frequent name used for God. However, rather than seeing an 'evolution' of this name from pagan origin to a title which is 'accommodated' by God and the patriarchs, it is possible to argue for a 'devolution' of this name, from a divinely instituted title to a name which, because of Man's increasing sinful rebellion against the true God, has become associated with idolatry and polytheism. As Vos writes, "Within Israel itself we can trace the downward shift of the natural Shemitic faith, not merely in the struggle with alien influences, but also in a gradual internal decline. What existed, and continued to keep alive, was the remnant of a purer knowledge of God, preserved from extinction by God himself."[109] Therefore we are to see the title *El* in its purest form as knowledge of the true God: "That name came to the fore in their times because Jehovah wished to stress his ability to transform his people and to perform his promises alone. *El* Shaddai means 'God Almighty' and points to divine omnipotence."[110]

However, such a name reveals nothing of the redemptive purposes of God. To validate a Christocentric continuity it would appear necessary to argue that the patriarchs did know something of God as Yahweh and something of the redemptive significance of this name. Is this possible? In the organic typological hermeneutic that I have argued for above, this is a definite possibility. In his seminal study, Alec Motyer persuasively argued that Exodus 6:2 and 3 does not deny that the patriarchs knew God as Yahweh, but that they did not know the significance of this name as God revealed it to Moses.[111] From the earliest times, God has revealed Himself as the redeeming Lord to His people. I have already noted that for Adam and Eve the significance of God's promise was barely discernible, but it was a promise nonetheless. Certainly the significance of the Name is revealed to Moses in an epochal way that brings new clarity and meaning to the Name (although, the ultimate fulfilment horizon would have to wait until Christ), but did not the covenanting God reveal something of His saving intentions to His chosen people before Moses: "Does not that evidence point to there being *some* connection in the minds of the people between the Name and the promise of a coming deliverer?"[112] If this is true then we have evidence that not only the saints in Genesis were ontologically saved by Christ, but that at some level, depending on their place in the development of divine disclosure, they confessed Christ through their confession of the Covenant-

---

[109] Vos, op. cit., p. 63.
[110] Jones, op. cit., p. 75f.
[111] J. Alec Motyer, *The Revelation of the Divine Name* (London, 1949).
[112] Jones, op. cit., p. 76.

Redeeming God.[113] Whether one places oneself within the covenant framework or the dispensational framework, both positions argue that in contrast to the lack of propositional content in Pinnock's 'faith principle,' there is a definite propositional content in the revelation of the divine name Yahweh which contains some knowledge not just of a God who exists, and not even the characteristics of the Creator God that can be discerned from the revelation of other divine names, but of a Redeeming God, a God who delivers His people and keeps His covenantal promises.

THE NOAHIC COVENANT

Pinnock claims that there is a "hermeneutical presupposition blocking truth out,"[114] in the minimalist way evangelicals have traditionally interpreted the meaning of the Noahic covenant. For him, this covenant is a universal promise of salvific blessing to all nations: "God announces in this covenant that his saving purposes are going to be working, not just among a single chosen nation, but among all peoples sharing ancestry with Noah... The call of Abram implements the promise of Noah."[115] I wish to make a number of points concerning the Noahic covenant and Pinnock's interpretation of it, concentrating on the themes of particularity and universality.

Firstly, it must be noted that God's revelatory promises to Noah begin before the flood (Gen. 6:17-22). Pinnock fails to note the events leading up to the sending of the flood and the particularistic nature of God's calling of Noah and the nature of His covenant with Noah. If there is an axiom of universality here, then it is a universalisation of God's wrath and judgement with His creation. The whole world is to be destroyed because of mankind's sin and rebellion, but God chooses to maintain His covenant with one man, Noah. I have already noted that God had revealed Himself in a particular way to Noah's line. This covenantal particularity manifests itself through a revelatory particularity. Noah still has to endure the flood of judgement, but he and he alone, has been given the information to be 'saved' from the flood. He is told to build an ark, an ark that will deliver him from the flood. Pinnock's study of universality would seem to demand that God had given everyone in the world this revelation and the opportunity to be 'saved.' However it appears that this saving revelation came uniquely to Noah.

It appears that with this particular revelation comes particularity in grace, for although God planned to destroy human beings because of their sin, Noah found grace in the eyes of the Lord (Gen. 6:8). As Vos comments: "The continuity of the race is preserved. God saves enough out of the wreck to enable Him to carry out his original purpose with the self-same humanity

---

[113] I will apply this to the New Testament 'name of the Lord' below.
[114] Pinnock, *Wideness*, p. 21.
[115] Ibid.

he had created."[116] But why is Noah chosen? Robertson notes the gratuity of Noah's calling. He writes:

> It may be that God's grace had kept Noah from sinking to the levels of depravity found among his contemporaries. But nothing indicates that Noah's favoured position arose from anything other than the grace of the Lord Himself... Although Gen. 6:9 affirms that Noah was 'a righteous man,' structural considerations characteristic of the book of Genesis forbid the conclusion that Noah received 'grace' because of a previously existing righteousness. The phrase "these are the generation of..." which begin Genesis 6:9 occurs 10 times in Genesis. Each time the phrase indicates the beginnings of another major section of the book. This phrase decisively separates the statement that "Noah found grace" (6:8) from the affirmation that Noah was a 'righteous man' (6:9). *God's grace to Noah did not appear because of man's righteousness, but because of the particularity of God's programme of redemption.*[117]

Secondly, while Pinnock is right to emphasise universality in God's later development of the covenant in Gen. 9:1-7, it is the nature of this universality that needs to be carefully defined. The Noahic covenant must be placed in the context of God's ante-diluvian revelation and the two spiritual lines of conflict, the seed of women of which Noah by that time was the sole representative, and the seed of Satan, which by Noah's time consisted of the rest of humanity. The cycle of human history as set down in Gen. 3, is not cancelled by the Flood, but works through this event:

> The Noahic covenant guarantees a stable universe, free from any threat of a global cataclysmic judgement such as the Flood was, even though sin continues to be practised in it. In such a world the gracious promises of the Abrahamic and the New covenants, and the promises made earlier in Genesis 1-5 are worked out throughout time and among all the nations.[118]

Here one sees the axioms of continuity and discontinuity. Although the Flood is literally and symbolically evidence of a new creation and a new beginning, the ontological effects of the Fall continue and the two spiritual lines are still present and can be seen soon after in the account of Noah's drunkenness and Ham's sin.[119] Pinnock's argument that God's saving pur-

---

[116] Vos, op. cit., p. 51.
[117] Robertson, op. cit., p. 112f (my emphasis).
[118] Jones, op. cit., p. 65f.
[119] For a different interpretation regarding the nature of Ham's sin, see O. Palmer Robertson, 'Current Critical Questions Concerning the "Curse of Ham" (Gen 9:20-27)' in *Journal of the Evangelical Theological Society* 41/2 (June 1988), pp. 177-188. Jones

poses are going to be working "not just among a single chosen nation but among all peoples sharing a common ancestry with Noah"[120] is incorrect when the Noahic covenant is seen in its proper place in the redemptive-historical index.

What then is the meaning of the Noahic covenant in Gen 9:1-7? Leaving aside the ethical theme of murder and the punishment of murder, evangelicals have traditionally interpreted this covenant in a purely physicalist (what Pinnock calls a 'minimalist') way, where God promises not to send another flood, precisely because the text calls for such an interpretation. As Grudem points out, "The covenant that God made with Noah after the Flood was not a covenant that promised all the blessings of eternal life or spiritual fellowship with God, but simply one in which God promised all mankind and the animal creation that the earth would no longer be destroyed by a flood."[121] The Noahic covenant cannot carry the weight of Pinnock's interpretation of universal *salvific* blessings.

In this sense the Noahic covenant has important disimilarities to the *protoevangelium* before it and the Abrahamic administration after it:

> the covenant with Noah, although it certainly does depend on God's grace or unmerited favour, appears to be quite different in the parties involved (God and all mankind, not just the redeemed), the condition named (no faith or obedience is required of human beings), and the blessing that is promised (that the earth will not be destroyed again by flood, certainly a different promise from that of eternal life.[122]

Vos notes that the universal and natural sign of the rainbow must be contrasted with the signs of redemption that "are bloody, sacramentally dividing signs."[123] However, as I have already noted this covenant is inextricably linked to what had come before and what would follow, for it promises the stability and preservation of creation through which God's redemptive promises can be fulfilled. In this sense, although Pinnock is wrong to say that this is a human salvific promise, he is right in his claim that the promise of God to Noah is still being maintained today. Firstly, it is being maintained in God's continuing gracious preservation of the earth into which God fulfills his redemptive promises. This is the explicit covenantal basis of a universal but nonsalvific 'common grace' that benefits believers and non-

---

argues that there are two alternatives regarding this sin, either it is the sin of disrespect or it was of a sexual nature. Robertson himself believes that "the more likely interpretation is that Ham committed a sexual sin, probably of a graver nature than merely "looking" on the nakedness of his father." (p. 180).

[120] Pinnock, *Wideness*, p. 21.
[121] Grudem, op. cit., p. 520.
[122] Ibid.
[123] Vos, op. cit., p. 51.

believers alike. But this is not all, for the doctrine of a universal 'general revelation' also finds its covenantal basis here. Robertson writes: "This universal character of the covenant with Noah provides the foundation for the world wide proclamation of the gospel in the present age. God's commitment to maintain faithfully the orderings of creation displays his longsuffering toward the whole of humanity. He desires to make known the testimony of his goodness throughout the universe."[124] Despite Man's universal rejection of this revelation, the creation is witness to the creating and preserving God: "The heavens declare the glory of God; the skies proclaim the work of his hands. Day after day they pour forth speech; night after night they display knowledge. There is no speech or language where their voice is not heard. Their voice goes out into all the earth, their words to the ends of the earth." (Ps. 19:1-4). Secondly, there is a sense in which this covenant has not found final historical fulfilment. If one wants to use the term 'salvation' regarding this covenant, then it is perhaps appropriate to refer to a 'cosmic' or creational salvation won by Christ, of which the new creation under Noah was but a type.[125]

GENEAOLOGICAL SUCCESSION AND THE CONCEPTS OF 'PRUNING' AND 'INGRAFTING'

If ante-diluvian saints were in the line of special redemptive revelation, and the universalistic overtones of the Noahic covenant do not pertain to salvation, how is one to deal with the list of post-diluvian 'pagan-saints' Pinnock refers to in his writing? Pinnock's case is that there are many men and women who were and are saved without any knowledge of Yahweh, or of the coming Messiah or of Jesus himself. If this can be proved then there is evidence that people can be saved from outside God's formal covenant communities. My argument is that there are no such examples because all the figures Pinnock lists were either pagans who became saints on coming into contact with special revelation, or, were always in contact with special revelation and so cannot be regarded as ever being 'pagans.' Shortly, I wish to deal with the figure of Melchizedek who Pinnock claims is the strongest evidence of a 'pagan saint.' However, I wish to briefly mention a theme

---

[124] Robertson, op. cit., p. 122.
[125] This makes sense of Isaiah's prophetic vision in Is. 11:1-9, and of Paul's words in Rom. 8:19-23 where he speaks of the groaning of the whole creation in eager expectation for the sons of God to be revealed. As Hanko, op. cit. puts somewhat poetically: "In the glory of Christ's mighty victory the new heavens and the new earth will be built. Christ as Head and Lord over all will take the entire creation to Himself with His people and into the fellowship of God... Now the wicked seem to be victorious. They seem to have gained God's creation for themselves to do with it as they will. But God's promise can never change. Presently the meek shall inherit the earth. Our God's salvation includes his whole creation" (p. 67). See also Robert Letham, op. cit., Ch. 10 - "The Mediatorial Kingship of Christ: the Cosmic Dimension," pp. 197-209.

that may help in understanding this issue of 'holy pagans' and also provide the background for the Melchizedek account.

From my perspective of 'covenant theology,' I have been arguing that the covenant of grace is particular in terms of the revelation and grace given in it. So far, I have argued that the covenant is maintained 'genealogically' from Adam and eventually to Christ. This is the 'seed of women' mentioned in Gen 3:15. While the 'succession of generations' may be the ordinary way through which God maintains His covenant, one must not totally equate God's spiritual genealogy with a physical genealogy. This is borne out in the concepts of 'pruning' and 'ingrafting.'

'Pruning' means that one may be genealogically/ethnically part of Israel and still yet not be part of true Israel (Rom. 9:6). True Israel is those "who in addition to being related to Abraham by natural descendency, also relate to him by faith, plus those Gentiles who are ingrafted by faith."[126] Here, Robertson notes that 'pruning' does not cancel the genealogical principle:

> While the 'pruning' principle may threaten any who would be presumptuous, it does not intend to suggest that God's grace works against the natural order of creation... The Christian must avoid being lured into a nature/grace dichotomy as he considers the work of God in salvation. Redemption has the effect of restoring the order of creation, and the solidarity of the family is one of the greatest of creation's ordinances. The genealogical character of redemption's activity underscores the intention of God to work in accord rather than in discord with the creational ordering.[127]

Conversely, while pruning takes away branches from the plant, ingrafting adds branches. Robertson writes:

> From the most ancient history of the Abrahamic covenant, the 'ingrafting' of those not of Israelite birth was made a possibility (Gen. 17:12,13). Through the incorporation of the proselyte, peoples of any nation could become Israelites in the fullest sense. Any definition of the 'biblical' significance must not fail to include this dimension. 'Israel' cannot be restricted in its essence to an ethnic community. Israel must include the proselyte who does not belong to 'Israel' according to the flesh, but is absorbed into Israel by process of ingrafting.[128]

Paul makes use of this when speaking of the ingrafting of the Gentiles: "If you belong to Christ then you are Abraham's seed, and heirs according to

---

[126] Ibid., p. 40.
[127] Ibid.
[128] Robertson, op. cit., p. 39.

the promise" (Gal. 3:29). This concept may help us to explain the status of figures such as Lot, Abimelech, Jethro, Rahab and Naaman. On coming into contact with 'Israel' they were ingrafted into the Israelite community. This 'ingrafting' meant that they would be saved as any other Israelite, through a 'forward-looking' faith in the promised deliverer.

In light of this, one should not minimize an important truth that Pinnock highlights that Israel was to be the channel of God's blessing to the nations: "I will also make you a light for the Gentiles, that you may bring my salvation to the ends of the earth" (Is. 49:6). However it appears that because of Israel's sin this light is hidden and often God has to work in spite of Israel:

> The story of Ruth is an illustration of the magnificence of God's grace to the nations. He brought Ruth into the covenant community as he had done earlier with Rahab... The story of Ruth is a perpetual warning to the covenant people that God is free to extend his blessing to the Gentiles. He fulfills his purposes in spite of his own people.[129]

VanGemeren also notes that the mediatory status of Israel is not a primary part of God's promise and throughout the patriarchal narratives the nature of the fulfilment of the blessings to the nations is never clearly defined. As I wish to demonstrate in a later section, this promise is fulfilled only in the coming of Christ. Certainly this theme appears unable to substantiate or sustain Pinnock's claim that "salvation history is co-extensive with world history"[130]

As regards the category of 'holy pagans' and concept of 'ingrafting,' one must ask whether it were possible to be 'ingrafted' into Israel without coming into geographical contact with Israel. To affirm this, while not demonstrating Pinnock's study that 'holy pagans' were necessarily saved outside special revelation, would show that God was working salvifically outside His formal covenant community. The figure of Melchizedek possibly provides such an example, and the Melchizedek account provides an excellent illustration to discuss this point and the previous points I have been making concerning 'holy pagans.'

---

[129] VanGemeren, op. cit., p. 205.
[130] Pinnock, *Wideness*, p. 23. For a more detailed treatment that discusses the precise nature of Israel's mission to the nations see John N. Oswalt, 'The Mission of Israel to the Nations' in eds. William V. Crockett and James G. Sigountos, *Through No Fault Of Their Own?* (Grand Rapids, 1991), pp. 85-97.

THE CASE OF MELCHIZEDEK IN GEN. 14:18-24

For Pinnock, Melchizedek is an important symbol:

> The story of his encounter with Abram shows that God was at work in the religious sphere of Canaanite culture… God seems to be teaching Abram that his election does not mean that he is in exclusive possession of God, but rather that God is calling him to be a means of grace to all nations among whom God is also and already at work. Melchizedek represents for me a larger group of pagan saints in Scripture among whom God worked.[131]

Pinnock uses the story of Melchizedek to support three distinct yet related arguments: firstly, that Melchizedek is evidence of the 'wider hope' and the *Heilsoptimismus*; secondly, that the Melchizedek story tells us something about God's positive attitude towards other religions as structures and cultures; and thirdly, that Melchizedek can be used in the analogy between 'pagan saints' and the unevangelised. Again, I have a number of points that I wish to raise concerning Pinnock's interpretation of this account concentrating primarily on Pinnock's third use of this account, although I will have recourse to mention the other two areas.[132]

Firstly, I want to outline what Pinnock must prove if his interpretation and use of this passage is to be deemed legitimate. Pinnock must demonstrate that Melchizedek was not in Abraham's lineage, that he was a 'pagan,' an 'outsider,' and not related to God's election of Abraham. Pinnock's argument is that Melchizedek worshipped a Canaanite deity, *El Elyon* but that Abram accepted the equivalence of this name with Yahweh: "God was giving Abraham a positive experience of the religious culture around him."[133] Of course this says nothing of the mode or source of revelation given to Melchizedek. However, if Pinnock wishes to draw an analogy with the unevangelised, and compare like with like, it would seem important that in terms of content, Melchizedek's revelation be that of the general kind mediated through creation and the *imago Dei*, for this is the mode through which the Spirit offers grace to the unevangelised. To question the validity of Pinnock's argument, and the analogy with the unevangelised, all that needs to be shown is that Melchizedek was the recipient of a special revela-

---

[131] Pinnock, 'An Inclusivist View,' p. 109.

[132] For two evangelical treatments which contextualise the Melchizedek incident within the literary debates concerning the historicity and unity of Genesis 14, see J. Gordon McConville, 'Abraham and Melchizedek: Horizons in Genesis 14' in eds. R. S. Hess, G. J. Wenham and P. E. Satterthwaite, *He Swore An Oath: Biblical Themes from Genesis 12-50* (Carlisle, 1994), pp. 93-118; Gordon Wenham, *Genesis 1-15* (Waco, 1987), pp. 301-322.

[133] Pinnock, *Wideness*, p. 94.

tion from God, or as Jones even more specifically states: "...Pinnock needs to prove that he [Melchizedek] was not a Semite in order to make his point, that he was a 'pagan' saint... If he were a Semite, he was an insider, a recipient of saving revelation and a member of the chosen line."[134]

However, in dealing with the Melchizedek story, one must immediately recognise that perhaps the most important feature of Melchizedek (especially to the writer of Hebrews) is his mysterious and enigmatic nature: "Without father or mother, without genealogy, without beginning of days or end of life, like the Son of God he remains a priest for ever" (Heb. 7:3). The Bible says nothing of his conversion or encounter with God, nor his parentage, but theologically this is the point of the story and his status as a type of Christ. This makes saying anything certain about Melchizedek and his origins, difficult, if not impossible. Because of this mysteriousness, one must question whether Melchizedek *can* be used as an example of a 'pagan saint' and as being analogous to the unevangelised, let alone that he is a representative and head of other religions traditions that God accepts as valid. Saying this, it must be also questioned as to whether he can be used to disprove the category of 'pagan saints' and to disprove the analogy with the unevangelised. Any statements made by Pinnock and his critics concerning Melchizedek would appear to belong to the realms of speculation and deduction. Interestingly, this is exactly what we see in the work of some commentators who explain the Melchizedek incident in a number of ways including arguments that he was an example of someone who led a sinless life, Shem, a theophany, an embodiment of the Holy Spirit, and a Christophany.[135]

The Melchizedek account is further complicated if we wish to discern whether Melchizedek's knowledge was fashioned from general revelation or special revelation as we are pre-empting the discussion we will have later concerning these two forms of revelation, their relationship to one another, their content, purpose and efficacy. In spite of all these cautions, it may be useful to outline some possible alternative lines of inquiry as regards the origins of Melchizedek and his knowledge of God.

It seems that at the centre of the debate surrounding Melchizedek is the meaning and referent of *El Elyon*. Several interpretations seem to emerge, all of which are based on wider presuppositions of the nature of religious belief and divine revelation at this time. If *El Elyon* is to be equated with a deity in the Canaanite pantheon and completely divorced from the monotheistic worship of Yahweh, then there would appear to be strong evidence regarding the acceptance of other religious traditions outside Israel. For

---

[134] Jones, op. cit., p. 81.

[135] For a good summary on the history of interpretation concerning the Melchizedek story, see P.E. Hughes, 'Excursus I: The Significance of Melchizedek' in *A Commentary on the Epistle to the Hebrews* (Grand Rapids, 1979), pp. 237-245.

example, in his commentary, Von Rad equates *El Elyon* with 'Baal of heaven' a deity known in Phoenicia.[136] This is precisely Pinnock's point concerning the salvation of Melchizedek: "Even faith-responses can be made in the context of other religions as in the case of Melchizedek and Jethro (both pagan priests). Their religions seem to have been the vehicle of salvation for them." [137] Other commentators such Hamilton,[138] Wenham,[139] and Goldingay and Wright link *El Elyon* to a god in the Canaanite pantheon and claim that Abram incorporated this name into his worship. Goldingay and Wright state:

> The implication seems to be that Abram and Genesis itself recognise that Malkisedeq *[sic]* (and presumably other people in Canaan who worship *El* under one manifestation or another) does serve the true God but does not know all there is to know about that God... The biblical view is that the living God, later disclosed as Yahweh, accommodated his dealings with the ancestors of Israel to the names and forms of deity then known in their cultural setting.[140]

Such a view appears to sit well with Wenham's argument that there is "an air of ecumenical *bonhomie* about the patriarchal religion which contrasts with the sectarian exclusiveness of the Mosaic age and later prophetic demands."[141] But what is the evidence of such *'bonhomie'*? There is no suggestion in the patriarchal narratives of involvement with Canaanite religion, and as Wenham himself points out, the patriarchs establish their own places of worship rather than making use of Canaanite shrines.[142] It is wrong to suggest an inclusive attitude towards other religions in this period of history, just because there are not the statements of exclusivism found later in the Old Testament. Indeed placed against the explicit exclusivity seen from the Mosaic epoch, such an attitude of tolerance seems out of place. However, is the Melchizedek story itself the primary evidence for this inclusive attitude found within patriarchal religion? Possibly, but again placed within the context of the rest of Israelite history, such an interpretation of the story would appear to be going against the tenor of exclusivity. Von Rad himself notes, "such a positive, tolerant evaluation of a Canaanite cult outside Israel

---

[136] G. Von Rad, *Genesis: A Commentary* (London, 1961), p. 175.
[137] Pinnock, *Wideness*, p. 107.
[138] V. P. Hamilton, *The Book of Genesis: Chapters 1-17* (Grand Rapids, 1990), p. 410.
[139] Gordon Wenham, *Genesis 1-15* (Waco, 1987), p. 316f.
[140] John E. Goldingay and Christopher J. H. Wright, '"Yahweh Our God Yahweh One": The Oneness of God in the Old Testament' in ed. Andrew D. Clarke and Bruce W. Winter, *One Lord, One God: Christianity in a World of Religious Pluralism* (Grand Rapids, 1992), p. 48.
[141] Wenham, 'The Religion of the Patriarchs,' p.184.
[142] Ibid.

is unparalleled in the Old Testament."[143] Commenting on Hess's fourfold typology of the Israelite religious outlook[144] and translating it into patriarchal history, Carson astutely comments that Wright and Goldingay's interpretation of the Melchizedek incident is a case of a confusion between description and prescription.[145]

In light of the preceding point, is it possible that *El Elyon* does not refer to another deity at all, but is simply another descriptive name for Abram's God? I have already argued that God had revealed Himself as *El* and Yahweh to ante-diluvian saints. After the Flood, God's covenant line with its revelation of God's name continues through Shem and not through Ham and Japheth. This is indicated by the prophecies of Noah in Genesis 9: 25-27, "'Cursed be Canaan! The lowest of slaves will he be to his brothers.' He also said, 'Blessed be the Lord, the God of Shem! May Canaan be the slave of Shem. May God extend the territory of Japheth; may Japheth live in the tents of Shem, and may Canaan be his slave.'" Here, God gives Himself to a particular people, the Semites, and they become the covenant line, the bearers of revelation and redemption. However, as Hanko notes: "...this does not mean that all the generations of Shem were included in the line of the covenant. Undoubtedly for a time this was true - and then not only for Shem but for Japheth. But rapidly that covenant line was narrowed down until it was limited to Abraham. All the other generations of Shem are forgotten in the sacred narrative, and the Scriptures concentrate their attention upon Abraham with whom God would establish his covenant."[146]

We begin to see, therefore, that after the Flood there was a stream of redemptive revelation:

Noah and Shem knew of the revelation and Japheth too. It did not die out with the Flood. It would therefore have been transmitted to posterity, diminishing in some families as time passed because of the increasing effects of sin, but being augmented in others by the onward unfolding of special revelation. In those years up to the pre-Sinai era, to be outside the

---

[143] Von Rad, op. cit. p. 175.
[144] Richard Hess, 'Yahweh and His Asherah?' in eds. Clarke and Winter, op. cit., pp. 13-42. Focusing on the period of the Northern and Southern Kingdoms, Hess notes four Israelite attitudes to religion: 1) the exclusive worship of Yahweh and an intolerance to the worship of any other god, as emphasised by the prophets. This Hess calls the 'official' attitude; 2) The attitude that although Yahweh was the Israelite God, the state deities of other nations were accepted and acknowledged "through political and marital alliances with the rulers of these foreign states."(p. 15); 3) the 'popular' view, that Yahweh was the state God, but that other local gods could be worshipped and that these could help with daily life; 4) The foreign cult is made the national cult e.g. in the reign of Ahab and Jezebel.
[145] Carson, *The Gagging of God*, p. 249-252.
[146] Hanko, op. cit., p. 70.

covenant line was not ipso facto to be destitute of *all* knowledge of Yahweh.[147]

Originally redemptive revelation came to Shem and then bifurcated into many lines of generation. God keeps alive a special knowledge of Himself to His chosen line, carrying on revealing Himself to Arphaxad, Salah, Eber, Peleg, Reu, Serug, Nahor, Terah and Abraham (Gen. 11:10-32). However outside this line, God does not preserve this special revelation and gradually it is forgotten, changed and perverted due to Man's sin and external influences.[148] Idolatry becomes more and more prevalent and monotheism devolves into henotheism, polytheism and animism. Could it be though, that for some reason God preserved some special knowledge of Himself to Melchizedek? Carson comments:

> It is far more natural in reading the account to suppose that there were still people who preserved some memory of God's gracious self-disclosure to Noah, people who revered the memory of the severe lesson of Babel... Of course, Abram was the one who received the special call to follow God and head up the race that would prove a blessing to all the nations of the earth. But that doesn't mean he was the only one who believed in the one true God.[149]

This too is Jones' conclusion:

> It is true that Melchizedek did declare himself to be priest of '*El* Elyon - God Most High.' But this does not have to be a deity other than the One whom Abram knew and worshipped. Melchizedek was a representative of the older religion fashioned in response to God's self-revelation in Crea-

---

[147] Jones, op. cit., p. 77.

[148] Geerhardus Vos argues that the Semites had a peculiar religious consciousness: "Significant ...is also the element that seems to lie uppermost in the Shemitic religious consciousness. This is the element of submission, cp. the word 'Islam,' meaning this very thing. This is, of course, an idea essential to all religion, but it is not everywhere developed with equal strength. Without it religion can never become the supreme factor in the life of the religious subject, which it must be in order to act as a great force. The Shemites have become leaders in the world of religion, because religion was the leading factor in their life whether for good or for evil." *Biblical Theology* (Edinburgh, 1985), p.62. This concurs with the historic evangelical view that Judaism and Islam are perversions and distortions of special revelation. See Bruce Demarest, 'General and Special Revelation' in eds. Andrew D. Clarke and Bruce W. Winter, *One God, One Lord: Christianity in a World of Religious Pluralism* (Grand Rapids, 1992), p. 199f.

[149] Carson, op. cit., p. 250.

tion, Fall and Flood, but from which all reference to Yahweh and the significance of the Name had dropped out.[150]

If this is the case, then Melchizedek cannot be considered as a 'pagan' saint as he was the recipient of special revelation, albeit a more primitive form.

Even if this argument is enough to show the tenuous nature of Pinnock's analogy with the unevangelised, we still have to offer an answer to the question as to the salvific state of Melchizedek prior to his meeting with Abram. Did Melchizedek have to come into contact with Abraham to be saved? The answer would seem to depend on the narrowness of the redemptive line at that time: was salvation to be found only in Abram's line? Or could it be only found in the Semitic line in general? Or did God save people outside the Semitic line? I will illustrate three contrasting arguments all of which claim that Melchizedek was the recipient of a 'special revelation.'

Firstly, there is a less speculative option that does not question Melchizedek's human origins (i.e. was he a Canaanite or a Semite?), but centres on the source of his knowledge of God. Richard wishes to place this story in its historical context. Although Pinnock states that this incident proves that religious experience is valid outside Judaism and Christianity, at this time there was no *formalised* Jewish or Christian religion: "Pinnock's observation may be able to carry some weight *before* Judaism and Christianity existed, but it has no force if applied completely outside of and apart from either religion. Too, he needs to demonstrate that his assertion would be valid after the establishment of these biblical religions."[151] Here I think Pinnock is guilty of the hermeneutical error which involves identification and universalizability: "what is stated to be true of a particular individual in Scripture is assumed to be true of the whole of humanity *mutatis mutandis*"[152] It is important to remember where this story is in the 'redemptive historical index.' It seems that God's way of revealing Himself at this time was not through one particular way, but through a multiplicity of ways: theophany (Gen. 15:17; 17:1); vision (Gen. 15:1; 46:2); dream (Gen. 20:3); angelic visitation (Gen. 16:7; 22:11).[153] Richard does not doubt that Melchizedek experienced a divine revelatory and salvific initiative but he notes that this was a time when such experiences were considered as normative: this is how God communicated with his people whether Adam, Noah or

---

[150] Jones, op. cit., p. 82.
[151] Richard, op. cit., p. 39.
[152] Sinclair Ferguson, *The Holy Spirit* (Leicester, 1996), p. 246.
[153] For more details on the various forms of revelation at this time, see Vos, op. cit., pp. 69-76. Commenting on the differing ways God revealed Himself in the patriarchal period, Vos notes: "On the whole we may say that revelation, while increasing in frequency, at the same time becomes more restricted and guarded in its mode of communication. The sacredness and privacy of the supernatural begin to make themselves felt." (p. 69).

Melchizedek. They all fall under God's salvific tradition. This, too, is the line taken by Demarest and Harpel[154] who contrast Melchizedek's knowledge of God with the limited knowledge of God that can be gleaned from general revelation. They suggest that God could have directly communicated with Melchizedek through a dream vision or theophany: "It seems reasonable, ...to assume that Melchizedek came to know the living God redemptively in the same way other early saints did (e.g. Abel, Enoch, Noah, Job)."[155] To compare, therefore, this stage of history with post-messianic history seems disanalogous especially when we consider the first verses of the Hebrews letter: "In the past, God spoke to our forefathers through various prophets at many times and in various ways, but in these last days he has spoken to us by his Son."[156]

What Richard and Demarest do consider as exceptional in the Melchizedek incident, is the origin of this direct special revelation because they concede that Melchizedek's knowledge of God was independent of the normative channel of revelation: in this case the Abrahamic line. Demarest states that figures like Melchizedek, "offer illustrations of God's activity outside of the usual vehicles of his saving purpose."[157] Therefore Pinnock is right to note God's activity outside the 'normal' or 'ordinary' channels of revelation. However both Demarest and Richard are quick to note that cases like Melchizedek's are exceptions to the rule and cannot prove a 'manyness' doctrine as Pinnock would like to believe. Just because God may have revealed Himself at a particular time, in a particular way, to a particular person, for a particular purpose, does not mean that this can be generalised into a universal principle working today. Furthermore, Richard suggests that these 'exceptions' always eventually came into contact with God's normative channel of revelation: "the others mentioned as standing under the Melchizedek umbrella were all divinely nudged into contact with Israel, the news-bearers of salvation, as she fulfilled her elective missionary role."[158] This idea is in accord with the notion of 'ingrafting' mentioned above.

Secondly, and referring back to the idea that Melchizedek was a recipient of an older source of revelation, Jones argues for the Semitic origin of Mel-

---

[154] Bruce A. Demarest and Richard J. Harpel, "Don Richardson's 'Redemptive Analogies' and the Biblical Idea of Revelation' in *Bibliotheca Sacra* 146 (1989), pp. 330-340.
[155] Ibid., p. 338.
[156] This point has close links to the debate over the means and modes of grace and revelation, and the relationship between the Spirit and the Word. See below pp. 249-256.
[157] Bruce A. Demarest, *General Revelation* (Grand Rapids, 1982), p. 261. See also R. Bryan Widbin 'Salvation for People Outside Israel's Covenant' in eds. William V. Crockett and James G. Sigountos, *Through No Fault Of Their Own?* (Grand Rapids, 1991), pp. 73-85.
[158] Richard, op. cit., p. 40. He cites Jethro with Moses, Balaam, Naaman with Elisha, the Queen of Sheba with Solomon, Nebuchadnezzar with Daniel and Ninevah with Jonah.

chizedek. He states that Pinnock assumes that Melchizedek was a Canaanite but that he provides no evidence of this. Certainly he was not a direct descendent of Abraham because he is not named in Abraham's genealogy. Is it possible he was a Semite? Jones claims that his name is Semitic (although he gives no evidence of this). If we are to argue that special redemptive revelation could only be found in Shem's line, and that Melchizedek was a recipient of this revelation of God prior to his meeting with Abram, then we must conclude that Melchizedek was a Semite. At this point, though, Jones is confusing. He says that Melchizedek was a Semite and a member of the chosen line and therefore not a pagan. However he then emphasises that Abram's knowledge was needed to supplement Melchizedek's inadequate knowledge:

> When Abram received a blessing and gave tithes, he did both in the Name of '*Yahweh El* Elyon.' What does this combination of the name of Melchizedek's god with the name of Yahweh mean?… Surely it means that he was supplementing the inadequate knowledge that Melchizedek possessed with the revelation that he himself had been given. The Creator of heaven and earth was in reality Yahweh, the deliverer. There is no word about Abram's crediting *Melchizedek's* religion or his worship. Abram was consciously worshipping Yahweh in submitting to Melchizedek's ministrations.[159]

Jones appears to be saying that contact with God's redemptive revelation (Abram and his knowledge of Yahweh) was necessary to fulfil Melchizedek's imperfect knowledge. He does not question (as is probably right not to) what the salvific status of Melchizedek would have been had he never met Abram. Vos' conclusion is similar, "Melchizedek stood outside the circle of election recently formed. He was a representative of the earlier pre-Abrahamic, knowledge of God. His religion though imperfect, was by no means to be identified with the average paganism of the tribes. Abraham recognised the *El Elyon*, whom Melchizedek worshipped, as identical with his own God (Gen. 14, 18,19)."[160] This returns us to our original point concerning the title of *El*.

---

[159] Jones, op. cit., p. 82.

[160] Vos, op. cit., p. 77. P.E. Hughes in his discussion on Melchizedek is even more certain of the validity of Melchizedek's worship: "That 'the Most High God,' whose priest Melchizedek was, was not the title of some heathen deity, but the same sovereign God whom Abraham worshipped, is evident from the manner in which, in the Genesis narrative, Abraham speaks to the king of Sodom of "the Lord God Most High, maker of heaven and earth," or "the Most High God Yahweh, maker of heaven and earth." This description corresponds to the "God Most High, maker of heaven and earth," whom Melchizedek invokes, and points to the conclusion that Melchizedek, like Abraham, was a worshipper of Yahweh, the one true God. The qualification "most high," then, should

Finally, I want to mention John Owen's theory as to the origin of Melchizedek, as it provides an intriguing alternative to the other two options. Owen discusses Melchizedek through the filter of Hebrews and through his unique representation as a type of Christ.[161] After noting the mysterious nature of Melchizedek's origin and dismissing the more speculative theories concerning his existence, he suggests three ideas concerning his existence: one of statement, one of judgement and one of conjecture.

Firstly, he claims that Melchizedek came to his office not by primogeniture or any other successive way, but was "raised up and immediately called of God thereunto."[162] This may suggest that Owen believes that Melchizedek should be viewed as a unique example and not as a representative of another religious culture. Secondly, he notes that although Melchizedek dwelt in Canaan, and that this land was possessed by the posterity of Ham that had been cursed by God, Melchizedek could not be Canaanite in origin, for

> God would not raise up among them, that is of their accursed seed, the most glorious ministry that ever was in the world, with respect unto typical signification; which was all that could be in the world until the Son of God came in his own person. This I take to be true, and do somewhat wonder that no expositors did ever take any notice of it, seeing it is necessary to be granted from the analogy of sacred truth.[163]

Finally, Owen suggests that Melchizedek came from the posterity of Japheth, who was regarded to be the Father of the Gentiles, and that God led

---

not be understood in a polytheistic sense, as though indicating the highest among many deities, but as designating the one and only God who is supreme in His sovereignty over the whole of existence. Accordingly, we see these two ancient personages united in the profoundest possible manner at the religious heart of their being." Hughes, op. cit., p. 246f.

[161] See John Owen, *An Exposition of Hebrews* Vol. 3 (Hebrews 4:12-8:12) (Delaware, 1969), pp. 291-343.

[162] Ibid., p. 298.

[163] Ibid., p. 298f. I must note a word of caution regarding the 'curse of Ham,' as historically it has been used to legitimate certain racist viewpoints. I agree with Robertson in his article 'Current Critical Questions Concerning the "Curse of Ham" (Gen 9:20-27),' pp. 177-188, that the 'curse' must be interpreted in a redemptive-historical context rather than a politico-ethnic context: "the substance of the curse itself indicates that the passage must be interpreted from a redemptive-historical perspective. It is not merely a case of political enslavement that is involved. Instead it is the curse of being separated from the redemptive activity of God that is implied in the passage. The Lord of the covenant will be the God of some of the descendants of Noah, bringing blessing to their lives. At the same time, others of the descendants of Noah will be cursed by the same God"(p. 183).

him and others to pursue the promise made to Shem and to claim the promise before Abraham, so claiming a superiority over Abraham. In Melchizedek we see an early claim of God's promise to Japheth that in due course he would dwell in the tents of Shem: "this signal prefiguration of Christ to the nations of the world, at the same time when Abraham received the promise himself and his posterity, gave a pledge and assurance of the certain future call of the Gentiles unto an interest in him and participation in him."[164] More than this though, Melchizedek manifests

> that the state of Gentile converts, in the promise and spiritual privileges of the church, should be far more excellent and better than were the state and privileges of the posterity of Shem whilst in their separate condition: "God having provided some better things for us, that they without us should not be made perfect."[165]

Interestingly in expounding the significance of Melchizedek, Owen supports the particular Christocentric faith of all believers that I have argued for above. Owen suggests that Melchizedek's priesthood, which was the "first instituted type of Christ," gave to Abraham a "great light and instruction into the nature of the first promise, and the work of the blessing Seed which was to be exhibited. For the faith of the church in all ages was so directed, as to believe that God had respect unto Christ and his work in all his institutions of worship."[166] In other words, Abraham understood something of Melchizedek's typological significance: "it was Abraham that gave a tenth of all to Melchizedek; whereby he acknowledged him to be priest of the most high God, and the type of the Son of God as incarnate, - every way superior unto him, who had but newly received the promises."[167]
Therefore Owen's interpretation of the Melchizedek account through the prism of Hebrews appears to point not to the truth of a generalised 'faith principle' in God, but to the uniqueness and particularity of Christ, the antitype of Melchizedek.

In conclusion, it can be seen that Melchizedek is an interesting and complex puzzle in the biblical narrative and no definite conclusions can be drawn as to his origins or the revelation he received. There is certainly no evangelical consensus in interpreting this incident and especially the nature and origin of Melchizedek's religiosity.[168] How one views this story ap-

---

[164] Ibid., p. 300.
[165] Ibid., p. 299.
[166] Ibid., p. 308.
[167] Ibid., p. 321.
[168] Some slightly different evangelical treatments of Melchizedek's worship are to be found in Gordon Wenham, *Genesis 1-15* Vol. 1 (Waco, 1987), pp. 302-322; John E. Goldingay and Christopher J. H. Wright, "'Yahweh Our God Yahweh One:" The Old

pears to depend on other *a priori* considerations, and because of its enigmatic nature, it is unlikely by itself to persuade one to commit to either Pinnock's inclusivism or an opposing exclusivism.

Post-Messianic Believers and the Nature of Saving Faith: Issues of Discontinuity/Diversity

The Preparatory Nature of the Old Testament

So far in this chapter, I have been arguing for a Christocentric continuity in soteriology, that essentially there is no difference between the faith of Old Testament believers and New Testament believers. Anyone and everyone who has been saved, has had to confess Christ according to their place in the 'redemptive-historical index.' Therefore Pinnock's analogy between Old Testament believers and the unevangelised, which is one of the main planks of evidence for his inclusivism, is invalid as there is no such thing as an Old Testament 'faith principle' with which to compare the salvation of the unevangelised.

In arguing for continuity, I do not want to minimize the discontinuity between the types and shadows of the Old Testament epochs, and the fulfilment of these types and shadows in the coming of Christ. I believe that affirming this discontinuity, further damages Pinnock's argument concerning the content of saving faith, because no matter how Old Testament believers were saved in their particular epochs, their faith was *sui generis*, and our post-Christ place in the redemptive historical index means that explicit confession of Jesus Christ is necessary for salvation. In this short sub-section I want to begin to unravel some of the implications of this discontinuity by focusing on the area of pneumatology. Pinnock's position on the unevangelised is 'pneumatological inclusivism' and so concentrating on the Spirit's person and work is entirely appropriate. This focus will serve a dual purpose. Firstly, it will provide the contextual background in which the relevant New Testament material on the unevangelised can be discussed. This material consists of Pinnock's interpretation of so-called 'restrictivist' texts, and the example of New Testament 'holy pagans,' especially the story of Cornelius in Acts 10. Secondly, and more importantly, it will begin to prepare us for the content of the next chapter that will explicitly concentrate on the relationship between the Spirit and the Word.[169] For now, all I want to highlight is one aspect of difference between the work of the Spirit in the Old Testament and the work of the Spirit in the New Testament.

Testament and Religious Pluralism' in eds. Clarke and Winter, *One God, One Lord in a World of Religious Pluralism* (Grand Rapids, 1992), pp. 38-39.

[169] I will have more to say on the complex issue of the work and understanding of the Holy Spirit in the Old Testament in Ch. 8, pp. 243-249.

I have already outlined the unity/continuity in the soteriology of the different redemptive epochs. However, I have also noted the crucial difference between the preparatory nature of the epochs leading up to Christ and the 'realised' nature of the epoch established after Christ. All these earlier epochs were united in that through their typologies, they looked forward to the antitype. The question that is raised at this point is this: How could the Spirit salvifically work in these past epochs if these past epochs only served a preparatory function? How was the Spirit given to these saints before Pentecost when we are told that the Spirit was only given at Pentecost?

Commenting on the work of the Spirit before the incarnation, Abraham Kuyper states that although the preparatory and saving work of the Spirit in earlier epochs are separate operations, they are in fact inextricably linked:

> The Holy Spirit so interwove and interlaced this twofold work that what was the preparing of redemption for us, was at the same time revelation and exercise of faith for the Old Testament saints; while, on the other hand, He used their personal life, conflict, suffering, and hope as the canvas upon which He embroidered the revelation of redemption for us.[170]

This 'preparatory' nature of the earlier epochs is re-enforced by B.B. Warfield:

> The old dispensation was a preparatory one and must be strictly conceived as such. What spiritual blessing came to it were by way of prelibation... The object of the whole dispensation was only to prepare for the outpouring of the Spirit upon all flesh... It was not that His work is more real in the new dispensation than in the Old. It is not merely that it was more universal. It is that it is directed to a different end - that it is no longer for the mere preserving of the seed unto the day of planting, but for the perfecting of the fruitage and the gathering of the harvest.[171]

In other words, the teleology of the Spirit's work in the Old Testament is different from the New Testament, preservation and preparation giving way to outpouring and fulfilment.

The above insight on teleology has an important bearing on the validity of Pinnock's analogy between pre-Messianic saints and the unevangelised, for this analogy appears to 'flatten' the contours of redemptive history forgetting the *sui generis* nature of Old Testament salvation:

---

[170] Kuyper, op. cit., p. 52.
[171] B.B. Warfield, 'The Spirit of God in the Old Testament' in *Biblical Doctrines* (Edinburgh, 1988), pp. 101-129, pp. 128f.

Before Christ, the entire service of types and shadows had significance that it lost immediately after the Advent. To continue it after the Advent would be equivalent to a denial and repudiation of His coming. One's shadow goes before him; when he steps into the light the shadow disappears. Hence the Holy Spirit performed a special work for the saints of God by giving them a temporary service of types and shadows... We repeat that the Holy Spirit had a special work in the days before Christ, which was intended for the saints of those days, but which lost for us all its former significance.[172]

With the coming of Christ, the focus of faith has sharpened in its intensity, vagueness has been replaced by specificity. The Christocentricity of salvation means salvation by Jesus Christ, the Christocentric nature of faith means faith in Jesus Christ himself. This is precisely what the New Testament affirms and it is to this area that I now turn.

No Other Name?

For both inclusivists and restrictivists, there are a number of specific texts appealed to which are thought to validate their respective positions. Pinnock is well aware of a number of 'restrictivist' New Testament texts that have always been cited as evidence that salvation requires an explicit confession of Christ (Rom. 10:9-10; Acts 4:12; Jn. 14:6; Jn. 1:12). However, Pinnock does not see these passages as a threat to his inclusivism for two main reasons; one logical and one theological. Logically, Pinnock uses the argument of another evangelical inclusivist, John Sanders. Sanders uses the argument: "If A, then B" does not guarantee the truth of "If not A, then not B." He applies this in the following way. A person will be saved if he confesses Christ as Lord. However, this does not necessarily mean that a person who does not confess Christ will not be saved.[173] Theologically, Pinnock separates the epistemological confession of Christ from ontological salvation by Christ: these texts are saying that salvation is by Christ alone, not through confession of Christ alone. Positively, Pinnock believes there to

---

[172] Kuyper, op. cit., p. 53. John Piper in his book, *Let the Nations Be Glad: The Supremacy of God in Missions* (Leicester, 1994), puts it even more starkly writing, "Something of immense historical significance happened with the coming of the Son of God into the world. So great was the significance of this event that the focus of saving faith was henceforth made to center on Jesus Christ alone. So fully does Christ sum up all the revelation of God and all the hopes of God's people that it would henceforth be a dishonor to him should saving faith repose on anyone but him"(p. 127).

[173] John Sanders, *No Other Name? Can Only Christians be Saved?* (London, 1994), p. 67. Pinnock uses a form of this argument in his essay, 'Acts 4:12: No Other Name Under Heaven' in eds. W. Crockett and J. Sigountos, *Through No Fault of Their Own?* (Grand Rapids, 1991), pp. 107-115.

be a number of texts which endorse his inclusivism, the most important ones being the evidence of New Testament 'holy pagans' especially Cornelius in Acts 10.

In my critique, I do not want to re-rehearse the detailed exegetical issues of every individual passage as I think this has been convincingly done elsewhere.[174] I do however, wish to make a number of more general points concerning both 'restrictivist' and 'inclusivist' texts. Before doing this, I should sound a note of caution concerning the use of these texts in ascertaining the validity/invalidity of Pinnock's inclusivism. It is difficult to see how, on their own, a few individual verses could prove or disprove either inclusivism or restrictivism. I have been trying to show throughout this study that these positions are based on a number of biblical and theological considerations, not just the exegesis of a few texts. Both restrictivists and inclusivists believe they can incorporate the others' 'proof texts' into their own paradigms. Pinnock is right to point out that none of these texts directly refer to the unevangelised and so any conclusions drawn on their fate are ones from inference and deduction. Having said this, I still wish to make some observations.

Firstly, on Rom. 10:9-10, (although the argument can apply to a number of texts), Pinnock and Sanders appeal to the logic that 'confession of Christ as Lord equals salvation does not necessarily mean non-confession of Christ equals non-salvation,' is a valid argument with one important exception. If all those who confess Jesus is Lord *are precisely identical* to all those who are saved, then it is true to say that if you do not confess Jesus you will not be saved. Carson notes:

> ...what Sanders has done is *assume* that the two classes do not precisely coincide - which is, of course, nothing other than assuming the conclusion. Of course, exclusivists for their part must not simply assume the opposite. But, in fact, it can be shown that the perfect coincidence of the two classes is precisely what Paul presupposes. This is clear not only from Paul's treatment of the entire biblical story line, but from this chapter of his epistle to the Romans.[175]

After saying there is no difference between Jew and Gentile, Paul asks, "How, then can they call on the one they have not believed in? And how can they believe in the one they have not heard? And how can they hear without someone preaching to them?" (Rom. 10:14,15). Carson notes, "For Paul, the impossibilities lurking behind these rhetorical questions are exactly the opposite of what inclusivists are proposing. For Paul, it is impos-

---

[174] See Carson, op. cit., p. 300-313; Richard, op. cit., pp. 57-68; Jones, op. cit., pp. 9-30, 117-136; Nash, op. cit., pp. 137-149.
[175] Carson, op. cit., p. 313.

sible to call on the true God without believing in Jesus."[176] In other words, these verses simply confirm the exclusivity and particularity of redemptive history that I have argued is present throughout the biblical narrative.

Secondly, in Pinnock's appeal to various 'inclusivist' texts, he has a tendency to read more into the text than is justified. For example, from Acts 14:16-17 which refers to God's universal 'testimony' in creation, Pinnock seems to infer that this testimony, which means that truth and goodness exist in pagan cultures, is necessarily a saving truth and a saving goodness.[177] Another illustration is Pinnock's idea that terms such as "God-fearing Greeks" refer to the salvific status of such people. However, as Bock notes "respect for those who seek God is not the same as acceptance of their faith as 'true' or 'saving.' Luke knows the difference."[178] One begins to see here a lack of nuance in Pinnock's argument that can be traced to his rejection of distinctions in revelation and grace. For him, all grace is saving grace, and all revelation potentially salvific. This is sharply contrasted to evangelicals who wish to distinguish between general and special revelation and common and special grace. So returning to Acts 14:16, Carson writes: "*A priori*, I am quite happy to accept that elements of truth and goodness exist in every culture: that is the fruit of common grace, of the *imago Dei*, of gen-

---

[176] Ibid. To put this in the context of intra-Pauline studies, we should say that Paul distinguishes between general revelation that is not salvific and special revelation that is salvific. The majority of evangelicals do not deny that general revelation contains true knowledge of God, but they do insist that it is not a saving knowledge. Incidents such as Paul's ministry in Lystra (Acts 14:8-18); and his Areopagus address (Acts 17:18-11) see Paul finding points of contact between himself and his audience. These points of contact are those of 'general revelation': Paul never declares this revelation to be salvific. Similarly with Rom. 1 and 2, the *locus classicus* for discussing general revelation. Paul does not deny that all people know God in some way. However this knowledge is not a saving knowledge. For more details of exegesis on these specific passages see: Lewis and Demarest, *Integrative Theology*, Vol. I, pp. 68-71; Demarest, 'General and Special Revelation,' pp. 190-199; Bruce W. Winter, 'In Public and in Private. Early Christians and Religious Pluralism' in *One God, One Lord. Christianity in a World of Religious Pluralism* eds. Andrew D. Clarke and Bruce W. Winter (Grand Rapids, 1992), pp. 125-148; Darrell L. Bock, 'Athenians Who Have Never Heard' in eds. W. Crockett and J. Sigountos, *Through No Fault of Their Own?* (Grand Rapids, 1991), pp. 115-124; Aída Besançon Spencer, 'Romans 1: Finding God in Creation' in eds. W. Crockett and J. Sigountos, *Through No Fault of Their Own?*, pp. 125-135; Douglas Moo, 'Romans 2: Saved Apart from the Gospel?' in eds. W. Crockett and J. Sigountos, *Through No Fault of Their Own?*, pp. 137-145; Jones, op. cit., pp. 45-50.
[177] In the same way Pinnock argues for the *Logos* theology of Justin Martyr. See pp. 61, 237 n. 38.
[178] Darrell L. Bock, 'Athenians Who Have Never Heard,' in eds. W. Crockett and J. Sigountos, *Through No Fault of Their Own*, p. 124.

eral revelation. But that does not mean their sins are forgiven and they are saved."[179]

Finally, it is difficult to give any convincing evidence as to whether the New Testament apostles made the inclusivist distinction between ontological salvation and an epistemological awareness of this salvation. Rather it seems that they did not separate salvation in Christ from an explicit confession of Christ. The apostles in Acts constantly preach repentance and forgiveness of sins *in the name of Jesus Christ*. Richard brings this out well in his exegesis of Acts 4:12.[180] He notes that it may be possible to make the distinction between the phrase '*in* Jesus' name' which refers to the ontological grounds of salvation, and the phrase '*by* Jesus' name' which refers to the epistemological grounds of salvation. Although he notes that translators have difficulty in keeping this distinction,[181] even if it is a valid distinction, Acts 4:12 states that salvation is both 'in' and 'by' Jesus' name alone:

> The first prepositional indicator permits the ontological force. But the latter indicator points to the necessary *(dei)* means or ground *(en)* and content *(ho)* of human salvation. Now whether the phrase shows the necessary ground or necessary means of salvation, it also shows the necessary content of salvation. Therefore, not only did the apostle not make a distinction between the ontology and epistemology of salvation, he went beyond the ontology of salvation to include the epistemology. The leaders (v. 8), all Israelites (v. 10) and all humans (v. 12), faced the *epistemological* issue of Jesus' name (cf. "made known," v. 10).[182]

Therefore "the given name" *(onoma to dedomenon)* of Jesus is the only means by which we receive the ontological ground of salvation: "Just as the unevangelised are among men and under heaven, this is the *given* name among men and under heaven."[183]

The Case of Cornelius in Acts 10

Pinnock describes Cornelius as "the pagan saint *par excellence* of the New Testament, a believer in God before he became a Christian."[184] In discussing this incident there appear to be two distinct questions that need to be addressed: firstly, is Cornelius an example of someone who was saved before coming into contact with the gospel? Secondly, is there a valid analogy

---

[179] Carson, op. cit., p. 307f.
[180] Richard, op. cit., pp. 57-60.
[181] Ibid., p. 59.
[182] Ibid.
[183] Ibid.
[184] Pinnock, *Wideness*, p. 165.

to be drawn between the experience of Cornelius and unevangelised believers today?

Dealing with the second question first, whether one believes that Cornelius was saved or not before he encountered Peter, there is enough dissimilarity between Cornelius' experience and that of the 'faith principle' to make Pinnock's analogy tenuous. The main dissimilarity is that Cornelius was in contact in some degree with special revelation through the channel of the Jewish faith and an angelic visitation, and not merely in contact with general revelation. Indeed in his commentary, Calvin in his exegesis of Acts 10:4 regards him as a believing proselyte and therefore not a pagan but a saint: "Whosoever came at that time into Judea he was enforced to hear somewhat of the Messiah, yea, there was some fame of him spread through countries which were far off. Wherefore, Cornelius must be put in the catalogue of the old fathers who hoped for the salvation of the Redeemer before he was revealed."[185] In this sense then, Cornelius is just another example of the other Old Testament cases I have described earlier in the chapter: they were never pagans but confessed Christ albeit in an embryonic way.

But even if this position is suspect, is Cornelius an example of someone who was ontologically saved by Christ but epistemologically unaware of him? Calvin's view suggests that Cornelius was not epistemologically unaware of Christ. However, I do not wish to take this line because to do so would appear to flatten the contours of redemptive history because as I have argued, with the coming of Christ, Christ becomes the focus of faith: the preparatory types and shadows become invalid. If one wants to make a connection between Cornelius and Judaism then an explanation which would retain the contours of redemptive history would place Cornelius in the same situation as Jewish believers at this time: they needed to know that the Messiah, the Antitype had come. Piper points out that in Acts (e.g. 2:5,38; 3:19; 13:38-39), there are many God-fearing and devout Jews who are still called to repentance and baptism in the name of Jesus.[186]

Like the Melchizedek account, the answer to this second question borders on the realms of speculation. The primary difficulty Pinnock has to overcome in the Cornelius story is that in direct contrast to the unevangelised who live and die without hearing the gospel, Cornelius does eventually come into contact with the gospel. Helm writes:

> It seems unacceptably abstract and hypothetical to say...that (for instance) if Cornelius had not met Peter he would have been saved. Scripture does not invite us to break up the causal nexus of events as revealed and to speculate about each link in the chain. For it might be counter-

---

[185] Quoted from Jones, op. cit., p. 93.
[186] Piper, op. cit., p. 138.

argued that the Holy Spirit produced the desire for Christ in each case as a first stage in their actually coming to Christ.[187]

Given that Cornelius did hear the gospel, is it legitimate to ask at what point in this 'causal nexus of events' was the point where Cornelius was saved? I believe that there is enough contextual exegetical evidence to shed doubt on Pinnock's conclusion that Cornelius was saved before he encountered the gospel through Peter's preaching. At the end of his sermon in Acts 10:43, Peter notes that to Christ "all the prophets bear witness that everyone who believes in him receives forgiveness of sins through his name" Piper notes: "Forgiveness of sins is salvation. No one is saved whose sins are not forgiven by God. And Peter says that forgiveness comes through believing in Christ, and it comes through the name of Christ."[188] In the next chapter of this study I will try to show the theological relationship between such concepts of forgiveness and why such concepts must be confessed through the name of *Christ* as opposed to some other object of faith (or in the 'ethical faith principle' no object at all). In Acts 11:14, Peter recalls the words of the angel to Cornelius, "Send to Joppa for Simon who is called Peter. He will bring you a message through which you and all your household will be saved." Here there seems to be no distinction between a believer's salvation as opposed to a messianic salvation, rather the emphasis is on the future tense, Cornelius will be saved through Peter's message. This is re-enforced a few verses later where the Jewish believers note that God has given the Gentiles 'repentance unto life' suggesting that before their repentance they did not have life.

In reaching the conclusion that Cornelius was saved only when he came into contact with the Gospel, we must speculate briefly as to what the Greek *dektos* (translated as 'accepted') means in Acts 10:34-35: "I now realise how true it is that God does not show favouritism, but accepts men from every nation who fear him and do what is right." Pinnock assumes that this word refers to salvation and then proceeds to base his 'faith principle' on this equivalence. But is this interpretation right? Critics of Pinnock have suggested other meanings of this word that do not equate *dektos* with salvation. Carson and Richard note that the NIV translation 'accepts' may be misleading, in that a more accurate translation is more likely 'acceptable' or 'welcome' as used, for example in Lk. 4:24: "It is never used in reference to

---

[187] Paul Helm, 'Are They Few That be Saved?' in ed. Nigel M. de S. Cameron, *Universalism and the Doctrine of Hell* (Edinburgh, 1992), p. 280. The last statement in this comment by Helm is reminiscent of the position that God regenerates the unevangelised person and then sends a messenger to take the gospel to this seeker. See Appendix 1.
[188] Ibid., p. 137f.

whether or not a person is accepted in some saving sense."[189] Within the context of the story, which concerns the inclusion of the Gentiles into God's salvific plans, Peter's statement refers, not to the salvific state of Cornelius but the principle that non-Jews are 'acceptable' or 'welcome' to God, i.e. "the international availability of salvation and acceptability to God regardless of ethnic origin."[190] As Richard concludes:

> First, instead of a universal salvific will, Peter submits a universal salvific welcome to anyone from any nation. Second, there is also a particularity axiom - the reception of forgiveness for everyone is through Jesus' name by belief in Him. God rejects no one on the basis of nationality… Now men from every nation were acceptable to Him and would be accepted by Him as they related to Jesus. Again, this divine acceptance is seen in the gift of the Holy Spirit that is given without ethnic partiality. Peter then did not refuse baptism to the Gentile believer in Christ. Inclusivists need to give more weight to Peter's conclusions from the Cornelius event, rather than reading the narrative through their prior conclusions.[191]

Conclusion

In this chapter I have put forward a particular hermeneutical framework called 'covenant' theology and which is redemptive-historical in its nature. I have tried to contrast this approach with Pinnock's hermeneutic of the biblical text as regards his inclusivism. Bringing together all the lines of argument I have put forward in this chapter, I wish to note the following conclusions all of which cast doubt on Pinnock's inclusivism. Firstly, the analogy that Pinnock draws between the salvation of Old Testament believers and the unevangelised is invalid. Old Testament believers confessed Christ as Christ was revealed to them in their place in the redemptive-historical index, and this cannot be compared to Pinnock's idea of a cognitive or ethical 'faith principle.' Secondly, and following on from this, there is no biblical evidence to suggest that anyone has been saved apart from God's special revelation. Although there can be different arguments as to the medium through which this revelation may come, 'special' revelation, as opposed to general revelation, has a specific propositional content which contains some knowledge of Christ. Therefore, I wish to argue that there is much evidence to suggest that everyone saved in the Bible confessed Christ, and that the distinction between being ontologically saved by Christ

---

[189] Carson, op. cit., p. 307. In Appendix 1, p. 316f., I note how John Piper uses this text to argue for his version of restrictivism.
[190] Richard, op. cit., p. 61f.
[191] Ibid., p. 64.

whilst being epistemologically unaware of him is not a biblical distinction but one created by Pinnock and other inclusivists. Finally, I have begun to put forward the idea that God's special revelation and grace are not universalistic concepts but are particularistic in their scope. Taking all this into account, I believe that concerning the biblical evidence, the burden of proof would seem to go firmly against Pinnock's position on the unevangelised. However, as I have already indicated, I not only want to demonstrate the biblical 'fact' that ontology and epistemology cannot be separated, that a confession of Christ is necessary for salvation, and that saving grace and special revelation are particular and not universal, but I want to indicate the theological reasons 'why' ontology and epistemology are inextricably linked, 'why' a confession of Christ is necessary for salvation, and 'why' saving grace and special revelation are particular. This is the subject of the next two chapters.

CHAPTER 7

Universality, Particularity and Incarnation: A Christological Critique of Pinnock's Inclusivism

In the next two chapters I wish to try and add further theological substantiation to the claims that I made from a biblical standpoint in the previous chapter, and show that in soteriology, ontology and epistemology cannot be separated, and that a confession of Christ is always necessary for salvation. As I described in Ch. 3, Pinnock's inclusivism is cradled in the two axioms of universality and particularity with the person and work of the Spirit representing universality, and the person and work of Christ representing particularity. In this chapter and the following one, I wish to critically explore a number of implications that arise from Pinnock's attempt to mediate these two axioms. This chapter will highlight what I see to be a number of lacunae and ambiguities in Pinnock's understanding of this relationship as regards the uniqueness of Christ and the nature of the atonement. Building on this, Ch. 8 will compare and contrast Pinnock's understanding of the Trinitarian relationship between the Second and Third Persons of the Trinity with that of a Reformed evangelical understanding of the relationship. A common thread running through the next two chapters is my contention that Pinnock's 'pneumatological inclusivism' significantly alters the meaning of solus Christus, sola fide, sola Scriptura, and sola gratia, all shibboleths of the evangelical faith.

Universality, Particularity, and the Person of Christ

Problems Concerning Christ's 'Derivative Uniqueness'

In Ch. 3, I noted how Pinnock related the universality axiom to the particularity axiom, where universality was theologically first but grounded in particularity, and that particularity was epistemologically and redemptively first but intelligible because of universality.[1] Pinnock criticises theological pluralism because it affirms a gracious, loving God while undercutting the

---

[1] Ch. 3, p. 56.

basis for knowing that God is personal, gracious, loving and forgiving - that is the incarnation. One can only affirm theocentricity if one affirms Christocentricity.[2]

Ironically, though, as Pinnock develops his 'faith principle' in order to demonstrate the principle of a universal accessibility to salvation, one wonders whether he is guilty of the very same pluralistic error which before he had criticised, for the very basis of the 'faith principle' is that God *can* be known redemptively outside Christ by the Spirit through general revelation. Note how Pinnock states that God's distinctive profile is not found exclusively in Christ but in the biblical God:

> Uniqueness belongs first of all to the God of the Bible; and, if it should be said that Jesus is unique, it will only be because of the special relation to God he is thought to enjoy as God's Son. Uniqueness and finality belong to God. If they belong to Jesus, they belong to him only derivatively.[3]

One can see why Pinnock wishes to take this line. By emphasising a theocentric uniqueness he can bypass the problems that Christocentricity has for access to salvation, for revelation referring to God is not limited to an event "in a thin slice of land in Palestine,"[4] but is universally accessible through a cosmic revelation. However, in stressing this theocentricity, there appear to be some sacrifices made regarding particularity. Concerning the previous quotation, what can a "derivative uniqueness" mean for Christology? As Wood points out:

> ...I confess my worry that Pinnock often seems more Jeffersonian that Trinitarian in his inclusivism. He repeatedly employs the indefinite article to make his main Christological claims... Jesus is "*a* decisive redemption" (15), "*a* self-characterization of God (45), and he thus plays "*a* distinctive role in the coming of God to rule" (64). Pinnock insists, far more tellingly, that the Bible is not Christocentric but theocentric. It begins, he says, "with God and not with Christ" - as if the Son were not the aboriginal Second Person of the Trinity... Though Pinnock calls his Christology 'high,' it strikes me as abysmally low.[5]

---

[2] See Clark Pinnock, *A Wideness in God's Mercy: The Finality of Jesus Christ in a World of Religions*, (Grand Rapids, 1992), pp. 44-46.

[3] Ibid., p. 53.

[4] Clark Pinnock, *Flame of Love: A Theology of the Holy Spirit.* (Downers Grove, 1996), p. 188.

[5] Ralph C. Wood, 'Whatever Happened to Baptist Calvinism? A Response to Molly Marshall and Clark Pinnock on the Nature of Salvation in Jesus Christ and in the World Religions' in *Review and Expositor* 91 (1994), pp. 593-608, p. 598f. The page references refer to Pinnock, *Wideness*, op. cit.

It would appear that Pinnock wishes to use terms such as 'finality' and 'uniqueness' while referring to Christ but at the same time deny that such terms imply exclusiveness. This is part of Pinnock's plan to "reenvisage categories like the uniqueness of Jesus"[6] whereby there is a "universal vision arising from a responsible understanding of Jesus' uniqueness."[7] But at this point there appears to be a tension in Pinnock's thought in trying to affirm uniqueness whilst denying exclusivity:

> But would the uniqueness of Jesus have to mean exclusivity? Not necessarily. Was not the Buddha a unique religious figure in his own way? There is room in the world for many unique people, even many religious leaders. Buddha points to truths and values that we would do well to weigh, just as Jesus does. Could not the claims of Jesus and the Buddha, though different be complementary rather than contradictory?... But it would be a mistake to deny a level of incompatibility and competitiveness too. Jesus proclaimed a loving personal deity, while Buddha considered such talk futile metaphysical speculation... This makes a choice between Jesus and Buddha difficult to avoid, however complementary they are in other ways.[8]

Part of the problem with a statement like this is knowing exactly what Pinnock means by 'exclusivity.' Does he simply mean that 'truth' is not limited to God's revelation in Christ and so some teaching of the Buddha was 'true'? If he means this, then he is in line with many evangelicals who would put such 'truths' down to God's general revelation in creation and the *imago Dei*.[9] However if by 'exclusivity' Pinnock is referring in any way to salvation, then he appears to be entering new territory for an evangelical theologian, for however strongly he claims uniqueness for Christ, one wonders if he wants to, or even can, make the seemingly crucial distinction between a qualitative uniqueness for Christ and a quantative uniqueness. One of the most fundamental ideas contained in the concept of the 'uniqueness' of Christ is that it is only in Christ that human beings can know the love of God as Saviour, this epistemology is not available in general revelation where human beings can only know God as Creator.

---

[6] Clark H. Pinnock, 'An Evangelical Response to Knitter's Five Theses' in eds. Leonard Swidler and Paul Mojzes, *The Uniqueness of Jesus: A Dialogue with Paul F. Knitter* (Maryknoll, 1997), p. 118.
[7] Ibid.
[8] Pinnock, *Wideness*, p. 63f.
[9] Sinclair Ferguson comments, "It is appropriate to believe, with Calvin and many others, that all truth is God's truth, even when it is found in the mouth of the ungodly, and that all good gifts come to us from above (Jas. 1:17)." Sinclair Ferguson, *The Holy Spirit* (Leicester, 1996), p. 246. I will be returning to the issue of truth and goodness in Ch. 9.

I am suggesting here that Pinnock's understanding of a 'derivative uniqueness' for Christ affects his Christological formulation. We saw in the previous chapter that Pinnock is willing to explore other avenues in a Christological formulation. In *Wideness* (1992), he distinguished between functional and ontological categories of Christology, stating that incarnation is only one category of Christology, and while he believes it to be true, "there are other ways of dealing with the significance of Jesus alongside it."[10] This led him to question whether one could be saved by confessing 'Jesus as Lord' in a functional sense but not necessarily in a metaphysical sense.[11]

Again one can see why Pinnock wishes to make a separation between the functional and the ontological because the confessional propositional boundaries are widened: "it would be easier for Jews and Muslims to accept Jesus in those terms [the functional] rather than under the incarnational category."[12] However in doing this, Pinnock unintentionally is weakening the particularity of Christ. Leaving aside the evidence that incarnation is far more prevalent in the Bible than Pinnock claims,[13] there are dangers in separating the functional and ontological. Richard points out that many 'heretical' Christian groups ascribe to a 'derivative uniqueness' of Christ:

> The 'derived uniqueness' of Jesus as different from cult versions of derived uniqueness needs to be explicated by Pinnock lest he and other inclusivists, in a sort of guilt by association, be lumped in with the error of the cultists... We must not attempt to dismantle essential intratrinitarian relationships, as inclusivists need to do when referring to uniqueness.[14]

I am not suggesting that Pinnock is in any way guilty of the error of unitarianism, but for a theologian who calls his theological paradigm '*trinitarian openness*' and who bases his inclusivism on the truth of the Trinity, it does seem somewhat strange for him to under-emphasise the category of incarnation. However, as I have already suggested this under-emphasis is in line with his desire to at the same time uphold uniqueness and deny exclusivity. What we see here is an ambivalence in Pinnock's thought and part of the tension in trying to mediate both universality and particularity.

---

[10] Pinnock, *Wideness* p. 62.
[11] For a brief analysis of this, see Richard, op. cit., pp. 48-52.
[12] Pinnock, *Wideness*, p. 60.
[13] See for example Phil. 2:6; Col. 1:3; 2:9. Richard, op. cit., comments, "it is evangelically inconsistent to set up John against the other gospel writers (the Synoptics). To see the Incarnation as only a Johannine model - merely one of several models in the Bible- does not make it any less authoritative. Inasmuch as one gospel writer mentions the Incarnation, it cannot but become a normative category to be included in a credible and comprehensive Christology. Pinnock has to let the whole Bible speak on the issue" (p. 48).
[14] Richard, op. cit., p. 51.

Problems Concerning 'Spirit-enriched' Christology and Kenosis

This same tension is even more apparent when the Holy Spirit enters into Pinnock's Christological formulation. Pinnock's intention is to see Christology as an aspect of pneumatology, therefore contextualising the particularity of Christ within the universality of the Spirit. Pinnock claims that he does not wish to challenge or critique traditional evangelical Christology, but merely to correct an imbalance in evangelical thinking which has neglected the work of the Holy Spirit in the life of Christ. Pinnock is right that this area has been neglected by evangelicals and deserves more emphasis.[15] However, Pinnock's own formulation of a 'Spirit-enriched Christology' is problematic because it is built on questionable foundations laid in his earlier work. The most important of these is his espousal of some form of *kenotic* theory which Pinnock supported originally because it could answer problems of incarnational intelligibility, but which more recently has been alluded to as being complimentary to his doctrine of the Spirit, the idea being that what the *Logos* gave up, the Spirit filled up: "The Son's self-emptying meant that Jesus was compelled to rely on the Spirit."[16]

While evangelical theologians do not seem afraid to speak about a 'self-emptying' with regard to the incarnation, this 'self-emptying' refers to the giving up of status and privilege rather than any ontological connotations. As Macleod notes: "over against *kenoticism*...we have to insist that it is perfectly possible to speak of real renunciation without defining it as renuncia-

---

[15] Pinnock looks outside the evangelical tradition for insight into this area of christology. See, for example his reference to Yves Congar, *The Word and the Spirit* (San Francisco, 1984) Ch. 6 'The Holy Spirit in Christology,' pp. 85-101, in *Flame of Love*, p. 81. However, some notable evangelicals have highlighted this deficiency in evangelical Christology. Abraham Kuyper writes that "the Church has never sufficiently confessed the influence the Holy Spirit exerted upon the work of Christ." *The Work of the Holy Spirit* tr. H. De Vries (New York, 1900), p. 97.

[16] Pinnock, *Flame of Love*, p. 88. The other area that I could have focused on is the claim that Christ took on a fallen human nature, and that: "his sinlessness was really due to his relation with the Spirit, not his own deity." (*Flame of Love*, p. 88). This idea again is disputed within evangelical theology. See Donald Macleod, *The Person of Christ* (Leicester, 1998), pp. 221-231. Macleod contends that the belief Christ took on a fallen human nature cannot counter the claims of Nestorianism or the idea that fallen must imply sinful so claiming that Christ was guilty of original sin. What I think is a more orthodox position is given by John Owen in *The Holy Spirit: His Gifts and Powers* (Grand Rapids, 1954). He writes, "Being not begotten by natural generation, it [the human nature of Christ] derived no taint of original sin from Adam; it was obnoxious to no charge of sin, but was absolutely innocent and spotless, as Adam was in the day he was created. But this was not all; it was positively endowed by the Holy Spirit with all grace."(p. 95).

tion of deity."[17] Macleod has noted a number of dangers inherent in *kenotic* theory which he believes possibly contravene Chalcedon orthodoxy. Firstly, there is the problem of how the world was being preserved and sustained, if the Word was totally self-emptied in the person of Jesus "Any form of *kenotic*ism which involves the idea of a depotentiated *Logos* ('one who had no power which a perfect manhood could not mediate') would be fatal to the Lord's competence to carry out his cosmic functions."[18]

Secondly, there is the danger of speaking in monophysitic language with the result of sacrificing the divine properties of the hypostatic union.[19] Thirdly, there is the problem of maintaining a continuity of consciousness between the pre-existent and the incarnate Son, the result of kenosis implying "a degree of amnesia to which there can be no parallel."[20] Fourthly, *kenotic* theory cannot account for the divine consciousness of Christ without driving "a fatal wedge between the Jesus of History and the Christ of faith."[21] What are we to make of Jesus' self-claims of divinity and of his disciples seeing his glory? "If the earthly Christ had disclosed nothing but 'human likeness' (Phil. 2:7) - Christ would never have been worshipped and Christianity would never had been born."[22]

In a wider context, both Berkhof and McGrath note the relationship between *kenotic* theory and the doctrine of divine immutability. Berkhof somewhat simplistically states that *kenosis* "is altogether subversive of the doctrine of the immutability of God... Absoluteness and mutability are mutually exclusive; and a mutable God is certainly not the God of Scriptures."[23] Pinnock himself realises the relationship between *kenosis* and immutability but his 'trinitarian openness' has made the necessary adjustment in its revision of divine immutability.[24] However, in Pinnock arguing for some form of *kenotic* theory, he does speak of Jesus being the 'agent' of God's salvation: "We could say that the human is a structure that is capable

---

[17] Macleod, op. cit., p. 219. For some evangelical treatments of *kenosis* see Macleod, op. cit., pp. 205-221; Wayne Grudem, *Systematic Theology* (Leicester, 1994), pp. 549-552; Gordon Lewis and Bruce Demarest, *Integrative Theology Vol. 2* (Grand Rapids, 1990), pp. 283-286, 343-345.
[18] Ibid., p. 209.
[19] Pinnock at times is guilty of such language, for example in *Theological Crossfire*, he writes "The eternal Son in his incarnation by a voluntary act limited himself to a historical human consciousness and to human faculties of knowledge and action." (p. 146).
[20] Macleod, op. cit., p. 216.
[21] Ibid., p. 210.
[22] Ibid., p. 211.
[23] Louis Berkhof, *Systematic Theology* (Grand Rapids, 1958), p. 328. See also, Alister McGrath, *Christian Theology: An Introduction* (Oxford, 1994), p. 307.
[24] See Pinnock, *Theological Crossfire*, p. 146.

of receiving the divine logos and of being a vehicle of the divine presence."[25] Bradley comments on the danger of language like this:

> Barth insisted that in the eternal decree of God, Christ is God and man (*Logos ensarkos*), and he believed that it is theologically disastrous to think of the second person of the Trinity as only *Logos*...it becomes hard in this view to avoid the idea that with the incarnation, there is a change in the Trinity. If on the other hand, in the eternal purpose of God there is only a *Logos ensarkos*, the Word in flesh, then there is no change in the Trinity, as if a fourth member came in after the incarnation. Pinnock's language betrays the reality of this problem, and raises doubts whether he actually possesses a clear doctrine of the Trinity. He writes of 'God's decision to deal with humanity through the agency of Jesus almost as if the incarnation was an afterthought.[26]

I would like to suggest that a more orthodox way to emphasise the role of the Spirit in the life of Christ, is by referring to the *communio gratiarium* (communion in graces) in the doctrine of the *communicato idiomatum* (communion in attributes).[27] Believing it to be appropriate to speak of the Holy Spirit as the agent or executor in creation, John Owen notes that Christ's humanity, being created, was subject to the Spirit's agency. This was also evidence that the hypostatic union itself did not lead to the communication of properties. As Trueman notes:

> This is made crystal clear in Owen's vigorous emphasis upon the fact that the assumption of the flesh is the only immediate act of the Son upon the human nature, and the only necessary consequence of this is the personal union. Then, in line with this view that the immediate agent in all acts within the created realm is the Spirit, Owen argues that all other actions of the Son on the human nature are performed *via* the Spirit as intermediary...although he does stress the concurrence of the Father and the Son.[28]

Owen argues that all Christ's charismata which made it possible for him to perform his threefold role as prophet, priest and king (the *triplex munus*),

---

[25] Ibid.
[26] James Bradley '*Logos* Christology and Religious Pluralism: A New Evangelical Proposal' in *Proceedings of the Wheaton Theology Conference: The Challenge of Religious Pluralism: An Evangelical Analysis and Response* (Wheaton, 1992), p. 202.
[27] For a basic description of this doctrine see Macleod, op. cit., pp. 193-199; Heinrich Heppe, *Reformed Dogmatics* (Grand Rapids, 1978), pp. 434-447.
[28] Carl R. Trueman, *The Claims of Truth: John Owen's Trinitarian Theology* (Carlilse, 1998), p. 177f.

was made possible by the dynamic ministry of the Spirit in his humanity.[29] Christ was the Anointed One, the man of the Spirit *par excellence*. For Macleod, "this accords well with such an incident as the agony in the garden, where Jesus appeals not to the 'grace of union' but to 'him who was able to save him' (Heb. 5:7), so that at last, through the eternal Spirit, he offered himself unblemished to God (Heb. 9:14)."[30] From within this context one can agree with Pinnock that "it was anointing by the Spirit that made Jesus "Christ," not the hypostatic union, and it was the anointing that made him effective in history as the absolute Savior."[31]

Relevant to the discussion concerning Pinnock's inclusivism, are his motivations behind these Christological developments. His aim is to affirm a high Christology *and* widen the access of salvation to unevangelised believers. Pinnock argues that these two statements are not 'either-or' but 'both-and' when viewed from the proposal of a 'Spirit-enriched Christology' where Christology is seen as an aspect of pneumatology. This is precisely the reason I have given so much space over to an exposition of Pinnock's Christology for it provides the bedrock for his own formulation of inclusivism. However, for the reasons outlined above, the success of this attempt must be questioned, for when he stresses universality, particularity appears to be compromised and a high Christology that has always been a fundamental tenet of evangelicalism, appears somewhat weakened and ambiguous. As Bradley notes, "Cosmic revelation is such a strong corrosive that it will tend to dissolve the ties one wishes to maintain with historic revelation, especially when those ties are maintained only with the thin thread of personal belief."[32]

Universality, Particularity and the Work of Christ

Understanding Pinnock's Model of Atonement

In *Flame of Love* (1996), Pinnock tries to solve the universality/ particularity tension by referring to the 'two hands of God': "I believe it would help if we recognised the twin, interdependent missions of Son and Spirit. It reduces the tension between universality and particularity and fosters a sense that they are complementary rather than contradictory. The two poles turn out to be both-and, not either-or."[33]

As described in Ch. 3, Pinnock bases his universality axiom on the social relations between the Persons of the Trinity (*ad intra*) where God invites

---

[29] See Owen, op. cit., Bk.2 Ch.3: 'Work of the Holy Spirit with Respect to the Human Nature of Christ, the Head of the New Creation.' pp. 90-107.
[30] Macleod, op. cit., p. 195.
[31] Pinnock, *Flame of Love*, p. 80.
[32] Bradley, op. cit., p, 203.
[33] Pinnock, *Flame of Love*, op. cit. p. 192.

everyone to participate in the fullness of triune life. More specifically Pinnock links the universal love of God with the cosmic work of the Spirit in creation. The implication of this is that God is sacramentally present in all of creation because of the Spirit's omnipresence. Pinnock wishes us to see that there is no discontinuity between creation and incarnation:

> Spirit prepares the way for Christ by gracing humanity everywhere. In such global activities Spirit supplies the prevenient grace that draws sinners to God and puts them on the path toward reconciliation. What one encounters in Jesus is the fulfilment of previous invitations of the Spirit. God's love is the ever-present ground and goal of created things. We know this from Jesus Christ, but this truth has always been so, always a possibility. One does not properly defend the uniqueness of Jesus Christ by denying the Spirit's preparatory work that preceded his coming. Let us try to see continuity, not contradiction, in the relation of creation and redemption.[34]

Statements like this generate a number of crucial questions concerning the precise nature of Pinnock's doctrine of atonement. If God's love is grounded in creation and the presence of the Spirit, then what exactly is the purpose of the incarnation and the atonement? If the cross is not the source of God's saving grace, then why is it needed? Does it effect salvation or does it merely reveal (albeit normatively) something already presupposed? Is it representative or constitutive? Is it, as Richard points out, not intrinsic to the structure of God's global grace but complementary?[35] Pinnock may wish to cover all possibilities by saying that divine grace is present everywhere, "since God has created the whole world, since Jesus Christ died for all, and since the Spirit gives life to creation,"[36] but it seems theologically crucial to know the relationships between these three truths and whether one is primary. Pinnock is unclear and ambiguous over these questions. I have already noted, that the significance of Pinnock's 'Spirit enriched Christology' is that it views Christ as an aspect of the Spirit's mission, instead of viewing the Spirit as a function of Christ's: "My desire is to emphasize that the Spirit is active in every aspect of the messianic mission - not as a substitute for Christ nor as an instrument of Christ but as the third person of the Trinity."[37] It is the Spirit who facilitates the Christ event: "something happened through the total journey of Jesus that literally

---

[34] Ibid., p. 63.
[35] Ramesh P. Richard, *The Population of Heaven. A Biblical Response to the Inclusivist Position on Who Will be Saved.* (Chicago, 1994), p. 51.
[36] Clark Pinnock , 'An Inclusivist View' in eds. D. Okholm and T. Phillips, *More Than One Way?* (Grand Rapids, 1995), p. 98.
[37] Pinnock, *Flame of Love*, p. 92.

changed the world and opened the door wide to union with God."[38] But what is this 'something' and why was it necessary? Pinnock seems unclear as to the objective efficacy of redemption in Christ, and appears confused in that he wants to posit *both* a definite disjunction between creation and redemption and a definite continuation. What exactly is his doctrine of the atonement?

Commenting on various models of atonement Begbie writes:

> In the evangelical constituency, the issue that has probably provoked more furore than any other in the evangelical world is that of substitution and representation... A large stream of evangelicalism has seen substitution as the centre around which the atonement revolves - Jesus endures the judgement of God in our place. Others have felt bound to lay the stress on representation: the heart of the matter is not that Jesus bore something instead of us, but that he accomplished something on our behalf.[39]

My description of Pinnock's 'recapitulation' model in Ch. 3 would appear to place him firmly in the language of representation. The key to it was that Christ represented humanity so that the effect of Adam's sin was reversed:

> God effected the conversion of humanity in Jesus, who represented the race and thereby altered the human situation. In his death and resurrection, humanity de jure passed from death to life, because God has included it in the event. Its destiny has been objectively realised in Christ - what remains to be done is a human response and salvation de facto... A new situation now exists: we have only to accept what has been done and allow the Spirit to conform our lives to Christ.[40]

However, does this help one understand the 'mechanics' of Pinnock's model? We know what Pinnock's model is not. It is not the penal substitution model which is too legalistic for Pinnock and which leads inexorably to ideas of limited atonement. We know also that the atonement is seen as only one part of the salvific act: we are saved by Christ's life of obedience and his resurrection as well as by the cross. It is an inclusive model, Christ represented the race as a generic whole, he died for all without exception, and that as a result of this its efficacy depends on a human response. We also know the results of the model, "It would expose man's injustice while revealing the righteousness of God. It would overcome the powers of dark-

---

[38] Ibid., p. 93.
[39] Jeremy Begbie, 'Editorial Matters: Rediscovering and Re-Imagining the Atonement' in *Anvil* 11/3 (1994), p. 199.
[40] Pinnock, *Flame of Love*, p. 96.

ness while delivering humankind from them. It would reveal God's heart definitively."[41]

In Pinnock's essay 'Salvation by Resurrection'(1993), he seems to align himself with Aulén's *Christus victor* model: "Humanity which was subject to the powers of darkness needs deliverance from sin, death, and Satan, and Christ set us free from them by his triumph in life, death and resurrection. Having disarmed the hostile powers and won a victory over them, the *Christus Victor* has freed us from our sins and made us alive to God."[42]

Such an exposition fits neatly into J. I. Packer's second type of how Christ's death has been explained.[43] Packer writes about this type:

> Through the cross, these hostile forces, however conceived - whether as sin and death, Satan and his hosts, the demonic in society and its structures, the powers of God's wrath and curse, or anything else - are overcome and nullified... The assumption here is that man's plight is created entirely by hostile cosmic forces distinct from God; yet, seeing Jesus as our champion, exponents of this view could still properly call him our substitute... Just as a substitute who involves others in the consequences of his action as if they had done it themselves is their representative, so a representative discharging the obligations of those whom he represents is their substitute.[44]

Such a categorisation explains Pinnock's references to Irenaeus who also saw the work of Christ as a cosmic conflict and drama; and his insistence that salvation should be seen not only in the context of the cross but in view of the totality of Jesus' life, death and especially resurrection.[45]

---

[41] Pinnock, *Theological Crossfire* (Grand Rapids, 1990), p. 149.
[42] Pinnock, 'Salvation By Resurrection' *Ex Auditu* 9 (1993), p. 3.
[43] See above, p. 76.
[44] J.I. Packer, 'What Did the Cross Achieve? The Logic of Penal Substitution' in *Tyndale Bulletin* 25 1974, pp. 3-46, p. 20.
[45] See Robert Letham, *The Work Of Christ* (Leicester, 1993), pp. 159-161. It is interesting to compare Irenaeus' belief in an ethical dualism that was the context for his idea of recapitulation, and Pinnock's idea of a 'cosmic drama' between God and the powers of darkness. The notion of 'spiritual warfare' is important for Pinnock and was briefly mentioned in the previous chapter, his 'doctrine of the powers' concerning other religions. It should also be noted that the idea of an ethical dualism is important in Pinnock's 'trinitarian openness,' for Pinnock wishes to distance himself from any view of God's sovereignty which suggests He purposes evil as well as good: "History is the scene of a real struggle between God and the powers of darkness in which man is a combatant, and this conflict is not a fake or mere appearance, one in which God is directing both sides." Clark H. Pinnock, 'Responsible Freedom and the Flow of Biblical History' in ed. Pinnock, *Grace Unlimited* (Minneapolis, 1975), p. 101.

However by *Flame of Love* (1996) with its stress on the Spirit's role in Christology, it is less clear that Pinnock fits neatly into this 'classic theory' and there seems a new ambiguity over the purpose of the cross and its objectivity. What we see is somewhat of an amalgamation of many known models: recapitulation; ransom; vicarious sacrifice; moral influence; governmental; vicarious sympathy; solidarity by abandonment; all subsumed under the theme of representation. However, one is left asking the question as to how Pinnock's model works. He never really explains the links between his overarching theme of Christ's participatory journey, and the new situation it allegedly creates.

While still referring to Irenaeus, some of his statements echo the contemporary neoorthodox theologian Hendrikus Berkhof.[46] Berkhof writes, "Representation signifies that in him the relationship is restored, that is, that which from our side obstructed the relationship simply does not count anymore in the light of his perfect love and obedience."[47] This is in line with Pinnock's insistence that it is humanity who needs reconciliation to God, not God to humanity. Interestingly though, Berkhof concedes that the exact connection between the cross and redemption is not clear, "The NT asserts the 'that,' but has no answer to the 'why' and the 'how.' That is God's secret."[48] This sounds remarkably like Pinnock when he questions whether his theory is a 'rational' one, "we know it is an effective medicine but are not certain how it works,"[49] and, "as for the substitution, only God really understands the atonement in its godward side and why it was necessary."[50]

The problem here seems to be one of theological comprehension. Helpful again, is Packer's threefold typology in which Christ's death has been historically explained. Each provides different explanations as to the necessity, purpose, perfection and extent of the atonement. Part of the problem with Pinnock's exposition is that he seems to want to draw insights from all these different models not fully realising that each model is answering different questions. So Pinnock claims that the atonement is necessary but he never really explains the primary reason for its necessity. He uses the motif of recapitulation that is rich in theological symbolism and imagery. Yet one is left with the question as to *how* Christ's participatory journey objectively provides salvation. There appear to be important pieces of exposition missing and, as a result, the coherence and precision of Pinnock's model suffers.

I believe that in part this ambiguity stems from the tension of trying to mediate universality and particularity. Pinnock appears to be in a theologi-

---

[46] Pinnock refers favourably to Berkhof in *Flame of Love*, p. 98.
[47] Hendrikus Berkhof, *Christian Faith* trans. Sierd Woudstra (Grand Rapids, 1979), p. 305.
[48] Ibid.
[49] Pinnock, *Flame of Love*, p. 105.
[50] Pinnock, *Theological Crossfire*, p. 149.

cal dilemma. He wishes to state that the incarnation and atonement create a new state of affairs: that grace flows from the Christ-event, that the human situation is turned around as a result, and that God has reconciled the world in Christ in an objective sense. However, he also strenuously denies that grace is conditional upon penal satisfaction, "evangelicals seem to think that, until the Cross, the divide had not been bridged, as if the Cross actually changed God in AD 32. Do we mean that there was no salvific will of God before that moment? Do we actually think that the cross changed God's wrath into love rather than being the gift of his love?"[51] The heart of Pinnock's universality axiom is that grace has always been present, through the omnipresence of the Spirit in creation. But if grace has always been present in and through creation, then what is there left for Christ to do on the cross? Pinnock says that "because Christ died as our representative, our status before God is changed and a new situation is created,"[52] but this 'new situation' cannot be the possibility of salvation, for this has always been universally possible through the Spirit.

Understanding the 'Penal Substitution' Model of Atonement

At this point, and before I move onto further consideration of the Spirit's activity with regards the work of Christ, I want to compare Pinnock's model of atonement with that of the 'penal substitution' model which has been for evangelicals, the central model for understanding the work of Christ. I not only want to defend this model against Pinnock's criticisms of it, but want to positively demonstrate how the 'penal' model can incorporate the themes of atonement that are important for Pinnock. From the perspective of the redemptive-historical framework that I have been proposing and the covenantal approach that I have adopted, I wish to make an observation concerning the work of Christ. It was Calvin who organised his discussion of the work of Christ into the *triplex munus*, the 'threefold office.' Based on the three offices in the Old Testament, Christ's work as Saviour is prophetic, priestly and kingly: "In short, the threefold office...highlights his role in (1) speaking and teaching the word of God which ultimately focused on himself; (2) offering himself as a vicarious sacrifice to God; and (3) reigning over his church and the world as risen Lord."[53] The detailed explanation of these offices can be found elsewhere.[54] What I wish to note is the connection between this way of understanding Christ's work and the model of atonement which evangelicals have traditionally favoured as being the

---

[51] Ibid., p. 149.
[52] Pinnock, *Flame of Love*, p. 105.
[53] Letham, op. cit., p. 22.
[54] See John Calvin, *Institutes of the Christian Religion* tr. Henry Beveridge (London, 1949), Bk. 2, Ch. 15; Letham, op. cit., pp. 91-225.

central 'metaphor' in interpretation: the penal substitution model. Having noted this view to be *the* distinguishing mark of evangelicalism, Pinnock writes: "the theory of penal substitution began its life in apologetics, not exegesis or theology. It originated as a rational explanation of the incarnation."[55] Pinnock believes this model to be based on a Latin judicial framework that is alien to the biblical understanding of atonement. But is this analysis correct?

The observation I wish to make concerns the genesis of the 'penal' model. I would like to suggest that evangelicals have stressed the 'penal substitution' model of atonement and all the concepts contained within it, sacrifice, propitiation, expiation, reconciliation, and redemption, because they are all concepts seen in various typological ways in God's revelation in the Old Testament, and as Christ is the fulfilment of these types, it is necessary to understand his work in this context. For Pinnock to suggest that the 'penal' model is not rooted in exegesis seems to either negate the continuity of Old Testament revelation, abstracting the work of the Christ from his historical context, or is simply a case of historical amnesia. There are a number of examples I could give to illustrate my point. Christ's death is the supreme realisation of Robertson's definition of covenant I adopted in the previous chapter: 'a bond-in-blood sovereignly administered:' "Christ dies in the place of the sinner. Because of covenantal violations, men were condemned to die. Christ took on himself the curses of the covenant and died in the place of the sinner."[56] This definition is illustrated by numerous typological examples; the ratification of the Abrahamic covenant where God alone walks through the sacrificed animals; the offering up of Isaac and the ram who is substituted in his place; the Passover story where the blood of the lamb causes God to pass over the houses. Possibly the clearest illustration is that of Israel's ceremonial law:

> First of all, the backcloth to the Old Testament ritual was always sin. The offerer was pronounced guilty, and he was liable to the wrath of God. His sin and guilt were then symbolically transferred to the animal through the laying on of hands. Then the animal was killed and its blood poured out, to be manipulated by the priest. The offerer was thus cleared of his sin and guilt, the animal incurring it on his behalf. Of course, no intrinsic efficacy could attach to animal sacrifices as such. They were provisional, proleptic ceremonies that foreshadowed the coming reality.[57]

Johnson puts it in this fashion:

---

[55] Pinnock, *Flame of Love*, p. 107.
[56] O. Palmer Robertson, *The Christ of the Covenants* (Phillipsburg, 1980), p. 12.
[57] Letham, op. cit., p. 129.

The sacrifices of animals had their beginning in the Garden of Eden (cf. Gen 3:21) and were enshrined in the law of Moses as emblems and types intended to teach men and women that forgiveness of sin was impossible without the satisfaction of divine justice in the payment of penalty of death. This payment was ultimately impossible for guilty men and women to make; thus, it could be made only by a divinely provided substitute to whom guilt was transferred.[58]

While not wishing to eradicate all mention of penalty, Pinnock does not see this theme as being primary in understanding the death of Christ. However, in not stressing this aspect, I think that Pinnock neglects the hermeneutical tools of God's preparation in Israel from where Christ emerges. I would argue that it is primarily in terms of the Old Testament conceptual framework that the New Testament writers expound the meaning and significance of the death of Christ and that this framework is what evangelicals call the 'penal substitutionary' model.[59] Pinnock may not like the concepts of law, wrath, guilt, appeasement and punishment, but it seems hard to escape such concepts in the context of Old Testament revelation.

But what of Pinnock's claims that such a view creates a strange impression theologically by firstly making grace conditional upon penal satisfaction and secondly giving the impression that the Father actually hates sinners and cannot love them until his wrath is appeased; and thirdly that there is a schism in the Trinity with the Father being pitted against the Son? In order to give an adequate answer to this, it would be necessary to move the terms of debate into the realm of harmartology. I will mention this area briefly in my final chapter. For now, I can only outline how the 'penal' view understands the issue. In the 'penal' view, the vindicatory justice of God is emphasised as strongly as the grace of God: "Sin is the contradiction of God and he must react against it with holy indignation. This is to say that sin must meet with divine judgement. It is this inviolable sanctity of God's law, the immutable dictate of holiness and the unflinching demand of justice that makes mandatory the conclusion that salvation from sin without expiation and propitiation is inconceivable."[60]

At this point I must strongly repudiate what I think is a caricature of the penal position when Pinnock asks: "Do we actually think that the cross

---

[58] S. Lewis Johnson Jr. 'Behold the Lamb: The Gospel and Substitutionary Atonement' in ed. John H. Armstrong, *The Coming Evangelical Crisis* (Chicago, 1996), pp. 119-138., p. 125.

[59] There are numerous verses and texts that can be referred to. Some of the more explicit ones are Matt. 20:28; Rom. 3:21-26, 5:10-11, 8:32; 2 Cor. 5:18-21; Col. 1:19-20; Tit. 2:14; 1 Pet 1:18-19, 3:18; 1 Tim. 2:4-6; 1 Jn 3:8, 4:10. Heb. 5-10 places the death of Christ in the context of Old Testament sacrifice.

[60] John Murray, *Redemption Accomplished and Applied* (Grand Rapids, 1961), p. 18.

changed God's wrath into love rather than being the gift of his love?"[61] Some evangelicals may have been guilty of suggesting such an idea, but the best expositions of the 'penal' model strongly repudiate such an idea. Wrath is not turned into love but rather the cross is where, in the words of the modern song, 'wrath and mercy meet.' There is no-one who explains this better than John Stott:

> The whole notion of a compassionate Christ inducing a reluctant God to take action on our behalf founders on the fact of God's love. There was no *Umstimmung* in God, no change of mind or heart secured by Christ. On the contrary, the saving initiative originated in him.[62]

> It cannot be emphasised too strongly that God's love is the source, not the consequence of the atonement... God does not love us because Christ died for us; Christ died for us because God loves us. If it is God's wrath that needed to be propitiated, it is God's love which did the propitiating. If it may be said that the propitiation 'changed' God, or that by it he changed himself, let us be clear he did not change from wrath to love, or from enmity to grace, since his character is unchanging. What the propitiation changed was his dealings with us.[63]

Having decided out of sovereign love to save a people for Himself, the atonement is absolutely necessary to accomplish this salvation, for in the cross we see the demands of holiness and justice vindicated. The point I want to stress here *contra* Pinnock's view that saving grace has been universally present through the Spirit in creation, is that saving grace and love flow exclusively from the atonement. Had it not been for Christ as the atypical 'bond-in-blood sovereignly administered' then we would be left in our sin to await the righteous wrath of God in judgement. This is not denying the gracious nature of the original creation, but that sin made the cross necessary, and saving grace and saving love stem from the cross. The theme of 'reconciliation' demonstrates this well. Both Pinnock's model and the 'penal' model see reconciliation as an important theme. But which party is

---

[61] Pinnock, *Flame of Love*, p. 149.
[62] John Stott, *The Cross of Christ* (Leicester, 1989), p. 151.
[63] Ibid., p. 174. In his book, *The Difficult Doctrine of the Love of God* (Leicester, 2000), Don Carson elaborates on the relationship between God's wrath and His love: "Our problem, in part, is that in human experience wrath and love normally abide in mutually exclusive compartments. Love drives wrath out, or wrath drives love out... But this is not the way it is with God. God's wrath is not an implacable blind rage. However emotional it may be, it is an entirely reasonable and willed response to offences against his holiness. But his love... wells up amidst his perfections *and is not generated by the loveliness of the loved*. Thus there is nothing intrinsically impossible about wrath and love being directed toward the same individual or people at the same time"(p. 80).

reconciled? Contrary to Pinnock, the 'penal' model emphasises that it is God's enmity that is removed in the cross as well as ours, "with God's righteous demands satisfied, then and only then is enmity withdrawn... By the atoning death of Christ, God is reconciled to us, since our sins are expiated and his wrath appeased. His justice and his grace are a harmonious whole."[64] Therefore, although we can call the atonement a "consequent absolute necessity,"[65] "the atonement does not win or constrain the love of God. The love of God constrains to the atonement as the means of accomplishing love's determinate purpose."[66]

But what of Pinnock's claim that the Father has to punish the Son in order to 'make' God love, so causing a rift in the Trinitarian relations? I think that such a criticism misunderstands the trinitarian unity of the 'penal model.' Recalling our discussion of covenant theology in the last chapter, it was noted that some covenant theologians posit the existence of a 'covenant of redemption' or *pactum salutis*[67] made *ad intra* between the Father, Son and Spirit and the ground for the covenant of grace *ad extra*. The idea here is that the Son as Mediator willingly and freely agrees with the Father and Spirit to bring salvation to men and women.[68] The motivation of this

---

[64] Letham, op. cit., p. 146. See also Murray, op. cit., pp. 33-42.

[65] Murray, op. cit., p. 12. Murray further defines this as follows: "The word 'consequent' in this designation points to the fact that God's will or decree to save any is of free and sovereign grace. To save lost men was not of absolute necessity but of the sovereign good pleasure of God. The terms 'absolute necessity,' however, indicate that God, having elected some to everlasting life out of his mere good pleasure, was under the necessity of accomplishing this purpose through the sacrifice of his own Son, a necessity arising from the perfections of his nature. In a word, while it was not inherently necessary for God to save, yet, since salvation had been purposed, it was necessary to secure this salvation through a satisfaction that could be rendered only through substitutionary sacrifice and blood-bought redemption."(p. 12).

[66] Ibid., p. 10.

[67] Berkhof, op. cit. notes that the term *pactum salutis* (counsel of peace) was first used by Coccejus and derives from a supposed reference to the agreement between Father and Son in Zech. 6:13.

[68] See Berkhof, op. cit., pp. 265-271; Macleod, op. cit., p. 77f; Grudem, op. cit., p. 518f. Grudem notes: "To refer to the agreement among the members of the Trinity as 'covenant' reminds us that it was something voluntarily undertaken by God, not something that he had to enter into by virtue of his nature. However, this covenant is also different from the covenants between God and man because the parties enter into it as equals, whereas in covenants with man God is the sovereign Creator who imposes the provisions of the covenant by his own decree. On the other hand, it is like the covenants God makes with man in that it has the elements (specifying the parties, conditions, and promised blessings) that make up a covenant" (p. 519). I should note that for differing reasons, not all covenant theologians are happy defining God's plan of redemption in covenantal terms. Robertson, op. cit. believes it to be an artificial construction (p. 54); and because he does not define covenant as an agreement (believing God lives a covenant life in Himself), Hanko, op. cit. also rejects the idea (p. 172f).

agreement is one of grace, the supreme demonstration of God's love to us: "There is no schism in the Trinity when redemption and its application is understood properly. Rather, there is perfect harmony, the Father sacrificing His Son, the Son willingly offering himself, and the Spirit applying the benefits of the sacrifice to God's elect."[69] The measure of God's love is shown by what Christ has to undergo to secure Man's salvation.[70]

In stressing the importance of the 'penal substitutionary' model of atonement, I do not deny the validity of Pinnock's own insights on recapitulation and participation, nor his stress on the 'saving' nature of Christ's life and the resurrection. He is possibly right when he says that there has been a tendency in evangelical treatments of the atonement to overstress the legal and forensic nature of atonement concentrating solely on the death of Christ. However, I do believe that without the idea of a penal substitution, Pinnock's treatment is insufficient and inadequate because saving grace can be seen as divorced from the cross rather than flowing from the cross. As well as raising questions as to the nature and severity of the Fall and sin in Pinnock's theology, there are again questions as to the necessity of the cross in Pinnock's argument, and perhaps more crucially the necessity of Christ in Pinnock's soteriology. As I shall demonstrate shortly, Pinnock's doctrine of salvation, especially when considering the unevangelised is more pneumatocentric that Christocentric.

As a positive piece of theological construction, if one cannot give up the fundamentals of the 'penal substitution' model, then is it possible to incorporate Pinnock's insights into the 'penal substitution' model of atonement? I believe that it is possible because the 'penal' model is very inclusive as regards other models of atonement providing they are seen in the right perspective. Commenting on his threefold typology, Packer says:

> It should be noted that though the two former views regularly set themselves in antithesis to the third [the penal view], the third takes up into itself all the positive assertions that they make; which raises the question whether any more is at issue here than the impropriety of treating half-

---

[69] Johnson, op. cit., p. 122.

[70] Carson, op. cit. echoes this point well: "when we us the language of propitiation, we are not to think that the Son, full of love, offered himself and thereby placated (i.e., rendered propitious) the Father, full of wrath. The picture is more complex. It is that the Father, full of righteous wrath against us, nevertheless loved us so much that he sent his Son. Perfectly mirroring his Father's words and deeds, the Son stood over against us in wrath – it is not for nothing that the Scriptures portray sinners wanting to hide from the face of him who sits on the throne and *from the wrath of the Lamb* - yet, obedient to his Father's commission, offered himself on the cross. He did this out of love both for his Father, whom he obeys, and for us, who he redeems. Thus God is necessarily both the subject and the object of propitiation... That is the glory of the cross" (p. 83). See also Packer, op. cit., pp. 39-41; Letham, op. cit., pp. 136-138.

truths as the whole truth, and of rejecting a more comprehensive account on the basis of speculative negations about what God's holiness requires as a basis for forgiving sins.[71]

There are two complimentary themes involved in the work of Christ that can possibly soften the legal harshness that Pinnock sees in the 'penal' model.

Firstly, there is the broad theme of Christ's obedience. It is common in evangelical theology to distinguish between Christ's passive obedience in which he endured the curse and penalty of the law and his active obedience whereby he fulfilled the positive requirements of the law.[72] It is Christ's active obedience that has some affinities with Pinnock's concerns because it is possible to use the language of recapitulation in discussing this aspect of Christ's vicarious obedience. As the second Adam, Christ recapitulated the steps of the first Adam, but this time succeeding where Adam failed. The important point to note is that Christ was acting like Adam "not merely as a private person but as the Head of a solidaric unit."[73] When both passive and active aspects of obedience are highlighted we can say that it is not merely in the incarnation that redemption is achieved, nor is it merely through Christ's death. Rather it is the whole of his life, death and resurrection that is vicarious: "Restoration of fallen man hinges on the one act of obedience of Christ, the second Adam."[74] In this sense it is impossible to separate Christ's work from his person, as they are mutually definitive:

> They are part of the one great movement of God's grace to humanity in Jesus Christ. It is not enough that we affirm the truth of the incarnation and then move on to affirm the truth of the atonement as two factors in isolation. They are integral parts of a great whole. The historical appearance of the incarnate Son in Christ was to atone for our sins. The atoning sufferings and death of Christ for our sins were those of the incarnate God himself.[75]

Secondly, there is the 'tie' that binds Christ's recapitulation to the believer. In his own construction of the penal model, as well as the themes of guilt and retribution Packer notes that the theme of solidarity (a theme which Pinnock highlights) is also important. He notes that the idea of a penal substitution is one 'moment' of the theme of Christ as the second Adam,

---

[71] Packer, op. cit, p. 21.
[72] For a useful summary of this idea, see Murray, op. cit., pp. 19-24.
[73] Letham, op. cit., p. 117.
[74] Robertson, op. cit., p. 85.
[75] Ibid., p. 29f.

and what is also known as the mystical union with Christ. In this idea Christ:

> ... carried our identity and effectively involved us all in his dying... Christ has taken us with him into his death and through his death into his resurrection. His death for us brought remission of sins committed 'in' Adam, so that 'in' him we might enjoy God's acceptance; our death 'in' him brings release from the existence we knew 'in' Adam, so that 'in' him we are raised to life and become new creatures.[76]

In this sense we can speak of Christ as our substitute and representative: "the appropriate formulation is that on the cross Jesus' representative relation, as the last Adam whose image we are to bear, took the form of substituting for us under judgement, as the suffering servant of God on whom the Lord 'laid the iniquity of us all.'"[77] Because the believer is 'in' Christ, all that Christ achieved in his life and death of obedience can be the believer's:

> Because of the inextricable connection between Christ and his people, his death and resurrection were also ours... We died and rose in him because he was our representative. We died and rose in him because his death and resurrection have dynamic power by the Holy Spirit, transforming us and raising us to new life. We died and rose in him because of the intimate personal union that prevails. All that he has done is ours by his grace just as all that was ours (our sins) became his on the cross.[78]

In contrast to what he calls the 'legal' theory, Pinnock believes that his participatory model "portrays a world in which humanity dies and is raised to life in Christ. It speaks of new creation and of the Spirit who invites us to enter into it by faith."[79] I believe that put in the context of the believer's union with Christ, the 'penal model' can affirm all that Pinnock wants to affirm but crucially what the 'penal model' stresses is that the union between Christ and the believer is only possible because of the 'penal' 'substitutionary' death of Christ on the cross, where both God and man are reconciled to one another. As such, I believe that Pinnock presents a false dichotomy when he compares and contrasts his 'personal' and 'relational' model with those that are 'impersonal' and 'legal.' The theme of the believer's union with Christ is intimately personal and relational, but only because the judicial and legal demands of a holy God have been met in Christ.

---

[76] Packer, op. cit., p. 33.
[77] Ibid., p. 34.
[78] Letham, op. cit., p. 84.
[79] Pinnock, *Flame of Love*, p. 111.

The Spirit's Role in Atonement as Regards the Unevangelised

Put alongside the 'penal substitution' model that sees the atonement as necessary for the dispensation of grace, are we in a better position to evaluate Pinnock's position as regards the necessity of the atonement? Pinnock hints that there may be a possible solution to his dilemma of wanting to stress on the one hand the necessity of atonement while on the other hand seeing grace in creation as well as re-creation, by placing the work of the Son within the context of the work of the Spirit and emphasizing the Spirit's role in atonement. Referring to Jn.16:7, he writes, "Why did the outpouring of the Spirit have to wait until Jesus died and was glorified? What was it about those events that made them a turning point in the history of redemption? How did the mission of Jesus trigger Pentecost?"[80] Pinnock suggests that the incarnation was the clearest and most decisive presentation of God in history but that Jesus was, in fact, the "fulfilment of a process"[81] which had been started by the Spirit. In an important passage Pinnock says:

> The incarnation should not be viewed as a negation of universality but as the fulfilment of what the Spirit had been doing all along. The birth of Jesus by the Spirit was the climax of a universal set of operations. Hovering over Mary, Spirit was engaged in new creation. Spirit, everywhere at work in the whole of history, was now at work in Jesus to make him head of the new humanity. Throughout history the Spirit has been seeking to create such an impression of God's true self in human beings and hear the response to God that would delight his heart. This is what happened in Jesus by the Spirit. The invisible became visible, and a yes was heard on behalf of the race. Jesus became the receptacle of God's self-communication, and in him God received complete acceptance. Therefore the Spirit filled Jesus without measure and opened up the possibility for us to share this fullness. The floodgates of grace were opened for the world.[82]

Clearly for Pinnock the incarnation is representative in that it unambiguously demonstrates the love of God, a love already presupposed in creation but which is opaque due to the effects of sin.

However, the incarnation is unique and pivotal in the history of the world in that it marks a new stage in the work of the Spirit, "Jesus did not represent the first offering of God's grace - rather, the offer reached its culmination and high point in Him. The offer was so intense and world-changing through his participatory power that the Spirit could then come in Pentecos-

---

[80] Pinnock, *Flame of Love*, p. 93.
[81] Ibid., p. 195.
[82] Ibid., p. 195f.

tal power."[83] Pinnock believes that Christ's participatory journey was necessary to realize God's purpose for creation, "The idea is that what took place in Christ paradigmatically will be applied to and realized in us."[84] Through the Spirit, Christ created a new sphere of existence, a "space for salvation to go forward,"[85] which all can enter into by virtue of solidarity with him, "God revealed the goal of creation in Christ and offers it as a gift to us."[86]

In this there definitely seems to be a shift of emphasis with more importance being put on the role of the Spirit in the accomplishment of salvation. The move is away from the objective, legal dimension of the atonement and to a more personal subjective interpretation that emphasises not so much what Christ did for humanity, but rather what Christ enables the Spirit to do for humanity. By emphasising this, Pinnock can demonstrate both the discontinuity of Christ's particularity and the continuity of the Spirit's universality. Discontinuity is present in that epistemologically Christ reveals in a normative way God's love for humanity. This is how Pinnock could call the particularity axiom epistemologically first while being theologically second to the universal salvific will of God, "The Incarnation is the means by which we have come to know the primordial mystery of the world. In this event that mystery is disclosed, and we know God to be the loving friend of sinners."[87] Even more than this though, discontinuity can be seen in that because of Christ the barriers of sin have been broken down and as a result there is a new freedom which the Spirit enjoys. This is what Pinnock means when he refers to the "floodgates of grace opening on the world."[88] However, from the perspective of the Spirit, there is a continuity in what the Spirit has always been doing in creation, and what we see in the incarnation, "Salvation can be a universal possibility if we recognise the universal, loving activities of the Spirit. God has always wanted friendship and reconciliation with sinners. *What Jesus made explicit and implemented has always been true.*"[89]

Does this help answer the question concerning the representative or constitutive nature of Pinnock's model of atonement? I would like to suggest that by bringing into this discussion Pinnock's position on the unevangelised, I am in a better position to answer this question. Firstly, there is the question concerning the theological grounds for a universally accessible grace. It would seem difficult to base a universal grace on the work of

---

[83] Ibid. p. 198.
[84] Ibid., p. 95.
[85] Ibid., p. 94.
[86] Ibid., p. 100.
[87] Pinnock, 'An Inclusivist View,' p. 103.
[88] Pinnock, *Flame of Love*, p. 196.
[89] Ibid., p. 105, (my emphasis).

Christ because Pinnock insists that creation itself is gracious and a natural sacrament. Christ was the fulfilment of a process in the history of the Spirit. Everyone who has ever lived has been able to respond to the Spirit's prevenient grace, including all those who lived before Christ. One wonders then, what are the benefits of Christ to the unevangelised if grace is universally present outside the incarnation and has always been universally present.

However, Pinnock stresses that the unevangelised are ontologically saved by Christ although they are epistemologically deficient. Even if we concede that this is true, we are still faced with the question, that in the light of the above discussion on the atonement, it is difficult to know what Pinnock means by 'ontological' salvation. It would seem strange if the unevangelised, who epistemologically are unaware of Christ, could be ontologically saved by Christ, if a key component of Pinnock's soteriology is the human response of solidarity with Christ in his representative journey. Surely if one is to 'die with Christ' and 'rise with Christ,' one must know what he has done, let alone know the fact that he exists? This point relates back to the objective and subjective dimensions of the atonement. For Pinnock, Christ died for everyone, but this does not imply universalism, for salvation is conditional on the human response, "a new situation now exists: we only have to accept what has been done and allow the Spirit to conform our lives to Christ."[90] But does this new situation exist for the unevangelised? Pinnock's soteriology that puts emphasis on the human response needs to show how the unevangelised are saved *by Christ*. It is true that the unevangelised may implicitly decide to respond to Prevenient Grace by turning from self-centredness and giving themselves to God and neighbour, and this may well involve a dying to self and rising to life. Indeed, Christ may well be the normative and unique revelation of this self-sacrifice and the unevangelised person may be implicitly mirroring, and so participating in, Christ's representative journey. But the question remains how the salvation of the unevangelised believer is related directly to the work of Christ and not merely to the work of the Spirit in creation, of which Christ is but the ultimate expression.

The above analysis leads me tentatively to the conclusion that although Pinnock confesses a high constitutive Christology, it would appear in reality that the unevangelised can be saved outside Christ (but of course not outside God's grace) because Christ's work and God's grace are identical. At an epistemological level, the incarnation is unique, final and exclusive, but ontologically it only represents (albeit normatively) what the Spirit has been doing always from creation. Pinnock confesses a constitutive Christology and an objective redemption but his position on the unevangelised appears to question whether in fact he can coherently hold on to both doc-

---

[90] Ibid., p. 96.

trines. Rather than being Christocentric in his inclusivism, which I believe he would claim to be, Pinnock's position is pneumatocentric and as a result the particularity of Christ is compromised.

Such an analysis may help one understand more clearly the ramifications and significance of the definition of inclusivism given earlier that Christ is ontologically necessary for salvation but not epistemologically necessary. In the previous chapter I attempted to show how the Bible never separates the ontological from the epistemological when referring to soteriology. However Pinnock's desire to universalise the particular has meant a separation of the epistemological from the ontological. What I want to suggest, is that for Pinnock this separation is *only* theologically possible because in reality not only is Christ not epistemologically necessary for the salvation of the unevangelised, but that there is a great deal of ambiguity as to how the unevangelised are *ontologically* saved by God's grace in Christ. Certainly they are saved by accepting God's grace through the Holy Spirit in creation. But ontologically what does this grace have to do with Christ? There is a major lacuna in the relationship between the work of Christ and the salvation of the unevangelised in Pinnock's inclusivism.

One begins to get the impression that in his desire to prove universal accessibility, Pinnock has proscribed two ways to salvation, one through the revelation of the Spirit in creation which brings salvation albeit opaque and incomplete, and one through the revelation of God in Christ which brings full messianic salvation. Let us explore the ramifications of this idea for a moment. Firstly, let us recall Pinnock's relationship to Vatican II and the notion of a *preparatio evangelica*. Pinnock does, on a number of occasions, state that the Spirit's role is a preparatory one and he does make the distinction between Christians who have experienced messianic salvation and 'not-yet Christians' who await this type of salvation. But what is the exact status of the 'not-yet Christian'? Is the difference between Christian and 'not-yet Christian' purely epistemological, or is there an ontological change when the 'not-yet Christian' comes into contact with the explicit Gospel?

Here Pinnock again is ambiguous. On the one hand he says, "A premessianic believer is, one might say, latently a member of Christ's body and destined to receive the grace of conversion and explicit knowledge of Jesus Christ at a later date, whether in this life or after death."[91] Pinnock states that the Gospel brings with it a clearer revelation of God's love and forgiveness and that this in turn brings assurance. Such people need to experience God in the dimension of Pentecost, "Those like Cornelius, who have responded to God in pagan contexts will need to turn to Christ to receive what Jesus alone can give them: the Holy Spirit, a portion in the Kingdom of God, and the experience of messianic salvation."[92] Pinnock does not

---

[91] Pinnock, 'An Inclusivist View,' p. 117.
[92] Pinnock, *Wideness*, p. 179.

Universality, Particularity and Incarnation 223

deny that 'not-yet Christians' are saved and that they have a relationship with God at some level. It must be asked though, as to what kind of a relationship it can be where one side is totally ignorant of the other, and in fact may be against the other at a propositional and cognitive level? What can 'salvation' mean in this context? I think Bradley is overstating the case when he says that, "'Salvation,' for Pinnock, tends to be reduced to the bare notion of escape from final judgement,"[93] because Pinnock claims that the 'not-yet Christian' can display the fruits of the Spirit which are the marks of salvation. However 'salvation' in this context would have to be a concept without firstly, the assurance that God had done something in history to save me (a concept which I will show shortly, is fundamental to saving faith), and secondly without the presence of a Christian community. To put it another way, how does Pinnock's notion of salvation here correspond to the definition of the believers 'union with Christ,' an idea I have already mentioned with regard to the atonement and one to which I will return in the next chapter. How is the 'not-yet Christian' united to Christ? Part of the idea of this union is that "Christ and His people become organically one by faith so that Christ and His people are one people, one living organism, one unity."[94] This idea has serious implications for ecclesiology. Pinnock wishes to see 'not-yet Christians' as belonging to the "larger people of God"[95] and latently a member of Christ's body. But is this possible without reference to Christ? Bradley notes the particular christological focus of ecclesiology:

> The historic and geographic location of Christ's humanity and suffering is inextricably linked to the humanity of Christ's body, the Church, and its suffering; making disciples is accomplished through this particular human vehicle, though bound to time and place and pain... If any place in the world can become the "epiphany of the divine and the pictorial transparency of the deity" - to borrow a phrase from Moltmann - then the importance of the community and the urgency of the Great Commission will be undermined.[96]

It is strange that Pinnock himself does not see this danger, for in *Flame of Love* (1996) he stresses the importance of corporateness to salvation:

---

[93] James E. Bradley, '*Logos* Christology and Religious Pluralism: A New Evangelical Proposal' in *Proceedings of the Wheaton Theological Conference* (Wheaton, 1992), p. 206.
[94] Hanko, op. cit., p. 178.
[95] Pinnock, *Wideness*, p. 104.
[96] Bradley, op. cit., p. 205.

Note that in the flow of this book I am choosing to treat the salvation of individuals after the doctrine of the Church. This is not due to a devaluation of the personal aspects of salvation... No, I place the personal after the corporate in view of the fact that individuals are shaped by communities. One becomes a person in relationship with other persons, not otherwise. John Donne was right to say that no man is an island, because the self is a delicate flower that requires a social context in order to flourish.[97]

When speaking of the criterion for discerning the Spirit's activity, Pinnock implies that truth incarnate is the canon for testing, "Wherever, for example, we find self sacrificing love...we know the Spirit of Jesus is present... Such things tell us where the brothers and sisters of Jesus indwelt by the Spirit are."[98] In this account rather than the Spirit preparing the way for Christ, it is Christ that identifies the Spirit. The 'not-yet Christian' can display all the characteristics of messianic salvation, the only difference being one of knowledge and propositional truth. In contrast, one might argue, though, that propositional truth itself must be evidence that the Spirit of Jesus is present. As Bradley comments:

> Here we see that worship in the Spirit... is possible apart from knowledge of Christ. In effect, a God who has no decisive meaning to the worshipper may be worshipped, and in this act the true God is being worshipped. All Pinnock wants to insist on is that the idea of God as a personal, loving God, comes to us uniquely from the Bible. Yet evidently, this unique God does not require that he be worshipped uniquely.[99]

But can one separate the propositional and the ethical like this? There must be some correlation between what a person thinks and what a person does. I will return to this discussion in the next chapter.

Summary

So far, my primary concern in this chapter has been to focus on issues relating to the coherence and comprehensibility of Pinnock's position. I believe that with regards to Christology, Pinnock has failed to mediate universality and particularity because the result of his argument is a subtle universalisation of the particular. So while Pinnock still thinks he maintains the finality, particularity and primacy of Christ in soteriology, the real consequences of his thinking is that the incarnation and atonement have been re-interpreted to conform with the universality axiom. This move poses questions con-

---

[97] Pinnock, *Flame of Love*, p. 152.
[98] Ibid., p. 210.
[99] Bradley, op. cit., p. 204.

cerning the normativity of the incarnation, the necessity and purpose of the atonement and more specifically the relationship between the work of Christ and the salvation of the unevangelised. In other words, concerning the salvation of the unevangelised, the notion of *solus Christus* in Pinnock's theology appears to have gone under a significant redefinition and one is left asking the meaning of this fundamental evangelical tenet. That Pinnock does not adequately deal with these areas leads one to two possible conclusions concerning his argument.

Firstly, it could be said that all the above points illustrate one of the main weaknesses of Pinnock's theology in general, which is a lack of precision and potential superficiality in argumentation. As I mentioned in my description of Pinnock at the beginning of Ch. 2, there are advantages to his style of theology, but there are disadvantages when one presses for details on key issues. Pinnock would probably concede this point admitting that a lot more work needs to be done in specific areas. He is only painting with broad brushstrokes. A more fundamental criticism concerns the issue of theological coherence. Pinnock does not hide the motives behind his inclusivism. For him, the universality axiom cannot be compromised. However, at the same time, he still wishes to hold to evangelical orthodoxy in his Christology, realising the dangers of pluralism to Christological formulation. The resulting synthesis, though, when seen from the perspective of his inclusivism and the salvation of the unevangelised, is theologically ambiguous and at times verges on the contradictory. In the coming chapter I will trace what I think is the genesis of this ambiguity, which is his construal of the relationship between the second and third Persons of the Trinity.

CHAPTER 8

Spirit and Son in the Accomplishment and Application of Redemption: A (Binitarian) Trinitarian Critique of Clark Pinnock's Inclusivism

At the end of the previous chapter, I suggested that in Pinnock's inclusivism, there was a theological ambiguity as regards the relationship between the person and work of Christ and the salvation of the unevangelised. Is it possible to locate the source of this ambiguity? In this chapter, I will suggest that this ambiguity stems from Pinnock's (mis)understanding of the trinitarian relations both economically and immanently. Underpinning Pinnock's proposal of a 'Spirit enriched Christology,' is his emphasis on "the two hands of God," the Son and the Spirit, where the Son safeguards particularity and the Spirit universality. Pinnock claims that his Christology gives greater recognition to the missions of both Son and Spirit, not exaggerating nor diminishing the role of either Person: "God uses his two hands in the work of redemption. Neither is subordinate to the other; neither supplants the other."[1] But what exactly are the dynamics of the relationship between Christ and the Spirit? Pinnock insists that what he is doing throughout his inclusivism is to redress an imbalance in evangelical theology and to re-assert the centrality of the Spirit in Christology and soteriology. However in his redressing, a specific pattern can be discerned in Pinnock's trinitarian theology concerning the relationship between Son and Spirit. It is this relationship that I wish to critique, as I believe it is an unevangelical way of understanding the relationship between the Son and Spirit.

Spirit and Son in the *Historia Salutis* and the Accomplishment of Redemption

In his attempt to mediate both the axioms of universality and particularity, Pinnock contextualises christology within pneumatology, not seeing the Spirit as 'tied' or subordinate to Christ as his substitute or instrument, but as being universally and salvifically present even where Christ is not known:

---

[1] Pinnock, *Flame of Love*, (Downers Grove, 1996), p. 92.

"Let us see what results from viewing Christ as an aspect of the Spirit's mission, instead of (as is more usual) viewing Spirit as a function of Christ's. It lies within the freedom of theology to experiment with ideas;"[2] [and], "God sends both Son and Spirit... The relationship is dialectical. The Son is sent in the power of the Spirit, and the Spirit is poured out by the risen Lord... It is not right to be Christocentric if being Christocentric means subordination of the Spirit to the Son. The two are partners in the work of redemption."[3]

Pinnock suggests that the *filioque* clause may threaten the Spirit's universality because it can promote Christomonism in that: "it does not encourage us to view the divine mission as being prior to and geographically larger than the Son's."[4] This picture accords well with Pinnock's inclusivist position on the unevangelised, which I labelled as being primarily 'pneumatological' in that it is by prevenient grace through the Spirit that the unevangelised can be saved. The point I have been trying to establish is that for Pinnock saving grace is universal because it is pneumatological and present in creation. The implication of this is that this grace is in some way separated from the Christ event.

It is precisely this salvific pneumatocentricity over Christocentricity which I wish to dispute, because as Badcock states:

> There is a strong sense in New Testament pneumatology, however, and indeed in the Christian theological tradition in general, that the gift of the Spirit is something that flows from the Christ-event, and that it is of decisive importance precisely because it is an eschatological event, something that ruptures the previous continuities of natural human existence... The fact that the Spirit appears...to be given fundamentally at creation, appears to conflict with the links of Scripture and tradition that are made both between Pentecost and Calvary and between the Messianic age and the life to come.[5]

In this section, I wish to compare and contrast Pinnock's reading of the story of the Spirit and His "entangled life history"[6] with the Son, with what I believe to be an orthodox evangelical reading of the story. My primary

---

[2] Ibid., p. 80.
[3] Ibid., p. 82.
[4] Ibid., p. 196.
[5] Badcock, op. cit., p. 153.
[6] Kevin Vanhoozer, 'Does the Trinity Belong in a Theology of Religions? On Angling in the Rubicon and the "Identity" of God' in ed. Kevin Vanhoozer, *The Trinity in a Pluralistic Age: Theological Essays on Culture and Religion* (Cambridge, 1997), p. 64. Referring to Ricoeur, Vanhoozer uses this phrase when speaking of the narrative identity of the triune God: "Each person's life history is 'entangled' in the history of others." (p. 64).

aim is to show why from trinitarian foundations, an evangelical theology cannot legitimise any form of inclusivism that separates salvation from an explicit confession of Christ. A secondary aim is to try and deal with a number of difficult questions concerning the activity of the Spirit before the incarnation.

Three Fundamental Trinitarian Truths: Homoousios, Autotheos, and Perichoresis.

Realising the complexity of the debate and the constant historical development of the terminology, Plantinga Jr. has given a useful threefold typology which highlights three basic responses to the question of unity/plurality of the Godhead: 1) God is one person existent as Father, Son and Holy Spirit; 2) God is three 'persons,' Father, Son, and Holy Spirit, who are also one (person?); 3) God is three persons, Father, Son and Holy Spirit, who exist in perichoretic union as one God.[7] In espousing some form of social analogy of the Trinity, Pinnock appears to fit most comfortably in the third typology. While this is not the place to discuss the merits and perils of the social analogy of the Trinity,[8] orthodox Evangelical theology which wishes to trace its heritage from the Magisterial Reformation is firmly placed within the second category: there is one essence (*ousia*) and three Persons (*personae*). Contrary to those who believe that such a schema collapses plurality into unity, both *De Deo uno* and *De Deo trino* are stressed although Blocher is probably right when he says that the Western tradition "has overprivileged unity of essence and understressed the threeness of God."[9] A balanced view might be that an evangelical Trinitarian theology traditionally based on the Western model, has, as its starting point or 'guiding principle,' the unity of the one essence of deity founded in biblical monotheism: "Hear, O Israel, Jehovah our God is One God." (Deut. 6:4).[10] However,

---

[7] Cornelius Plantinga Jr., *The Hodgson-Welch Debate and the Social Analogy of the Trinity* (PhD. diss., Princeton Theological Seminary, 1982), pp. 31-35. quoted in Thomas R. Thompson, 'Trinitarianism Today: Doctrinal Renaissance, Ethical Relevance, Social Redolence' in *Calvin Theological Journal* 32 (1997), pp. 9-42. p. 27.

[8] See, for example, Thompson, op. cit., pp. 31-42; Henri Blocher, 'Immanence and Transcendence in Trinitarian Theology' in ed. Vanhoozer, *The Trinity in a Pluralistic Age*, p. 106f. Blocher states, "The trend toward 'social' views of the Trinity looks dangerously unaware of the gravity of tritheism: assigning to the three a generic or corporative unity equals tritheism, it *is* tritheism." (p. 107).

[9] Blocher, op. cit., p. 106.

[10] It is worth noting that Gerald Bray in *The Doctrine of God* (Leicester, 1993), p. 199, lists as his first characteristic of Reformed trinitarianism that "the essence of God is of secondary importance in Christian theology...they [the Reformers] said only that God speaks sparingly of his essence, because he wants us to focus our attention and our

with Macleod, evangelicals equally hold the three Persons "are not simply modalistic or chronological distinctions. They are real ontological distinctions. In other words, there are *differentia* in the depths of God's own being that correspond to these three *personae*, Father, Son and Holy Spirit."[11]

The above preamble is necessary because it sets the scene to discuss the nature of the divine unity. Firstly, Evangelicals have traditionally stressed both the generic and numerical identity of the *homoousios*.[12] The unity of the Trinity is substantial and necessary and based on the one divine essence. Secondly, there is the idea, championed by Calvin to dispel any form of ontological subordinationism, that each person is *autotheos*: that is "God in his own right, and not merely by divine appointment:"[13]

> Calvin's position rested on a clear distinction between *person* (*hypostasis*) and *essence* (*ousia*). It was perfectly correct, according to Calvin, to describe Christ as 'God of God' (*theos ek theou*) if we were referring to the former. As Son he was from the Father... But the essence of the Son was not from the Father. Simply as essence it was ingenerate and unbegotten. It could not be subordinate to that of the Father for the simple reason that it was not only generically but numerically identical with that of the Father (and, of course, the Holy Spirit).[14]

Bray notes that an implication of *autotheos* is that terms such as 'generation' and 'procession' cannot have any implications of causality or derivation:

> It is true that he [Calvin] admits that the person of the Son has his beginning in God (*Institutes*, I, 13, 25), but his words are carefully chosen as to avoid any hint of causality in this expression. What he means is that everything the Son is and does must be understood with reference to the Fa-

---

worship elsewhere (Calvin, *Institutes*, I, 13,1)." By this he means that God's essence cannot be discussed apart from a predicate of the three persons.

[11] Donald Macleod, 'The Doctrine of the Trinity' in *Scottish Bulletin of Evangelical Theology* 3/1 (Spring, 1985), pp. 11-21, p. 12.

[12] For a summary of these terms see, Macleod, *The Person of Christ*, pp. 136-140; idem. 'The Doctrine of the Trinity,' p. 16f. Here he writes: "There is one *ousia*, one *substantia*, one *theiotes*, one divine nature, one godhead. Hence, the *homoousios* must be numerical. There is one God, one being who is God, and Christ's deity must be fitted into that fundamental perspective. The three do not form three Gods having a merely generic identity. They form one God with a numerical identity" (p. 16f).

[13] Gerald Bray, *The Doctrine of God*, p. 201. The seminal exposition of this concept is to be found in B.B. Warfield's essay 'Calvin's Doctrine of the Trinity' in *Calvin and Augustine* (Philadelphia, 1956), pp. 189-284.

[14] Macleod, *The Person of Christ*, p. 151.

ther, because that is the way the Son understands himself - not because he is ontologically dependent on the Father, as the only true *autotheos*.[15]

This raises the more controversial question as to what, for example 'begottenness' means. Who is the Son? What does it mean for the Son to be Son? Macleod's answer is that the *persona* is to be defined by what he does in redemption. Here the functional and the ontological are brought together: "In the last analysis, form and colour are given to the only begotten by the fact that, as the Son, he did things, and suffered things, which were not done or suffered by the Father."[16]

Thirdly, there is the Western understanding of co-inherence, the doctrine of *perichoresis* (Latin: *circuminsessio, circumincessio*)[17] that in the Western form must be seen as a function of the substantial unity of the *homoousios*. The idea is that each person dwells in the other, and occupies the same space as the other, and communicates everything that is common to the other apart from that which distinguishes them:

> So far as our human experience goes, God comes to us as one. Yet the one in whom he comes is the Father, the Son and the Holy Spirit. The coming is such that in the one the three come; and that in each the other come... The three co-inhere in a single being so that there is no relation with the being apart from a relationship with the persons; no action of one person which does not involve the action of the others; and yet no action

---

[15] Bray, *The Doctrine of God*, p. 204. Another implication of *autotheos* brought out by Macleod and to which I will refer again later in this chapter, is the language with which the New Testament writers refer to the Persons. Macleod argues that because there is no connotation of causality or derivation in *autotheos*, then a certain 'liberty' can be taken in how we speak of the Persons. Firstly, the language of Father-Son is not the only way of speaking of the first and second persons: the Second Person is called Word or Lord: "In particular, we should not read off from the designation 'Son' ideas of derivation and subordination which would be entirely inappropriate to the equally valid designation 'Lord'" (p. 146). Secondly, the traditional order of 'Father, Son and Spirit' is not sacrosanct and in a number of places is reversed (2 Cor. 13:14; Lk. 1:35; 1 Cor. 12:4-6;1 Pet. 1:2).

[16] Macleod, *The Person of Christ*, p. 138.

[17] Leonardo Boff in his *Trinity and Society* (New York, 1988), pp. 135-136, gives a good definition of these Latin terms noting that the Greek *perichoresis* has a double meaning: "Its first meaning is that of one thing being contained in another, dwelling in, being in another - a situation of fact, a static state. This understanding was translated by *circuminsessio*...this signified: one Person is in the others, surrounds the others on all sides (*circum-*), occupies the same space as the others, fills them with its presence. Its second meaning is active and signifies the interpenetration or interweaving of one Person with the others and in the others. This understanding seeks to express the living eternal process of relating intrinsic to the three Persons, so that each is always penetrating the others."

which does not have his own distinctive mark upon it. The external acts of the triune God are indeed common to all three persons, but that does not mean that each acts in the same way... Each acts in his own proper way.[18]

Applying these fundamental rules of Trinitarian discourse to Pinnock's inclusivism, I wish to note the following points.

Firstly, if we are to take seriously the truth of the triune God working in the *opera ad extra*, for example, soteriology, then we must see the person and work of all three Persons in the soteriological act. In Evangelical orthodoxy, we see this triune element: the Father orders salvation, the Son accomplishes salvation, and the Spirit applies salvation. However in Pinnock's stressing the Spirit's 'independent' mission of offering prevenient grace in creation to the unevangelised, one is left asking where the Son is in the economy of salvation. Again I return to the question I asked of Pinnock in the previous chapter: if saving grace has always been available in creation by the Spirit, then why is Christ needed for salvation? In Pinnock's inclusivist position on the salvation of the unevangelised, the *opera* appear to have divided, the person and work of the Spirit has been severed from the person and work of Christ. Is it possible to translate this point into epistemology?

Bray claims a principle of Reformation theology stemming from the notions of *homoousios* and *perichoresis* is that "knowledge of one of the persons involves knowledge of the other two at the same time."[19] I think that by 'knowledge' Bray means experiential and applicatory acquaintance. In other words, he is merely affirming what I have just stated above: if a consequence of *perichoresis* is that where the Spirit is the Son is, then where is the Son in Pinnock's soteriology of the unevangelised? However, could 'knowledge' here mean self-conscious cognition? I would tentatively like to suggest that if saving revelation is an act of the triune God, and that God is present *perichoretically*, then there could be such a notion as an epistemological or revelatory *perichoresis*, the idea being that it is not possible to know only the Father, or the Son, or the Spirit, but rather in knowing one, the others are revealed. God reveals himself as he is: he is the triune God.

Bray's idea seems to be that one of the truths about salvation is that we come to know God personally, and knowing God personally means knowing his triunity as this is one of the fundamental 'facts' of God's existence. Bray claims that as long as God's presence remains external to the worshipper, "the latter would see his acts of creation, redemption and sanctification only in the undivided unity of the will common to all three per-

---

[18] Macleod, *The Person of Christ*, p. 142.
[19] Bray, *The Doctrine of God*, p. 202.

sons."[20] However because salvation is the indwelling of God in our hearts, God reveals to the believer "the secret of his own internal relations."[21] This would appear to point us back in the direction of Christocentricity, because it is only in the revelation of Christ, that we begin to *clearly* see the revelation of God's triunity.[22]

---

[20] Ibid.

[21] Ibid.

[22] If I am to remain consistent on this point then must I argue that there is this epistemological *perechoresis* in special revelation before Christ? What about the salvation of Old Testament believers? Did they not only confess Christ in an embryonic form (as argued in the previous chapter), but did they perceive the triunity of God in their confession and see in some way the work of Father, Son and Spirit? Some kind of answer to this issue lies in the axioms of continuity and discontinuity between the Old Testament and New Testament as described in the previous chapter. Bray seems to want to emphasise discontinuity here because he makes the common distinction between an external and internal revelation, so God reveals himself *among* his people in the Old Testament, but not *within* them as he does after Pentecost. But this is not entirely satisfactory because, as I shall show shortly, the nature of Old Testament salvation is essentially the same as the New Testament: that is an internal work of the Spirit which renews the heart of believers giving them the faith to believe in Christ. B.B. Warfield in his essay 'The Spirit of God in the Old Testament,' in *Biblical Doctrines* (Edinburgh, 1988), pp. 101-129, holds to this internal working of the Spirit in the Old Testament, but as regards the Old Testament conception of the hypostatization of the Spirit, Warfield believes that in Old Testament times it was important to stress the monotheistic unity of God over the plurality of God which might have led to polytheism "A premature revelation of the Spirit as a distinct hypostasis could have wrought nothing but harm to the people of God... Not until the whole doctrine of the Trinity was ready to be manifested in such a visible form as at the baptism of Christ ...could any part of the mystery be safely uncovered" (p. 127). This too is Ferguson's conclusion: "the nature of the Spirit's ministry in the Old Testament adumbrates the hypostatization which emerges in the New. But it is doubtful whether we are justified in holding that the Old Testament unequivocally clarifies that the *ruach* Yahweh is a distinct hypostasis within a Trinitarian being," p. 30. Certainly the Old Testament revelation is shadowy, incomplete, partial, enigmatic, and preparatory and it should be stressed that the Trinity is fully revealed to us only in and through incarnation. However, having noted all these provisos, if one is to argue for the continuous, progressive and organic character of revelation, is there any way in which Old Testament believers perceived something of the triunity of God? I believe that there is, because the difference between Old and New Testaments is essentially one of degree (even if there is vast difference) and not of kind. Possible evidence for this could be: 1. References to the Spirit of God even if this is only understood as an objectification; 2. Old Testament Christophanies; 3. Prophecies concerning the coming of the Messiah and the outpouring of the Spirit. In spite of his caution regarding this matter Warfield, op. cit. says that "it is pragmatic in Isidore of Pelusium to say that Moses knew the doctrine of the Trinity well enough, but concealed it through fear that polytheism would profit by it. But we may safely affirm this of God the Revealer, in the gradual delivery of the truth concerning himself to men"(p. 127).

Secondly, in Trinitarian discourse we must take note of the full maxim: *opera ad extra indivisa servato discrimine et ordine personarum*. Implied in this are two ideas, the doctrines of appropriation and proper actions. Although all the members of the Trinity are involved in all the *opera ad extra*, it is appropriate to associate a particular person with a particular action. So traditionally it is appropriate to attribute the act of creation to the Father, revelation and redemption to the Son, and efficacy and sanctification to the Spirit. Proper action means that, for example, incarnation is proper only to the Son, since only he became incarnate. Because the economic Trinity analogically reflects the immanent Trinity, these roles are not arbitrary because they define who the persons are. My question concerning Pinnock's inclusivism is whether the Spirit is acting in an inappropriate manner especially with regards salvation. I have suggested that in Pinnock's inclusivism, God's salvation comes not so much from the work of the Son but from the work of the Spirit in creation. The result of this is that the Son's role diminishes (and almost disappears) while the Spirit's role is exaggerated. This configuration, while fitting into Pinnock's universal concerns, is certainly not an 'evangelical' configuration.

The Filioque

Pinnock suggests that the *filioque* can promote Christomonism, and that in setting aside the clause, one can uphold the divine mission of the Spirit as being prior to and geographically larger than the Son's. That is to say, Pinnock believes that by claiming that the Spirit proceeds from the Father only, the Spirit has a 'freer' role as one of the 'two hands of God,' not being subordinate to the Son in the divine economy, but fulfilling His own mission. What is one to make of this implication of the *filioque* clause? Certainly, there does seem to be a line of thinking within Protestant thinking in general and evangelical thinking in particular, that the *filioque* clause is directly linked to how Son and Spirit relate to each other in the divine economy of salvation. So, for example, Bavinck,[23] Berkhof,[24] and Grudem[25] in their respective systematic theologies, believe that the Eastern Church in abandoning the clause is susceptible to mysticism where mind and heart are placed in an antithetical relationship because Son and Spirit are "more or less independent of each other; each leads to the Father in His own peculiar way."[26] It would seem that on this line of thinking, Pinnock is being theologically consistent in his desire to set aside the clause, so allowing the Spirit to work where Christ is not named. Discussion of the *filioque* clause

---

[23] Herman Bavinck, *The Doctrine of God* (Edinburgh, 1977), pp. 313-317.
[24] Louis Berkhof, *Systematic Theology* (Grand Rapids, 1976), p. 98.
[25] Wayne Grudem, op. cit., p. 247.
[26] Bavinck, op. cit., p. 317.

would appear to be central in assessing the validity of Pinnock's inclusivism.

I would like to argue that this equivalence of the *filioque* to the separation of Son and Spirit is too simple an association and that denying the *filioque* does not necessarily lead to the 'freeing' of the Spirit from the Son, although it can be used as supplementary evidence to re-enforce the bond between Christ and the Spirit. I believe that the *filioque* clause is an important doctrine because it highlights a number of fundamental trinitarian issues including the relationship between the economic and immanent Trinity; the truth/falsity of affirming the Father as the *fons deitatis*, and whether this implies an inherent subordinationism; and the precise meaning of terms like 'procession' and 'begetting'. However, there is evidence to suggest that if one rejects the *filioque*, it is still possible to affirm a strong relationship between the Spirit and Christ in the economy of salvation, a relationship which questions the legitimacy of Pinnock's use of the clause.

Pinnock claims that Eastern Orthodox theology is his inspiration and support for his reading of the *filioque* clause. On this point, I want to note two things. Firstly, the trinitarianism of the Cappadocian Fathers struggled with the relationship between Son and Spirit. Bray notes that although Gregory of Nazianzus struggled to define the difference between generation and procession, he did not want to suggest that the Spirit was in any way an alternative to the Son as mediator between God and humanity. Bray states "The idea that the Holy Spirit can produce 'anonymous Christians,' or bring people to a saving knowledge of God without explicit reference to Christ, ...receives no support from Cappadocian theology."[27] Secondly, Pinnock makes no reference to the distinctive Eastern Orthodox doctrine of the divine *energies*, the "livingness of God - Father, Son and Holy Spirit."[28] With this doctrine, Eastern Orthodoxy can state that although the Spirit proceeds from the Father alone at the level of the divine essence, at the level of the divine *energies*, he proceeds from the Father through the Son, or from both Father and Son. Although Vladimir Lossky strongly rejects the *filioque* and emphasises the work of the Spirit in the Orthodox doctrine of *theosis*, he still appears to hold together both Spirit and Son:

> The redeeming work of the Son is related to our nature. The deifying work of the Holy Spirit concerns our persons. But the two are inseparable. One is unthinkable without the other, for each is a condition of the other, each is present in the other... This double dispensation of the Word and of the Paraclete has as its goal the union of created beings with God.[29]

---

[27] Bray, op. cit., p. 161.
[28] Gary Badcock, *Light of Truth and Fire of Love: A Theology of the Holy Spirit* (Cambridge, 1997), p. 82.
[29] Vladimir Lossky, *In the Image and Likeness of God* (New York, 1974), p. 109.

A fundamental tenet of evangelical trinitarian theology is that the economic Trinity analogically reflects the immanent Trinity,[30] and this tenet is one of the reasons why evangelicalism cannot accept the doctrine of the *energies*. It has also been the foundation for accepting the *filioque*, for many see the Spirit proceeding from the Son in the economic relations and so believe that this procession must be true of the intra-trinitarian relations. The evangelical theologian Nick Needham agrees with this parallel between economic and immanent Trinity, but believes that there is not the exegetical evidence for believing in the double procession. Rather he suggests that the New Testament points to a relationship that sees the Holy Spirit proceeding from the Father to the Son and then from the Son to the believer:

> If the economic Trinity is truly grounded in the ontological Trinity, could we not say that the Holy Spirit is the Spirit of the Father by original possession, and the Spirit of the Son by an eternal proceeding of the Spirit to the Son from the Father, so that from all eternity the Spirit rests on the Son and abides in him - that the Son is the eternal abode, the timeless holy temple, of his Father's Spirit?[31]

Needham claims that the Western fears of a 'non-Christ-centred mysticism' are unfounded because "the Spirit rests upon and abides in the Son; or in John of Damascus' phrase, the Spirit is the Son's eternal companion."[32] He also claims that the *filioque* has not prevented the West from adopting forms of charismatic behaviour that for him are far nearer to a Christless mysticism.[33] In fact he claims that in adopting the Eastern view he has a

---

[30] Badcock, op. cit. distinguishes two different senses regarding the axiom that the economic Trinity is the immanent Trinity, what could be called the literal and the analogical. I think that Evangelicals fall into the analogical position, defined by Badcock thus: "there is a clear and close relation of identity between the economic and immanent Trinity, but a relation that is best understood as analogical, according to the traditional theological conception, and that thus lays emphasis upon their unity-in-*difference*, rather than as a radical sublation of distinction through the idea that the Trinity in itself is what it is in the economy as such... From this point of view, Rahner's axiom could be understood to assert that the economic Trinity contains in a mode appropriate to its representation in the created order, the reality of the heavenly, or immanent Trinity, and in a corresponding sense, that the immanent Trinity is a reality contained in the economic... The mystery [of the Trinity], in this case, would be disclosed but not *completely* disclosed"(p. 224f).

[31] Nick Needham, 'The *Filioque* Clause: East or West?' in *Scottish Bulletin of Evangelical Theology* 15/2 (Aut. 1997), pp. 142-162, p. 155.

[32] Ibid., p. 159.

[33] Ibid., p. 160. Needham even suggests that the Western understanding of the Trinity may encourage mysticism: "It is arguable that the real mystical trap actually lies in the

"deeper appreciation of the Son as the One through whom the Spirit comes to believers - the Son as 'Spirit - bestower'... I see the Son as distinct from the Father as fountain, but through the Son as the Father's medium and channel."[34]

In summary then, I would like to suggest that based on very different evidence (given on the one hand by an Eastern Orthodox theologian like Lossky, and on the other hand by an evangelical like Needham), that a denial of the *filioque*, while perhaps being evangelically unorthodox, firstly does not necessarily lead to nonchristocentric mysticism, and more important secondly, does not theologically legitimize Pinnock's attempt to 'free' the Spirit from the Son in the divine economy enabling the third person to work independently from the Son.

A Functional Economy: The Glorification of the Son by the Spirit

Whether one wishes to hold to the *filioque*, or one holds to the idea that the Spirit proceeds from the Father and abides in the Son, there appears to be strong biblical and theological evidence for positing an inextricable relationship between Son and Spirit.

I want to further suggest that in this relationship there is a particular functional economy in salvation that leads to a definite Christocentricity and not a pneumatocentricity. Although I wish to concentrate mainly on the role of the Spirit after Christ's glorification, I think it is necessary to comment briefly on the activities of Spirit and Word in creation and in special revelation before the incarnation.[35]

WORD AND SPIRIT IN CREATION

I have been arguing that the *opera ad extra* are the work of the triune God and that because of their *perichoretic* relations, where one person is present so are the other two. Affirming this means that Pinnock is wrong to associate a universality to the Spirit and a particularity with Son and then attempt a mediation. Rather, it seems more appropriate to say that both Spirit and Son are associated with universality and particularity depending on how

---

preoccupation with 'the one Godhead' behind or even beyond the Trinitarian Persons, a mysticism of the divine essence, such as we do indeed find in great Western mystics like Meister Eckhart. This is something no Easterner would dream of; it is ruled out by the overwhelmingly Person-orientated structure of Eastern Trinitarianism" (p. 160).

[34] Ibid., p. 162.

[35] To organise my material in this order may seem strange epistemologically as there is a clearer revelation of the relationship between Son and Spirit in the New Testament than in the Old Testament and in revelation in creation. Indeed I have indicated that for many evangelicals one can only understand the Old from the perspective of the New. However I wish to organise my material chronologically keeping in view the contours of redemptive history that have been an important factor throughout this critique.

one defines these terms. If this construal is correct, then creation itself must show evidence of the activity of Son and Spirit as well as re-creation. This has been traditionally affirmed by seeing creation as from the Father, through the Son and by the Holy Spirit. Pinnock bases his inclusivism on the omnipresence of the Spirit and the universality of revelation in this creative act. Where there is the Spirit, there is prevenient grace, where there is prevenient grace there is the opportunity to turn to God explicitly or implicitly. The problem with this argument is that it confuses and conflates the universal work of the Word and Spirit in creation and the particular work of the Word and Spirit in re-creation. This is not, as Pinnock claims, a neo-Marcionite tendency to see two Gods, one in creation and one in re-creation, but merely recognises that the one Word and Spirit have different spheres of activity in creation and re-creation. This point needs further justification.

Warfield discerns a threefold typology in the Spirit's activity: the immanence of the universal cosmic Spirit in the world, the particular inspiring theocratic Spirit in the Church, and the salvific indwelling individual Spirit in the soul.[36] In terms of general revelation, while a number of themes are seen as important by evangelicals (e.g. the *imago Dei*, and the *sensus divinitatis*), a number of evangelicals parallel the activities of the Spirit with the activities of the Word (*Logos*). Nash says that it is possible to speak of Christ as the cosmological Logos: the agent through whom God brought the world into existence; the epistemological Logos: the ground of all human knowledge; and the soteriological Logos: who as both priest and sacrifice brings salvation.[37] The first two activities come under the sphere of God's 'general revelation,' while the third belongs to special revelation.[38] The

---

[36] Warfield, 'The Spirit of God in the Old Testament,' p. 106. This threefold typology is also used by John C. J. Waite, *The Activity of the Holy Spirit within the Old Testament Period* (London, 1961).

[37] Ronald Nash, *The Word of God and the Mind of Man: The Crisis of Revealed Truth in Contemporary Theology* (Phillipsburg, 1982), p. 66. Other Evangelicals who make use of this idea of the *Logos* are Bruce Demarest, *General Revelation: Historical Views and Contemporary Issues* (Grand Rapids, 1982), p. 228; Carl Henry, *God, Revelation and Authority* Volume 3 (Waco, 1979), p. 192f. See also Terry C. Muck, 'Is There Common Ground Among Religions?' in *Journal of the Evangelical Theological Society* 40/1 (March 1997), pp. 99-112.

[38] Pinnock cites the *Logos* theology in some of the Early Fathers as supporting an optimism in salvation and universal accessibility to all. It is not possible here to prove this claim one way or the other, only to say that Pinnock's reading is just *one* possible interpretation, and that other interpretations claim that these Fathers were far more exclusive than Pinnock would like to believe. These interpreters claim that the *Logos spermatikos* was not primarily concerned with issues of salvation but issues of truth: the purpose of the doctrine was not to answer questions on the unevangelised. See, for example, Gerald Bray, 'Explaining Christianity to Pagans' in *The Trinity in a Pluralistic*

relationship between Word and Spirit is that they work together, objective revelation is the means through which the Spirit subjectively works, the Spirit illuminates and testifies to God's revelation.

In the axiom, *opera ad extra indivisa servato discrimine et ordine personarum*, it is appropriate to associate the Spirit with God's immanence. The cosmic Spirit of God is omnipresent in the whole of creation "as the executive of the Godhead...the divine principle of activity everywhere."[39] Therefore it is possible to agree with Pinnock concerning the universal presence of the Spirit. However, as Blocher points out, the idea of 'divine presence' is no simple easy notion but is complex and nuanced.[40] I want to suggest that Pinnock's argument concerning the divine gracious presence is too simplistic and that it is this simplicity leads to a number of erroneous conclusions concerning a universal salvific presence.

Firstly there is the nature of the divine presence. I noted in Ch. 4, that Pinnock's paradigm of 'trinitarian openness' has a particular emphasis on divine immanence which I claimed at times could be interpreted as bordering on the panentheistic. Although this is not the place to go into a detailed critique of transcendence and immanence in Pinnock's 'trinitarian openness,' I do want to note that evangelical orthodoxy has been very careful to equally balance both God's otherness from creation and His involvement in creation. In his *Institutio Theologicae Elencticae* (1679-85), the Reformed scholastic Francis Turretin makes a number of distinctions concerning God's immensity and omnipresence. He notes that God can be said to be

---

Age. Theological Essays on Culture and Religion. ed. Kevin Vanhoozer (Grand Rapids, 1997), pp. 9-25; James G. Sigountos, 'Did Early Christians Believe Pagan Religions Could Save?' in *Through No Fault of Their Own?* eds. W. Crockett and J. Sigountos (Grand Rapids, 1992), pp. 229- 241; Graham A. Keith, 'Justin Martyr and Religious Exclusivism' in *One God, One Lord. Christianity in a World of Religious Pluralism* eds. Andrew D. Clarke and Bruce W. Winter (Grand Rapids, 1992), pp. 161-185. Keith notes that even though Justin may have hinted that figures like Socrates may have been saved, all these figures were in the past and Justin gives no broader hope to his contemporaries, "Nor did Justin believe in any category of contemporaries who had never heard the gospel and yet would be saved since they remained faithful to the light they had been given; for Justin thought every nation had in fact heard the gospel (*Dial. C. Tryth.* 117)" (p. 172 f.). This optimistic ethos cannot be simply assumed, at best it is disputed and at worst it is a misinterpretation, although we should note that Pinnock's interpretation is by no means unique or eccentric. Examples of two other theologians who take Pinnock's line and whom we have mentioned elsewhere in this study are Sullivan, op. cit., pp. 14-16; and Richard Henry Drummond, *Toward a New Age in Christian Theology* (New York, 1985), p. 28.

[39] Warfield, 'The Spirit of God in the Old Testament,' p. 105. For more on the Spirit's omnipresent immanence see Ferguson, op. cit., pp. 15-23; Badcock, op.cit., pp. 8-11; Edwin Palmer, *The Holy Spirit* (Phillipsburg, 1971), pp. 19-29; David F. Wells, *God The Evangelist* (Exeter, 1987), pp. 16-18.

[40] Blocher, op. cit., p. 110.

present in three modes: by power; by knowledge; and by essence.[41] Commenting on this third mode he defines God's presence not circumscriptively (as in bodily presence), nor definitively (as in finite spirits), but repletively - it completely fills all space.[42] He writes:

> Therefore God is said to be repletively everywhere on account of the immensity of his essence, that this should be understood in a most different manner from the mode of being in place of bodies (i.e., beyond the occupation of space, and the multiplication, extension, division of itself, or its mingling with other things, but independently and indivisible). For wherever he is, he is wholly; wholly in all things, yet wholly beyond all; included in no place and excluded from none; and not so much in a place (because finite cannot comprehend infinite) as in himself... This only is to be held as certain [that God's immensity and omnipresence consists] in the simple and to us incomprehensible infinity of divine essence, which is so intimately present with all things that is both everywhere in the world and yet is not included in the world.[43]

Blocher notes that immanence implies transcendence and vica versa: "The pervasive and indwelling presence, *praesentia* with the Latin connotations of power and command, involves no confusion with created being: it *expresses* the other side of transcendence. Both immanence and transcendence tell of the divine *more*, and *beyond*, the true *akbar*"[44] Blocher's trinitarian formulation appropriates transcendence to the Father, immanence to the Spirit, with "the Son, the second Person in trinitarian order, prevent[ing] us from understanding transcendence and immanence in dialectical fashion."[45] Despite his claims to the contrary, without further explanation by Pinnock, it is difficult to know whether in a statement like "...God is in the world and the world is in him"[46] Pinnock is guilty of firstly, disrupting the very careful balance between God's transcendence and immanence and secondly, not delineating clearly enough the boundary between Creator and created.[47]

---

[41] Francis Turretin. *Institutes of Elenctic Theology* Vol. 1 trans. G.M. Giger, ed. J.T. Dennison Jr. (Phillipsburg, 1992), p. 197.
[42] Ibid.
[43] Ibid., p. 198.
[44] Blocher, op. cit., p. 111. Interestingly, Blocher notes that "if etymology were the key to meaning, "panentheism" would be acceptable (Acts 17:28); but, since the word was coined by Krause, it is used to soften resistance to pantheism, to decorate a milder and more timid form of pantheism"(p. 118).
[45] Ibid., p. 123.
[46] Pinnock, *Flame of Love*, p. 61.
[47] Blocher, op. cit., notes that this boundary is not always easy to draw: "He [the Spirit] is so intimately united with created being that many passages remain ambiguous:

Secondly, and more pertinently to our discussion, I noted in my description of Pinnock's view of presence that there was a certain uniformity of God's presence in that all presence is a saving presence. As Pinnock says, "there is no special sacred realm, no sacred-secular split - practically anything in the created order can be sacramental of God's presence."[48] However, orthodox evangelical theology has distinguished a variety of different ways God is present in creation:

> Though God is distinct from the world and may not be identified with it, He is yet present in every part of his creation, not only *per potentiam* but also *per esstiam*. This does not means, however, that He is equally present and present in the same sense in all his creatures. The nature of His indwelling is in harmony with that of his creatures, He does not dwell on earth as He does in heaven, in animals as He does in man, in the inorganic as he does in the organic creation, in the wicked as he does in the pious, nor in the Church as he does in Christ. There is an endless variety in the manner in which He is immanent in His creatures, and in the measure in which they reveal God to those who have eyes to see.[49]

It is crucial to distinguish between God's universal presence in sustaining and preserving all things, His presence to bless, and His presence to punish.[50] When we make these distinction we can say with Turretin: "God is far off from the wicked (as to the special presence of his favour and grace), but is always present with them by his general presence of essence. Where God is, there is indeed his grace originally and subjectively, but not always effectively because its exercise is perfectly free."[51] On this nuanced understanding of presence, we do not have to conclude with Pinnock that God's presence is necessarily a 'redemptive' presence. I think that in his desire to prove universal accessibility, Pinnock has blurred and confused the general

---

do they speak of man's created breath or of God's own like-giving breath? We may never identify the two, but how close they are!"(p. 122).

[48] Pinnock, *Flame of Love*, p. 62.

[49] Berkhof, op. cit., p. 61.

[50] Grudem, op. cit., makes this threefold distinction but claims that most of the time that the Bible talks about God's presence, it is referring not to God's sustaining presence, but God's presence to bless: "For example, it is in this way that we should understand God's presence above the ark of the covenant in the Old Testament. We read of "the ark of the covenant of the Lord of Hosts, who is *enthroned on the cherubim*" (1 Sam. 4:4; cf. Ex. 25:22), a reference to the fact that God made his presence known and acted in a special way to bring blessing and protection to his people at the location he had designated as his throne... It is not that God was not present elsewhere, but rather that here he especially made his presence known and here he especially manifested his character and brought blessing to his people" (p. 176).

[51] Turretin, op. cit., p. 200.

and universal operations of the Spirit in creation and the specific and particular operations of the Spirit in salvation.

Thirdly, while I want to distinguish clearly between God's sustaining presence and God's redemptive presence, it is still possible to speak of God's universal *gracious* presence providing we make one final distinction. Here we come to the role of the Spirit as dispenser of divine grace. Pinnock is not necessarily wrong to link grace with creation and not just re-creation, providing he defines this grace as universal common grace and not particular saving grace. The manifestation of common grace is *essentially* different from salvific grace.[52] While saving grace is seen as being supernatural and flowing from the cross: "Common grace, on the other hand, is natural...it does not remove sin or set men free, but merely restrains the outward manifestations of sin and promotes outward morality and decency, good order in society and civic righteousness, the development of science and art and so on. It works only in the natural, and not the spiritual sphere."[53]

---

[52] I should note a position usually associated with the Protestant Reformed Church, who deny that there is a 'common grace.' For a representative example, see the series of articles by Herman C. Hanko, entitled, 'Another Look at Common Grace' published in nine parts in the *Protestant Reformed Theological Journal* April 1992-April 1997. Hanko gives a good presentation of the Protestant Reformed Position as well as interacting with the classic Reformed statements of common grace. Their argument is that 'grace' in the Bible is always associated with 'salvation' and is not only an attitude of God, but an attribute: it always achieves its end. In this view, God shows no grace or favour to reprobate humanity. It is argued by Hanko, 'Another Look at Common Grace (3) What is Grace?' in *Protestant Reformed Theological Journal* April, 1993, pp. 28-44, that grace is always rooted in ethical goodness and perfection (Prov. 22:11; Ps. 45:2; Eph. 4:29; Col. 4:6)[p. 33]. Scripture also speaks about certain individuals finding grace in the sight of God (Acts 7:46; Lk. 1:30) But how can this be true when both individuals like David and Mary were in the same sinful state as all humanity? How could God be favourably inclined to them. Hanko writes, "God is favourably inclined to them... because they were ethically perfect for another reason than the kind of people they actually were. They were ethically pure objectively in Christ who died for them so that God sees them in Christ. But that great attitude of God's favour towards them made them ethically pure." (p. 34). For Hanko, what Pinnock and the 'common grace' theologians have confused is grace and providence. God sends rain on just and unjust but this is not grace but His providential presence in His creation. See Hanko, 'Another Look at Common Grace (4) Blessings For All Men?' in *Protestant Reformed Theological Journal* November, 1993, pp. 13-28; and 'Another Look at Common Grace (5) Blessings For All Men?' in *Protestant Reformed Theological Journal*, April, 1994, pp. 21-44.

[53] Louis Berkhof, *Systematic Theology* (Grand Rapids, 1976), p. 439. It is wrong to state that all who posit a non-saving 'common grace,' believe its source to be solely in creation. There has been much discussion as to the relationship between 'common grace' and the atonement: see Berkhof, op. cit., pp. 437- 439; Grudem, op. cit., p. 657f. John Murray believed that 'common grace' was a non-salvific benefit of the cross. In 'The Atonement and the Free-offer of the Gospel' in *Collected Writings of John Murray*

In the doctrine of common grace, God does not let the effects of the Fall go unchecked but restrains Mankind by common grace. The relationship between common grace and Christ's cosmic and epistemological revelation is outlined by Hodge: "'Common grace' is the restraining and persuading influences of the Holy Spirit acting...through the natural light of reason and of conscience, heightening the natural moral effect of such truth upon the understanding, conscience, and heart. It involves no change of heart, but simply an enhancement of the natural powers of the truth."[54] Common grace enables human beings to see God's revelation in creation and in this sense this revelation is itself a fruit of common grace as it gives human beings a rationality and makes understanding possible. However, general revelation is epistemologically inadequate because it can only speak of God as Creator and not of God as Re-creator. The act of re-creation has to deal with the penalty of sin as well as establishing a new creation. Here we see a new activity of Word and Spirit, the particular act of re-creation.[55]

(Edinburgh, 1976) Vol. 1, he writes, "The non-elect enjoy many benefits that accrue *from* the atonement but they do not participate *of* the atonement." (p. 69). See also his paper, 'Common Grace' in *Collected Writings of John Murray* Vol. 2 (Edinburgh, 1976), pp. 93-123. Bruce Demarest also sees two purposes in the atonement, "The universal intent of Christ's death mediates general benefits for all people: preservation in existence, the common blessings of life, restraint of evil, an objective provision sufficient for all, and the future resurrection of the body. The particular intent of Christ's death imparts saving benefits to the 'sheep' *viz*., ransom, redemption, and reconciliation," in 'General and Special Revelation,' p. 204. Whether the source of common grace is believed to be creation and/or atonement, both positions are definite that common grace is a 'non-salvific grace' and to symbolize this, the doctrine is usually thought of as belonging to creation related doctrine and not to soteriology proper.

[54] A. A. Hodge, *Outlines of Theology* Ch. 28, section 13, quoted in Murray, 'Common Grace,' p. 95f. For Demarest, op. cit., it is the combination of general revelation and common grace which explains the presence of other religions: "On the basis of God's universal general revelation and common enabling grace, undisputed truths about God, man, and sin lie embedded to varying degrees in the non-Christian religions. In addition to elements of truth, the great religions of the world frequently display a sensitivity to the spiritual dimension of life, a persistence in devotion, a readiness to sacrifice, and sundry virtues both personal (gentleness, serenity of temper) and social (concern for the poor, nonviolence). But in spite of these positive features, natural man, operating in the context of natural religion and lacking special revelation, possesses a fundamentally false understanding of spiritual truth" (p. 259). I believe that this link between common grace, general revelation and the presence of other religions is an area that demands further investigation by evangelicals. I will mention this point again at the end of this study.

[55] If I want to argue for an epistemological *perichoresis* in special revelation, then must I say that the Trinity is perceivable in general revelation? To be consistent it would seem that I have to say yes. This is a very contentious and complicated issue but I can make a few brief observations. Firstly, it must be noted that Demarest, op. cit., in his

WORD AND SPIRIT IN RE-CREATION

In the previous chapter I argued for the particularity of saving revelation, it was not universally given but limited to a particular people. I want to argue that the same must be said of the Spirit's redemptive activity. Kuyper reit-

---

otherwise comprehensive survey of general revelation, makes no mention of this area. He has quite a positive view of the epistemological content of general revelation and notes twenty characteristics of God that can be discerned in general revelation. However in this list there is no mention of the fact that there is plurality in the one God. If triunity is a fundamental and basic truth about God, then it is strange that there is no mention of this fact. Similar to the distinction he makes between the external presence of the Spirit among his people in the Old Testament as opposed to the internal Spirit within his people in the New Testament, Gerald Bray in 'The *Filioque* Clause in History and Theology' *Tyndale Bulletin* 34 (1983), pp. 91-145, draws a sharp distinction between the work of the Trinity in creation and redemption: "The work of creation is external to the Trinity, but the work of redemption is internal. This is why unregenerate man can have some knowledge of God even to the extent of acknowledging Him as a personal being, yet remain in ignorance of the Trinity" (p. 142). What does Bray mean here by the terms 'external' and 'internal'? This is hard to discern as I do not think Bray means that redemption is somehow 'necessary' for God. Possibly by the word 'internal' he is referring to the believers' intimate relationship to the Godhead when united to Christ. Whatever his meaning, Bray's comment demonstrates yet again the difficulties in mediating the axioms of continuity and discontinuity. While it is true to say that the work of the Trinity in creation is distinct from that of re-creation, it is not entirely separate and discontinuous because firstly it is the same Persons who accomplish their appropriate roles in both works, and secondly, because the background of re-creation is creation, as it is creation that is renewed. Colin Gunton hints at a possible answer to the question. Firstly, he believes that general revelation does not operate in parallel with biblical revelation but is derived from it: because of our sin we can only see general revelation through the 'spectacles' of the Bible and the eyes of faith. There is therefore a distinction between the objectivity of revelation and the subjective ability to appropriate this revelation. Added to this subjective blindness due to the effects of sin, I could also add that objective revelation has also been marred significantly by sin. However in spite of these significant provisos, Gunton notes that "The world reveals the hand that made it in the remarkable combination of unity and diversity, of relationality and particularity, that it manifests, marks that can be recognised by their analogy to the unity and diversity of the Triune God...the plurality in unity of the triune revelation enables us to do justice to the diversity, richness and openness of the world without denying its unity in relativist versions of pluralism" Colin Gunton, 'The Trinity, Natural Theology, and a Theology of Nature' in ed. Vanhoozer, *The Trinity in a Pluralistic Age*, p. 103. Could it be that there are trinitarian motifs in creation, in, for example, concepts such as family, society? Even through the prism of special revelation, there may only be glimmerings of the triunity of God in creation. However this is very different from saying there are no glimmerings at all. On this issue the difference would appear to be quantative rather than qualitative, although on the issue of redemption there is a crucial qualitative distinction because while general revelation may reveal a hint of the Trinity, it does not reveal the Trinitarian God as Redeemer. For this truth, special revelation is essential.

erates what I have just said regarding the divine presence noting that omnipresence refers to local presence in space, not to the world of spirits:

> God's omnipresence has reference to all space, but not to every spirit. Since God is omnipresent, it does not follow that He also dwells in the spirit of Satan. Hence it is clear that the Holy Spirit can be omnipresent without dwelling in every human soul; and that He can descend without changing place, and yet enter a soul hitherto unoccupied by Him; and that He was present among Israel and among the Gentiles, and yet manifested Himself among the former and not among the latter. From this it follows that in the spiritual world He can come among Israel, not having been among them before, and that he manifested Himself among them less powerfully and in another way than on and before the day of Pentecost.[56]

This particular manifestation of the Spirit is distinguished by external and internal activities. Firstly, there are the theocratic gifts of the Spirit given to God's people: "The theocratic Spirit appears to be represented as the executive of the Godhead within the sacred nation, the divine power working in the nation for the protection, governing, instruction and leading of the people to its destined goal."[57] The most prominent evidence of this activity is the gift of prophecy.[58] These gifts are temporary, they come and go as the Spirit wills. However, as well as this theocratic activity, there is also an internal work of the Spirit by which he renews and sanctifies the people's hearts.[59] This activity is that of saving grace. In the framework of Christocentric continuity that I outlined in the previous chapter, there is not only a continuity in the propositional element of saving faith (i.e. a confession of Christ), but also in the nature of this salvation. The re-creating Spirit was at work in the hearts of Old Testament believers, applying "the objective truth of God's revelation to the hearts of God's people in such a way that they are given eyes to see that truth and ears to hear and faith to believe."[60] The point I wish to make is that in the Old Testament one can see in embryonic form, the relationship between the Spirit and revelation. In the sphere of creation, the universal operations of the Spirit accompany universal revelation. However in the sphere of re-creation, the saving operations of the Spirit accompany special revelation. Salvation always consists of saving grace through saving revelation. Spirit and the Word are linked as both are equally needed for salvation. Pinnock's error is that he confuses and con-

---

[56] Kuyper, op. cit., p. 118f.
[57] Warfield, 'The Spirit of God in the Old Testament,' p. 115.
[58] Ibid., p. 114; Waite, op. cit., p. 18-20.
[59] Warfield, 'The Spirit of God in the Old Testament,' pp. 119-129; Waite, op. cit., pp. 20-22; Kuyper, op. cit., p. 119; Ferguson, op. cit., pp. 23-26.
[60] Herman Hanko, *God's Everlasting Covenant of Grace* (Grand Rapids, 1988), p. 48.

flates these universal non-salvific operations with the particular saving operations.

What is significant in this summary of the Spirit's activity in the Old Testament, and a point I began to make in the previous chapter, is that similar to the issue of revelation, the salvific activities of the Spirit have a Christocentric climax and fulfilment. Strangely, the incompleteness of the pre-incarnational dispensations of the Spirit can highlight for us the reality of the Spirit's work in Christ and make sense of a statement like John 7:39 "Up to that time the Spirit had not been given, since Jesus had not yet been glorified."[61] Concerning the theocratic activity, Warfield notes:

> all the theocratic endowments that had been given separately to others unite upon him; so that all previous organs of the Spirit appear but as partial types of Him to whom as we are told in the New Testament, God "giveth not the Spirit by measure" (John iii:34)... By Him accordingly the kingdom is consummated... His endowment also was not for himself but for the kingdom; it, too, was official.[62]

More important than this theocratic activity is the idea that when the Messiah comes, there will be a new outpouring of the Holy Spirit where he will abide in the heart of the believer. This is part of Christ's function as Mediator of the covenant. In Christ "all the mediatorial externalities are removed, and the substance of the law itself lives in the heart of the new covenant participant."[63] Because Christ is the mediator of the covenant we can know God im-mediately: "in the coming of Jesus, the Day of the Spirit had finally dawned."[64] The paradox is that what had been particular to Israel and those ingrafted to Israel, now becomes 'universally particular' in the sense that the Spirit is poured upon all flesh. Here Kuyper makes a crucial point. He notes that whereas in the Old Testament the Spirit works in a preparatory way on individual persons, on the day of Pentecost this no longer suffices "for His particular operation, on and after that day, consists in extending of His operation to a company of men organically united."[65] This organic relation is the body of Christ:

> The mild showers of the Holy Spirit descended upon Israel of old in drops of saving grace... So it continued until the coming of Christ. then there

---

[61] Both Don Carson, *The Gospel of John* (Leicester, 1991), p. 329; and Hanko, op. cit., p. 180, translate this verse even more starkly by stating that a more accurate translation is 'for the Spirit was not yet.'
[62] Warfield, 'The Spirit of God in the Old Testament,' p. 119.
[63] Robertson, op. cit., p. 292.
[64] Ferguson, op. cit., p. 33.
[65] Kuyper, op. cit., p. 120.

came a change; for He gathered the full stream of the Holy Spirit for us all, *in His own Person*. With him all saints are connected by the channels of faith... Hence there can be no doubt that there exists a mystic union between Christ and believers which works by means of an organic connection, uniting the Head and the members in a for us invisible and incomprehensible manner. By means of this organic union, the Holy Spirit was poured out on Pentecost from Christ the Head into us, the members of the body.[66]

I will mention in more detail the idea of the believer's mystical union with Christ shortly. The point I wish to make is that in this new activity of the Spirit we see, possibly at its most acute, the discontinuity between the Spirit's work in preparation and his work after Christ's glorification. Both Kuyper and Gaffin note that while the Old Testament believers were regenerated, justified and sanctified proleptically, the mode of covenant fellowship in which they experienced these blessings was provisional and lacked the finality and permanence of union with (the glorified Christ). The momentous, unprecedented reality of this union can hardly be overemphasised: "it involves a relationship to the covenanting God that is nothing less than eschatological in its intimacy and perfections."[67] While noting the manifold activity of the Spirit before Pentecost, it is the 'newness' or 'radicality' of the dispensation of the Spirit after Christ's exaltation that enables us to make sense of John's words that up until that time 'the Spirit was not yet.'

We have already noted that Jesus received the Spirit without measure and that the Spirit prepared Christ for his threefold role of prophet, priest and king. However as well as Christ receiving the Spirit, there is also the idea that Jesus will dispense the Spirit. Jesus himself describes what the work of the Spirit is to be in the Farewell Discourses of John. As the Paraclete, the role of the Spirit is to bear witness to the Son and serve as his advocate. The Spirit's task is one of testimony, but it is not to testify concerning Himself, but concerning Christ. However is it possible to say more, for not only is the Spirit's role to testify concerning Christ, but it appears that the Spirit's role must be seen as part of the continuing work of Christ? As Gaffin notes:

> The work of the Spirit is not some addendum to the work of Christ. It is not some more or less independent sphere of activity that goes beyond or supplements what Christ has done... Rather the coming of the Spirit brings to light not only that Christ *has* done certain things but that he, as

---

[66] Ibid., p. 123.
[67] Richard B. Gaffin Jr. *Perspectives on Pentecost: New Testament Teaching on the Gifts of the Holy Spirit* (Grand Rapids, 1979), p. 36

the source of eschatological life, *now* lives and is at work in the church. By and in the Spirit Christ reveals himself as present.[68]

The Spirit is the Spirit of Christ, a point that Paul clearly brings out in Romans 8:9-10. There is an economic (not ontological) equivalence between the Spirit and Christ in the heart of the believer: "With respect to his economic ministry to us, the Spirit has been imprinted with the character of Jesus. This is precisely what it means for Jesus to send *allos parakletos*."[69] The Spirit's ministry then is inextricably linked to the ministry of Christ, and is in reality defined by the ministry of Christ. It is Christ who dwells in the believer by the Spirit. Vanhoozer notes that taking into account the diverse relationship between Father, Son and Spirit "configures the Spirit as the deputy of Christ rather than as an independent itinerant evangelist."[70] This Christocentricity defines the Spirit's role in salvation.

The above insight seems to be neglected in Pinnock's inclusivism for it is difficult to see in the 'faith principle' how the Spirit performs the role of Christ's advocate and witness. Ironically, Pinnock himself highlights this testifying function of the Spirit. In discussing the title 'Spirit' he notes that the Spirit takes no special name and chooses to remain anonymous: "Deferentially he turns away from himself and graciously points to the others."[71] But how can the Spirit point to Christ where Christ is not known? In reality, Pinnock's actual construal of the relationship between Spirit and Christ is shown in his argument about Christ being the criterion of the Spirit's activity. Here he appears to reverse the configuration of the Spirit witnessing to Christ as it is Christ who becomes the advocate and witness of the Spirit.

Is it possible to re-enforce this point further by commenting on the role of the Spirit in the immanent Trinity? Here I wish to return to the *filioque* debate by noting one of Macleod's arguments in favour of the clause. Macleod strongly affirms the *homoousioi* and *autotheos* and rejects any notion of causality or derivation in the Godhead that would lead to subordinationism. For him the idea of the Father as the *fons deitatis* implies subordination and so he rejects such language. He realises though that in affirming the *filioque* he may lay himself open to the charge of subordinationism because neither the Father nor Son proceed from the Spirit. He therefore asks whether it is possible to speak of a procession of the Son from the Father and the Spirit. He notes, as I have already noted, the dynamic role of the Spirit in the life of Christ. Secondly, and more importantly, he ponders on John 16:14 where Jesus states that the Paraclete will bring him glory.

---

[68] Ibid., p. 19f.
[69] Ferguson, op. cit., p. 55.
[70] Vanhoozer, op. cit., p. 66.
[71] Pinnock, *Flame of Love*, p. 26.

Macleod asks whether this economic statement is a revelation of the immanent Trinity. He says:

> If the Father begets the Son, and if from the Father and the Son together there proceeds the Holy Spirit, why may we not introduce as a third movement 'the Spirit glorifies the Father and the Son'? This brings symmetry into Trinitarian relations. Without that, we have one person (the Holy Spirit) who is always a recipient and never a doner.[72]

Macleod notes that Barth could not accept this idea as for him it would imply a further notion of 'an origin of the Father from the Son and from the Spirit.' However Macleod believes that such a statement is only problematical if procession and begetting imply origination, something that he himself rejects. He notes:

> Begetting and proceeding are descriptions of relationships, not accounts of origins. The subsistences are as eternal as the essence itself...it is clear that the Father owes it to the Son and the Spirit that he is what he is (Father) as much as they owe to him and to each other that they are what they are (respectively Spirit and Son). Only thus can we say that *none* is greater and *none* is lesser. The Father begets the Son. The Father and Son breathe the Spirit. The Spirit glorifies the Father and Son.[73]

Bringing this into the sphere of interest of this study, I would like to make two points. Firstly, I want to suggest that in the *ad extra* and *ad intra* there is an economic/functional subordinationism. The Spirit's role is one of glorification, His peculiar or proper role is to point to the other two Persons, and to illuminate what they have done. Indeed if we want to argue that the Persons are identified by the functions they perform, then this role of the Spirit defines who He is as a Person. To deny this functional subordinationism is to de-Personalize the Spirit. Therefore we must affirm that the presence of the Spirit is the presence of the Son (*allos parakletos*) and the presence of the Father. This simply returns us to the notion of *perichoresis*: "to have the Spirit is to have Christ; to have Christ is to have the Spirit. Not to have the Spirit of Christ is to lack Christ. To have the Spirit of Christ is to be indwelt by Christ."[74]

Secondly, the teleological theme of the glorification of Christ returns me to the question of the particularity of the atonement. I have been arguing that the Spirit's peculiar role is to glorify Christ. Mirroring this action is Reformed theology's emphasis that the ultimate purpose of human beings

---

[72] Macleod, *The Person of Christ*, p. 148.
[73] Ibid., p. 149.
[74] Ferguson, op. cit., p. 54.

(and of everything for that matter) is to glorify God (*soli Deo gloria*), God being most glorified through His redemptive acts when He brings to life that which was dead.[75] It can be argued, therefore, that God's work in Christ is the apex of God being glorified. However Pinnock's inclusivism dilutes this principle somewhat. As Barrett notes:

> Redemptive history was initiated for the glory of God. If the 'hard' inclusivists' schema is permitted then logically the concept of 'redemptive history' focussed upon the uniqueness of Israel and Jesus Christ is, to all intents and purposes, abolished. If salvation is obtainable *apart* from the outworking of special revelation through God's covenant with Israel and subsequently the gospel, then the particularity of the Christ event is no longer seen as decisive... God is not glorified *in* Christ as was God's intention through redemptive history (Jn. 13:31; 14:12; 17:1). It is hard to escape the impression that in following the inclusivist line, the incarnation has been robbed of its unique significance.[76]

The Spirit and the Word Agraphon and Engraphon: Pinnock's Inclusivism and Sola Scriptura.

I have been arguing on Trinitarian grounds that perichoretically where there is the Spirit, so there is the Son and the Father, and that economically the role of the Spirit is to bear witness to the Son and glorify him. The question to be asked is this: How is the Spirit able to bear witness to the Son, and how is Christ present to the human individual? The Reformed tradition has argued that just as the Spirit and the Word *agraphon* (that is the Second Person of the Trinity) are inextricably linked, so are the Spirit and the Word *engraphon* (that is Scripture).[77]

---

[75] On the subject of God's own glory being the ultimate purpose for both human beings and God see John Piper, *Let the Nations Be Glad: The Supremacy of God in Missions* (Grand Rapids, 1994), pp. 15-30. The first question of the Shorter Westminster Catechism clearly displays this teleology of glorification. It is possible to say that this idea of God's self-glorification being the chief end of everything does not descend into a selfish egocentricism as Pinnock believes because of the Trinitarian nature of God and the fellowship of the Persons which means that each glorifies the other. See also J.I. Packer, *Concise Theology: A Guide to Historic Christian Beliefs* (Leicester, 1993), pp. 59-61.

[76] John K. Barrett, 'Does Inclusivist Theology Undermine Evangelism?' in *The Evangelical Quarterly* 70:3 (1998), p. 241.

[77] For a detailed analysis see Richard A. Muller, *Post-Reformation Reformed Dogmatics: Volume 2 - Holy Scripture: The Cognitive Foundation of Theology* (Grand Rapids, 1993), pp. 147-231.

Letham argues that the Word *engraphon* can be seen as an aspect of Christ's office as prophet.[78] Christ assures he will be present to the disciples through the Spirit. I have already commented on the economic equivalence between Christ and the Spirit. How, though, is this presence manifested? Here again it is important to distinguish between the objective and subjective activity of the Spirit. Objectively, the same Spirit that theocratically inspired the prophets in the Old Testament to speak about the coming Messiah, the same Spirit who was intimately associated with Christ throughout his ministry, is now the one who inspires the writers of Scriptures to testify about Christ:

> In terms of the economy of salvation and behind that, the relations between the persons of the Godhead, the Bible is a work in which the Son shares also. In terms of the history of salvation, Scripture throughout witnesses to the Son incarnate... It is the incarnate Son himself who, exalted at God's right hand, has sent the Spirit to his church, the same Spirit who is the primary author of Scripture.[79]

Because the Spirit inspires the Scriptures we can say that they are the Word of God. In this sense although Christ is sufficient for salvation, we must say also that the Scriptures are sufficient, because we only learn of Christ through the Scriptures. This does not mean a competition between Christ and the Scriptures because "In trusting ourselves to the Saviour, we believe, trust and obey his Word to us, given by the Holy Spirit through the mouths of prophets and apostles."[80] Trueman comments on John Owen's view of this:

> The Son reveals the Father, and that revelation is appropriated by human beings through the work of the Spirit. Because of the close connection between Word *agraphon* and Word *engraphon*, the Scriptures can act as a cognitive substitute in this arrangement for the second person of the Trinity and thus stand as the revelation of the Father witnessed to by the Spirit. For Owen, the Holy Spirit is preeminently the Spirit of Christ and is thus to be understood as working within the framework established by the person and work of Christ... Owen's Trinitarianism means that Spirit and Word, subjective and objective, must be held together.[81]

---

[78] Letham, op. cit., pp. 100-102.
[79] Ibid., p. 101.
[80] Ibid., p. 102.
[81] Trueman, op. cit., p. 78f.

Owen grounds this in a strong affirmation of the *filioque*, but I believe that an equally strong affirmation of *perichoresis* could equally be grounds for this connection.

It is possible to say that not only are the Scriptures sufficient for salvation but that they are essential because they must be seen as not only containing the gospel of Christ, but are themselves part of the gospel. This is because through the Spirit's inspiration, the events surrounding the life, death and resurrection of Christ are given a divine interpretation. Because of the Spirit's "confluent action"[82] upon the biblical writers, we know not only the bare facts that a man called Jesus lived and died but the significance of these events for our salvation. This relates back to what was said earlier concerning the inextricable link between God's acts and God's words.[83]

This is not all though. Once again I return to the distinction between the objective and subjective. The Spirit objectively inspired the Scriptures so they are the very Word of God. Now the Spirit subjectively illuminates the Word so the believer is able to understand the truths contained within it. This is not considered to be a new act of revelation or inspiration but one of enlightenment: "The sum of the matter is, then, that when the Holy Spirit comes into people's lives he enlightens them, gives them understanding, teaches them, opens their eyes, removes the veil from their hearts, and softens their hearts so that they can know the things of the Spirit of God. Without him, man is blind to see the truths of revelation."[84] In saying this, I are merely re-affirming the Spirit's role as Paraclete, witnessing concerning Christ and thereby glorifying him.

I believe that the above argument raises serious questions regarding Pinnock's inclusivism because his argument concerning the salvation of the unevangelised is based on the divorce of Word and Spirit. I also believe that this separation of Word and Spirit is a decidedly unevangelical position to take. However, there is another issue that must be addressed; that is the exclusivity of the tie between the Word and the Spirit. With such a strong link between Christ and the medium of knowledge we have of Christ (Scripture), the conclusion that has been reached by many evangelicals, and especially Reformed Evangelicals, is that the Spirit cannot be divorced from the Word written, just as it cannot be divorced from the Word incarnate. The task of the Spirit of the Father and Son is to bear witness to Christ as the revelation of the Father. The Spirit bears witness through the Bible and does not work apart from the Word. Badcock notes that for Reformation theology: "...the Spirit can only be named or known, and his presence in some sense validated, by reference to other things. If experience of the

---

[82] Wells, op. cit., p. 31.
[83] See p. 146.
[84] Palmer, op. cit., p. 58.

Spirit comes through the written and preached Word...if these are, in Luther's vivid terms, the "very bridge by which the Holy Spirit can come" - then it is pointless to attempt to speak of the Spirit in any other way."[85]

This same point can be stated from a different perspective. Reformed theology especially speaks about the 'means of grace'.[86] Within the sphere of 'special grace' which we described above, the ordinary way the Spirit acts is not immediately, but mediately through particular means: "God is a God of order, who in the operation of His grace ordinarily employs the means which He Himself has ordained."[87] It is the written Word of God which is the principle means of grace: "the Reformers maintained the Word alone is not sufficient to work faith and conversion; that the Holy Spirit can, but does not ordinarily work without the Word; and therefore in the work of redemption the Word and Spirit work together."[88]

We therefore have two issues: one concerning the relation between the Spirit and revelation, the second concerning the Spirit and the mediation of grace. It is no coincidence that these are precisely the two issues involved in two of the most important ongoing debates within evangelicalism, the nature of biblical authority,[89] and the split between the charismatics and cessationists.[90] Pinnock's positions on these issues are well known and have been treated extensively elsewhere.[91]

---

[85] Badcock, op. cit., p. 95. Historically, with regards the Magesterial Reformers, Badcock contextualises this issue within the debate between the Magesterial Reformers and 'radicals' such as Munzter (pp. 86-95). Similarly Trueman, op. cit. in his exposition of Owen, notes that his connection between Spirit and Word arose from his debates with the Quakers who "in their emphasis upon the direct leading of the Spirit and the 'inner light' tended to downgrade the role of Scripture as a source of knowledge of God and his leading"(p. 67).

[86] For example, Berkhof, op. cit., pp. 604-615; Hoeksema, op. cit., pp. 631-655.

[87] Berkhof, op. cit., p. 608. Note below the qualifications of this, p. 254 n. 96.

[88] Ibid., p. 611. To the criticism that this denies the freedom of the Spirit, Gaffin, op. cit., notes that what is at stake here is not the issue of freedom "but the pattern by which God chooses to reveal his Word to the church, the *structure* or *order* which the Spirit has set for himself in his *freedom*"(p. 118).

[89] For a representative survey see Grudem, *Systematic Theology*, pp. 47-138; Demarest and Lewis, op. cit., pp. 131-171.

[90] Very broadly, this issue revolves around firstly, the question as to how God speaks today; and secondly, the presence (or not) in today's church of miraculous spiritual gifts. Charismatics argue that New Testament gifts such as healing, prophecy and tongues are present in today's church; cessationists believe such gifts ceased with the death of the Apostles and the completion of the canon of Scripture. They argue that charismatics do not properly distinguish between the *historia salutis* and the *ordo salutis*. Since the canon was completed, the Spirit only works through Scripture. For a general survey of the main issues and protagonists involved see Grudem, *Systematic Theology,* pp. 1016-1047; idem *The Gift of Prophecy in the New Testament* (Eastbourne, 1988); ed. Grudem, *Are Miraculous Gifts for Today? Four Views* (Leicester, 1996). This book is a dialogue

Roennfeldt in his PhD thesis concerning Pinnock's bibliology, notes that Pinnock possibly fails to adequately distinguish between revelation, inspiration, and illumination: "Conservative theologians have customarily differentiated between divine revelation, the inspiration of the Scriptures, and the illumination of the Bible by the Holy Spirit, in order to protect the uniqueness and normativeness of Scripture as once-for-all inscripturation of revelation."[92] Pinnock is a fervent advocate of charismatic renewal,[93] and these two points put together pose an interesting question as to how one is to assess him. Erickson comments (possibly too charitably):

> One does not want to be unfair to Pinnock here, for it is apparent that his aim is not to propound a Barthian view of revelation but to revitalize the evangelical doctrine of illumination of Scripture by the Holy Spirit. Yet, at some points, he clearly goes beyond the traditional form of that doctrine, insisting that what the Holy Spirit speaks today is not limited to the

---

between four positions: cessationist, 'open but cautious;' third wave; and Pentecostal/charismatic; John Yates, 'How Does God Speak to us Today?: Biblical Anthropology and the Witness of the Holy Spirit' in *Churchman* 107/2 (1993), pp. 102-129. For a survey from a cessationist theologian, see R. Fowler White 'Does God Speak Today Apart From The Bible?' in *The Coming Evangelical Crisis. Current Challenges to the Authority of Scripture and the Gospel.* ed. John H. Armstrong (Chicago, 1996), pp. 77-91. Two of the more important treatments representing both sides are: on the charismatic side, Jack Deere, *Surprised by the Power of the Holy Spirit* (Grand Rapids, 1993); and on the cessationist side, O. Palmer Robertson, *The Final Word* (Edinburgh, 1993). It should also be noted that "there is a large 'middle' group with respect to this question, a group of 'mainstream evangelicals' who are neither charismatics nor Pentecostals on the one hand, nor 'cessationists' on the other, but are simply undecided, and unsure if this question can be decided from Scripture." Grudem, *Systematic Theology*, p. 1031.

[91] In his biographical essay, 'Clark H. Pinnock: A Theological Odyssey' *Christian Scholars Review* 3 (1990), pp. 252-270, Robert Rakestraw comments that, "Pinnock has become more known for his doctrine than for any other of theological thought"(p. 255). The most important work on Pinnock's bibliology is Ray C. W. Roennfeldt's PhD study, *Clark H. Pinnock on Biblical Authority. An Evolving Position* (Michigan, 1993) who analyses the changes in Pinnock's bibliology throughout his career. Interestingly his conclusion is that Pinnock's move from an 'intrinsicalist' inerrancy position to a more 'functional' inerrancy position is due to his paradigm shift from Calvinism to Arminianism, the latter allowing for more of a balance between divine initiative and human response (p. 364). Pinnock's most recent work on Scripture is *The Scripture Principle* (San Francisco, 1984). See also Millard Erickson, *The Evangelical Left. Encountering Postconservative Evangelical Theology* (Grand Rapids, 1997), pp. 78f.

[92] Roennfeldt, op. cit., p. 335.

[93] In his writing of *Flame of Love*, Pinnock acknowledges the influence the Toronto Blessing has had on him: "The flow of grace and love in this remarkable awakening can only be marveled at."(p. 250 n. 10).

original intent of the text, and that revelation may come to us, not merely through the Bible, but through contemporary prophets as well.[94]

The point I wish to make concerning Pinnock's inclusivism is that in these intra-evangelical debates, all parties have agreed (albeit implicitly) that the context of discussion falls within the realms of special revelation and special grace. These nuanced and complex arguments revolve around how God speaks in His special revelation and whether or not He speaks today apart from the Bible and if He does whether this is revelation as authoritative as Scripture, or a more fallible revelation, or something else completely. Regarding the unevangelised, if one believes that the means of the Spirit's grace and special revelation is today solely confined to the Word,[95] then the most likely conclusion must be that God does not reveal Himself through the medium of visions, dreams or theophanies and so the unevangelised, that is those people who have not come into contact with the Word cannot be saved.[96] However, and still within the boundaries 'special revelation' if

---

[94] Millard J. Erickson, *The Evangelical Left. Encountering Postconservative Evangelical Theology* (Grand Rapids, 1997), p. 79.

[95] Hoeksema, op. cit., narrows this even further by insisting that the Word is not a means of grace, but only the Word *preached*: "a preacher is not a person who merely speaks concerning Christ, but one through whom it pleases Christ Himself to speak and to cause His own voice to be heard by His people" (p. 638).

[96] Hence the position known as restrictivism. Having said this, I do not want to give the impression that from the Reformed cessationist position, the issue is totally unambiguous. There are two areas that need further clarification and explanation as to whether they could allow the possibility that the unevangelised can be saved. Firstly, theologians like Berkhof, op. cit. are careful to note that although God 'ordinarily' works through the means of grace, and is pleased to bind Himself to these means, He is free to work without these means and in fact does in the case of infant baptism (p. 608). The case of 'ordinary' as opposed to 'extraordinary' is also indicated in the Westminster Confession of Faith 5/3 "God, in his ordinary providence, maketh use of means, yet is free to work without, above, and against them at his pleasure;" and 10/3: "Elect infants, dying in infancy, are regenerated, and saved by Christ, through the Spirit, who worketh when, and where, and how he pleaseth: so also are all other elect persons who are incapable of being outwardly called by the ministry of the Word." Secondly, and related to the first point is the intra-Reformed debate of whether in the *ordo salutis* in terms of logical priority the Spirit always works through the instrumentality of the Word or works immediately, that is not through these means. The issue here would be whether this logical distinction could be applied temporally, that is could God regenerate (and therefore save), someone and there be a temporal gap before this seed blossoms. For a fascinating interpretation of Jonathan Edwards in this regard see, Anri Morimoto, *Jonathan Edwards and the Catholic Vision Salvation* (Pennsylvania, 1995), pp. 61-69. I briefly describe Morimoto's argument in Appendix 1, p. 313f. The Reformed view of paedo-baptism adds a further dimension to this debate, for it is believed that covenant children are immediately regenerated, although within the bounds of the visible church and therefore

one holds that the Spirit's activity is not solely confined to the Word *engraphon*, then there may be the possibility of arguing that in certain circumstances the Spirit might reveal Himself through another 'special' medium other than Scripture.[97]

Concerning Pinnock, the point I wish to make, is that his inclusivism would appear to take these issues into a new arena because he does not distinguish between special and general revelation or common and special grace: "practically anything in the created order can be sacramental of God's presence. God is present to us in the creation, and the world is a natural sacrament."[98] Again the importance of the Spirit is emphasised: "Revelation is pregnant, and development arises from the presence of the Spirit in community. There are authoritative sources - Scripture and tradition, ecumenical councils, reason and experience, elders and bishops - but authority is ultimately charismatic. There is no law of development other than dependence of the Spirit."[99]

We must ask whether Pinnock in his merging of different types of revelation and grace, has departed significantly from a central belief of evangelicalism, for the criticism I levelled at him concerning the separation of Christ and Spirit seems equally applicable concerning the Spirit and the Word:

> While desiring to hold to Scripture as authority… Pinnock's theology of religions portrays salvific revelation in the realm of history, outside special normative revelation. God salvifically reveals Himself, at least indirectly, in ordinary *and* special events of universal history. This salvific revelation is uncovered by the 'faith principle'. A question related to this version of 'neoorthodoxy' may be asked. If salvation is possible outside the Bible, why is the Bible treated *as if* it were special at all?[100]

What does this say about Pinnock's understanding of *sola Scriptura*? If cessationist evangelicals criticise charismatics for compromising this foundational belief[101] and of being guilty of a vague mysticism that devalues the primacy of the Word,[102] how is one to assess Pinnock where in his pneumatology everything is a medium to convey saving grace? What we are seeing is that Pinnock's pneumatology, developed to prove his belief in the univer-

---

within the ministry of the Word. For the terms of this debate see Murray, *Redemption Accomplished and Applied*, pp. 95-105; Hoeksema, op. cit., pp. 635-655; Jones, op. cit., pp. 113-115; Berkhof, op. cit., pp. 604-615.

[97] Again this is another area that needs further research.
[98] Pinnock, *Flame of Love*, p. 62.
[99] Ibid., p. 232.
[100] Richard, op. cit., p. 142 n. 32.
[101] See, for example, White, op. cit.
[102] See Yates, op. cit., p. 107.

sality axiom, has significant ramifications not only for the doctrine of the Trinity, but for the doctrine of revelation, a defining tenet of evangelicalism.

Spirit and Word in the *Ordo Salutis* and the Application of Redemption

So far in this chapter, I have mainly been concentrating on the 'objective' *historia salutis*, that is the events and Trinitarian relationships before, during and immediately after the incarnation. I have argued that although the Spirit was intimately associated with these events, He has a specific role of witnessing to perform, a role which with varying levels of clarity can be seen in the Old Testament, in creation and can analogically be applied to the relationships *ad intra*. In this final section I want to bring together several ideas that I have presented in the chapter, and concentrate on what is known as the *ordo salutis* that is the subjective application of these events to believers today, because as Calvin comments: "So long as we are without Christ and separated from him, nothing which he suffered and did for the salvation of the human race is of the least benefit to us."[103] Here I want to show that although the Spirit's role is central to the application of salvation, this role is one of testimony, witness and illumination to Christ, that is, that the whole of the *ordo salutis* is Christocentric in orientation.

Salvation as Union with Christ

What is salvation? Evangelicals have argued that salvation consists of a number of elements: regeneration, effectual calling, faith, repentance, justification, adoption, sanctification, perseverance and glorification. However underlying all these facets and uniting them under a broader rubric is the doctrine of the mystical union with Christ. Grudem defines it as follows: "Union with Christ is a phrase used to summarize several different relationships between believers and Christ, through which Christians receive every benefit of salvation. These relationships include the fact that we are in Christ, Christ is in us, we are like Christ, and we are with Christ"[104] Commenting on Calvin's exploration of this theme, Badcock notes that union with Christ is the context in which the rest of Calvin's soteriology is to be understood "Calvin speaks openly...in this context of a sharing through Christ in the life of God - which is self-evidently far more than the soteriological 'legal fiction' of which he is often accused."[105] My interest in this doctrine is the Spirit's role in this union. Far from playing a minor role, it is

---

[103] John Calvin, *Institutes of the Christian Religion* tr. Henry Beveridge (London, 1949), Bk. 3, Ch.1, Sec.1.
[104] Grudem, op. cit., p. 840.
[105] Badcock, op. cit., p. 100.

the Holy Spirit who effects this union, Christ is present to us by the Spirit. "The Holy Spirit was in a special capacity a part of the Mediator's reward, as such was poured out on the day of Pentecost for the formation of the spiritual body of Jesus Christ. Through the Holy Spirit Christ now dwells in believers, unites them to Himself, and knits them together in a holy unity."[106] There are a number of points I wish to make. Firstly, there appears to be an interesting comparison between union with Christ and Pinnock's espousal of the Orthodox idea of *theosis*, a point evangelicals have recently begun to explore.[107] In my analysis of Pinnock, I commented on the distinction between created and uncreated grace, noting that Pinnock seemed to want to argue for the uncreated idea, that grace is the presence and power of the Spirit in our lives. Union with Christ affirms this idea that believers are changed into the image of Christ. Interestingly Bray makes this point about Calvin in Bray's strong affirmation of the *filioque*:

> Our relationship with the Son is secured by the Holy Spirit, who is the bond by which Christ effectually binds us to Himself. In language that might have been borrowed from Palamas, Calvin says that '...by means of him we become partakers of the divine nature, so as in a manner to feel his quickening energy within us.' What else can this mean but that by the Holy Spirit we share in the uncreated grace of God?[108]

However, while noting this similarity between Calvin and Orthodoxy, there is an important dissimilarity that Bray notes:

> The work of the Holy Spirit is to remake us in the image of Christ so that we might enjoy the benefits of Christ's relationship to the Father. We are not being transformed into God by nature, but being raised into the fellowship of the Trinity as persons united with Christ by faith. If the Holy Spirit is the one who makes this possible, it is obvious that he must have the capacity to do so. If he were remaking us in the image of Christ's nature, as Palamas and his followers maintain, it would not be necessary for him to share in Christ's hypostasis. But according to Calvin He is remaking us in the image of Christ's person, so that we may too be sons of God by adoption. To do this, the Holy Spirit must share in the hypostasis of the Son, and therefore proceed from Him.[109]

---

[106] Berkhof, op. cit., p. 450.
[107] See Daniel B. Clendenin, 'Partakers of Divinity: The Orthodox Doctrine of Theosis' in *Journal of the Evangelical Theological Society* 37/3 (Sep. 1994), pp. 365-379; Robert V. Rakestraw, 'Becoming Like God: An Evangelical Doctrine of Theosis' in *Journal of the Evangelical Theological Society* 40/2 (June, 1997), pp. 257-269; Don Fairbairn, 'Salvation as Theosis: The Teaching of Eastern Orthodoxy' in *Themelios* 23/3 (1998), pp. 42-54.
[108] Gerald Bray, 'The *Filioque* Clause...,' p. 140.
[109] Ibid., p. 142.

The seemingly crucial distinction to make between union with Christ and *theosis* is that our transformation in Christ is according to his human nature, not his divine nature: "The goal of the Spirit is transformation into the image of God as that is expressed in Christ's humanity, so that believers become progressively more and more truly and fully human."[110] In this sense evangelicals have preferred to speak of union with Christ and the doctrine of sanctification, rather than the idea of deification. Through the progressive work of the Spirit in the believer, sanctification means that we become more and more like Christ in our lives.[111]

This may be an interesting point to make, but how is it relevant to Pinnock's inclusivism and his claim that people can be saved without confessing Christ? Pinnock's soteriology coheres well with this inclusivism: The universal Spirit offers prevenient grace, the believer explicitly or implicitly allows the Spirit to transform the person, the 'fruits of the Spirit' become evident in this person's life and so we can say that they are not-yet Christians awaiting messianic salvation. This process is one of mutuality, both God and human beings co-operate. While I wish to agree with Pinnock concerning the presence of the Spirit as the uncreated grace of God (although stressing union with Christ and sanctification rather than *theosis*), my contention is that Pinnock's soteriology is too narrow in its definition. Still under the broad rubric of union with Christ, Evangelicals and especially those from the Reformed tradition have stressed the distinction between sanctification that is an internal work of the Spirit, and justification which refers to our legal standing before God. While it is not possible to describe in detail the doctrine of justification, I want to sketch a brief definition because I believe that when justification is seen as an integral part of soteriology, then an explicit confession of Christ becomes necessary for salvation.

The Centrality of Justification by Faith

Evangelicals whose roots are in the Magesterial Reformation have argued that our guilty legal status before God is not reversed by a change to our nature, but that we are acquitted of our guilt and made righteous by the passive and active obedience of Christ. Badcock notes the importance of the

---

[110] Ferguson, op. cit., p. 112.

[111] See Murray, op. cit., pp. 141-151. There is a further implication of this union that might bring one close to the idea of *theosis*. Because of the doctrine of *perichoresis*, the mutual indwelling of the Persons in the others, it is legitimate to say that when we are united with Christ, we are also united with the Father and the Spirit (Jn. 14:23; 14:16). In this sense, "we are introduced in Christ to the fellowship of God himself," (Letham, op. cit., p. 84) we are raised up in Christ and sit with him in the heavenly places (Eph. 2:6).

role of the Spirit in this: "rather than being the agent of renewal by which we are made righteous, the Spirit becomes the means by which we come to Christ, who alone justifies, and only secondarily the agent of moral renewal - moral renewal that is located only at the periphery of soteriological theory."[112] From this we come to the classic distinction between the concepts of imputation and impartation in soteriological theory. Impartation is the idea that the Spirit changes our nature so we can be righteous before God. However Reformed theology has argued that this impartation cannot be the grounds of our forgiveness and salvation because sin still remains and therefore our guilt still remains. Imputation, has two aspects, firstly, the nonimputuation of sin, that is Christ's punishment is ours, and secondly, the imputation of Christ's righteousness that we 'put on' and so we are declared righteous even though we still continue to sin. Our justification therefore is located and grounded not in ourselves but in Christ. We are declared righteous before God being clothed in the righteousness of Christ.[113]

This idea has significant implications for the meaning of *sola gratia* and *sola fide*. While acknowledging an uncreated aspect of grace in the presence of the Spirit, an equal emphasis must be on created grace that Berkhof describes as follows:

> ...it is God's free, sovereign, undeserved favour or love to man, in his state of sin and guilt which manifests itself in the forgiveness of sin and deliverance from its penalty...grace is used as a designation of the objective provision which God made in Christ...the term is applied not only to what Christ is, but what he merited for sinners...'grace' is used to designate the favour of God as it is manifested in the application of the work of redemption by the Holy Spirit. It is applied to the pardon which we receive in justification.[114]

Contrary to Pinnock's argument, this grace is located not in creation but in the cross where as our substitute, Christ endures the punishment and wrath of God so we can be acquitted of guilt and clothed with righteousness. In this sense grace is not pneumatocentric, simply being the presence of the omnipresent Spirit in the world, but is Christocentric, emanating from the work of Christ. The 'gratuity' of this grace means that there is nothing we can do to earn or merit this gift. Contrary to Pinnock's synergistic under-

---

[112] Badcock, op. cit., p. 97.
[113] For some more detailed treatments of justification see Philip Eveson, *The Great Exchange: Justification by Faith Alone in the Light of Recent Thought* (Bromley, 1996); Murray, op. cit., pp. 117-132; Letham, op. cit., pp. 177-194; ed. Don Kistler, *Justification by Faith Alone: Affirming the Doctrine by which the Church and the Individual Stands or Falls* (Morgan, 1996).
[114] Berkhof, op. cit., p. 427.

standing, Reformed evangelicals have stressed monergism: salvation is wholly a work of God.

The Holy Spirit still plays a vital role in this doctrine because as an aspect of union with Christ, it is the Spirit who is the instrumental cause of justification. The Spirit effects union and through the gift of faith justifies the sinner which Calvin argues is the primary function of the Spirit in the application of salvation.[115] Justification by grace through faith is a gift of the Spirit. Seen in the context of union with Christ, concepts like justification and imputation can be seen to be more personal concepts. As Calvin writes:

> ...that joining together of Head and members, that indwelling of Christ in our hearts - in short, that mystical union - are accorded by us the highest degree of importance, so that Christ, having been made ours, makes us sharers with him in the gifts which he has been endowed. We do not, therefore, contemplate him outside ourselves from afar in order that his righteousness may be imputed to us, but because we put on Christ and are engrafted into his body - in short, because he designs to make us one with him.[116]

Here we can see the practical outworking of the Spirit's role as *Paraclete*. Through the gift of faith, the Spirit who embodies uncreated grace, dwells in the believer and unites us to Christ, gradually transforming us into Christ's likeness. However this same Spirit is also called the Spirit of Christ, and testifies, illuminates, regenerates and applies the created grace won by Christ on the cross. In this sense then under the overarching theme of union with Christ, the believer is objectively and legally justified and subjectively sanctified.

But what specifically does this tell us about the nature and content of saving faith? Firstly, and seen within the context of the Spirit's work in uniting us to Christ, Evangelicals who stress the 'deadness' of the sinner to respond to God, argue that although the sinner exercises faith, this faith is a gift of the Spirit and does not effect regeneration and union with Christ but is itself the first tangible sign of this regeneration and union.[117] In this sense there is a mysterious work of the Spirit that precedes conversion:

> We are not born again by faith or repentance or conversion; we repent and believe because we have been regenerated. No one can say in truth that

---

[115] Calvin, op. cit., 3.1.1.
[116] Calvin, op. cit., 3.11.10.
[117] In discussing revelation, it is important to distinguish between 'regeneration' as the external effects of conversion and the 'internal' initial impartation of new life by the Spirit. In my argument I am referring to the latter usage.

Jesus is the Christ except by regeneration of the Spirit and that is one of the ways by which the Holy Spirit glorifies Christ. The embrace of Christ in faith is the first evidence of regeneration and only thus may we know that we have been regenerated.[118]

While Reformed evangelicals state that Word and Spirit are inseparable, a major question that I alluded to earlier is whether in this initial work of regeneration, the Spirit works mediately through the instrumentality of the Word (*per verbum*), or whether He acts immediately accompanying the Word (*cum verbo*).[119]

In Ch. 5, I described how Pinnock had changed the object of faith from 'Jesus' to 'God,' but that he still wanted to hold onto the traditional elements of faith: *notitia, fiducia and assensus*. The question, though, is how one can hold onto these elements without the object of faith being Christ. The name 'Jesus' means 'saviour from sins' and it is knowledge of who Christ is and what he has done that defines saving faith:

> ...faith is a matter first and foremost of looking outside and away from oneself to Christ and his cross as the sole ground of present forgiveness and future hope...faith grasps the reality of God's free gift of righteousness, i.e. 'rightness' with God that the righteous enjoy (cf. Rom. 5:16), and with it the justified man's obligation to live henceforth 'unto' the one who died for his sake and rose again. (cf. 2 Cor. 5:14).[120]

Looking outside ourselves to the objective work of Christ, tells us also something of the role of faith and its efficacy:

> It is to be remembered that the efficacy of faith does not reside in itself. Faith is not something that merits the favour of God. All the efficacy unto salvation resides in the Saviour. .., it is not faith that saves but faith in Je-

---

[118] Murray, *Redemption Accomplished and Applied*, p. 103.

[119] Ferguson, op. cit., holds to the mediate position, "Regeneration and the faith to which it gives birth are seen as taking place not by revelationless divine sovereignty, but within the matrix of preaching the word and the witness of the people of God (*cf.* Rom. 10:1-15). Their instrumentality in regeneration does not impinge upon the sovereign activity of the Spirit. Word and Spirit belong together"(p. 126). However Berkhof, op. cit. favours the immediate view. He quotes from the confessional standard, the *Conclusions of Utrecht*: "regeneration is not effected through the Word or sacraments as such, but by the almighty regenerating work of the Spirit; that this regenerating work of the Holy Spirit, however, may not in that sense be divorced from the preaching of the Word, as if both were separated from each other...the gospel is a power of God unto salvation for every one who believes, and that in the case of adults the regenerating work of the Holy Spirit accompanies the preaching of the gospel" (p. 476).

[120] Packer, 'What Did the Cross Achieve?,' p. 30.

sus Christ; strictly speaking, it is not even faith in Christ that saves but Christ that saves through faith. Faith unites us to Christ in the bonds of abiding attachment and entrustment and it is this union which ensures that the saving power, grace, and virtue of the Saviour become operative in the believer. The specific character of faith is that it looks away from itself and finds its whole interest and object in Christ. He is the absorbing preoccupation of faith.[121]

Here, faith is merely the instrument through which God justifies. Faith itself does not save.

Pinnock's 'faith principle' cannot give propositional knowledge needed for holistic biblical faith because it does not contain information about the source of salvation, that is the life, death and resurrection of Christ: "...faith comes from hearing the message, and that message is heard through the word of Christ" (Rom. 10:17). More than this though, I wish to contend that to change the object of faith is to change the nature of faith, for without its Christocentric focus, faith in Pinnock's theology is not merely the instrument through which we receive God's justification, but the ground of justification itself: we are saved by our acceptance of the Spirit's prevenient grace.

This discussion highlights one of the *reasons* why general revelation is insufficient for salvation. For *even if* sin has not totally destroyed our subjective interpretation of this revelation, as some maintain, objectively there is not enough propositional revelation to stimulate saving faith. General revelation speaks of God's nature and His demands but offers no knowledge as to how humanity can be saved. This is the point of special revelation: "In the divine mercy this came through the revealed utterances of certified prophets and apostles and through the life of the incarnate Christ, all of which are preserved in inspired Scripture. This fuller knowledge of God's nature and redemptive purposes provides the objective basis for faith's informed decision."[122]

Calvin talks about nature revealing the hands and feet of God but not his heart. It is only knowledge of Christ that gives faith the essential quality of *notitia*, "Whoever aspires to know God, and does not begin with Christ,

---

[121] John Murray, *Redemption Accomplished and Applied* p. 112. Grudem, op. cit. asks why it is 'faith' in particular that is the instrument of justification rather than some other action such as joy, or love. He writes: "It is apparently because faith is the one attitude of the heart that is the exact opposite of depending on ourselves...and therefore it is the attitude that perfectly fits salvation that depends not at all on our own merit but entirely on God's free gift of grace"(p. 730).

[122] Bruce Demarest, 'General and Special Revelation. Epistemological Foundations of Religious Pluralism' in *One God, One Lord. Christianity in a World of Religious Pluralism*, p. 199.

must wander as it were in a labyrinth,"[123] and, "there is no having knowledge of God without Christ."[124] It would appear that if faith in God as revealed in general revelation is insufficient as the object of faith, then to have faith in another god, or to have no object of faith (as in the atheist who can be saved by the ethical faith principle), is even further removed from the biblical idea of saving faith.

Summary

In the last two chapters, I have ranged over a wide area of doctrine looking at the implications Pinnock's 'pneumatological inclusivism' has for topics such as Christology, the doctrine of the Trinity and soteriology. Clark Pinnock still wishes to remain within the evangelical wing of Christianity and offers his inclusivism as a viable position for evangelicals to take regarding the salvation of the unevangelised. However, I have tried to show how Pinnock's mediation of universality and particularity in the form of his 'pneumatological inclusivism' significantly redefines the orthodox interpretation of the four *solas* of the evangelical faith: (*solus Christus, sola fide, sola gratia,* and *sola Scriptura*), as well as reconfiguring the relationship between the second and third persons of the Trinity. As a result of his departure from foundational evangelical tenets, my conclusion here is that because of the ramifications it has for other doctrinal loci, Pinnock's version of inclusivism cannot be considered as a viable evangelical argument for both Reformed and Arminian evangelicals.

However, given the evangelical invalidity of Pinnock's actual formulation of how the unevangelised can be saved, all evangelicals are still left with some questions to be answered concerning the foundational presuppositions of Pinnock's inclusivism. Pinnock does not hide the theological motives behind his inclusivist formulation. For him, the universality axiom comprising of God's universal salvific will, universal atonement and universal accessibility, are fundamental truths that cannot be compromised. Even if one is to reject Pinnock's actual argument on the unevangelised, his formulation of the universality axiom together with the particularity axiom, would still appear to demand some mediation especially when focusing on the unevangelised: If God desires all to be saved, and if Christ dies for all,

---

[123] John Calvin, commentary on Jn. 8:19. Quoted in Bruce Demarest, *General Revelation* (Grand Rapids, 1982), p. 58.
[124] John Calvin, *Institutes of the Christian Religion* (Grand Rapids, 1949), II. Vi. 4. Quoted from Bruce Demarest, *General Revelation*, p. 58.

what are we to say concerning the unevangelised and the possibility of their salvation? It is to the universality axiom and the way Pinnock and other evangelicals construe it that becomes the subject of my final chapter.

CHAPTER 9

The Universality Axiom and the 'Problem' of the Unevangelised

In the previous two chapters, I have argued, primarily from the perspective of Reformed evangelicalism, that Pinnock's inclusivist position regarding the salvation of the unevangelised, significantly redefines and even compromises the four *solas* of the evangelical faith, and as a result cannot be regarded as a legitimate 'evangelical' argument. My claim was that although Pinnock believes he can mediate the axioms of particularity and universality, on a number of doctrinal loci, Pinnock has universalised the particular with significant implications for Christology, Trinitarian formulation, the doctrines of revelation and soteriology.

However, while it may be concluded that Pinnock's own particular formulation of inclusivism is invalid, the axioms of universality and particularity are still in place and demand some kind of mediation. In this final chapter, I wish to widen my focus somewhat, concentrating not so much on the details of Pinnock's inclusivism, but rather on the axiom which I believe generates his inclusivism: the universality axiom consisting of God's universal salvific will, Christ's universal provision in the atonement, universal accessibility to salvation, and the *Heilsoptimismus*. Bearing in mind everything that I have already argued in the previous two chapters, my aim in this chapter is to question the validity of this axiom and so move towards eliminating the tension that generates Pinnock's inclusivism in the first place. In questioning the universality axiom, I intend not only to interact with Pinnock, but also to raise a number of questions concerning more orthodox 'evangelicals' who, while rejecting Pinnock's own formulation of inclusivism, hold to one or more of the tenets of the universality axiom.

This questioning of the universality axiom will lead to my final conclusion: It could perhaps be thought that the questions Pinnock asks concerning the unevangelised are genuine questions, although ultimately Pinnock himself has failed to give an adequate 'evangelical' answer to these questions. His positive contribution to the debate has been to map out the territory to explore these questions, highlighting the area of systematic theology that needs to be tackled if the problem of the unevangelised is to be satisfactorily resolved. However, this study has highlighted throughout the relationship between the pertinent areas of doctrine that need to be explored in any discussion of the unevangelised (Pinnock's theology has been an extremely apposite vehicle to highlight this), and the questions generated from a particular construal of these issues. My conclusion will ask whether the questions Pinnock and many evangelicals ask concerning the unevangelised, and which were the primary motivation for his inclusivism and the other theories outlined in Appendix 1, are real questions at all, or, are in fact a number of 'pseudo-questions' inextricably linked to and generated by the theological paradigms within which they work, paradigms which have been discussed and rejected at an earlier juncture in my argument. I will argue that the 'Reformed' evangelical paradigm does not ask the same questions as Pinnock concerning the unevangelised, and does not see there to be the same kind of biblical, theological or ethical 'problems' surrounding their existence and status which Pinnock claims there to be. That is to say, there is no 'problem' of the unevangelised.

The Universality of Sin

Two Different Harmatologies

In my critique of Pinnock, I have purposefully not dealt explicitly with the very different harmatological structures at work in Pinnock's theology and in Reformed evangelicalism. However, the question of the nature, depth and extent of the Fall demands some attention here as it has been uncomfortably present throughout the discussion on the necessity and purpose of the atonement; and the doctrine of salvation. One could argue that the fundamental differences between Pinnock's inclusivism and the Reformed critique that I have advocated, stem from the different starting points concerning sin. It is not my intention to give a detailed exposition of this area but rather in a broad way to indicate, in contrast to Pinnock's understanding of the Fall, what I believe to be the tenor of the Reformed interpretation of the biblical narrative on this issue. I hope that this will pull together a number of separate doctrinal strands that I have been arguing for throughout this critique.

Pinnock's universality axiom concentrates on the universality of God's saving love and his universal gracious presence by the Spirit in creation, the ultimate demonstration of this being the incarnation. I have argued that because the unevangelised can freely accept or reject the Spirit's overtures of prevenient grace, and because the source of this grace and the ability to respond to it are located in creation and not in re-creation, that there are major questions concerning the necessity and purpose of the atonement. In contrast to this, Reformed theology has argued that one cannot understand the atonement without understanding its necessity, and the Bible constantly refers to the universal depth of human sin as making Christ's penal substitution absolutely necessary in God's provision of salvation: "Adam's sin plunged the entire human race into sin and condemnation. So humanity outside Christ is described as dead in sin, without God and without hope (Eph. 2:1, 11-12), destined for judgement (Heb. 9:27) and eternal condemnation (Mt. 25:31-46; Rom. 5:12-21). Underlying this grim reality is the basic truth that God's justice requires the punishment of sin and the sinner."[1]

This theme cannot be ignored or minimized. We are 'objects of wrath' (Eph. 2:3), 'dead in transgressions and sin' (Col. 2:3), slaves to sin who wilfully conform to the sinful nature.[2] Wright summarises the Reformed doctrine of Man's sinful condition in five statements:

> 1. Since the Fall of Adam and Eve, all are born spiritually dead in their sin nature, and therefore require regeneration to a life they do not naturally possess...
> 2. Being fallen, the natural heart and mind is sinfully corrupt and unenlightened...
> 3. Because the whole of nature is involved in the Fall and its results, sinners are slaves to sin.
> 4. No one escapes the unrighteous tendencies of the sinful Adamic nature...
> 5. Left to themselves, those dead in trespasses and sins have no spiritual ability to reform themselves, or to repent, or to savingly believe...[3]

The doctrines of original sin and total depravity articulate the reality of the human condition.[4] Sin is universal and crippling. This is the 'bondage of the will,' a moral inability to do good.[5]

From this starting point, the rest of the Reformed soteriological structure (the so-called 'doctrines of grace' or 'five points of Calvinism') falls into place.[6] Salvation is therefore an act of divine monergism where God gives

---

[1] Robert Letham, *The Work of Christ* (Leicester, 1993), p. 125.
[2] Jn. 8:34; Rom. 6:17-20; 2 Pet. 2:19.
[3] R. K. McGregor Wright, *No Place for Sovereignty: What's Wrong with Freewill Theism* (Downers Grove, 1996), pp. 112-116.
[4] See Wayne Grudem, *Systematic Theology* (Leicester, 1994), pp. 490-514; Gordon Lewis and Bruce Demarest, *Integrative Theology*, Vol. 2 (Grand Rapids, 1990), pp. 190-224; John Murray, *The Imputation of Adam's Sin* (Grand Rapids, 1959). Some of the more important verses are: Job. 14:4; Jer. 13:23; Mt. 7:16-18, 12:33; Rom. 5:12-19, 11:35-36; I Cor. 2:14, 4:7; 2 Cor. 3:5.
[5] See Gen. 6:5, 8:21; Ecc. 9:3; Jer. 17:9-10; Mk. 7:21-23; Jn. 3:19; Rom. 8:7-8; 1 Cor. 2:14; Eph. 4:17-19, 5:8; Tit. 1:15.
[6] These are denoted by the mnemonic T.U.L.I.P: Total Depravity; Unconditional Election; Limited Atonement; Irresistible Grace; Perseverance of the Saints. I made reference to these points earlier on in the study, see p. 9.

new life to that which was dead. This is the regeneration by the Holy Spirit that was spoken about in the previous chapter. From this perspective we must tackle Pinnock on a number of issues. Firstly, there is the subjective reception of revelation. Objectively, we have noted the non-salvific nature of general revelation: it only tells human beings about God the Creator, not God the Redeemer. This discussion took place, though, without placing this objective revelation in the context of the Fall that has veiled and distorted not only the revelation itself but our reception of it. The argument is that *even if* general revelation was salvific, no-one would ever avail themselves of it due to their sinful natures.[7]

Secondly, Arminian soteriology is often accused by Reformed theology of diluting *sola gratia* because saving faith originating from the freewill of the individual becomes the "hinge on which the atonement depends,"[8] and the ground of justification: "The Arminian teaching on justification is in effect, if not intention, legalistic, turning faith from a means of receiving from God into a work that merits before God."[9] Evangelical Arminians like John Wesley have attempted to respond to this by adopting a doctrine of universal prevenient grace which is an effect of the atonement and which mitigates the effect of Adam's sin making a free response to God possi-

---

[7] This point is put forward by Reformed evangelicals in varying degrees of force depending on their views regarding the depth of the Fall ontologically and noetically. So, for example, Hanko in 'Another Look at Common Grace (8) Restraint of Sin and General Revelation' in *Protestant Reformed Theological Journal* April, 1996, pp. 31-50, who denies a common grace, also denies general 'revelation' preferring to translate the word which Paul uses in Rom. 1:18ff as 'manifestation'. He argues that this word means to uncover that which is hidden as in a public unveiling of a painting. He writes, "Now it is clear already from the term itself that such 'revelation' or unveiling implies the ability on the part of the audience to see what is unveiled. If among the throng there are fifty blind people, it is obvious that, as far as the unveiling is concerned, there is no 'revelation' of the work of art to these blind folk. The work of art may be unveiled, but the blind are unable to see it" (p. 36). This he claims is the exact situation of sinners as presented in the Bible. They need the eyes of faith to see creation, and this God only gives to His elect. Like grace, it is particular. Of course, this view and its less extreme counterparts, have to answer the accusation that such a view takes away human being's responsibility. However, as in soteriology, the Reformed position does not hold the basic philosophical presupposition of Arminianism that 'inability limits responsibility.' This issue is one of the fundamental areas of debate between Reformed theology and Pinnock's 'trinitarian openness.' A good overview of the issues from within the Reformed tradition can be found in John Frame's *The Doctrine of the Knowledge of God*, (Phillipsburg, 1987), pp. 49-61 in a section entitled 'The Unbelievers Knowledge.' Frame's own formulation attempts to steer through the Scriptural truth that the unbeliever knows God and does not know God at the same time.

[8] Letham, op. cit., p. 231.

[9] J. I. Packer, 'Arminianisms' in eds. R. Godfrey and T. Boyd, *Through Christ's Word: A Festshrift for P.E. Hughes*. (Phillipsburg, 1985), p. 134.

ble.[10] However, as we saw in Ch. 4, Pinnock's version of prevenient grace is more in line with Karl Rahner's supernatural existential than Wesley's doctrine because Pinnock denies a total depravity claiming that *from creation* human beings made in the *imago Dei*, have always been able to say yes or no to the Spirit's overtures: "freedom is essential to the image of God in us...salvation requires the operation of both grace and the human will."[11] This underestimation of the ontological and noetic effects of the Fall, and the merging of nature and grace Post-Fall, goes directly against the majority of 'evangelical' teaching, Arminian and Reformed. On this point Gary Badcock's comments on Rahner can be equally applied to Pinnock. Is it:

> ... possible to maintain that God is close to all, so close that his presence is almost indistinguishable from the self, in view of the biblical teaching that all alike are objects of divine wrath? The fact that in Rahner the God of wrath has entirely given place to the God of love may be theologically welcome from a certain perspective, but can it be justified in biblical terms? Rahner himself does not provide such a justification, and it must be questioned whether one could ever be provided from strict exegesis of either the Old or the New Testaments. At the very least, one must say that while there are biblical themes relating to the *imago dei*, for example, that lend support to his position, there are plenty of others that do not.[12]

Pinnock seems to be even more susceptible than traditional Arminianism to the accusation of semi-Pelagianism especially when one considers the ethical 'faith principle' where good works are a positive response to the Spirit's overtures.

Finally, it is appropriate at this point to note the relationship between the work of the Spirit and the universality and extent of sin. Pinnock's stress on the cosmic activity of the Spirit is the main feature of his 'pneumatological' inclusivism and while my critique has not denied this cosmic feature, it has criticised Pinnock for not distinguishing between general and special operations of the Spirit and between salvific and nonsalvific operations of the Spirit. The whole tenor of Pinnock's argument is optimistic and positive:

---

[10] The main arguments against this view are 1) the lack of explicit biblical evidence supporting such an operation of grace; and 2) that the efficacy of grace is weakened as it can be accepted or rejected. See Thomas R. Schreiner, 'Does Scripture Teach Prevenient Grace in the Wesleyan Sense?' in eds. Thomas R. Schreiner and Bruce A. Ware, *The Grace of God, The Bondage of the Will. Historical and Theological Perspectives on Calvinism* (Grand Rapids, 1995), pp. 365-383.
[11] Clark Pinnock, *Flame of Love: A Theology of the Holy Spirit* (Downers Grove, 1996), p. 160.
[12] Gary Badcock, 'Karl Rahner, the Trinity, and Religious Pluralism' in ed. Kevin J. Vanhoozer, *The Trinity in a Pluralistic World: Theological Essays on Culture and Religion* (Cambridge, 1997), p. 152f.

the Spirit embodies grace, "the cosmic breadth of Spirit activities can help us conceptualise the universality of God's grace. The Creator's love for the world, central to the Christian message, is implemented by the Spirit."[13] However, Pinnock's positive emphasis on the relationship between the Spirit and world is perhaps too optimistic. Note Ferguson's comment:

> When we consider this emphasis on the cosmic and universal ministry of the Spirit in light of the explicit statements of the New Testament, we immediately encounter a surprising datum. The New Testament places the Spirit and the world in an antithetical, not a conciliatory, relationship. The world cannot see or know the Spirit (Jn. 14:17); the Spirit convicts the world (Jn. 16:8-11); the spirit of the world and the Spirit of God stand over against each other (1 Cor. 2:12-14; 1 Jn. 4:3).[14]

There are many aspects to the Spirit's work, dispensing grace being only one facet. While judging and convicting the world of guilt in regard to sin may be one of the more negative aspects of the Spirit's universal work, in order to gain a true biblical perspective on the world, it must not be under-emphasised or forgotten. The same Spirit that issues grace also brings judgement to a sinful humanity.

Defining 'good'

But how should one respond to Pinnock's question of existential viability - the 'fact' that many of the unevangelised perform acts of love and mercy and are 'holy' people? For Pinnock this is a sign of a response to grace, an implicit acceptance of the mystery of one's being. I have already offered one explanation of 'good' acts in our discussion of common grace. There it was said that the Spirit restrains sin in a non-salvific way and this is the cause of much 'good' we see both individually and culturally. However, in the context of our discussion of sin, we should raise the question as to whether acts that Pinnock calls 'good' are in fact 'good.' Here one must ask what is the biblical definition of sin? Although from one perspective sin can be defined as the failure to keep the law of God, Romans 1:21-25 hints that the root of sin is not the performance of evil but primarily a failure to glorify God as God. It is an idolatry that exchanges the glory of God for lesser created things. With this in mind, Schreiner writes:

> Such a conception of sin helps us to understand how people can perform actions that externally conform with righteousness yet remain slaves of sin. These actions are not motivated by a desire to honor and glorify God

---

[13] Pinnock, *Flame of Love*, p. 187.
[14] Ferguson, *The Holy Spirit* (Leicester, 1996), p. 246.

as God. They are not done out of an attitude of faith, which brings glory to God (Rom. 4:20). Faith brings glory to God because he is seen to be the all powerful one who supplies our every need, and thus deserving of praise and honour... The necessity of faith is underscored by Romans 14:23, where Paul notes that "everything that does not come from faith is sin." Slavery to sin does not mean that people always engage in reprehensible behaviour. It means that the unregenerate never desire to bring glory to God, but are passionately committed to upholding their own glory and honour.[15]

As outlined in the previous chapter, the question for Pinnock to answer is how God can be the object of glorification, (or perhaps more specifically how can God glorify Himself in His Son Jesus Christ through the witness of the Spirit), when propositionally He is misunderstood or not even not known? The marks of true faith must include both propositional and ethical elements, both are inextricably linked and cannot be separated (1 Jn. 4:1-6).

An Optimism in Salvation?

Perhaps it is now appropriate, having briefly discussed the nature and extent of sin, to deal with Pinnock's belief in the *Heilsoptimismus* and the 'hermeneutic of hopefulness:' his reading of the biblical narrative from Genesis through to Revelation. We must remember that an optimism in salvation is a *reason* Pinnock gives for the salvation of the unevangelised:

Premiss 1: The Bible issues hope that the majority of mankind will be saved.
Premiss 2: The majority of mankind constitute the unevangelised.

---

[15] Schreiner, op. cit., p. 367f. Hanko, op. cit., who denies that there is such a thing as God's common grace, puts it in even starker terms arguing that because (on the analogy that a bad tree can produce only bad fruit) of man's sinful nature, all acts deriving from this nature are sinful: "The Scriptures teach that man is incapable of doing any good. All his works are evil continually. No matter what he does, it is wrong. Does he observe in some outward fashion the law of God so that perhaps he does not go around shooting at his neighbor? He really only does this for his own good, not for the love of God. And God says this is sin. Does he build hospitals, institutions of learning? It is also corrupt, for God demands truth within, and man does these things for his own honor and fame, that his name may live after him. Does he give his surplus food to the poor and attempt to feed the hungry in the world? It is wicked, for he forgets God in his pride. Does he advance with giant strides on the frontiers of science and subject the forces of creation to his use with powerful inventions? Yet he does this to establish a kingdom which stands in opposition to God. Does he seek peace on earth? God hates his efforts, for he wants peace without the blood of the cross. Does he develop mighty systems of philosophy? Even Augustine called all these works of the heathen "splendid vices.""(p. 156f).

Therefore conclusion 3: it must be possible for the unevangelised to be saved.

Pinnock would agree that it is a futile exercise to speculate on the exact number of people who will eventually be saved. What I wish to discuss, is whether the Bible issues hope or pessimism as to the numbers who will be saved. We have already mentioned Pinnock's problem of affirming a *Heilsoptimismus* (or a *Heilspessimismus* for that matter) because of his denial of exhaustive divine foreknowledge. Here, I will make a few comments on his hermeneutic of the biblical text.

Firstly, Pinnock seems quite selective in his interpretation of Genesis and early biblical history. He appears to overlook the explicit theme of retribution coupled with a definite *Heilspessimismus*. With creation came accountability: "These pre-flood days show not only mercy but judgments on all creation - nature (cf. the Edenic curse) and humans (cf. the curse, Cain's banishment and his godless line)."[16] The reality of a sinful humanity and a retributive God cannot be ignored. Although Pinnock stresses the universality of the Noahic covenant, he forgets the tremendous venting of God's wrath which precedes the covenant: the Flood where all flesh is destroyed save for Noah and his family who too would have been destroyed were it not for God's mercy. Rather than demonstrating universality, there is an exclusivity about this event that cannot be ignored:

> ...most of those who should have heard Noah's message were not in geographical proximity to Noah. Neither does it seem that all wilfully rejected Noah's message. They unknowingly ignored Noah but were still judged. Further, Jesus uses "Noah's day" to speak of judgement and not salvation (Matt. 24:36-41; cf. Luke 17:37, which provides Jesus' interpretation of the event). On this event, Hebrews 11:7 has a manyness doctrine of *condemnation*. In fear and faith "Noah prepared an ark for the salvation of his household, by which he condemned the *world*." Eventually, no one was spared except for the preacher of righteousness and his family who entered the exclusive ark.[17]

There was a particularity of revelation here: Noah's safety depended on a special revelation from God and him faithfully obeying the specific commands God gave him, the rest of humanity died in the Flood God sent. This 'tenor' continues throughout the Bible: sinful humanity rejects the one holy and loving God, and what one sees is a 'righteous remnant' not a 'righteous majority,' God punishing the wicked and blessing the faithful.

---

[16] Ramesh Richard, *The Population of Heaven: A Biblical Response to the Inclusivist Position on Who Will be Saved* (Chicago, 1994), p. 31.
[17] Ibid., p. 33.

Secondly, Pinnock refers to a number of texts that speak about multitudes being saved, Lk. 13:29; Rev. 7:9, 15:3. While no evangelical doubts that on an absolute scale there will be a great number of people saved, there is no indication as to relative numbers of saved and unsaved. The only explicit indications are Jesus' statements in Matt. 7:13-14: "Enter through the narrow gate. For wide is the gate and broad is the road that leads to destruction, and many enter through it. But small is the gate and narrow the road that leads to life, and only a few find it;" and Lk. 13:23-24: "Someone asked him, "Lord, are only a few people going to be saved?" He said to them, "Make every effort to enter through the narrow door, because many, I tell you, will try to enter and will not be able to." These verses hardly support a *Heilsoptimismus*.[18] Carson writes:

> Pinnock does not think "that this text about fewness can be used to cancel out the optimism of salvation which so many verses seem to articulate." [*Wideness*, p. 154]. But are there any texts where the question of *relative* proportions is directly addressed and the proportions go the other way? Hermeneutically, one should not attempt to set aside texts that directly respond to a specific question by appealing to themes that answer the question, if they answer it at all, at best indirectly. Moreover, the proportionality envisaged by Jesus in this passage is entirely in line with the entire history of the people of God across the Bible's story-line.[19]

---

[18] I should note that it is not only Pinnock who argues against a *Heilspessimismus* from these verses. Helm notes that B.B. Warfield held to a similar hermeneutic, regarding these verses to be ethical rather than prophetic in their intent, "They are concerned with changing people's attitudes rather than predicting the final numbers or proportions of the saved and the lost. How could Luke 13:23 be interpreted otherwise, Warfield asks, when it is found alongside parables which teach the inexorable growth of the kingdom of God throughout the world... In defending this interpretation Warfield says: 'It is, in other words, not the number of the saved that is announced, but the difficulty of salvation. The point of the remark is that salvation is not to be assumed by any one as a matter of course, but is to be sought with earnest and persistent effort.'" Paul Helm, 'Are They Few That be Saved?' in ed. Nigel M. de S. Cameron, *Universalism and the Doctrine of Hell* (Edinburgh, 1992), p. 273. The quotation from Warfield comes from his essay 'Are They Few That be Saved?' in *Biblical and Theological Studies* (Philadelphia, 1952), p. 341.

[19] Don Carson, *The Gagging of God: Christianity Confronts Pluralism* (Leicester, 1996), p. 300. As a footnote to this section I wish to say something of Pinnock's 'historical' hermeneutic of hopefulness. To support his argument for a 'wideness in God's mercy,' Pinnock notices three broad historical trends in Western theology (see Clark Pinnock, *A Wideness in God's Mercy* (Grand Rapids, 1992), pp. 35-43. I described these briefly in Ch. 4). Firstly, he states that the early Church and early Fathers were optimistic in the scope of salvation, this being epitomised in Justin's doctrine of the *Logos spermatikos*. However with Augustine came a new restrictive paradigm which was pessimistic and "which would eat its way into the consciousness of the Western churches

Understanding the Wider Context

Relating Universal Accessibility to a Universal Salvific Will and a Universal Atonement.

Pinnock states that it is a challenge of theological interpretation to mediate the tension that holds that God loves the whole world (universality) and that Jesus is the only way to God (particularity). Specifically the problem concerns access to God's grace. Here Pinnock makes the following claim: "If God really loves the whole world and desires everyone to be saved, it follows logically that everyone must have access to salvation. There would have to be an opportunity for all people to participate in the salvation of

---

and erode the positive biblical spirit in their thinking." (Ibid., p. 39). This Augustinian tradition strongly influenced Reformation theology that in turn has influenced contemporary evangelicalism. Finally Pinnock believes that recently God Himself has prompted a shift back to optimism, "The more lenient approach, seen in the Greek fathers, is fast coming back into favour, and the cloud which has darkened theology in the West for centuries is finally passing over" (Ibid., p. 41). This is seen most clearly in the statements of the Second Vatican Council. A number of observations can be made on this historical hermeneutic. Firstly, Pinnock must be careful not to regard the popularity of a particular position as a test of truth. As Geivett points out: "There may be better explanations for the perceived popularity of inclusivism - explanations that have less to do with the impulse of the Holy Spirit or with biblical exegesis and more to do with the sociological aspects of a pluralistic culture... Premature announcements about the emergence of some new 'consensus' is a feature of paradigm shifting that can precipitate broad acceptance of a novel theory." (W. Gary Phillips and R. Douglas Geivett, 'Response to Clark H. Pinnock' in *More Than One Way? Four Views on Salvation in a Pluralistic World.* (Grand Rapids, 1995), p. 136). Secondly, if Pinnock wishes to interpret the Augustinian paradigm as being conditioned primarily from historical and political factors rather than theological ones, he must be self-critically aware that his own thought can be interpreted as being equally conditioned by the pluralistic climate of the West. Richard asks, "How Pinnock has access to this divine corrective extra-biblical reading of history is in itself a reasonable question" (Richard, op. cit., p. 20) Thirdly, Pinnock regards the problem of the unevangelised to be a relatively new area in systematics, and that had Western 'orthodox' theologians realised the pressure caused by the questions it raises, the restrictivist hermeneutic might not have arisen and become established. However, there is evidence to show that theologians throughout Christian history have realised the presence of other faiths and the existence of the unevangelised. John Sanders himself a prominent evangelical inclusivist, has in his book, *No Other Name. Can Only Christians Be Saved?* (London, 1994) surveyed Christian responses to the question of the unevangelised giving historical bibliographies on all the major positions from restrictivism to universalism. Francis A. Sullivan traces historically Catholic responses to the presence of other religions in *Salvation Outside the Church? Tracing the History of the Catholic Response* (London, 1992). A fairer assessment is that of Phillips who states that "while Christian theologians have not ignored the task of developing theology of religions, the present social context has pushed this issue to the front *and, at the same time, invited an attitude of leniency*"(Phillips and Geivett, op. cit., p. 137).

God... God's universal salvific will implies the equally universal accessibility of salvation for all people."[20]

But is there a logical link between God's universal salvific will and a universally accessible salvation? Like Carson[21] and Nash,[22] I believe this implication to be problematical because of its relation to Pinnock's trinitarian openness. Pinnock holds to a qualified definition of a 'universal salvific will' because he believes that God's will can be frustrated by human libertarian freedom. Hence, soteriologically speaking, God may desire everyone to be saved, but such a desire can be frustrated by a rejection of God's grace. Could not though the same argument be used concerning universal accessibility? God may desire everyone to hear the gospel, but this desire for everyone to hear can be frustrated. At this point we must note that this has indeed been the view of many evangelical Arminians: God may desire the salvation of all men, but getting the gospel to those people is our task, and this task can succeed or fail. One of the primary motivations for two thousand years of mission and evangelism has been the belief that Christian men and women are the means by which the unevangelised hear the gospel and the fact that many have not heard is their responsibility. That people never hear the gospel is a 'risk' God takes in deciding to create a world of conditionality and mutuality. This argument alone would seem to prove that while God's universal salvific will and universal accessibility may complement one another, there is no necessary link from the former to the latter. If universal accessibility is to be theologically proved, then it must be on other grounds.[23]

However, Pinnock does not only link a universal salvific will to universal accessibility, but he also links unlimited atonement to universal accessibility: "If Christ died for all, while yet sinners, the opportunity must be given for all to register a decision about what was done for them. They cannot lack the opportunity merely because someone failed to bring the gospel

---

[20] Clark H. Pinnock, *A Wideness in God's Mercy: The Finality of Christ in a World Of Religions* (Grand Rapids, 1992), p. 157.
[21] Don Carson, op. cit., p. 289.
[22] Ronald Nash, *Is Jesus the Only Saviour?* (Grand Rapids, 1994), pp. 130-135.
[23] Carson, op. cit. believes that there is a problem in linking God's universal salvific will to universal accessibility in light of Pinnock's denial of exhaustive divine omniscience. He states: "Since Pinnock's God...is necessarily ignorant of the outcome of future free human decisions - including, presumably, the decision to have children, where they will live, what they will eat and read and so forth - it is far from clear what Pinnock means by insisting that God must give access to all of them. He cannot even know how many will exist. Or is the universal provision of access effected by general revelation and/or by the *imago Dei*, regardless of how many human beings there are, what they are like, where they live, and so on? If so, Pinnock's argument needs much more substantiation" (p. 289 n. 53). I have tried to show in Part 2 of this study, that Pinnock does substantiate this argument.

of Christ to them."[24] If the notion of a universal salvific will proves a dead-end in proving universal accessibility, then what about the notion of unlimited atonement, the belief that Christ's death includes everyone in its scope?[25] Although, in the last two chapters I have raised questions concerning the representative rather than constitutive nature of the atonement in Pinnock's inclusivism and the tenuous relationship between the work of Christ and the salvation of the unevangelised, I want for the moment to take Pinnock's belief that it is the work of Christ which is the objective ground of salvation for the unevangelised.

There seems to be a close connection between God's universal salvific will and unlimited atonement as the saving will of God is revealed in Christ's work on the cross. However there would also appear to be some important differences between the two concepts because in the atonement, we are not dealing with an abstract 'wish' that can be frustrated, but in the making of this wish come true, a reality that has occurred in history: Christ died for all. Is there a necessary link between Christ dying for everyone, and everyone hearing about Christ dying for everyone?

The question therefore is not whether a universal redemptive provision is universal in its efficacy, for Pinnock and the Arminian theologians admit that man's freedom to resist salvific grace limits the efficacy. Rather the question is whether a universal redemptive provision can be limited in its scope in some way or another, for example the failure of Christian mission to take the gospel to certain parts of the world. All the treatments of unlimited atonement that I have looked at (apart from Pinnock's), do not answer this question. I would briefly like to offer what I think must be the response.

Let me describe in a little more detail the contours of the doctrine of unlimited atonement. Here, for the moment I want to focus on the scope or extent of the atonement rather than on its purpose and meaning, of course realising that both areas impinge on the other. At the heart of this doctrine are two sets of linked ideas: objective accomplishment and subjective application, and universal possibility and particular actuality. Whatever Jesus' death accomplished, only Jesus could accomplish it, but each individual must still accept that free gift: "It is clear...that Christ's death is universal in sufficiency and intention, but it is limited in its application. This limitation is imposed not by God but by man. The individual human being, created in the image of God with free will, must accept the benefits of the atonement."[26] Therefore one sees a mutual reciprocity between objective and subjective sides in Arminian soteriology: a positive subjective response is

---

[24] Pinnock, *Wideness*, p. 157.

[25] Strangely, neither Carson, op. cit. or Nash, op. cit. mention this connection in their critiques of Pinnock.

[26] Terry L. Miethe, 'The Universal Power of the Atonement' in ed. Clark H. Pinnock, *The Grace of God and Will of Man* (Minneapolis, 1995), p. 75.

needed to make effective the objective accomplishment, but there could not be the possibility of a subjective response without the objective provision. Because there is a degree of conditionality in this schema, an objective universalism is avoided, for unlimited atonement only leads to universalism if "God's sovereignty means that every act of God must be 'efficacious' and 'cannot be frustrated by man,' thereby negating any possible human freedom as being consistent with divine sovereignty."[27] There is enough biblical evidence to suggest that not everyone has accepted God's free gift in Christ. Conversely while there is the possibility that no-one would accept Christ's free offer of grace, this is only a logical possibility since the Bible suggests that many do indeed accept this offer.

It is the inextricable link between the objective and subjective sides of the Arminian soteriology, which seems to tie universal atonement to universal accessibility. For although Christ's death has achieved something objectively independent of the believer (i.e. a possibility of salvation which did not exist before Christ's death), in terms of its salvific potential, the subjective offer of this objective achievement would seem to be necessary to make the provision truly 'universal.' It would appear that to make a genuine 'universal' offer one needs every recipient to be in a position to accept or reject the offer. But can a universal offer be genuine yet frustrated? It can in terms of efficacy (acceptance or rejection) but what about scope? One can say that the atonement is potentially universal in efficacy but can it be only potential in scope? To affirm this would appear to disrupt the delicate balance between objective and subjective with the subjective totally defining the objective. I do not, though, think that this is what Arminian theologians mean when they claim that Christ's death is objectively unlimited and universal, for without the universal possibility to accept or reject Christ, Christ's death becomes limited to those who hear about it and of no use to those who don't.

I would like to suggest, then, that whereas a belief in God's universal salvific will does not necessarily imply universal accessibility, a belief in universal atonement does, and although in practice Pinnock may fail to demonstrate this idea, in principle he is correct. Pinnock also sees the implication of this belief: "This raises a difficult question. How is salvation within the reach of the unevangelised? How can anyone be saved without knowing Christ? The idea of universal accessibility, though not a novel theory, needs to be proven. It is far from self-evident, at least biblically speaking. How can it best be defended?"[28]

I have spent the greater part of this study trying to show that Pinnock's attempt to prove universal accessibility is fundamentally flawed precisely because of its divorce from the work of Christ, and at the same time indi-

---

[27] Ibid.
[28] Pinnock, *Wideness*, p. 157.

cated the particular doctrinal issues that need to be addressed in formulating a position on the unevangelised. This said, if one wants to argue that universal atonement implies universal accessibility, then there would have to be some theory that would demonstrate the principle that universal accessibility, and all such theories have a number of weaknesses.[29]

The Case for an Effective and Particular Atonement

The need to provide some theory only exists if one wishes to accept the doctrine of unlimited atonement. Reformed theology has the resources to be able to deny universal accessibility because it denies unlimited atonement. Rather than adopt Pinnock's model of atonement, if one is to believe that the 'penal substitution' model is the biblical way of understanding the atonement, then there are some conclusions concerning its intent and extent that must be mentioned, conclusions which Pinnock himself sees.[30] There is much material on this subject and the debate is well-rehearsed within evangelicalism, so I will only briefly mention the relevant issues as regards the unevangelised.[31]

The 'penal' model is a totally objective model: that is, it does not make salvation merely possible, but accomplishes and secures it with the Holy Spirit applying its benefits to the believer:

> Should we not think of Christ's substitution for us on the cross as a definite, one-to-one relationship between him and each individual sinner? ...But if Christ specifically took and discharged my penal obligation as a sinner, does it not follow that the cross was decisive for my salvation not only as its sole meritorious ground, but also in guaranteeing that I should be brought to faith, and through faith to eternal life? For is not the faith which receives salvation part of God's gift of salvation...and implied in what Paul says of *God's calling* and John of *new birth*? And if Christ by his death on my behalf secured reconciliation and righteousness as gifts for me to receive (Rom. 5:11,17), did not this make it certain that the faith which receives this gifts would also be given to me, as a direct consequence of Christ's dying for me?[32]

---

[29] I survey a number of these theories in Appendix 1.

[30] See p. 78.

[31] For a more detailed discussion of the extent of the atonement see G. Michael Thomas, *The Extent of the Atonement: A Dilemma for Reformed Theology from Calvin to the Consensus* (Carlilse, 1997); Letham, op. cit., pp. 225-249; Louis Berkhof, *Systematic Theology* (Edinburgh, 1958), pp. 292-399; Grudem, op. cit., pp. 594-603; John Murray, *Redemption Accomplished and Applied* (Edinburgh, 1961), pp. 59-76.

[32] Packer, 'What Did the Cross Achieve? The Logic of Penal Substitution' in *Tyndale Bulletin* 25 (1974), p. 36.

I come here to the question of the extent of the atonement. For if Christ died for everyone, then logically all *must* be saved, for the cross *secures* salvation. This would imply universalism, a conclusion which Pinnock rejects and a belief that we rejected because it falls outside the parameters of an 'evangelical' theology. But having rejected universalism we are left with limited efficacy (the cross only made salvation possible), which strict penal substitution cannot accept, or a limited extent (Christ only died for a particular people). Pinnock himself realises that a strict penal substitution necessarily must lead to particular redemption as do the majority of evangelicals who call themselves 'Reformed.' For Pinnock, his biblical presuppositions concerning the universal salvific will of God and Man's freedom cannot lead him to particular redemption and so his model of atonement has been revised to an inclusive model, indeed revised to the extent that the necessity and purpose of the atonement have become ambiguous.[33]

The idea of a particular effective atonement coheres very well with two of the major themes I have been advocating in previous chapters. Firstly this position is entirely consistent with the nature of the covenant established earlier: It is not a bilateral pact which depends on both sides for ratification, but a unilateral covenant which God establishes and maintains unconditionally.[34] Also there is the notion of Christ being the second Adam. If we are to believe that the first Adam was humanity's representative and that both legally and organically he represented humanity, then we must view Christ as the second Adam:

> Christ is the head of the new humanity as the second Adam, and he imparts a real personal union to his people. His life is communicated to them by the Holy Spirit... His actions were done on their behalf and in their place...a provisional and universal atonement would undermine the vital

---

[33] I should comment on those passages that say that Christ died for 'all' and which for Pinnock are foundational in proving the unlimited extent of the atonement. Here the exegetical dispute centres on the meaning of the words 'all' and 'world.' Expressions like 'all men' could mean *all without exception*, or *all without distinction*. So for example, commenting on Titus 2:11, Carson, op. cit. believes that to hold to the *all without exception* exegesis is false because the grace of God as seen in the incarnation was only seen by a relatively small number of people: "... the point of the Titus passage is that the grace of God has appeared 'to all men *without distinction*' i.e. not to Jews only, but to Jews and Gentiles alike, without distinction, to slave and free alike, without distinction. So in the context, Christian slaves are told they are to live in such a way that 'they will make the teaching about God out Saviour attractive. For the grace of God that brings salvation has appeared to all men (Titus 2:10-11)."(p. 288) Similarly, passages referring to 'the world,' do not mean every individual, rather they are referring to the cosmic side of the atonement and the renewal of creation.

[34] See Hanko, 'The Idea of Covenant' in *God's Everlasting Covenant of Grace*, pp. 13-27.

union with Christ that lies at the heart of biblical soteriology... He is no longer anybody's representative. He is not acting vicariously. In practice, if he is in the place of everyone provisionally, he is in the place of no-one specifically... Scripture holds before, however, the corporate nature of humanity and its salvation. We belong in Adam by nature and, as Christians by grace. Therefore, it is not first and foremost a question of Christ dying for certain individuals. He dies for *his people* (Mt. 1:21).[35]

Secondly, a particular extent of the atonement reaffirms trinitarian unity and order of the Persons where the Father plans the salvation of some, the Son, by his passive and active obedience, objectively accomplishes the redemption of some in the *historia salutis*, and the Spirit, by uniting the believer to Christ and giving the gift of faith, subjectively applies salvation to some in the *ordo salutis*.[36]

The 'Problem' of the Unevangelised?

In this study I have explicitly focused on Pinnock's inclusivist argument concluding that there is no biblical evidence that the unevangelised can be saved through an unspecific 'faith principle.' I have shown that throughout the biblical story there is a particularity of revelation and a particularity of grace and that a universalisation of these themes leads Pinnock away from traditional evangelical moorings.

In critiquing Pinnock's particular construal of inclusivism, I have been led into critiquing other areas of Pinnock's theology, particularly certain facets of Pinnock's soteriology, a soteriology which is part of Pinnock's theological framework he calls 'trinitarian openness.' This framework with its presuppositions of mutuality and conditionality between God and human beings dictate Pinnock's view of salvation. For human beings to be responsible agents, they must have libertarian freedom and a degree of autonomy. This means that they can always choose or reject God's grace. To be able to choose, human beings must have some knowledge, and so there must be a universal access to salvation. For God to be just and fair, He must give everyone the chance to respond to God's overtures. It should be apparent that the critique levelled at Pinnock over the atonement and faith is part of the wider conflict between Reformed evangelicalism and 'trinitarian openness.'

My point is this: In Pinnock's theology, his adherence to 'trinitarian openness' with its stress on mutuality and reciprocity between God and human beings, generates his construal of the universality axiom. With the

---

[35] Letham, op cit., p. 236.

[36] Letham, op. cit., believes that universal atonement introduces disorder into the Trinity because the Father and Spirit have different goals from the Son: "The tendency is towards tritheism, and the unity of the Godhead is undermined" (p. 237).

universality axiom as a presupposition, Pinnock is pressured to find a mediation that shows a universal accessibility. As has been seen, though, a universalisation of particular themes such as revelation, grace and atonement, changes the whole nature of these themes so removing them from their biblical meaning. I suggest that with this in mind, one should look at whether there is the tension between universality and particularity that Pinnock suggests.

The issue seems to be one of perspective. Pinnock has stressed the love, grace and mercy of God so much, that other equally important themes, the depth of sin, the righteous wrath and judgement of God, have been neglected. This reductionism results in a misunderstanding of the love of God and its complex nature. As Carson notes:

> The tone of the Bible...is that if we human beings are lost, it is because of our sin. Our guilt before God justly earns his wrath. If we are not consumed, it is of the Lord's mercy... The love of God is presented as surprising, undeserved, unmerited, lavish...the condemnation of guilty rebels that seems so transparently obvious in the Bible's story-line is now transmuted into a different kind of story, a 'pity the perpetrator' story: they may be guilty, but if they do not have free access to a way of escape surely it would be unjust to condemn them?[37]

Biblical anthropology presents the effects of the Fall as being so severe that the only universal thing we merit is judgement, wrath and condemnation, *not* love:

> The justice of God is questioned by some critics who protest that election-love is discriminatory and therefore a violation of justice. But all love is preferential or it would not be love... The modern misjudgment of God flows easily from contemporary theology's occupation with love as the core of God's being, while righteousness is subordinated and denied equal ultimacy with love in the nature of deity.[38]

Packer is not being 'unfair' when he comments that Pinnock's argument seems more influenced by 'American principles of fairness' than anything else.[39] Pinnock believes that the unevangelised pose questions concerning the justice of God. But as Henry points out, "God's justice is not based on empirical considerations but reflects his own essential nature: he is intrinsi-

---

[37] Ibid., p. 289f.
[38] Carl Henry, 'Is it Fair?' in eds. Crockett and Sigountos, *Through No Fault of Their Own?* (Grand Rapids, 1992), p. 253f.
[39] Quoted from Nash, op. cit., p. 164.

cally just (Ps. 85:11)... God does not stand under justice as a norm but is himself the norm."[40]

The problem with the question of the unevangelised is that it is wrongly construed as being about 'those who have never heard *through no fault of their own*,' or those who are 'invincibly *ignorant*.' However the biblical worldview tells us that no-one is spiritually guiltless and that while there are degrees of light and of responsibility, everyone has spurned the light they have, whether this be the light of general revelation or special revelation. This is the universality of sin. Seen from this perspective, there is less pressure and urgency to try and mediate universality and particularity. Indeed we are now finally in a position to question whether there is a universality axiom.

This question has already been answered in our discussion on atonement and the scope of its saving provisions. But this discussion is only one part of a wider picture that ultimately comes down to one's view of God and His sovereignty. A statement of the issue is simple: Pinnock believes in God's universal salvific will and believes that this implies a universal accessibility, the assumption in Pinnock's proposal is that God's desire to save everyone *obliges* Him to send enough revelation and grace to save everyone. Once again I refer to the comment of W. Gary Phillips, "In relation to the attributes of God, holiness (a constant) and justice (a constant) have priority over redemption (a contingent). If God were not holy and just, he would not be God. But redemption is not an attribute but an action; that is, God could have chosen not to manifest his mercy through redemption, and still be God."[41]

There is, though, another position that is possible. If one believes in a total depravity and a particular redemption based on God's sovereign electing grace, then one is in a position to question whether God's salvific will is 'universal.' As Henry states: "Nowhere does the Bible teach that God plans to save all human beings; it indicates rather that God in His sovereign will elects certain individuals to Christ (Jn. 6:37; Eph. 1:4-5). Some would seek to invert predestination by conditioning it on foreseen faith or good works, but biblical salvation rests distinctively on God's merciful intervention and not on human merit."[42] The 'Reformed' soteriological structure I have outlined is but a subset and microcosm of the 'Reformed' worldview, "The five points [which I described on pp.15f.] assert no more than that God is sovereign in saving the individual, but Calvinism, as such, is concerned with the much broader assertion that he is sovereign everywhere."[43] Here

---

[40] Carl Henry, 'Is it Fair?' in eds. Crockett and Sigountos, op. cit., p. 255.
[41] W. Gary Phillips, 'Evangelicals and Pluralism: Current Options' in *Proceedings of the Wheaton Theology Conference*, 1992, p. 188.
[42] Ibid., p. 254.
[43] Packer, 'Introductory Essay' p. 5.

we are into areas such as providence, predestination, election, determinism and human responsibility that fall outside the scope of this study but areas that define Pinnock's 'trinitarian openness' framework as well as Reformed theology.

How do the unevangelised fit into a Reformed framework? The answer to this question has not been the purpose of this study although it is perhaps the next step to make from this study. I can only hint at how the argument might run. Donald Lake claims that the doctrine of unconditional election solves the question of the unevangelised for Calvinists in the following way: "The doctrine of election has served to solve the problem of those who have died without ever hearing the gospel: if they were part of the elect, they were saved without hearing; if not numbered among the elect, their not hearing was of no consequence."[44] I believe that such an argument unnaturally divides the ends and the means to that ends, that is the decree of election and the implementation of that decree. It seems more natural to see election and predestination together with the scope of Christ's death and with providence. This appears to be Calvin's own view on the unevangelised as explained by G. Michael Thomas:

> God's providential deprivation of such people is to be viewed as an expression of the predestination that has destined salvation for only a part of the human race: "The covenant of life is not preached equally among all men... This variety...also serves the decision of God's eternal election." It must be a matter of causal determination of individual destinies revealed by effects (the conversion of some and the nonconversion of others). Scope is thereby given for understanding God's intention concerning the scope of redemption in terms of its effects in time.[45]

> Predestination and providence are closely allied, and in matters of both providence and predestination God's will may be judged from its result. From the fact that not all hear the gospel, and of those that hear not all believe, Calvin read the particularism of God's ultimate intentions.[46]

What is systematically interesting here, and following Calvin's line, is a number of Reformed theologians who use the simple fact that not everyone hears the gospel as evidence in their defence of a particular extent to the atonement. John Owen in *The Death of Death in the Death of Christ* is one who uses this line of argument:

---

[44] Donald M. Lake, 'He Died for All: The Universal Dimensions of the Atonement' in ed. Clark H. Pinnock, *Grace Unlimited* (Minneapolis, 1975), p. 43.
[45] G. Michael Thomas, op. cit., p. 15f.
[46] Ibid., p. 34.

If the Lord intended that he should, and [he] by his death did, procure pardon of sin and reconciliation with God for all and every one, to be actually enjoyed upon condition that they do believe, then ought this goodwill and intention of God, with this purchase in their behalf by Jesus Christ, to be made known to them by the word, that they might believe ... for if these things be not made known and revealed to all and every one that is concerned in them, namely, to whom the Lord intends, and for whom he hath procured so great a good, then one of these things will follow; either, first, That they may be saved without faith in, and the knowledge of, Christ (which they cannot have unless he be revealed to them), which is false, and proved so; or else, secondly, That this good will of God, and this purchase made by Jesus Christ, is plainly in vain, and frustrate in respect of them, yea, a plain mocking of them, that will neither do them any good to help them out of misery, nor serve the justice of God to leave them inexcusable, for what blame can redound to them for not embracing and well using a benefit which they never heard of in their lives? Doth it become the wisdom of God to send Christ to die for men that they might be saved, and never cause these men to hear of any such thing; and yet to purpose and declare that unless they do hear of it and believe it, they shall never be saved?[47]

In a more recent work, Robert Reymond cites 'The Limited Number of People, by Divine Arrangement, Who Actually Hear the Gospel' as one evidence for the doctrine of particular redemption. He writes: "Clearly, the matter of who hears the gospel is under the providential governance of the sovereign God, and he has so arranged gospel history that many people will never hear about Christ. It is unthinkable to suppose then that God sent his Son to save people who, by the ordering of his own providence, never hear the gospel in order that they may believe and be saved."[48]

If God wishes to save the unevangelised (and in this theological framework it is now difficult to know what the term 'unevangelised' means), He will provide the means for them to be saved. As the ordinary means is traditionally thought to be *fides ex auditu* through the human messenger, then those who never hear must lie outside God's salvific will and Christ's atoning provisions. God has prescribed certain means by which people can be

---

[47] Owen, John. The Death of Death in The Death of Christ: A Treatise in Which the Whole Controversy About Universal Redemption is Fully Discussed (1648) (with an introductory essay by J.I Packer.) (Edinburgh, 1983), p. 126.

[48] Robert L. Reymond, *A New Systematic Theology of the Christian Faith* (Nashville, 1998), p. 676f. Reymond cites biblical evidence to indicate that "God, by determining as he has the recipients of special revelation and by governing the geographic directions of missionary history, determined that some people would not hear the gospel," including Acts 16:6-8 where he writes "as a result the gospel spread westward into Europe and not eastward toward Asia, and many Asians died never having heard of Christ" (p. 676).

saved. One *could* say that the unevangelised cannot be saved because they are not within the redemptive stream of salvation where God brings salvation. God does not wish to save them and so there is no need to construct a theology that includes them.

Equally, though, it is logically possible to say one would not compromise God's sovereignty or the monergism of salvation by saying that God may have a variety of means to bring special revelation and saving grace to the unevangelised although there are other issues to be noted here, particularly the relationship between the Spirit and the Word.[49]

Of course as I have noted, the issue in a Reformed framework is far more sophisticated and nuanced than I have portrayed, for many wish to distinguish different connotations of God's 'will,'[50] of God's love,[51] of God's grace (as was seen in the common grace debate), and of God's revelation (as was seen in the general revelation debate). All I wish to assert at the moment is that in Reformed theology, the pressure to resolve universality and particularity is not as acute as it is (and must be) in Pinnock's theology because the universality axiom is not a presupposition of that paradigm.

---

[49] I noted at the end of the previous chapter p. 254 n. 96 the issues involved here. For some Reformed theologians (including W. G. T. Shedd, Zanchius, Richard Baxter, and Zwingli) who believe that God can and indeed does work extraordinarily without the Word see Paul Helm, 'Are They Few That Be Saved' in ed. Nigel M. de S. Cameron, *Universalism and the Doctrine of Hell* (Edinburgh, 1992), pp. 255-281. Referring to the biblical examples that Shedd uses as evidence for such a view (including Cornelius), Helm writes: "In going back beyond human authorities we cannot afford to neglect what Scripture *may* teach. For the history of the Church has shown that the conflict, or apparent conflict, between Scripture and experience has often led to a more comprehensive understanding of Scripture and so, in turn, to a firmer faith in God's revealed truth. And it would be most unfortunate to allow prejudice or tradition, however hallowed, which may strongly dispose us to believe that...a knowledge of Christ is indispensable to salvation, to prevent a true appreciation of the biblical data" (p. 272). In fact, Helm's own tentative argument suggests that the Holy Spirit can regenerate someone through the medium of general revelation (pp. 275-281).

[50] The traditional Reformed distinction has been made between God's secret and revealed will. See, Grudem, op. cit., pp. 211-216, 332; Berkhof, op. cit., pp. 41-81; Lewis and Demarest, *Integrative Theology Vol. 1*, pp. 291-337; John Piper 'Are There Two Wills in God? Divine Election and God's Desire for All to be Saved' in eds. Thomas R. Schreiner and Bruce A. Ware, *The Grace of God, The Bondage of the Will*. Vol. 1. (Grand Rapids, 1995). pp. 107-133.

[51] See, for example, J. I. Packer, 'The Love of God: Universal and Particular' in eds. Thomas R. Schreiner and Bruce A. Ware, *The Grace of God, The Bondage of the Will*. Vol. 2. Grand Rapids, 1995), pp. 413-429; Don Carson, 'On Distorting the Love of God' in *Bibliotheca Sacra* 156 (Jan.-Mar.), pp. 3-12; idem 'God is Love' in *Bibliotheca Sacra* 156 (Apr.-June), pp. 131-142.; idem *The Difficult Doctrine of the Love of God* (Leicester, 2000).

Concluding Remarks

Assessing Pinnock's Inclusivism

In the previous section, I began the important task of relating both Pinnock's inclusivism and the counter Reformed view to the wider theological frameworks that are operating in both positions. Like Clarke, I believe that these wider frameworks run on two continuums, the first being between God's transcendence and immanence and the second between human sinfulness and godlikeness:

> For those accustomed to Reformed modes of thinking, the need to maximise the distance between God and human beings leads to stressing the transcendence and sinfulness poles, a depreciation of general revelation, and a skittishness about any human involvement in the process of salvation. These emphases spin a web of beliefs that inevitably lead to a denial of point 1 *[God's universal salvific will]*... For those attracted to the implicit-faith view *[what I have called inclusivism]*... They believe it is better to admit a richer sense of the godlikeness of the human person...and a fuller understanding of the immanence of God through his action in the world.[52]

Having described and critiqued Pinnock's inclusivism I would like to conclude that the basic impulses behind his pneumatological inclusivism, that is the universality axiom (consisting of God's salvific will for everyone, Christ's death for everyone, salvation accessible for everyone and the *Heilsoptimismus*) are in line with Pinnock's wider theological framework called 'trinitarian openness.' However when one begins to analyse the 'mechanics' of his inclusivism, there are internal tensions due to Pinnock's desire to affirm universality and particularity. This in turn leads to lacunas in his argument and imprecision over crucial areas of doctrine.

Possibly a more serious failure, concerns the exegetical test and Pinnock's hermeneutical assumptions. My conclusion here is the same as Carson: "We begin to suspect that we are not dealing with a well thought out theological synthesis, backed by careful exegesis and evenhanded reason, but with a mindset that is no longer comfortable with the constraints of the biblical story-line, but cannot quite let go of it."[53]

This quotation highlights for me a real ambiguity in Pinnock's thinking which makes assessment of him from an evangelical point of view difficult. I think the cause of this ambiguity can be explained by an unresolved tension running throughout his position on the unevangelised. Pinnock still

---

[52] David. K. Clarke, 'Is Special Revelation Necessary for Salvation?' in eds. Crockett and Sigountos, op. cit., pp. 35-45, p. 44.
[53] Carson, op. cit., p. 300.

wishes to remain within the boundaries of evangelical orthodoxy in terms of his belief in the particularity and finality of Christ. However his desire to prove the universality axiom puts strain on, and at times compromises, both particularity and orthodoxy. This is visible at key stages of his argument (Christology, atonement, Trinitarian processions, revelation and soteriology) and is epitomized in his failure to properly relate Spirit (who for him represents universality) and Son (who represents particularity). For this tension to be resolved, Pinnock would seem to have a choice to make. He could re-affirm evangelical orthodoxy realising the detrimental ramifications this would have for his inclusivism. Alternatively he could follow his inclusivist impulses, realising that this would mean the giving up of certain tenets of evangelical orthodoxy. Pinnock's constant emphasis on universality and his willingness to look outside the evangelical tradition to resource his inclusivist argument is possibly an indication that he is not perturbed about the claim that his position goes outside the boundaries of orthodox evangelicalism. Even under a broad definition of evangelicalism, I believe that I have shown that there are too many problems both internally and biblically to make Pinnock's doctrine of the unevangelised a viable 'evangelical' option.

Towards an Evangelical 'Theology of Religions': Tasks and Topics Ahead

Clark Pinnock's inclusivist attempt may be fatally flawed, but at least he has attempted to engage with some important contemporary theological questions that demand some kind of answer. I think that all evangelicals, from whatever theological background, have some constructive theologizing to do in the areas I have been exploring. Having rejected Pinnock's inclusivism, evangelicals must not be left with a theological vacuum, but give some sustained attention and reflection to a number of issues, some of which I have hinted at throughout the study. Firstly, I think my analysis has highlighted the areas of doctrine that need to be discussed in any theology of the unevangelised and raised questions as to whether *any* inclusivism can be compatible with evangelicalism; and furthermore the difficulties for evangelicals who adopt the principle of universal accessibility. Certainly within Reformed parameters within which I have based my critique, there are not the same theological or emotional pressures generated as there are in other evangelical doctrinal systems and which make the unevangelised and the possibility of their salvation a 'problem' seeking a theological answer.

However, and secondly, I readily concede that in my own argumentation there are several areas that require much more critical reflection, detail and substantiation. I think here particularly of my trinitarian suggestions concerning an 'epistemological *perichoresis*' in revelation which is definitely still at an embryonic stage.[54] More generally I think that Reformed evangelicals need to give much more critical reflection to the doctrine of the means of grace, and in particular the distinctions between 'ordinary' and 'extraordinary' means and immediate and mediate means in the *ordo salutis*. While these distinctions have traditionally arisen with regard to the doctrine of baptism and children in the church, I have noted various Reformed thinkers who wish to apply these categories when speculating on the possibility outside of the visible church.

Finally, and what is possibly the most pressing need, is for a comprehensive evangelical 'theology of religions' which not only says what other religions are not, but offers some detailed suggestions as to what other religions are. As Conn states: "Affirming the finality of Christ does not relieve us of the responsibility to explain the relationship between Christianity and other religions. Sadly, the evangelical world seems almost silent on this crucial issue... No, extensive, systematic model has appeared in recent years."[55] Such an exploration will raise crucial questions: How exactly is God present in other religions? From a biblical perspective what are the genesis of other religions? What is the origin of religious experiences in other religions? Based on my research in this study, I would like to suggest that a rich vein to mine in looking for answers to these questions are the doctrines of general revelation and common grace, again both areas which need contemporary evangelical restatements.

---

[54] This whole area of epistemology can be neatly summarised as the need to differentiate different types of knowledge. In correspondence, my friend Allen Baird has outlined one way of formulating the issue:
1. The knowledge of a regenerate man - in creation - of the ontological Trinity
- of the economic Trinity
- in the gospel - of the ontological Trinity
- of the economic Trinity
2. The knowledge of an unregenerate man - in creation - of the ontological Trinity
- of the economic Trinity
- in the gospel - of the ontological Trinity
- of the economic Trinity

[55] Harvie M. Conn 'Do Other Religions Save?' in eds. W. Crockett and J. Sigountos *Through No Fault of Their Own? The Fate of Those Who Have Never Heard.* (Grand Rapids, 1991), p. 207. As to one evangelical thinker who has attempted a systematic treatment in this area, Conn mentions the work of J. H. Bavinck and his "exciting 'possessio' model"(p. 207). Certainly Bavinck's work needs more careful analysis and could well be the foundation for the type of approach I am advocating. See John H. Bavinck, *An Introduction to the Science of Missions* trans. David H. Freeman (Grand Rapids, 1960), pp. 169-90, 221-272; *idem* 'Human Religion in God's Eyes: A Study of Romans 1:18-32' *Scottish Bulletin of Evangelical Theology* 12/1 (Spring 1994), pp. 44-52.

The Universality of Mission

Finally, I wish to conclude my study by re-affirming a defining tenet of evangelicalism: the necessity of evangelism and missions. I have purposefully not dealt with the missiological implications of Pinnock's inclusivism, and other positions regarding the salvation of the unevangelised in general, as I believe this has been tackled ably elsewhere.[56] All I want to say is that from a Reformed evangelical perspective, a perspective that I have been advocating throughout this study, rather than succumbing to a predestinarian paralysis which is sometimes levelled at the Reformed position,[57] one must take with utmost seriousness the belief that God has not only ordained the way of salvation through the Gospel, but also the means for this Gospel to be proclaimed: through the human messenger. It is at this point that one must embrace a belief in universality, a universal vision for disseminating the Word of God. As the Canons of Dordt state, "The command to repent and believe ought to be declared and published to all nations and to all persons promiscuously and without distinction, to whom God out of his good pleasure sends the Gospel"(II/5). Commenting on Rom. 10:14,15[58] John Piper writes the following:

---

[56] See John K. Barrett, 'Does Inclusivist Theology Undermine Evangelism?' in *Evangelical Quarterly* 70/3 (1998), pp. 219-245; John Piper, *Let the Nations Be Glad: The Supremacy of God in Missions* (Leicester, 1994), pp. 115-167; Nash, op. cit., pp. 165-169; William V. Crockett and James G. Sigountos, 'Are the "Heathen" Really Lost?' in eds. William V. Crockett and James G. Sigountos, *Through No Fault of Their Own?* (Grand Rapids, 1991), pp. 257-265; John D. Ellenberger, 'Is Hell a Proper Motivation for Missions?' in eds. William V. Crockett and James G. Sigountos, *Through No Fault of Their Own?* (Grand Rapids, 1991), pp. 217-227; Charles VanEngen, 'The Uniqueness of Christ in Mission Theology' in eds. Edward Rommen and Harold Netland, *Christianity and the Religions: A Biblical Theology of World Religions* (Pasadena, 1995), pp. 183-217.

[57] For example John Sanders writing on the importance of missions for restrictivists states "An example of restricitivists who do not subscribe to this argument would be those in the Reformed tradition, who have traditionally not evidenced much interest in missions despite their belief that the unevangelised are damned to hell." *No Other Name*, p. 48 n. 24. For a refutation of Sanders' claim, see William Travis, 'William Carey: The Modern Missions Movement and the Sovereignty of God' in eds. Thomas R. Schreiner and Bruce A. Ware, *The Grace of God, the Bondage of the Will. Volume 2: Historical and Theological Perspectives on Calvinism* (Grand Rapids, 1995), pp. 323-336. For a strong Calvinist position which stresses the importance of mission over and against hyper-Calvinists who do not, see David J. Engelsma, *Hyper-Calvinism and the Call of the Gospel* (Grand Rapids, Reformed Free Publishing Association), pp. 67-127.

[58] "How, then, can they call on the one they have not believed in? And how can they believe in the one of whom they have not heard? And how can they hear without someone preaching to them? And how can they preach unless they are sent? As it is written, 'How beautiful are the feet of those who bring good news!'"

Charles Hodge is right that "the solemn question, implied in the language of the apostle, "HOW CAN THEY BELIEVE WITHOUT A PREACHER? should sound day and night in the ears of the churches." It is our unspeakable privilege to be caught up with him in the greatest movement in history - the ingathering of the elect "from all tribes and tongues and peoples and nations."[59]

As an evangelical, I fervently believe that God commands all evangelicals to take this *evangel* into all the world, just as the king says to his servants in Jesus' parable of the wedding banquet, "Go to the street corners and invite to the banquet anyone you find."(Mat.11:9). That it has pleased God to bring His salvation through the instrumentality of the preached Word, is at the same time an 'unspeakable privilege,' and an awesome responsibility, a responsibility that is truly universal in its scope.

---

[59] Piper, op. cit., pp. 158. Piper is quoting from Charles Hodge, *Commentary on the Epistle to the Romans* (New York, 1893), p. 553.

APPENDIX, BIBLIOGRAPHY AND INDEX

APPENDIX 1

EVANGELICAL RESPONSES TO THE FATE OF THE UNEVANGELISED

Introduction

In my definition of inclusivism in Ch. 1, I hinted at a particular typology of evangelical responses to the unevangelised. The purpose of this Appendix is one of contextualisation: to outline this typology in more detail and outline the theological geography of evangelical responses to the question of the unevangelised.[1] The Appendix will be divided into two parts. The first part will set out a typology for delineating various evangelical responses to the question of the unevangelised, the second part will actually describe these responses.

As outlined in Ch. 1, the question of the unevangelised is an emotive and controversial issue that intersects many areas of evangelical theology and raises many basic questions. It was remarked that, at an academic level, it is only recently that the issue has been systematically treated in its own right. Compared to the important non-evangelical typologies on the question of non-Christian salvation I would like to say the following. As evangelicals presuppose the finality, particularity and salvific ontological necessity of Christ, and deny universalism,[2] the range of options available concerning non-Christian salvation is more narrow in scope than non-evangelical typologies. In Ch. 1 I refer to Alan Race[3] and Gavin D'Costa's[4] threefold typology concerning the relationship between Christianity and other religions. Although the focus for evangelicals relates to non-Christian salvation rather than the status of other religions *per se*, evangelical responses to the unevangelised correspond to both the exclusivist and inclusivist paradigms as

---

[1] I have decided to include this section as an Appendix rather than in the main body of the text because the subject of my study concerns the particular position of inclusivism rather than a survey of evangelical responses.
[2] I explain these presuppositions in more detail in Ch. 1, pp. 28-32.
[3] Alan Race, *Christians and Religious Pluralism* (London, 1982).
[4] Gavin D'Costa, *Theology and Religious Pluralism* (Oxford, 1986).

outlined by Race and D'Costa. This threefold typology has been adapted by two evangelicals Dennis L. Okholm and Timothy R. Phillips, who edit *More Than One Way? Four Views on Salvation in a Pluralistic World*.[5] This book contains a four way conversation between John Hick who represents pluralism, the evangelical theologian Clark H. Pinnock who represents inclusivism, and two forms of particularism[6] represented by the evangelicals Alister McGrath, and R. Douglas Geivett and W. Gary Phillips. Paul Knitter in his book *No Other Name*[7] outlines four Christian attitudes toward Religious Pluralism: "The Conservative Evangelical Model: One True Religion;"[8] "The Mainline Protestant Model: Salvation only in Christ;"[9] "The Catholic Model: Many Ways, One Norm;"[10] "the Theocentric Model: Many Ways to the Center."[11] The evangelical spectrum I will outline certainly compares to the first and second of Knitter's groupings and regarding the form of inclusivism I focus on in my study, may well encroach into the third grouping.

Finally and within Catholic theology, J. Peter Schineller[12] outlines a spectrum of four views on the relationship between Christology and ecclesiology:

1. Ecclesiocentric universe, exclusive Christology: Jesus Christ and Church constitutive and exclusive way of salvation.
2. Christocentric universe, inclusive Christology: a) Jesus Christ and Church constitutive but not exclusive way of salvation; b) Jesus Christ constitutive but Church nonconstitutive way of salvation.
3. Theocentric universe, normative Christology: Jesus Christ and Church normative but not constitutive way of salvation.
4. Theocentric universe, nonnormative Christology: Jesus Christ one of many ways of salvation.[13]

---

[5] eds. Dennis L. Okholm and Timothy R. Phillips, *More Than One Way? Four Views on Salvation in a Pluralistic World* (Grand Rapids, 1995), pp. 7-27.

[6] Okholm and Phillips, op. cit., choose the term 'particularism' over 'exclusivism' or 'restrictivism' because they believe that a term like 'exclusivism' "is so prejudicial that it precludes true dialogue"(p. 16).

[7] Paul Knitter, *No Other Name: A Critical Survey of Christian Attitudes Toward the World Religions* (Maryknoll, 1985).

[8] Ibid., pp. 75-96.

[9] Ibid., pp. 79-119.

[10] Ibid., pp. 120-144.

[11] Ibid., pp. 145-168.

[12] Peter J. Schineller, 'Christ and the Church: A Spectrum of Views' in *Theological Studies* 37 (1976), pp. 545-566.

[13] Ibid., p. 550.

Compared to the evangelical spectrum, certainly Schineller's first two positions correspond, and again my study argues that certain theologians move into the third category.

Moving into the evangelical community, and before I concentrate on what I consider to be the most important typology on this question, I would briefly like to mention the typology outlined by David K. Clark in his essay, 'Is Special Revelation Necessary for Salvation,'[14] because I will adapt some of Clark's ideas when constructing my own typology. Clark outlines five beliefs:

> 1) God desires all persons to have an opportunity to experience salvation...
> 2) If one is to experience salvation, it can only be by knowing Christ.
> 3) If one is to know Christ, it can only be by coming into contact with special revelation...
> 4) God is powerful enough to see to it that everyone comes into contact with special revelation.
> 5) Not all persons in human history have had contact with special revelation.[15]

He continues:
> Unless we accept the disputed idea of 'middle knowledge,' [see below] these five statements cannot all be true; at least one of them is false. Evangelicals consider
> (2) nonnegotiable although some liberals cast it aside, and they accept (4) although it is regularly doubted by process theologians. Given the evangelical view of special revelation, (5) is true. So while some undoubtedly live with the tension, those evangelicals who have resolved the dilemma must do so by denying (1) or (3). Either they claim that God does not desire to save all persons or they suggest that knowledge about God through modes of revelation other than Christ or the Bible can provide sufficient knowledge for the Holy Spirit to elicit faith.[16]

Clark describes three positions, the 'Traditional Reformed View' that denies (1); the 'Universalist Alternative' which denies (5); and the 'Implicit-Faith' view which denies (3).

---

[14] in eds. W. Crockett and J. Sigountos, *Through No Fault of Their Own?* (Grand Rapids, 1991), pp. 35-45.
[15] Ibid., p. 35f.
[16] Ibid., p. 36.

John Sanders' Typology of Evangelical Responses on the Fate of the Unevangelised

The work of the American evangelical John Sanders remains the most comprehensive and detailed on the subject of the unevangelised in evangelical theology, and it is his understanding of the question and his terminology that has been most widely adopted in the general discussion.[17]

Laying aside the inclusion of universalism in his typology, and which I have already deemed untenable for evangelicals,[18] Sanders describes two

---

[17] Sanders has written extensively on this subject. See the following 'Is Belief in Christ Necessary for Salvation?' *Evangelical Quarterly* 60 (1988), pp. 241-259; 'The Perennial Debate' *Christianity Today* (May 14th 1990): 20-21; 'Mercy to All: Romans 1-3 and the Destiny of the Unevangelised' in *Proceedings of the Wheaton Theology Conference*, pp. 216-229; 'Evangelical Responses to Salvation Outside the Church' *Christian Scholars Review* 24/1 (1994), pp. 45-58; ed. Sanders, John E. *What About Those Who Have Never Heard? Three Views on the Destiny of the Unevangelised.* (Downers Grove, 1995). By far the most important work is Sanders' booklength study, *No Other Name: An Investigation Into the Destiny of the Unevangelised.* (London, 1994). For other evangelicals who use and adapt Sanders' typology see W. Gary Phillips, 'Evangelicals and Pluralism: Current Options' in *Proceedings of the Wheaton Theology Conference. The Challenge of Religious Pluralism: An Evangelical Analysis and Response* (Wheaton, 1992), pp. 174-190; Alan Linfield, 'Sheep and Goats: Current Evangelical Thought on the Nature of Hell and the Scope of Salvation' *Vox Evangelica* 24 (1994), pp. 63-75; 'The Destiny of The Unevangelised.' *Bibliotheca Sacra* 1) 152. Jan-Mar. 1995. pp. 3-15; 2) 152. Apr-Je. 1995. pp. 113-144; 3) 152. Jly-Sept. 1995. pp. 259-272.

[18] As well as being an untenable position for evangelicals to take, I think that including universalism in his typology is unhelpful for two reasons. Firstly if universalism is the doctrine that everyone will be saved, then surely the opposite of this doctrine would be that no-one is saved. But restrictivism (which Sanders claims is the opposite of universalism) does not hold to this view, indeed I know of no theologian who holds to this. Therefore with regards to the unevangelised, universalism can maintain that they are all saved, because *everyone* is eventually saved, both evangelised and unevangelised. This does not seem helpful in dealing with the unevangelised as a separate community, because as suggested in Ch. 1 p. 30f, universalism is not an option for evangelicals. Now if Sanders wanted to define a particular type of universalism which maintained that the unevangelised are saved *because* they are unevangelised, then I feel he would have a more interesting argument to work on and logically this could be an 'evangelical' position because doctrines such as judgement and hell could still be maintained (but only for those who have heard the gospel). However this is not the way he defines universalism and there is no theologian in any of the literature that maintains a saved/unsaved distinction as regards the evangelised, but believes that all the unevangelised are automatically saved. Although I know of no-one who holds this position, it is logically possible to hold to it. The obvious problem with it would be the classical debate over determinism and free-will i.e. critics would say that to automatically save the unevangelised would be to contravene a person's freedom to accept or reject the Gospel. There could be no response to this because as soon as someone held a possibility that some could reject the gospel, it could no longer be called unqualified universalism and would have to call

types of position. Restrictivism maintains that "access to salvation is not universal but is restricted to those who hear the gospel from a human agent before death. Restrictivists hold that those who die never hearing the gospel of Christ are necessarily damned, due to their rejecting God the creator."[19] It is important to note that Sanders uses the term restrictivism rather than exclusivism for a very good reason:

> In the literature on religious pluralism, *exclusivism* designates the view that Christianity offers the only valid means of salvation... Though exclusivism affirms the particularity and finality of Jesus, it does not necessarily entail restrictivism, since some exclusivists are universalists, while other exclusivists affirm an opportunity after death for salvation. Both Karl Barth and Carl F. H. Henry are exclusivists regarding the relationship between Christianity and other religions, but they disagree strongly when it comes to the destiny of the unevangelised. Henry is a restrictivist, whole Barth hoped for universal salvation.[20]

Therefore all restrictivists are exclusivists but not all exclusivists are restricitivists.

In contrast to restrictivism are several "Wider Hope"[21] positions: "these positions disagree with restrictivism in that they affirm that God makes salvation universally accessible; every human being is given sufficient grace for salvation."[22] In *No Other Name*, Sanders describes three types of position within 'the Wider Hope': "Universal Evangelisation - before Death;" "Eschatological Evangelization;" and "Universally Accessible Salvation apart from Evangelisation" which he calls inclusivism. On Sanders' typol-

---

itself something else. Another perceptive criticism could be that in this position it would be always better *not* to evangelise and *not* to hear the gospel as this could jeopardise a person's salvation who was already saved when they were classed as unevangelised. This would have serious ramifications for missions! Secondly, including universalism leads to Sanders conflating two related but ultimately separate questions, the first concerning the *source/channel* of salvation, and the second concerning the *scope* of salvation. Universalism is primarily concerned with the scope of salvation and can include many formulations as to how this salvation is mediated. Sanders other categories though are defined by how salvation is mediated and subsequently deals with the scope of salvation. Many people could be saved by many means or few or one; few people could be saved by many or few or one. In Sanders' essay, 'Evangelical Responses to Salvation Outside the Church,' op. cit. he makes no reference to universalism. In my own typology that I outline below, I primarily focus on the question of accessibility of salvation, and subsequently deal with the means of salvation.

19   Sanders, 'Evangelical Responses to Salvation Outside the Church,' p. 46.
20   Sanders, *What About Those Who Have Never Heard?*, p. 12f.
21   Sanders, *No Other Name?*, p. 131.
22   Sanders, 'Evangelical Responses to Salvation Outside the Church,' p. 50.

Appendix 1: Evangelical Responses to the Fate of the Unevangelised 299

ogy there is one main point I wish to make and which will also serve as an introduction into my own typology.

In one of his introductions, Sanders notes the relationship between one's position concerning the unevangelised and one's view on other areas of doctrine. Here he makes a puzzling statement:

> ...many theological categories that separate Christians on other issues are, for the most part, irrelevant here. Whether I am a Calvinist, Arminian, dispensationalist, covenant theologian, charismatic, high church or low church may give a particular colouring to the model I choose, but these factors do not determine which model I favour regarding the destiny of those who have never heard the gospel. Some Calvinists for example, affirm restrictivism while others defend inclusivism and still other post-mortem evangelisation.
> What *is* significant for determining one's position on the unevangelised is one's particular view of the nature of God (especially the relationship between divine law and justice), the nature of the church, the significance of physical death, the value of God's revelation in creation, the nature of saving faith, the means of grace, and what is the best method for doing theology. The stand we take on these issues decisively affect the answer we give to the question of the destiny of the unevangelised.[23]

While Sanders in his historical bibliographies gives evidence of a wide range of theologians with differing backgrounds all named under one particular position, the problem with the above statement is that Sanders appears to forget that *partly* what distinguishes the Calvinist, from the Arminian, from the postconservative evangelical, are the issues he lists as being decisive in how one determines one's view on the unevangelised, most noticeable the nature of God and His salvific will, revelation in creation, nature of saving faith and the means of grace. If this is the case, then it would seem that whether one is a Calvinist or Arminian would have a bearing on what position is taken on the unevangelised.

Sanders, I think, would maintain that one can only really evaluate a theologian's position on the unevangelised, when it is placed into their broader theological framework that leads to the very position they are advocating. One position cannot be taken out of context as an isolated belief but must be viewed as part of a larger picture. This is not to say that outlining some broad positions is an unhelpful exercise, but that this can only be done on the understanding that any position one outlines contains theologians who are coming to this position by completely different routes.

What Sanders does, though, when he comes to describe, analyse and critique the different positions, is to only concentrate on *one* way in which this

---

[23] John Sanders, *What About Those Who Have Never Heard?*, p. 17.

position can be construed. This description not only outlines the position on the unevangelised, but states a certain theological framework that the position fits into. He therefore gives the impression that if one wants to adopt this position, one has to also adopt other theological baggage. The reason Sanders does this, is because there appears to be a subtext in his work, not concerned specifically with the unevangelised but with the certain theological framework that some evangelicals believe in. Sanders seems to reject restrictivism as much for the theological framework he believes restrictivists employ, as for their actual position on the unevangelised. As Caneday states: "Sanders so closely identifies restrictivism with 'Calvinism' that he mishandles restrictivism, virtually equating it with Calvinism (witness the three leading defenders he identifies: Augustine, Calvin, R.C. Sproul). Though it may be granted that most evangelicals are 'restrictivists,' only a minority would identify themselves as Calvinists."[24]

This strict alignment of Calvinism with restrictivism skews the issue, firstly, because it is difficult to know whether Sanders' real target is Calvinism, restrictivism, or both, and secondly because, apart from a few sentences, he forgets that there are many restrictivists who are not Calvinists. This same criticism applies to Sanders' definition of the 'wider hope' positions which he states more adequately uphold his two biblical axioms: Jesus as the only Saviour and God's universal salvific will. In his historical bibliography of this position, he mentions some Reformed theologians who he believes can come under this category, e.g. William Shedd.[25] However in his analysis of the 'wider hope' and the subsequent positions subsumed under it, Sanders describes the position in a such way as to question whether any Reformed theologian could align himself to the 'wider hope.' This is epitomised by Sanders' original definition of the 'wider hope' in terms of the biblical axioms. The first axiom dealing with the finality of Jesus has already been established as an evangelical fundamental with which all would agree. However it is Sanders' interpretation of the second axiom that causes a problem. He defines God's universal salvific will as affirming that, "God, in grace, grants every individual a genuine opportunity to participate in the redemptive work of the Lord Jesus, that no human being is excluded from the possibility of benefiting from salvific grace."[26] Whether this is a right or wrong interpretation of God's universal salvific will is not the point. What is at issue is that not all evangelicals would believe the claim, 'God wants all to be saved,' let alone the subsequent claim that God wanting all to be saved necessarily leads to the statement, 'God gives every hu-

---

[24] A.B. Caneday, 'Evangelical Meltdown "To Go Beyond What is Written" An Exercise in Speculative Theology' *Contra Mundum* No. 5 Fall 1992, pp. 1-11.
[25] Sanders, *No Other Name*, p. 144. See William Shedd, *Dogmatic Theology* 3 Vols. (New York, 1888-94), Vol. 2, pp. 706-708.
[26] Ibid., p. 131.

Appendix 1: Evangelical Responses to the Fate of the Unevangelised 301

man a chance to benefit from his saving grace' (what Sanders calls the principle of "universal accessibility").[27] Indeed those from a Reformed background would take issue with this interpretation. My point is that unless Sanders wishes to omit Reformed theology from his definition of evangelicalism, this interpretation of God's will cannot, to my mind, simply be *assumed* as a control-belief, but has to be *proven* as *part* of an argument. To set it up as a fundamental axiom, seems to be a flawed piece of thinking, as not all evangelicals would agree with this particular interpretation. Therefore, while Sanders lists certain Reformed thinkers as believing in the 'wider hope,' it is debatable whether a true Reformed position could adhere to Sanders' interpretation of the 'wider hope' (even though certain Reformed theologian do believe that the unevangelised can be saved), for he defines it in a way that constricts it to a certain interpretation of the second axiom.

I think that this alignment has led to a shift in the issues concerning the unevangelised. Both the terms 'restrictivist' and 'inclusivist' have become so closely linked to particular theological traditions, that the debate has moved from a discussion of the unevangelised to a re-opening of an older debate which has always divided evangelicalism. This debate concerns the tension between Divine Sovereignty and human freedom sometimes polarised into two camps, Calvinism and Arminianism. Despite the difficulty of defining such terms, restrictivism has become associated with traditional Reformed thinking and "wider hope" positions have become associated with Arminian thinking. This alignment is intensified by the fact that Sanders and Pinnock, the two main proponents of inclusivism (the most prominent "wider hope position"), are also associated in the evangelical world, with re-statements of the Arminian position[28] and even more so, with a new departure which aligns them with a position called the 'trinitarian openness of God' which has caused controversy within the evangelical community.[29]

---

[27] Ibid., p. 132.

[28] See Clark Pinnock, 'Responsible Freedom and the Flow of Biblical History' in ed. Clark Pinnock, *Grace Unlimited* (Minneapolis, 1974), pp. 95-110; ed. Pinnock, *The Grace of God, the Will of Man. A Case for Arminianism* (Minneapolis, 1995). Both Pinnock and Sanders write essays in this latter book. See Sanders, 'God as Personal' pp. 165-180 and Pinnock's 'From Augustine to Arminius: A Pilgrimage in Theology,' pp. 15-31. This latter collection of essays shows that there are differences within the term 'Arminianism.' For example Cottrell's essay, 'The Nature of Divine Sovereignty' does not deny God's omniscience, whereas both Pinnock's and Hasker's do. For Pinnock's view see his essay, 'Between Classical and Process Theism' in ed. Nash, *Process Theology* (Grand Rapids, 1987), pp. 309-327.

[29] ed. Clark Pinnock [et al], *The Openness of God. A Biblical Challenge to the Traditional Understanding of God* (Downers Grove, 1994). For some initial reviews and responses to this collection see, editorial, David Neff, 'Has God been held hostage by Philosophy? A forum on free-will theism, a new paradigm for Understanding God.' in

It is the debates surrounding these issues that have taken over the discussion of the unevangelised, and this is more evidence to show why the issue is so polemical in the evangelical community and has become a mark of orthodoxy. There are two points I wish to make concerning this alignment of restrictivism with Reformed theology and "Wider Hope" with more Arminian theology.

Firstly, I do not think the alignment of a Reformed outlook with a certain construal of restrictivism is wrong and as I have already stated, part of this study is to examine the relationship between fundamental doctrine and one's position on the unevangelised. However to *necessarily* link them appears too constricting for Reformed theologians who wish to move out of restrictivism into another position, and for those restrictivists who are not Reformed in their thinking. As Clarke comments: "Now it is by no means logically necessary...that the implicit-faith view [inclusivism] compromises God's sovereignty and the totally gracious character of salvation. Yet it is surely true that the strength of the Traditional Reformed view lies in its stout defence of these ideas."[30] It may well be that the only possible position a Reformed theologian can take is a restrictivist one and similarly the only position an Arminian can take is an inclusivist one. But here one must be very clear what one means by 'restrictivist' and 'inclusivist.'

This leads into a second point: that one has to be very careful in our theological labelling. Here I think Sanders is guilty of two forms of oversimplification. Firstly, as I have already mentioned, he has aligned a general category that he calls 'restrictivism' with a particular construal of that position (what I will call 'Reformed 'hard' restrictivism') and so leaves out a number of theologians who would fall under the restrictivist definition but who are not 'Reformed.' Secondly, though, I think there are category problems due to how one defines the unevangelised. Sanders, in a footnote, defines the unevangelised as "those who have died without hearing about or understanding the work of Christ - among whom I would include those who are too young to understand the gospel and those who are mentally or psychologically incapable of understanding it..."[31] Sanders then defines restrictivism as saying that all the unevangelised are damned because salvation can only come through hearing the gospel preached by a human messenger in this life. However I would question whether, on this definition of the un-

---

Christianity Today 39:30-34, Jan. 9 1995; Alister E. McGrath, 'Whatever Happened to Luther? A Response to the Openness of God' in *Christianity Today* 39:34 Jan. 9. 1995, p. 34. For a more recent and critical collection of essays that cover biblical, historical and systematic issues surrounding Pinnock's own 'openness theology' see eds. Tony Gray and Christopher Sinkinson, *Reconstructing Theology: A Critical Assessment of the Theology of Clark Pinnock* (Carlisle, 2000).

[30] David K. Clarke, 'Is Special Revelation Necessary for Salvation?' in eds. Crockett and Sigountos, op. cit., p. 45.

[31] Sanders, *No Other Name*, p. 15 n.2.

evangelised, the majority of theologians Sanders labels as restrictivists (who for Sanders are Reformed in their outlook) in fact come under this position. Let me give an example. Sanders lists John Calvin as being one of the main proponents of restrictivism.[32] However, in his exposition of Calvin he notes:

> This is not to say that Calvin believed God limited himself to using human messengers to communicate saving knowledge, however; he held that preaching is the "ordinary dispensation" or means of bringing faith but that it should never be used to "prescribe a law for the distribution of his grace". In other words, all those who are *truly elect* can be saved even without preaching: God will miraculously send them the message of Christ. According to Calvin, if God had decreed that a certain person living prior to Jesus was to be saved, then God saw to it that the individual received the gospel message about the coming Savior.[33]

If Sanders' interpretation of Calvin is correct, then he certainly falls outside the restrictivist definition that the Gospel *must always* be preached by a human messenger in this life, because there is evidence that Calvin believed that the means of grace could be widened to save some who did not come into contact with a human messenger. Similarly Sanders himself notices in his bibliographical section on the 'Wider Hope,' that many Reformed evangelicals do believe that children dying in infancy can be saved.[34] He quotes the Westminster Confession (10:3): "Elect infants dying in infancy, are regenerated, and saved by Christ, through the Spirit, who worketh when and where, and how he pleaseth: so are all other elect persons who are incapable of being outwardly called by the ministry of the Word." Sanders appears to have defined restrictivism in terms of only one category of people who constitute the unevangelised (let us say 'adults who never hear the gospel') forgetting the other categories he outlined himself in his definition of the term. If the 'wider hope' means that a person believes that some children in infancy can be saved, then a statement like the Westminster Confession (10:3) belongs to the 'wider hope.' My argument is, though, that the majority of Reformed theologians would fall into this category on the topic of infants, while issuing less hope for other groups of people. Note what the Westminster Confession (10:4) states in the subsequent paragraph to the one pertaining to infants: "Much less can men not professing the Christian religion be saved in any other way whatsoever, be they ever so diligent to

---

[32] Ibid., pp. 56-58.
[33] Ibid., p. 57. The references to Calvin here are *Commentary on the Catholic Epistles* trans. John Owen (Grand Rapids, 1948), p. 113; *Commentary on Romans* trans. John Owen (Grand Rapids, 1948), p. 398.
[34] Sanders, *No Other Name*, p. 143.

frame their lives according to the light of nature and the law of that religion they do profess; and to assert that they may, is very pernicious, and to be detested."[35]

I would suggest that to be very clear, categorisation could be attempted in one of three ways:

1) That one should keep a very narrow definition of terms and create new terms for those who fall outside. So, for example, Sanders could keep his definition of restrictivism acknowledging that many he includes in that term would constitute a new category.

2) That one should broaden the definition of say 'restrictivism' to include statements like that of Calvin and the Westminster Confession. So, for example, instead of equating restrictivism with having to hear the gospel from a human messenger in this life, one could widen the definition to say that there is no salvation outside 'special revelation' in this life.

3) That when outlining a particular position, it should be made clear what groups of people are meant when using the term 'the unevangelised.'

A Typology and Description of Evangelical Responses on the Fate of the Unevangelised.

Introduction

Throughout my study I stress the organic nature of doctrine and the way different doctrines fit into a particular theological system. In setting out, therefore, my own typology regarding responses to the unevangelised, I believe that any such typology should not only concentrate on questions of whether it is possible for the unevangelised to be saved, but to widen the frame of reference to salvation in general and the different soteriological frameworks employed by evangelicals. The following diagram illustrates what I think are the important areas of systematic theology that need to be considered:

---

[35] Interestingly Sanders (ibid.) is unsure as to whether this statement categorically rules out the idea that unevangelised adults can be saved.

Appendix 1: Evangelical Responses to the Fate of the Unevangelised 305

Divine Salvific Will **B1**: Particular **B2**: Universal	**EVANGELICAL** **PRESUPPOSITION:**
Divine Salvific Provision **B3**: Particular **B4**: Universal	**THE FINALITY** **PARTICULARITY** **and SALVIFIC NECESSITY**
Salvific Hope **B5**: Heilspessimismus **B6**: Heilsoptimismus	**OF JESUS CHRIST**

SALVIFIC ACCESSIBILITY **B7**: PARTICULAR **B8**: UNIVERSAL

SALVIFIC MEANS	
B9: Christ Epistemologically Necessary Means: Special Revelation	**B10**: Christ Not Epistemologically Necessary Means: Special and General Revelation

SALVIFIC ESCHATOLOGICAL OPPORTUNITY	
B11: Determined by Acceptance / Rejection of Christ in this life	**B12**: Not Necessarily Based on Acceptance / Rejection of Christ in this life

Given that a fundamental presupposition of evangelicalism is an affirmation of the finality, particularity and salvific ontological necessity of Christ, the primary axiomatic question I wish to focus on in my typology concerns the accessibility of salvation: Is salvation universally accessible (**B8**) or is it only accessible to a particular group of people (**B7**)? It will be helpful if I say a little more on what I mean precisely by the term accessibility. In terms of soteriology in general, irrespective of whether one is 'evangelised' or 'unevangelised,' a belief in universal accessibility would maintain that "salvation is not genuinely universally accessible...unless all people have an opportunity of being redeemed by God's grace after they have sinned."[36] The key word here is 'opportunity.' As such a view presupposes certain construals of divine sovereignty and human freedom, it is my contention that no Reformed theology (as I have defined Reformed in Ch.1) can hold to a belief in universal accessibility because in Reformed theology, the gift of salvation is given only to those predestined to be saved. As everyone is not predestined to be saved (i.e. the denial of universalism), salvation cannot be universally accessible. Therefore all positions that affirm universal accessibility come from within the Arminian and postconservative evangelicalism as defined in Ch. 1.

In contrast to universal accessibility, a belief in particular accessibility would argue that for some reason salvation is not available to all. In my analysis I discern two related but distinct reasons why accessibility may be restricted, depending on one's soteriological framework. Firstly, if one is working from within a Reformed framework, salvation is restricted to those whom God wills to save: the elect. The question Reformed theologians have to answer is whether the elect are always from within the 'evangelised,' or whether the elect can be 'unevangelised' persons. I will note how Reformed theologians deal with this question shortly. However, a position of particular accessibility is not exclusively the property of Reformed theology, because again as I will show, non-Reformed theology can hold that salvation is restricted not by divine election, but by other factors, e.g. the failure of evangelism.

As I will demonstrate, how one decides on the accessibility question determines how one believes salvation is mediated and whether or not the unevangelised can be saved. For if one believes salvation is universally accessible, one cannot believe that salvation is mediated through a means that is not available universally. However, I tried to point out in the previous section, the question of accessibility itself rests on more basic theological questions: Does God want everyone to be saved (**B2**) or only a particular group of people (**B1**)? Is Christ's death universal in its provision (**B4**) or particular (**B3**)? Can we be optimistic about salvation (**B6**) or must we be pessimistic (**B5**)? In the study I try to demonstrate that the answers we give to these questions determines our stance on accessibility that in turn determines our position on the unevangelised.

In the remaining part of this Appendix I wish to describe various evangelical responses to the question of the unevangelised. I split these responses into two groups, those who affirm a particular accessibility to salvation and those who affirm a universal accessibility. Within these two groupings I delineate a number of variations.

---

[36] Sanders, *No Other Name*, p. 131f.

Appendix 1: Evangelical Responses to the Fate of the Unevangelised   307

Positions of Particular Accessibility

Those views that are included within particular accessibility refer to any view that asserts the particularity of salvific accessibility **(B7)**, that is to say, that salvation is not universally accessible but for whatever reason is restricted in some way.

In defining positions of particular accessibility in this way I do not necessarily state that:
1) all proponents believe necessarily that the unevangelised are not saved (although many do assert this).
2) all proponents believe that Christ is epistemologically necessary for salvation **(B9)** (although many do assert this).
3) all proponents necessarily believe in a *Heilspessimismus* **(B5)** over a *Heilsoptimismus* **(B6)** (although many do believe this).

THEME: REFORMED 'HARD' RESTRICTIVISM[37]

Because of their belief in God's absolute sovereignty, Reformed theologians do not wish to say that the will of God can be frustrated through the failure of evangelism which is the only modality of special revelation through which humanity can know Christ. They therefore affirm **(B1)** and say that God in His 'hidden' or 'secret' will does not wish to save all persons or wish them to have the opportunity to be saved **(B7)**. This statement coheres well with the Reformed doctrine of 'limited atonement' or 'particular redemption' **(B3)** which maintains that Christ did not die for every person who has ever lived, but only for those whom God has predestined to salvation: the elect.

In the 'hard' restrictivist scheme, the means and end to salvation are inextricably linked to the means defining the 'restrictivness' of restrictivism. God has prescribed a certain way in which human beings may be saved, namely, by believing in Christ as heard from a human messenger in this life. Had God wanted to save persons from among the unevangelised, He would have providentially arranged matters so that they would have received special revelation (that is the revelation necessary for salvation) through the human messenger. That in God's providence they do not receive this revelation is an expression of God's predestination of some to salvation.

Although this position is logically coherent, it is offensive to many, and Sanders in describing such a position uses emotive terms describing restrictivism, "God automatically damns all the unevangelised to hell,"[38] and, "the unevangelised are indiscriminately damned."[39] I do not believe that any

---

[37] I am borrowing the term 'hard' restrictivism from Okholm and Phillips, op. cit., p. 19.
[38] Sanders, *No Other Name*, p. 6.
[39] Ibid., p. 7.

theologically responsible restrictivist would put their position in these terms, and I agree with Caneday that, "neither responsible traditionalists nor Calvinists affirm that events are determined by causal necessity or that human beings are condemned against their will."[40] However it does seem that this form of restrictivism must answer the question of the distributive justice of God. To show how they do respond, I will outline the argument of Carl Henry who to my mind represents the 'hard' restrictivist position clearly.

Carl Henry sees the heart of the critique against his position: "After all is said and done, is it fair - so the query is often phrased - that the unreached heathen should perish."[41] In responding to this query he divides his answer into three parts: Who are the heathen? Is anyone totally unreached? How is 'fairness' to be defined and by whom? Henry defines the unevangelised as those who remain outside the 'channel' of revealed religion, that is special revelation that demands personal faith in the Christ. In his definition he does not include the Jewish nation in the Old Testament because they stood in this channel, the sacrificial system looked forward to the atonement of Christ. He also does not include children who die before the age of accountability believing them to be in a separate category: "they are embraced by covenant-theology as members of the family of faith. Other communions hold that, just as children are counted guilty in Adam without volition of their own, so God accounts them justified in Christ without personal exercise of faith."[42]

Henry believes that the unevangelised are condemned not for explicitly rejecting Christ, but are judged for their response to the light they did have in the *imago Dei*. All humans have knowledge of God and God confronts them in general revelation: "Even before any human being hears the name of Jesus Christ, the eternal Logos confronts all human beings internally with the Creator's claim on human conscience and life and consigns mutinous humankind to a fearsome sense of impending judgement (see Rom. 1:18-32)."[43]

To the claim that some outside special revelation may realise their guilt and throw themselves on the mercy of God, Henry responds by saying that this has no biblical support and that repentance and faith are gifts of God only found in special revelation. He does concede though that there are levels of rebellion and that the final judgement will include 'few blows' and 'many blows,' but that everyone suppresses the light they have and are so rendered accountable and culpable.

---

[40] Caneday, op. cit., p. 3.
[41] Henry, op. cit., p. 245.
[42] Ibid., p. 247 n.2.
[43] Ibid., p. 248.

But can general revelation provide a genuine knowledge of God? Henry refers to G.C. Berkouwer who like Barth believed that the unevangelised were ignorant of God.[44] In contrast, Henry agrees with theologians like Bruce Demarest who claim that if general revelation contains only a "misty pseudo-knowledge of God,"[45] then God would be unjust for condemning people for ignorance. For Henry, general revelation contains objective knowledge of God, "a knowledge that renders every person guilty for revolt against light, in view of humankind's attempted suffocation of that revelatory content."[46] But because of the extent of the Fall, even the content of general revelation cannot be deduced apart from God self-revealing Himself in special revelation:

> General revelation, however, does not provide sinful humanity with a comprehensive, reliable view of God. Because of humanity's sinful condition, a proper understanding even of the content of general revelation rests in the divinely inscripturated special revelation. Scripture objectively identifies valid and invalid claims made by rebellious sinners on the basis of the supposed *indicia* in nature and humankind...divine condemnation of sinful humankind presupposes some objectively reliable knowledge of God that rebellious human beings can consciously reject. Demarest's repeated insistence that general revelation penetrates the human mind everywhere with objective knowledge is sound. Also sound is his insistence that sin is inexcusable because sinners consciously spurn God and thus have no right to plead ignorance.[47]

In summary, all humans are without excuse and cannot plead ignorance. When judgement comes it will not be a surprise to any person.

Finally, Henry deals with questions that arise about God's justice: is it just for God to condemn people who have never heard of Christ? Henry believes that the unevangelised are in the same position as fallen angels who have not been provided with a redeeming revelation. He states: "God is not obliged to save any morally rebellious creature. His nonprovision of redemption for some fallen humans does not compromise his justice, any more than does his nonprovision of redemption for all fallen angels. God is

---

[44] See G.C. Berkouwer, 'General and Special Divine Revelation' in *Revelation and the Bible*, ed. Carl F.H. Henry (Grand Rapids, 1976), p. 15.

[45] Ibid., p. 250. See also Bruce Demarest, *General Revelation: Historical Views and Contemporary Issues* (Grand Rapids, 1982), p. 145.

[46] Ibid., p. 251.

[47] Ibid., 251f. For a more detailed analysis of the paradoxical claim that the unbeliever 'knows' God and yet at the same time 'does not know' God, see John Frame, *The Doctrine of the Knowledge of God* (Phillipsburg, 1987), pp. 49-60.

not obliged to redeem all or any rebels; his elective intervention is a voluntary expression of holy love."[48]

This elective love is not based on any human merit but purely on God's preferential love to some creatures. However this is not a double-predestination where God's decree to elect is symmetrical with his decree to damn, because the non-elect are not condemned for being non-elect, but for their total rebellion against God who created them. So God has every ground to condemn but no ground to save. Amazingly God does choose to save some creatures through Christ. To claim that God is unjust in this, is to forget that justice is defined not by Western human society, or any human society, but by God Himself where justice and righteousness constitute the very core of His Being. Henry concludes, "God's fairness is demonstrated because he condemns sinners not in the absence of light but because of their rebellious response. His mercy is demonstrated because he provides fallen humans with a privileged call to redemption not extended to fallen angels."[49] Although this position is seen by evangelicals like Sanders to be a misunderstanding of the biblical narrative and therefore wrong, I do think that such a view on the unevangelised is inconsistent with Henry's Reformed framework and is not 'automatic' or insensitive in condemning the unevangelised.

VARIATION I: REFORMED 'AGNOSTIC' RESTRICTIVISM

I believe there to be levels or degrees of strength with which the restrictivist position can be held, and that because the 'unevangelised' are not explicitly or directly mentioned as a specific group in Scripture, many Reformed restrictivists wish to safeguard the sovereignty of God by adopting a more agnostic stance on the issue. As Okholm and Phillips note:

> One can...be a pessimistic agnostic toward the unevangelised, acknowledging that special revelation is necessary for salvation but choosing to go no further than Scripture (which admittedly does not seem to offer much hope to those who have not heard)... But this agnostic stance toward the unevangelised can also be construed optimistically, though such optimism can only be held tentatively and as a secondary theme, never to encroach on or revise the salvation-history scheme.[50]

Louis Berkhof writes, "There is no Scripture evidence on which we can base the hope that adult Gentiles [by this he means those Gentiles who do not hear], or even Gentile children that have not yet come to years of dis-

---

[48] Ibid., p. 253.
[49] Ibid., p. 255.
[50] Okholm and Phillips, op. cit., p. 20.

cretion, will be saved."[51] Possibly the best example here is that of Loraine Boettner. A strong believer in the Reformed doctrine of predestination, he believes that in the providential workings of God, the fact that the majority of the human race has not come into contact with special revelation must mean that God does not intend to save them. Note his infamous declaration: "When God places people in such conditions we may be sure that He has no more intention that they shall be saved than He has that the soil of Northern Siberia, which if frozen all the year round, shall produce crops of wheat. Had he intended otherwise He would have supplied the means leading to the desired end."[52] However, even he appears to step back slightly from complete assurance of his view:

> We do not deny that God can save some even of the adult heathen people if he chooses to do so, for His Spirit works when and where and how He pleases, with means or without means… Certainly God's ordinary method is to gather His elect from the evangelised portion of mankind, although we must admit the possibility that by an extraordinary method some of His elect may be gathered from the unevangelised portion.[53]

The same sentiment is portrayed by W. Gary Phillips who calls himself a 'negative agnostic' with regards to the unevangelised.[54] For him the biblical evidence gives him every reason to believe firmly that 1) Jesus is the ontological *and* epistemological basis of salvation; 2) the Bible's statements pertaining to salvation are exclusivistic; 3) that unlike holiness and justice which are attributes of God and constant, redemption is contingent and not an attribute of God but an action (that is, it need not happen for God to continue being God). However in spite of these three statements, he believes there remains the bare possibility that God *may* have special arrangements for the unevangelised although he is not optimistic, "While one may hope that God indeed does have special arrangements, what is conceivable to human sensibilities is not a criterion of truth and must always remain open to divine correction."[55] As Paul Helm notes:

> It is always important to distinguish what is abstractly possible from what is warranted in believing. Perhaps there is some abstract sense in which it

---

[51] Louis Berkhof, *Systematic Theology* (Grand Rapids, 1958), p. 693.
[52] Loraine Boettner, *The Reformed Doctrine of Predestination* (Grand Rapids, 1954), p. 120.
[53] Ibid., p. 119.
[54] W. Gary Phillips, 'Evangelicals and Pluralism: Current Options' in *Proceedings of the Wheaton Theological Conference* 1992, pp. 188.
[55] Ibid.

is possible for people to be saved in ignorance of the revealed truth of God. This is, after all, how God is believed to convey his grace to those who die in infancy and for all we know, to those adults who live and die demented. But is there any warrant from Scripture to believe that God has in fact conveyed his grace to rational adults in this way?[56]

VARIATION II: REFORMED 'SOFT' RESTRICTIVISM

Although I labelled him as agnostic, Berkhof is careful to note that although God 'ordinarily' works through specific means of grace (i.e. the Word and sacraments), and is pleased to bind Himself to these means, He is free to work without these means and in fact does in the case of infant baptism. The Reformed theologian W.G.T. Shedd believed that although ordinarily the Spirit worked through the instrumentality of the Word, there could be *extraordinary* instances where the Holy Spirit in his sovereignty could immediately (as opposed to mediately), create the habit of faith in a person who had never heard of Christ. After noting that the 'heathen' have no claims upon the Divine mercy he states the following:

> It does not follow, however, that because God is not obliged to offer pardon to the unevangelised heathen, either here or hereafter, therefore no unevangelised heathen are pardoned. The electing mercy of God reaches to the heathen. It is not the doctrine of the Church, that the entire mass of pagans, without exception, have gone down to endless impenitence and death. That some unevangelised men are saved, in the present life, by an extraordinary exercise of redeeming grace in Christ, has been the hope and belief of Christendom. It was the hope and belief of the elder Calvinists, as it is of the later.[57]

Shedd then goes onto list a number of Reformed sources to evidence his claim. Firstly, he quotes the Second Helvetic Confession (1566): "We recognise that God can illuminate whom and when he will, even without the external ministry, for that is in his power"(I.7); and the Westminster Confession of Faith (5:3) "God, in his ordinary providence, maketh use of means, yet is free to work without, above, and against them at his pleasure;" and (10:3): "Elect infants, dying in infancy, are regenerated, and saved by Christ, through the Spirit, who worketh when, and where, and how he pleaseth: so also are all other elect persons who are incapable of being outwardly called by the ministry of the Word." Concerning this latter reference

---

[56] Paul Helm, 'Are They Few That be Saved?' in ed. Cameron, *Universalism and the Doctrine of Hell* p. 274f.
[57] W.G.T. Shedd, *Dogmatic Theology* Vol. 2. (New York, 1888-1894), p. 706.

Shedd notes that "this is commonly understood to refer not merely, or mainly, to idiots and insane persons, but to such of the pagan world as God pleases to regenerate without the use of the written revelation."[58] Secondly, he quotes "one of the strictest Calvinists of the sixteenth century"[59] Girolamo Zanchius (1516-1590) in his famous treatise *Absolute Predestination*. In Ch. 4, Position 1: 'Of Reprobation or Predestination as it respects the ungodly,' Zanchius notes that "the much greater part of mankind have been destitute even of the external means of grace, and have not been favoured with the preaching of God's Word or any revelation of his will."[60] However, having said this he then states: "it is not indeed improbable, that some individuals in these unenlightened countries may belong to the secret election of grace, and the habit of faith may be wrought in them."[61] Commenting on this Shedd notes:

> By the term 'habit' (habitus) the elder theologians meant an inward disposition of the heart. The 'habit of faith' involves penitence for sin, and the longing for its forgiveness and removal. The 'habit of faith' is the broken and contrite heart, which expresses itself in the prayer, 'God be merciful to me a sinner.' It is certain that the Holy Ghost can produce, if he pleases, such a disposition and frame of mind in the pagan, without employing, as he commonly does, the written word.[62]

In his study of Jonathan Edwards, Anri Morimoto formulates a possible theory on the salvation of the unevangelised along the same lines of Zanchius.[63] He speaks about Edwards' belief in the "infused habit of grace"[64] and that contrary to Aristotelian philosophy, the existence of this habit does not depend on its prior exercise. Edwards believed that a saving habit could be present before it was exercised through the act of faith in Christ and that

---

[58] Ibid., p. 708.
[59] Ibid.
[60] Girolamo Zanchius, *Absolute Predestination*, http://www. straitgate.com /books /zanchius/doctrine.htm, 21st December 2000, p. 20f.
[61] Ibid., p. 21. What Shedd doesn't note is another earlier statement in his treatise that too seems to allow for the salvation of the unevangelised. On defining reprobation Zanchius notes that "the word may be taken in another sense as denoting God's refusal to grant some nations the light of the Gospel revelation. This may be considered as a national reprobation, which yet does not imply that every individual who lives in such a country must therefore unavoidably perish for ever, any more than that every individual who lives in a land called Christian is therefore in a state of salvation. There are, no doubt, elect persons among the former as well as reprobate ones among the latter"(p. 4).
[62] Shedd, op. cit., p. 708.
[63] Anri Morimoto, *Jonathan Edwards and the Catholic Vision of Salvation* (Pennsylvania, 1995).
[64] Ibid., p. 61.

this helped to explain the salvation of infants and Old Testament saints.[65] Morimoto now asks "One can and should ask, what reasonable consequences can be drawn from [Edwards] theological perspective for today's pluralist society."[66] Applying Edwards' idea to the situation of non-Christian salvation he writes:

> If infants and the Old Testament faithful are saved on account of their unexercised dispositions, one must also conclude that non-Christians can be saved on the same grounds. They may not as yet manifest their saving disposition into a faith that is specifically Christian, but they might as well be given the disposition and counted as saved because of that disposition. They may even remain non-Christian for their whole lifetime, and still be saved; if the conditions and circumstances do not arise, their saving dispositions will remain unexercised. The point is whether they *have* the saving disposition, not whether they *exercise* it or not... Edwards is by no means a universalist. The fact remains that salvation depends on the presence of the saving disposition. One may or may not be given that disposition, and it rests with the divine counsel to determine who is to receive the infusion of the disposition... Those who appear to be non-Christian now might well be its members, being given the saving disposition but not manifesting it in exercise.[67]

Another theologian who has looked at Edwards' theology in this area and who then has attempted a contemporary appropriation is Gerald McDermott.[68] Concentrating on Edwards' writings in his private notebooks (the *Miscellanies*), McDermott attempts to show that Edwards may have been far more open to truth, revelation and even salvation outside the ordinary means of grace, than has been traditionally believed on the evidence of his published writings. McDermott builds his case on three theological ideas present in Edwards' writing: the *prisca theologia;*[69] the use of typology;[70]

---

[65] Ibid., p. 63.
[66] Ibid., p. 64.
[67] Ibid., p. 66.
[68] See Gerald R. McDermott, *Jonathan Edwards Confronts the Gods: Christian Theology, Enlightenment Religion and Non-Christian Faiths* (Oxford, 2000); idem *Can Evangelicals Learn From World Religions* (Downers Grove, 2000).
[69] McDermott defines this as: "a tradition in apologetic theology... that attempted to prove that vestiges of true religion were taught by the Greeks and other non-Christian religions. Typically it alleged that all human beings were originally given knowledge of true religion (monotheism, the Trinity, *creatio ex nihilo*) by the Jews or by traditions going back to Noah's good sons (Shem and Japheth) or antediluvians such as Enoch or Adam... In his own appropriation of the *prisca theological*, Edwards said that the heathen learned these truths by what could be called a trickle-down process of revelation. In the 'first ages' of the world the fathers of the nations received revelation of the great religious truths, directly or indirectly, from God himself. These truths were then passed

and (as already outlined above) the idea of a dispositional soteriology.[71] McDermott comments on a number of the *Miscellanies* the most cryptic being *Misc.* 1162, where on commenting on the fact the certain heathen philosophers including Socrates and Plato were subjects of divine revelation, Edwards writes: "We know not what evidence God might give to the men themselves that were the subjects of these great inspirations that they were divine and true... and so we know not of how great benefit the truths suggested might be to their own souls." On this, McDermott writes:

> Edwards is hesitant and tentative, but he nevertheless clearly opens the possibility that these heathen could have used revelation for their own spiritual benefit – a notion that is incoherent unless it means they can be saved. When we recall that Edwards wrote this entry during a period in which he was frequently quoting from writers who explicitly argued for the salvation of the virtuous heathen, it is difficult to believe that Edwards did not include salvation among the possible benefits to human souls.[72]

Having noted this, however, McDermott's conclusion on Edwards is somewhat ambivalent:

> We are left with a curious tension in Edwards's thinking about the salvation of the heathen. On the one hand, in most of his explicit commentary on the topic, he took a negative view characteristic of his Reformed predecessors... But that is not the whole picture. Edwards made a series of important theological moves beyond his Reformed predecessors that could have opened the door for a more hopeful view of the salvation of the heathen. The advances he made in typology, the extensive use he made of the *prisca*

---

down, by tradition, from one generation to the next. Unfortunately, there is also a religious law of entropy at work. Human finitude and corruption inevitably cause the revelation to be distorted, resulting in superstition and idolatry." McDermott, *Jonathan Edwards Confronts the Gods*, p. 93ff.

[70] In *Can Evangelicals Learn from the World Religions*, McDermott summarises his interpretation of Edwards' use of typology: "By that he [Edwards] meant a system of representation by which God points human beings to spiritual realities. For centuries Christians had seen in the Old Testament 'types' that pointed to the New Testament 'antitypes'... Edwards endorsed this traditional reading but pushed it beyond its traditional limits, arguing that God's typology extended to nature and history – and, I would add, the history of religions... Edwards also believed that God had planted types of true religion even in religious systems that were finally false. God outwitted the devil, he suggested, by using diabolically deceptive religion to teach what is true. For example, the practice of human sacrifice was the result of the devil's mimickry of the animal sacrifice that God had instituted after the Fall" (p. 104ff). For McDermott's detailed argument on this see *Jonathan Edwards Confronts the Gods*, pp. 110-130.

[71] See McDermott, *Jonathan Edwards Confronts the Gods*, pp. 132-141.

[72] McDermott, *Jonathan Edwards Confronts the Gods*, p. 141.

theologia, and his development of a dispositional soteriology prepared the theological way for a more expansive view of salvation. Edwards used these developments primarily to argue for a greater knowledge of religious truth among the heathen than his favorite Reformed predecessors... On the question of salvation, he usually only conceded the *possibility* that heathen could be saved and never spoke in the expansively hopeful terms of a Watts, Ramsey, or Skelton, or even a Baxter of Wesley. So while he built the theological foundations upon which a more hopeful soteriology could quite naturally have been erected, he himself never chose to do so.[73]

VARIATION III: JOHN PIPER'S REFORMED *PREPARATIO EVANGELICA*[74]

In Ch. 6 of this study, I discuss in some detail the story of Cornelius in Acts 10. I note that a number of evangelicals believe that before Cornelius came into contact with Peter and his message he was not saved, thus upholding the restrictivist idea that one must come into contact with the message of Christ in order to be saved. On dealing with v. 35 "In every nation one who fears God and does what is right is acceptable to him," I note that restrictivist commentators maintain that within the context of the story, (which concerns the inclusion of the Gentiles into God's salvific plans), Peter's statement refers, not to the salvific state of Cornelius but the principle that non-Jews are 'acceptable' or 'welcome' to God.

While he believes that Cornelius had to hear the Gospel before he was saved, John Piper takes a slightly different line regarding v. 35.[75] He distinguishes between the phrase "any man" in v. 28 and which refers universally to everyone, and the phrase "In every nation" in v. 35 that he believes refers to particular people 'within' every nation. So what does 'acceptable to God' mean? Piper notes that the answer lies midway between being saved and merely being an acceptable candidate for evangelism:

> My suggestion is that Cornelius represents a kind of unsaved person among an unreached people group who is seeking God in an extraordinary way. And Peter is saying that God *accepts* this search as genuine... and works wonders to bring that person the gospel of Jesus Christ the way

---

[73] Ibid., p. 143f.
[74] In *No Other Name*, Sanders calls this kind of position 'God Will Send the Message' and is located under the 'wider hope' category of universal evangelism before death. Sanders writes, "Proponents of this view believe that God ensures that the gospel is directed to those who are searching for the truth but those individuals are not saved until they hear and believe the word of Christ"(p. 152).
[75] John Piper, *Let the Nations Be Glad: The Supremacy of God in Missions* (Leicester, 1994), pp. 135-145.

he did through the visions of both Peter on the housetop and Cornelius in the hour of prayer.[76]

So the fear of God that is acceptable to God in verse 35 is a true sense that there is a holy God, that we have to meet him some day as desperate sinners, that we cannot save ourselves and need to know God's way of salvation, and that we pray for it day and night and seek to act on the light we have. This is what Cornelius was doing. And God accepted his prayer and his groping for truth his life (Acts 17:27), and worked wonders to bring the saving message of the gospel to him. Cornelius would not have been saved if no one had taken him the gospel. And no one who can apprehend revelation will be saved today without the gospel.[77]

I include Piper's position under particular accessibility because I still believe Piper to be working broadly within the Reformed soteriological framework and so would deny a universal accessibility to salvation in terms of universal opportunity. Also it is restrictive because those who live and die without hearing the gospel must be people showing no positive inclination to general revelation. Had they shown this inclination, they would have received the gospel. Piper's argument merely adds another stage to the Reformed soteriological process. In this scheme, general revelation acts as *preparatio evangelica*: general revelation cannot save but starts a chain of events that finishes in the reception of the gospel.

THE IMPLICIT-FAITH VIEW: 'SOFT' INCLUSIVISM/ 'OPAQUE' EXCLUSIVISM

Although Sanders, Clarke and Phillips in their typologies categorise the following views in the 'wider hope' inclusivist category, I have included them in the particular accessibility camp because, and this point is crucial, although they do suggest that the unevangelised can be saved outside special revelation and have a more positive assessment of general revelation than do restrictivist positions (which maintain that salvation can only be found within special revelation, unlike my own definition of the inclusivist camp), these views do not explicitly state that salvation is universally accessible in terms of opportunity, and in the main are cautious rather than bold in speculating on the numbers saved in this way. Carson calls such views 'soft' inclusivism. He writes:

This view is barely distinguishable from exclusivism. It holds that people must place their faith in Jesus Christ and his redemptive work to be saved, but allows the possibility, the bare possibility, that God in his grace may

---

[76] Ibid., p. 140.
[77] Ibid., p. 142.

save some who have never heard of Christ, assuming that in response to his grace in their lives they cast themselves in repentance and faith upon the God discernible, however dimly in creation.[78]

To avoid confusion with the title 'inclusivism' which is the subject of my study, I will adopt Clark's title of "implicit-faith,"[79] noting that I would not include Pinnock in this category as Clark does. Clark says of this position:

> ... people in a culture that has no contact with Christ or the Bible see through nature that a God exists and through conscience that they are out of touch with him. Although they know nothing of Christ specifically, God prompts them to cast themselves into his hands for safekeeping ... They are saved *objectively* on the basis of Christ's work of atonement; they are saved *subjectively* in that God elicits a faith response to the glimmer of light in natural revelation.[80]

In his seminal work, *Christianity and World Religions*,[81] Norman Anderson speculates that individuals from among the unevangelised could possibly be saved as Old Testament believers were saved: "Might it not be true of the follower of some other religion that the God of all mercy had worked in his heart by his Spirit, bringing him to some measure to realize his sin and need for forgiveness, and enabling him, in his twighlight as it were, to throw himself on God's mercy?"[82]

A different way of evaluating general revelation is an argument outlined by Paul Helm.[83] Within a Reformed soteriological framework (hence the position is called restrictivist), Helm offers a way to speculate how an individual could be saved without coming into contact with God's special revelation. He asks us to consider God's individual essential and unique properties (e.g. being underivedly just, being supremely good, being the Creator of the universe). From here he says:

> Suppose that a person, ignorant of God's special revelation in Scripture, were to pray using words that mean any of God's individual essential properties... Suppose, then, a person with little or no acquaintance with special revelation, but in deep personal need and despair, who cries out 'O most merciful one, have mercy on me.' I suggest that this is a prayer

---

[78] Donald Carson, *The Gagging of God: Christianity Confronts Pluralism* (Leicester, 1996), p. 279.
[79] Clark, op. cit., p. 41.
[80] Ibid., p. 42.
[81] Norman Anderson, *Christianity and World Religions* (Downers Grove, 1977).
[82] Ibid., p. 144.
[83] Helm, op. cit., pp. 275-281.

that is sincerely addressed to God and sincerely addressed to the only true God, even though the one who is speaking may not realise the fact. And I, for one, find it hard to imagine that such a prayer could not or would not be answered.[84]

Helm calls his position 'opaque exclusivism' because it qualifies the exclusivity of the Christian faith. He concludes, "Whether they qualify the particularism of the faith in a significant way, and give us reason for thinking that a majority of humankind will be saved, depends upon how many such cases there are. In the nature of things the answer to that question is at present, known only to God."[85]

EXCURSUS: PARTICULARITY AND PARSIMONY IN SALVATION

This last quotation of Helm's brings one into a discussion on the scope of salvation. In his discussion of Warfield and Shedd, Helm notes that both of these theologians are considering separate questions: "Are any saved by the Holy Spirit using means which do not causally arise out of God's revelation of himself in Scripture? Are there more saved than lost? An affirmative answer to the first question by Shedd is then used as some evidence in favour of an affirmative answer to the second question."[86] In outlining the above positions I have not explicitly commented on whether these positions of particular accessibility affirm a *Heilspessimismus* or a *Heilsoptimismus*. Which position one takes depends on how large one defines the unevangelised. For 'hard restrictivists' salvation can only come from hearing the gospel through a human messenger and so one could deduce from such a position that because many people have not come into contact with special revelation, 'hard restrictivists' would believe that the final number of the lost will be far greater than the number of the redeemed. However, this is not the only position to hold on this matter. Reformed theologians like B.B. Warfield and Charles Hodge, whilst still holding to a 'hard' restrictivist position, maintained that in terms of the numbers of redeemed, the lost would be insignificant to the redeemed. How is this possible considering that billions of people have never come into contact with special revelation? The answer is fashioned as part of their eschatological beliefs. As Sanders comments, "Warfield and Hodge appeal to the Postmillennial doctrine that a tremendous surge of evangelism and conversion will occur in the future. Since the future population of the earth will be greater that the total population throughout history, more will be saved than lost."[87]

---

[84] Ibid., p. 277.
[85] Ibid., p. 281.
[86] Helm, op. cit., p. 275.
[87] Sanders, 'Is Belief in Christ Necessary for Salvation?' in *Evangelical Quarterly* 60: 1988, pp. 241-259. See B.B. Warfield, 'Are They Few That Be Saved?' in *Biblical*

What can we say on this matter concerning 'agnostic' and 'soft' restricitivists as well as those who hold to some form of 'implicit-faith?' While in principal there is nothing to stop proponents of these positions from affirming that multitudes will be saved this way, the stress is firmly on God saving apart from human missionary endeavour as *extraordinary* occurrences. Referring to Norman Anderson's position, Jim Packer speculates that such an argument may be true "but that we have no warrant to *expect* that God will act thus in any single case where the gospel is not known or understood."[88] This too is Demarest's conclusion:

> ...the overwhelming biblical datum is that all people are lost and need to come to Christ for salvation. Let the church be reminded that in the plan of God the customary means by which sinners should come to know and love God is through the preached message of the cross. The number of those who might be brought to Christ through extraordinary means is small at best... Let the Church know that if the heathen are to be saved, in overwhelming measure it will be through the instrumentality of the message entrusted to it.[89]

Commenting on any position that affirms that God may save many rather than few through means other than through the preached gospel of Christ, Philips notes that:

> ...in application, these exceptions become the rule; they become paradigmatic - rather than exceptions - of how God has dealt and presently deals

---

and Theological Studies (Philadelphia, 1952), pp. 334-350; and Charles Hodge, *Systematic Theology* 3 Vols. (Grand Rapids, 1940), 3:879-80. Commenting on Warfield. Helm notes, "In Warfield's view God's saving purposes widen through history, rather as a ripple in a pool. By a process of development, first Israel and then the Christian Church, which is the 'internationalised' Israel of the New Testament era, enlarge the circle of God's saving grace until it embraces the vast majority and women, 'the world.' The lost are 'the prunings' as Warfield put it." Paul Helm, 'Are They Few That Be Saved' in ed. Nigel M. de S. Cameron, *Universalism and the Doctrine of Hell* (Edinburgh, 1992), p. 267. Warfield himself writes, "It must be borne well in mind that particularism and parsimony in salvation are not equivalent conceptions; and it is a mere caricature of Calvinistic particularism to represent it as finding its centre in the proclamation that there are few to be saved." B.B. Warfield, *The Plan of Salvation* (1915), p. 97. quoted in Helm, op. cit., p. 268.

[88] J.I. Packer, 'Good Pagans and God's Kingdom' in *Christianity Today* 30/1 (17 Jan. 1986), pp. 25. Other advocates of this position include. Bruce A. Demarest, *General Revelation: Historical Views and Contemporary Issues* (Grand Rapids, 1982), p. 259-262; Milliard J. Erickson, 'Hope for those who haven't heard? Yes, but...' in *Evangelical Missions Quarterly* 11 (Apr. 1975), pp. 122-126.

[89] Demarest, op. cit., p. 261.

with the bulk of humanity. This is curious: while explicit faith in Christ should be the norm, in effect (because of all those who have lived over the millennia) the *functionally normative* means by which most people in the eschaton will have been redeemed will be through some method other that that described in Romans 10:14-15![90]

NON-REFORMED RESTRICTIVISM

One does not have to deny God's universal salvific will (**B2**), nor believe in the doctrine of limited atonement to be a restrictivist, indeed one can hold to unlimited atonement which holds that Christ died for every person, and still maintain that one must explicitly confess Christ to be saved.[91] However, I know of no published evangelical who argues along this line. Any such position would presumably have to concede that although God may desire to save all persons, such a desire can be frustrated by the failure of evangelisation to spread the gospel: God is unable to save them. Such a position would therefore lay the responsibility of the unevangelised not being saved at the feet of the Christian and the Church. Therefore the motivation for mission would become greater as Christians would realise that the unevangelised were being lost because they had not taken the Gospel to them in time. For this position the principle of universal accessibility becomes something that is determined by Christians. However, such a view would have to believe that although God desires everyone to be saved, He limits Himself (or is limited) in the way salvation is mediated. I assess the viability of this position in Ch. 9 arguing that while a belief in the universal salvific will of God does not necessarily a universal accessibility of salvation, a belief in universal atonement does.

Positions of Universal Accessibility

This second group of positions equate to Sanders' 'Wider Hope' category that he defines:

> All of the positions discussed...affirm that God, in grace, grants every individual a genuine opportunity to participate in the redemptive work of the Lord Jesus, that no human being is excluded from the possibility of benefiting from salvific grace. The views differ regarding the nature and timing of the opportunity for salvation - specifically, on the issues of whether people must be aware that their salvation is in Jesus and whether the opportunity for salvation is given only before physical death or also after death.[92]

---

[90] Phillips, op. cit., p. 186.
[91] Sanders, *No Other Name*, p. 37, 50f.
[92] Sanders, *No Other Name*, p. 131.

Theologians who represent this second group of positions believe, that for whatever reason, salvation is universally accessible and not restricted to a particular people or type of revelation. In defining positions of universal accessibility in this way I do not necessarily state that:

1) all proponents believe necessarily that all the unevangelised are saved because only the opportunity of salvation is universal. Whether this is accepted or rejected depends on the subject.

2) all proponents believes that Christ is epistemologically necessary for salvation **(B9)** (although many do assert this).

3) all proponents necessarily believe in a *Heilsoptimismus* **(B6)** over a *Heilspessimismus* **(B5)** (although based on God's will to save and Christ's provision many do believe that the majority of the human race will be saved).

POST-MORTEM EVANGELISM / DIVINE PERSEVERENCE

Proponents of Post-mortem Evangelism (P.M.E.) wish to uphold universal accessibility but also believe that salvation can only come via special revelation and an explicit confession of faith in Jesus Christ **(B9)**. In this sense they can be properly still called exclusivists. But how can salvation be universally accessible when in this life not everyone has come into contact with special revelation? Here advocates of P.M.E. do the only thing they can to uphold these two axioms - they postpone an acceptance or rejection of Christ and hold that everyone of the unevangelised will come into contact with special revelation, not in this life but in a post-mortem encounter with Christ when they will be able to accept or reject him **(B12)**.[93]

There is also a third principle at work here. Whereas the restrictivist position maintains that the unevangelised are condemned for their rejection of God made manifest to them through general revelation and the *imago Dei*, proponents of P.M.E. believe that the only reason anyone is condemned to Hell is because they have explicitly rejected the invitation of Christ, "from this it is deduced that everyone must have an encounter with Jesus Christ in order to make a final decision about him. It is not ignorance that sends one

---

[93] For a full exposition of this position see the following: Sanders, *No Other Name*, Ch. 6; Gabriel Fackre, 'Divine Perseverance' in ed. Sanders, *What About...*, pp. 71-102; Milliard J. Erickson, 'Is There Opportunity for Salvation After Death' in *Bibliotheca Sacra* 152 April-June, 1995, pp. 131-144; Stephen T. Davis, 'Universalism, Hell, and the Fate of the Ignorant' in *Modern Theology* 6:2 Jan. 1990, pp. 173-186. Although Clark Pinnock is a major proponent of a post-mortem encounter with Christ, I have decided not to deal with his own position at this juncture in the study, as I treated Pinnock's inclusivism and his P.M.E. together in Ch. 5.

to Hell, but refusing Jesus Christ."[94] A post-mortem encounter with Christ would give this opportunity to the unevangelised.

This position, though, is not only based on a logical deduction. Proponents believe that there is explicit biblical evidence which supports this theory, most noticeably 1 Pet. 3:18-20; 4:6 which is the much debated text referring to Christ's descent into Hell and his proclamation of the gospel to the spirits in prison. There is not the space here to discuss the exegetical and hermeneutical debates concerning this text, and this has been done elsewhere.[95] Suffice it to say that these verses are regarded as being some of the most difficult to interpret in the New Testament, and there appears to be no consensus regarding them. This leads critics of P.M.E. to point out that to base an important belief regarding the unevangelised on such a controversial reading of a notoriously difficult verse is not a good ground for believing it. They also point out that elsewhere in the biblical narrative, there are less difficult verses that speak clearly of humankind's destiny being fixed at death.[96]

The belief in P.M.E. must be not be confused with the doctrine of the 'second chance' or 'free-will restorationism' which maintains that everyone will have one or more chances after death to accept the grace of God.[97] Rather what is maintained here, is the universality of a 'first chance,' and so most commonly refers specifically to the unevangelised. Here, though, the issue becomes confusing as different theologians are divided on what constitutes a 'first chance.' Stephen T. Davis includes in his definition of the unevangelised the fourth category of people that I listed earlier, namely those who have not heard a full and adequate presentation of the Gospel in this life. He believes that some who rejected the gospel in this life will respond positively to it after death, because when they heard it in this life they were psychologically unable to view it positively because of their circumstances. He asks: "Does this bring in universalism by the back door? Certainly not. I have little doubt some will say no to God eternally (the Bible predicts this, in fact), nor do I see any need for a 'second chance' for

---

[94] Sanders, *No Other Name*, p. 179. Some biblical texts seeming to support this are Mk. 16:15-16; Matt. 10:32-33; 2 Thes. 1:8; Jn. 3:18. See Sanders, *No Other Name*, p. 179-181.

[95] For a summary of the interpretations given see Erickson, op. cit. who mentions all the relevant positions concerning this text and its relationship to P.M.E. For a more detailed bibliographical history concerning this text, see Sanders, *No Other Name*, pp. 177-189 who notes all the major Protestant and Catholic treatments concerning these verses.

[96] See Heb. 9:27; Matt. 7:13-23; Rev. 20:11-15; Jn. 5:29. For a restrictivist criticism of P.M.E. see Ronald Nash, op. cit. pp. 150-158, and his response to Fackre in ed. Sanders, *What About...*, pp. 96-101. For a more general evaluation see Sanders, *No Other Name*, pp. 205-211.

[97] This argument is usually the basis to come to a universalist position where everyone eventually will repent and yield to the grace of God.

those who have freeingly and knowingly chosen in this life to live apart from God."[98] For Davis, only God can know what circumstances would enable a person to receive an opportunity to respond after death.

Sanders points out that some proponents of P.M.E. also deal with the problem of children who die in infancy. He quotes the nineteenth century Puritan Egbert Smyth who was troubled by the problem of infant salvation. He argued for a version of P.M.E. that held that, "since acceptance of Christ is a requisite for salvation, it follows that such infants should 'grow up' and accept Christ as Saviour in the next life."[99]

One evangelical who has defended P.M.E. is Gabriel Fackre. Fackre calls his position, 'universal particularity' for he wishes to uphold the axioms of God's universal salvific will and the *solus Christus*.[100] He compares the question of the unevangelised with the problem of evil because he sees them to have similarities in the tensions that arise in affirming three biblical truths, God is almighty, God is loving and all good, and evil is real. He believes that the other responses to the unevangelised compromise one of these truths. Universalism denies the reality of evil, restrictivism denies the goodness of God, and inclusivism restricts the power of God because it sets worldly limits on people coming to Christ.[101] He therefore advocates, "*eschatological evangelism* - the divine perseverance in bringing together the goodness and power of God in the face of the unreached."[102] The reality of sin has meant that the Word has not been spread throughout the world. However the power of God is not limited by our weakness or by the boundary of death because of the victory of Christ in the cross and resurrection. But the nature of God's power means that no-one is forced to accept His

---

[98] Stephen T. Davis, op. cit., p. 184. For an analysis of this same point see R.R. Cook's paper, 'Is Universalism an Implication of the Notion of Post-Mortem Evangelism?' in *Tyndale Bulletin*, 45.2 1994, pp. 395-409. Cook deals with Pinnock's argument to which I referred in Ch. 5, pp. 162-165.

[99] See Sanders, *No Other Name,* p. 191f. For some more conceptual difficulties concerning the nature of a post-mortem encounter with Christ, see K. Surin's essay on George Lindbeck's postliberal version of post-mortem evangelism, 'Many Religions and the One True Faith' in *Modern Theology* Jan. 1988. For Lindbeck's version of post-mortem evangelism and how it fits into his cultural-linguistic model of religion, see his *The Nature of Doctrine. Religion and Theology in a Postliberal Age.* (Philadelphia, 1984), pp. 46-72, and '*Fides ex auditu* and the salvation of non-Christians: Contemporary Catholic and Protestant Positions' in ed. Vilmos Vajta, *The Gospel and the Ambiguity of the Church* (Minneapolis, 1974), pp. 92-123.

[100] See Gabriel Fackre, 'The Scandals of Particularity and Universality' in *Midstream* 22 Jan. 1983:, pp. 32-52; *The Christian Story: A Narrative Interpretation of Basic Christian Doctrine* (Grand Rapids, 1984), pp. 219-221, 229-241; 'Divine Perseverance' in ed. Sanders, *What About...* pp. 71-107.

[101] Fackre, 'Divine Perseverance,' p. 76.

[102] Ibid., p. 79.

offer of grace, "While the power of God will patiently *persist* in that desire, it will not *insist* upon our compliance. We are free to say no into eternity itself."[103]

Fackre believes that this view is supported by specific passages of Scripture[104] but more important it is in line with the themes of the whole biblical story, namely God's indefatigable desire to save and our freedom to resist. He also wishes to re-state two traditional evangelical affirmations. Firstly, he wishes to retain the distinction between 'common grace' which is given to all creation and which sustains human life and 'special grace' which is concerned with the revelation of Jesus Christ. Both can be called 'salvation,' the former is "'horizontal' salvation - before and in the midst of temporal suffering", the latter is 'vertical' salvation - how you and I stand before the eternal God.[105] These two cannot be confused although they are both salvations by grace. Horizontal grace cannot justify us before God because of our sin and finitude; we need God's vertical grace for justification. This leads to Fackre's second affirmation that retains the *fides ex auditu* in appropriating this salvific grace. But this offer of vertical grace is made to everyone, even after death.

Finally, and as a footnote, Fackre wishes to retain with a belief in divine perseverance, something of the mystery of God. Although he believes that eschatological evangelism best upholds the truths found in the biblical narrative, he concedes that there is still mystery concerning the 'paradox of grace': "we cannot catch God in the nets of human logic."[106] We must admit that the mysteries of God that are present in all of theology can be explored but they cannot always be totally explained.

MIDDLE KNOWLEDGE

Like P.M.E. those who hold to middle knowledge[107] believe that our destiny is not determined by our acceptance/rejection in this life **(B12)**, but argue for this in a completely different way from those who hold to some form of P.M.E.. Because of its philosophical nature, I will briefly sketch out the basics of this argument before putting it into the context of the unevangelised. 'Middle knowledge' attempts to combine a strong view of God's

---

[103] Ibid., p. 81.
[104] He mentions those already discussed above, 1 Pet. 3:19-20, 4:6; Jn. 10:16, 5:25.
[105] Ibid., p. 92.
[106] Ibid., p. 95.
[107] Although Sanders views 'middle knowledge' as somewhat of a minor position concerning the unevangelised, I include it here, because it highlights some of the tensions concerning God's providence and human free-will which is a theme constantly referred to in this study.

providence (what Helm calls a 'no-risk' view)[108] *and* an indeterministic view of human freedom. Originally devised by the Jesuit, Luis De Molina, it distinguishes between three truths of God's omniscience. There are 'necessary truths' which include the laws of logic and which could not be false, 'free knowledge' which are truths because God has willed them to be true, and finally there is God's 'middle knowledge' which stands in the middle of these other two truths. Helm describes this truth as, "the knowledge that God has of all possibilities which he does not will, but which remain abstract possibilities."[109] The original step of this position comes when this 'middle knowledge' is used to show how God can ordain events through non-deterministic human action. God knows many propositions of the form: "(A) In circumstances C, if Jones freely chooses between X and Y, he will choose Y."[110] Therefore as William Lane Craig says: "Since God knows what any free creature would do in any situation, he can, by creating the appropriate situations, bring it about that creatures will achieve his ends and purposes and that they will do this so *freely*."[111]

In the philosophical debate, the main area of discussion is whether it is possible for God to know what totally free creatures would do under any circumstances. Philosophers who believe in indeterministic human freedom believe that God cannot have such knowledge either because He denies Himself middle knowledge, or because there is nothing for God to know before a free human decision.[112] Leaving this discussion behind and presuming that middle knowledge *is* possible for God, and that it entails genuine freedom, I wish to show two different positions that use the basic idea of middle-knowledge to formulate a solution to the issues surrounding the unevangelised.

Middle Knowledge and Universally Accessible Salvation

In this position, God knows all possible worlds and so knows how any persons would have responded had they heard the gospel in this world. As Phillips says, "God elects the individual to salvation according to his knowledge of a *potential* present world rather than according to decisions

---

[108] Paul Helm, *The Providence of God* (Leicester, 1993), p. 55. I will use Helm's description of 'middle-knowledge' because I find it to be clear and concise for my purposes.
[109] Ibid., p. 56.
[110] Ibid., p.57.
[111] William Lane Craig, *The Only Wise God* (Grand Rapids, 1987), p. 135. cited in Helm, op. cit., p. 57.
[112] See William Hasker, 'A Refutation of Middle-Knowledge' in *Nous* 20 1986, pp. 545-557; and Robert Merrihew Adams, 'Middle Knowledge and the Problem of Evil' in *American Philosophical Quarterly* Vol. 14, No.2, April 1977, pp. 109-117; Richard Swinburne, *The Coherence of Theism* (Oxford, 1977), p. 175f. For more discussion see the references in Helm, op. cit.

made in this *actual* world."[113] One theologian who holds such a view is Donald Lake.[114] Lake believes in the doctrine of unlimited atonement, that is that Christ died for all without exception and that his death has potential salvific significance for all mankind. He says that for Reformed theologians with their view of limited atonement, God always provides the means through which the elect can be saved. But what about those who believe in unlimited atonement? He writes:

> When the atonement, however, is understood as having potential significance for all mankind, this radically changes the perspective. A valid offer of grace has been made to mankind, but its application is limited by man's response rather than God's arbitrary selection. God knows who would, under ideal circumstances, believe the gospel, and on the basis of his foreknowledge, applies that gospel even if the person never hears the gospel during his lifetime.[115]

Providing one holds to the philosophical presuppositions of middle knowledge, Sanders correctly notes that there are a number of questions left unanswered with regards to this position, "Do they in fact mean to assert that people can be saved without any sort of act of faith toward God? Can people be saved without any actual faith of their own? Can people be saved apart from any knowledge of Christ?"[116] Phillips states that this position is not an exegetical insight but theological behaviourism, "and negates the clear meaning of too many passages which anchor faith to *this* life (e.g. Jn. 3:18, 1 Jn. 2:23)."[117] Phillips also notes that it is hard to hold this view without lapsing into universalism, "Since the mind of God knows an infinite number of possible worlds, what is to stop one from arguing that every human would be saved in *some* possible world...and therefore no-one will be in hell? This is a happy thought, but hardly biblical."[118]

Middle Knowledge and the Fairness of God

This is a much more sophisticated use of the doctrine of middle knowledge which holds that the unevangelised will not be saved, but which still believes in human choice and the distributive fairness of God. The main pro-

---

[113] Phillips, op. cit., p. 180.
[114] Donald Lake 'He Died For All: The Universal Dimensions of the Atonement' in ed. Pinnock *Grace Unlimited* (Grand Rapids, 1975), pp. 31-51.
[115] Ibid., p. 43.
[116] Sanders, *No Other Name*, p. 174.
[117] Phillips, op. cit., p. 181.
[118] Ibid.

ponent of this view is William Lane Craig.[119] Craig's proposal is quite complex, but I will attempt to explain his basic argument.

Like Fackre, Craig comes to the problem of the unevangelised through the soteriological problem of evil that arises from claiming that salvation is exclusively through Christ. Here there is a tension between two propositions:

1. God is omniscient, omnipotent, and omnibenevolent.
2. Some persons do not receive Christ and are damned.[120]

Critics of orthodox Christianity maintain that these two statements are inconsistent in a broadly logical sense, and that there is no possible world where both can be true. Lane comments:

> Now in order to show this, the objector must supply some further premise(s) that meet the following conditions:
> (i) its conjunction with (1) and (2) formally entails a contradiction,
> (ii) it is either necessarily true, essential to theism, or a logical consequence of propositions that are, and
> (iii) its meeting conditions (i) and (ii) could not be denied by a right-thinking person.[121]

Lane now looks at and analyses six possible premises and finally rests with the following one which he believes to be consistent with (1) and (2): "God has actualised a world containing an optimal balance between saved and unsaved, and those who are unsaved suffer from transworld damnation."[122]

For Lane, this can help answer the three questions that prompted his enquiry. Firstly, it is not feasible for God to create a world where everyone freely accepts His grace because He would have done it if it were feasible. However, every world realisable by God contains some creatures who will always freely reject His grace. Secondly, to the question, 'Why did God create this world when He knew that so many persons would not receive Christ and would therefore be lost?' Lane answers that, "given the truth of certain counterfactuals of creaturely freedom, it was not feasible for God to actualise a world having as many saved as but with no more damned that in

---

[119] See William Lane Craig, '"No Other Name": A Middle Knowledge Perspective on the Exclusivity of Salvation through Christ' in *Faith and Philosophy* Vol.6 No.2 April 1989, pp. 172-188.
[120] Ibid., p. 180.
[121] Ibid., p. 180.
[122] Ibid., p. 184. Transworld damnation refers to a person who does not respond to God's grace, "and is lost in every world feasible for God in which that person exists" (p. 184).

Appendix 1: Evangelical Responses to the Fate of the Unevangelised 329

the actual world."[123] Thirdly, and most pertinent to this discussion, is the question of why God did not provide special revelation to those who rejected general revelation *but who would have responded to special revelation had they had the opportunity to hear it*. Lane answers by stating that there are no such persons. In every world that feasibly exists, God wishes to save these people and presents them with His grace. However every time they freely reject this grace. Here I quote Lane in detail:

> If there were anyone who would have responded to the gospel if he had heard it, then God in his love would have brought the gospel to such a person... God in His providence has so arranged the world that...all who would respond to his gospel, were they to hear it, did and do hear it. Those who only respond to general revelation and do not respond to it would also not have responded to the gospel had they heard it. Hence, no one is lost because of lack of information due to historical or geographical accident. All who want or would want to be saved will be saved.[124]

Sanders regards such an argument as a modified version of restrictivism but questions whether restrictivists would accept it because it goes against a common missionary belief that, "there are indeed people who would not have been saved and would have gone to hell had they never heard of Christ."[125]

These middle-knowledge positions seem logically possible providing one believes that middle-knowledge is a theological and biblical truth. As was mentioned, though, it is a disputed position philosophically and theologians like Sanders and Pinnock do not accept it because they believe it goes against their own particular construals of human freedom.[126]

POSITIVE AGNOSTICISM

In the section on restrictivism, I mentioned a view propounded by some restrictivists that one cannot be dogmatic on the question of the unevangelised, but that one can be dogmatic on what the Bible says about the restrictive way of salvation which by inference alludes to the destiny of the unevangelised. The reason for this was to protect the sovereignty of God. Phillips called this 'negative agnosticism'[127] but I think it is more of a restrictivist position because it clearly defines the way in which people are saved.

---

[123] Ibid., p. 185.
[124] Ibid.
[125] Sanders, *No Other Name*, p. 175.
[126] See Sanders, *No Other Name*, p. 111 n.64, 173-175, 216; Pinnock, op. cit., pp. 160-161.
[127] Phillips, op. cit., p. 188.

A different kind of 'agnosticism' is that of John Stott's. Phillips calls his view 'positive agnosticism' because it believes that some of the unevangelised will be saved while being agnostic about how God will bring this about.[128] Stott makes three statements that he believes are fundamental evangelical tenets, **1.** all human beings are perishing, **2.** human beings cannot save themselves, **3.** Jesus Christ is the only Saviour.[129] He now enquires about the unevangelised in light of these previous statements and asks whether they can be saved. After briefly surveying the range of answers, he concludes that the most Christian stance is to remain agnostic on the issue, "We have to leave them [the unevangelised] in the hands of the God of infinite justice and mercy, who manifested these qualities most fully in the cross. Abraham's question, 'will not the Judge of all the earth do right?' (Genesis. 18:25) is our confidence too."[130] However in spite of this agnosticism, Stott still believes that there is solid biblical evidence to support the view that the majority of the human race will be saved,[131] "this is the hope I cherish, and that is the vision that inspires me, even while I remain agnostic about how God will bring it to pass."[132] The question that arises from this statement is whether Stott must revise or qualify his three fundamental tenets in the light of this hope. It appears that Stott wishes to be more restrictive concerning the defined nature of salvation, but at the same time, maintain the, 'wider hope' over the 'fewness doctrine.' At an emotional level this seems to be a very satisfactory position to hold. Intellectually, though, I am not so sure that it is so satisfactory because it does not seem to work out consistently the implications of Christian exclusivity for those eventually saved. On a view like Stott's I am inclined to agree now with Sanders' statement about relieving the tension on the issue without paying the theological price.[133]

Bridging the gap between agnosticism and 'inclusivism' that is the focus of my study, is the position of Alister McGrath. Defining his position as "A Particularist View: A Post-Enlightenment Approach,"[134] Alister McGrath affirms both the particularity of Christ and the universality of God's salvific will. From here he moves to the idea that salvation must be universally accessible.

---

[128] Ibid., p. 189.
[129] John Stott and David Edwards, *Essentials, A Liberal-Evangelical Dialogue.* (London, 1988), pp. 320-323.
[130] Ibid., p. 327.
[131] He bases this view on inferences of the character of God that shows Him to be infinitely patient and compassionate to all His creation.
[132] Ibid., p. 328.
[133] Sanders, *No Other Name*, p. 77.
[134] Alister McGrath, 'A Particularist View: A Post-Enlightenment Approach' in Okholm and Phillips, op. cit., pp. 149-181.

But what about those who never hear the gospel? He writes that "a human failure to evangelise cannot be transposed into God's failure to save. In the end, salvation is not culturally conditioned or restricted accomplishment; it is God's boundless sovereign gift to his people."[135] He continues: "God is not inhibited from bringing people to faith in him, even if that act of hope and trust may lack the fully orbed character of an informed Christian faith."[136] He also mentions Muslim converts who have encountered the risen Christ through a dream or vision and notes that although Christians "may have failed to make the Good News available to all; this does not mean that God will fail in his intention to make salvation a universal possibility."[137]

---

[135] Ibid., p. 178.
[136] Ibid., p. 179.
[137] Ibid.

BIBLIOGRAPHY

ed. Abbott, Walter M. *The Documents of Vatican II.* New Jersey: New Century Publishers, 1966.

Adams, Robert. 'Middle Knowledge and the Problem of Evil' *American Philosophical Quarterly* 14 (1977): 109-117.

Aldenhoven, Herwig. 'The Question of the Procession of the Holy Spirit and its Connection with the Life of the Church' in *Spirit of God, Spirit of Christ: Ecumenical Reflections of the Filioque Controversy.* ed. Lukas Vischer, 121-133. London: SPCK, 1981.

Allchin, Donald. 'The *Filioque* Clause: an Anglican Approach' in *Spirit of God, Spirit of Christ: Ecumenical Reflections of the Filioque Controversy.* ed. Lukas Vischer, 85-97. London: SPCK, 1981.

Allen, Diogenes. *Christian Belief in a Postmodern World: The Full Wealth of Conviction.* Louisville: Westminster/John Knox, 1989.

Anderson, Norman. *Christianity and the World Religions.* Leicester: Inter-Varsity Press, 1984.

Anderson, Ray S. 'Evangelical Theology' in *The Modern Theologians.* Vol. 2. ed. David F. Ford, 131-152. Oxford: Blackwell, 1993.

Aulen, Gustaf. *Christus Victor: An Historical Study of the Three Main Types of the Idea of Atonement.* London: SCPK, 1953.

Badock, Gary. 'The Anointing of Christ and the *Filioque* Doctrine' *Irish Theological Quarterly* 60 (1994): 241-258.

___. 'Karl Rahner, the Trinity, and Religious Pluralism' in *The Trinity in a Pluralistic Age: Theological Essays on Culture and Religion.* ed. Kevin J. Vanhoozer, 143-155. Cambridge: Eerdmans, 1997.

___. *Light of Truth and Fire of Love: A Theology of the Holy Spirit.* Cambridge: Eerdmans, 1997.

Barker, Kenneth L. 'False Dichotomies Between the Testaments' *Journal of the Evangelical Theological Society* 25/1 (1982): 3-16.

Barrett, John K. 'Does Inclusivist Theology Undermine Evangelism?' *Evangelical Quarterly* 70/3 (1998): 219-245.

Barth, Karl. *Church Dogmatics.* 1.1: 'The Doctrine of the Word of God' Edinburgh: T&T Clarke, 1975.

eds. Basinger, David and Randell Basinger, *Four Views on Predestination and Free Will.* Downers Grove: Inter-Varsity Press, 1986.

Baugh, Steven M. ' "Saviour of All People": 1 Tim 4:10 in Context' *Westminster Theological Journal* 54 (1992): 331-340.

Bavinck, Herman. 'Common Grace' trans. and intro. by Raymond C. Van Leeuwen *Calvin Theological Journal* 24/1 (1989): 35-66.
___. *The Doctrine of God*. Edinburgh: Banner of Truth Trust, 1977.
___. *Our Reasonable Faith*. Grand Rapids: Eerdmans, 1956.
Bavinck, J. H. 'Human Religion in God's Eyes: A Study of Romans 1:18-32' *Scottish Bulletin of Evangelical Theology* 12/1 (Spring 1994): 44-52.
___. *An Introduction to the Science of Missions*. trans. David H. Freeman. Grand Rapids: Baker Book House, 1960.
Bebbington, David. *Evangelicalism in Modern Britain: A History from the 1730's to the 1980's*. Grand Rapids: Baker Books, 1989.
Begbie, Jeremy. 'Rediscovering and Re-Imaging the Atonement' *Anvil* 11/3 (1994): 193-202.
Benz, Ernest. *The Eastern Orthodox Church, Its Thought and Life*. New York: Doubleday, 1963.
Berkhof, Hendrikus. *The Christian Faith*. trans. Sierd Woudstra Grand Rapids: Eerdmans, 1979.
Berkhof, Louis. *Systematic Theology*. Edinburgh: Banner of Truth, 1958.
Blackham, Paul. 'Did the NT Writers Misunderstand the OT,' *http://freespace.virgin.net/lizzy.blackham/Papers/NTwritersonOT.htm,* September 27th 2000.

Blocher, Henri. 'Immanence and Transcendence in Trinitarian Theology' in *The Trinity in a Pluralistic Age*. ed. Kevin J. Vanhoozer, 104-124. Cambridge: William B. Eerdmans, 1997.
___. 'The Scope of Redemption and Modern Theology' *Scottish Bulletin of Evangelical Theology* 9/2 (Autumn 1991): 80-103.
Bloesch, Donald. *Essentials of Evangelical Theology*. 2 Vols. New York: Harper, 1978.
Bock, Darrell L. 'Athenians Who Have Never Heard' in *Through No Fault of Their Own? The Fate of Those Who Have Never Heard*. eds. W. Crockett and J. Sigountos, 117-123. Grand Rapids: Baker Books, 1991.
Boettner, Loraine. *The Reformed Doctrine of Predestination*. Grand Rapids: Eerdmans, 1954.
___. *Studies in Theology*. Grand Rapids: Eerdmans, 1947.
Boff, Leonardo. *Trinity and Society*. Maryknoll: Orbis Books, 1988.
Bolt, John. 'A Smouldering Ember: Harry Boer's Continuing Battle with the Reformed Tradition' *Calvin Theological Journal* 26/1 (1991): 11-125.
Borland, James. 'A Theologian Looks at the Gospel and the World Religions.' *Journal of the Evangelical Theological Society* 33/1 (1990): 3-11.
Braaten, Carl E. *No Other Gospel! Christianity Among the World's Religions*. Minneapolis: Fortress Press, 1992.
Bradley, James E. '*Logos* Christology and Religious Pluralism: A New Evangelical Proposal' in *Proceedings of the Wheaton Theological Conference. The Challenge of Religious Pluralism: An Evangelical Analysis and Response*. (Wheaton, 1992): 190-208.
Bray, Gerald. *Creeds, Councils and Christ*. Fearn: Mentor, 1997.
___. *The Doctrine of God*. Leicester: Inter-Varsity Press, 1993.
___. 'The Double Procession of the Holy Spirit in Evangelical Theology Today: Do we still need it?' *Journal of the Evangelical Theological Society* 41/3 (1998): 415-426.
___. 'Eastern Orthodox Theology in Outline' *Evangel* (Spring 1999): 14-22.

___. 'Explaining Christianity to Pagans' in *The Trinity in a Pluralistic Age: Theological Essays on Culture and Religion.* ed. Kevin J. Vanhoozer, 9-26. Cambridge: Eerdmans, 1997.
___. '*Filioque* and Anglican-Orthodox Dialogue' *Churchman* 93 (1979): 123-136.
___. 'The *Filioque* Clause in History and Theology' *Tyndale Bulletin* 34 (1983): 91-145.
___. *The Personal God: Is the Classical Understanding of God Tenable?* Carlisle: Paternoster, 1998.
___. 'The Significance of God's Image in Man' *Tyndale Bulletin* 42.2 (1991): 195-225.
Brobinsky, Boris. 'The *Filioque* Yesterday and Today' in *Spirit of God, Spirit of Christ: Ecumenical Reflections of the Filioque Controversy.* ed. Lukas Vischer, 133-149. London: SPCK, 1981.
Brow, Robert. 'Evangelical Megashift' *Christianity Today* (Feb. 19th, 1990): 12-17.
Brown, Harold, O. J. 'How Crowded Will Hell Be?' *Christianity Today* (Sep. 14th, 1992): 39-40.
Buhlman, Walbert. *The Chosen Peoples.* Slough: St. Paul Publications, 1982.
Butler, Diane. 'God's Visible Glory: The Beauty of Nature in the Thought of John Calvin and Jonathan Edwards' *Westminster Theological Journal* 52 (1990): 13-26.
Calvin, John. *Institutes of the Christian Religion.* 2 Vols. trans. Henry Beveridge. London: James Clarke, 1949.
Caneday, A.B. 'Evangelical Meltdown "To Go Beyond What is Written" An Exercise in Speculative Theology' *Contra Mundum* No. 5 (Fall 1992): 1-11.
Carson, Don. *The Difficult Doctrine of the Love of God.* Leicester: IVP, 2000.
___. *Divine Sovereignty and Human Responsibility: Biblical Perspectives in Tension.* Grand Rapids: Baker Books, 1994.
___. *Exegetical Fallacies.* Grand Rapids: Baker Books, 1996.
___. *The Gagging of God: Christianity Confronts Pluralism.* Leicester: Apollos, 1996.
___. 'God is Love' *Bibliotheca Sacra* 156 (Apr.-June 1999): 131-142.
___. *The Gospel According to John.* Leicester: Inter-Varsity Press, 1991.
___. *New Testament Commentary Survey.* (4th ed.) Grand Rapids: Baker Books, 1993.
___. 'On Distorting the Love of God' *Bibliotheca Sacra* 156 (Jan.-Mar. 1999): 3-12.
eds. Carson, D.A. and John D. Woodbridge, *Scripture and Truth.* Grand Rapids: Zondervan, 1983.
___. *Hermeneutics, Authority and Canon.* Grand Rapids: Zondervan, 1986.
Chapman, Colin. 'The Riddle of Religions' *Christianity Today* 34/8 (14th May, 1990): 16-22.
Ciocchi, David M. 'Reconciling Divine Sovereignty and Human Freedom' in *Journal of the Evangelical Theological Society* 37/3 (1994): 395-412.
___. 'Understanding Our Ability to Endure Temptation: A Theological Watershed' *Journal of the Evangelical Theology Society* 35/4 (1992): 463-468.
Clark, Gordon H. *Predestination.* (The combined edition of Biblical Predestination and Predestination in the Old Testament). Phillipsburg: Presbyterian and Reformed Publishing Company, 1987.
eds. Clarke, Andrew D. and Bruce W. Winter, *One God, One Lord in a World of Religious Pluralism.* Grand Rapids: Baker Book House, 1992.
Clarke, David K. 'Is Special Revelation Necessary for Salvation?' in *Through No Fault of Their Own? The Fate of Those Who Have Never Heard.* eds. W. Crockett and J. Sigountos, 35-45. Grand Rapids: Baker Books, 1991.

___. 'Warfield, Infant Salvation, and the Logic of Calvinism' *Journal of the Evangelical Theological Society* 27/4 (1984): 459-464.

Clendenin, Daniel B. 'Partakers of Divinity: The Orthodox Doctrine of Theosis' *Journal of the Evangelical Theological Society* 37/3 (1994): 365-379.

Clowney, Edmund P. *The Unfolding Mystery: Discovering Christ in the Old Testament.* Leicester: Inter-Varsity Press, 1990.

eds. Cobb, John B. and Clark H. Pinnock, *Searching for an Adequate God: A Dialogue Between Process and Free Will Theists.* Cambridge: Eerdmans, 2000.

Colquhoun, John. *Repentance.* London: Banner of Truth Trust, 1965.

Colwell, John 'The Contemporaneity of the Divine Decision: Reflections on Barth's Denial of 'Universalism' in *Universalism and the Doctrine of Hell.* ed. Nigel M. de S. Cameron, 139-161. Carlisle: Paternoster, 1992.

Congar, Yves. *The Word and the Spirit.* London: Geoffrey Chapman, 1986.

Conn, Harvie M. 'Do Other Religions Save?' in *Through No Fault of Their Own? The Fate of Those Who Have Never Heard.* eds. W. Crockett and J. Sigountos, 195-208. Grand Rapids: Baker Books, 1991.

Cook, E. David. 'Hick and Christianity's Uniqueness' in *One God, One Lord: Christianity in a World of Religious Pluralism.* eds. Andrew D. Clarke and Bruce W. Winter, 237-246. Grand Rapids, Baker Book House, 1992.

Cook, Robert, R. 'Is Universalism an Implication of the Notion of Post-Mortem Evangelism?' *Tyndale Bulletin* 45 (N. 1994): 395-409.

Cotterell, Jack. 'The Fate of the Unreached: Are They Lost Without Special Revelation?' *International Journal of Frontier Mission* 10 (1993): 67-72.

Cotterell, Peter. 'The Unevangelised: An Olive Branch to the Opposition' *International Review of Mission* 77 (1988): 131-135.

Covell, Ralph, R. 'The Christian Gospel And World Religions: How Much Have American Evangelicals Changed?' *International Bulletin of Missionary Research* 15 (1991): 12-17.

Craig, William. 'Does Omitting the *Filioque* Clause Betray Traditional Anglican Thought?' *Anglican Theological Review* 78/3 (1996): 420-439.

Craig, William Lane. ' 'No Other Name': A Middle-Knowledge Perspective on the Exclusivity of Salvation Through Christ' *Faith and Philosophy* 6 (1989): 172-188.

ed. Crockett, William. *Four Views on Hell.* Grand Rapids: Zondervan, 1992.

Dahms, John V. 'The Subordination of the Son' *Journal of the Evangelical Theological Society* 37/3 (1994): 351-364.

Danielou, Jean. *History of Early Christian Doctrine.* Vol. 2 'Gospel Message and Hellenistic Culture' London: Darton, Longman and Todd, 1973.

Davis, Stephen. 'Universalism, Hell, and the Fate of the Ignorant' *Modern Theology* 6 (1990): 173-186.

D'Costa, Gavin. 'Against Religious Pluralism' in *Different Gospels.* ed. Andrew Walker, 139-154. London: SPCK, 1993.

___. 'Christ, the Trinity and Religious Plurality' in *Christian Uniqueness Reconsidered: The Myth of a Pluralistic Theology of Religions.* ed. Gavin D'Costa, 16-30. Maryknoll: Orbis Books, 1990.

___. *The Meeting of Religions and the Trinity.* New York: Orbis, 2000.

___. 'Revelation and Revelations: Discerning God in Other Religions - Beyond a Static Valuation' in *Modern Theology* 10/2 (1994): 165-183.

___. *Theology and Religious Pluralism.* Oxford: Blackwell, 1986.

___. 'Theology of Religions' in *The Modern Theologians*. ed. David F. Ford, 274-290. Vol. 2. Oxford: Blackwell, 1993.
Del Colle, Ralph. *Christ and the Spirit: Spirit Christology in Trinitarian Perspective*. Oxford: Oxford University Press, 1994.
Demarest, Bruce. 'General and Special Revelation: Epistemological Foundations of Religious Pluralism' in *One God, One Lord: Christianity in a World of Religious Pluralism*. eds. Andrew D. Clarke and Bruce W. Winter, 189-206. Grand Rapids: Baker Books, 1992.
___. *General Revelation*. Grand Rapids: Zondervan, 1982.
Demarest, Bruce and R. J. Harpel, 'Don Richardson's Redemptive Analogies and The Biblical Idea of Revelation' *Bibliotheca Sacra* 146 (July-Sept. 1989): 583-592.
Demarest, Bruce and Gordon R. Lewis, *Integrative Theology*. 3 Vols. Grand Rapids: Zondervan, 1987-1992.
Dowsett, Dick. *God That's Not Fair: How Do you Square God's Love With Everlasting Punishment?* Harpenden: Overseas Missionary Fellowship, 1993.
Drummond, Richard. *Toward a New Age in Christian Theology*. Maryknoll: Orbis Books, 1985.
Duffy, Stephen J. *The Graced Horizon: Nature and Grace in Modern Catholic Thought*. Minnesota: The Liturgical Press, 1992.
Dumbrell, W. J. *Covenant and Creation*. Carlisle: Paternoster Press, 1997.
Dupuis, J. 'The Cosmic Christ in the Early Fathers' in *Indian Journal of Theology* 15 (1966): 106-120.
Dye, Wayne. 'Towards a Cross-Cultural Definition Of Sin' *Missiology* 4 (1976): 32.
Edwards, David and John Stott. *Essentials: A Liberal - Evangelical Dialogue*. London: Hodder and Stoughton, 1988.
Ellenberger, John D. 'Is Hell a Proper Motivation for Missions?' in *Through No Fault of Their Own?* eds. William V. Crockett and James G. Sigountos, 217-227. Grand Rapids: Baker Book House, 1991.
Engelsma, David J. *Hyper-Calvinism and the Call of the Gospel*. Grand Rapids: Reformed Free Publishing Association, 1994.
Erickson, Millard. *Christian Theology*. Grand Rapids, Baker Books, 1983.
___. 'The Destiny of The Unevangelised.' *Bibliotheca Sacra* 1) 152. Jan-Mar. 1995: 3-15; 2) 152. Apr-Jne. 1995: 113-144; 3) 152. Jly-Sept. 1995: 259-272.
___. *The Evangelical Left: Encountering Postconservative Theology*. Grand Rapids: Baker Books, 1997.
___. 'Hope For Those Who Haven't Heard: It Depends' *Evangelical Missions Quarterly* 11 (1975): 122-126.
___. 'Is Universalistic Thinking Now Appearing Among Evangelicals?' *United Evangelical Action* 48 (1989): 35-42.
Evangelical Alliance. 'The Salvation of The Gentiles: Implications for Other Faiths' *Evangelical Review of Theology* 15 (1991): 36-43.
Eveson, Phillip H. *The Great Exchange: Justification by Faith Alone in the Light of Recent Thought*. Bromley: DayOne Publications, 1996.
Fackre, Gabriel. 'An Evangelical Megashift? The Promise and Peril of an Open View of God' *Christian Century* 112 (May 3rd. 1995): 484-487.
___. 'The Scandals of Particularity and Universality' *Midstream* 22 (1983): 32-52.
Fairbairn, Don. 'Not Just 'How' But Also 'Who': What Evangelicals Can Learn From the Orthodox' *Evangel* (Spring, 1999): 10-13.

___. 'Salvation as *Theosis*: The Teaching of Eastern Orthodoxy' *Themelios* 23/3 (1988): 42-54.
Feinberg, John S. 'Systems of Discontinuity' in *Continuity and Discontinuity: Perspectives of the Relationship Between the Old and New Testaments*. ed. John S. Feinberg, 63-86. Westchester: Crossway, 1988.
Ferguson, Sinclair. *The Holy Spirit*. Leicester: Inter-Varsity Press, 1996.
Fernando, Ajith. *The Christian's Attitude Toward World Religions*. Wheaton: Tyndale House, 1987.
Ferrante, Joseph M. 'The Final Destiny of Those Who Have Not Heard The Gospel' *Trinity Studies* 2 (1980): 55-62.
Ford, David F. *The Modern Theologians: An Introduction to Christian Theology in the Twentieth Century*. 2 Vols. Oxford: Blackwell, 1989.
Frame, John. *The Doctrine of the Knowledge of God*. Phillipsburg: Presbyterian and Reformed, 1987.
Fudge, Edward. 'How Wide Is God's Mercy?' *Christianity Today* 36 (April 27th 1992): 30-33.
Gaffin Jr., Richard B. *Perspectives on Pentecost: New Testament Teaching on the Gifts of the Holy Spirit*. Grand Rapids: Baker Book House, 1979.
Geisler, Norman. *Creating God in the Image of Man? The New "Open" View of God - NeoTheism's Dangerous Drift*. Minneapolis: Bethany House Publishers, 1997.
Geivett, R. Douglas. 'John Hick's Approach to Religious Pluralism' in *Proceedings of the Wheaton Theological Conference. The Challenge of Religious Pluralism: An Evangelical Analysis and Response*. (Wheaton, 1992): 39-56.
___. '"Misgivings" and "Openness": A Dialogue on Inclusivism Between R. Douglas Geivett and Clark Pinnock' *The Southern Baptist Journal of Theology* 2/2 (Summer 1998): 26-40.
Gill, John. *The Cause of God and Truth*. Grand Rapids: Sovereign Grace Publishers, 1971.
Gillis, Chester. 'Evangelical Inclusivism: Progress or Betrayal?' *Evangelical Quarterly* 68/2. (1996): 139-150.
Gingrich, F. Wilbur. *Shorter Lexicon of the Greek New Testament*. (2nd ed.) rev. Frederick W. Danker. London: University of Chicago Press, 1983.
Glenny, W. Edward. 'Typology: A Summary of the Present Evangelical Discussion' *Journal of the Evangelical Theological Society* 40/4 (1997): 627-638.
Gnanakan, Ken. *Kingdom Concerns: A Theology of Mission Today*. Leicester: Inter-Varsity Press, 1993.
Goldingay. John E. *Old Testament Commentary Survey*. Leicester: Religious and Theological Studies Fellowship, 1994.
Goldingay, John E. and Christopher J. H. Wright, ' 'Yahweh Our God Yahweh One': the Old Testament and Religious Pluralism' in *One God One Lord in a World of Religious Pluralism*. eds. Andrew D. Clarke and Bruce W. Winter, 34-52. Grand Rapids: Baker Books, 1992.
Gootjes, N. H. 'General Revelation and Science: Reflections on a Remark in Report 28' *Calvin Theological Journal* 30 (1995): 94-107.
___. 'General Revelation in its Relation to Special Revelation' *Westminster Theological Journal* 51 (1989): 359-368.
___. 'The Sense of Divinity: a Critical Examination of the Views of Calvin and Demarest' *Westminster Theological Journal* 48 (1986): 337-350.

Grenz, Stanley J. 'Toward an Evangelical Theology of Religions' *Journal of Ecumenical Studies* 31 (Winter-Spring 1995): 49-65.
Griffiths, Paul J. 'Modalizing the Theology of Religions' in *Journal of Religion* 73 (1993): 382-389.
Groothuis, Douglas. 'Proofs, Pride, and Incarnation: Is Natural Theology Theologically Taboo?' *Journal of the Evangelical Theological Society* 38/1 (1995): 67-76.
Grudem, Wayne. T*he Gift of Prophecy in the New Testament and Today*. Westchester: Crossway, 1988.
___. *Systematic Theology: An Introduction to Biblical Doctrine*. Grand Rapids: Zondervan. 1994.
___, ed. *Are Miraculous Gifts For Today? Four Views*. Leicester: Inter-Varsity Press, 1996.
Gundry, Robert. 'Salvation According To Scripture: No Middle Ground.' *Christianity Today* (Dec. 9th 1977): 14-16.
Gunton, Colin. 'The Trinity, Natural Theology, and a Theology of Religions' in *The Trinity in a Pluralistic Age: Theological Essays on Culture and Religion*. ed. Kevin J. Vanhoozer, 88-104. Cambridge: Eerdmans, 1997.
Hackett, Stuart. *The Reconstruction of The Christian Revelation Claim*. Grand Rapids: Baker Book House, 1984.
Haight, Roger, 'The Case for Spirit Christology' *Theological Studies* 53 (1992): 257-287.
Hamilton, V. P. *The Book of Genesis: Chapters 1-17*. Grand Rapids: Eerdmans, 1990.
Hanko, Herman. 'Another Look at Common Grace' published in nine parts in the *Protestant Reformed Theological Journal* Pt. 1: Apr. 1992: 24-31; Pt. 2: Nov. 1992: 46-62; Pt. 3: Apr. 1993: 28-44; Pt. 4: Nov. 1993: 13-28; Pt. 5: Apr. 1994: 21-44; Pt. 6: Nov. 1994: 25-38; Pt. 7: Apr. 1995: 3-18; Pt. 8: Apr. 1996: 31-50; Pt. 9: Apr. 1997: 27-39.
___. *God's Everlasting Covenant of Grace*. Grand Rapids: Reformed Free Publishing Association, 1988.
Hart, Trevor A. 'Irenaeus, Recapitulation and Physical Redemption' in *Christ in Our Place: The Humanity of God in Christ for the Reconciliation of the World* eds. Trevor Hart and Daniel Thimell, 152-181. Exeter: Paternoster, 1989.
___. 'Universalism: Two Distinct Types' in *Universalism and the Doctrine of Hell*, ed. Nigel M. de S. Cameron, pp. 15-35. Carlisle: Paternoster, 1992.
Hasker, William. 'A Refutation of Middle Knowledge' *Noûs* 20 (1986): 545-547.
Hastings, Adrian. 'Your High Priest, Melchizedek' *Missionalia* 18 (1990): 271-276.
Helm, Paul. 'Are They Few That Be Saved?' in *Universalism and the Doctrine of Hell*. ed. Nigel M. de S. Cameron, 256-281. Carlisle: Paternoster, 1991.
___. *Calvin and the Calvinists*. Edinburgh: Banner of Truth Trust, 1982.
___. *Eternal God: A Study of God Without Time*. Oxford: Oxford University Press, 1988.
___. *The Providence of God*. Leicester: Inter-Varsity Press. 1993.
Henry, Carl F. *God, Revelation and Authority*. Vols. 1, 2, 5 and 6. Waco: Word, 1976 (Vol. 1), 1978 (Vol. 2), 1982 (Vol. 5), 1983 (Vol. 6).
___. 'Is it Fair?' in *Through No Fault of Their Own? The Fate of Those Who Have Never Heard*. eds. W. Crockett and J. Sigountos, 245-256. Grand Rapids: Baker Books, 1991.
___. 'Justification: a Doctrine in Crisis' in *Journal of the Evangelical Theological Society* 38/1 (1995): 57-65.

Heppe, Heinrich. *Reformed Dogmatics*. Grand Rapids: Baker Books, 1978.
Heron, A. I. C. 'The *Filioque* Clause' in *One God in Trinity*. eds. Peter Toon and James D. Spiceland, 62-78. London: Samuel Bagster, 1980.
___. 'The *Filioque* in Recent Reformed Theology' in *Spirit of God, Spirit of Christ: Ecumenical Reflections of the Filioque Controversy*. ed. Lukas Vischer, 110-121. London: SPCK, 1981.
___. '"Who Proceedeth from the Father and the Son:" The Problem of the Filioque' *Scottish Journal of Theology* 24 (1971): 149-166.
Hess, Richard S. 'Yahweh and His Asherah? Religious Pluralism in the Old Testament World' in *One God, One Lord: Christianity in a World of Religious Pluralism*. eds. Andrew D. Clarke and Bruce W. Winter, 13-42. Grand Rapids: Baker Books, 1992.
Hick, John. *God and the Universe of Faiths*. Oxford: Oneworld Publications, 1993.
Hodge, Charles. *Systematic Theology*. Vol. 2. New York: Scribner, Armstrong and Co., 1873.
___. *Systematic Theology*. Vol. 3. Grand Rapids: Eerdmans, 1940.
Hoeksema, Herman. *Reformed Dogmatics*. Grand Rapids: Reformed Free Publishing Association, 1973.
Hook, Richard. 'A Biblical Definition of Saving Faith' *Bibliotheca Sacra* (Apr.-Jne. 1964): 135-151.
ed. House, Paul R. *The Southern Baptist Journal of Theology: Responses to Universalism and Inclusivism* 2/2. (Summer 1998).
Hughes, Dewi. 'An Evangelical Theology of Pluralism' *Evangelical Review of Theology* 14 (1990): 179-188.
Hughes, P. E. *A Commentary on the Epistle to the Hebrews*. Grand Rapids: Eerdmans, 1979.
Hunter, James D. *Evangelicalism: the Coming Generation*. Chicago: University of Chicago Press, 1987.
Inch, Morris A. *Saga of the Spirit: A Biblical, Systematic and Historical Theology of the Holy Spirit*. Grand Rapids: Baker Book House, 1985.
Johnson, Garrett P. 'The Myth of Common Grace' *The Trinity Review* 54 (Mar.-Apr. 1987): 1-8.
Johnson Jr., Lewis S. 'Behold the Lamb: The Gospel and Substitutionary Atonement' in, *The Coming Evangelical Crisis*. ed. J. H. Armstrong, 119-139. Chicago: Moody Press, 1996.
Johnston, Robert K. *The Use of the Bible in Theology: Evangelical Options*. Atlanta: John Knox Press, 1985.
Jones, Hywel R. *Only One Way: Do You Have to Believe in Christ to be Saved?* Kent: Day One Publications. 1996.
Kane, Herbert. *Christian Missions In Biblical Perspective*. Grand Rapids: Baker Book House, 1976.
eds. Kantzer, Kenneth and Carl F. Henry, *Evangelical Affirmations*. Grand Rapids: Acadamie Press, 1990.
Karlberg, Mark W. 'Legitimate Discontinuities Between the Testaments' *Journal of the Evangelical Theological Society* 28/1 (1985): 9-20.
Kasper, Walter. *The God of Jesus Christ*. London: SCM Press, 1983.
Keith, Graham A. 'Justin Martyr and Religious Exclusivism' in *One God, One Lord: Christianity in a World of Religious Pluralism*. eds. Andrew D. Clarke and Bruce W. Winter, 161-185. Grand Rapids: Baker Books, 1992.

Khodr, Georges. 'Christianity in a Pluralistic World - The Economy of the Holy Spirit' *Ecumenical Review* 23 (1971): 118-128.
Kidner, Derek. *Genesis.* London: Tyndale Press, 1971.
Kingdon, David. *Children of Abraham: A Reformed Baptist View of Baptism, the Covenant and Children.* Larne: James Drummond, 1973.
ed. Kistler, Don. *Justification by Faith Alone: Affirming the Doctrine by which the Church and the Individual Stands or Falls.* Morgan: Soli Deo Gloria Publications, 1995.
Klein, William W. *The New Chosen People: a Corporate View of Election.* Grand Rapids: Zondervan, 1990.
Klooster, Fred H. 'The Biblical Method of Salvation' in *Continuity and Discontinuity: Perspectives of the Relationship Between the Old and New Testaments.* ed. John S. Feinberg, 131-160. Westchester: Crossway, 1988.
Knitter, Paul F. *No Other Name? A Critical Survey of Christian Attitudes Toward the World Religions.* Maryknoll: Orbis Books, 1985.
Kraemer, Hendrik. *Religion and the Christian Faith.* London: Lutterworth Press, 1961.
Kraft, Charles. *Christianity in Culture.* London: Orbis, 1979.
Kuyper, Abraham. *The Work of the Holy Spirit.* trans. H. De Vries. New York: Funk and Wagnalls, 1900.
LaCugna, M. *God For Us: the Trinity and Christian Life.* San Francisco: HarperSanFransisco, 1991.
Lake, Donald. 'He Died for All: The Universal Dimensions of the Atonement' in *Grace Unlimited.* ed. Clark H. Pinnock, 31-51. Minneapolis: Bethany, 1975.
Lamadrid, Lucas. 'Anonymous or Analogous Christians? Rahner and Von Balthasar on Naming the Non-Christian' *Modern Theology* 11/3 (1995): 363-384.
Lampe, Geoffrey. 'The Holy Spirit and the Person of Christ' in *Christ, Faith and History.* eds. S. W. Sykes and J. P. Clayton, pp. 111-131. Cambridge: Cambridge University Press, 1972.
Letham, Robert. *The Work of Christ.* Leicester: Inter-Varsity Press, 1993.
Lewis, C. S. *The Last Battle.* New York: Macmillan, 1970.
___. *Mere Christianity.* New York: Macmillan, 1967.
___. *The Problem of Pain.* New York: Macmillan, 1962.
Lindbeck, George. 'Fides ex auditu and the Salvation of Non- Christians: Contemporary Catholic and Protestant Positions' in *The Gospel and the Ambiguity of the Church.* ed. Vilmos Vajta, 92-123. Minneapolis: Fortress Press, 1974.
___. *The Nature of Doctrine: Religion and Theology in a Postliberal Age.* Philadelphia: Westminster Press, 1984.
Linfield, Alan. 'Sheep and Goats: Current Evangelical Thought on the Nature of Hell and the Scope of Salvation' *Vox Evangelica* 24 (1994): 63-75.
Lints, Richard. *The Fabric of Theology: a Prolegomenon to Evangelical Theology.* Grand Rapids: Eerdmans. 1993.
Lopes, Augustus Nicodemus. 'Calvin, Theologian of the Holy Spirit: The Holy Spirit and the Word of God' *Scottish Bulletin of Evangelical Theology* 15/1 (Spring 1997): 38-49.
Lorenzen, Thorwald. 'Baptists and the Challenge of Religious Pluralism' *Review And Expositor* 89 (Winter 1992): 49-69.
Lossky, Vladimir. *In the Image and Likeness of God.* New York: St. Vladimir's Seminary Press, 1974.

McConville, J. Gordon. 'Abraham and Melchizedek: Horizons in Genesis 14' in *He Swore an Oath: Biblical Themes from Genesis 12-50*. eds. R. S. Hess, G. J. Wenham and P. E. Satterthwaite, 67-92. Carlisle: Paternoster, 1994.

McGrath, Alister E. 'The Challenge of Pluralism for the Contemporary Church' *Journal of the Evangelical Theological Society* 35 (1992): 361-373.

___. 'The Christian Church's Response to Pluralism' *Journal of the Evangelical Theological Society* 35 (1992): 487-501.

___. *Christian Theology: An Introduction*. Oxford: Blackwell, 1994.

___. *Evangelicalism and the Future of Christianity*. London: Hodder and Stoughton, 1994.

___. *A Passion for Truth: The Intellectual Coherence of Evangelicalism*. Leicester: Apollos, 1996.

___. 'Whatever Happened To Luther? [a response to the Openness of God]' *Christianity Today* 39 (Jan 9th 1995): 34.

McIntosh, John. 'Biblical Exclusivism: towards a Reformed Approach to the Uniqueness of Christ' *Reformed Theological Review* 53 (Jan-Apr. 1994): 13-27.

Macleod, Donald. 'The Doctrine of the Trinity' *Scottish Bulletin of Evangelical Theology* 3/1 (Spring 1985): 11-21.

___. *The Person of Christ*. Leicester: Inter-Varsity Press, 1998.

McVeigh, Malcolm. 'The Fate of Those Who've Never Heard? It Depends' *Evangelical Missions Quarterly* 21 (1985): 367- 372.

Maddox, Randy L. *Responsible Grace: John Wesley's Practical Theology*. Nashville: Kingswood, 1994.

Marsden, George M. *Evangelicalism and Modern America*. Grand Rapids: Eerdmans, 1984.

Marshall, Howard. Kept by the Power of God: A Study of Perseverance and Falling Away. London: Epworth, 1969.

Marshall, Molly Truman. 'The Doctrine of Salvation: Biblical-Theological Dimensions' *Evangelical Review of Theology* 23/3 (1999): 196-204.

___. *No Salvation Outside the Church? A Critical Inquiry*. Lewiston: Edwin Mellen Press, 1993.

McDermott, Gerald R. *Can Evangelicals Learn From World Religions*. Downers Grove: Inter-Varsity Press, 2000.

___. *Jonathan Edwards Confronts the Gods: Christian Theology, Enlightenment Religion and Non-Christian Faiths*. Oxford: OUP, 2000.

Miethe, Terry L. 'The Universal Power of the Atonement' in *The Grace of God and the Will of Man: A Case for Arminianism*. ed. Clark H. Pinnock, 71-97. Minneapolis: Bethany House Publishers, 1995.

Milne, Bruce. *Know the Truth: A Handbook of Christian Belief*. Leicester: Inter-Varsity Press, 1982.

Minns, Denis. *Irenaeus*. London: Geoffrey Chapman, 1994.

Mohler Jr., R. Albert. 'The Eclipse of God at Century's End: Evangelicals Attempt Theology Without Theism' *The Southern Baptist Journal of Theology* 1/1 (Spring 1997): 6-16.

___. '"Evangelical:' What's in a Name?' in *The Coming Evangelical Crisis* ed. John H. Armstrong, 29-45. Chicago: Moody Press, 1996.

Moo, Douglas. 'Romans 2: Saved Apart from the Gospel?' in *Through No Fault of Their Own? The Fate of Those Who Have Never Heard.* eds. W. Crockett and J. Sigountos, 137-145. Grand Rapids: Baker Books, 1991.
Moody, Dale. *The Word of Truth: A Summary of Christian Doctrine Based on Biblical Revelation.* Grand Rapids: Eerdmans, 1981.
Morimoto, Anri. *Jonathan Edwards and the Catholic Vision of Salvation.* Pittsburgh: Penn State University Press, 1995.
Morris, Leon. *The Atonement: Its Meaning and Significance.* Leicester: Inter-Varsity Press, 1983.
Motyer, J. A. *Look to the Rock: An Old Testament Background to our Understanding of Christ.* Leicester: Inter-Varsity Press, 1996.
___. *The Revelation of the Divine Name.* London: Tyndale Press, 1959.
Muck, Terry C. 'Is There a Common Ground Among Religions?' *Journal of the Evangelical Theological Society* 40/1 (1997): 99-112.
Muller, Richard A. 'Grace, Election, and Contingent Choice: Arminius' Gambit and the Reformed Response' in *The Grace of God, the Bondage of the Will: Historical and Theological Perspectives on Calvinism.* Vol. 2. eds. Thomas R. Schreiner and Bruce A. Ware, 251-279, Grand Rapids: Baker Books, 1995.
___. *Post-Reformation Reformed Dogmatics.* Vols. 1 and 2. Grand Rapids: Baker Book House, 1987 and 1983.
Munlochy, W. C. Campbell-Jack. 'Common Grace and Eschatology' *Scottish Bulletin of Evangelical Theology* 7/2 (Autumn 1989): 100-115.
Murray, John. *Christian Baptism.* Phillipsburg: Presbyterian and Reformed, 1980.
___. *Collected Writings of John Murray.* Vol. 2. Edinburgh: Banner of Truth, 1976.
___. *The Covenant of Grace: A Biblico-Theological Study.* London: Tyndale Press, 1961.
___. *The Imputation of Adam's Sin.* Grand Rapids: Eerdmans, 1962.
___. *Redemption Accomplished and Applied.* Edinburgh: Banner of Truth, 1961.
Nash, Ronald. *Is Jesus the Only Savior?* Grand Rapids: Zondervan, 1994.
___. *The Word of God and the Mind of Man: The Crisis of Revealed Truth in Contemporary Theology.* Phillipsburg: Presbyterian and Reformed, 1982.
Needham, Nick. 'The *Filioque* Clause: East or West?' *Scottish Bulletin of Evangelical Theology* 15/2 (Autumn 1997): 142-162.
Neff, David.. 'A Call to Evangelical Unity' (including the document 'The Gospel of Jesus Christ: An Evangelical Celebration') in *Christianity Today* (June 14th 1999): 51-56.
___. 'Has God Been Held Hostage By Philosophy? A Forum on Free-will Theism, A New Paradigm for Understanding God' *Christianity Today* 39 (Jan. 9th 1995): 30-34.
Neilands, David L. *Studies in the Covenant of Grace.* Phillipsburg: Presbyterian and Reformed, 1980.
Netland, Harold. *Dissonant Voices: Religious Pluralism and the Question of Truth.* Grand Rapids: Zondervan, 1991.
___. 'Exclusivism, Tolerance, and Truth' *Missiology* 15 (1987): 77-95.
Newbigin, Lesslie, *The Gospel in a Pluralist Society.* Grand Rapids: Eerdmans, 1991.
Newman, Paul W. *A Spirit Christology: Recovering the Biblical Paradigm of Christian Faith.* Maryland: University Press of America, 1987.
Nicholls, Bruce J. 'The Salvation and Lostness of Mankind' *Evangelical Review of Theology* 15 (1991): 4-21.

Nicole, Roger. 'Covenant, Universal Call and Definite Atonement' *Journal of the Evangelical Theological Society* 38/3 (1995): 403-412.

___. 'John Calvin's View of the Extent of the Atonement' *Westminster Theological Journal* 47 (1985): 197-225.

___. 'The Meaning of the Trinity' in *One God in Trinity*. eds. Peter Toon and James D. Spiceland, 1-11. London: Samuel Bagster, 1980.

___. 'The Uniqueness of Jesus Christ' *Evangelical Review of Theology* 17 (1993): 3-109.

Noll, Mark., Cornelius Plantinga Jr. and David F. Wells. 'Evangelical Theology Today' *Evangelical Review of Theology* 21/2 (1997):176-187.

Noll, Mark A. and David F. Wells, eds. *Christian Faith and Practice in the Modern World*. Grand Rapids: Eerdmans. 1988.

eds. Okholm, Dennis L. and Timothy R. Phillips, *More Than One Way? Four Views on Salvation in a Pluralistic World*. Grand Rapids: Zondervan, 1995.

Osbourne, Grant R. *The Hermeneutical Spiral: A Comprehensive Introduction to Biblical Interpretation*. Downers Grove: Inter-Varsity Press, 1991.

Osburn, Evert D. 'Those Who Have Not Heard: Have They No Hope?' *Journal of the Evangelical Theological Society* 32 (1989): 370-379.

Oswalt, John N. 'The Mission of Israel to the Nations' in *Through No Fault of Their Own? The Fate of Those Who Have Never Heard*. eds. W. Crockett and J. Sigountos, 85-97. Grand Rapids: Baker Books, 1991.

Owen, John. *The Death of Death in The Death of Christ: A Treatise in Which the Whole Controversy About Universal Redemption is Fully Discussed (1648)* (with an introductory essay by J.I. Packer.) Edinburgh: Banner Of Truth Trust, 1983.

___. *An Exposition of Hebrews* Vol. 3 (Hebrews 4:12-8:12) Delaware: The National Foundation for Christian Education, 1969

___. *The Holy Spirit: His Gifts and Power*. Grand Rapids: Kregal Publications, 1954.

Packer, J.I. 'Arminianisms' in *Through Christ's Word: A Festshrift for P.E. Hughes*. eds. R. Godfrey and T. Boyd, 121-148. Phillipsburg: Presbyterian and Reformed, 1985.

___. *Concise Theology: A Guide to Historic Christian Beliefs* Leicester: Inter-Varsity Press, 1993.

___. 'Good Pagans and God's Kingdom' *Christianity Today* 30/1 (Jan 17th 1986): 22-25.

___. 'Introductory Essay' to John Owen's, *Death of Death in the Death of Christ: A Treatise in Which the Whole Controversy about Universal Redemption is Fully Discussed (1648)*, 1-25. Edinburgh: Banner of Truth Trust, 1983.

___. 'The Love of God: Universal and Particular' in *The Grace of God, The Bondage of the Will*. Vol. 2 eds. Thomas R. Schreiner and Bruce A. Ware, 413-429. Grand Rapids: Baker Books, 1995.

___. 'What Did the Cross Achieve? The Logic of Penal Substitution' *Tyndale Bulletin* 25 (1974): 3-46.

Palmer, Edwin H. *The Holy Spirit*. Philadelphia: Presbyterian and Reformed, 1971.

Phillips, W. Gary. 'Evangelical Pluralism: a Singular Problem' *Bibliotheca Sacra* 151 (April-June 1994): 140-154.

___. 'Evangelicals and Pluralism: Current Options' *Evangelical Quarterly* 64 (1992): 229-244.

Pinnock, Clark H. 'Acts 4:12: No Other Name Under Heaven' in *Through No Fault of Their Own? The Fate Of Those Who Have Never Heard* eds. W. Crockett and J. Sigountos, 107-115. Grand Rapids: Baker Books, 1991.

___. 'An Arminian Option' [a reply] *Christianity Today* 34 (Feb. 19th 1990): 15.

___. 'Between Classical and Process Theism' in *Process Theology*. ed. Ronald Nash, 309-329. Grand Rapids: Baker Books, 1987.

___. *Biblical Revelation: the Foundation of Christian Theology*. Chicago: Moody Press, 1971.

___. 'The Destruction of the Finally Impenitent' *Criswell Theological Review* 4 (1990): 243-259.

___. 'An Evangelical Response to Knitter's Five Theses' in *The Uniqueness of Jesus: A Dialogue with Paul Knitter* eds. Leonard Swidler and Paul Mojzes, 116-121. Maryknoll: Orbis, 1997.

___. 'Evangelical Theologians Facing the Future: An Ancient and a Future Paradigm' *Wesleyan Theological Journal* 33 (Fall 1998): 7-28.

___. 'The Finality of Jesus Christ in a World of Religions' *Christian Faith and Practice in the Modern World*. eds. Mark A. Noll and David F. Wells, 152-171. Grand Rapids: Eerdmans. 1988.

___. *Flame of Love: a Theology of the Holy Spirit*. Downers Grove: IVP, 1996.

___. 'Foreword' in *Clark H. Pinnock on Biblical Authority*. Ray C.W. Roennfeldt, xv-xxviii. Michigan: Andrews University Press, 1993.

___. 'From Augustine to Arminius: A Pilgrimage in Theology' in *The Grace of God, the Will of Man: a Case for Arminianism*. ed. Clark H. Pinnock, 15-31. Minneapolis: Bethany House Publishers, 1995.

___. 'Fuller Seminary and The Nature of Evangelicalism' *Christian Scholars Review* 23/1 (1993): 44-47.

___. 'God Limits His Knowledge' in *Four Views on Predestination and Freewill*. eds. David Basinger and Randell Basinger, 143-162. Downers Grove: Inter-Varsity Press, 1986.

___. 'God's Sovereignty in Today's World' in *Theology Today* 53 (1996): 15-21.

___. 'An Inclusivist View' in *More Than One Way? Four Views on Salvation in a Pluralistic World*. eds. Dennis L. Okholm and Timothy R. Phillips, 93-124, 141-149. Grand Rapids: Zondervan, 1995.

___. 'Reason and Reasonable Faith' *Crux* 29 (Spring 1993): 39-42.

___. 'Responsible Freedom and the Flow of Biblical History' in *Grace Unlimited*. ed. Clark H. Pinnock, 95-109. Minneapolis: Bethany Books, 1975.

___. 'The Role of The Spirit in Interpretation' *Journal of the Evangelical Theological Society* 36 (1993): 491-497.

___. 'Salvation by Resurrection' *Ex Auditu* 9 (1993): 1-11.

___. *The Scripture Principle*. London: Hodder and Stoughton, 1985.

___. 'Systematic Theology' in *The Openness of God: a Biblical Challenge to the Traditional Understanding of God*. eds. Clark H. Pinnock with Richard Rice, John Sanders, William Hasker and David Basinger, 101-126. Downers Grove: IVP, 1994.

___. 'Toward an Evangelical Theology of Religions' *Journal of the Evangelical Theological Society* 33 (1990): 359-368.

___. *Tracking the Maze: Finding Our Way Through Modern Theology From an Evangelical Perspective*. San Fransisco: Harper Collins, 1990.

___. 'Why is Jesus the Only Way?' *Eternity* (December 1976): 13-15, 32.

___. *A Wideness in God's Mercy: The Finality of Jesus Christ in a World of Religions*. Grand Rapids: Zondervan, 1992.

Pinnock, Clark H. and Robert C. Brow. *Unbounded Love: a Good News Theology for the 21st Century*. Downers Grove: Inter-Varsity Press, 1994.

eds. Pinnock, Clark H. and Delwin Brown, *Theological Crossfire: an Evangelical/Liberal Debate*. Grand Rapids: Zondervan, 1990.

eds. Pinnock, Clark H. with Richard Rice, John Sanders, William Hasker and David Basinger. *The Openness of God: a Biblical Challenge to the Traditional Understanding of God*. Downers Grove: IVP, 1994.

Piper, John. *Let the Nations Be Glad! The Supremacy of God in Missions*. Leicester: IVP, 1994.

___. 'Are There Two Wills in God? Divine Election and God's Desire for All to be Saved' in *The Grace of God, The Bondage of the Will*. Vol. 1. eds. Thomas R. Schreiner and Bruce A. Ware, 107-133. Grand Rapids: Baker Books, 1995.

Poythress, Vern Sheridan. 'Indifferentism and Rigorism in the Church: With Implications for Baptizing Small Children' *Westminster Theological Journal* 59 (1997): 13-29.

___. 'Linking Small Children with Infants in the Theology of Baptizing' *Westminster Theological Journal* 59 (1997): 143-58.

___. *Understanding Dispensationalists*. Phillipsburg: Presbyterian and Reformed, 1994.

Price, Robert M. 'Clark H. Pinnock: Conservative and Contemporary' *The Evangelical Quarterly* 60 (1988): 157-183.

Proceedings of the Wheaton Theology Conference: the Challenge of Religious Pluralism: an Evangelical Analysis and Response. Vol. 1. Wheaton, 1992.

Race, Alan. *Christians and Religious Pluralism* London: SCM, 1983.

Rahner, Karl. *Foundations of the Christian Faith*. London: Darton, Longman and Todd, 1978.

___. *Theological Investigations*. Vols. 1, 2, 5 and 10. London: Darton, Longman and Todd, 1963-1992.

___. *The Trinity*. trans. Joseph Donceel. London: Burns and Oats, 1970.

___, ed. *Sacramentum Mundi: An Encyclopedia of Theology*. New York: Herder and Herder, 1968.

Rakestraw, Robert V. 'Becoming Like God: An Evangelical Doctrine of Theosis' *Journal of the Evangelical Theological Society* 40/2 (1997): 257-269.

___. 'Clark H. Pinnock: A Theological Odyssey' *Christian Scholars Review* 3 (1990): 252-270.

___. 'John Wesley as a Theologian of Grace' *Journal of the Evangelical Theological Society* 27 (1984): 193-203.

Reichenbach, Bruce R. 'Freedom, Justice, and Moral Responsibility' in *The Grace of God and the Will of Man: A Case for Arminianism*. ed. Clark H. Pinnock, 277-305. Minneapolis: Bethany House Publishers, 1995.

Reymond, Robert L. *A New Systematic Theology of the Christian Faith*. Nashville: Thomas Nelson, 1998.

Richard, Ramesh P. *The Population of Heaven: A Biblical Response to the Inclusivist Position on Who Will Be Saved*. Chicago: Moody Press, 1994.

___. 'Soteriological Inclusivism and Dispensationalism' *Bibliotheca Sacra* 151 (Jan.-Mar. 1994): 85- 108.

Richardson, Don. *Eternity in Their Hearts*. Ventura: Regal, 1981.

Ritchie, Bruce. 'Theological Logic' *Scottish Bulletin of Evangelical Theology* 4/2 (1986): 109-122.

Robertson, O. Palmer. *The Christ of the Covenants*. Phillipsburg: Presbyterian and Reformed, 1980.

___. 'Current Critical Questions Concerning the "Curse of Ham" (Gen. 9:20-27)' *Journal of the Evangelical Theological Society* 41/2 (1988): 177-188.

___. *The Final Word: a Biblical Response to the Case for Tongues and Prophecy Today*. Edinburgh: Banner of Truth Trust, 1993.

Roennfeldt, Ray C.W. *Clark H. Pinnock on Biblical Authority*. Michigan: Andrews University Press, 1993.

Rommen, Edward. 'Synthesis' in *Christianity and the Religions: A Biblical Theology of World Religions*. eds. Edward Rommen and Harold Netland, 241-254. Pasadena: William Carey Library, 1995.

Ross, Allen P. 'The Biblical Method of Salvation: A Case for Discontinuity' Discontinuity' in *Continuity and Discontinuity: Perspectives of the Relationship Between the Old and New Testaments*. ed. John S. Feinberg, 131-160. Westchester: Crossway, 1988.

Roth, Robert Paul. 'The Unique but Inclusive Christ' *Areopagus* 4/2 (1991): 3-4.

Runia, Klaas. 'The Gospel and Religious Pluralism' *Evangelical Review of Theology* 14 (1990): 341-379.

___. 'What is Evangelical Theology?' *Evangelical Review of Theology* 21/4 (1997): 292-305.

___. 'Why Christianity of All Religions?' *Evangelical Review of Theology* 22/3 (1998): 244-263.

Ruokanen, Miikka. *The Catholic Doctrine of Non-Christian Religions According to the Second Vatican Council*. New York: E. J. Brill, 1992.

Sanders, John E. 'Evangelical Responses to Salvation Outside the Church' *Christian Scholars Review* 24/1 (1994): 45-58.

___. 'Is Belief in Christ Necessary for Salvation?' *Evangelical Quarterly* 60 (1988): 241-259.

___. *No Other Name: Can Only Christians be Saved?* London: SPCK, 1994.

___. 'The Perennial Debate' *Christianity Today* (May 14th 1990): 20-21.

___, ed. *What About Those Who Have Never Heard? Three Views on the Destiny of the Unevangelised*. Downers Grove: IVP, 1995.

Sanders, J. Oswald. *What of Those Who Have Never Heard?* Crowborough, East Sussex: Highland Books, 1966.

Satyavrata, Ivan. 'God Has Not Left Himself Without a Witness' *AETEI Journal* 5 (1992): 2-9.

Schaeffer, Francis. *Genesis in Space and Time*. Downers Grove: IVP, 1972.

Schineller, J. Peter. 'Christ and Church: A Spectrum of Views' *Theological Studies* 37 (1975): 545-565.

Schreiner, Thomas R. 'Did Paul Believe in Justification By Works? Another Look at Romans 2' *Bulletin for Biblical Research* 3 (1993): 131-158.

___. 'Does Scripture Teach Prevenient Grace in the Wesleyan Sense?' in *The Grace of God, The Bondage of the Will*. Vol. 2. eds. Thomas R Schreiner and Bruce A. Ware, 365-383. Grand Rapids: Baker Books, 1995.

Schleiermacher, Friedrich. *The Christian Faith*. 2 Vols. New York: Harper and Row, 1963.

Schmidt, Frederick W. 'Jesus and the Salvation of the Gentiles' ' in *Through No Fault of Their Own? The Fate of Those Who Have Never Heard.* eds. W. Crockett and J. Sigountos, 97-105. Grand Rapids: Baker Books, 1991.
Shank, Robert. *Elect in the Son: A Study of the Doctrine of Election.* Springfield: Westcott, 1970.
Shedd, William G. T. *Dogmatic Theology* Vol. 2. New York: Scribner's, 1888-94.
Sigountos, James G. 'Did Early Christians Believe Pagan Religions Could Save?' in *Through No Fault of Their Own? The Fate of Those Who Have Never Heard.* eds. W. Crockett and J. Sigountos, 229-241. Grand Rapids: Baker Books, 1992.
ed. Silva, Moisés. *Foundations of Contemporary Interpretation.* Leicester: Apollos, 1997.
Sinkinson, Chris. *John Hick: An Introduction to his Theology.* Leicester: RTSF, 1995.
Smith, Gordon T. 'Religions and the Bible: An Agenda for Evangelicals' in *Christianity and the Religions: A Biblical Theology of World Religions.* eds. Edward Rommen and Harold Netland, 9-30. Pasadena: William Carey Library, 1995.
Spencer, Aída Besançon. 'Romans 1: Finding God in Creation' in *Through No Fault of Their Own? The Fate of Those Who Have Never Heard.* eds. W. Crockett and J. Sigountos, 125-135. Grand Rapids: Baker Books, 1991.
Stackhouse Jnr., John G. 'Evangelicals Reconsider World Religions: Betraying or Affirming the Tradition' *Christian Century* 110 (1995): 858-865.
Staniloae, Dumitru. 'The Procession of the Holy Spirit from the Father and his Relation to the Son, as the Basis of our Deification and Adoption' in *Spirit of God, Spirit of Christ: Ecumenical Reflections of the Filioque Controversy.* ed. Lukas Vischer, 174-186. London: SPCK, 1981.
Stott, John. *The Cross of Christ.* Leicester: IVP, 1989.
Stott, John and David L. Edwards, *Essentials, A Liberal-Evangelical Dialogue.* London: Hodder and Stoughton, 1988.
Strange, Daniel. 'Biographical Essay: Clark H. Pinnock: The Evolution of an Evangelical' in *Reconstructing Theology: A Critical Assessment of the Theology of Clark Pinnock.* eds. Tony Gray and Christopher Sinkinson, 1-18. Carlisle: Paternoster, 2000.
___. 'Clark H. Pinnock: The Evolution of a Theological Maverick' *Evangelical Quarterly* 71/4 (Oct. 1999): 349-358.
___. 'The Possibility of Salvation Among the Unevangelised: An Analysis of 'Opaque Exclusivism' in Recent Evangelical Theology' *World Faiths Encounter* 17 (July 1997): 43-52.
___. 'Presence, Prevenience, or Providence? Deciphering the Conundrum of Pinnock's Pneumatological Inclusivism' in *Reconstructing Theology: A Critical Assessment of the Theology of Clark Pinnock.* eds. Tony Gray and Christopher Sinkinson, 184-258. Carlisle: Paternoster, 2000.
___. 'The Price of Internal Consistency?' *Tyndale Bulletin* 51/1 (2000): 139-150.
___. 'Salvation, Atonement and Accessibility: Towards a Solution of the Soteriological Problem of Evil' *Foundations* 44 (2000): 9-20.
Strehle, Stephen. 'The Extent of the Atonement and the Synod of Dort' *Westminster Theological Journal* 51 (1989): 345-357.
___. 'Universal Grace and Amyraldianism' *Westminster Theological Journal* 51 (1989): 345-357.

Strickland, Wayne G. 'Isaiah, Jonah, and Religious Pluralism' *Bibliotheca Sacra* 153 (Jan.- Mar. 1995): 24-33.
Strimple, Bob. 'What Does God Know?' in *The Coming Evangelical Crisis*. ed. J. H. Armstrong, 139-155. Chicago: Moody Press, 1996.
Sullivan, Frances. *Salvation Outside the Church? Tracing the History of the Catholic Response*. London: Geoffrey Chapman, 1992.
Thiselton, Anthony C. *New Horizons in Hermeneutics*. London: Harper Collins, 1992.
Thompson, Mike. 'Extra Christum Nulla Salus?' *Churchman* 111/3 (1997): 227-238.
Thompson, Thomas R. 'Trinitarianism Today: Doctrinal Renaissance, Ethical Relevance, Social Redolence' *Calvin Theological Journal* 32 (1997): 9-42.
The Three Forms of Unity: The Heidelberg Catechism, The Belgic Confession, The Canons of Dordrecht and the Ecumenical Creeds. Reprinted in 1996 by the Mission Committee of the Protestant Reformed Churches in America
Tidball, Derek. *Who are the Evangelicals?: Tracing the Roots of Today's Movements*. London: Marshall Pickering, 1994.
Tiénou, Tite. 'Eternity in Their Hearts?' in *Through No Fault of Their Own? The Fate of Those Who Have Never Heard*. eds. W. Crockett and J. Sigountos, 209-215. Grand Rapids: Baker Books, 1991.
Tiessen, Terrance. 'Can the Unevangelised be Saved? A Review Article' *Didaskalia* 5 (Fall 1993): 77-91.
___. 'Divine Justice and Universal Grace: A Calvinistic Proposal' *Evangelical Review of Theology* 2/11 (1997): 63-83.
Torrance, Thomas F. 'The Atonement. The Singularity of Christ and the Finality of the Cross: The Atonement and the Moral Order' in *Universalism and the Doctrine of Hell*. ed. Nigel M. de S. Cameron, 223-255. Carlisle: Paternoster, 1992.
___. *The Christian Doctrine of God, One Being Three Persons*. Edinburgh: T&T Clark, 1996.
The Three Forms of Unity: The Heidelberg Catechism, the Belgic Confession, the Canons of Dordrecht. Reprinted by the Mission Committee of the Protestant Reformed Churches in America, 1996.
Travis, Stephen. *Christian Hope and the Future of Man*. Leicester: IVP, 1980.
Travis, William. 'William Carey: The Modern Missions Movement and the Sovereignty of God' in *The Grace of God, the Bondage of the Will. Volume 2: Historical and Theological Perspectives on Calvinism*. eds. Thomas R. Schreiner and Bruce A. Ware, 323-336. Grand Rapids, Baker Books, 1995.
Trueman, Carl R. *The Claims of Truth: John Owen's Trinitarian Theology*. Carlisle: Paternoster, 1988.
Turnbull, Richard. 'Evangelicalism: the State of Scholarship and the Question of Identity' *Anvil* 16/2 (1999): 95-106.
Turretin, Francis, *Institutes of Elenctic Theology*. Vol. 1. trans. G. M. Giger; ed. J. T. Dennison Jr. Phillipsburg: Presbyterian and Reformed, 1992.
Unger, Walter. 'The Destiny of Those Who Have Never Heard: a Bibliographical Essay' *Direction* 23 (Spring 1994): 54-63.
VanEngen, Charles. 'The Uniqueness of Christ in Mission Theology' in *Christianity and the Religions: A Biblical Theology of World Religions*. eds. Edward Rommen and Harold Netland, 184-217. Pasadena: William Carey Library, 1995.
VanGemeren, Willem. *The Progress of Redemption: From Creation to New Jerusalem*. Carlisle: Paternoster, 1995.

___. 'Systems of Continuity' in *Continuity and Discontinuity: Perspectives of the Relationship Between the Old and New Testaments*. ed. John S. Feinberg, 37-62. Westchester: Crossway, 1988.
Vanhoozer, Kevin J. 'Does the Trinity Belong in a Theology of Religions? One Angling in the Rubicon and the "Identity" of God' in *The Trinity in a Pluralistic Age: Theological Essays on Culture and Religion*. ed. Kevin J. Vanhoozer, 41-72. Cambridge: William B. Eerdmans, 1997.
___. 'Effectual Call or Causal Effect? Summons, Sovereignty and Supervenient Grace' *Tyndale Bulletin* 49/2 (1988): 213-251.
Van Til, Cornelius. *Common Grace and the Gospel*. Phillipsburg: Presbyterian and Reformed Publishing Company, 1972.
Veenhof, Jan. 'Holy Spirit and Holy Scripture: Considerations Concerning the Character and Function of Scripture in the Framework of Salvation History' *Scottish Bulletin of Evangelical Theology* 4/2 (Autumn 1986): 69-84.
ed. Vischer, Lukas. *Spirit of God, Spirit of Christ: Ecumenical Reflections of the Filioque Controversy*. London: SPCK, 1981.
Vos, Geerhardus. *Biblical Theology*. Edinburgh: Banner of Truth, 1975.
Waite, John C. J. *The Activity of the Holy Spirit within the Old Testament Period*. London: London Bible College, 1961.
Ware, Bruce A. 'An Evangelical Reformulation of the Doctrine of the Immutability of God' in *Journal of the Evangelical Theological Society* 29/4 (1986): 431-446.
___. 'An Exposition and Critique of the Process Doctrines of Divine Mutability and Immutability' in *Westminster Theological Journal* 47 (1995): 175-196.
Ware, Timothy. *The Orthodox Church*. London: Penguin, 1963.
Warfield, B.B. *Biblical and Theological Studies*. Philadelphia: Presbyterian and Reformed, 1952.
___. *Biblical Doctrines*. Edinburgh: Banner of Truth Trust, 1988.
___.*Calvin and Augustine*. Philadelphia: Presbyterian and Reformed Publishing Company, 1956.
___. *Studies in Theology*. New York: Oxford University Press, 1932.
Watson, Gordon. 'The Filioque - Opportunity for Debate?' *Scottish Journal of Theology* 41 (1988): 313-330.
Webster, John. 'Karl Rahner's Theology of Grace' *Evangel* (April 1983): 9-11.
Weinandy, Thomas G. *The Father's Spirit of Sonship*. Edinburgh: T&T Clark, 1995.
Wells, David F. *God the Evangelist: How the Holy Spirit Works to Bring Men and Women to Faith*. Exeter: Paternoster, 1987.
Wenham, Gordon J. *Genesis 1-15*. Waco: Word Books, 1987.
___. 'The Religion of the Patriarchs' in *Essays in the Patriarchal Narratives*. eds. A. R. Millard and D. J. Wiseman, 157-189. Leicester: IVP, 1980.
Wenham, John W. *Christ and the Bible*. Leicester: IVP, 1984.
Widbin, R. Bryan. 'Salvation for People Outside Israel's Covenant?' in *Through No Fault of Their Own? The Fate of Those Who Have Never Heard*. eds. W. Crockett and J. Sigountos, 73-85. Grand Rapids: Baker Books, 1991.
Wilken, Robert L. 'Religious Pluralism and Early Christian Theology' *Interpretation*
Williams, Rowan. 'Balthasar and Rahner' in *The Analogy of Beauty: The Theology of Hans Urs Von Balthasar*. ed. John Riches, 11-35. Edinburgh: T&T Clark, 1986.
___. 'Eastern Orthodox Theology' in *The Modern Theologians*. Vol. 2 ed. David F. Ford, 152-171, Oxford: Blackwell, 1993.

eds. Willis, David and Michael Welker, *Towards the Future of Reformed Theology: Tasks, Topics and Traditions*. Cambridge: Eerdmans, 1999.

Wood, Ralph C. 'Whatever Happened to Baptist Calvinism?' *Review and Expositor* 91 (1994): 593-608.

Wright, Christopher J. H. 'The Christian and Other Religions: The Biblical Evidence' *Themelios* 9/2 (1994): 4-15.

___. 'P for Pentateuch, Patriarchs and Pagans' *Themelios* 18 (1993): 3-4.

Wright, David. 'The Watershed of Vatican II: Catholic Approaches to Religious Pluralism' in *One God, One Lord: Christianity in a World of Religious Pluralism*. eds. Andrew D. Clarke and Bruce W. Winter, 207-226. Grand Rapids: Baker Books, 1992.

Wright, N. T. 'Towards a Biblical View of Universalism' *Themelios* 4 (1979): 54-58.

Wright, R. K. McGregor. *No Place for Sovereignty: What's Wrong with Freewill Theism*. Downers Grove: IVP, 1996.

Yates, John. 'How Does God Speak to us Today?: Biblical Anthropology and the Witness of the Holy Spirit' *Churchman* 107/2 (1993): 102-127.

Zanchius, Girolamo. *AbsolutePredestination*, http://www.straitgate.com/books/zanchius/doctrine.htm, 21st December 2000.

INDEX

Abbott, W.M, 63, 117, 118, 332
Abel, 166, 168-169, 185
Abimelech, 110, 178
Abraham, 53, 57-58, 110, 115, 120-121, 152-154, 160, 163, 165-167, 170-171, 173, 174-175, 177, 179, 181-186, 188, 190, 203, 212, 330, 340
Adam, 33, 79-80, 83, 93, 116, 155, 156, 163, 165-169, 171-172, 177, 184, 203, 208, 217-218, 267, 268, 279, 308, 314, 342
Adams R., 326, 332
Ahab, 182
Aldenhoven, H., 332
Allchin, D., 332
Amos, 120
analogia, 149
analogy, 29, 34, 51, 64-66, 84, 101, 110-111, 116, 122, 134, 149, 151-153, 162, 165, 167, 179-180, 184, 187, 189-190, 194-195, 197, 228, 233, 235, 243, 256, 271
Anderson, N., 4, 16, 19, 24, 108, 111, 135, 318, 320, 332
annihilation, 80, 83
annihilationism, 19
Anselm, 78
antediluvian saints, 167, 174, 176, 182, 314
antinomy, 48
antitype, 150, 161-162, 166, 188, 190
Aquinas, 65, 104
archetype, 68
Arminianism, 10-11, 13, 43, 44, 49, 50, 52, 77-78, 96, 253, 263, 268-269, 275-277, 299, 301-302, 306, 341, 343-345
Arminius, J., 10-11, 43, 47-48, 50, 53, 78, 96, 301, 342, 344

Armstrong, J.H., 4, 10, 213, 253, 339, 341, 347
Arphaxad, 183
Athenagoras, 61
Athenians, 121, 193, 333
Athens, 123
atonement, 28-29, 46, 50, 67-68, 73, 76-79, 81-84, 93, 164, 199, 206-208, 210-212, 214, 216-217, 219-221, 223-224, 241, 248, 263, 265-266, 268, 275-283, 287, 307-308, 318, 321, 327
  constitutive, 28, 83, 102, 106, 159, 207, 220-221, 276, 295
  extent of, 19, 24, 26, 31, 34, 46, 79, 144, 210, 243, 266, 269, 271, 276, 278-280, 283, 309
Augustine, xvii, 43, 47-48, 53, 61-62, 65, 78, 96, 165, 167, 229, 271, 273, 300-301, 344, 349
Augustinianism, 30, 58, 61-62, 111, 274
Aulen G., 76, 332
autotheos, 229-230, 247

Badcock, G., 65, 102, 227, 234-235, 238, 251-252, 256, 258-269, 332
Bagnell, W.R., 10-11
Baillie, D., 69
Balaam, 185
Balthasar, H. Urs Von., 340, 349
Barker, K.L., 332
Barrett, J.K., 26, 249, 289, 332
Barth, K., 8, 12, 31, 65, 78, 107, 111, 205, 248, 298, 309, 332, 335
barthianism, 8, 32, 253
Basil, 66
Basinger, D., 43, 47, 50, 332, 344
Basinger, R., 43, 332, 344
Baugh, S.M., 332
Bavinck, H., 233, 332,

Bavinck, J.H., 288, 333
Baxter, R., 285, 316
Bebbington, D., 4, 25, 333
Begbie, J., 208, 333
Benz, E., 106, 333
Berkhof, H., 8, 210, 333
Berkhof, L., 10, 98, 99, 156, 157, 159, 168, 169, 204, 215, 233, 240, 241, 252, 254, 257, 259, 261, 278, 285, 310, 311, 312, 333
Berkouwer, G.C., 309
Beyerhaus, P., 23
Beza, T., 10
Blackham, P., 164, 333
Blaising, C., 153
Blocher, H., 66, 228, 238-239, 333
Bloesch, D., 32, 62, 333
Bock, D.L., 153, 193, 333
Boettner, L., 33, 311, 333
Boff, L., 230, 333
bond-in-blood, 158-159, 212, 214
Borland, J., 333
Braaten, C.E., 333
Bradley, J.E., 88, 152, 205-206, 223-224, 333
Bray, G., 5, 228-232, 234, 237, 243, 257, 333
Brobinsky, B., 334
Brow, R., 13, 47, 64, 78, 334, 344
Brown, H.O.J., 64, 68, 140, 334, 344
Brunner, E., 8
Buhlman, W., 334
Butler, D., 334

Calvinism, xiii, 8-11, 13, 46, 48-50, 52, 77-78, 93, 96, 98, 132, 134, 200, 253, 267, 269, 282-283, 289, 299-301, 308, 312-313, 320, 334, 336, 338, 342, 348-349
Canaanite, 179-181, 184, 186-187
Caneday, A.B., 300, 308, 334
Cappadocian Fathers, 65-66, 234
Carnell, E.J., 6
Carson, D., 3-5, 14, 16-19, 29, 32, 39, 47, 129, 132, 141-142, 149, 182-183, 192-194, 196-197, 214, 216, 245, 273, 275-276, 279, 281, 285-286, 317-318, 334
Catholicism, 93, 95, 122, 135
cessationism, 252, 254-255
Chalcedon, 5, 69, 75, 204

Chapman, C., 334-335, 341, 347
charismata, 205
charismatic, 235, 252-253, 255, 299
Christ, viii-xi, xvii, 5, 7-11, 13, 15-16, 19-25, 28-38, 45, 47-48, 50, 56-57, 59-60, 63, 67-89, 93-94, 97, 100, 103, 105-108, 110-111, 113-116, 119-121, 123, 125-135, 139, 150-157, 159, 161-172, 176-180, 187-197, 199-218, 220-237, 240-251, 254-263, 265, 267-268, 271, 275, 276-280, 282-289, 294-298, 302-303, 305-310, 312-313, 316-349
  finality of, 28-29, 36, 38, 47, 56, 68, 70-71, 84, 101, 135, 200-201, 224, 246, 287-288, 294, 298, 300, 305
Christic, 123
Christocentricity, 21, 37, 73, 161-163, 171-172, 188-189, 191, 200, 216, 222, 227, 232, 236, 244-245, 247, 256, 259, 262, 295
Christology, x, xviii, 13, 37, 46, 56-57, 63, 67-75, 80, 83-84, 87-89, 101, 105, 107, 152, 199-200, 202-203, 205-207, 210, 221, 223-226, 263, 265, 287, 295, 333, 335, 338, 342
Christomonism, 106-107, 111, 227, 233
Christophany, 88, 164, 180, 232
Ciocchi, D.M., 47-48, 334
circumincessio, circuminsessio, 230
Clarke, A.D., 16, 18, 24, 86, 104, 112, 119, 134, 170, 181-183, 189, 193, 238, 286, 302, 317, 332, 334-337, 339, 349
Clayton, J.P., 74, 340
Clement, 61
Clendenin, D.B., 257, 334
Clowney, E., 161, 168, 335
Cobb, J., 92, 335
Coccejus, 215
co-inherence, 230
Coleman, R.J., 13
Colle, R.D., 74, 335
Colquhoun, J., 335
Colwell. J., 31, 335
communicato idiomatum, 205
Congar, Y., 74, 106, 203, 335
Conn, H.M., 288, 335

Index 353

continuity, 148, 155, 160, 162-163, 165, 170-174, 189-190, 204, 207, 212, 220, 232, 243-244
Cook, E.D., 16, 335
Cook, R.R., 133, 324, 335
Cornelius, x, 3, 13, 59, 109, 117, 121, 189, 192, 194, 195, 196, 197, 222, 228, 285, 316, 317, 343, 348
Cotterell, P., 335
Cottrell, J., 12, 301, 335
Covell, R.R., 335
covenant, 34, 47, 57-58, 60, 68, 86-87, 107, 110, 114, 117, 143, 146, 148, 150-163, 165-170, 172-178, 182-183, 187, 197, 211-212, 215, 240, 245-246, 249, 254, 272, 279, 283, 299, 308
covenant-theology, 308
Craig, W.L., 37, 153, 326, 328, 335
creation, 28, 51-52, 60, 64, 66, 73, 80-81, 83, 89-93, 95, 98-101, 103-106, 109, 111-114, 118-119, 121, 123, 125, 128, 130, 143, 149, 153, 156, 162, 173-177, 179, 193, 201, 205, 207, 211, 214, 218-222, 227, 231, 233, 236-238, 240-244, 255-256, 259, 266, 268-269, 271-272, 279, 288, 299, 318, 325, 330
Crockett, W., 18, 24, 31, 33, 35, 39, 59, 86, 178, 185, 191, 193, 238, 281-282, 286, 288-289, 296, 302, 333-336, 338, 341, 343, 346-348, 349
cross, 7, 21, 23, 76-77, 79, 81-83, 94, 116, 145, 169, 207-211, 213-214, 216, 218, 241, 259, 260-261, 271, 276, 278-279, 320, 324, 330

Dahms, J.V., 335
Danielou, J., 80, 88, 110, 335
Darby, J.N., 153
David, 160
Davis, S., 322-324, 335
Deere, J., 253
deification, 258
Demarest, B., 10, 70, 76, 77-78, 103-104, 111-113, 115-116, 124, 125, 141, 143-144, 153, 155, 183, 185, 193, 204, 237, 242, 252, 262-263, 267, 285, 309, 320, 336-337
Deogratias, xvii

disanalogy, 185
discontinuity, 113, 154-155, 160, 162, 171, 174, 189, 207, 220, 232, 243, 246
dispensation, 110, 148, 152-154, 156-157, 160-161, 164, 170-171, 173, 190, 219, 234, 245-246, 303
dispensationalism, 148, 153-155, 299
disunity, 162
divinization, 102-103, 119
Dowsett, D., 336
Drummond, R., 61-62, 238, 336, 340
Duffy, S.J., 100, 102-103, 336
Dumbrell, W.J., 155, 157, 336
Dunning, H.R., 93
Dupuis, J., 87, 336
Dye, W., 336

ectype, 157
Eden, 213, 272
Edwards, J., 6, 10, 23, 145, 254, 313, 314-315, 330, 334, 336, 341-342, 347
El Elyon, 121, 179-180, 182-183, 186
election, 8-11, 29-30, 32, 35, 49, 58, 77-78, 85, 93, 99, 134, 179, 186, 216, 242, 254, 268, 281, 283, 290, 303, 306-307, 310-313, 327
Elisha, 185
Ellenberger, J.D., 289, 336
energies, 95, 234, 235
Engelsma, D., 289, 336
engrafted, 260
Enoch, 110, 166, 169, 185, 314
Enosh, 171
epistemology, 39, 56, 67, 110, 113, 151-152, 154, 162, 165, 170-171, 191, 194-195, 198-199, 201, 220-222, 231-232, 236-237, 242, 287-288, 307, 311, 322
epoch, 148-151, 154, 160, 166, 171-172, 181, 190
Erickson, M., 4, 10, 12-13, 24-26, 112, 116, 253-254, 320, 322-323, 336
eternal, 16, 20, 23, 66, 69, 77, 101, 123-124, 129, 156-157, 175, 204-206, 230, 235, 248, 267, 278, 283, 308, 325
Eusebius, 165
evangel, 5, 290

evangelical, xiii, xviii, 3-7, 10-14, 16-18, 21-32, 35-38, 42-43, 46, 50, 53, 57, 60, 62, 66, 68-69, 71, 75-78, 84-85, 87-88, 99-101, 104, 109-112, 114-116, 119, 121, 125, 127, 131, 135-136, 139-143, 145, 147-153, 155, 161, 168, 170-171, 173, 175, 179, 183, 188, 191, 193, 199, 201, 203-204, 208, 211-214, 216-217, 225-228, 233, 235-238, 240, 242, 251, 253-255, 257-258, 260-261, 263, 265, 268-269, 273-275, 279-280, 286-290, 294, 296-297, 299-301, 303-304, 306, 310, 316, 321, 324-325, 330

evangelicalism, xviii, 3-8, 12, 14, 16-19, 21-26, 28, 32, 43-44, 61-62, 72, 76, 87, 93, 104, 111, 135, 139-140, 154, 202, 206, 208, 212, 235-236, 252, 255-256, 265-266, 274, 278, 280, 287, 289, 301, 305-306

evangelised, 131, 133, 297, 303, 305-306, 311

evangelism, 7, 33, 127, 130, 132, 275, 289, 306, 307, 316, 319, 324-325

evangelistic, 5

Eve, 163, 165, 168-169, 171-172, 267

Eveson, P.H., 259, 336

exclusivism, 15-18, 21, 23, 111, 118, 181, 189, 192, 294-295, 298, 311, 317, 319, 322

exclusivity, 18, 20, 23, 61-62, 73, 92, 135, 154, 179, 181-182, 193, 201-202, 204, 214, 221, 237, 251, 272, 295, 319, 330

Fackre, G., 30, 111, 322-325, 328, 336
Fairbairn, D., 257, 336
faith, xv, xvii, 6-7, 9-11, 16-23, 26-30, 33, 47, 50, 58, 62, 77, 78, 86, 93, 97-98, 101, 103, 106-111, 113-119, 122-127, 129, 131-134, 136, 141, 149, 151-154, 156, 159-160, 162-167, 169-173, 175, 177-178, 181, 188-191, 193, 195-197, 199-200, 204, 218, 223, 232, 243-244, 246, 247, 252, 255, 256, 257, 260-263, 265, 268-269, 271-272, 278, 280, 282, 284-285, 296, 299, 303, 308, 312-314, 317-319, 321-322, 327, 331

implicit, 116, 286, 302, 318, 320
faith principle
  cognitive, ix, 109-110, 117, 118, 122, 123, 125, 126, 132, 197, 223, 250
  ethical, ix, 104, 116-118, 122, 124-126, 129, 133, 196-197, 263, 269
Fall, 13, 45, 89, 94, 96-98, 139, 156, 167, 174, 184, 216, 242, 266-269, 281, 300, 309, 315, 334, 344, 348
Feinberg, J., 48, 141, 154-155, 163, 165, 337, 340, 346, 348
Ferguson, S., 184, 201, 232, 238, 244-245, 247-248, 258, 261, 270, 337
Ferrante, J.M, 337
filioque, 106-107, 126, 227, 233-236, 247, 251, 257
foedus, 155
fons deitatis, 234, 247
Ford, D.F., 4, 10, 15, 21, 33, 92, 104, 332, 335, 337, 349
Frame, J., 143, 145, 147, 150, 268, 309, 337
fundamentalism, 63
fundamentals, 26, 216

Gaffin Jr., R.B., 143, 246, 252, 337
Geisler, N., 92, 141, 337
Geivett, R.D., 16, 38, 274, 295, 337
genealogy, 177
generate, 207
Genesis, 57, 147, 167-168, 171-172, 174, 179, 181-182, 186, 188, 271-272, 330, 338-340, 346, 349
Gentiles, 33, 58-59, 110, 112, 152, 177-178, 187-188, 192, 196-197, 244, 279, 310, 316, 336, 346
Gillis, C., 135, 337
Gingrich, F., 337
Glenny, W.E., 151, 161, 337
Gnanakan, K., 25, 337
God
  anger of, 78
  immanence of, 38, 51, 64-65, 70, 91- 92, 99-101, 103, 124, 233-235, 237-240, 247, 286
  immutability of, 51-52, 70, 75, 92, 204, 213
  impassibility of, 51-52, 70

Index 355

justice of, 19-20, 86, 94, 126, 135, 146, 213-214, 243, 267, 281-282, 284, 299, 308-311, 330
love of, xv, 20, 30, 47, 52, 56-61, 63-66, 68, 73-76, 79, 82, 86, 89-90, 92-95, 99-100, 106-107, 113, 115-117, 120, 123-127, 132, 201, 207, 210-211, 213-216, 219-220, 222, 224, 253, 259, 262, 266, 269-271, 281, 285, 310, 320, 329
mercy of, 20, 57, 61, 85, 108, 110, 113-114, 129, 132, 134, 166, 214, 262, 270, 272-273, 281-282, 308, 310, 312, 318, 330
omnibenevolence of, 328
omnicompetence of, 51
omnipotence of, 328
omnipresence of, 89-90, 107, 123-124, 207, 211, 237, 238-239, 244, 259
omniscience of, 51-53, 70, 275, 301, 326, 328
presence of, 38, 62, 75, 87, 89, 90, 92-93, 99-100, 103-105, 121-124, 126, 128, 132, 205, 207, 223, 230-231, 238-244, 248, 250-252, 255, 257-259, 266, 269, 274, 314
providence of, 11, 20, 99, 241, 283-284, 311
salvific will of, 16, 34, 36-37, 39, 47, 56-57, 60, 63, 78-79, 86, 92, 101, 103-104, 107, 109-111, 113, 119, 124, 127-129, 173, 175, 184, 186, 193, 197, 208, 211, 220, 227, 237-238, 241, 245, 255, 263, 265, 268-270, 275-277, 279, 282, 284, 286, 294, 299-300, 305, 307, 316, 321, 324-325, 327, 330
sovereignty of, 8, 26, 32, 35, 46-52, 61, 67, 141, 187, 209, 261, 277, 282, 285, 302, 306-307, 310, 312, 329
triunity, 52, 64, 66, 87, 100-101, 114, 124, 157, 207, 227, 231-232, 236, 243
wrath of, 79, 81-82, 127-128, 173, 209, 211-214, 216, 259, 267, 269, 272, 281

Goldingay, J.E., 170, 181-182, 188, 337
Gootjes, N.H., 112-113, 337
Gore, C., 70
grace, 9-11, 13, 26, 28, 31-32, 34-35, 37-38, 46-49, 57, 59-60, 61, 63, 73, 80, 82-83, 86-87, 89-105, 107-108, 113-115, 117-133, 156-160, 162-163, 165-166, 171-175, 177-179, 185, 193, 198, 203, 206, 207, 211-222, 227, 231, 237, 240-242, 244-245, 252-255, 257-260, 262, 266-271, 274-277, 279-282, 285, 288, 298-300, 303, 306, 312-314, 317, 320-321, 323, 325, 327-328
 common, 98-99, 130, 175, 193, 241-242, 255, 268, 271, 285, 288, 325, 332, 338-339, 342, 348
 special, 99, 101, 193, 252, 325
grafted, 102
Gray, T., 42, 302, 347
Grenz, S.J., 12-13, 337
Griffiths, P.J., 118, 338
Groothuis, D., 338
Grotius, 78
Grudem, W., 5, 9-12, 48, 76-77, 99, 141, 153, 157, 168, 175, 204, 215, 233, 240-241, 252, 256, 262, 267, 278, 285, 338
Gunton, C., 65, 243, 338

Hackett, S., 85, 338
Haight, R., 75, 338
Ham, 174, 182, 187, 345
Hamilton, V.P., 42, 181, 338
Hanko, H., 156-158, 161, 176, 182, 215, 223, 241, 244-245, 268, 271, 279, 338
harmartology, 213, 266
Harpel, R., 185, 336
Hart, T., 31, 80, 338
Hartshorne, C., 92
Hasker, W., 47-50, 52, 301, 326, 338, 344
Hastings, A., 338
heathen, 33, 108, 186, 271, 308, 311-312, 314-315, 320
Heidegger, M., 104
Hell, 16, 18-19, 23, 26, 31, 62, 116, 120, 289, 297, 307, 327, 329

Helm, P., 47, 52, 77, 195, 196, 273, 285, 311-312, 318-320, 326, 338
henotheism, 183
Henry, C.F., 6-7, 10, 13, 33, 35, 61, 112, 166, 211, 237-238, 256, 281, 282, 298, 308-310, 334, 338-339
Heppe, H., 205, 338
Heraclitus, 87
Heron, A.I.C., 338
Hess, R.S., 179, 182, 339-340
Hick, J., xiii, 16, 20-21, 23, 38, 63, 295, 335, 337, 339, 347
Hodge, C., 10, 156, 164-165, 242, 290, 319-320, 339
Hodgson-Welch debate, 228
Hoeksema, H., 156, 252, 254-255, 339
Holy Spirit, viii-xi, 7, 9, 43, 47, 64-65, 67, 70,72-75, 79-84, 86-87, 89-93, 95, 97-102, 104-108, 110, 113-115, 120-130, 133, 141, 153, 160, 179-180, 189-191, 196-197,199-200, 203, 205-211, 215-216, 218-231, 233-244, 235-261, 268-271, 278-280, 287, 296, 303, 311-312, 318-319, 332-335, 337-340, 342-344, 347, 349-350
homoousios, 229-231, 247
Horner, N., 21
House, P.R., 333-339, 341-345
Hughes, D., 339
Hughes, P.E., 10, 50, 180, 186, 268, 339, 343
Hunter, J.D., 12, 16-17, 21-22, 339
hypostatization, 232

imago Dei, 49, 97, 111-112, 119, 130, 179, 193, 201, 237, 269, 275, 308, 322
imputation, 95, 168, 259-260
incarnation, 7, 15, 19, 28, 63, 67, 69-71, 74-75, 79-80, 82-84, 87-88, 101, 105-106, 113, 126, 130, 162, 164, 188, 190, 200, 202-205, 207, 211-212, 217, 219-221, 224, 228, 232-233, 236, 249-251, 256, 262, 266, 279
Inch, M., 339
inclusive, 5, 21, 28, 37, 57, 61-62, 68, 80, 181, 208, 216, 279, 295
inclusivism, xvii, 3, 15, 17, 19-20, 22, 34-35, 37-38, 42-47, 51, 67, 70, 87, 89, 95, 100, 109, 118, 129-132, 134-136, 139-140, 145, 148, 151-154, 157, 162, 189, 191-194, 197, 199-200, 202, 206, 222, 225-228, 231, 233, 234, 237, 247, 249, 251, 254-255, 258, 263, 265-266, 269, 274, 276, 280, 286, 287, 289, 294, 298-299, 301-302, 317, 318, 322, 324, 330
infralapsarianism, 10
ingrafting, 167, 177-178, 185, 245
Irenaeus, 61-62, 73, 79-80, 105, 114, 209-210, 338, 341
Isaac, v, xv, 160, 163, 212
Isaiah, 163, 176, 347
Isidore, 232
Islam, 183
Israel, 54, 58-59, 68, 110, 122, 125, 153-154, 160-161, 165, 167, 169, 172, 177-178, 180-181, 185, 212-213, 228, 244-245, 249, 320, 343, 349
Israelite, x, 163, 166-167, 170, 177, 178, 181-182

Japheth, 182, 187, 314
Jehovah, 172, 228
Jesus, viii, 5, 7-8, 13, 15-16, 19, 21-25, 28, 31-35, 37-38, 45, 47, 56-57, 59, 63, 67-83, 85, 87-88, 93, 97, 105-106, 108, 111, 113, 116, 122-128, 130-132, 147, 150, 152-153, 156, 160, 163, 165, 171, 176, 189, 191-195, 197, 200-209, 217-220, 222, 224, 245-247, 249, 251, 257, 261, 271-275, 276, 284, 290, 295, 298, 300, 303, 308, 311, 316-317, 321-322, 325, 330, 339, 342-344, 346
Jethro, 110, 178, 181, 185
Jews, 58-59, 71, 110, 133, 152-153, 195, 197, 202, 279, 314, 316
Jezebel, 182
Job, 58, 110, 185, 267
Joel, 170
Johnson Jr., L.S, 154, 212-213, 216, 339
Johnston, R.K., 140, 339
Jonah, 54, 185, 347
Jones, H.R., 7, 24, 167, 169, 171-172, 174, 180, 183-186, 192-193, 195, 255, 326, 339
Judaism, 183-184, 195

Index

judgement, 19, 31, 60, 76, 83, 113, 133, 142, 156, 158, 173, 174, 187, 208, 213-214, 218, 223, 267, 270, 272, 281, 297, 308-309
justification, 7, 46, 79, 114-115, 159, 237, 256, 258-260, 262, 268-269, 325
Justin Martyr, 61, 87, 193, 238, 339

Kane, H., 25, 339
Kant, I., 104
Kanzter, K., 7, 339
Karlberg, M.W., 339
Kasper, W., 339
kenosis, 69-70, 72-75, 79, 203-204
Khodr, G., 63, 106, 339
Kidner, D., 339
Kingdon, D., 340
Kistler, D., 259, 340
Klein, W.W., 58, 340
Kline, M., 143
Klooster, F.H., 163, 165, 340
Knitter, P., 13-14, 63, 75, 104, 119, 120, 201, 295, 340, 344
Kraemer, H., 340
Kraft, C., 340
Kuyper, A., 165-166, 190-191, 203, 243-246, 340

Ladd, G., 12
Lake, D., 283, 327, 340
Lamadrid, L., 340
Lamech, 169, 170
Lampe, G., 74, 340
Langford, T., 95, 98-99
Lausanne, 23, 33
Lee, U., 98, 103
Letham, R., 76-78, 157, 159-161, 176, 209, 211-212, 215-218, 250, 258-259, 267, 268, 278, 280, 340
Lewis, C.S., 10, 62, 70, 76-78, 92, 112, 115, 135, 141, 143-144, 153, 155, 193, 204, 213, 252, 267, 285, 336, 339-340
libertarian freedom, 11, 48-50, 52-53, 77, 96-97, 132, 275, 280
Lindbeck, G., 324, 340
Lindsell, H., 21, 23
Linfield, A., 297, 340
Lints, R., 29, 142-151, 160, 340
logos, 205

logos spermatikos, 237, 273
Lopes, A.N., 340
Lorenzen, T., 340
Lossky, V., 98, 106, 234, 236, 340
Lubac, H., 102, 130
Luther, M., 30, 62, 111, 165, 252, 302, 341
lutheran, 9, 10

Macleod, D., 70, 203-206, 215, 229-231, 247-248, 341
Maddox, R., 93-95, 98, 341
Marsden, G.M., 4, 27, 341
Marshall, H. 48, 341
Marshall, M.T., 124-125, 200, 341
Melanchthon, 10
Melchizedek, 58, 110, 120-121, 176, 178-181, 183-188, 195, 338, 340
Messiah, 126, 153, 164-166, 176, 195, 232, 245, 250
middle-knowledge, 52, 326, 329
Miether, T.L., 77, 276, 341
Milne, B., 341
Minns, D., 80, 341
mission, xi, 9, 21, 23, 25, 178, 289, 335, 337, 343, 347-348
modal inclusivism, 65, 118
Mohler Jr., R.A., 4, 7, 341
Molina, L., 326
Moltmann, J., 8, 44, 65, 92, 223
monotheism, 180, 232
Moo, D., 193, 341
Moody, D., 113, 339, 341, 343, 345, 347
Morimoto, A., 254, 313, 342
Morris, L., 76, 165, 339, 342
Motyer, J.A., 161, 172, 342
Muller, R.A., 11, 50, 249, 342
Munlochy, W.C., 342
Murray, J., 10, 48, 76-77, 157, 168, 213, 215, 217, 241, 242, 255, 258-259, 261-262, 267, 278, 342

nature and grace debate, 100
Neoorthodoxy, 12, 255
neotheism, 92
Netland, H., 14-19, 22, 25, 33, 289, 342, 346-348
Newbigin, L., 14, 342
Newman, P.W., 74, 342
Nicholls, B.J., 342

Nicole, R., 77, 342
Noah, 57, 59, 60, 67, 108, 110, 114, 121, 152-153, 166, 170-171, 173-175, 182-184, 187, 272, 314

Ockenga, J., 6
Ogden, S., 92
Okholm, D.L., 8, 15-16, 23-24, 37-38, 42, 45, 88, 108, 152, 207, 295, 307, 310, 330, 343-344
Olevianus, 155
ontic, 74, 102
ontology, 14, 28, 38, 64, 67-69, 71, 73, 81, 91, 100, 103, 107, 114, 151, 165, 172, 174, 191, 194-195, 197, 199, 202-203, 221-222, 229-230, 235, 247, 268-269, 288, 294, 305, 311
openness theology, 12, 43, 45-47, 50-51, 53, 61, 64, 70, 78, 84, 91-92, 202, 204, 209, 238, 243, 268, 275, 280, 283, 286, 301-302
Origen, 61, 76
Osbourne, G.R., 29, 142-145, 149-150, 343
Osburn, E.D., 121, 343
Oswalt, J.N., 178, 343
Owen, J., 9, 50, 77, 112, 165, 187-188, 203, 205-206, 250, 251-252, 283-284, 303, 343, 348

Packer, J.I., 5, 8-11, 50, 76-77, 116, 209, 210, 216-218, 249, 261, 268, 278, 281-285, 320, 343
pactum salutis, 157, 215
pagan saint, 176, 180, 184, 194-195
pagans, 33, 59, 110, 114, 120, 126, 133, 167, 169, 172, 176, 178-181, 184, 186, 189, 192-195, 222, 312-313
Palamas, 257
Palmer, E.H., 155, 174, 212, 238, 251, 253, 343, 345
panentheism, 91-92, 104, 238-239
Pannenberg, W., 8, 65
pantheism, 239
Paraclete, 247, 248
particularism, 8, 38, 283, 295, 319-320
Patriarchs, 170, 181, 349
Paul, 147, 193
Peacocke, A., 92

Pelag, 183
Pelagius, 61
penal substitution, 76-79, 82, 84, 208, 211-219, 267, 278-279
perechoresis, 228, 230-232, 236, 242, 248-249, 251, 258, 287
Phillips, W.G., 8, 15-16, 20, 23-24, 29, 37-39, 42, 45, 88, 108, 152, 207, 274, 282, 295, 297, 307, 310-311, 317, 321, 326-327, 329-330, 343-344
Pinnock, C.H., vii-xi, xiii, xv, xvii, 3, 8, 11-13, 24-27, 31-32, 35, 38-39, 41-102, 104-111, 113-137, 139-141, 143, 145, 147-148, 150-154, 157-158, 162-163, 167, 173-176, 178-181, 184-186, 189, 190-197, 199-228, 231, 233-234, 236-241, 244, 247, 249, 251-255, 257-259, 261-263, 265-266, 268-283, 285-287, 289, 295, 301, 318, 322, 324, 327, 329, 335, 337, 340-341, 343, 344-345, 347
Plantinga, Jr. C., 3-4, 19, 228, 343
Plato, 315
pluralism, xvii, 14-18, 20-21, 29, 38, 45, 53, 56-57, 62-63, 66, 70-72, 107, 111, 118, 135, 199-200, 225, 243, 274, 295, 298, 314
pneumatocentricity, 216, 222, 227, 236, 259
pneumatological, 67, 89, 101, 139, 152, 189, 199, 227, 263, 269, 286
pneumatology, 63, 129, 189, 203, 206, 226, 227, 255
polytheism, 187
postconservatism, 12-13, 299, 306
postliberalism, 324
postmodernism, 142
post-mortem encounter with Christ, 47, 129, 131-133, 299, 322-325
Poythress, V.S., 154, 156, 345
predestination, 8, 10, 62, 282-283, 307, 310, 311
premessianic believers, 34, 110-111, 126, 128, 130, 133, 151-153, 162, 222
preparatio evangelica, 129, 222, 317
prevenient grace, 47, 93-102, 104-105, 107-108, 114-115, 118-119, 121-

Index 359

127, 131, 133, 207, 221, 227, 231, 237, 258, 262, 266, 268
propitiation, 76, 79, 212-214, 216
protoevangelium, 168-169, 171, 175

Quebedeaux, R., 12-13, 32

Race, A., 37, 118, 294, 345
Rahab, 178
Rahner, K., xiii, 56, 65, 86, 100, 102-104, 109, 120, 124-125, 129-130, 235, 269, 332, 340, 345, 349
Rakestraw, R.V., 42-44, 253, 257, 345
Ramm, B., 12, 32
recapitulation, 61, 80, 83, 116, 208-210, 216, 217
redemption, 9-10, 60, 66, 72-73, 77, 80, 85, 88-89, 102, 105, 113, 115, 128, 142-143, 146-148, 156-157, 161-162, 165, 169, 174-175, 177, 182, 190, 200, 207-208, 210, 212, 215, 217, 219, 221, 226-227, 230-231, 233, 242-243, 252, 259, 279, 280, 282-284, 306-307, 309-311, 319, 321
redemptive-historical index, 58, 68, 71, 85, 89, 112-113, 129, 142, 145-146, 148-150, 155, 161, 163, 166, 171-172, 175-176, 182-184, 186-187, 189-190, 193, 195, 197, 211, 236, 240-241, 243, 249, 262, 276, 285, 300, 317, 321
Reformed, 8
Reichenbach, B., 86, 345
religion, xiii-xiv, xvii, 13-19, 21, 23, 37, 59, 89, 107, 109-110, 114, 124-126, 129-131, 136, 170, 179-184, 186, 209, 242, 294, 298, 303, 308, 314, 315, 318, 324
  theology of religions, xiv, xvii, 14, 16, 18-19, 21, 43-44, 56, 71, 117-118, 121-122, 255, 274, 288
religiosity, 188
repentance, xvii, 14-16, 19, 21, 52-53, 56, 59, 63, 66, 70, 111, 118-122, 142-143, 161, 164, 170, 179, 180, 182-184, 187, 201, 288, 298, 314-316
reprobation, 313
restrictivism, 25, 34-35, 56, 59, 68, 134-135, 155, 189, 191-192, 197,
254, 274, 289, 295-304, 307, 310, 316-324, 329
revelation, xviii, 13, 15-16, 19-20, 26, 28, 35, 49, 59, 63, 65, 67-69, 73, 87, 92, 94, 97, 99, 101-102, 129, 130, 133, 141-148, 150, 153-155, 157-158, 161, 163-167, 169-174, 176-180, 182-186, 188, 190-191, 193, 195, 197, 206, 212-213, 220-222, 231-233, 236-237, 242-245, 248-256, 260, 262-263, 265, 268, 272, 275-276, 280-288, 296, 299, 304
  general, 36-38, 90, 103-104, 107, 111-114, 116, 118, 120-121, 125, 130, 153, 176, 180, 185, 193-195, 197, 200-201, 237, 240, 242, 255, 262-263, 268-269, 282, 285-286, 288, 305, 308-309, 317-318, 322, 329, 336-7
  special, 36-39, 86, 98, 104, 107, 111-114, 125, 153, 165-167, 176, 178-180, 182-186, 193, 195, 197-198, 236-237, 242, 244, 249, 254-255, 262, 272, 284-285, 296, 304-305, 307-311, 317-319, 322, 329, 334, 335-337
Reymond, R., 284, 345
Rice, R., 47, 50, 52, 344
Richard, R.P., 154, 163, 169, 170, 182, 184, 185, 192, 194, 196, 197, 202, 207, 238, 246, 249, 255, 272, 274, 285, 326, 345
Richardson, D., 121, 185, 336, 345
Riches, J., 349
Ricoeur, P., 227
Ridderbos, H., 143
righteousness, 95, 99, 110, 115, 156, 166, 174, 208, 241, 259-261, 270, 272, 278, 281, 310
Ritchie, B., 345
Robertson, O.P., 150, 155, 157-160, 162, 168, 174, 176-177, 187, 212, 215, 217, 245, 253, 345
Robinson, J.A.T., 31
Roennfeldt, R.C.W., 42, 44, 49, 141, 253, 344-345
Rommen, E., 289, 346-348
Roth, R.P., 346
Runia, K., 4, 5, 346

Ruokanen, M., 101-103, 119, 122, 124, 128-130, 346
Ryrie, C.C., 154

salvation, xiii-xiv, xvii, 9, 11, 13, 15, 16, 19-20, 22-23, 25, 27-32, 34-38, 43, 47-48, 50, 56-64, 66-67, 71-73, 76-81, 85-89, 91, 94-95, 99, 101, 106-111, 113-121, 123, 125, 127-130, 132-135, 139, 141-142, 148, 150-154, 156-159, 161-168, 170-173, 176-178, 181, 184-185, 189-192, 194-197, 199-202, 204, 206-211, 213-216, 220-228, 231-234, 236-237, 241, 244, 247, 249-251, 254-256, 258, 259, 260-263, 265-267, 269, 271-280, 282-287, 289-290, 294-298, 300, 302-307, 309-322, 324-330
   accessibility of, 36-39, 85-86, 89, 104, 107-108, 116, 131, 153, 200, 220, 222, 237, 240, 263, 265, 275, 277-278, 281-282, 286, 287, 298, 301, 305, 306-307, 317, 319, 321-322, 330
   monergism in, 10, 13, 78, 115, 158, 259, 267, 285
   of infants, 23, 33-34, 134, 254, 303, 312, 314, 324
   particularity of, xiii, xvii, 21, 28-29, 36, 47, 56-57, 67-68, 70, 72, 85, 102, 105-106, 126-127, 135, 162, 168, 173-174, 188, 193, 197-200, 202-203, 206, 210, 220, 222, 224, 226, 236, 243, 248-249, 263, 265, 272, 274, 280-282, 285-287, 294, 298, 305, 307, 324, 330
   universality of, xvii, 21, 56-57, 59, 60, 62-64, 66, 67-68, 70, 72, 85, 87, 90, 102, 105-107, 126-127, 135, 140, 152, 168, 173-174, 199, 202-203, 206, 210, 219-220, 224-227, 236, 263, 265-266, 269, 272, 274, 280, 282, 285-287, 289, 323, 330
salvation-history, 310
Sanders, J., xii, xvii, 21, 22, 23, 24, 25, 26, 27, 28, 29, 30, 31, 34, 37, 47, 50, 51, 111, 191, 192, 274, 289, 297, 298, 299, 300, 301, 302, 303,

304, 306, 307, 310, 316, 317, 319, 321, 322, 323, 324, 325, 327, 329, 330, 344, 346
Sanders, J.O., 30, 346
Satterthwaite, P.E., 179, 340
Satyavrata, I., 113, 346
Schaeffer, F., 13, 346
Schaff, P., xvii
Schineller, J.P., 28-29, 37, 295-296, 346
Schleiermacher, F., 31, 69, 100, 346
Schmidt, F.W., 346
Schreiner, T., 10-11, 48, 50, 93, 269-271, 285, 289, 342-343, 345-346, 348
seed, 81, 148-149, 163, 168-170, 174, 177, 187, 190, 254
semi-pelagianism, 61
Semites, 180, 182-184, 186
sensus divinitatis, 237
Shedd, W.G.T., 285, 300, 312-313, 319, 346
Shem, 170, 180, 182-183, 186, 188, 314
Shemites, 172, 183
Sigountos, J., 18, 24, 31, 33, 35, 39, 59, 86, 178, 185, 191, 193, 238, 281-282, 286, 288-289, 296, 302, 333-336, 338, 341, 343, 346-349
Sinkinson, C., xv, 16, 42, 302, 347
Smith, G.T., 347
Smyth, E., 324
Sodom, 186
solus Christus, 5, 16-18, 20-21, 27-28, 56, 76, 79, 199, 209, 225, 263, 324, 332
soteriology, xviii, 8-9, 17, 20, 25-26, 35, 38, 44, 49, 61, 79, 81, 94, 98-99, 114, 149, 158, 189, 190, 199, 216, 221-222, 224, 226, 231, 237, 242, 256, 258-259, 263, 265, 267-268, 275-277, 280, 282, 287, 304-306, 315-318, 328
Spencer, A.B., 193, 347
Spiceland, J.D., 338, 342
Sproul, R.C., 5, 8, 300
Stackhouse Jr., J.G., 347
Staniloae, D., 347
Stott, J., 7, 23, 62, 214, 330, 336, 347
Strange, D., 42, 44, 72, 75, 347
Strehle, S., 77, 347

Index 361

Strickland, W.G., 347
Strimple, B., 347
substitution, 76-78, 82, 208, 210-212, 216-217, 219, 267, 278-279
Sullivan, F., 88, 238, 274, 347
supralapsarianism, 10
Swidler, L., 75, 201, 344
Swinburne, R., 326
Sykes, S., 74, 340

theocentricity, 63, 70, 200
theophany, 166, 180, 184, 254
theosis, 114, 234, 257, 258
Thimell, D., 80, 338
Thiselton, A., 142, 347
Thomism, 101, 104
Thompson, T.R., 64-65, 228, 347
Tidball, D., 4, 348
Tiessen, T., 348
Tillich, P., 69, 100
Torrance, T.F., 8, 348
Travis, S., 132-133, 289, 348
Travis, W., 348
trinitarian procession, 34, 130, 247, 257, 287
Trinity, 43, 45-47, 50-51, 53, 61-62, 64-65, 70, 74, 78, 84, 86-87, 91-92, 99, 106, 153, 202, 204, 209, 215, 226, 228, 234-235, 238-239, 243, 268, 275, 280, 283, 286-287, 301
  economic, 65, 233-235, 247, 248, 250, 288
    immanent, 70, 92, 64-65, 70, 92, 233-235, 247-248
tritheism, 65-66, 228, 280
Trueman, C., 205, 250, 252, 348
Turnbull, R., 4, 348
Turretin, F., 238-240, 348
typology, 5, 15, 35-37, 76, 95, 118, 150-151, 160-163, 166, 172, 182, 188, 210, 212, 216, 228, 237, 294, 296-297, 299, 304-305, 314-315

unevangelised, xv, xvii, 3, 12, 14, 16, 18-19, 21-23, 25-35, 42-49, 53, 55-57, 59, 67, 73, 83-86, 89, 94, 107-111, 116, 118, 121-122, 124, 126-136, 139-140, 143, 151, 153-154, 157, 163, 165, 167, 179-180, 184, 189-190, 192, 194-197, 206, 216, 220-222, 225-227, 231, 237, 251, 254, 263, 265-266, 270-272, 274-278, 280-287, 289, 294, 297, 298-313, 317-319, 321-330
Unger, W., 348
union with Christ, 73, 80-83, 114, 204, 205-206, 208, 218, 223, 228, 234, 246, 256, 258, 260, 262, 279
universal, 13, 20, 36-38, 47, 56, 58-60, 63, 71-72, 78-79, 85-87, 89, 93-94, 97-100, 102, 104, 106, 107, 110-113, 120, 126-128, 130-131, 153, 157, 167, 173, 175, 185, 190, 193, 197-198, 200-201, 207, 211, 214, 219-220, 222, 226-227, 233, 237-238, 240-245, 255, 258, 263, 265-268, 270, 275-282, 286-287, 289-290, 298, 300, 305-307, 316-317, 321-322, 324, 330
universalisation, 167, 173, 224, 280-281
universalism, 23, 25, 30-32, 63, 77-78, 134, 176, 198, 221, 274, 277, 279, 294, 297, 298, 306, 314, 323, 327
Ursinus, 155

Van Til, 13, 348
VanGemeren, W., 143
Vanhoozer, K., 66, 92, 99, 100, 102, 115, 227-228, 238, 243, 247, 269, 332-333, 338, 348
Vatican II, 43, 62-63, 100-101, 109, 117-118, 120, 123-124, 128-129, 135, 222, 274, 332, 346, 349
Veenhof, J., 349
Vischer, L., 106, 332, 334, 339, 347, 349
Von Rad, G., 181-182
Vos, G., 143, 145-149, 157, 172-175, 183-184, 186, 349

Waite, J.C., 237, 244, 349
Ware, B., 10, 12, 48, 50, 93, 106, 269, 285, 289, 342-343, 345-346, 348-349
Warfield, B.B., 10, 134, 190, 229, 232, 237-238, 244-245, 273, 319, 334, 349
Watson, G., 349
Webster, J., 349
Weinandy, T.G., 349
Welker, M., 8, 349

Wells, D.F., 3, 4, 5, 6, 19, 67, 108, 238, 251, 343-344, 349
Wenham, G., 7, 170, 179, 181, 188, 340, 349
Wesley, J., 6, 11, 93-98, 268, 316, 341, 345
Wesleyanism, 13, 45, 93, 95-96, 98-99, 139, 269, 344, 346
Whitehead, A.N., 92
Whitlefield, G., 6, 165
Widbin, R.B., 185, 349
Wilken, R.B., 349
Williams, R., 349
Willis, D., 8, 349
Winter, B., 16, 18, 24, 104, 112, 119, 170, 181-183, 189, 193, 238, 334, 335-337, 339-340, 349
Wiseman, D., 170, 349
Wood, R.C., 200, 349
Woodbridge, J., 141-142, 149, 334
Word
   agraphon, 249-250
   engraphon, 249-250, 255
   inerrancy of, 12, 141, 253
   infallibility of, 125
Wright, C.J.H., 170-171, 181-182, 188
Wright, D., 119,
Wright, N.T., 349
Wright, R.K., 10, 267, 350

Yahweh, 169-172, 176, 179-184, 186, 188, 232, 337, 339
Yates, J., 253, 255, 350

Zanchius, G., 285, 313, 350
Zwingli, U., 155, 285

Paternoster Biblical Monographs

(All titles uniform with this volume)
Dates in bold are of projected publication

Joseph Abraham
Eve: Accused or Acquitted?
A Reconsideration of Feminist Readings of the Creation Narrative Texts in Genesis 1–3
Two contrary views dominate contemporary feminist biblical scholarship. One finds in the Bible an unequivocal equality between the sexes from the very creation of humanity, whilst the other sees the biblical text as irredeemably patriarchal and androcentric. Dr Abraham enters into dialogue with both camps as well as introducing his own method of approach. An invaluable tool for any one who is interested in this contemporary debate.
2002 / 0-85364-971-5 / xxiv + 272pp

Octavian D. Baban
Mimesis and Luke's on the Road Encounters in Luke-Acts
Luke's Theology of the Way and its Literary Representation
The book argues on theological and literary (mimetic) grounds that Luke's on-the-road encounters, especially those belonging to the post-Easter period, are part of his complex theology of the Way. Jesus' teaching and that of the apostles is presented by Luke as a challenging answer to the Hellenistic reader's thirst for adventure, good literature, and existential paradigms.
2005 */ 1-84227-253-5 / approx. 374pp*

Paul Barker
The Triumph of Grace in Deuteronomy
This book is a textual and theological analysis of the interaction between the sin and faithlessness of Israel and the grace of Yahweh in response, looking especially at Deuteronomy chapters 1–3, 8–10 and 29–30. The author argues that the grace of Yahweh is determinative for the ongoing relationship between Yahweh and Israel and that Deuteronomy anticipates and fully expects Israel to be faithless.
2004 / 1-84227-226-8 / xxii + 270pp

Jonathan F. Bayes
The Weakness of the Law
God's Law and the Christian in New Testament Perspective
A study of the four New Testament books which refer to the law as weak (Acts, Romans, Galatians, Hebrews) leads to a defence of the third use in the Reformed debate about the law in the life of the believer.
2000 / 0-85364-957-X / xii + 244pp

Mark Bonnington
The Antioch Episode of Galatians 2:11-14 in Historical and Cultural Context

The Galatians 2 'incident' in Antioch over table-fellowship suggests significant disagreement between the leading apostles. This book analyses the background to the disagreement by locating the incident within the dynamics of social interaction between Jews and Gentiles. It proposes a new way of understanding the relationship between the individuals and issues involved.

2005 / 1-84227-050-8 / approx. 350pp

David Bostock
A Portrayal of Trust
The Theme of Faith in the Hezekiah Narratives

This study provides detailed and sensitive readings of the Hezekiah narratives (2 Kings 18–20 and Isaiah 36–39) from a theological perspective. It concentrates on the theme of faith, using narrative criticism as its methodology. Attention is paid especially to setting, plot, point of view and characterization within the narratives. A largely positive portrayal of Hezekiah emerges that underlines the importance and relevance of scripture.

2005 / 1-84227-314-0 / approx. 300pp

Mark Bredin
Jesus, Revolutionary of Peace
A Non-violent Christology in the Book of Revelation

This book aims to demonstrate that the figure of Jesus in the Book of Revelation can best be understood as an active non-violent revolutionary.

2003 / 1-84227-153-9 / xviii + 262pp

Robinson Butarbutar
Paul and Conflict Resolution
An Exegetical Study of Paul's Apostolic Paradigm in 1 Corinthians 9

The author sees the apostolic paradigm in 1 Corinthians 9 as part of Paul's unified arguments in 1 Corinthians 8–10 in which he seeks to mediate in the dispute over the issue of food offered to idols. The book also sees its relevance for dispute-resolution today, taking the conflict within the author's church as an example.

2006 / 1-84227-315-9 / approx. 280pp

Daniel J-S Chae
Paul as Apostle to the Gentiles
His Apostolic Self-awareness and its Influence on the Soteriological Argument in Romans
Opposing 'the post-Holocaust interpretation of Romans', Daniel Chae competently demonstrates that Paul argues for the equality of Jew and Gentile in Romans. Chae's fresh exegetical interpretation is academically outstanding and spiritually encouraging.
1997 / 0-85364-829-8 / xiv + 378pp

Luke L. Cheung
The Genre, Composition and Hermeneutics of the Epistle of James
The present work examines the employment of the wisdom genre with a certain compositional structure and the interpretation of the law through the Jesus tradition of the double love command by the author of the Epistle of James to serve his purpose in promoting perfection and warning against doubleness among the eschatologically renewed people of God in the Diaspora.
2003 / 1-84227-062-1 / xvi + 372pp

Youngmo Cho
Spirit and Kingdom in the Writings of Luke and Paul
The relationship between Spirit and Kingdom is a relatively unexplored area in Lukan and Pauline studies. This book offers a fresh perspective of two biblical writers on the subject. It explores the difference between Luke's and Paul's understanding of the Spirit by examining the specific question of the relationship of the concept of the Spirit to the concept of the Kingdom of God in each writer.
2005 / 1-84227-316-7 / approx. 270pp

Andrew C. Clark
Parallel Lives
The Relation of Paul to the Apostles in the Lucan Perspective
This study of the Peter-Paul parallels in Acts argues that their purpose was to emphasize the themes of continuity in salvation history and the unity of the Jewish and Gentile missions. New light is shed on Luke's literary techniques, partly through a comparison with Plutarch.
2001 / 1-84227-035-4 / xviii + 386pp

Andrew D. Clarke
Secular and Christian Leadership in Corinth
A Socio-Historical and Exegetical Study of 1 Corinthians 1–6
This volume is an investigation into the leadership structures and dynamics of first-century Roman Corinth. These are compared with the practice of leadership in the Corinthian Christian community which are reflected in 1 Corinthians 1–6, and contrasted with Paul's own principles of Christian leadership.
2005 / 1-84227-229-2 / 200pp

Stephen Finamore
God, Order and Chaos
René Girard and the Apocalypse
Readers are often disturbed by the images of destruction in the book of Revelation and unsure why they are unleashed after the exaltation of Jesus. This book examines past approaches to these texts and uses René Girard's theories to revive some old ideas and propose some new ones.
2005 / 1-84227-197-0 / approx. 344pp

David G. Firth
Surrendering Retribution in the Psalms
Responses to Violence in the Individual Complaints
In *Surrendering Retribution in the Psalms*, David Firth examines the ways in which the book of Psalms inculcates a model response to violence through the repetition of standard patterns of prayer. Rather than seeking justification for retributive violence, Psalms encourages not only a surrender of the right of retribution to Yahweh, but also sets limits on the retribution that can be sought in imprecations. Arising initially from the author's experience in South Africa, the possibilities of this model to a particular context of violence is then briefly explored.
2005 / 1-84227-337-X / xviii + 154pp

Scott J. Hafemann
Suffering and Ministry in the Spirit
Paul's Defence of His Ministry in II Corinthians 2:14–3:3
Shedding new light on the way Paul defended his apostleship, the author offers a careful, detailed study of 2 Corinthians 2:14–3:3 linked with other key passages throughout 1 and 2 Corinthians. Demonstrating the unity and coherence of Paul's argument in this passage, the author shows that Paul's suffering served as the vehicle for revealing God's power and glory through the Spirit.
2000 / 0-85364-967-7 / xiv + 262pp

Scott J. Hafemann
Paul, Moses and the History of Israel
The Letter/Spirit Contrast and the Argument from Scripture in 2 Corinthians 3
An exegetical study of the call of Moses, the second giving of the Law (Exodus 32–34), the new covenant, and the prophetic understanding of the history of Israel in 2 Corinthians 3. Hafemann's work demonstrates Paul's contextual use of the Old Testament and the essential unity between the Law and the Gospel within the context of the distinctive ministries of Moses and Paul.
2005 / 1-84227-317-5 / xii + 498pp

Douglas S. McComiskey
Lukan Theology in the Light of the Gospel's Literary Structure
Luke's Gospel was purposefully written with theology embedded in its patterned literary structure. A critical analysis of this cyclical structure provides new windows into Luke's interpretation of the individual pericopes comprising the Gospel and illuminates several of his theological interests.
2004 / 1-84227-148-2 / xviii + 388pp

Stephen Motyer
Your Father the Devil?
A New Approach to John and 'The Jews'
Who are 'the Jews' in John's Gospel? Defending John against the charge of antisemitism, Motyer argues that, far from demonising the Jews, the Gospel seeks to present Jesus as 'Good News for Jews' in a late first century setting.
1997 / 0-85364-832-8 / xiv + 260pp

Esther Ng
Reconstructing Christian Origins?
The Feminist Theology of Elizabeth Schüssler Fiorenza: An Evaluation
In a detailed evaluation, the author challenges Elizabeth Schüssler Fiorenza's reconstruction of early Christian origins and her underlying presuppositions. The author also presents her own views on women's roles both then and now.
2002 / 1-84227-055-9 / xxiv + 468pp

Robin Parry
Old Testament Story and Christian Ethics
The Rape of Dinah as a Case Study

What is the role of story in ethics and, more particularly, what is the role of Old Testament story in Christian ethics? This book, drawing on the work of contemporary philosophers, argues that narrative is crucial in the ethical shaping of people and, drawing on the work of contemporary Old Testament scholars, that story plays a key role in Old Testament ethics. Parry then argues that when situated in canonical context Old Testament stories can be reappropriated by Christian readers in their own ethical formation. The shocking story of the rape of Dinah and the massacre of the Shechemites provides a fascinating case study for exploring the parameters within which Christian ethical appropriations of Old Testament stories can live.

2004 / 1-84227-210-1 / xx + 350pp

Ian Paul
Power to See the World Anew
The Value of Paul Ricoeur's Hermeneutic of Metaphor in Interpreting the Symbolism of Revelation 12 and 13

This book is a study of the hermeneutics of metaphor of Paul Ricoeur, one of the most important writers on hermeneutics and metaphor of the last century. It sets out the key points of his theory, important criticisms of his work, and how his approach, modified in the light of these criticisms, offers a methodological framework for reading apocalyptic texts.

2006 / 1-84227-056-7 / approx. 350pp

Robert L. Plummer
Paul's Understanding of the Church's Mission
Did the Apostle Paul Expect the Early Christian Communities to Evangelize?

This book engages in a careful study of Paul's letters to determine if the apostle expected the communities to which he wrote to engage in missionary activity. It helpfully summarizes the discussion on this debated issue, judiciously handling contested texts, and provides a way forward in addressing this critical question. While admitting that Paul rarely explicitly commands the communities he founded to evangelize, Plummer amasses significant incidental data to provide a convincing case that Paul did indeed expect his churches to engage in mission activity. Throughout the study, Plummer progressively builds a theological basis for the church's mission that is both distinctively Pauline and compelling.

2006 / 1-84227-333-7 / approx. 324pp

David Powys
'Hell': A Hard Look at a Hard Question
The Fate of the Unrighteous in New Testament Thought
This comprehensive treatment seeks to unlock the original meaning of terms and phrases long thought to support the traditional doctrine of hell. It concludes that there is an alternative—one which is more biblical, and which can positively revive the rationale for Christian mission.

1997 / 0-85364-831-X / xxii + 478pp

Sorin Sabou
Between Horror and Hope
Paul's Metaphorical Language of Death in Romans 6.1-11
This book argues that Paul's metaphorical language of death in Romans 6.1-11 conveys two aspects: horror and hope. The 'horror' aspect is conveyed by the 'crucifixion' language, and the 'hope' aspect by 'burial' language. The life of the Christian believer is understood, as relationship with sin is concerned ('death to sin'), between these two realities: horror and hope.

2005 / 1-84227-322-1 / approx. 224pp

Rosalind Selby
The Comical Doctrine
The Epistemology of New Testament Hermeneutics
This book argues that the gospel breaks through postmodernity's critique of truth and the referential possibilities of textuality with its gift of grace. With a rigorous, philosophical challenge to modernist and postmodernist assumptions, Selby offers an alternative epistemology to all who would still read with faith *and* with academic credibility.

2005 / 1-84227-212-8 / approx. 350pp

Kiwoong Son
Zion Symbolism in Hebrews
Hebrews 12.18-24 as a Hermeneutical Key to the Epistle
This book challenges the general tendency of understanding the Epistle to the Hebrews against a Hellenistic background and suggests that the Epistle should be understood in the light of the Jewish apocalyptic tradition. The author especially argues for the importance of the theological symbolism of Sinai and Zion (Heb. 12:18-24) as it provides the Epistle's theological background as well as the rhetorical basis of the superiority motif of Jesus throughout the Epistle.

2005 / 1-84227-368-X / approx. 280pp

Kevin Walton
Thou Traveller Unknown
The Presence and Absence of God in the Jacob Narrative
The author offers a fresh reading of the story of Jacob in the book of Genesis through the paradox of divine presence and absence. The work also seeks to make a contribution to Pentateuchal studies by bringing together a close reading of the final text with historical critical insights, doing justice to the text's historical depth, final form and canonical status.
2003 / 1-84227-059-1 / xvi + 238pp

George M. Wieland
The Significance of Salvation
A Study of Salvation Language in the Pastoral Epistles
The language and ideas of salvation pervade the three Pastoral Epistles. This study offers a close examination of their soteriological statements. In all three letters the idea of salvation is found to play a vital paraenetic role, but each also exhibits distinctive soteriological emphases. The results challenge common assumptions about the Pastoral Epistles as a corpus.
2005 / 1-84227-257-8 / approx. 324pp

Alistair Wilson
When Will These Things Happen?
A Study of Jesus as Judge in Matthew 21–25
This study seeks to allow Matthew's carefully constructed presentation of Jesus to be given full weight in the modern evaluation of Jesus' eschatology. Careful analysis of the text of Matthew 21–25 reveals Jesus to be standing firmly in the Jewish prophetic and wisdom traditions as he proclaims and enacts imminent judgement on the Jewish authorities then boldly claims the central role in the final and universal judgement.
2004 / 1-84227-146-6 / xxii + 272pp

Lindsay Wilson
Joseph Wise and Otherwise
The Intersection of Covenant and Wisdom in Genesis 37–50
This book offers a careful literary reading of Genesis 37–50 that argues that the Joseph story contains both strong covenant themes and many wisdom-like elements. The connections between the two helps to explore how covenant and wisdom might intersect in an integrated biblical theology.
2004 / 1-84227-140-7 / xvi + 340pp

Stephen I. Wright
The Voice of Jesus
Studies in the Interpretation of Six Gospel Parables
This literary study considers how the 'voice' of Jesus has been heard in different periods of parable interpretation, and how the categories of figure and trope may help us towards a sensitive reading of the parables today.
2000 / 0-85364-975-8 / xiv + 280pp

Paternoster
9 Holdom Avenue,
Bletchley,
Milton Keynes MK1 1QR,
United Kingdom
Web: www.authenticmedia.co.uk/paternoster

Paternoster Theological Monographs
(All titles uniform with this volume)
Dates in bold are of projected publication

Emil Bartos
Deification in Eastern Orthodox Theology
An Evaluation and Critique of the Theology of Dumitru Staniloae
Bartos studies a fundamental yet neglected aspect of Orthodox theology: deification. By examining the doctrines of anthropology, christology, soteriology and ecclesiology as they relate to deification, he provides an important contribution to contemporary dialogue between Eastern and Western theologians.
1999 / 0-85364-956-1 / xii + 370pp

Graham Buxton
The Trinity, Creation and Pastoral Ministry
Imaging the Perichoretic God
In this book the author proposes a three-way conversation between theology, science and pastoral ministry. His approach draws on a Trinitarian understanding of God as a relational being of love, whose life 'spills over' into all created reality, human and non-human. By locating human meaning and purpose within God's 'creation-community' this book offers the possibility of a transforming engagement between those in pastoral ministry and the scientific community.
2005 */ 1-84227-369-8 / approx. 380 pp*

Iain D. Campbell
Fixing the Indemnity
The Life and Work of George Adam Smith
When Old Testament scholar George Adam Smith (1856–1942) delivered the Lyman Beecher lectures at Yale University in 1899, he confidently declared that 'modern criticism has won its war against traditional theories. It only remains to fix the amount of the indemnity.' In this biography, Iain D. Campbell assesses Smith's critical approach to the Old Testament and evaluates its consequences, showing that Smith's life and work still raises questions about the relationship between biblical scholarship and evangelical faith.
2004 / 1-84227-228-4 / xx + 256pp

Tim Chester
Mission and the Coming of God
Eschatology, the Trinity and Mission in the Theology of Jürgen Moltmann
This book explores the theology and missiology of the influential contemporary theologian, Jürgen Moltmann. It highlights the important contribution Moltmann has made while offering a critique of his thought from an evangelical perspective. In so doing, it touches on pertinent issues for evangelical missiology. The conclusion takes Calvin as a starting point, proposing 'an eschatology of the cross' which offers a critique of the over-realised eschatologies in liberation theology and certain forms of evangelicalism.
2006 / 1-84227-320-5 / approx. 224pp

Sylvia Wilkey Collinson
Making Disciples
The Significance of Jesus' Educational Strategy for Today's Church
This study examines the biblical practice of discipling, formulates a definition, and makes comparisons with modern models of education. A recommendation is made for greater attention to its practice today.
2004 / 1-84227-116-4 / xiv + 278pp

Darrell Cosden
A Theology of Work
Work and the New Creation
Through dialogue with Moltmann, Pope John Paul II and others, this book develops a genitive 'theology of work', presenting a theological definition of work and a model for a theological ethics of work that shows work's nature, value and meaning now and eschatologically. Work is shown to be a transformative activity consisting of three dynamically inter-related dimensions: the instrumental, relational and ontological.
2005 / 1-84227-332-9 / xvi + 208pp

Stephen M. Dunning
The Crisis and the Quest
A Kierkegaardian Reading of Charles Williams
Employing Kierkegaardian categories and analysis, this study investigates both the central crisis in Charles Williams's authorship between hermetism and Christianity (Kierkegaard's Religions A and B), and the quest to resolve this crisis, a quest that ultimately presses the bounds of orthodoxy.
2000 / 0-85364-985-5 / xxiv + 254pp

Keith Ferdinando
The Triumph of Christ in African Perspective
A Study of Demonology and Redemption in the African Context
The book explores the implications of the gospel for traditional African fears of occult aggression. It analyses such traditional approaches to suffering and biblical responses to fears of demonic evil, concluding with an evaluation of African beliefs from the perspective of the gospel.
1999 / 0-85364-830-1 / xviii + 450pp

Andrew Goddard
Living the Word, Resisting the World
The Life and Thought of Jacques Ellul
This work offers a definitive study of both the life and thought of the French Reformed thinker Jacques Ellul (1912-1994). It will prove an indispensable resource for those interested in this influential theologian and sociologist and for Christian ethics and political thought generally.
2002 / 1-84227-053-2 / xxiv + 378pp

David Hilborn
The Words of our Lips
Language-Use in Free Church Worship
Studies of liturgical language have tended to focus on the written canons of Roman Catholic and Anglican communities. By contrast, David Hilborn analyses the more extemporary approach of English Nonconformity. Drawing on recent developments in linguistic pragmatics, he explores similarities and differences between 'fixed' and 'free' worship, and argues for the interdependence of each.
2006 / 0-85364-977-4 / approx. 350pp

Roger Hitching
The Church and Deaf People
A Study of Identity, Communication and Relationships with Special Reference to the Ecclesiology of Jürgen Moltmann
In *The Church and Deaf People* Roger Hitching sensitively examines the history and present experience of deaf people and finds similarities between aspects of sign language and Moltmann's theological method that 'open up' new ways of understanding theological concepts.
2003 / 1-84227-222-5 / xxii + 236pp

John G. Kelly
One God, One People
The Differentiated Unity of the People of God in the Theology of Jürgen Moltmann

The author expounds and critiques Moltmann's doctrine of God and highlights the systematic connections between it and Moltmann's influential discussion of Israel. He then proposes a fresh approach to Jewish–Christian relations building on Moltmann's work using insights from Habermas and Rawls.

2005 / 0-85346-969-3 / approx. 350pp

Mark F.W. Lovatt
Confronting the Will-to-Power
A Reconsideration of the Theology of Reinhold Niebuhr

Confronting the Will-to-Power is an analysis of the theology of Reinhold Niebuhr, arguing that his work is an attempt to identify, and provide a practical theological answer to, the existence and nature of human evil.

2001 / 1-84227-054-0 / xviii + 216pp

Neil B. MacDonald
Karl Barth and the Strange New World within the Bible
Barth, Wittgenstein, and the Metadilemmas of the Enlightenment

Barth's discovery of the strange new world within the Bible is examined in the context of Kant, Hume, Overbeck, and, most importantly, Wittgenstein. MacDonald covers some fundamental issues in theology today: epistemology, the final form of the text and biblical truth-claims.

2000 / 0-85364-970-7 / xxvi + 374pp

Keith A. Mascord
Alvin Plantinga and Christian Apologetics

This book draws together the contributions of the philosopher Alvin Plantinga to the major contemporary challenges to Christian belief, highlighting in particular his ground-breaking work in epistemology and the problem of evil. Plantinga's theory that both theistic and Christian belief is warrantedly basic is explored and critiqued, and an assessment offered as to the significance of his work for apologetic theory and practice.

2005 / 1-84227-256-X / approx. 304pp

Gillian McCulloch
The Deconstruction of Dualism in Theology
With Reference to Ecofeminist Theology and New Age Spirituality
This book challenges eco-theological anti-dualism in Christian theology, arguing that dualism has a twofold function in Christian religious discourse. Firstly, it enables us to express the discontinuities and divisions that are part of the process of reality. Secondly, dualistic language allows us to express the mysteries of divine transcendence/immanence and the survival of the soul without collapsing into monism and materialism, both of which are problematic for Christian epistemology.
2002 / 1-84227-044-3 / xii + 282pp

Leslie McCurdy
Attributes and Atonement
The Holy Love of God in the Theology of P.T. Forsyth
Attributes and Atonement is an intriguing full-length study of P.T. Forsyth's doctrine of the cross as it relates particularly to God's holy love. It includes an unparalleled bibliography of both primary and secondary material relating to Forsyth.
1999 / 0-85364-833-6 / xiv + 328pp

Nozomu Miyahira
Towards a Theology of the Concord of God
A Japanese Perspective on the Trinity
This book introduces a new Japanese theology and a unique Trinitarian formula based on the Japanese intellectual climate: three betweennesses and one concord. It also presents a new interpretation of the Trinity, a co-subordinationism, which is in line with orthodox Trinitarianism; each single person of the Trinity is eternally and equally subordinate (or serviceable) to the other persons, so that they retain the mutual dynamic equality.
2000 / 0-85364-863-8 / xiv + 256pp

Eddy José Muskus
The Origins and Early Development of Liberation Theology in Latin America
With Particular Reference to Gustavo Gutiérrez
This work challenges the fundamental premise of Liberation Theology, 'opting for the poor', and its claim that Christ is found in them. It also argues that Liberation Theology emerged as a direct result of the failure of the Roman Catholic Church in Latin America.
2002 / 0-85364-974-X / xiv + 296pp

Jim Purves
The Triune God and the Charismatic Movement
A Critical Appraisal from a Scottish Perspective
All emotion and no theology? Or a fundamental challenge to reappraise and realign our trinitarian theology in the light of Christian experience? This study of charismatic renewal as it found expression within Scotland at the end of the twentieth century evaluates the use of Patristic, Reformed and contemporary models of the Trinity in explaining the workings of the Holy Spirit.
2004 / 1-84227-321-3 / xxiv + 246pp

Anna Robbins
Methods in the Madness
Diversity in Twentieth-Century Christian Social Ethics
The author compares the ethical methods of Walter Rauschenbusch, Reinhold Niebuhr and others. She argues that unless Christians are clear about the ways that theology and philosophy are expressed practically they may lose the ability to discuss social ethics across contexts, let alone reach effective agreements.
2004 / 1-84227-211-X / xx + 294pp

Ed Rybarczyk
Beyond Salvation
Eastern Orthodoxy and Classical Pentecostalism on Becoming Like Christ
At first glance eastern Orthodoxy and classical Pentecostalism seem quite distinct. This ground-breaking study shows they share much in common, especially as it concerns the experiential elements of following Christ. Both traditions assert that authentic Christianity transcends the wooden categories of modernism.
2004 / 1-84227-144-X / xii + 356pp

Signe Sandsmark
Is World View Neutral Education Possible and Desirable?
A Christian Response to Liberal Arguments
(Published jointly with The Stapleford Centre)
This book discusses reasons for belief in world view neutrality, and argues that 'neutral' education will have a hidden, but strong world view influence. It discusses the place for Christian education in the common school.
2000 / 0-85364-973-1 / xiv + 182pp

Hazel Sherman
Reading Zechariah
The Allegorical Tradition of Biblical Interpretation through the Commentary of Didymus the Blind and Theodore of Mopsuestia
A close reading of the commentary on Zechariah by Didymus the Blind alongside that of Theodore of Mopsuestia suggests that popular categorising of Antiochene and Alexandrian biblical exegesis as 'historical' or 'allegorical' is inadequate and misleading.
2005 / 1-84227-213-6 / approx. 280pp

Andrew Sloane
On Being a Christian in the Academy
Nicholas Wolterstorff and the Practice of Christian Scholarship
An exposition and critical appraisal of Nicholas Wolterstorff's epistemology in the light of the philosophy of science, and an application of his thought to the practice of Christian scholarship.
2003 / 1-84227-058-3 / xvi + 274pp

Damon W.K. So
Jesus' Revelation of His Father
A Narrative-Conceptual Study of the Trinity with Special Reference to Karl Barth
This book explores the trinitarian dynamics in the context of Jesus' revelation of his Father in his earthly ministry with references to key passages in Matthew's Gospel. It develops from the exegeses of these passages a non-linear concept of revelation which links Jesus' communion with his Father to his revelatory words and actions through a nuanced understanding of the Holy Spirit, with references to K. Barth, G.W.H. Lampe, J.D.G. Dunn and E. Irving.
2005 / 1-84227-323-X / approx. 380pp

Daniel Strange
The Possibility of Salvation Among the Unevangelised
An Analysis of Inclusivism in Recent Evangelical Theology
For evangelical theologians the 'fate of the unevangelised' impinges upon fundamental tenets of evangelical identity. The position known as 'inclusivism', defined by the belief that the unevangelised can be ontologically saved by Christ whilst being epistemologically unaware of him, has been defended most vigorously by the Canadian evangelical Clark H. Pinnock. Through a detailed analysis and critique of Pinnock's work, this book examines a cluster of issues surrounding the unevangelised and its implications for christology, soteriology and the doctrine of revelation.
2002 / 1-84227-047-8 / xviii + 362pp

Scott Swain
God According to the Gospel
Biblical Narrative and the Identity of God in the Theology of Robert W. Jenson
Robert W. Jenson is one of the leading voices in contemporary Trinitarian theology. His boldest contribution in this area concerns his use of biblical narrative both to ground and explicate the Christian doctrine of God. *God According to the Gospel* critically examines Jenson's proposal and suggests an alternative way of reading the biblical portrayal of the triune God.
2006 / 1-84227-258-6 / approx. 180pp

Justyn Terry
The Justifying Judgement of God
A Reassessment of the Place of Judgement in the Saving Work of Christ
The argument of this book is that judgement, understood as the whole process of bringing justice, is the primary metaphor of atonement, with others, such as victory, redemption and sacrifice, subordinate to it. Judgement also provides the proper context for understanding penal substitution and the call to repentance, baptism, eucharist and holiness.
2005 / 1-84227-370-1 / approx. 274 pp

Graham Tomlin
The Power of the Cross
Theology and the Death of Christ in Paul, Luther and Pascal
This book explores the theology of the cross in St Paul, Luther and Pascal. It offers new perspectives on the theology of each, and some implications for the nature of power, apologetics, theology and church life in a postmodern context.
1999 / 0-85364-984-7 / xiv + 344pp

Adonis Vidu
Postliberal Theological Method
A Critical Study
The postliberal theology of Hans Frei, George Lindbeck, Ronald Thiemann, John Milbank and others is one of the more influential contemporary options. This book focuses on several aspects pertaining to its theological method, specifically its understanding of background, hermeneutics, epistemic justification, ontology, the nature of doctrine and, finally, Christological method.
2005 / 1-84227-395-7 / approx. 324pp

Graham J. Watts
Revelation and the Spirit
A Comparative Study of the Relationship between the Doctrine of Revelation and Pneumatology in the Theology of Eberhard Jüngel and of Wolfhart Pannenberg

The relationship between revelation and pneumatology is relatively unexplored. This approach offers a fresh angle on two important twentieth century theologians and raises pneumatological questions which are theologically crucial and relevant to mission in a postmodern culture.

2005 / 1-84227-104-0 / xxii + 232pp

Nigel G. Wright
Disavowing Constantine
Mission, Church and the Social Order in the Theologies of John Howard Yoder and Jürgen Moltmann

This book is a timely restatement of a radical theology of church and state in the Anabaptist and Baptist tradition. Dr Wright constructs his argument in dialogue and debate with Yoder and Moltmann, major contributors to a free church perspective.

2000 / 0-85364-978-2 / xvi + 252pp

Paternoster
9 Holdom Avenue,
Bletchley,
Milton Keynes MK1 1QR,
United Kingdom
Web: www.authenticmedia.co.uk/paternoster

www.ingramcontent.com/pod-product-compliance
Lightning Source LLC
Chambersburg PA
CBHW071437300426
44114CB00013B/1479